One-Win Wonders

Edited by Bill Nowlin
Associate editors Len Levin, Carl Riechers, and Bruce Slutsky

Society for American Baseball Research, Inc.
Phoenix, AZ

One-Win Wonders
Edited by Bill Nowlin
Associate editors Len Levin, Carl Riechers, and Bruce Slutsky

Front cover design: Gilly Rosenthol
Cover photograph: Copyright Yobro10 / Dreamstime.
Design: Gilly Rosenthol

ISBN 978-1-960819-13-0 (paperback)
ISBN 978-1-960819-12-3 (ebook)
Library of Congress Control Number: 2023918450

"Topps® trading cards used courtesy of The Topps Company, Inc."
Thanks to Michael and Linda Hanks.

Copyright © 2023 Society for American Baseball Research, Inc.
All rights reserved. Reproduction in whole or in part without permission is prohibited.

Cronkite School at ASU
555 N. Central Ave. #416
Phoenix, AZ 85004
Phone: (602) 496-1460
Web: www.sabr.org
Facebook: Society for American Baseball Research
Twitter: @SABR

TABLE OF CONTENTS

1	**Introduction**	72	**ED COLE** *by Gregory H. Wolf*
12	**NICK ADENHART** *by Ray Danner*	77	**BOB COONEY** *by Mike Cooney*
17	**FRED APPLEGATE** *by Phil Williams*	85	**REESE DIGGS** *by Eric Vickrey*
22	**PHILLIPPE AUMONT** *by Clayton Trutor*	89	**TOM "SUGAR BOY" DOUGHERTY** *by Tim Newby*
26	**JOHN BAKER** *by Sean Kolodziej*	93	**DICK EGAN** *by Glen Sparks*
32	**FRED BESANA** *by Malcolm Allen*	100	**STEVE ELLSWORTH** *by David Laurila*
37	**DRAKE BRITTON** *by Bill Nowlin*	105	**EDWIN ESCOBAR** *by Tony S. Oliver*
43	**SCOTT BROWN** *by Steve Heath*	111	**CLAY FAUVER** *by Mark Hodermarsky*
49	**IKE BUTLER** *by Paul Proia*	116	**MIGUEL FUENTES** *by Tony S. Oliver*
57	**FRED CAMBRIA** *by John Paul Hill*	121	**RYAN GARTON** *by Bill Hickman*
63	**JIM CLINTON** *by Mark Pestana*		

129	**TOM GILLES** by Tom Hawthorn	220	**BRENT MAYNE** by Paul Hofmann
133	**BILL GING** by William H. Brewster	227	**ED McCREERY** by Chad Moody
140	**GEORGE GOETZ** by Richard Bogovich	233	**TOM METCALF** by Michael Trzinski
151	**KENNY GREER** by Rory Costello	241	**CRAIG MINETTO** by Bob Webster
156	**CHARLIE GUTH** by Jeff Findley	245	**WILLIE MUELLER** by Dennis D. Degenhardt
160	**JORDAN JANKOWSKI** by John Fredland	253	**SHANE NANCE** by Alan Cohen
167	**JIM JOHNSON** by Jim Moyes	258	**EDDIE O'BRIEN** by Tim Herlich
174	**JOSH KINNEY** by Josh Kaiser	266	**JOHNNY O'BRIEN** by Tim Herlich
181	**BRANDON KNIGHT** by Steve Sisto	274	**DON O'RILEY** by Paul White
190	**GEORGE KORINCE** by Jerry Nechal	280	**JOHN POLONI** by John Watkins
194	**JACK KULL** by Jack V. Morris	288	**ROBERT RAMSAY** by Steve Friedman
199	**LARRY LANDRETH** by Gary Belleville	294	**HARRY RAYMOND** by Philip H. Dixon
209	**WILLIAM J. MADIGAN** by Richard Riis	298	**C.J. RIEFENHAUSER** by Peter M. Gordon
213	**RALPH MAURIELLO** by Alan Cohen	304	**RALPH "BLACKIE" SCHWAMB** by Glen Sparks

312	**ATAHUALPO SEVERINO**
by Luis Blandón	344	**GEORGE TSAMIS**
by Chris Hicks
319	**JOE STRONG**
by Joe Schuster	354	**WILSON VALDÉZ**
by Len Pasculli
325	**DENNIS TANKERSLEY**
by Gerard Kwilecki	362	**CHARLIE VAUGHAN**
by Eric A. Simonsen
329	**JAY TESSMER**
by Alan Raylesberg	369	**WILBUR "BIGGS" WEHDE**
by William H. Johnson
336	**CARL THOMAS**
by Tim Otto	373	**AL YEARGIN**
by Bill Nowlin
		378	**CONTRIBUTORS**

INTRODUCTION

This book, *One-Win Wonders*, is a companion book to the 2021 SABR book *One-Hit Wonders*.

The data that provided the basis for the book was provided in mid-2020 by the late Tom Ruane of Retrosheet. Figures are thus complete through the 2019 season. Thus, while Aaron Bummer of the Chicago White Sox was on Tom's list for his one win in 2017, he lost out on the opportunity to be featured in this book because he won a second big-league game on July 29, 2020. He was still active in the 2023 season and as of the beginning of September had won 13 games. He's no longer a "one-win wonder."

In early September 2023, Joe Callahan of Retrosheet updated this list, with a cutoff date at the end of the 2019 season.

The 58 players whose biographies presented here are among those whose major-league career comprised only one win. On the list Joe supplied, there are some 915 players. (This listing does not include players in Negro Leagues baseball, as those statistics are still quite incomplete.) An astonishing 229 of those 915 players never lost a game; each of them had a career record of 1-0. Clearly, most of those simply had very brief careers. In a few cases, they were position players who wound up on the mound at one point or another and left with a victory. It is surprising that 26 of the 915 players with just one win threw shutouts – but never won even one more game.

Plumbing the data can be interesting. The age of the players as of the date of their own win ranges considerably. The youngest were both 17 years old – Roger McKee, a World War II-era pitcher for the Phillies, and William J. Madigan, 1-13 for the Washington Nationals, with a win in 1886. The oldest was Joe Strong, who was over age 37 in the year he was 1-1 for the Florida Marlins in 2000. (There had been another Joe Strong, years earlier, but he won 69 games in the Negro Leagues between 1922-37.)

We wanted to encourage new research by featuring players who did not yet have a SABR biography. Thus this book does not include the surprising Jack Nabors (with a career record of 1-25), but his biography by Stephen V. Rice can be found on the www.sabr.org website, or indirectly via other sites such as Baseball-Reference.com and Retrosheet.org.

Each of the current 30 major-league franchises is represented by at least one such "wonder," as are a number of other teams, some dating back to the nineteenth century.

There were 26 players who threw shutouts for their one and only win:

Herb Bradley
Bob Clark
Bill Cristall
Morrie Critchley
Dave Downs
Don Fisher
Claral Gillenwater
John Hibbard
Bill Lattimore
Don Loun
Paul Marak
John McPherson
Spike Merena
Mike Modak
Pidgey Morgan
Grover Powell
Lefty Russell
Dick Rusteck
Jack Scheible
John Singleton
Oad Swigart
Claude Thomas
Andy Van Hekken
George Walker
Ed Warner
Jesse Whiting

Those aren't household names. That's to be expected, of course – they each only won one game, even if that one win represents an accomplishment that rather few legitimate star pitchers can boast today.

There are some names on the list of one-win wonders who are more well-known – for instance, Hall of Famer Jimmie Foxx. He had pitched once for the Red Sox in 1940, throwing one inning, but then worked in nine games for the Phillies in 1945. On August 19, he threw 6⅔ innings and earned the win, holding the visiting Cincinnati team to just one hit and one run through the first six innings, then yielding three hits and another run before being relieved. The Phillies won, 4-2.

There were 36 players who only appeared in one game and won that very game.

On the other end of the spectrum was Jack Nabors, who pitched for the Philadelphia Athletics in the years 1915-17 and holds a career won-lost record of 1-25. His biography is not included in this book because it had already been written, and one of our goals with the book was to inspire new research and writing, to add to the more than 6,000 biographies that SABR members have already written. Stephen V. Rice had previously written the Nabors biography and it can be found on the BioProject portion of the SABR website at: https://sabr.org/bioproj/person/Jack-Nabors/.

There have been 20 other pitchers whose one win is balanced by 10 or more losses. Biographies of some of those players are included in this book: Ike Butler (1-10 in 16 games), Jim Clinton (1-15 in 19 games), William J. Madigan (1-13 in 14 games), Dennis Tankersley (1-10 in 27 games), and Al Yeargin (1-12 in 33 games).

There were 293 who never started a major-league game.

Jhan Mariñez, who appeared in a total of 103 games for seven major-league clubs while winning only one game (for the Florida Marlins in 2010), is the leader in that category, tied with Sean Runyan, whose one win was for the Detroit Tigers in 1988, a year in which he led the majors in appearances.

Mariñez holds another first among one-win wonders. He hit 13 opposing batters with pitches, having faced 596. Second in HBP is Harry Colliflower with 11. He pitched for the 1899 Cleveland Spiders.

Mike Thompson struck out a group-leading 113 batters but won just once – for the Washington Senators in 1971. Just one strikeout behind Thompson was Chris Smith, who won one game for the 2008 Boston Red Sox but struck out 112 batters over the course of a 77-game career that also included time with Milwaukee and Oakland.

Jack Nabors allowed the most base hits to opposing batters – 266 of them, almost 100 more than second-place Jim Clinton, who allowed 178.

Nabors also threw the most innings while pursuing his one win – 269⅔ innings of work. He threw 13 complete games, the same number as Jim McElroy. He led in bases on balls, too – walking 131, three more than Mike Thompson. A distant third was Craig Minetto, who walked 72.

Three of the one-win wonders threw only one big-league inning each – John Baker, Brent Mayne, and Wilson Valdéz. Baker and Mayne were both catchers. Baker threw a perfect inning in his one appearance. Wilson Valdéz was an infielder who played in 439 games for seven teams; in his one inning of mound work, he hit a batter, retired three others, and won the game.

Some of the others one will encounter in this book:

Nick Adenhart won his game at age 22; a month before he would have turned 23, he was killed in an automobile accident.

Dick Egan pitched in 74 games from 1963 into 1967, closing 29 of them. Only in his final year did he get a win.

Miguel Fuentes won his game at age 23; less than five months later, he was shot and killed.

Tom Gilles's two-pitch victory was his only decision in a two-game, 14-pitch major-league career.

Charlie Guth's one win came in the last game of the season, and he won despite giving up eight runs.

Josh Kinney had just one regular-season win, but had pitched scoreless ball in three 2007 NLCS games with a win in Game Two.

Ed McCreery allowed five earned runs, six hits, and three walks in only two innings pitched, for a game ERA of 22.50 and a WHIP of 4.50, but he got the win.

Twins Eddie and Johnny O'Brien, who both pitched for the Pirates in the 1950s. Johnny got his one and only win, in relief against the Phillies, at home on July 3, 1956. Eddie got his on September 14, 1947, a complete game on the road against the Cubs.

Jay Tessmer won only one game but was a member of three World Series Championship Yankees teams (1998, 1999, 2000).

Charlie Vaughan's sole victory was the only game he ever pitched in the major leagues and he did it not long before he turned 19.

Where you can read about each of these wins

This book offers the biographies of the 58 players selected for inclusion. We are also pleased to present accounts of the games each of these players won. In each case, the author who wrote the player biography was also asked to write up the account of the game for SABR's Games Project. These write-ups do not appear in the book itself, but are available online at SABR's Games Project page. A complete listing of the games is presented here, along with hyperlinks for those who are reading this book in electronic form. Those who are reading the physical book can find each game by going to the SABR website and entering the date of the game into the "Search the Research Collection" window at www.sabr.org. There may be more than one game that occurred on that date, but the game you are seeking should be fairly easy to locate.

This book represents the collaborative work of nearly 60 researchers, authors, and editors from the Society for American Baseball Research.

—Bill Nowlin

Nick Adenhart

Nick Adenhart earns first and only career win for Angels

By Ray Danner

May 12, 2008: Los Angeles Angels of Anaheim 10, Chicago White Sox 7, at Angel Stadium of Anaheim, Anaheim

https://sabr.org/gamesproj/game/may-12-2008-nick-adenhart-earns-sole-victory-in-angels-win/

Fred Applegate

Rube Waddell salutes last-place Senators; Philadelphia's Fred Applegate earns sole major-league win

By Phil Williams

October 10, 1904: Philadelphia Athletics 7, Washington Senators 6, at American League Park, Washington DC (game one of a doubleheader)

https://sabr.org/gamesproj/game/october-10-1904-rube-waddell-salutes-last-place-senators-philadelphias-fred-applegate-earns-sole-major-league-win/

Phillippe Aumont

Phillippe Aumont earns only career win for Phillies

By Clayton Trutor

April 12, 2013: Philadelphia Phillies 3, Florida Marlins 1 (10 innings), at Marlins Park, Miami

https://sabr.org/gamesproj/game/april-12-2013-phillippe-aumont-earns-only-career-win-for-phillies/

John Baker

Cubs backup catcher John Baker records a win in Colorado

By Sean Kolodziej

July 29, 2014: Chicago Cubs 4, Colorado Rockies 3 (16 innings), at Wrigley Field, Chicago https://sabr.org/gamesproj/game/july-29-2014-cubs-backup-catcher-john-baker-records-a-win-in-colorado/

Fred Besana
Orioles' Fred Besana settles down to beat Senators
By Malcolm Allen
April 22, 1956: Baltimore Orioles 7, Washington Senators 3, at Memorial Stadium, Baltimore (game one of doubleheader)
https://sabr.org/gamesproj/game/april-22-1956-orioles-fred-besana-settles-down-to-beat-senators/

Drake Britton
Jonny Gomes' unassisted double play helps Drake Britton earn first major-league win
By Bill Nowlin
July 31, 2013: Boston Red Sox 5, Seattle Mariners 4 (15 innings), at Fenway Park, Boston
https://sabr.org/gamesproj/game/july-31-2013-jonny-gomes-unassisted-double-play-helps-drake-britton-earn-first-major-league-win/

Scott Brown
Reds' Scott Brown records his only major-league win as Fernando Valenzuela's struggles continue
By Steve Heath
August 11, 1981: Cincinnati Reds 7, Los Angeles Dodgers 6, at Dodger Stadium, Los Angeles
https://sabr.org/gamesproj/game/august-11-1981-reds-scott-brown-records-his-only-major-league-win-as-fernando-valenzuelas-struggles-continue/

Ike Butler
Ike Butler earns only major-league win for Orioles
By Paul Proia
September 20, 1902: Baltimore Orioles 9, Washington Senators 6 (second game of doubleheader), at American League Park, Washington, DC
https://sabr.org/gamesproj/game/september-20-1902-ike-butler-earns-only-major-league-win-for-orioles/

Fred Cambria
Pirates rookie Fred Cambria beats Phillies for only major-league win
By John Paul Hill
September 5, 1970: Pittsburgh Pirates 6, Philadelphi Phillies 4, at Three Rivers Stadium, Pittsburgh
https://sabr.org/gamesproj/game/september-5-1970-pirates-rookie-fred-cambria-beats-phillies-for-only-major-league-win/

Jim Clinton
Journeyman outfielder Jim Clinton notches his only major-league pitching victory
By Mark Pestana
May 26, 1875: Brooklyn Atlantics 14, New Haven Elm Citys 4, at Union Grounds, Brooklyn
https://sabr.org/gamesproj/game/may-26-1875-journeyman-outfielder-jim-clinton-notches-his-only-major-league-pitching-victory/

Ed Cole
Ed Cole wins only big-league game as Buster Mills, Red Kress star at plate
By Gregory H. Wolf
August 30, 1938: St. Louis Browns 9, Boston Red Sox 5, at Fenway Park, Boston
https://sabr.org/gamesproj/game/august-30-1938-ed-cole-wins-only-big-league-game-as-buster-mills-red-kress-star-at-plate/

Bob Cooney
It was a "dark and stormy day" for Browns, Red Sox
By Mike Cooney
July 31, 1932: St. Louis Browns 7, Boston Red Sox 3 (second game of doubleheader), at Sportsman's Park, St. Louis
https://sabr.org/gamesproj/game/july-31-1932-it-was-a-dark-and-stormy-day-for-browns-red-sox/

Reese Diggs
From sandlots to big leagues, Reese Diggs earns first win in Senators blowout
By Eric Vickrey
September 17, 1934: Washington Senators 13, Cleveland Indians 6, at League Park, Cleveland
https://sabr.org/gamesproj/game/september-17-1934-from-sandlots-to-big-leagues-reese-diggs-earns-first-win-in-senators-blowout/

Tom Dougherty
White Sox beat Cleveland on fierce rally as Tom Dougherty picks up only career win
By Tim Newby
April 24, 1904: Chicago White Sox 5, Cleveland Naps 4, at South Side Park, Chicago
https://sabr.org/gamesproj/game/april-24-1904-white-sox-beat-cleveland-on-fierce-rally-as-tom-dougherty-picks-up-only-career-win/

Dick Egan
Dodgers finally knock out Cardinals' Jaster; Dick Egan gets his only big-league win
By Glen Sparks
April 24, 1967: Los Angeles Dodgers 6, St. Louis Cardinals 5 (13 innings), at Dodger Stadium, Los Angeles
https://sabr.org/gamesproj/game/april-24-1967-dodgers-finally-knock-out-cardinals-jaster-dick-egan-gets-his-only-big-league-win/

Steve Ellsworth
Boston's Steve Ellsworth tames Tigers for sole big-league win
By Bill Nowlin
April 21, 1988: Boston Red Sox 12, Detroit Tigers 3, at Tiger Stadium, Detroit
https://sabr.org/gamesproj/game/april-21-1988-bostons-steve-ellsworth-tames-tigers-for-sole-big-league-win/

Edwin Escobar
Diamondbacks beat Reds in 11th inning as Edwin Escobar earns sole major-league win
By Tony S. Oliver
August 26, 2016: Arizona Diamondbacks 4, Cincinnati Reds 3 (11 innings), at Chase Field, Phoenix
https://sabr.org/gamesproj/game/august-26-2016-diamondbacks-beat-reds-in-11th-inning-as-edwin-escobar-earns-sole-major-league-win/

Clay Fauver
Louisville Colonels' 'Mysterious Twirler' Clay Fauver defeats Pirates for only big-league win
By Mark Hodermarsky
September 7, 1899: Louisville Colonels 7, Pittsburgh Pirates 4, at Exhibition Park, Pittsburgh
https://sabr.org/gamesproj/game/september-7-1899-louisville-colonels-mysterious-twirler-clay-fauver-defeats-pirates-for-only-big-league-win/

Miguel Fuentes
The first of many that were not to come for Pilots' Miguel Fuentes
By Tony S. Oliver
September 8, 1969: Seattle Pilots 5, Chicago White Sox 1 (second game of doubleheader), at Sick's Stadium, Seattle

https://sabr.org/gamesproj/game/september-8-1969-the-first-of-many-that-were-not-to-come-for-pilots-miguel-fuentes/

Ryan Garton

Evan Longoria's homer lifts Rays to comeback victory; Ryan Garton earns only big-league win

By Bill Hickman

June 4, 2016: Tampa Bay Rays 9, Seattle Mariners 7, at Tropicana Field, St. Petersburg

https://sabr.org/gamesproj/game/june-14-2016-evan-longorias-homer-lifts-rays-to-comeback-victory-ryan-garton-earns-only-big-league-win/

Tom Gilles

Toronto's Tom Gilles earns first and only career win on two pitches

By Tom Hawthorn

June 8, 1990: Toronto Blue Jays 11, Milwaukee Brewers 5, at County Stadium Milwaukee

https://sabr.org/gamesproj/game/june-8-1990-toronto-rookie-earns-first-and-only-career-win-on-two-pitches/

Bill Ging

Beaneaters' Bill Ging earns only big-league win against Giants

By Bill Brewster

September 25, 1899: Boston Beaneaters 2, New York Giants 1 (8 innings), at Polo Grounds, New York

https://sabr.org/gamesproj/game/september-25-1899-beaneaters-bill-ging-earns-only-big-league-win-against-giants/

George Goetz

George Goetz's only major league win extends Louisville's losing streak to 21

By Rich Bogovich

June 17, 1899: Baltimore Orioles 10, Louisville Colonels 6 (first game of doubleheader), at Oriole Park, Baltimore

https://sabr.org/gamesproj/game/june-17-1889-george-goetzs-only-major-league-win-extends-louisvilles-losing-streak-to-21/

Kenny Greer

From Greer to Eternity

By Rory Costello

September 29, 1993: New York Mets 1, St. Louis Cardinals 0 (17 innings), at Shea Stadium, New York

https://sabr.org/gamesproj/game/september-29-1993-from-greer-to-eternity/

Charlie Guth

Amateur Charlie Guth wins in only professional appearance for White Stockings

By Jeff Findley

September 30, 1880: Chicago White Stockings 10, Buffalo Bisons 8, at White Stocking Park, Chicago

https://sabr.org/gamesproj/game/september-30-1880-amateur-guth-wins-in-only-professional-appearance/

Jordan Jankowski

Astros erupt with 11-run eighth inning to rout Twins, give Jankowski only big-league win

By John Fredland

May 29, 2017: Houston Astros 16, Minnesota Twins 8, at Target Field, Minneapolis

https://sabr.org/gamesproj/game/may-29-2017-astros-erupt-with-11-run-eighth-inning-to-rout-twins-give-jankowski-only-big-league-win/

Jim Johnson

Giants-Reds slugfest yields Jim Johnson's sole major-league win

By Jim Moyes

April 18, 1970: San Francisco Giants 16, Cincinnati Reds 9, at Crosley Field, Cincinnati

https://sabr.org/gamesproj/game/april-18-1970-giants-reds-slugfest-yields-jim-johnsons-sole-major-league-win/

Josh Kinney

Josh Kinney earns first major-league victory behind Pujols' power

By Josh Kaiser

June 27, 2009: St. Louis Cardinals 5, Minnesota Twins 3, at Busch Stadium, St. Louis

https://sabr.org/gamesproj/game/june-27-2009-josh-kinney-earns-first-and-only-major-league-victory-behind-pujols-power/

Brandon Knight

New York Mets' Brandon Knight records first and only major-league win

By Steve Sisto

September 17, 2008: New York Mets 9, Washington Nationals 7, at Nationals Park, Washington D.C.

https://sabr.org/gamesproj/game/september-17-2008-new-york-mets-brandon-knight-records-first-and-only-major-league-win/

George Korince

Tigers' George Korince earns first major-league win

May 13, 1967: Detroit Tigers 10, Boston Red Sox 8, at Fenway Park, Boston

By Jerry Nechal

https://sabr.org/gamesproj/game/may-13-1967-tigers-george-korince-earns-first-major-league-win/

Jack Kull

Jack Kull records only major-league win as Athletics beat Walter Johnson on final day of 1909 season

By Jack V. Morris

October 2, 1909: Philadelphia Athletics 6, Washington Senators 5 (first game of doubleheader), at Shibe Park, Philadelphia

https://sabr.org/gamesproj/game/october-2-1909-jack-kull-records-only-major-league-win-as-athletics-beat-walter-johnson-on-final-day-of-1909-season/

Larry Landreth

Larry Landreth, Expos' first Canadian starting pitcher, wins big-league debut

By Gary Belleville

September 16, 1976: Montreal Expos 4, Chicago Cubs 3, at Parc Jarry, Montreal

https://sabr.org/gamesproj/game/september-16-1976-larry-landreth-expos-first-canadian-starting-pitcher-wins-big-league-debut/

William J. Madigan

Washington's plucky "Pony" Madigan is a phenom at 17, out of the majors at 18

By Richard Riis

July 19, 1886: Washington Nationals 7, Philadelphia Quakers 5, at Swampoodle Grounds, Washington, DC

https://sabr.org/gamesproj/game/july-19-1886-washingtons-plucky-pony-madigan-is-a-phenom-at-17-out-of-the-majors-at-18/

Ralph Mauriello

Dodgers rookies take center stage

By Alan Cohen

September 19, 1958: Los Angeles Dodgers 5, Chicago Cubs 1, at Wrigley Field, Chicago

https://sabr.org/gamesproj/game/september-19-1958-dodgers-rookies-take-center-stage/

Brent Mayne
In Rockies' exciting rally, the winning pitcher was the catcher
By Paul Hofmann
August 22, 2000: Colorado Rockies 7, Atlanta Braves 6 (12 innings), at Coors Field, Denver
https://sabr.org/gamesproj/game/august-22-2000-in-rockies-exciting-rally-the-winning-pitcher-was-the-catcher/

Ed McCreery
Ed McCreery becomes a dubious "one-win wonder" in bizarre debut
By Chad Moody
August 16, 1914: Detroit Tigers 13, Cleveland Naps 6, at League Park, Cleveland
https://sabr.org/gamesproj/game/august-16-1914-ed-mccreery-becomes-a-dubious-one-win-wonder-in-bizarre-debut/

Tom Metcalf
Yankees' Tom Metcalf gets sole major-league win, aided by home runs
By Michael Trzinski
September 1, 1963: New York Yankees 4, Baltimore Orioles 4, at Memorial Stadium, Baltimore
https://sabr.org/gamesproj/game/september-1-1963-yankees-tom-metcalf-gets-sole-major-league-win-aided-by-home-runs/

Craig Minetto
Oakland's Craig Minetto picks up only major league win
By Bob Webster
April 28, 1979: Oakland Athletics 1, New York Yankees 0. At Oakland-Alameda County Stadium, Oakland
https://sabr.org/gamesproj/game/april-25-1979-oaklands-craig-minetto-picks-up-only-major-league-win/

Willie Mueller
Cecil Cooper stars, rookie Willie Mueller earns first win for Brewers
By Dennis Degenhardt
August 22, 1978: Milwaukee Brewers 5, Cleveland Indians 4 (second game of doubleheader), at County Stadium, Milwaukee
https://sabr.org/gamesproj/game/august-22-1978-cecil-cooper-stars-rookie-willie-mueller-earns-first-win-for-brewers/

Shane Nance
Arizona's Shane Nance earns only big-league win
August 23, 2004: Arizona Diamondbacks 5, Pittsburgh Pirates 4, at PNC Park, Pittsburgh
By Alan Cohen
https://sabr.org/gamesproj/game/august-23-2004-arizonas-shane-nance-earns-only-big-league-win/

Eddie O'Brien
"Startling performance" earns lone victory for Pirates' Eddie O'Brien
By Tim Herlich
September 14, 1957: Pittsburgh Pirates 3, Chicago Cubs 1 (first game of doubleheader), at Wrigley Field, Chicago
https://sabr.org/gamesproj/game/september-14-1957-startling-performance-earns-lone-victory-for-pirates-eddie-obrien/

Johnny O'Brien
"Best batting-practice pitcher" Johnny O'Brien saves Bucs
By Tim Herlich
July 3, 1956: Pittsburgh Pirates 6, Philadelphia Phillies 5, at Forbes Field, Pittsburgh
https://sabr.org/gamesproj/game/july-3-1956-best-batting-practice-pitcher-johnny-obrien-saves-bucs/

Don O'Riley
Royals come back three times to defeat White Sox
By Paul White
July 11, 1969: Kansas City Royals 8, Chicago White Sox 5, at Municipal Stadium, Kansas City
https://sabr.org/gamesproj/game/july-11-1969-royals-come-back-three-times-to-defeat-white-sox/

John Poloni
Rangers end season with franchise's best record and rookie John Poloni's only career win
By John J. Watkins
October 2, 1977: Texas Rangers 8, Oakland Athletics 7, at Arlington Stadium, Arlington, Texas
https://sabr.org/gamesproj/game/october-2-1977-rangers-end-season-with-franchises-best-record-and-rookie-john-polonis-only-career-win/

Robert Ramsay
Mike Cameron powers Mariners as Robert Ramsay wins first game
By Steve Friedman
June 15, 2000: Seattle Mariners 12. Minnesota Twins 5, at Metrodome, Minneapolis
https://sabr.org/gamesproj/game/june-15-2000-mike-cameron-powers-mariners-as-robert-ramsay-wins-first-game/

Harry Raymond
Harry Raymond's wild win
By Philip H. Dixon
July 27, 1889: Louisville Colonels 6, Columbus Solons 2, at Recreation Park, Columbus, Ohio
https://sabr.org/gamesproj/game/july-27-1889-harry-raymonds-wild-win/

C.J. Riefenhauser
C.J. Riefenhauser earns his only major-league win for Rays
By Peter M. Gordon
June 14, 2015: Tampa Bay Rays 2, Chicago White Sox 1, at Tropicana Field, St. Petersburg
https://sabr.org/gamesproj/game/june-14-2015-c-j-riefenhauser-earns-his-only-major-league-win-for-rays/

Blackie Schwamb
Ralph "Blackie" Schwamb earns his only win in major leagues
By Glen Sparks
July 31, 1948: St. Louis Browns 10, Washington Senators 8, at Sportsman's Park, St. Louis
https://sabr.org/gamesproj/game/july-31-1948-ralph-blackie-schwamb-earns-his-only-win-in-major-leagues/

Atahualpa Severino
Michael Morse's clutch 9th-inning homer seals victory for Atahualpa Severino
By Luis A. Blandón Jr.
September 26, 2011: Washington Nationals 6, Florida Marlins 4, at Sun Life Stadium, Miami
https://sabr.org/gamesproj/game/september-26-2011-michael-morses-clutch-9th-inning-homer-seals-victory-for-atahualpa-severino/

Joe Strong
37-year-old rookie Joe Strong records first major-league win
By Joe Schuster
June 24, 2000: Florida Marlins 7, Chicago Cubs 4, at Pro Player Stadium, Miami
https://sabr.org/gamesproj/game/june-24-2000-37-year-old-rookie-joe-strong-records-first-major-league-win/

Dennis Tankersley
Padres' Dennis Tankersley records only career win and homer
By Gerard Kwilecki
May 26, 2002: San Diego Padres 8, Milwaukee Brewers 7, at Miller Park, Milwaukee
https://sabr.org/gamesproj/game/may-26-2002-padres-dennis-tankersley-records-only-career-win-and-homer/

Jay Tessmer
August 27, 1998: Yankees blow 9th-inning lead before beating Angels in 11th
By Alan Raylesberg
August 27, 1998: New York Yankees 6, Anaheim Angels 5 (11 innings), at Yankee Stadium, New York
https://sabr.org/gamesproj/game/august-27-1998-yankees-blow-9th-inning-lead-before-beating-angels-in-11th/

Carl Thomas
Score vs. Latman duel is short-lived
By Tim Otto
May 14, 1960: Cleveland Indians 10, Chicago White Sox 9, at Cleveland Stadium, Cleveland
https://sabr.org/gamesproj/game/may-14-1960-score-vs-latman-duel-is-short-lived/

George Tsamis
George Tsamis records a win in "wet and wild" matchup with Athletics
By Chris Hicks
May 26, 1993: Minnesota Twins 12, Oakland Athletics 11, at Oakland-Alameda County Coliseum, Oakland
https://sabr.org/gamesproj/game/may-26-1993-george-tsamis-gets-career-win-in-wet-and-wild-matchup-with-athletics/

Wilson Valdéz
Infielder Wilson Valdéz pitches the 19th inning and records the win for Phillies
By Len Pasculli
May 25, 2011: Philadelphia Phillies 5, Cincinnati Reds 4 (19 innings), at Citizens Bank Park, Philadelphia
https://sabr.org/gamesproj/game/may-25-2011-infielder-wilson-valdez-pitches-the-19th-inning-and-gets-the-win/

Charlie Vaughan
Braves' 18-year-old Charles Vaughan masters Astros in first major-league start
By Eric A. Simonsen
September 3, 1966: Atlanta Braves 12, Houston Astros 2 (game one of doubleheader), at Atlanta Stadium, Atlanta
https://sabr.org/gamesproj/game/september-3-1966-braves-18-year-old-charles-vaughan-masters-astros-in-first-major-league-start/

Biggs Wehde
Bob Fothergill leads White Sox in 11-run rally to beat Yankees
By Mike Huber
July 28, 1931: Chicago White Sox 14, New York Yankees 12, at Yankee Stadium, New York
https://sabr.org/gamesproj/game/july-28-1931-bob-fothergill-leads-white-sox-in-11-run-eighth-inning-rally-to-beat-yankees/

Al Yeargin
Al Yeargin earns only career win for Braves before losing 11 in a row
By Bill Nowlin
May 16, 1924: Boston Braves 8, Cincinnati Reds 3, at Redland Field, Cincinnati
https://sabr.org/gamesproj/game/may-16-1924-al-yeargin-earns-only-career-win-for-braves-before-losing-11-in-a-row/

NICK ADENHART

BY RAY DANNER

Baseball is a young man's game. A game of quick reflexes, short memories and the daily grind. In the opening week of the 2009 season, 22-year-old Nick Adenhart had already overcome an untimely Tommy John surgery and four seasons in the minor leagues to make the Los Angeles Angels' Opening Day roster as their number-three starter. The Angels' top pitching prospect, he pitched six shutout innings in his season debut and appeared to be in the first act of a prosperous career as a big leaguer from a small town.

Instead, the end came immediately after the beginning and Adenhart's young life was cut short just hours after his season debut in a tragic car accident, leaving Angels fans and his followers back home in Washington County, Maryland, wondering, "What if?"

Nicholas James Adenhart was born on August 24, 1986, in Silver Spring, Maryland, a city bordering Washington, D.C. He was the only child of James, a United States Secret Service agent, and Janet Adenhart, who worked in finance. Janet and James divorced when Nick was a child but he was raised by both parents, and Janet remarried Duane Gigeous, with whom she had a son, Henry.

Adenhart was raised in Williamsport, Maryland, a small town in the outskirts of Hagerstown where visitors can stand upon Doubleday Hill, a Civil War monument that overlooks the Potomac River into West Virginia; a town of about 2,000 people where local baseball is everything.

Like many big-league ballplayers, Adenhart began to make his name in local youth leagues. At the ages of 11 and 12, he pitched his team in the Halfway Little League to consecutive District One championships, going 9-0 on the mound in that two-year run.

When Adenhart was 12, his best friend, David Warrenfeltz, became his catcher and chief competitor. The boys would play backyard Wiffle Ball between games, testing their skills against each other at anything they could think of. "He was the most competitive person times five," Warrenfeltz remembered. "When he was younger, he was borderline cocky."[1] Warrenfeltz would catch Adenhart through their high-school careers and has been interviewed about Adenhart in subsequent years.

In 2001, at the age of 15, Adenhart joined an amateur showcase team called the Oriolelanders, a team of top local players sponsored by the Baltimore Orioles. Nick played in the summer and fall after PONY League season against high-school sophomores, juniors, and seniors. He played with the Oriolelanders for four years and continue to impress locally.

Longtime Hagerstown sportswriter Bob Parasiliti remembered when he first started covering Adenhart: "Even at a young age, he had the focus to compete and he had the very precise mechanics that he carried all the way through his pitching career. Those were the attributes that gave everyone the impression he was going places."[2]

Adenhart initially attended high school at St. Maria Goretti in Hagerstown and played baseball and basketball but transferred to hometown Williamsport High School for his junior and senior years; there he focused solely on baseball. Recalling Adenhart's competitive fire on the court, Warrenfeltz said, "Janet pulled him out because it was too risky. Plus, he talked so much trash." At Williamsport High Adenhart encountered his first pro scout.

To cap his junior year, Adenhart lost a legendary 1-0 duel with Allegany High School (Cumberland, Maryland) senior Aaron Laffey in the Class-1A West Regional despite pitching a no-hitter. Laffey pitched a two-hitter (one by Adenhart) and struck out 19 while Adenhart fanned 14 and allowed one unearned run, in front of scouts from 11 major-league teams. It was Adenhart's only loss of the season. "After that game, Nick thought he let the team down because he didn't win. That haunted yet motivated him," Parasiliti recalled.[3] Adenhart would start his senior season with a perfect game against Allegany, striking out 15 of 21 batters.

Adenhart signed a letter of intent with the University of North Carolina early in his senior year even though he was unlikely to go to college because of his professional draft prospects. Entering his senior year at Williamsport, he was a projected first-round pick in the 2004 amateur draft and *Baseball America's* number-one high-school prospect.[4] Remembering the flurry of activity, his coach Rod Steiner said, "He put us on the map. When he pitched, we'd have 500, 1,000 people here. You're lucky to see 20 people at a normal high school game. But he was special."[5]

Adenhart had a dominant senior season and entered the final regular-season game of his high-school career with a 5-1 record, a 0.73 ERA, and 2.2 K's per inning.[6] On May 11, 2004, just two weeks before the amateur draft, Adenhart's season finale was cut short when he felt a pop in his elbow while facing the third batter of the game.

"He threw a curve and waved me out," remembered Warrenfeltz. "He told me 'No more curves.'

Nick Adenhart. Courtesy of Los Angeles Angels of Anaheim.

I felt like I could have thrown up." It was a partial ligament tear, and Adenhart's high-school pitching career was over.

Adenhart became the team's designated hitter in the Maryland 1A playoffs, homering over 360 feet to dead center field in his first at-bat.[7] Williamsport lost the state title and Adenhart appeared to have lost his chance at being a first-round draft pick as his arm injury required Tommy John surgery, performed by Dr. James Andrews.[8]

In June 2004 the Los Angeles Angels selected Adenhart in the 14th round of the amateur draft, the 413th player selected overall. Rather than let Adenhart slip away to UNC, the Angels gave him first-round money and signed him for $710,000 on July 28. Angels scout Dan Radcliffe was credited with the signing. Adenhart reported to Arizona to rehab with the Anaheim training staff. "Being hurt, rehabilitation is the most important part of coming back strong," Adenhart said at the time. "Being with the Angels gives me the best shot."[9] The Angels also selected future ace Jered Weaver

Nick Adenhart. Courtesy of Los Angeles Angels of Anaheim.

(12th overall) as well as future big leaguers Mark Trumbo (18th round) and Martín Maldonado (27th round) in the 2004 draft.

In 2005, after rehabbing from his Tommy John surgery, Adenhart pitched in 14 games across two levels, pitching in 13 games in the rookie Arizona League and making one start with the Orem Owls of the rookie Pioneer League. Overall, he was 3-3 with a 3.24 ERA in 50 innings pitched, striking out 59.

Adenhart went to major-league spring training in 2006 as a nonroster invitee. He was assigned to the Class-A Cedar Rapid Kernels, where he went 10-2 with a 1.95 ERA in 16 starts, striking out 99 in 106 innings and earning a roster spot on the 2006 All-Star Futures Game. He was moved up to the Advanced-A Rancho Cucamonga Quakes (California League) for nine more starts and finished the 2006 season with 15 wins and a 2.56 ERA in 158⅓ innings.

Nick's family recalled later that his time spent in Cedar Rapids was his favorite on his way to the major leagues. "I think it was where the dream kind of started," his mother, Janet Gigeous, remembered. "I think it was a happy time for him. This place has a lot of really good memories."[10]

Adenhart's repertoire at this time, according to an internet scouting report, consisted of fastballs "in the high-80s-to-low-90s, topping out at 94 on a few occasions. He is an extreme groundball pitcher."[11] He also threw a curveball in the mid-70s and a circle changeup in the 80s. "My changeup tends to be the strikeout pitch," Adenhart said at the time, while also reporting that his surgically repaired elbow felt no pain two years after his surgery.

Adenhart spent the entire 2007 season in the Double-A Texas League with the Arkansas Travelers, going 10-8 with a 3.65 ERA. He was 20 years old for most of the season and was the Angels' top pitching prospect.

In 2008, an injury to John Lackey in spring training opened up a rotation spot in Anaheim and Adenhart battled Dustin Moseley for the role. Mosely got the job and Adenhart was assigned to the Triple-A Salt Lake Bees.

At the end of April, Adenhart was 4-0 with a 0.87 ERA for Salt Lake, which was 21-1, the best start in franchise history.[12] After Moseley's April struggles, Adenhart was called up to make his major-league debut on May 1 in Anaheim in a starting assignment against the Oakland Athletics. Pitching on three days' rest for the first time in his career, he lasted just two innings, giving up five runs on three hits and five walks, getting a no-decision in a 15-8 loss. "There was not much feel out there," said Adenhart after the game. "I was a little numb."[13]

His next start was in Kansas City on May 6; another no-decision in a 5-3 win. Adenhart went 4⅓ innings and allowed three runs on six hits and five walks with three strikeouts.

Adenhart earned his first and only big-league victory on May 12 at home against the Chicago White Sox. He pitched into the sixth inning and allowed four runs on nine hits and three walks with one strikeout. He was then sent down to Triple A, where he regressed to 1-5 with an 8.80 ERA[14] and finished the minor-league season at 9-13 with a 5.76 ERA in 145⅓ innings. His major-league totals for 2008 were 1-0 with a 9.00 ERA in 12 innings pitched.

In 2009, spring-training injuries to established veterans Lackey, Ervin Santana, and Kelvim Escobar put all three on the disabled list and opened the door for Adenhart, still the Angels' top pitching prospect, to open the season as the Angels' number-three starter. He made his first start on April 8 in the finale of the season-opening three-game set in Anaheim against Oakland.

Summoning his father to Los Angeles, saying "You better come here, because something special is going to happen,"[15] Adenhart had his most effective start yet in the major leagues, going six shutout innings while scattering seven hits and three walks and striking out five. He left the game with a 3-0 lead but the Angels' bullpen allowed six runs in the last two innings in a 6-4 loss, costing Adenhart his second major-league victory.

After his successful season debut, Adenhart went out with friends to celebrate. He was riding in a Mitsubishi Eclipse driven by a friend, Courtney Frances Stewart, along with passengers Henry Pearson and Jon Wilhite when the car was struck at the corner of Lemon and Oglethorpe in Fullerton at 12:20 A.M., less than seven miles from Angels Stadium. A Toyota Sienna minivan, driven under the influence by Andrew Thomas Gallo, went through a red light at 65 mph and broadsided the Eclipse.[16] Gallo, who had a suspended license from a previous DUI, fled the scene and was apprehended a mile away. Stewart (20 years old) and Pearson (25) were killed while Wilhite miraculously survived critical injuries. Adenhart was transported to the UC Irvine Medical Center, where he died in the early morning hours of April 9, 2009, at the age of 22 years and 228 days.

The Angels franchise and Adenhart's family were stunned. The series finale with Oakland was canceled and a makeshift shrine was erected by fans outside Angels Stadium while the Angels hosted a somber news conference. "His life's goal was to be a major league baseball player, and he certainly achieved that standard," said his agent, Scott Boras. The quotes from team officials and teammates were unanimous in their grief for the loss of the promising young man. "I'm at a loss," Oakland pitcher Dallas Braden, who had pitched against Adenhart in the minors, said. "Talk about a guy who was on his way, about to take baseball by storm. He was ready to bring it to the main stage, and it was all cut short for no reason whatsoever."[17]

Adenhart's family, the Angels franchise, and many of his stops along his path to the major leagues have honored his memory throughout the years.

After struggling to a sub-.500 April in the aftermath of Adenhart's death, the Angels maintained his locker all season and rallied to win the American League West by 10 games in 2009. They eventually lost the American League Championship Series to the New York Yankees but voted to send a full share of playoff money, $138,039, to Adenhart's estate.

The Angels created the "Nick Adenhart Pitcher of the Year" award in June of 2009, to be awarded each season to the Angels' most outstanding pitcher. The player receives a bronze statue of Adenhart with a larger one on display in the team's trophy case. Jered Weaver, who in 2013 named his son Aden in Nick's honor, won the first Adenhart Award.[18]

The Adenhart family created the Adenhart Memorial Fund to raise funds to support youth baseball organizations. The Little League field where Adenhart played in Williamsport was renamed the Nicholas James Adenhart Memorial Field.[19] The Cedar Rapids Kernels set up an annual $1,000 scholarship in his memory funded by the Adenhart Memorial Fund.

Adenhart is remembered in his hometown in various ways. He was buried a mile from Williamsport High in Greenlawn Memorial Park. The Williamsport High School gym prominently displays Adenhart's number 34 on the wall; and the grandstand behind home plate on the field where he excelled in high school has his name and number 11.

Nicholas James Adenhart Memorial Field has a picture of Adenhart in mid-delivery in an Angels uniform hung on the wall in right field. Signs on the concession stand at the Halfway fields recognizing past Division I champions include Adenhart's 1998 and 1999 teams listing full rosters and coaching staff. And every year in late May the Nick Adenhart 5K is run in Williamsport to raise money for local youth programs.

SOURCES

In addition to the sources cited in the Notes, the author consulted www.baseball-reference.com, www.ancestry.com, and the Nick Adenhart player file at the National Baseball Hall of Fame Library. The author is particularly grateful for the time granted by David Warrenfeltz and Bob Parasiliti in Williamsport, Maryland.

Halfway Little League (https://www.leaguelineup.com/topnews.asp?url=halfwayll&itemid=369534)

Find a Grave (https://www.findagrave.com/memorial/35686684/nick-adenhart)

Mike Matthews, "Laffey vs. Adenhart: A Battle to the Finish, a Game for the Ages," *Cumberland Times-News*, May 13, 2003. Accessed online October 6, 2021, at https://www.times-news.com/sports/local_sports/laffey-vs-adenhart-a-battle-to-the-finish-a-game-for-the-ages/article_27d6f20c-769b-52fd-9075-9633205bc3e6.html

Mike Matthews, "Allegany: 1 Run, 0 Hits, 1 Victory," *Cumberland Times-News*, May 13, 2003. Accessed online October 6, 2021, at https://www.times-news.com/sports/local_sports/allegany-1-run-0-hits-1-victory/article_f0dbeedf-d1e7-5e84-9244-931047571bbe.html

Cedar Rapids Community Scholarship (https://www.milb.com/cedar-rapids/community/adenhart-scholarship)

Nick Adenhart 5K (https://runsignup.com/Race/MD/Williamsport/NickAdenhart5K)

NOTES

1. Author interview with David Warrenfeltz on May 22, 2021. Unless otherwise attributed, all direct quotations come from this interview.

2. Rick Maese, "Remembering Nick Adenhart," *Baltimore Sun*, April 16, 2009. Accessed October 6, 2021, at https://www.baltimoresun.com/bs-mtblog-2009-04-remembering_nick_adenhart-story.html.

3. Maese, "Remembering Nick Adenhart."

4. Dan Steinberg, "When You Get a Good Kid ... It's Sad," *Washington Post*, May 29, 2004. Accessed October 6, 2021, at https://www.washingtonpost.com/archive/sports/2004/05/29/when-you-get-a-good-kid-its-sad/843a5519-d63c-4eb2-baf3-77f231f75a85/.

5. Rick Maese, "Back Home, There's No Letting Go of Adenhart," *Baltimore Sun*, April 11, 2009: 17.

6. Steinberg, "When You Get a Good Kid ... It's Sad."

7. Steinberg, "When You Get a Good Kid ... It's Sad."

8. Roch Kubatko, "Top Prospect Adenhart to Have Elbow Surgery," *Baltimore Sun*, May 22, 2004: 5C.

9. Mike DiGiovanna, "Moreno: Price May Be Too High for Johnson," *Los Angeles Times*, July 27, 2004: D5.

10. Jim Ecker, "Special Funds Keeps Adenhart's Memory Alive," perfectgame.org. Accessed October 6, 2021, at https://www.perfectgame.org/Articles/View.aspx?article=4871&mode=full.

11. Rich Lederer, "Nick Adenhart: A Rising Star (Once Again)," baseballanalysts.com. Accessed October 6, 2021, at http://baseballanalysts.com/archives/2006/07/nick_adenhart.php.

12. Mike DiGiovanna, "Angels Report," *Los Angeles Times*, April 28, 2008: D7.

13. Mike DiGiovanna, "Angels' Rookie Has Wild Debut," *Los Angeles Times*, May 2, 2008: D1.

14. Bill Shaikin, "Angels FYI," *Los Angeles Times*, June 15, 2008: D12.

15. A quote widely attributed in the following days' reports with subtle variations.

16. In December 2010 Gallo was sentenced to 51 years to life in prison.

17. Mike DiGiovanna, "Pitcher Had Fought Back After Injuries," *Los Angeles Times*, April 10, 2009: A26.

18. As of 2021, the winners of the Adenhart Award have been Weaver (2009-2012), C.J. Wilson (2013), Garrett Richards (2014), Huston Street (2015), Matt Shoemaker (2016), Yusmeiro Petit (2017), Andrew Heaney (2018), Hansel Robles (2019), Dylan Bundy (2020), and Shohei Ohtani (2021, 2022).

19. Kevin Baxter, "Painful Anniversary for Angels," *Los Angeles Times*, April 9, 2010: C6.

FRED APPLEGATE

BY PHIL WILLIAMS

Frederick Romaine Applegate, who won one of three decisions pitching for the Philadelphia Athletics in 1904, was born on May 9, 1879. His father, James, emigrated from England to America in 1871. James settled in Williamsport, Pennsylvania's timber-industry hub, where he worked as a grocer. In April 1878 he married New York native Mary Williams.[1] The newlyweds moved to Tarport, a village just east of Bradford, Pennsylvania, where James opened a grocery.[2] Fred arrived a year later.[3] The family had returned by 1883, settling south of the Susquehanna River, an area soon incorporated as South Williamsport.[4] Eight years later a second son, James, arrived.

Fred Applegate's baseball career first gained attention in 1894, as he pitched for the Burlingame Juniors.[5] Locals nicknamed him Snitz, after the Pennsylvania Dutch treat of dried apples.[6] Williamsport possessed a thriving baseball scene and, in the years ahead, Applegate honed his skills alongside Jimmy Sebring, Bucky Veil and Johnny Lush. A genial sort, who eventually gained a reputation as "a real humorist," Applegate played football alongside these mates during the fall and hunted with them in the winter.[7] The right-hander grew into a 6-foot-2, 180-pound frame.

By 1899, Williamsport's Demorest Manufacturing Company employed Snitz as a machinist. He also starred as their team's pitcher.[8] Prior to the Demorests' season-opener, at Lewisburg on April 15 vs. Bucknell University, Applegate cut his left hand on the job.[9] Bandaged, he played left field and pitched in relief the next day. Bucknell, with Christy Mathewson starting in the box, romped, 12-4.[10] Two weeks later in Williamsport, Applegate bested Mathewson, 7-6.[11]

Blood poisoning sent Applegate to the hospital in June. Whether this was attributable to a re-infection or a new injury is unclear. Applegate returned home by late July, but typhoid fever returned him to the hospital for nearly two months. In November, doctors amputated his right little finger to address its "chronic affliction."[12]

For the next two seasons, Applegate played company or semipro ball in Billtown (as Williamsport residents often called their city) or in nearby towns. Then, in April 1902, he signed with the North Carolina League's New Bern Truckers.[13] Applegate was winless in five decisions before New Bern released him in May. The circuit's Charlotte team promptly signed him.[14] With Applegate's assistance, the Hornets won 25 games in a row before disbanding on July 9.[15] Applegate then signed with Newark, the Eastern League's cellar dwellers, went 1-5, and was released.[16]

Applegate began the 1903 campaign with the Eastern League's Worcester Riddlers. In late June, adrift in the standings and seeking to raise capital, Worcester sold Applegate and Charlie Frisbee to the New Orleans Pelicans of the Southern League for $1,500.[17] On August 17 Applegate told skipper Zeke Wrigley he was too overworked to take the ball that afternoon in Memphis. The last-place Pelicans released the pitcher. Memphis picked him up, and he pitched sporadically for the first-place Egyptians. Applegate's 1903 ledger: 5-4 with Worcester and a combined 4-12-1 with New Orleans and Memphis.[18]

Despite the unimpressive beginning to his professional career, Applegate demonstrated potential. Employing a side-arm crossfire delivery, he used "speed across the inside corner mixed with springy shoots that slant across the outer edges of the plate."[19] Observers consistently noted the effectiveness of his drop curve.[20] He only lacked control. "Applegate is the great untamed," a Worcester sportswriter commented. "He is the wildest there is that isn't behind bars."[21]

Applegate returned to the Eastern League in 1904, signing with Toronto in February. His first start, in Newark on May 4, did not bode well: Despite allowing only three singles, he walked four in the fifth inning and suffered a 5-1 defeat. But Applegate pitched better that summer, three-hitting Jersey City en route to a 2-1 win on July 30 and throwing a two-hit shutout against Rochester on August 9.

Meanwhile, Connie Mack's Philadelphia Athletics were battling for the AL pennant. In mid-August Chief Bender and Eddie Plank missed time to illness, and Rube Waddell and Weldon Henley tired picking up the extra starts. Mack recalled Andy Coakley and Jim Fairbank. For a reported $2,000, he also purchased Applegate from Toronto, with an understanding that the pitcher would report to the Athletics on September 29.[22]

Applegate went 1-5 with Toronto in September, to finish 1904 with a 12-16 record for the 67-71 Maple Leafs.[23] He joined the Mackmen during a lengthy season-concluding road trip. When they ventured into Detroit's Bennett Park on September 30, the Athletics were out of the race, in fifth place, 9½ games behind the Boston Americans.[24] It was the fourth of nine doubleheaders the season's final two weeks held for them.

In the first game on September 30, Detroit's defense gave Plank a victory. In the second, Applegate took the mound. His wildness surfaced in the second inning, as a hit batsman, a single, and a walk loaded the bases. Applegate retired his rookie pitching counterpart, Charlie Jaeger, for the third out. In the next inning, he wasn't so fortunate: His two walks fueled a four-run frame. The Athletics rallied in the seventh to cut the Tigers' lead to 5-4. Umpire Tommy Connolly then called the game as darkness overtook the field.[25]

Three days later, at Cleveland's League Park, Coakley began another doubleheader by shutting down the Naps, 2-0. In the second game, Mack again handed Applegate the ball. Cleveland pounced upon his crossfire and capitalized on his wildness. After six innings, umpire Silk O'Loughlin sent the chilled crowd home in the dusk. Applegate's line in the 7-2 loss: 10 hits, a hit batsman, a wild pitch, two walks, all runs earned.[26]

Applegate's third start came in Washington on October 10, opening another twin bill. It was the season's final day. Via the "big blackboard in left field," fans followed the pennant-deciding doubleheader between Boston and New York as they humored their last-place Senators.[27] Applegate pitched scoreless ball for six innings as the Athletics, aided by one of his two hits in the game, put five runs across the plate in the fourth. Washington hit him hard in the final three frames – and Philadelphia's fielding behind him weakened – but he held on for a 7-6 victory. The Senators beat Waddell in the abbreviated second game, 4-3, concluding a dreadful 38-113 season.

The Athletics finished in fifth place, 12½ games behind Boston. After Applegate's start in Cleveland, Mack declared that "the loss of [Danny] Hoffman and Harry Davis put us out of the championship."[28] Certainly their absences hurt; both the dynamic young outfielder Hoffman (badly beaned on July 1) and the veteran field general Davis (a broken hand sliding into home on September 9) were among the league's OPS leaders when they were lost.

But a lack of pitching depth also characterized Philadelphia's 1904 campaign. After Waddell and Plank, who both set career highs in innings pitched, the staff was uncertain. In their sophomore seasons, neither Henley (15-17, with an ERA+ of 107) nor Bender (10-11, an ERA+ of 94) demonstrated great promise. Coakley (4-3, an ERA+ of 144) had not yet experienced a full major-league season's competition.

Consequently, Mack planned on bringing Applegate to spring training in March 1905.[29] Perhaps his delivery could be refined, his composure steadied, his wildness tamed. If not, he could be returned to Toronto.

Yet when Mack's contract reached him in Williamsport, Applegate balked at the offer, which was reportedly less than what Toronto had paid him in 1904.[30] Conveniently for the pitcher, the fledgling Tri-State League was outside the National Commission's orbit and had a well-backed Williamsport Millionaires franchise. Applegate agreed to terms with the Millionaires; then Toronto manager Dick Hartley visited him in Williamsport in March.[31] Several weeks later he signed a six-month Maple Leafs contract at $325 per month.[32] Mack, who had signed 20-year-old spitballer Jimmy Dygert in February, released Applegate to Toronto.[33]

Applegate pitched for Toronto for two months, compiling a 3-4 record. In early June, Williamsport manager Max Lindheimer recruited the pitcher back to the Millionaires fold, reportedly at a monthly salary of at least $350.[34] Billtown fans enjoyed a memorable summer. After beginning August in fourth place with a 43-37 record, their team roared to the pennant by winning 35 of its final 42 games.[35] Jimmy Sebring's midseason arrival provided the key spark. Lew Richie paced the staff with a 24-9 record.[36] Walter Manning came over from the Tri-State's Lebanon squad and won 15 straight for Williamsport.[37] Applegate, 8-7 with the Millionaires, was a lesser light.

Just before the Millionaires caught fire, Toronto sold Applegate's rights to the Boston Beaneaters.[38] Several months later, the National Commission confirmed Boston's rights to him, and the team announced plans to bring him to their 1906 spring training.[39] Applegate re-signed with Williamsport.[40]

After battling injuries early in the 1906 season, Applegate asked for and was granted a release from the Millionaires.[41] Several weeks later he signed with the Johnstown (Pennsylvania) Johnnies, one of Williamsport's Tri-State rivals.[42] He concluded the campaign with an overall 11-15 record.[43]

Fred Applegate played four seasons for the Toronto Maple Leafs.

In January 1907, negotiations brought the Tri-State League into Organized Baseball. Applegate was awarded to Toronto. The Leafs won the Eastern League pennant. Applegate, with a 9-9 record, added rotational depth. In a postseason series with the American Association's Columbus Senators, he won the fifth and deciding game.[44] Remaining with Toronto in 1908, Applegate contributed an 8-12 record as the team tumbled into sixth place.

Snitz started the 1909 season back with the Millionaires, but after an 0-2 beginning, he was released.[45] The New York State League Wilkes-Barre Barons picked him up. The Barons, like the 1905 Millionaires, caught fire to win the pennant. Languishing in seventh place with a 10-16 record on June 5, Wilkes-Barre went 78-37 the rest of the way. Unlike 1905 in Williamsport, Applegate drove this surge, leading the Barons' staff with a 22-7 record.[46]

For the 1910 season, Applegate returned to Wilkes-Barre. Then, in early 1911, he began to plan for a post-baseball career, purchasing 97 acres north of Williamsport to start a fruit orchard business and announcing his candidacy for county auditor.[47] He spent the 1911 summer in Nebraska, pitching for the Western League's Lincoln Railsplitters. He returned home that autumn to win, as a Republican in a mostly Democratic county, one of the three auditor seats.[48]

Applegate bounced around lesser teams over the next two seasons: Elmira (New York State League), York (Tri-State League), and Guelph (Canadian League) in 1912, Newport News (Virginia League) and Newburgh (New York-New Jersey League) in 1913. In 1914 he umpired in the Tri-State League.

In March 1915, Applegate married Mary Noll, a Williamsport native. The marriage did not produce any children. Applegate settled into a politician's life. In 1933 a taxpayers' committee accused several local officials, including Applegate, then a county commissioner, of misusing public funds for private home improvements.[49] The allegations cost Applegate re-election two years later.[50] He stayed active in his local fire department and Elks lodge. Mary died in 1962. Fred Applegate followed her on April 21, 1968, dying from heart disease in Williamsport. He rests in the city's Wildwood Cemetery.

SOURCES

In addition to the sources cited in the Notes, the author accessed Ancestry.com, the *Encyclopedia of Minor League Baseball*, and the following sites:

archive.org/details/orangeandblue_01_reel01

canadiana.ca

jvbrownpublic.advantage-preservation.com.

NOTES

1. "Married," *Williamsport Sun and Lycoming Democrat*, April 17, 1878: 5.
2. "Minor Locals," *Williamsport Sun and Lycoming Democrat*, June 12, 1878: 5. See also Luella A. Harris, "A History of Bradford, PA," *Back to Bradford*, www.backtobradford.com/HistoryOfBradford.pdf, accessed January 13, 2022.
3. His death certificate lists East Bradford as his birthplace.
4. This is the first post-1878 city directory in which James Applegate is listed.
5. "The Ball Field," *Williamsport Sun and Banner*, June 18, 1894: 1; "Demorest's Big Benefit," *Pennsylvania Grit* (Williamsport), July 29, 1894: 8.
6. For the origins of the nickname, see "Harrisburg Was Retarded," *Williamsport Sun*, August 9, 1905: 6.
7. "Sporting Review," *Lincoln* (Nebraska) *Star*, October 5, 1911: 9.
8. "Now for Baseball," *Williamsport Sun and Banner*, April 18, 1899: 1. For his employment as a machinist, see the 1899 Williamsport city directory.
9. "Has a Badly Cut Hand," *Pennsylvania Grit*, April 16, 1899: 1.
10. "Bucknell-Demorest," *Orange and Blue* (Bucknell student newspaper), April 18, 1899: 1.
11. "Demorest-Bucknell," *Orange and Blue*, May 2, 1899: 1.
12. For these events, see "South Williamsport Events," *Pennsylvania Grit*, July 16, 1899: 2; "South Side Notes," *Williamsport Evening News*, April 18, 1899: 4; "South Side," *Williamsport Sun and Banner*, September 23, 1899: 2; "South Williamsport Affairs," *Pennsylvania Grit*, November 5, 1899: 2.
13. "The Newbern Team," *Charlotte Observer*, April 13, 1902: 12.
14. "Wilmington Shut Out," *New Bern Observer*, July 1, 1902: 4; "Home Runs," *Charlotte News*, May 22, 1902: 5.
15. "They All Want Ashenback," *Charlotte Observer*, July 25, 1902: 6.
16. "Louis Bruce Is Premier Artist," *Worcester* (Massachusetts) *Spy*, September 22, 1902: 3; "Jersey City Club Defeated Buffalo," *Jersey City Journal*, August 2, 1902: 8.
17. "Two Go to New Orleans," *Pittsburgh Press*, June 25, 1903: 14.
18. Henry Chadwick, ed., *Spalding's Base Ball Guide 1904* (New York: American Sports Publishing Co., 1904), 148, 168.
19. "Pelicans Take Second," *New Orleans Times-Democrat*, July 30, 1903: 11; "Baseball Chat," *New Orleans Item*, July 20, 1903: 8.
20. "Eastern League Season Opens," *Jersey City Journal*, April 30, 1903: 9; "Pelicans Playing a Winning Game," *New Orleans Picayune*, July 21, 1903: 14.
21. "Sporting Notes," *Worcester Spy*, June 18, 1903: 2.
22. "Athletics Suffer a Setback," *Philadelphia North American*, August 29, 1904: 13; "Base Ball," *Philadelphia Item*, August 31, 1904: 4; "Right Off the Bat," *Buffalo Evening News*, September 1, 1904: 24.
23. Applegate's 1904 season record per Chadwick, *Spalding's Base Ball Guide 1905*, 163. Applegate's September ledger with Toronto: a 3-1 loss at Buffalo on September 2; a 6-4 loss vs. Montreal on September 6; a 6-2 loss vs. Buffalo on September 10; a 5-2 loss in Montreal on September 15; a 4-2 loss vs. Newark on September 22; and a 4-3 victory over Providence on September 26.

24 For more on the A's 1904 season, see Norman Macht, *Connie Mack and the Early Years of Baseball* (Lincoln: University of Nebraska Press, 2007), 325-332.
25 "Custom Called for Division," *Detroit Free Press*, October 1, 1904: 9.
26 "Winning Streak Was Broken," *Cleveland Plain Dealer*, October 4, 1904: 10; "Athletics Stop Winning Streak," *Cleveland Leader*, October 4, 1904: 8.
27 "Sports of All Sorts," *Washington Evening Star*, October 11, 1904: 9. See also, "Closed with Victory," *Washington Post*, October 11, 1904: 8.
28 "Notes of the Game," *Cleveland Plain Dealer*, October 4, 1904: 10.
29 "Mack's Athletics," *Williamsport Evening News*, December 1, 1904: 5; "Mack Will Take 22 Players to Train," *Philadelphia North American*, January 30, 1905: 4.
30 "Applegate May Stay," *Williamsport Evening News*, January 26, 1905: 5; "The Unjust Draft Rule," *Williamsport Evening News*, January 31, 1905: 8.
31 "Are After Our 'Snitz,'" *Williamsport Evening News*, March 15, 1905: 1.
32 "Promised Lindheimer," *Williamsport Evening News*, April 5, 1905: 1; "Applegate Has a Nice Contract," *Williamsport Sun*, April 8, 1905: 6.
33 "Hurrah! They Come to Toronto," *Toronto World*, April 13, 1905: 3.
34 "'Snitz' Joins Grays," *Williamsport Evening News*, June 7, 1905: 1; "Baseball Bunts from Many Sources," *Buffalo Evening News*, January 8, 1906: 10.
35 George M. Graham, "Millionaires Captured Thirty-Five Out of Forty-Two Games, Including Strings of Eight and Fourteen Consecutive Victories," *Philadelphia North American*, September 17, 1905: 13.
36 "A Few Season's Records," *Pennsylvania Grit*, September 17, 1905: 2.
37 "Manning Is Signed," *Pennsylvania Grit*, January 7, 1906: 2.
38 "Baseball Brevities," *Toronto World*, August 25, 1905: 3.
39 "Will Try Out Applegate," *Boston Globe*, November 18, 1905: 8.
40 "Local Stars Signed," *Pennsylvania Grit*, November 26, 1905: 2.
41 "Sporting News," *Williamsport Sun*, June 4, 1906: 6; "Tri-State Notes," *Williamsport Evening News*, June 5, 1906: 5.
42 "Sporting News," *Williamsport Sun*, June 27, 1906: 6.
43 "The Tri-State Averages," *Sporting Life*, January 5, 1907: 14.
44 "Class A Battle," *Sporting Life*, October 12, 1907: 17.
45 Applegate's 1909 Williamsport record per Francis C. Richter, ed., *The Reach Official American League Base Ball Guide for 1910* (Philadelphia: A.J. Reach Co., 1910), 283. For his release, "Evidence Will Show Carpenter Decision Wrong," *Williamsport Evening News*, June 16, 1909: 1.
46 "Applegate Leading Pitcher in League," *Wilkes-Barre Times Leader*, September 29, 1909: 16.
47 "Social Realm and Social Mention," *Williamsport Sun*, March 22, 1911: 10; "South Side," *Williamsport Gazette and Bulletin*, March 7, 1911: 6.
48 "Samuel Stabler Next Mayor of Williamsport," *Williamsport News*, November 8, 1911: 1.
49 "Says Officials Used Fund to Improve Homes," *Wilkes-Barre Evening News*, February 4, 1933: 3.
50 "Offices Are Divided in Lycoming County," *Scranton Tribune*, November 7, 1935: 3.

PHILLIPPE AUMONT

BY CLAYTON TRUTOR

Phillippe Aumont pitched in 46 big-league games over the course of four seasons for the Philadelphia Phillies (2012-2015). A tall (6-feet-7), powerfully-built (265 pounds), and hard-throwing (fastball in the high 90s) right-hander, Aumont is as of 2022 the player from Quebec selected highest in the amateur free-agent draft. The Seattle Mariners made the 18-year-old hurler from Gatineau, Quebec, the 11th overall selection in the first round of the 2007 draft. Aumont pitched professionally for 13 years, spending time in the Mariners, Detroit Tigers, Toronto Blue Jays, and Chicago White Sox organizations as well as for the Phillies, where he completed the entirety of his major-league service. He worked almost exclusively as a relief pitcher for the Phillies, starting just one game in his career. Aumont posted a 1-6 career record with an ERA of 6.80 during a major-league career highlighted not only by his status as an important milestone holder in Canadian baseball history but also the 2012 and 2013 campaigns, when he served as a key stopper in Philadelphia's bullpen.

Aumont was born on January 7, 1989, in Gatineau, a city of more than 275,000 that sits across the Ottawa River from Canada's capital city. The future major leaguer grew up in a working-class Francophone neighborhood and was raised primarily by his father, Jean-Pierre Aumont, who worked as a laborer for a moving company.[1]

"Where I come from, we speak French. English is something you start to learn in school and past that, nobody really uses it," Aumont said of his upbringing in a 2021 interview.[2] He spent most of his time as a young man outside, playing with other children from his neighborhood. At age 11, he started playing baseball competitively and soon joined up with Canada's national baseball program, playing in junior tournaments across North America. As Aumont grew during his adolescence, the baseball-mad teenager started to draw interest from baseball scouts.

"My style of pitching was more power pitching than anything else. I never wanted you to touch the ball. All I was shooting for was a strikeout. Period," Aumont said.[3] His size and strength helped make his approach to pitching highly successful.

"My high-school career was great. I won many trophies and many medals," Aumont recalled.[4] As a junior in high school, he first realized that scouts were following his games closely, but this came as a surprise to him despite his success.

"I had no vision on going further and playing pro. The dream wasn't really something I had coming up. I love to compete and when I do, I always want to win," Aumont said.[5]

When the Mariners made Aumont their first-round pick in 2007, selecting him from high school (Ecole du Versant in Gatineau), it was a significant milestone in the baseball history of Quebec. Never before had a native son of La Belle Province been selected so highly in the first round. The most recent Quebecer selected in the first round previous to Aumont was Ntema Ndungidi of Montreal, an outfielder selected 36th overall in the 1997 draft by the Baltimore Orioles. Only two previous Canadians, pitchers Adam Loewen and Jeff Francis (both selected in 2002), had been selected higher than Aumont in baseball's amateur draft.

"I had great support locally. People were really happy about it and I certainly gained a little bit more fame," Aumont said of the experience.[6]

The Mariners, too, were excited to get their hands on the robust young prospect.

"The first time I saw him last summer, he was throwing 92-93 [MPH] at the time, with the makings of a slider and some sink on his fastball," Mariners scout Dave May said of Aumont to the *Seattle Times*. "This spring, he was up to 96 on his fastball with heavy sink and his slider got better. With him getting better and better, I think he has one of the highest ceilings of anyone in this draft."[7]

Aumont signed with the Mariners and progressed rapidly in their minor-league organization. At just 20 years of age, he advanced to Double A, spending much of the summer of 2009 with the West Tennessee Diamond Jaxx of the Southern League. The trajectory of Aumont's career changed in December 2009 when he was one of three players (the other two being minor-league outfielder Tyson Gillies and pitcher JC Ramírez) sent to the Philadelphia Phillies in exchange for 2008 Cy Young Award winner Cliff Lee. The trade didn't really pan out for either club. Lee spent less than half a season in Seattle while Aumont, Ramírez, and Gillies all failed to turn into long-term big leaguers.

For the next three seasons, Aumont bounced around the Philadelphia organization before debuting for the Phillies on August 23, 2012. In 2010 the Phillies organization tried Aumont out as a starter in Double-A Reading with little success. In 2011 he made a combined 43 relief appearances in Reading and Triple-A Lehigh Valley with much greater success. Before making his big-league debut in August, Aumont was again a stalwart in Lehigh Valley's bullpen, making 41 appearances with an ERA of 4.26.

Aumont recalled the jitters he felt when he entered his first major-league game at Citizens Bank Park. He came in for the eighth inning against the Cincinnati Reds.

"The gut feeling when you get the phone call in the bullpen to start warming up. The adrenaline kicks in and it just feels surreal," Aumont recalled.[8] The 23-year-old rookie did great in his debut, pitching a scoreless inning while surrendering a walk to Miguel Cairo. The Phillies went on to win 4-3 in 11 innings that evening.[9] Aumont's strong debut presaged a strong rookie campaign. Over the next two months, he made 18 appearances for Philadelphia, earning two saves and garnering a 3.68 ERA as a middle reliever.

The Gatineau native split the 2013 between Triple-A Lehigh Valley (International League) and Philadelphia. He again performed admirably for the Phillies, making a career-high 22 appearances, all in relief. In 2013, Aumont had a 4.19 ERA for the season and a 1-3 overall record.

Aumont gained his first and only career victory on April 12, 2013, against the Miami Marlins. He entered a 1-1 game in the bottom of the ninth inning at Marlins Park and faced three batters. He retired Plácido Polanco on a groundout, walked Justin Ruggiano, and got Greg Dobbs to hit into a double play. Chase Utley and Michael Young drove in runs for the Phils in the top of the 10th and Jonathan Papelbon finished off Miami in the bottom of the inning, earning the save to Aumont's win.

"I came out, did my job to put up a zero on the board and we scored the next inning with Papelbon closing it out," Aumont recalled.[10]

For whatever reason, Aumont could never break out of his status as a borderline big-league pitcher in the Philadelphia organization. Both at the major- and minor-league levels, he had a tendency to give up walks and home runs – both were certainly a product of his power-pitching approach to the game. The 2014 and 2015 seasons proved to be particularly frustrating ones for Aumont. During both campaigns, he pitched well for Lehigh Valley but struggled in his rare appearances at the major-league level.

In all, Aumont made just five appearances for the Phillies in 2014, posting an ERA of 19.06 for the season. In 2015 he made just one major-league appearance.

On June 19, 2015, Aumont started his first game in the majors. He surrendered six earned runs to the St. Louis Cardinals in four innings, taking the loss in a 12-4 Cards win. The defeat proved to be not only Aumont's first career start but also his final major-league appearance and his only appearance of the 2015 major-league season. The Phillies released Aumont shortly thereafter, thus beginning a more than half-decade odyssey throughout Organized Baseball.

On June 28, 2015, Aumont signed with the Toronto Blue Jays and made five appearances for the Buffalo Bisons, the club's Triple-A affiliate. Toronto released him in late August. He joined the Chicago White Sox organization during the offseason and spent the first half of the 2016 campaign with the Triple-A Charlotte Knights before being released. In 2017 Aumont returned to his old stamping grounds, pitching for the Ottawa Champions of the independent Canadian-American Association.

The Detroit Tigers were sufficiently impressed with Aumont's performance in Ottawa to sign him to a minor-league contract in January 2018. The then 29-year-old pitcher spent the vast majority of the season with the Triple-A Toledo Mud Hens and was released after the season.

After his release by the Tigers, Aumont re-signed with Ottawa of the Canadian-American Association in 2019 and enjoyed a renaissance season. Working exclusively as a starter, he was named the league's Pitcher of the Year, going 8-4 with a 2.65 ERA. In one outing, Aumont struck out a league-record 18 batters.[11] His production in 2019 earned Aumont another opportunity to make it back to the big leagues.

In December 2019 Aumont signed with the Toronto Blue Jays and gave it another shot in spring training. Before Major League Baseball shut down due to the COVID-19 pandemic in mid-March of 2020, Aumont made two appearances for the Blue Jays in spring training. Amid the shutdown, he decided to retire from baseball and pursue family farming on a farmstead just outside Gatineau. As of the June 2021 interview, he and his wife, Frederique, were still settling into the 12-hour workday on the farm.

"This is our first year growing crops in greenhouses. We plan to grow fully organic in high tunnels and outside in the fields within the next three to five years," Aumont said of his life after baseball. "We want to create a bit of an ecosystem on the farm where we can develop self-sufficiency and also feed our community with organic foods and get away from industrial chemicals foods."[12]

Looking back on his big-league career, Aumont said he felt a great sense of pride.

"From where I come from to where I am now, not many people in the world can say they did and experienced what I did. I'm proud to be part of that."[13]

Phillippe Aumont won his game during four seasons with the Philadelphia Phillies. Courtesy of Phillippe Aumont.

NOTES

1. Phillippe Aumont, interview by the author, June 14, 2021; David Singh, "Why Phillipe Aumont Gave Up Pro Baseball to Become a Pitcher," Sportsnet, September 13, 2020. Accessed September 14, 2020: https://www.sportsnet.ca/mlb/longform/phillippe-aumont-gave-pro-baseball-become-farmer/.

2. Aumont interview.

3   Aumont interview.
4   Aumont interview.
5   Aumont interview.
6   Aumont interview.
7   Scott Hanson, "M's Pick Up Aumont at No. 11," Seattle Times, June 8, 2007. Accessed on September 14, 2020: https://www.seattletimes.com/sports/ms-pick-up-aumont-at-no-11/.
8   Aumont interview.
9   "Phillies Slip Past Reds in 11th on RBI Single from John Mayberry Jr.," ESPN.com, August 23, 2012. Accessed September 14, 2020: https://www.espn.com/mlb/recap?gameId=320823122.
10 Aumont interview.
11 "Champions Hurler Sets Single-Game Strikeout Record," CBC.com, July 17, 2019. Accessed September 14, 2021: https://www.cbc.ca/news/canada/ottawa/phillippe-aumont-gatineau-strikeout-record-champions-1.5214601.
12 Aumont interview.
13 Aumont interview.

JOHN BAKER

BY SEAN KOLODZIEJ

The Chicago Cubs have a long history of famous games. There was "Merkle's boner," which helped the Cubs eventually win the 1908 NL pennant. There was also Babe Ruth's called shot, which helped the Cubs eventually lose the 1932 World Series. "The Homer in the Gloamin'" is one of the most famous home runs in baseball history. The "Ryne Sandberg Game" helped put the 1984 Cubs in the national spotlight. Unfortunately, the "Bartman Game" helped put the 2003 Cubs in the national spotlight for all the wrong reasons. Then, of course, there is the "John Baker Game" – the game where the backup catcher got the win.

John David Baker was born on January 20, 1981, in Alameda, California, to David and Stephanie Baker. Both parents have master's degrees from Stanford, his mother in philosophy and his father in business. He is the oldest of three children.

John's father, David, played baseball growing up and was drafted out of high school in the 36th round of the 1972 free-agent draft by the Los Angeles Dodgers. Electing to go to Stanford University instead, he was then drafted in the sixth round of the 1975 draft by the Philadelphia Phillies. He was a catcher in their minor-league system for the 1975 and 1976 seasons, playing as high as Double A before settling in to a career as a CPA.

Because of his father's history with playing baseball, the game played a prominent role in John's childhood. "It was a sport that I grew up playing as a kid," he once said. "My dad played baseball and some of my earliest memories are of my dad playing softball as a kid in Walnut Creek, California. It was always a game I enjoyed."[1] His father would hang a Wiffle Ball from a tree in their backyard, and right after John could walk, he was hitting that ball with a Wiffle Ball bat. His father coached his T-ball team when John was 4 years old and continued coaching his teams all the way up to and including his high-school team.[2]

The Oakland Athletics were John's favorite team growing up. After his grandfather retired from the Pacific Bell phone company, he worked in concessions at the Oakland Coliseum. His family would go to the ballpark often and he could name every member of the 1980s Athletics teams.[3] As a left-handed hitter, John's favorite player was Will Clark.[4] He loved watching Clark swing the bat left-handed. But Clark, a six-time All-Star, played in San Francisco. Though he collected all of Clark's baseball cards, he was the only San Francisco Giants player that John liked.[5]

Baker graduated from De La Salle High School in Concord, California, in 1999 as the class salutatorian with a 4.0 grade-point average. On the baseball field, he was a pitcher and played a lot of first base. He had a .433 batting average and earned All-Bay Valley Athletic League honors as a junior and a senior.

After high school, Baker signed up to go to UCLA for political science. He wanted to go to law school. Baseball was "always something I did on the side. I always focused on school," he said.[6] He felt he was never the best player on any of his baseball teams.[7] But a phone call from Dave Esquer, the new baseball coach at the University of California, Berkeley, convinced him otherwise.

"He called me and said I think you have a good enough swing to play college baseball and how would you like to go to Cal and play? That was fantastic, as I lived 20 to 25 minutes away from Berkeley. I walked into his office and he said have you played catcher before? I said not really and he said, well, here's the gear. We'll teach you how to play catcher."[8] Baker practiced every chance he had, and once caught both games of a doubleheader.[9]

Baker majored in American Studies. "I definitely enjoyed my classes," he said. "I did not feel like baseball got in the way."[10] Based on his statistics, it doesn't seem that his classes got in the way of baseball either. It also helped that he could now see properly. During his senior year in high school, his baseball coach, thinking Baker had a vision problem, recommended that he go to an ophthalmologist. It turned out that his vision was so bad that he wasn't legally supposed to be driving. The first at-bat he had with glasses on, he hit a home run over the center-field fence.[11]

As a junior in 2002, Baker led the Pac-10 with a .383 batting average and was selected to the All-Pac-10 team. He spent his summers playing for the Yarmouth-Dennis Red Sox of the Cape Cod Baseball League.

While playing on Cape Cod, Baker realized he had a chance to play professional baseball. He was surrounded by the best prospects in the country and he was playing great. He wasn't supposed to catch there, but Yarmouth-Dennis's top catching prospect broke his ankle and the other catcher on the team had a sore arm, so Baker ended up catching 40 games in a row.[12]

On June 4, 2002, Baker was drafted by the Oakland A's in the fourth round of the amateur draft. This draft was immortalized in the book *Moneyball*.[13] Baker is mentioned several times in the book; he was one of the players targeted by the Oakland A's to draft.

Since he grew up as an A's fan, being drafted by them was one of the biggest thrills of Baker's life. He was also really enjoying his time at college, so he wasn't sure if he should finish his senior year or go play professional baseball. After going through a workout with the A's, though, he knew he was going to choose baseball over college.[14] He officially signed with the team on June 28.

Later that year, Baker made his professional debut at Vancouver in the short-season Class-A Northwest League. He hit .235 with one home run and 13 RBIs while playing in 39 games. The biggest adjustment for him there was that he was now surrounded by international players. Seated near a player from the Dominican Republic, Baker tried his hardest to speak with him, with what little Spanish he knew at the time. For two days he struggled to communicate, but still tried his hardest. On the third day, the other player said, "Hey, I speak English." He had tested Baker to see what he was really like. That other player was Nelson Cruz, and they became good friends.[15]

In 2003 Baker split his first full professional season between Class-A Kane County (Midwest League) and Double-A Midland (Texas League). In all, he hit .286 with 7 home runs and 70 RBIs in 125 games. That batting average was good enough to rank 11th among all minor-league catchers.

Baker spent most of 2004 in Double-A Midland, but was promoted to Triple-A Sacramento (Pacific Coast League) on August 13. He combined at both stops to hit .287 with 15 home runs and 88 RBIs in 131 games. That batting average was once again ranked 11th among all minor-league catchers. He appeared in three playoff games for Sacramento. He went hitless in five at-bats, but walked twice and scored three runs.

Baker learned a lot at his time in Sacramento. Webster Garrison and Brian McArn were two coaches who went out of their way to make sure the players felt supported, no matter what happened on the field. They were two of the first people Baker reached out to when he was eventually called up to the major leagues.[16]

After the 2004 minor-league season, Baker played for the Arizona Fall League champion Phoenix Desert Dogs. He hit .318 in 18 games.

Baker's entire 2005 season was spent at Triple-A Sacramento. He hit .234 with 5 home runs and 41 RBIs in 103 games. He threw out 28 of 96 attempted basestealers and made only four errors, good for a .995 fielding percentage.

After that 2005 performance, Baker had an eventful offseason. On December 15 he was selected off waivers by the Florida Marlins. Less than a month later, on January 5, 2006, he was back in the Oakland A's organization, as they selected him off waivers from the Marlins. This experience taught Baker that baseball was a business. He was actually designated the day before his wedding and was claimed by the Marlins while on his honeymoon. He had met his wife, Meghan, while they both attended De La Salle High School.[17]

In 2006 Baker was invited to the A's spring training. He wasn't sent down to the minor leagues until the very end of camp. He spent the entire season at Triple-A Sacramento. He batted .273 with 4 home runs and 38 RBIs in 83 games, and tossed out 25 of 90 attempted basestealers.

On March 30, 2007, Baker was traded to the Marlins for Jason Stokes. Stokes was a first baseman who battled wrist problems and other injuries throughout his career. This trade ended up helping Baker greatly because he was able to be coached by Tim Cossins. Cossins changed his approach to catching. "Without Tim, I would have never played a day in the major leagues," Baker said.

Baker played at Triple-A Albuquerque for the 2007 season. He hit .285 with 8 home runs and 41 RBIs in 89 games. After the season, Baker worked at St. Isidore School in Danville and volunteered with youth baseball programs in Lafayette and the Livermore-Castro Valley area.[18]

Baker began the 2008 campaign with Triple-A Albuquerque. He was named to the PCL all-star team after batting .321 with 6 home runs and 31 RBIs in 59 games. He was called up to the Marlins on July 9, 2008, after Florida catcher Matt Treanor went on the disabled list.

In his second major-league game, on July 10, Baker became the 10th Marlins player to hit a home run for his first major-league hit. He did this in Los Angeles against the Dodgers' Chan-Ho Park. He also doubled in the game, finishing with two runs and an RBI.

That day is a day that Baker will never forget. He had to remind himself to move his legs as he rounded the bases on his home run. After he got to the dugout, Luis Gonzalez said to Baker, "Hey, 499 more of those and you'll have a good career."[19]

John Baker broke in with the Marlins, winning his game during his seventh big-league season.
Courtesy The Topps Company, Inc.

Baker was kept on the Marlins' roster for the rest of the 2008 season and ended up hitting .299 with 5 home runs and 32 RBIs in 61 games (54 starts.) He drew 30 walks while striking out 48 times, and finished with a .392 OBP.

Baker platooned with Ronny Paulino for the 2009 season. Baker played against right-handed pitchers while Paulino generally played against left-handed pitchers. Baker started 99 games behind the plate and posted a .271 average with 9 home runs and 50 RBIs. His five home runs in May tied for the most home runs that month by an NL catcher. He batted .319 with runners in scoring position, which ranked second among NL catchers.

On May 3 the Marlins played the Cubs at Wrigley Field. Baker's grandfather, Arthur, flew out from California to Chicago to see him play. Baker hit a home run off Carlos Mármol. As he rounded second base, he saw the fan who caught the home-run ball throw it back onto the field. This was a highlight for him. After the game, he was able to hug his grandfather, who had seen him play at every level of baseball. To have him see this home run at Wrigley Field was special.[20]

In January of 2010, Baker went on an eight-day trip to Kuwait and Iraq with other Marlins personnel. The group visited US troops, saw the Iran border, and met Kuwaiti Little Leaguers. He wanted to go see for himself what it was like for these soldiers.[21]

After returning, Baker wrote in a letter to the *Miami Herald*, "I made a commitment … to do the best I could to support veterans in our community."[22] During spring training, he spent time with residents of the Stand Down House in Palm Beach County. He provided tickets for veterans to come out to games and he spent time with them at the ballpark.

Baker saw very limited playing time in the 2010 season. On May 13 he was placed on the 15-day disabled list with a strained flexor tendon in his right arm. It ended up being a season-ending injury, and Baker had Tommy John surgery on his right elbow in September.

While on the disabled list, Baker was part of a Marlins contingent that traveled to Haiti in July to visit families affected by an earthquake that struck earlier in the year. He then served as the spokesman for the Marlins Homes for Haiti campaign, which helped raise funds to build a 25-home village just outside of Port-au-Prince.

In September of 2010, Baker was named the Marlins' nominee for the Roberto Clemente Award, given annually to the major leaguer who combines a dedication to giving back to the community with outstanding skills on the baseball field. He said, "I am incredibly honored to be mentioned in the same sentence as the great Roberto Clemente. I wear the number 21 proudly in his honor."[23] As of 2021, Baker was on the board of a charity called Lost Boyz, Inc., which seeks "to decrease violence, improve the social and emotional conditions, and provide financial opportunities among the youth in Chicago's South Shore community."[24]

Most of Baker's 2011 season was spent rehabbing. After the Tommy John surgery, his arm hurt for a few more years and he would never feel the same way when swinging a bat.[25] He rejoined the Marlins in September, and made 16 appearances as a pinch-hitter.

On November 22, 2011, Baker was traded to the Padres for Wade LeBlanc. "We believe John fits well into our catching situation," Padres GM Josh Byrnes said.[26] "As a left-handed hitter with a good history of getting on base, he will provide us with depth and will help balance the roster from a left-right perspective."[27] Baker was also happy about the trade. His friends on the Marlins were all the leaving the team, and he felt the organization was in disarray, going through a lot of coaches and managers.[28]

For the 2012 season, Baker mainly served as a backup to Padres catchers Nick Hundley and Yasmani Grandal. He played in 63 games, hitting .238 with no home runs and 14 RBIs. He enjoyed his time in San Diego. He loved living in the city and playing at Petco Park.[29]

At San Diego, Baker started to catch with one knee down. He realized that it gave the umpire a tougher look at the bottom of the strike zone, and the pitchers were getting more called strikes. It started when Huston Street told Baker to put his knee on the ground and hold his glove out with two strikes.[30] This style of catching is becoming more popular today.

Baker made the Padres team coming out of spring training of 2013 mainly because Grandal was serving a 50-game suspension for testing positive for a high testosterone level. On May 28, the day Grandal returned to the Padres, Baker was optioned to the Triple-A Tucson Padres. After he played just four games there, the Padres designated him for assignment.

Needing catching depth, the Los Angeles Dodgers claimed Baker off waivers on June 15 and optioned him to Triple A Albuquerque. Baker struggled there, hitting just .203 in 40 games. On August 5, the Dodgers cut Baker from their 40-man roster and he became a free agent on October 1.

On December 18, 2013, Baker signed a minor-league deal with the Chicago Cubs, with an invitation to spring training. At spring training, Baker won a roster spot as a backup catcher to Welington Castillo. He batted only .192 with no home runs and 15 RBIs in 68 games. But one game stood out for him – the game that has become known in Cubs' history as "The John Baker Game."

The Cubs played the Colorado Rockies on July 29. The game lasted 16 innings and ended up taking 6 hours and 27 minutes to complete; through the 2021 season it remained the Cubs' longest game by time. Notably, after the Cubs used all of their available relief pitchers, Baker was called upon in the 16th inning to pitch. According to him, he pitched the world's worst batting practice.[31] But not only did he get out of the top half of the inning allowing no runs (he retired the Rockies on a pop foul, a walk, and a double play), he himself walked to start the bottom of the 16th and came around to score the winning run on a sacrifice fly.

In his only major-league pitching appearance, John Baker, a backup catcher, was credited with the win and became the first position player to earn a win for the Cubs since Fred Pfeffer in 1885. His career pitching stats are 1-0, 0.00 ERA.

Every July 29 is now known as John Baker Day to Cubs fans. There is always an organized event he attends which includes raffles and live music. The proceeds go to charity. Past charities have included the Hazleton Integration Project and the Chicago Metropolitan Battered Women's Network.

Even with those unblemished pitching stats, the Cubs did not re-sign Baker after the 2014 season. He was released on December 2, 2014. Theo Epstein, then president of baseball operations with the Cubs, told Baker that whenever he was done playing, there would be a home for him with the Cubs.[32]

Baker then signed a minor-league deal with the Seattle Mariners on January 29, 2015, and started the season playing for the Triple-A Tacoma Rainiers. After playing just 17 games and hitting .161 with no home runs and five RBIs, the organization tried to put him on the disabled list even though he was not injured. After explaining to the team that he wanted to play baseball and not just watch, he was released on May 20. After receiving a few minor-league offers that he felt would go nowhere, Baker decided that he was done playing professional baseball.[33]

Once Baker stopped playing baseball, he needed something to pursue physically. He started competing in Brazilian Jiu-Jitsu. As of 2021, he had achieved a purple belt, with hopes of achieving a black belt.[34]

At the end of 2015, Baker rejoined the Cubs organization as a baseball operations assistant. True to his word, Theo Epstein hired him once Baker's playing career ended. He rose through the organization, serving as a mental skills coordinator from 2017 to 2019, and becoming head mental skills coach in 2020. He also went back to school, receiving his bachelor's degree in liberal science from Arizona State University and his master's degree in performance psychology from National University.

On November 10, 2020, Baker was hired to be the Pittsburgh Pirates director of coaching and player development. Going from the big-budget Cubs to a smaller-market Pirates team had its challenges. But Baker was up for the task. "I like to chase challenges, and this seemed like the appropriate challenge with the appropriate people," he said. "I really feel like we can do some cool things."[35] Baker uses his degree in performance psychology to help guide the players in the Pirates organization. He likes to always think what is best for the person. "We don't like to say these are baseball players, we like to say these are people who play baseball."[36]

After the 2021 season, Baker began to prepare for the 2022 season. According to MLB Pipeline, the Pirates' minor-league system ranked in baseball's top five.[37] The expectations for 2022 were to do better than in 2021. But Baker said he doesn't want to be trapped into having the same mindset: "We can't let success get in the way of improvement."

SOURCES

In addition to the sources cited in the Notes, the author consulted baseball-reference.com and Retrosheet.org.

NOTES

1. TwistNHook, "CGB Interviews Former Golden Bear and Current Florida Marlin, John Baker," *California Golden Blogs*, CGB Interviews Former Golden Bear And Current Florida Marlin, John Baker Part I – California Golden Blogs, June 14, 2010, accessed May 11, 2021.
2. John Baker, Zoom interview with author, October 24, 2021. Unless otherwise attributed, all direct quotations are from this interview.
3. Author interview with John Baker.
4. "CGB Interviews Former Golden Bear and Current Florida Marlin, John Baker."
5. Author interview with John Baker.
6. "CGB Interviews Former Golden Bear and Current Florida Marlin, John Baker."
7. Author interview with John Baker.
8. "CGB Interviews Former Golden Bear and Current Florida Marlin, John Baker."
9. Author interview with John Baker.
10. "CGB Interviews Former Golden Bear and Current Florida Marlin, John Baker."
11. Author interview with John Baker.
12. Author interview with John Baker.
13. Michael Lewis, *Moneyball: The Art of Winning an Unfair Game* (New York: W.W. Norton and Company, 2003).
14. Author interview with John Baker.
15. Author interview with John Baker.
16. Author interview with John Baker.
17. Author interview with John Baker.
18. Laurence Miedema, "For Cal and De La Salle Star Baker Has Huge Homecoming," *East Bay Times*, August 20, 2008. For Cal and De La Salle star Baker has huge homecoming – East Bay Times. Accessed May 11, 2021.
19. Author interview with John Baker.
20. Author interview with John Baker.
21. Author interview with John Baker.
22. "Open Letter from Marlins Catcher John Baker," *Miami Herald*, September 23, 2010. Open Letter from Marlins Catcher John Baker | Fish Bytes (typepad.com). Accessed May 11, 2021.
23. "Open Letter from Marlins Catcher John Baker."
24. Lost Boyz Inc.
25. Author interview with John Baker.
26. "San Diego Padres Acquire Catcher John Baker from Miami," MLB.com, San Diego Padres acquire catcher John Baker from Miami | MLB.com. Accessed May 11, 2021.
27. "San Diego Padres Acquire Catcher John Baker from Miami."
28. Author interview with John Baker.
29. Author interview with John Baker.
30. Author interview with John Baker.
31. Author interview with John Baker.
32. Author interview with John Baker.
33. Author interview with John Baker.
34. Author interview with John Baker.
35. Jason Mackey, "Why John Baker Left the Cubs to Help the Pirates," *Pittsburgh Post-Gazette*, November 12, 2020. Why John Baker left the Cubs to help the Pirates | Pittsburgh Post-Gazette. Accessed May 11, 2021.
36. Author interview with John Baker.
37. Jim Callis, Sam Dysktra, and Jonathan Mayo, "Here's Where All 30 Farm Systems Rank," MLB.com, Pipeline Farm System Rankings (mlb.com). Accessed October 26, 2021.

FRED BESANA

BY MALCOLM ALLEN

A wild southpaw, Fred Besana spent the first month of the 1956 season with the Baltimore Orioles, appearing in seven games and winning one of his two starts. Besana also played parts of eight seasons in the minors and starred in semipro leagues around four years of Air Force service.

Frederick Cyril Besana was born on April 5, 1930, in Lincoln, California, about 30 miles north of Sacramento in Placer County. He was the only child of Cyril "Cedo" and Clara (Lappens) Besana. The family had Italian and Dutch ancestry.[1] Cedo worked for Gladding, McBean and Co., a terracotta and clay manufacturing company. Gladding, McBean also sponsored a baseball team in the semipro Placer-Nevada League. In 1926 Cedo's pitching led the Lincoln Cubs to the PNL championship.[2] Less than a month after Fred's ninth birthday, his mother died in her early 30s. After Cedo remarried, Frank's half-brother Keven was born in 1948. Keven became the Placer County sheriff.

Fred learned to pitch by throwing stones against the family barn. He played baseball and basketball at Lincoln Union High School. In one memorable duel, he beat Richie Myers of rival Elk Grove, 1-0, in a contest in which both pitchers hurled no-hitters. "When we played Elk Grove at home, it was such a big deal that the whole town shut down and all the grammar school kids were let out of class for the day to go to the game," Besana recalled. As a 1947 senior, Fred notched 107 strikeouts in 65 innings to lead the Zebras to the Sacramento County League Championship.[3] He was also the president of his graduation class.[4]

Besana continued his education at Placer Junior College.[5] In addition to earning his two-year associate of arts degree, he continued to star in two sports. As he matured closer to his full 6-foot-3, 200-pound size, Besana helped the Spartans basketball squad win the state basketball championship. After they won their league baseball title, Besana pitched Placer College to a 1-0 victory in the opener of the best-of-three Northern California playoffs. In the decisive third game, he hurled 13 innings and hit a two-run homer, but the Spartans fell to San Mateo, 3-2, in 16.[6] On summer Sundays, Besana pitched and played the outfield in the Placer Nevada League, suiting up for Roseville and his hometown Lincoln Potters.[7]

Before the 1950 season, Oakland Oaks owner Brick Laws signed Besana for his Pacific Coast League club.[8] The pitcher received $5,000 plus the promise of an additional $5,000 should his contract be purchased by a major-league franchise.[9] After spring training with the Oaks, Besana was assigned to the Class-D Longhorn League, where he was 3-1 with a 4.64 ERA in five starts for the Sweetwater (Texas) Swatters. On May 19 he advanced to the Class-C West Texas-New Mexico League and went 15-11 in 33 games (25 starts) for the Albuquerque Dukes. Clubs averaged more than seven runs per game in the circuit, and the collective batting average was .306, so Besana's 9.2 hits allowed per nine innings was second-best in the league. Among pitchers with at least 100 innings, his 5.23 ERA ranked 10th. Overall, Besana worked 205 innings and won 18 games in his first year of professional baseball.

His advance to the majors would have to wait. "I joined the Air Force instead of getting drafted into the Army," Besana explained. He spent most of 1951 and 1952 at Fort Campbell's Clarksville Base in Tennessee along the Kentucky border. When the owner of the Hartsville Sun semipro team learned that a professional pitcher was stationed there, he convinced the base commander that granting the lefty weekend passes to pitch would benefit both the base and the town. Besana earned $10 per game, until the Clarksville Moose club found out and offered him $25. He recalled a memorable experience playing in Harlan, Kentucky. "I remember rounding third, heading for home and plowing over the catcher," Besana recalled. "When I sat down in the dugout, this hillbilly in farmer's overalls walks up to me and says, 'That's my son you knocked down boy, and I don't want to see that happen again.' As he walked away, he pulled back his coat to show me he was packing a pistol."[10]

In 1953 Besana was transferred to Travis Air Force Base in Fairfield, California, about 45 miles southwest of Sacramento. On June 21, 1953, he married Sylvia Rastler, a physical-education instructor at Placer High School. Being near home also allowed Besana to pitch for the independent Marysville Giants, often to former White Sox catcher Vince Castino, with future American League umpire Merle Anthony manning second base. Besana set semipro records for the Yuba-Sutter area that still stood, as of 2021, with his 23-2 regular-season record, .920 winning percentage, six shutouts, and average of 13 strikeouts per game. He no-hit the Sacramento Solons rookies club, tossed three one-hitters, and whiffed 18 batters twice. On May 11, 1953, Besana struck out 17 Hatzell Radio hitters and homered in the bottom of the ninth to win, 1-0. He didn't taste his first regular-season defeat until a perennially strong House of David club beat him on August 14. In the National Baseball Congress playoffs for the northern part of the state, he struck out 17 Atwater Plumbers to set a tournament record. Overall, Marysville went 33-5 and Besana's record – including tournament games – was 24-3. Besana was named a Northern Division All-Star, but he had to return to base before the final contest and a Ford Ord Warriors team featuring J.W. Porter and Bobby Winkles prevailed.[11]

Also in 1953, with first place in the Placer-Nevada League at stake, Besana's hometown Lincoln club asked him to join them for their game against the Roseville Happy Hour and former minor-league southpaw LeRoy Stevens. "I don't really want to, but I will," Besana replied. He saved a Lincoln victory.[12] While stationed in California, Besana also visited Folsom Prison to play exhibitions with the Sacramento Stars.[13] Looking back on his four years in the Air Force, Besana said, "All I ever did was play baseball and basketball."[14]

Besana's son Fred Jr. was born on March 9, 1954. Fred Sr. was discharged from the service that summer and joined the Oakland Oaks for the end of their Pacific Coast League season. In his debut on August 18 in Portland, Besana permitted only one unearned run in the first eight innings before surrendering a pair of scores in the ninth. In his home debut, four nights later, the San Francisco Seals clobbered him for six runs in the second inning.[15] In seven appearances (five starts), Besana was 0-4 with a 6.83 ERA.

When Besana returned to the PCL in 1955, the Oaks' new manager was former major leaguer Lefty O'Doul. Though 29 of Besana's 41 games were in relief, he walked 100 batters in 146⅓ innings to rank second in the circuit, and his 11 wild pitches tied for third. He finished 6-10 with a 3.75 ERA. Besana split his last six decisions, beginning with a two-hit shutout of San Diego on August 10 in which he carried a no-hit bid into the seventh inning. Dick Sisler's one-out single broke it up.[16] Besana blasted a grand slam against the Seals to aid his own cause in a 10-3 win on August 30.[17] For pitchers with at least 100 innings, Besana's rate of 6.3 strikeouts per

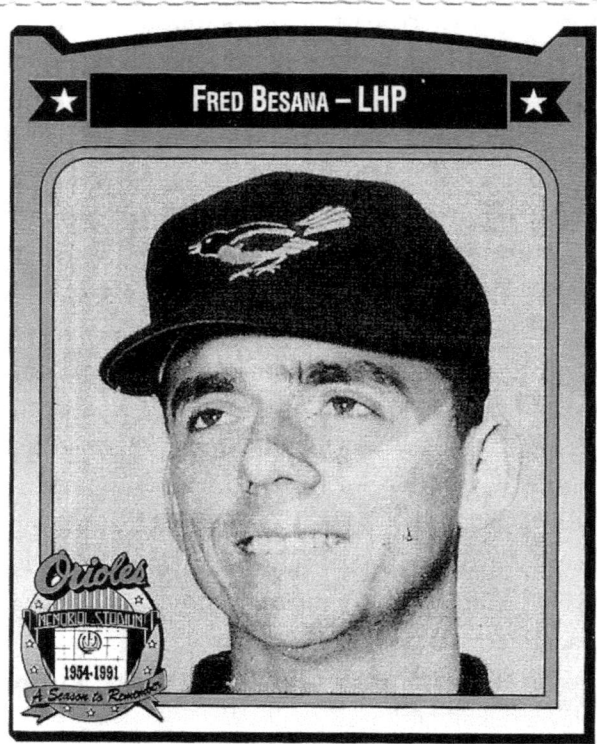

Fred Besana was a perfect 1-0 for the 1956 Baltimore Orioles. Courtesy The Topps Company, Inc.

nine innings was fourth-best in the circuit, and his 0.3 homers allowed ranked third.

At the conclusion of the season, the Oakland Oaks announced that they'd begin a working agreement with the Baltimore Orioles and move to Vancouver in 1956.[18] In the first transaction with their new affiliate, the Orioles swapped outfielder Carl Powis for Besana. West Coast scouts Mike Catron and Don McShane had recommended the southpaw to Baltimore skipper Paul Richards.[19]

At Orioles spring training in Scottsdale, Arizona, in 1956, Richards noted that Besana "can go in there and get out those lefty batters."[20] On March 16 he handled a righty – two-time All-Star Clyde McCullough – for the final out of an exhibition victory over the Cubs.[21] Besana was named Baltimore's "Best Young Pitcher" in a poll of *The Sporting News*'s correspondents.[22] He and fellow rookie southpaw Don Ferrarese made the team as relievers.

Baltimore's Opening Day loss in Boston was the first major-league game that Besana witnessed in person. He debuted in the second one, entering to pitch the bottom of the seventh at Fenway Park with the Orioles trailing 8-4. Besana retired Sammy White and Bob Porterfield on fly outs to right. After Billy Goodman reached on an error, Billy Klaus walked to bring up the third spot in the Red Sox' batting order. Normally, that would've meant Ted Williams, but a badly bruised instep had forced Williams to depart for a pinch-runner two innings earlier. Instead, Dick Gernert grounded back to the mound for the third out. "All I ever wanted was to be able to tell my son and grandson Ted Williams hit one off me that's still going," Besana lamented more than a half-century later.[23] In the eighth, Besana walked Jackie Jensen leading off, but he caught Don Buddin looking for his first big-league strikeout to complete two scoreless innings of hitless work.

Baltimore lost four of five to begin the season with Opening Day pitcher Bill Wight failing to survive the first inning in either of his two starts. The 34-year-old southpaw's struggles were so severe that Richards decided to give Besana an opportunity. On April 22 the rookie pitched the first game of a doubleheader against the visiting Washington Senators. Besana walked three of the first four hitters and surrendered three runs in the top of the first. By the time he departed after his sixth walk put two aboard to start the seventh, however, the Orioles had come back to lead 4-3. Relievers Fritz Dorish and George Zuverink recorded the last nine outs and Baltimore pulled away, 7-3, to hand Besana his first (and only) major-league victory. "I thought Besana looked real good today," Richards insisted.[24] The manager said he intended to give more opportunities to Besana and Ferrarese.[25]

Five nights later at Griffith Stadium, Besana faced the Senators again. Baltimore trailed 5-0 when he departed for a sixth-inning pinch-hitter. Four of the five runners who scored against him had reached via hit batsman or walks. The Orioles rallied to tie, so Besana received a no-decision in a game that his team ultimately lost, 8-5.

In May Wight found his form and Ferrarese's first two starts were a 13-strikeout complete game and a no-hit bid spoiled in the bottom of the ninth at Yankee Stadium. Besana, on the other hand, relieved four times and was pounded for 11 hits in 4⅔ innings. His fate was sealed when Baltimore purchased veteran lefty reliever Johnny Schmitz from the Red Sox. On May 16 Besana was optioned to Vancouver with a 1-0 record, 5.60 ERA, 14 walks, and 7 strikeouts in 17⅔ innings pitched in seven appearances. The Orioles offered no explanation. "They didn't have to," Besana remarked in 2013. "I knew. I was so damn wild I couldn't get the ball over the plate."[26]

Back in the PCL, Besana endured a nightmarish season. After losing his first seven decisions for the Mounties, he won once, then lost six more.[27] In addition to his unsightly 1-13 record and 6.62 ERA in 25 games (16 starts), Besana's peripheral statistics were poor: 116 hits and 65 walks allowed in 100⅔ innings with only 43 strikeouts. The Orioles sold his contract to Vancouver that offseason.[28]

In 1957 Besana made only seven appearances for Vancouver before he was optioned to the Knoxville Smokies in the Class-A South Atlantic League on May 10. He was returned after going 1-4 in five outings. Vancouver then transferred Besana's option to the Amarillo (Texas) Gold Sox of the Class-A Western League.[29] In Amarillo on July 24, in front of 2,601 fans, he beat the Sioux City Soos, 7-4, after Sylvia Besana pitched the Silver Anklets – the Gold Sox wives' team – to victory over their husbands in a pregame exhibition.[30] In 23 games (14 starts) for Amarillo, Besana was 10-3 with a 4.26 ERA. The Louisville Colonels of the Triple-A American Association purchased his contract after the season.[31]

Besana appeared in 37 games (28 starts) for Louisville in 1958 and recorded a 3.59 ERA in 203 innings. His 11-12 record included some memorable efforts. In a 3-2 win over Omaha on May 9, he drove in one run and scored the other two to support his own seven-hitter.[32] On May 29 he hurled one of his two shutouts to best Indianapolis's Barry Latman.[33]

A June 15 duel against Omaha's Bob Blaylock went 11 innings before Besana fell, 3-0.[34] In the final inning of his four-hit victory over Minneapolis on August 20, Besana retired Art Schult at first base after taking a line drive to the belt buckle. "I never even saw it coming," the pitcher insisted. "If the ball had hit me on the leg or in the ribs, it would have broken something for sure."[35]

In 1959 Besana returned to Vancouver and got off to his best start as a pro. When he allowed a home run to Sacramento's Nippy Jones on May 1, it was the first earned run he'd allowed in 21⅔ innings.[36] By May 26, his record was 5-1 with a 1.11 ERA.[37] Four days after Besana improved to 9-5, 2.37 by beating Seattle's Claude Osteen, 1-0, he started the PCL All-Star Game in San Diego for the North team. Besana was charged with the loss after allowing four runs in three innings.[38] With the bases loaded, however, he struck out Willie McCovey 10 days before the future Hall of Famer debuted in the majors. Besana finished the season with a 9-8 record and 2.77 ERA in 32 games (24 starts). He decided to retire. "I had had enough," he explained. "Baseball just wasn't fun anymore."[39]

In 1960 Besana completed the required courses at Sacramento State College to earn his teaching certification.[40] Not ready to completely change careers, he returned to Vancouver in 1961 and appeared in 13 games for the Mounties, then a Milwaukee Braves affiliate. In June he moved to the Dodgers' Spokane Indians farm team in the same circuit and pitched in his final 26 games as a professional.

From 1962 to 1964, Besana taught at his wife's alma mater, Roseville High School. He also coached junior-varsity basketball and baseball. By the time Sylvia returned to become Roseville's vice principal in 1966, Fred had moved on to start a baseball program at Oakmont High School for one year, followed by a quarter-century at American River College. Besana taught there until his 1990 retirement and coached the baseball team until 1985.[41] John Vukovich played for Besana at ARC.

According to *The Sporting News* Player Contract Cards database, Besana spent one year as a Houston Astros scout before joining the Atlanta Braves in the same role from 1968 to 1970. Though his son Fred Besana Jr. never appeared in an NFL game, he was briefly on the rosters of the Buffalo Bills and New York Giants. A quarterback, Fred Jr. spent three years (1983-1985) with the USFL's Oakland Invaders. In the league's inaugural season, he was the second-rated passer.

Predeceased by his wife in 2008, Fred Besana Sr. was 85 when he died on November 7, 2015, in Roseville. He is buried in Roseville Cemetery.

SOURCES

In addition to sources cited in the Notes, the author consulted www.ancestry.com and www.baseball-reference.com.

NOTES

1. Fred Besana, publicity questionnaire for William J. Weiss, September 4, 1954.
2. "History of the Potters," https://lincolnpotters.com/about/history/, last accessed February 15, 2021.
3. Mark McDermott, "Fred Besana, Former Major-Leaguer and Area Coach, Dies at 85," *Sacramento Bee*, November 7, 2015, https://www.sacbee.com/sports/mlb/article43656207.html, last accessed February 13, 2021.
4. *El Eco 1947*: 13.
5. In 1954 the institution was renamed Sierra College.
6. McDermott, "Fred Besana, Former Major-Leaguer and Area Coach, Dies at 85."
7. "Placer-Nevada League," https://www.northerncaliforniabaseball.com/placer-nevada-league.html, last accessed February 15, 2021.
8. Fred Besana, publicity questionnaire for William J. Weiss, February 6, 1958.
9. McDermott, "Fred Besana, Former Major-Leaguer and Area Coach, Dies at 85."
10. McDermott, "Fred Besana, Former Major-Leaguer and Area Coach, Dies at 85."
11. "Fantastic Freddie and the 1953 Marysville Giants," https://www.northerncaliforniabaseball.com/yuba-sutter-baseball.html, last accessed February 15, 2021.
12. Mark McDermott, "Fond Memories of the Placer-Nevada League," *Lake Tahoe News*, July 6, 2015, https://www.laketahoenews.net/2015/07/fond-memories-of-the-placer-nevada-league/, last accessed March 1, 2021.
13. "Folsom Prison," https://sactownbaseball.org/folsom-prison/, last accessed February 15, 2021.
14. McDermott, "Fred Besana, Former Major-Leaguer and Area Coach, Dies at 85."
15. "Oakland," *The Sporting News*, September 1, 1954: 24.
16. "Briggs Gives Major Scouts Eyeful," *The Sporting News*, August 24, 1955: 27.
17. "Oakland," *The Sporting News*, September 14, 1955: 40.
18. Jesse A. Linthicum, "Orioles Sign '56 Working Agreement with Vancouver," *The Sporting News*, October 19, 1955: 16.
19. Jesse A. Linthicum, "Besana Acquired from Vancouver," *The Sporting News*, October 26, 1955: 18.
20. Carl Lundquist (United Press), "No One Knows Who'll Be in Oriole Lineup" *Herald Journal* (Logan, Utah), April 5, 1956: 4.
21. Jim Ellis, "Bird Seed," *The Sporting News*, March 28, 1956: 7.
22. "Infielders Lead as 'Hot Prospects,'" *The Sporting News*, April 18, 1956: 21.
23. McDermott, "Fred Besana, Former Major-Leaguer and Area Coach, Dies at 85."
24. Bob Maisel, "Bird Hurling List Revised," *Baltimore Sun*, April 23, 1956: S15.
25. Gordon Beard (Associated Press), "Rookie Fred Besana Shines in Major Loop Mound Debut," *La Crosse* (Wisconsin) *Tribune*, April 23, 1956: 11.
26. McDermott, "Fred Besana, Former Major-Leaguer and Area Coach, Dies at 85."
27. "Vancouver," *The Sporting News*, June 27, 1956: 28.
28. "Deals of the Week," *The Sporting News*, February 27, 1957: 32.
29. "Deals of the Week," *The Sporting News*, July 3, 1957: 30.
30. "Winning Pitchers: Husband and Wife – in Double-Bill," *The Sporting News*, August 7, 1957: 43.
31. "Transactions," *The Sporting News*, December 25, 1957: 27.
32. "Louisville," *The Sporting News*, May 21, 1958: 30.
33. "Indianapolis," *The Sporting News*, June 11, 1958: 54.
34. "Omaha," *The Sporting News*, June 25, 1958: 36.
35. John Carrico, "Belt Buckle Saves Hurler Hit by Liner from Injury," *The Sporting News*, September 3, 1958: 34.
36. "Vancouver," *The Sporting News*, May 13, 1959: 30.
37. "Coast Averages," *The Sporting News*, June 3, 1959: 28.
38. Ben Foote, "Solon Trio Leads South to Triumph," *The Sporting News*, July 29, 1959: 29.
39. McDermott, "Fred Besana, Former Major-Leaguer and Area Coach, Dies at 85."
40. In 1972 the school's name changed to California State University, Sacramento.
41. McDermott, "Fred Besana, Former Major-Leaguer and Area Coach, Dies at 85."

DRAKE BRITTON

BY BILL NOWLIN

Left-hander Drake Britton had one win and one loss in his time in the big leagues, but he has a World Championship ring to treasure forever as a member of the 2013 Boston Red Sox. It was a year in which he almost lost the opportunity to pitch.

John Drake Britton was born in Waco, Texas, on May 22, 1989. His parents were Craig and Cathy Britton. Drake had an older sister, Taylor, and a younger brother, Chance. Cathy Britton had been a high-school math teacher who became a stay-at-home mom to look after the children. Craig was an architect who worked in commercial architecture for companies like CDI Engineering and ConocoPhillips. His work frequently took him overseas to such places as Dubai and Saudi Arabia.

Drake grew up with a Magnolia, Texas, address, in a Houston suburb. "We were right on the line between Tomball and Magnolia," he said in a May 2021 interview, "but I went to Tomball High School."[1]

He is no relation to three major-league pitchers Zack Britton, Chris Britton, or Jim Britton, or to 1913 Pittsburgh Pirates shortstop Gil Britton.

Other unrelated Brittons in baseball were Helene Robison Britton, who owned the St. Louis Cardinals from 1911 to 1916, and John Britton, an infielder who played for the Birmingham Black Barons in Negro League baseball.

Drake went to high school in Tomball. In 2006 he was named to the roster of the 2006 Aflac All-American Classic, played in San Diego.[2] That same year, he was selected to participate in the Junior Olympics operated by USA Baseball; though he didn't make the final team, he went through the workouts and played in some of the scrimmages in Arizona.

On graduation from Tomball High, Drake was selected by the Red Sox in the 23rd round of the June 2007 major-league draft, the 714th pick overall. He signed on August 15 for a reported $700,000 bonus later that year.[3] He had made a commitment to Texas A&M, but did not attend. "I signed with the Red Sox at the deadline, at 11:59." Red Sox scout Jim Robinson is credited with the signing, under team scouting director Jason McLeod, who said the Red Sox had followed Britton for about a year. He had what McLeod said was "a bad spring, but we saw him throw this summer and he has what we determine to be very good makeup. We've had him up to 94 [miles per hour.]"[4]

Britton said of Robinson, "Jim's great. He was our area scout." One of the other players Robinson signed, Britton noted, was Will Middlebrooks, a fifth-round selection in that year's draft.

Britton's first year in pro ball was not until the following year, 2008, when he pitched in eight games for the Single-A Lowell Spinners, working 33⅔ innings, striking out 26 but walking 16. His ERA in the short season was 4.28, with a record of 1-2, but late in the season he suffered an injury that required Tommy John surgery in October.

Britton didn't pitch much in 2009 because of the surgery, but came back relatively quickly, getting in a few innings before the season was over, with both the Spinners and the rookie league Gulf Coast Red Sox. He worked fewer than 12 innings, facing just 51 batters.

The 2010 season was Britton's first full year. He pitched for the Class-A South Atlantic League's Greenville Drive, starting 21 games for the Red Sox affiliate. He struck out 78 batters in 75⅔ innings and recorded an ERA of 2.97. He pitched and won the first game of the league playoffs. His fastball had gotten up to 96, post-surgery.[5] *Baseball America* ranked him fifth among Red Sox prospects.[6]

He had a rough year in 2011, going by statistics. His 2011 season was with the Salem (Virginia) Red Sox, in the Advanced-A Carolina League. Britton started 26 games and won only one of them, losing 13. His 1-13 record reflected to some extent his 6.91 earned-run average, significantly higher than the team's 4.16 ERA. His WHIP (walks and hits per inning pitched) was 1.70. The total of 13 losses was more than that of any other pitcher in the league, and the ERA was the worst among league starters.

Britton was, nonetheless, promoted. The Red Sox weren't ready to give up on either him or fellow prospect Stolmy Pimentel, who had been considered perhaps Boston's top two pitching prospects. Pimentel had gone 0-9 with a 9.12 ERA for Portland and then 6-4 (4.53) for Salem. Mike Hazen, Red Sox VP of player development, said, "We've told these guys that this season has to be the most important one in terms of development. They need to learn from what happened."[7] The following spring both were placed on the Red Sox' 40-man roster and signed to major-league contracts at the major-league minimum of $480,000, representing a further investment.[8]

Why did Britton seem to fare so poorly? Reminded of the statistics, he laughed and said of the ERA, "That was lower than I thought! It was a humbling year." He had a bad game and then another, and then a third, and found himself wrestling with anxiety about his performance. "It was the first time I'd experienced that. I just kind of let it consume me, snowball on me. Letting it get in my head. Over-thinking." Being placed on the 40-man roster let him know the Red Sox had confidence in him.

Britton was placed with Salem again in 2012. He was 3-5 in 10 games with an ERA of 5.80 but in early June he was promoted to Double-A Portland. In his June 5 debut he walked six batters in the first three innings, but didn't allow a hit through five, and earned a 6-1 win over Bowie.

He had the support of his family throughout but three coaches stood out for their support and encouragement during his early years. "Kevin Walker, my pitching coach from Low A to High A, he was always huge. Always positive. Left-handed pitcher. He always had my back. Kevin Boles, who I played for manager-wise, he always had my back. Bob Kipper, Double A. He was incredible. Always tried to keep the glass half-full for me and let me see the positive. To help train my mind to not dwell on the negatives. They're the three main people who stick out."

Britton was invited to 2013 spring training with the Red Sox but early in March was optioned to Portland. He was also arrested for driving under the influence. The arrest occurred on March 2 in Estero, Florida, at 4:42 A.M. He was timed driving 111 mph in a 45-mph zone and faced the possibility of up to a year in jail.[9] Alex Speier of WEEI radio quoted Britton as saying, "I'm extremely remorseful. … I'm sorry for the negativity that I brought, but that's about all I can say right now. I'd really rather not say anything else."[10]

Britton had several good outings with Portland, including the first complete game of his professional career, a June 11 win over Erie. He was named to the Eastern League All-Star team, along with batterymate Christian Vázquez. In early July, with a 7-6 record and a 3.51 ERA, he was promoted to Triple-A Pawtucket. In his first start for the PawSox, on July 9 against Lehigh Valley, he worked 5⅓ innings and allowed five earned runs.

The Red Sox were coming off a last-place finish in 2012 but were in first place under new manager John Farrell. The pitching staff was in some degree of flux, however, and Farrell – a former pitching coach – allowed that he would like to see Britton given a shot in the big leagues, perhaps in the bullpen. "A lefthander that has power stuff. We would like see Drake Britton here. Even if it's just initially getting his feet."[11] The Red Sox were looking for someone who could work multiple innings in relief. He was called up on July 14; to make room, outfielder Jackie Bradley Jr. was optioned out.

"I didn't know what to think at first," a surprised Britton said. "My mind was going a million miles an hour. I was really excited." He added, "It's awesome. I had the biggest smile on my face. Nobody could knock it off."[12]

Drake Britton's win helped Boston remain in first place during the championship 2103 season.
Courtesy The Topps Company, Inc.

The Boston pitching staff was going through changes. Britton was the sixth Red Sox pitcher to make his major-league debut in 2013.[13] His first appearance came on July 20 at Fenway Park against the New York Yankees. With his parents in the stands, he was called into the game in the top of the ninth, New York leading 4-2. There was nobody out and runners were on first and second. The first batter he faced was Ichiro Suzuki. While Britton was pitching, Luis Cruz stole third base. Britton got Suzuki to pop up to shortstop. Robinson Canó lined out to center, Cruz tagging and scoring. Brett Gardner was thrown out trying to steal second.

The Red Sox rookie was back on the mound the next night, throwing a scoreless 10th inning against the Yankees in a game the Red Sox won in the 11th. Reflecting back on his debut several months later, he said, "I had to remember to breathe."[14]

Britton threw scoreless innings against Tampa Bay on the 24th and in Baltimore against the Orioles on the 26th. On July 29 he worked two scoreless innings against the Rays. He'd thrown six innings in five appearances without giving up an earned run.

Britton got his first decision on July 31, working the 14th and 15th innings of a game tied 4-4 against the visiting Seattle Mariners. Once more, he held the opposition scoreless. He gave up a single in the 14th and two singles in the 15th, but saw left fielder Jonny Gomes execute a rare unassisted double play to close out the inning, catching a line drive to left and then running to the bag at second base to double up Raúl Ibañez, who had taken off on contact. Stephen Drew singled in the winning run for the Red Sox in the bottom of the 15th.

Britton pitched a scoreless eighth against the Arizona Diamondbacks on August 4 as four Red Sox pitchers combined on a 4-0 shutout.

His scoreless streak came to an end in his eighth appearance, in Houston on August 6. He worked 2⅓ innings in the game and the one run he gave up was only one among the 10 runs the Astros scored off Boston pitching, but it was still disappointing to see the streak snapped.

Three days after that, Britton lost his first game, on the road against the Kansas City Royals, charged with two runs in a 9-6 loss.

At the end of August, after 14 appearances, he was 1-1 with an ERA of 3.12.

He worked in four September games and finished the season 1-1 (3.86). He had worked 21 innings and given up 21 hits, only one of them a home run (by Houston's Jake Elmore in the August 6 game). He'd struck out 17 and only walked seven. It had been his best stint statistically – and it was achieved in the major leagues.

Britton pitched in seven more big-league games and never gave up another earned run. But that didn't come until September 2014.

In October 2013 the Red Sox won the World Series, their third championship in 10 years. Britton was not named to the postseason roster. He was sent to Fort Myers, the Red Sox' spring-training headquarters, to work out, to be ready in case he was needed. He came frustratingly close to joining the team. In fact, he got the call – but then was called off. Franklin Morales had gotten hurt. "I get a call from Juan Nieves [the Red Sox pitching coach]. He says, 'Hey, tomorrow when you get to the field, have all your stuff packed and dress ready to meet us.' So I'm all jacked up. I come walking in there. I've got my suitcase all packed. I'm dressed in my suit. Brandon Snyder was with me. They call us into the office and sit us down and put us on the speakerphone with [Red Sox GM] Ben Cherington. He basically just said, 'Thanks for your hard work down there, but we're going to take it from here and you all have a safe trip back home.'"

He returned home and watched the rest of the playoffs on television with his good friend and apartment mate Ryan Pressly, very happy that the Red Sox won but understandably disappointed at not being invited to Boston for the championship parade. The following spring, he was included in the world-championship ring ceremony at Fenway Park, driven up from Pawtucket with a few others who had been on the 2013 team.

Britton spent pretty much the full 2014 season with Pawtucket. He worked in 45 games, all in relief, closing 22 games. In contrast to 2013, when he had struck out more than double the number of batters he had walked, regardless of the level at which he pitched, in 2014 he walked 38 and struck out 37. His ERA for the season at Triple A was 5.86 (the staff ERA was 3.60). It was not an impressive season, but he still did get called up to Boston in early September. (He'd been called up once before, at the beginning of May, but not used.)

The Red Sox, though reigning world champions, were once again in the cellar, last place in the American League East.

Britton worked in seven games, for a total of 6⅔ innings. He did not give up any runs – earned or unearned. He allowed five scattered hits, walked two, and struck out four. With an ERA of 0.00 in 2014, his career ERA became 2.93.

When the Red Sox signed Alexi Ogando in early 2015, they made room by designating Britton for assignment. He was claimed off waivers by the Chicago Cubs on February 4. Why had the Red Sox seemed to lose interest in Britton? It might have been a simple matter of a personality difference with one or two people in the front office. John Farrell had told him he wanted him on the staff.[15]

Britton pitched the full season in Triple A, for the Iowa Cubs, and had another so-so year in the minors: he was 7-8 (5.08). The Cubs had him start 11 games and relieve in 17 others. A shoulder injury shelved him for a while at the end of the season. Why he performed so much better in the major leagues than in minor-league ball perhaps remains one of those baseball mysteries. The Cubs allowed him to become a free agent that November.

In December Britton signed with the Detroit Tigers organization for 2016 and worked exclusively in relief; in 37 games, he posted a record of 0-3 (4.57) with the Triple-A Toledo Mud Hens. In early August, however, he tested positive for amphetamines and was suspended for 50 games, without pay.[16] Needless to say, that put an end to his

2016 and with the suspension due to last well into 2017, he was not attractive as a pickup for any team.

Oddly, one could say he was suspended for taking fewer amphetamines than prescribed for him. "I had a TUE, a temporary therapeutic use exemption. I had a TUE granted by Major League Baseball to take amphetamines. I had two different types of amphetamines. You're supposed to take the medication exactly as prescribed. That's the rule by Major League Baseball. I was taking them both and then I realized I was having some problems sleeping, and things like that. I found that one of my medications worked better than the other and so – without consulting the doctor for the Tigers at the time – I chose on my own to stop taking one medication and only take the other one." Testing showed just the one, and not both. That was the violation.

He pitched the next two years in independent baseball, in the Atlantic League. In 2018 he worked for the Bridgeport Bluefish, relieving in 34 games. He recorded a 4-1 mark with a 3.68 ERA. In 2019 he worked for the Southern Maryland Blue Crabs, for whom he was 4-6 in 27 games, 14 of them starts. His earned-run average was 6.35.

The wear and tear of pitching caught up with Britton. "I had torn my flexor muscle off the bone in my elbow. I had to have surgery for that. While I was doing the MRIs prior to that surgery, they saw that I had torn my labrum and my rotator cuff was 85 percent torn.

"So six months after having flexor forearm surgery, I turned around and went back in for full labrum and rotator cuff surgery. I was in the elbow brace and the sling, and the shoulder brace, for a good seven months."

It was time to find some other ways to earn money to finance a growing family. He had met his future wife, Jacqueline, while living in Boston after the 2014 season. She is a registered nurse who was working at Boston Children's Hospital at the time, working in the ICU with newborns and small babies. They got married and as of the time of the May 2021 interview had two daughters – Belle, age 4½, and Blake, who had just turned 3. Jacqueline Britton took up work at a med spa, working with Botox, lip filler, and lasers – obviously working with an older clientele.

Drake Britton, while rehabbing from the first of the multiple surgeries, started work with the National Scouting Report at the beginning of 2019.

"They basically scout for every college baseball program in the country. I'll go out to a game, or someone will fill out an evaluation form to be evaluated by one of our scouts. If they're in my area in north Texas or anywhere around me, they'll be forwarded to me. I'll go out and evaluate that athlete and get them enrolled with NSR. Once they do that, they're available to be seen by every college in the country, but to be recruited by the schools that they fit into – for coaches who never would have known about that kid had not National Scouting Report connected them." The goal is to match the player to a program, to get a good fit.

He also got into coaching youth baseball. His friend Blake Beaven – who had been drafted by the Texas Rangers in the same June 2007 draft as Britton – had become the director of the Dallas Tigers West. Britton helped out Beaven at one tournament and really loved it. Britton now has two showcase baseball teams he coaches, one of 12-year-olds and starting in the spring of 2021 a team of 15-year-olds.

There's a big part of Britton that still wishes for one more shot. "Some guys, they can feel it when they just don't have the drive or the passion for it. They might have the stuff for it, but that drive and that passion goes away. It hasn't left me. I would still like to get back to a place to try to play in at least one more game, pain-free.

"I left so many stones unturned throughout my career. I made some mistakes. Maybe I let immaturity and things like that blind my vision of what I could have done in the game. That drive and that passion is still there.

"Deep down and in all honesty, I think that I have more to give. Whether that means physically playing, or mentally – like how I know the game. … I think that's why I am successful, and like being a coach, like working with younger athletes."

It's something he can convey to other players who are just starting out.

"That's why I feel good and why I like what I'm doing. I have the opportunity to do all those things with the next wave, the next generation of baseball players. I get the opportunity to speak and work with some damn good ballplayers. I get some fulfillment, a sense of still mattering in this game, by doing what I'm doing."

SOURCES

In addition to the sources cited in the Notes, the author consulted Baseball-Reference.com and Retrosheet.org. Thanks to Rod Nelson of SABR's Scouts and Scouting Research Committee.

NOTES

1. Author interview with Drake Britton on May 24, 2021. Unless otherwise indicated, all direct quotations attributed to Britton come from this interview.
2. Others on the roster included Madison Bumgarner, Freddie Freeman, Yasmani Grandal, Matt Harvey, Jason Heyward, DJ LeMahieu, and Rick Porcello.
3. First-round pick Nick Hagadone got $571,000. Britton got more than sixth-rounder Anthony Rizzo (reported at $325,000). Amalie Benjamin and Gordon Edes, "Disagreement Showed Their Signs of Discontent," *Boston Globe*, August 20, 2007: 32.
4. Amalie Benjamin and Gordon Edes, "Disagreement Showed Their Signs of Discontent."
5. Peter Abraham, "Top 10 Places to Get Better," *Boston Globe*, September 10, 2010: C5.
6. Peter Abraham, "Decision Is Due on Ortiz Option," *Boston Globe*, November 4, 2010: C7.
7. Peter Abraham, "Mostly, a Year of Seasoning," *Boston Globe*, September 9, 2011: C2.
8. Peter Abraham, "A Smart Move by Bailey," *Boston Globe*, March 10, 2012: C5. Being placed on the roster protected the Red Sox against having him claimed by another team.
9. Andrew Martin, "Boston Red Sox Prospect Drake Britton Faces Up to One Year in Jail," *USA Today*, March 19, 2013. https://bleacherreport.com/articles/1574279-boston-red-sox-prospect-drake-britton-faces-up-to-one-year-in-jail. Accessed March 9, 2021.
10. Martin. Because he had refused to take a field sobriety test, he had automatically been arrested. Out on bail, he played through the season, then returned to Florida for a court date and ended up charged with reckless driving. "Just because the charge was reduced to a lesser charge doesn't mean the judge or anybody took it easy on me. If anything, they made an example out of me." He was fined and had to do 150 hours of mandatory community service. "They got their point across to me." Author interview May 24, 2021. It may be of interest to note that Britton forthrightly acknowledged smokeless tobacco use. He wasn't the only one – David Ortiz, Mike Napoli, and Jonny Gomes were among other users on the team. Britton said, "I know I need to quit. I don't want to be one of those guys who never quits, dips the rest of my life, and gets cancer." See Peter Abraham, "Routines Outweighing Disdain, Players Cling to the Tobacco Habit," *Boston Globe*, March 7, 2014: A1, 10.
11. Peter Abraham, "Lefthander Thornton Added to Pen," *Boston Globe*, July 13, 2013: C5.
12. Peter Abraham, "Lester Is Being Dropped Back," *Boston Globe*, July 15, 2013: C3.
13. Alex Wilson, Allen Webster, Steven Wright, Jose de la Torre, and Brandon Workman had been the previous five.
14. Peter Abraham, "Going Up," *Boston Globe*, March 30, 2014: F14.
15. Author interview.
16. Chris McCosky, "Tigers Minor Leaguer Britton Suspended 50 Games," *Detroit News*, August 2, 2016.

SCOTT BROWN

BY STEVE HEATH

If it weren't for two relatively rare events, Cincinnati Reds reliever Scott Brown might not have been a "One-Win Wonder." One of those events delayed his major-league debut by four months, costing him multiple opportunities to earn more than one win. The other enabled the Reds' big right-hander from backwoods Louisiana to receive credit for that one win, even though he had not yet thrown his first big-league pitch when the game's winning run was scored.

Scott Edward Brown was born on August 30, 1956, the third child of Harvey Edward and Betty Lou (Allen) Brown, both lifelong residents of DeQuincy, Louisiana. They were married 59 years and had five children – four sons and a daughter: Danny, Ricky, Scott, Becky, and Tracey. DeQuincy, population 3,235, is a lumber and railroad town on the western edge of Cajun country, about 230 miles west of New Orleans and 130 miles east of Houston. Harvey was a railroad man who worked 42 years for the Missouri Pacific. Betty Lou taught English and home economics for 40 years at DeQuincy High School, where Scott did not excel in baseball, because the school didn't have a baseball team.[1]

Scott grew up playing Little League, Dixie Youth, and Sheriff's League baseball. He was big (6-feet-2 and 220 pounds) and could throw hard, but professional baseball was not on his mind. "I wanted to try out for LSU (Louisiana State University), but they weren't interested, because I hadn't played high school ball," he said, frustration still evident in his voice. "But after I made it to the big leagues, guess who was the first ones to call. I told 'em how to 'eat the cabbage.'"[2]

Brown may not have had his eyes on the pros, but the pros had their eyes on him. He was selected by Cincinnati in the fourth round of the June 1975 amateur draft, the 94th overall pick and the first athlete from DeQuincy ever drafted by any major-league team. He found out from his mother that he'd been drafted. The Reds called the high school and talked to her. Scott was momentarily baffled. "I said, 'Drafted? What does that mean?' I'd never heard of that." A whole new world was about to open up for the strapping 18-year-old from Louisiana's Gulf Coast lowlands.

Cincinnati sent Brown to its rookie-level Pioneer League affiliate in Billings, Montana. "What a trip that was!" he exclaimed. "I'd never been on an airplane. I'd never left my mom and dad. You know, I'd gone camping or things like that, but … I went over to Lake Charles, and that little airplane come in for me to get on, and I literally had to get on my hands and knees to get in. It held about six people. I was thinking, 'Oh, what the hell have I gotten into?' But it wasn't too bad. I mean, I made it all the way to Billings before I puked."

There, he joined future major leaguers Frank Pastore, Paul Moskau, and Larry Rothschild on the Mustangs' pitching staff. "I didn't know nothing about baseball, but I had fun," said Brown. "It was awesome! We were up in the mountains. I'd never seen any mountains. All I knew was Louisiana. Once we all got to know each other, we had a blast." When not exploring his new world, Brown appeared in 10 games, amassed a 6.50 ERA and walked 21 while striking out 13 in 18 total innings. "When I went to Billings, I didn't even know what a balk was," he admitted. "I'd never heard of it. I was in a game and, all of a sudden, the baserunner was going to second. I said, 'What the hell's going on?' [Manager Joe Hoff] said, "You balked.' I said, 'What the hell does that mean?' He told me, and I said, 'OK.'" Until then he had pitched only in local sandlot leagues in rural Louisiana, where the umpires were generally selected on the basis of "whoever wanted to do it" and they pretty much stuck to balls, strikes, and outs.

In 1976 Brown moved up a notch, to the Eugene (Oregon) Emeralds of the low Class-A Northwest League. He completed seven of 12 starts and had two shutouts. His ERA was an impressive 2.56, his strikeout-to-walks ratio an improved 1.35, and his walks-and-hits-to-innings-pitched ratio (WHIP) 1.363. He was growing more sophisticated as a ballplayer, but the small-town guy was still a bit naïve, and it was in Eugene that the legend of his quest for a curveball was spawned.

The legend was that Brown had never heard of a curveball until he got to the pros, and that his teammates had convinced him he should go to a local sporting-goods store to buy one.[3] As with most legends, there was some truth to the story. In DeQuincy, people didn't call them curveballs. They called them "drop balls" and "round-houses," which sort of made sense in a railroad town. However, Brown said, he did not go to a store to buy a curveball. "They made that crap up," he maintained, but also confessed, "They did get me to go into the clubhouse to look for the 'keys to the batter's box.' I went in there, and when I opened my mouth, the trainer looked at me funny, and then I knew what they'd done. When I come back out, I was going to kill every damn one of 'em, but I couldn't catch 'em."

Brown's performance in Eugene earned him a spot with Tampa of the Class-A Florida State

Scott Brown won the first big-league game of his career. Courtesy The Topps Company, Inc.

League in 1977. With the Tarpons, he began developing a breaking pitch and things began coming together for him. He had five complete games and two shutouts with a 3.82 ERA in 24 starts. But instead of being promoted, Brown was sent back to Tampa to start the 1978 season. He was not a happy camper.

"I almost quit baseball that year," Brown said. "I outpitched all of them (in '77). I told [the Reds], 'If this is the way y'all do it, hell, I don't need you. I'll go back and get me a job on the railroad. I don't need you people.' I was packing my stuff when Scotty Breeden (Reds roving pitching coach) come to the hotel and stopped me. We had a talk, but I was pissed. I didn't care. After all that work, there I was, still in A-ball, and I had a family to feed. I figured, 'The hell with this. I can go home and make more money working for the railroad.' I had my bags packed, but Scotty talked me out of it."

Determined to show the Reds they'd made a mistake, Brown started 16 games for the Tarpons, completed six of them, had two shutouts and posted a gaudy 1.31 ERA, with an even gaudier 0.974 WHIP and gaudier-yet 3.32 strikeout-to-walk ratio. The Reds saw the light and, about midseason, promoted Brown to Nashville of the Double-A Southern League. Brown arrived in Music City in time to make 13 starts for the Sounds and post a 4-3 record with a 4.50 ERA, 1.682 WHIP, and 1.62 strikeout-to-walk ratio.

The 1979 season was better. Still with Nashville, Brown had a 9-2 record, but more impressively, he dropped his ERA to 2.40 (best in the league) and his WHIP to 1.115. He upped his strikeout-to-walk ratio to 2.53 with three complete games and a shutout in 19 starts. "It's where I shoulda been in the first place," said Brown. "I was kicking ass in Nashville. I'd learned how to pitch, and I'd learned how to finesse hitters. But I wasn't a finesse pitcher. I was a power pitcher. And so George Scherger (Nashville manager) began putting me in the bullpen, which I … I hated him for that! But that's what got me to the big leagues. Otherwise, I'd have never made it."

No starter likes getting sent to the bullpen, but in 1980, that helped get Brown elevated to the Indianapolis Indians of the Triple-A American Association. While transitioning from starting to relieving, he put up decent numbers. He had six wins against seven losses, a 3.44 ERA, 1.325 WHIP and a 1.49 strikeout-to-walk ratio. He also pitched one complete game and had two saves, but wasn't called up during the annual September roster expansion.

Brown, now 24 years old, would have made the big-league roster coming out of 1981 spring training, but baseball's labor unrest reared its ugly head. Manager John McNamara went to Brown and offered a difficult choice. "During spring training, he said, 'It looks like there's going to be a strike. There's nothing we can do about that. What would you rather do? Draw a paycheck or go on strike?'" I said, 'Well, sir, I need to draw a paycheck. …' So it was back to Indianapolis.

It turned out to be a good decision. The strike started on June 12 and big-league play didn't resume until August 10. But the minors kept on going and Brown kept on drawing paychecks. He appeared in 51 games for Indianapolis, but started only three before being moved to the bullpen permanently. He finished 35 games and had 13 saves to go with a 6-5 record, a 2.28 ERA, 1.161 WHIP, and 2.05 strikeout-to-walk ratio. And when the strike finally ended, Brown was ordered to report to the Reds in Los Angeles, where they were working out in preparation for their season restart against the Dodgers on August 10. He got there in time to pitch in one of the Reds' practice games against the Angels.

It was the night of August 11 that Brown, three weeks shy of his 25th birthday, finally got his chance to pitch in a big-league game. There were 45,000-plus spectators at Dodger Stadium, 10,000 more than for the previous night's game, mostly because of Fernandomania. It was just the second game after the strike ended and regular-season play resumed, and attendance in Los Angeles was down significantly – just like everywhere else – because fans were mad at the owners and players over the strike.[4] Regardless, the Dodgers' rookie pitcher, Fernando Valenzuela, had taken baseball by storm before the strike. When play stopped, he had a 9-4 record with a 2.45 ERA and had pitched eight complete games and five shutouts. But he had also lost four of his last six starts. LA fans turned out despite their ire over the work stoppage, hoping Valenzuela would regain his early-season form. But his struggles continued that chilly August evening in Chavez Ravine.[5]

Cincinnati scored first. A bases-loaded single by Ray Knight in the top of the first drove in Dave Collins and Ken Griffey. Los Angeles tied it in the bottom half of the frame. Ken Landreaux tripled to right field, then Dusty Baker homered to left. Dave Concepción led off the third with a solo home run for a 3-2 Reds lead, but the Dodgers tied it in the bottom of the fourth on doubles by Pedro Guerrero and Bill Russell. Valenzuela exited in the top of the fifth after giving up one-out walks to Concepcion and George Foster. Terry Forster replaced him and got Dan Driessen to ground into an inning-ending double play.

In the bottom of the fifth, Cincinnati starter Mario Soto walked Baker with one out. Steve Garvey singled Baker to third and Ron Cey doubled to left, sending Baker home and Garvey to third. That was it for Soto. Doug Bair came in to face Guerrero. His first pitch went wild, enabling Garvey to score and Cey to take third. Guerrero then teed off on Bair for a double to right-center, and when the dust finally settled, Los Angeles was ahead, 6-3. Bair had given up two runs, but they were charged to Soto.

Bair retired the Dodgers in order in the bottom of the sixth, but he was due to be the leadoff hitter for Cincinnati in the seventh. Instead, McNamara had Rafael Landestoy pinch-hit for him. "I saw that they were going to pinch-hit for Bair, and was thinking, 'Oh (bleep)!' And sure as (bleep), McNamara called down there and told them to get me ready. I about to (bleep)," recalled Brown.

While Brown was warming up, Landestoy grounded out to second and Collins struck out looking. It appeared Brown needed to warm up faster. But then Griffey singled to right and Concepcion pushed him to second with a single to center. Next up was Foster, and he singled to right-center, scoring Griffey and moving Concepcion to third. That set the stage for a three-run homer just inside the right-field foul pole by Driessen that put the Reds ahead, 7-6.

When Brown took the mound, he found himself in front of a crowd 15 times larger than the population of DeQuincy. "You know what?" said Brown, "Remember when they used to have you come in from the bullpen on that little cart? Well, I ran. And when I got to the mound, my knees were like rubber. I was terrified. All I remember is McNamara saying, 'Just rear back and chunk it.' That was it. Once I threw the first pitch, [the fans] wasn't there no more. Once I started throwin', they were gone. All I saw was my catcher (Joe Nolan)."

Baker, the first batter Brown faced, grounded out to second. Next up was Garvey, and he grounded out to short. Cey poked a single to left, but was left stranded on first base when Brown got Guerrero on a routine fly to right. Bobby Castillo replaced Forster for the Dodgers in the top of the eighth and got Ron Oester and Nolan out on infield grounders. That made it Brown's turn to bat. McNamara, happy with his performance so far, elected not to replace Brown with a pinch-hitter. "I was sitting there (in the dugout) and I figured I'm out. McNamara looked over at me and said, 'You going to get on deck or what? So, I went out there and found a bat. I have no idea whose bat it was." It was Brown's first (and only) major-league at-bat and alas, there was no fairytale ending to this part of the story. Castillo struck out Brown, who wasn't exactly known for his hitting prowess. "I never saw the ball," Brown admitted.

Asked about it later, McNamara told reporters, "He was outstanding. We only wanted one inning out of him, but he was so sharp, we stayed with him. The Dodgers aren't the easiest lineup to face in your major-league debut."[6]

Brown rewarded McNamara's gamble by setting down the Dodgers in order in the bottom of the eighth. He got Mike Scioscia to ground out to short. Then Russell grounded back to Brown for out number two and pinch-hitting Rick Monday grounded out to Driessen unassisted to end the inning.

Brown again took the mound in the bottom of the ninth, with the Reds still up by one. He got Davey Lopes to fly out to center, but then Landreaux singled to right. With the hot-hitting Baker due up next, McNamara decided not to give the Dodgers hitters another look at Brown, and brought in Tom Hume, the Reds' closer. Brown's night was over. Hume got Baker to fly out to center, then struck out Garvey to record his sixth save of the season.

After the game, Brown learned that the scorekeeper had awarded him the win, even though Bair technically had been the pitcher of record when the Reds tallied the winning run in the seventh. Rule

9.17(c) gives the official scorer discretion to award a win to a subsequent relief pitcher if in the view of the scorer that pitcher was more integral to achieving the win.[7] Bair had given up two runs on a wild pitch and a double – both runners inherited from Soto – in his inning and two-thirds. Brown held the Dodgers scoreless on two harmless singles in 2⅓ innings. "I had no idea they were going to give me the win," said Brown. "I think it was my buddy, Dave Collins, who come to me and told me about it in the locker room after the game. Bair wasn't real happy about that, but hell, I had no clue that could happen." And that's how Brown got what turned out to be his only big-league win.

He made nine more appearances in 1981, three against the Expos, two against the Giants and Padres, and one vs. the Phillies and Braves – but all were no-decision outings for him. Including his debut against Los Angeles, Brown pitched a total of 13 innings and gave up four runs, all of them earned. He struck out seven, walked one, and, of the 16 hits he yielded, only one went for extra bases – a double by Padres catcher Terry Kennedy. He had a 2.77 ERA, 1.308 WHIP and 7.0 strikeout-to-walk ratio. He'd finally made it to "The Show," and was looking forward to going to spring training with the Reds as a roster player in 1982. And then he was traded.

In December of 1981, the Reds swapped Brown for Kansas City right fielder Clint Hurdle. Brown was surprised, and not particularly happy, but had little control over the situation. Appropriately enough, when he reported to the Royals' spring-training facility the following February, it was in Surprise, Arizona. "I pitched several innings in spring training with KC, and did all right," said Brown. "Then … I don't remember who we was playing, the Texas Rangers maybe, but anyway, I went in for just one inning, and God, I wished I hadn't. When I went to throw a curveball, [his arm] just went. That's all I can tell you. They come running out there and I tried to throw the ball and I couldn't even reach the plate. I knew I was in trouble. The medial collateral ligament tore, come to find out. They sent me all over the place to try to get somebody to rehabilitate it, but they couldn't do it. They finally sent me to (Dr. Frank) Jobe in Inglewood." Brown had Tommy John surgery, a procedure pioneered by Jobe, and it worked. "I was back! When I went back, I was throwing just as hard. It took me a while, but I was doing good in spring training (in 1983)," Brown recalled. "Then, all of a sudden, the ulnar nerve snapped, and that was it. My hand went halfway numb. I tried to pitch with it, but had no coordination. I went and got it fixed in Houston. The doctor told me he could get my hand back, but that my career was over. And he was right. I got my hand back, but I couldn't throw the ball 88 miles an hour. I tried and tried, but just couldn't get 90 mph, and I'd thrown a hell of a lot harder than that."

Brown briefly tried for a comeback, visiting several training camps in Arizona, but got no offers and so he went home to DeQuincy and became a railroad man like his dad. "First, I was with the bridge gang for six or seven years. That was terrible!" he said. "I had back problems and it was manual labor. Spiking stuff down. I had to get on my hands and knees. Then, I went into transportation and became an engineer. I did that for the last, oh, I don't know how many years; 20 or so. I went from Houston to New Orleans to Alexandria. That was my territory."

As of 2023, Brown was retired from the railroad, too. He and his wife of 45 years, Cheryl, still resided in DeQuincy and were active in church and community. Scott was taking it a little easier, having been hospitalized with pneumonia and COVID-19 during the pandemic. Their son, Matthew, also lives in DeQuincy. Their daughter, Alicia Ortagus, is married and lives in San Antonio. She and her husband bring Lucian Scott Ortagus, their son, to visit his grandparents as often as possible.

One thing Scott no longer did much is sing. And there's a baseball story behind that as well: "We (the Indianapolis Indians) were in Des Moines, Iowa, and it was like 11 degrees and that's when I got hit in the throat (by a line drive). It crushed my Adam's apple. Mine's flat. Most people's is round. Mine's kind of oval. I can't remember who hit the ball. (It was first baseman Chris Nyman,[8] who played for the White Sox in 1982 and '83.) They told me later the bastard was laughing over at first base. I said, 'OK, I'll get him.' It took me about a month. He knew when he walked up to the plate. I hollered at him, 'You ain't gonna laugh no more.' I hit him in the ribs as hard as I could throw and it sounded like when people thump a watermelon to see if it's ripe. Of course, the dugouts emptied and all that, but I got that sum*****." Brown could rear back and chunk a baseball.

SOURCES

In addition to the sources cited in the Notes, the author accessed BaseballAlmanac.com, Retrosheet.org, Baseball-Reference.com, and Statscrew.com.

NOTES

1. Author interviews with Scott Brown on November 22 and November 29, 2021.
2. Brown interviews. Unless otherwise indicated, all direct quotations attributed to Brown come from these interviews.
3. Hal McCoy, "The Real McCoy-Remembering Scott Brown," blog post, *Dayton Daily News*, February 23, 2012.
4. https://www.baseball-reference.com/leagues/majors/1981-misc.shtml
5. "Fernandomania Isn't Same; Neither Is He as Reds Win," *Los Angeles Times*, August 12, 1981: D1.
6. "Reds Rookie Wins Despite 'Pure Terror,'" *Columbus Dispatch*, August 12, 1981: D1.
7. Official Baseball Rules, 9.17(c)
8. "Frazier-Led Oaks Topple Indians, 8-4," *Des Moines Register*, April 15, 1980: 1S.

IKE BUTLER

BY PAUL PROIA

Ike Butler is a one-year major-league baseball anecdote – a player whose inclusion in a baseball encyclopedia was made possible by an opportunistic telegram sent during a franchise upheaval. However trivial his two-month major-league career was, Butler's minor-league career, especially the decade spent on the West Coast, included more than 200 professional wins and at least two minor-league records.

Named after his father's brother,[1] Isaac Burr Butler arrived in Langston, Michigan, on August 22, 1873, to Harrison H. and Mary A. (Kent) Butler just a little over a year after the farmer and his bride married. Harrison Butler served the Union during the Civil War as a private in the 80th Ohio Infantry; he served nearly four full years from late 1861 through the Confederate surrender in 1865. After the war, Harrison toiled at a number of jobs: farmer, day laborer, and timberman. After Isaac's arrival, Harrison and Mary had two daughters, Ethyl and Elizabeth.

Ike learned the sport playing baseball with his Traverse City, Michigan, friends at the city fairgrounds.[2] After spending time pitching for the Traverse City Hustlers and later Owosso in the Michigan Base Ball League,[3] Butler first pitched professionally in 1895 with Detroit in the old Western League, where he got a one-game tryout on August 10. The starting pitcher, Alex (or Alec) Whitehill, gave up 10 runs to Indianapolis in the first three innings. Ike Butler entered and gave up 10 more runs over the next six innings.[4]

Good enough for a look, but not good enough to stay, Butler found work pitching for Seattle in the Pacific Northwest League in 1896. The sturdy right-handed pitcher won nine of 15 decisions despite being swatted around a bit. "It was a pleasure to see Butler pitch the remaining innings," wrote a reporter for the *Seattle Post-Intelligencer*. "He was as cool as a cucumber, and every time Catcher (Ralph) Frary said, 'Put 'em over, Ike,' over they went. ... Every time they thought Butler was in danger of becoming a bit nervous he would be told to split the plate and let the fielders take care of the hits."[5] In that game, Butler gave up five runs in the first three innings, but pitched pretty well the rest of the way for an 11-6 win over Victoria. Butler did the bulk of the pitching for Seattle as the league called for just 32 games played per team.

His winning record earned Butler a tryout with St. Paul in the Western League. Getting a start on June 26, 1896, Butler allowed eight runs in four innings to Milwaukee, but his team rallied for 10 runs in the ninth to win the game.[6] In 1897, he pitched for Dubuque in the Western Association, leading the team with 13 wins and 18 losses, before returning home to pitch in Traverse City.[7] During the 1890s, Butler frequently pitched semipro games with the Hustlers as seasons elsewhere ended.[8]

Continuing this nomadic theme, Burlington (Iowa) in the Western Association hired Butler for the 1898 season. Despite not pitching all that well, he somehow earned a tryout with a last-place and desperate Omaha team in the Western League. Butler couldn't have impressed anyone (one start, three appearances, nearly a run allowed per inning) as he didn't survive Omaha. On the other hand, Omaha didn't survive the season; the franchise moved to St. Joseph, Missouri, halfway through 1898. For 1899, Butler signed a contract with Toledo and for the first time in his professional career he played two full seasons with the same club. His 15 wins in 1900 was a new career high.[9] Butler also threw his first true gem, a one-hitter to blank Youngstown on May 25, 1900.[10]

Kansas City of the Western League added Butler to the 1901 roster, but a week into the season he was loaned to Denver, where Butler alternated between good and bad outings.[11] Manager George Tebeau turned down cash offers from Colorado Springs and Omaha so he could recall Butler if he needed him later in the season. Indeed, Kansas City needed Butler to make a couple of starts in June. It didn't work out and he was again tossing for Denver.[12] Denver released Butler in July and a month later Butler signed with Shreveport in the Southern Association.[13] Making a good impression, Butler agreed to come back to Shreveport for 1902 and quickly became the ace of the Shreveport staff.[14]

In 1902 the war between the upstart American League and National League reached its zenith, with manager John McGraw and outfielder Joe Kelley jumping the Baltimore Orioles and taking several stars with them to the New York Giants and Cincinnati Reds. In fact, thanks to McGraw, New York Giants owner John T. Brush wrested away a majority ownership in the AL club. Having a National League owner now an owner of an American League franchise was the biggest threat to what had otherwise been a very successful American League organization. American League President Ban Johnson worked with the other owners to take back control of the Baltimore franchise and stock the team with enough players to finish the season. Some teams loaned a player or two to help with the cause, while other players were gathered from around various leagues to help play games.

Ike Butler was one of these gathered players. Butler had fairly good seasons in low-level minor leagues but little success in his brief stays in the better minor leagues. Still, Butler recognized an opportunity to play on a major-league team at a major-league salary and sent a telegram to Baltimore manager Wilbert Robinson offering his services.[15] Robinson, in desperate need of pitching, bought the sales pitch and agreed to purchase his rights from Shreveport. Most importantly, Butler was going to earn a lot more money. Shreveport paid Butler $125 per month for his mound work. Wilbert Robinson offered Butler $400 a month to pitch for Baltimore.

Butler's time in Shreveport for 1902 was bookended by the headlines "Pitcher Butler Is Here" and "Butler Is Gone" in the *Shreveport Times*.[16] In between, Butler pitched essentially .500 ball for a team that was 28-46 when he left. (He is credited with an 11-12 record on Baseball-Reference.com; the *Shreveport Times* said he had 12 wins in 24 appearances.) A *Times* reporter caught Butler after he told the club he was leaving. Butler said, "I dislike very much to part with friends, but baseball is a business to me. The offer made me by Baltimore is too great an opportunity to turn down. ... If I should ever play in a minor league again and I can secure a position with Shreveport, I will return."[17] Butler would return to the minors, but he would never pitch for Shreveport again.

In joining Baltimore, Butler took over Harry Howell's or Joe McGinnity's spot in the Orioles rotation. McGinnity was no longer with the team; Howell stopped pitching regularly and became a position player – he was a versatile defender and he could genuinely hit. At one point in July, the Orioles were 31-34 and competitive. After the upheaval of the summer, which stripped the team of most of its best players, the rotation included Snake Wiltse, Jack Katoll, and Ike Butler – Baltimore won just 19 games in the last 12 weeks of the season.

when there are men on the bags and he is forced to twirl without a preliminary gyration. ..."[19]

As August became September, Butler continued to pitch and lose. He gave up 12 runs to Detroit on September 6, nine more to a Philadelphia squad that was rolling toward the pennant (Rube Waddell won his 20th game in relief that day), and 13 runs on 20 hits to Boston in the first game of a doubleheader. That Baltimore had to play so many doubleheaders in September likely kept Butler on the roster. Ike started one game of a doubleheader in each of his last eight starts – including back-to-back days against the Athletics. The Orioles needed live arms.

Predictably, Baltimore fell from fifth place toward the bottom of the standings. Then they started losing in in ways not seen since the Cleveland Spiders gave up on the 1899 season. From August 26 through Butler's loss to Boston on September 17, Baltimore went 1-21 with two ties. Robinson needed a new good-luck charm and got it in a gift from O.P. Chase, who hailed from Robinson's hometown of Hudson, Massachusetts. Chase offered to send Wilbert a beagle hound puppy named May. The puppy arrived in Washington on September 20 before a doubleheader with the Senators.[20] With the new mascot (and future hunting companion), Baltimore won the first game, 6-5.

Butler's record stood at 0-8 when he took the hill against the Senators for game two. Washington drew first blood, but Baltimore put up a pair of runs in both the second and third innings. After scoring a run in the third, Washington bunched luck and hits into a three-run inning and a 5-4 lead in the fourth. Butler walked Lew Drill, who had himself been loaned to Baltimore for a couple of games earlier in the season. Then Bill Carrick reached out with his bat and caught just enough of a pitch to flip the ball into right field for a fluke double. Jack Doyle crushed a double of his own, scoring both runners. He later scored on Bill Keister's single and Washington now led. After this, Butler braced up and kept Washington scoreless for the next four innings. Meanwhile, Baltimore tallied one in the

Pitcher/outfielder Ike Butler with the Tacoma Tigers in 1908. Courtesy of David Eskenazi.

A day after signing his Baltimore contract in St. Louis, Butler took to the mound against the Browns, who smacked him around some. Butler smacked back – he singled and scored a run in the fifth. The Browns scored five runs on nine hits and two walks (and two errors) – three runs were earned.[18] Butler got no decision, as errors helped St. Louis plate the winning run in the 10th inning. Robinson himself caught Butler in his next outing; Butler lost to Cleveland, 6-3, but he pitched better. In fact, Butler wasn't awful but he wasn't always well-supported – in one outing he allowed 11 runs but only three were deemed earned. At the same time, Butler didn't help himself, especially when men were on base. The *Detroit Free Press* noted "Ike Butler, an Oriole recruit who has speed when he has time to wind himself up … is positively harmless sixth, two in the eighth – Butler contributed a run-scoring groundout – and two more in the ninth. When Butler got Ed Delahanty to fly out to deep right field, he and Baltimore got the win.[21]

Butler's outing was no gem. He allowed 16 hits and walked four batters, and three of his players made errors behind him. Butler won just one decision in his major-league career – this was it. The sweep got Baltimore temporarily out of last place, landing just percentage points ahead of Detroit. The Orioles won the first game of the next doubleheader, making it a three-game winning streak and four out of five. And then they lost the last six games, to Philadelphia and Boston – with Butler losing two of those decisions. In his last start, Butler fanned four Boston batters – his career-best game and nearly a third of his major-league career strikeouts.

Butler's 1-10 record, with 168 hits allowed in 116⅓ innings and just 13 strikeouts, is part of an inglorious – and yet amazingly courageous, from a league standpoint – conclusion to the Orioles season. Ban Johnson, angered by McGraw and Brush, arranged to put a team in New York, certainly to spite the Giants but also to get in the nation's largest city. The Orioles were dead; the Highlanders (eventually renamed the Yankees) were the new team in the American League.

Ike Butler wasn't kept when the franchise moved to New York. Shreveport claimed his rights, a story hit the wires saying that Butler signed with Milwaukee in the American Association,[22] and another story said he was ready to return to Shreveport.[23] Instead, he headed west to join a Portland team that was added when the California League expanded to become the Pacific Coast League in 1903.[24] Butler, now approaching his 30th birthday, was a thick and sturdy pitcher. He is listed as 6-feet and 175 pounds in Baseball-Reference.com, but in Portland, his weight was noted as 190 pounds.[25] While he wasn't the ace of the staff based on his record, he certainly was the "Old Reliable" of the staff based on his usage.[26] Butler appeared in 54 games, starting 50 of them. He threw 440⅔ innings and led the team with 22 wins and 27 losses. Butler threw strikes – his 104 walks represented one of the lowest walk rates in the league, though he didn't strike out that many batters (124).[27] And he occasionally took a turn in right field when needed. When the *Oregon Daily Journal* listed the final Pacific Coast League standings, Portland finished in fifth place at 95-107, but that didn't include ties. (Butler's last outing finished tied, 2-2.)[28] Two players appeared in more than 200 games, with Deacon Van Buren playing in 205 games and Phil Nadeau appearing in 204.

After wintering in Bakersfield, California, where he could train throughout the winter and join the team in better shape, Butler joined Portland for a second season. He was awarded the Opening Day start.[29] Daniel Dugdale took over the reins of the team early in the campaign, but as injuries and illnesses ripped through the roster, Dugdale became less enthusiastic about managing. In October Dugdale left and Butler, who remained healthy and respected throughout the season, took over at the helm.[30] Butler was the third manager that season as Portland limped home to an 80-136 record. Three pitchers lost 30 games, with Butler's 32 losses (against 17 wins) setting a PCL record that will never be challenged.

Not likely to be retained by changing management for the 1905 season, Butler chose not to stay with Portland.[31] He considered a two-month stint pitching for Skagway in Alaska,[32] but ended up signing with Atlanta (despite his reputation for jumping Shreveport),[33] which then moved him to Birmingham.[34] After winning two of three decisions there, he was sold to Charleston[35] but returned to Birmingham over a case of mistaken identity. Charleston management thought they were buying an outfielder who previously played for Memphis.[36] Released, Butler considered other opportunities and wound up returning to Michigan and pitching for Grand Rapids.[37]

Butler was about to enter the most stable period of his baseball career. Signed to pitch for Tacoma of the Northwestern League, he spent three years as the team's top pitcher. In 1906 he won 20 of 29 decisions, including one stretch of 12 wins in a row.[38] Then, in 1907, he completed the extremely rare 30-30 combination by winning 32 games against 18 losses – making him one of just a handful of pitchers to have a season with 30 wins and a season of 30 losses.[39] Two of those wins came in a doubleheader against Vancouver on July 1. In the morning game, he blanked the Canucks 8-0. Then he pitched the afternoon game and threw a second shutout, winning 5-0.[40] Not quite three weeks later, he threw a no-hitter to beat Seattle, 5-1.[41] His own throwing error on an Ed Bruyette grounder made the lone run possible. Butler agreed to join a winter league in San Diego where he shared pitching duties with Luther Taylor.[42] While there, he acted as a scout, signing players for Tacoma.[43]

So what changed for Butler to make him more successful? A writer for the *Butte Miner* explained Butler's success as being tied to his control and subtle movement in the strike zone: "One sitting behind the catcher cannot tell what Ike puts on the ball that keeps the batters from belting it out of the lot, but that he has something is evident from the fact that men who have proved themselves good hitters in swell company cannot meet the ball fairly when Ike is right. He has no wide sweeping curves and no ball he pitches will miss the plate more than six inches, but the ball either curves or jumps enough to keep the batsman from hitting it in the middle and the result is a popup or hitting the ball on top for a high bounder."[44]

Butler fell back to 19-14 in 1908, the season after his first wife, Mina, died. He started off pitching really well, but at some point the heavy usage and approaching age (35) caught up with him. He injured a leg, was frequently hit harder than in previous weeks, and he was starting to look for work outside of baseball. At the end of 1908, for example, he got involved in the ownership of a San Diego saloon.[45]

After managing a really good San Diego winter team, Butler returned to Tacoma a different pitcher. He was a late arrival, had issues getting in shape, and got frustrated with teammates after a couple of lousy outings. So Butler announced he was leaving the team to pitch for the Santa Cruz Sand Crabs of the independent California League.[46] Tacoma writers, used to calling Butler "Old Reliable" now called him "Unreliable," forgetting that jumping contracts was something Butler did from time to time.[47] Santa Cruz had financial problems by mid-July, so Butler returned to Tacoma, where his paycheck would be more dependable.[48] Happy to see their old pitcher back, Tacoma named Butler the team's manager a week later.[49] Butler frequently pitched in relief rather than starting – and his team never improved. Two months later, he was relieved himself – of the management job.[50] Butler fell up, though, asking for his release so he could pitch for Los Angeles of the Pacific Coast League for the remainder of the season.[51] Los Angeles kept the veteran around for a month of the 1910 season, but released him in early May.[52] Butler signed one more time with Tacoma and trudged his way through the remainder of the season.

In 1911 Butler made one more run back east and agreed to a contract with Grand Rapids. Upon landing in Michigan, he ran into a winter storm and was forced to purchase a winter coat for the first time in several years.[53] He pitched once, lost, and was released.[54] Back to San Diego, Ike pitched semipro baseball there until he was hired to be a battery coach for Tacoma in 1912.[55] Among the things Butler taught his new pitching staff was how to throw both the knuckleball and the spitball.[56] While it's not listed on his Baseball-Reference.com page, he made at least one relief appearance for Tacoma before asking for his release in May.[57] He next moved to Oregon, pitching independent ball for Salem and Medford, earning a car for his efforts on Medford's behalf.[58] He finished the 1912 season pitching for a semipro team in Maricopa, California.

After his West Coast career came to an end, Butler moved to Butte, Montana. He operated a saloon in Anaconda and pitched in a few semipro games. His last pitched game appears to be around 1916 when he would have been approaching 43 years old.[59] Less than three years after marrying (and quickly divorcing) his third wife, he decided to take a vacation and left Anaconda on a six-week tour of the West Coast.[60] Butler liked what he saw in California and decided to stay in Oakland permanently.

Butler first married Mina C. Maes on March 29, 1896. Maes hailed from Traverse City, Michigan, where the two were living when they hitched their lives together at a nearby Congregational church. A year later, on May 7, 1897, their daughter, Caroline Fay, arrived.[61] After the Butlers moved west, Mina and Caroline followed Ike to Tacoma's spring training prior to the 1907 season. She caught a cold in Walla Walla, Washington – whatever she caught turned into tuberculosis. So while Ike was winning a Northwestern League-record 32 games and pitching more than a third of Tacoma's games in a fight for the pennant, his wife was home fighting for her life. Part of the reason the Butlers moved to San Diego, one figures, is that it might have helped Mina's chances to survive. Instead, she died on November 4, 1907.[62]

During his later Tacoma days, Butler married Julia Averill, on July 24, 1909.[63] Julia was listed as his wife in the 1910 US Census, but she wouldn't be around long. (Butler was, if nothing else, a contract jumper.) In 1916, while living in Butte, Montana, Isaac married Hannah Gertrude Shaner. That marriage didn't last either – Butler and Shaner parted ways and Ike moved to Oakland. In July 1920 he married Grace May (Waters) McDonald, a recent divorcee – both listed that each was on marriage number two, and by the looks of it both were shading their age.[64] In the 1930 US census, their record shows they had a five-year-old son (whose name is illegible on the film) – that son is not living with them in the 1940 US census. Grace died in October 1946.

Butler managed saloons and bars after his baseball days. In 1920 he took a job as a sales clerk while advertising in an Oakland newspaper that he was interested in buying his own business. He also worked as a laborer into the 1940s. In addition to a lifelong interest in baseball, Butler loved flowers and was a member of the Elks Club dating back to his days in Traverse City.[65]

In 1920 Butler avoided death in a car accident in Oceanside, California, when the driver of a car in which he was a passenger swerved to avoid another car and the car rolled over twice. Butler was mildly injured but William Kelly, the driver, was killed.[66] The second time death called, Butler answered. He was attending a chrysanthemum auction in Oakland when he suffered a fatal heart attack and died on March 17, 1948.[67] His body was taken back to Michigan, where he was buried near his father in Forest Hill Cemetery in Stanton, Michigan.

SOURCES

In addition to the sources cited in the Notes, the author consulted Baseball-Reference.com, Retrosheet.org, FindAGrave.com, and genealogical records.

Notes

1   Inferred from relationship identified in the 1850 and 1860 US Census (Ohio).

2   "The Observer," *Traverse City Record-Eagle*, March 19, 1948: 4. Ironically (coincidentally?), this memory was published a couple of days after Butler's death.

3   "Local News," *Owosso Times*, April 26, 1895: 5; "They are in Manistee," *Traverse City Morning Record*, September 5, 1897: 1.

4   "Dissensions Again," *Detroit Free Press*, August 11, 1895: 6.

5   "Campau on the Line," *Seattle Post-Intelligencer*, May 14, 1896: 3.

6   "Four Straight Now," *St. Paul Globe*, June 27, 1896: 6.

7   "They Are in Manistee," *Traverse City Morning Record*, September 5, 1897: 1.

8   "Some More Old Time Pictures," *Traverse City Record-Eagle*, May 15, 1946: 8. Includes photo of the 1898 Traverse City Hustlers team, except that Butler is wearing his Burlington uniform from 1898.

9   "Players Released," *Cincinnati Enquirer*, February 23, 1899: 8; "Base Ball News," *Mansfield* (Ohio) *News*, March 16, 1900: 6.

10 "Notes of the Diamond," *Mansfield News*, December 1, 1900: 7; woodcut image in paper.

11 "Pitcher Ike Butler Has Been Loaned to Denver," *Kansas City Times*, May 16, 1901: 7. For examples of different games, see "Denver Won by Hitting the Ball," *Denver Post*, June 21,

1901: 8, and "Butler Was Dead Easy for Blues," *Denver Post*, June 11, 1901: 6.

12 "Bunts and Line Drives," *Kansas City Times*, June 28, 1901: 7.

13 "New Men Signed," *Shreveport Times*, August 20, 1901: 6.

14 "Butler Gone Home," *Shreveport Times*, September 25, 1901: 8.

15 "Orioles Fly Today," *Baltimore Sun*, July 30, 1902: 6.

16 "Pitcher Butler Is Here," *Shreveport Times*, March 6, 1902: 8; "Butler Is Gone," *Shreveport Times*, August 3, 1902: 6.

17 "Butler Is Gone." The standings appear on page 3.

18 "Orioles' Game Trial," *Baltimore Sun*, August 6, 1902: 6. The *Sun* said he was pulled after five innings; the *St. Louis Globe-Democrat* says he pitched the sixth, which is the record kept on Butler's Retrosheet page.

19 "Took Both of Double Header," *Detroit Free Press*, September 7, 1902: 8.

20 "Beagle Pup for 'Robbie,'" *Baltimore Sun*, September 21, 1902: 6.

21 The entirety of the game summary comes from the following newspapers: "Senators Drop Two Games to the Weakened Orioles," *Washington Times*, September 21, 1902: 10; "Baltimore Took Two Games from the Senators," *Washington Evening Star*, September 22, 1902: 9; "Not Tail-Enders Now," *Baltimore Sun*, September 21, 1902: 6. Also, "Baltimore Orioles 9, Washington Senators 6 (2)," Retrosheet.org, https://www.retrosheet.org/boxesetc/1902/B09202WS11902.htm, accessed March 3, 2021.

22 "Baseball Chat," *Louisville Courier-Journal*, January 4, 1903: Section 3, Page 4.

23 "Two Pitchers Added to Team," *Shreveport Journal*, February 23, 1903: 5. A story in the *Oregon Daily Journal* suggested that he actually did sign with Milwaukee, but Shreveport objected based on a rights claim that was upheld by the baseball commission. "I.B. Butler," *Oregon Daily Journal* (Portland), October 31, 1903: 8. Ultimately, Butler twice jumped Shreveport for better offers.

24 "Baseball Dustings," *Oregon Daily Journal*, February 14, 1903: 7.

25 "Ike Butler," *Oregon Daily Journal*, February 28, 1903: 9.

26 "I.B. Butler," *Oregon Daily Journal*, October 31, 1903: 8.

27 "Portland Leads in Team Batting," *Oregon Daily Journal*, December 29, 1903: 5.

28 Standings, *Oregon Daily Journal*, November 30, 1903: 5.

29 "Baseball Season Formally Opened," *Oregon Daily Journal*, March 24, 1904: 9.

30 Dugdale Becomes Tired of the Portland Team," *Anaconda* (Montana) *Standard*, October 16, 1904: 3; "Dugdale Has Resigned," *Oakland Tribune*, October 17, 1904: 7.

31 "Butler and Castro Will Be Traded," *Bakersfield Morning Echo*, January 12, 1905: 3.

32 "Butler May Pitch for Skagway," *Bakersfield Morning Echo*, February 25, 1905: 2.

33 "In the Realm of Sports," *Birmingham News*, February 7, 1905: 9; "Ike Butler Declines to Comes South," *Birmingham News*, March 10, 1905: 9.

34 "Butler Made Debut in Little Rock," *Birmingham News*, May 17, 1905: 12.

35 "Ike Butler, Pitcher, Has Been Sold," *Birmingham News*, June 5, 1905: 9.

36 "Butler Still a Member of Birmingham Team," *Birmingham News*, June 9, 1905: 14.

37 "Base Ball Notes," *Fort Wayne Sentinel*, June 14, 1905: 6; "Dope Drippings," *Birmingham News*, June 10, 1905: 21; "Ike Butler Released," *Chattanooga Daily Times*, June 10, 1905: 4.

38 "Butler and Downey Stay with Tacoma," *Spokane Chronicle*, March 1, 1907: 13.

39 As best as I can tell, few pitchers did this after 1892 when Bill Hutchinson went 36-36 and Amos Rusie went 32-31. A few other pitchers are members of this exclusive club (including George Bradley and Jim McCormick, who have seasons with 40 wins and 40 losses), but most of them pitched well before the mound was moved back to 60 feet 6 inches. In saying that, the early PCL was among the only leagues where this would have been possible based on the length of its seasons. For example, Roy Hitt is one of them – winning 31 games with San Francisco in 1906 and losing 30 with Vernon in 1909.

40 "Butler Blanks Canucks Twice," *Spokane Chronicle*, July 2, 1907: 5.

41 "Ike Butler Gets Away Without a Single Hit," *Butte* (Montana) *Miner*, July 21, 1907: 8.

42 "Will Play Winter Ball," *Spokane Chronicle*, September 20, 2007: 5.

43 "Albert Carson Signed," *San Francisco Call*, December 2, 1907: 3.

44 "Isaac's Dope," *Butte Miner*, May 9, 1908: 2.

45 "Tacoma Will Lose Pitcher Ike Butler," *Vancouver* (British Columbia) *Daily Province*, October 3, 1908: 19.

46 *Stockton* (California) *Evening Mail*, May 13, 1909: 4; "Ike Butler, Leading Tacoma Pitcher in the Northwest League, Joins Santa Cruz Outlaws," *Oakland Tribune*, May 21, 1909: 17.

47 "Old Reliable Ike Butler Joins Outlaws," *Tacoma Times*, May 19, 1909: 2.

48 "Swanton Settles with the Players," *Santa Cruz Sentinel*, July 15, 1909: 5.

49 "Ike Butler Made New Tiger Boss," *Spokane Spokesman-Review*, July 21, 1909: 13.

50 "Blankenship in Charge," *Spokane Spokesman-Review*, September 19, 1909: 16.

51 "Ike Butler to Los Angeles Club," *Tacoma Times*, September 21, 1909: 2; "Butler Leaves for Angel City," *Los Angeles Record*, September 21, 1909: 7. Also, "Two New Players of Vernon and Los Angeles Leagues [sic]," *Los Angeles Herald*, October 3, 1909: Part III, 1.

52 "Butler Released," *Los Angeles Times*, May 5, 1910: 6.

53 "First Overcoat in Six Winters," *Fort Wayne Sentinel*, April 1, 1911: 8.

54 "Dolly Gray to Grand Rapids, Release Two," *Fort Wayne Journal-Gazette*, May 17, 1911: 6.

55 "Ike Butler to Assist Mike," *Tacoma Times*, November 1, 1911: 2.

56 "Fodder for Hungry Fans," *Tacoma Times*, April 5, 1912: 2.

57 "Tigers Release Pitcher Butler," *Spokane Chronicle*, May 7, 1912: 3.

58 "Base Ball Briefs," *Washington Evening Star*, August 29, 1912: 15.

59 "Walkerville to Have Strong Team," *Butte Miner*, May 23, 1916: 10.

60 "Anaconda News," *Anaconda Standard*, January 2, 1919: 9.

61 "Brevities," *Traverse City Morning Record*, May 8, 1897: 2.

62 "Sports," *Butte Daily Post*, November 12, 1907: 7.

63 "Ike Butler Takes a Bride," *Spokane Spokesman-Review*, July 25, 1909: 14.

64 The California marriage certificate lists Isaac as being 39 (instead of 42) and Grace as 30 (instead of 31).

65 "Locals," *Traverse City Record-Eagle*, March 22, 1948: 3.

66 "Oakland Man Killed in Automobile Crash," *San Francisco Examiner*, February 22, 1920: 7; "1 Dead, 3 Injured When Auto Runs Off Road," *Pasadena Post*, February 21, 1920: 1.

67 Old Ball-Player Dies," *Santa Rosa Press Democrat*, March 18, 1948: 2; "Locals," *Traverse City Record-Eagle*, March 22, 1948: 3.

FRED CAMBRIA

BY JOHN PAUL HILL

Although there are many hard-luck cases in the annals of baseball history, Fred Cambria's story is one of the most memorable. A highly touted college and minor-league pitcher, Cambria made his major-league debut with the Pittsburgh Pirates late in the 1970 season. Only 22 years old, he pitched effectively, going 1-2 with a 3.51 ERA. However, arm injuries prevented him from ever winning another game in the big leagues. Despite this setback, Cambria maintained a long association with baseball and looks back fondly on his time in the game.

Frederick Dennis Cambria was born on January 22, 1948, in Cambria Heights, a neighborhood in the New York City borough of Queens. (There is no connection between his last name and the name of the neighborhood.) He was the first of three children born to George Cambria, a lithographer, and Rita (Thomas) Cambria, a homemaker.[1] Growing up, he attended Brooklyn Dodgers games with his father and uncle, an experience that nourished his interest in sports.[2] When the Dodgers left for Los Angeles before the 1958 season, Cambria refused to switch his allegiance to the New York Yankees, leaving him temporarily without a team. He said, "I didn't like [the Yankees] because they were always winning and I liked the underdog." After the Mets arrived in 1962, he quickly fell in love with the expansion team.[3]

As a youth, Cambria played baseball in the Sacred Heart Parish, Cambria Heights, Catholic Youth Organization league. Starting out as a catcher, he pitched for the first time when he was 12 years old. He played both baseball and basketball at St. Pascal Baylon High School in Queens.[4] Cambria did not take his studies seriously enough; as a result, his chances of going to college seemed remote. However, St. Leo College (now St. Leo University), a small Catholic institution near Tampa, Florida, admitted him in the fall of 1966 on the condition that he maintain at least a 2.5 grade point average.[5] Intending to play basketball, he switched to baseball after making the team following an open tryout. Cambria fondly recalled the move: "I don't think I had a career in basketball, so I went with baseball, and it's the best decision I ever made."[6]

The 6-foot-2, 195-pound right-hander enjoyed an impressive freshman season for the Monarchs in 1967. He pitched back-to-back shutouts to begin his collegiate career – the second was a one-hitter against the University of Tampa.[7] His talents central to the team's success, Cambria was the winning pitcher in five of the Monarchs' first seven victories.[8] Although his pitching stood out, Cambria also enjoyed some noteworthy performances at the plate. On March 15, for instance, he had a single, triple, and four RBIs while pitching St. Leo to an 8-1 victory over Stetson University; one month later, he slammed two home runs while playing the field in the nightcap of a doubleheader sweep of Florida Presbyterian College (now Eckerd College).[9]

Cambria continued to hone his skills during his sophomore and junior years. In particular, he

Fred Cambria of the Pittsburgh Pirates. Courtesy National Baseball Hall of Fame.

improved his slider and learned to change speeds and pitch inside effectively.[10] He also gained a reputation as a giant killer and began to attract attention from big-league teams. On March 27, 1968, in arguably the most impressive outing of his sophomore year, Cambria scattered three hits while striking out 13 and walking only two in an 8-0 shutout at home against Duke University.[11] After the game, Duke coach Tom Butters commented, "I'm not happy. But I'm not upset. We ran into a mighty good pitcher Wednesday."[12] Indeed, Butters, who pitched for the Pittsburgh Pirates from 1962 to 1965, was so impressed by Cambria that he recommended him to Pirates general manager Joe L. Brown.[13] On March 9, 1969, 37 pro scouts saw Cambria, then a junior, strike out 14 on his way to a 3-2 complete-game upset victory over Florida State University.[14] After the game, an unnamed San Francisco Giants scout asserted, "It looks like the kid has all of the potential to be a major league star."[15]

After his junior year, Cambria attended a tryout at Shea Stadium, hoping to be picked by his boyhood favorite team in the June 1969 draft.[16] He was instead chosen by the Pirates in the third round (the 58th pick overall).[17] Signed by scout Mark "Dutch" Deutsch, he was assigned to the York (Pennsylvania) Pirates of the Double-A Eastern League, Cambria made his professional debut against the Waterbury Indians at home on June 14, 1969. He pitched well, giving up only two hits and two unearned runs but came away with a no-decision in the Pirates' 14-inning, 4-3 victory.[18] His first win came against the Reading Phillies on June 25.[19] Thereafter, Cambria established himself as one of York's premier pitchers. He finished the season with a 9-2 record and a 2.16 ERA. His wins included a seven-inning perfect game against Waterbury in the first half of a twin bill on July 15.[20] In the stands that day was former Pirates manager Danny Murtaugh, who had come to watch his son, Tim, catch for York. Cambria believed that pitching the gem in front of Murtaugh quickened his path to the majors: "That's what gave me some ... leverage in the organization. My name was used and [the Pirates] said, 'Maybe he can do something.'"[21]

In the fall of 1969, like other elite prospects, Cambria pitched for the Florida Instructional League Pirates, compiling a 2-1 record with a 3.82 ERA. In 1970 he attended spring training with the Pirates as a nonroster invitee. Murtaugh, who was back managing the Pirates after a stint in the front office, was impressed by Cambria's talents – he said the 22-year-old was "really going to be some pitcher" – but cautioned that Cambria might be sent to the minors for further seasoning.[22] Cambria received notice on March 30 that he was being farmed to the Columbus Jets of the Triple-A International League.[23]

The proximity of the Florida Instructional League and spring training to St. Leo College allowed Cambria to finish his degree. Upon signing with the Pirates, he had promised his parents that he would graduate.[24] He was also determined to prove that his subpar high-school grades had been an aberration. He graduated from St. Leo in the spring of 1970 with a degree in political science, earning dean's list honors in four of his eight semesters.[25]

Cambria took the mound for Columbus on April 17 as the Opening Day starter against the Rochester Red Wings but gave up six unearned runs in six innings in a losing effort.[26] He dropped two more decisions before he beat the Buffalo Bisons on May 3 for his first win.[27] Hitting his stride, Cambria won nine of his next 13 decisions to take his record to 12-7.

While Cambria was enjoying success with the Jets, the Pirates were locked in a tight race in the National League East Division. They moved into first place by one game over the Mets on August 2, but reaching that point had not been easy. Several Pirates had missed playing time because of injury, with the pitching staff suffering the most setbacks. Lamenting the Pirates' predicament, Joe L. Brown commented, "We've had more pitching injuries than any club I have ever been connected with, and a lot of our regulars have been hurt, too."[28] The Pirates' pitching woes worsened in mid-August when the club pulled Dock Ellis from the rotation for two starts to rest his ailing elbow.[29] Moreover, reliever Orlando Peña had been hit hard in several consecutive outings. Against this backdrop, the Pirates put Peña or waivers and purchased Cambria's contract from Columbus on August 19.[30]

Cambria made his big-league debut on August 26, 1970, in a start against the Padres in San Diego. He learned he was starting only an hour and a half before game time after scheduled starter Bob Veale complained of shoulder pain. Despite the late notice, the young rookie pitched well, holding the Padres scoreless for six innings. San Diego took a 2-1 lead in the seventh, however, when third baseman Ed Spiezio homered with no outs to drive in center fielder Ivan Murrell, who had reached on an error. Cambria got the next batter to fly out to center, but Danny Murtaugh removed him after he walked pitcher Pat Dobson. Neither team scored the rest of the way, giving the Padres the win. Although he was the losing pitcher, Cambria's solid performance earned him the starting nod against the Giants in San Francisco on August 30.[31]

Cambria pitched well against the Giants but came away with a no-decision in the Pirates' 2-1 loss. His third appearance came on September 5. Starting against the Philadelphia Phillies at Three Rivers Stadium in Pittsburgh, Cambria and the Pirates trailed 1-0 entering the third. The Pirates put two runs on the board in the bottom of the inning to take the lead. The Phillies knotted the score in the top of fourth, only to see the Pirates come back and score another run in their half of the inning. In the next frame, the Pirates seemingly broke the game open when they scored three times on four hits to take a 6-2 lead. However, Cambria and the Pirates struggled to put the game away. After surrendering a run in the sixth, Cambria pitched a scoreless seventh. He then ran into trouble in the eighth, jeopardizing what could become his first career win. He allowed a single to start the inning. He got the next batter out, but second baseman Denny Doyle followed with a single to center to drive in a run. With the score now 6-4, Murtaugh took Cambria out of the game. Reliever George Brunet promptly gave up a double, forcing Murtaugh to go back to the bullpen. Dave Giusti held the Phillies scoreless the rest of the way to preserve the Pirates' 6-4 win and, with it, Cambria's first major-league victory.

Cambria struggled in his next start. Lasting only 5⅓ innings, he gave up five earned runs on six walks and eight hits in the Pirates' 6-4 loss to the St. Louis Cardinals at home on September 9. His last start of the year came against the New York Mets, his old favorite team, at Shea Stadium on September 20. With his family looking on, he outpitched future Hall of Famer Tom Seaver.[32] The Pirates scored five runs off Seaver in 5⅓ innings, while Cambria held the Mets to three runs, two of them earned, in the same number of innings. However, the Mets tied the game in the seventh, denying Cambria his second win. The Pirates went on to prevail 9-5 in 10 innings.

Cambria pitched one final time that season, recording two scoreless innings in relief against the St. Louis Cardinals at Busch Stadium on October 1. The Pirates won the game, the last of the regular season, good for an 89-73 record and first place in the National League East Division, five games ahead of the second-place Chicago Cubs. Cambria did not appear for the Pirates in the National League Championship Series, which the Cincinnati Reds swept in three games. Cambria finished the season with a 1-2 record and a 3.51 ERA in 33⅓ innings pitched.

Cambria seemed to have a promising future. After the 1970 season, he pitched for the San Juan Senators, a team managed by Pirates great Roberto Clemente in the Puerto Rican Winter League. He then joined the Pirates for spring training in 1971. He pitched effectively but was optioned to the Charleston (West Virginia) Charlies, the Pirates' new Triple-A affiliate, at the end of spring training.[33] Cambria struggled to find his stride with his new team, and he began experiencing pain in his pitching shoulder. He went 0-3 in seven starts before he was shut down for the season to rest his arm.[34] The time off did little to improve his shoulder, however. He experimented with different deliveries to ease the pain, but he pitched only marginally better the following season with the Charlies, going 2-0 with a 5.54 ERA in 17 relief appearances.[35]

Cambria's arm troubles were most likely due to an accumulation of factors. He recalled straining his arm during his standout win in college against Florida State University. Determined to defeat a team that expected "to beat up on us," Cambria had relied excessively on his slider in that start.[36] His time in winter ball was also probably a culprit. Looking back on his time there, he observed, "I hate to say it, but all that extra pitching [in Puerto Rico] might have had a bearing on my arm trouble."[37] Finally, his arm was never the same after he pitched in cold weather in his first start with the Charleston Charlies in 1971.[38]

In 1973, Cambria joined the Pirates again for spring training. His arm still ailing him, he failed to make the club once more. He began the year in Charleston but did not make an appearance and was released in June. Trying to prolong his career, Cambria called the Mets and Yankees, hoping they might be interested in him. The Yankees took a chance, signing him to a minor-league contract with West Haven of the Double-A Eastern League.[39] Cambria pitched only seven games for West Haven, all in relief, going 0-0 with a 4.24 ERA in 17 innings. He never pitched another game.

Following his pitching days, Cambria worked in sales for Izod for over a dozen years, but he never ventured far from baseball.[40] In the late 1980s, he worked as a marketing specialist for the Class-A Columbia (South Carolina) Mets, and in 1990, he returned to his alma mater, St. Leo College, as head baseball coach.[41] (The college renamed itself St. Leo University in 1999.[42]) In his two years at the helm, Cambria took the Knights (now known as the Lions) to a 55-46 record.[43] He later served as pitching coach for the Spokane Indians of the Northwest League for two years. He also coached for the Brisbane Bandits of the Australian Baseball League and was commissioner of both the Atlantic Collegiate Baseball League and the Hamptons Collegiate Baseball League.[44] His number, 22, was retired by St. Leo University in 2018, and he is a member of both the St. Leo University Athletics Hall of Fame and the Suffolk Sports Hall of Fame.[45]

Although his arm injury limited him to one win in the majors, Cambria considers himself fortunate. "I have no regrets. Baseball was great to me," he commented in a 2011 interview, "and I still love it today."[46] He is also fiercely loyal to St. Leo University and takes pride that he not only developed his baseball skills at the college but also applied himself and earned a degree after having struggled academically in high school.[47]

Acknowledgments

The author wishes to thank Fred Cambria for speaking to him about his life and career as well as Bill Nowlin of SABR and Joe Billetdeaux of the Pittsburgh Pirates for helping arrange the interview with Cambria.

SOURCES

In addition to the sources found in the Notes, the author consulted Baseball-Reference.com and Retrosheet.org.

NOTES

1. Fred Cambria, telephone interview, April 6, 2023. In addition, Fred Cambria's father and his two younger siblings are mentioned in Murray Chass, "A Former Mets Fans Returns as a Foe," *New York Times*, September 20, 1970: 200. His mother's obituary can be found at https://nolanfh.com/tribute/details/1075/Rita-Cambria/obituary.html (accessed February 2023).
2. "Baseball Still the Life for Former MLB Pitcher," *Brooklyn Tablet*, August 11, 2011, https://thetablet.org/baseball-still-the-life-for-former-mlb-pitcher/.
3. Chass, "A Former Mets Fan Returns as a Foe."
4. "Baseball Still the Life for Former MLB Pitcher."
5. Cambria, telephone interview.
6. Kevin Weiss, "Saint Leo Baseball to Retire Jersey of Its First MLB Draftee," *Laker/Lutz News* (Land o' Lakes, Florida), April 11, 2018, https://lakerlutznews.com/lln/2018/04/56028/.
7. "Cambria Pitches Second Shutout for St. Leo," *Tampa Bay Times*, March 5, 1967: 17.
8. "Cambria Leads St. Leo 2-0," *Tampa Bay Times*, April 8, 1967: 31.
9. "Cambria, St. Leo Whip Stetson 8-1," *Tampa Bay Times*, March 16, 1967: 25; "Pitchers Hit, Monarchs Rout Tritons Twice," *Tampa Bay Times*, April 16, 1967: 22. Newspaper accounts of St. Leo College's doubleheader sweep of Florida Presbyterian College on April 15, 1967, do not specify what position Cambria played in the night cap. He pitched in the first game.
10. Weiss, "St. Leo Baseball to Retire Jersey of Its First MLB Draftee."
11. "Monarchs Halt Blue Devils," *Tampa Bay Times*, March 28, 1968: 29.
12. Dick Brusie, "Blue Devils Lose; Tim Teer Stars," *Durham (North Carolina) Sun*, March 28, 1968: 26.
13. "Baseball Still the Life for Former MLB Pitcher."
14. "St. Leo Stuns FSU 3-2," *Tallahassee Democrat*, March 10, 1969: 10.
15. "A King-Size Step for Monarchs," *Tampa Bay Times*, April 18, 1969: 36.
16. "Baseball Still the Life for Former MLB Pitcher."
17. U.S., Baseball Questionnaire, 1945-2005 for Frederick Dennis Cambria, https://www.ancestry.com/discoveryui-content/view/74189:61599 (accessed April 2023).
18. "York Pirates Open 8-Game Road Trip at Elmira Tonight," *York (Pennsylvania) Dispatch*, June 16, 1969: 21.
19. "York Pirates Top Phils, Hike EL Lead," *York Dispatch*, June 26, 1969: 25.
20. "Pirates' Rookie Hurls Perfect Game in Double Win," *York Dispatch*, July 16, 1969: 36.
21. Fred Cambria, interview with Danny Torres, Talking 21, podcast audio, https://talkin-21-podcast.castos.com/episodes/s2-ep-11-fred-cambria.
22. "Major League Prospects for 1970," *York Dispatch*, March 16, 1970: 28.
23. "Chris-Crossing," *Pittsburgh Press*, March 31, 1970: 35.
24. Cambria, interview with Danny Torres.
25. John Agnello, "Major League Lesson," *Spirit Magazine*, https://spirit.saintleo.edu/tag/fred-cambria/ (accessed February 2023); "St. Leo Jersey of Former Pittsburgh Pirate Fred Cambria '70 Retired," *Community: News for the St. Leo University Community*, https://community.saintleo.edu/2018/04/saint-leo-jersey-of-former-pittsburgh-pirate-fred-cambria-70-retired/ (accessed April 2023).
26. Craig Stolze, "Wings Whip Jets in Opener," *Rochester (New York) Democrat and Chronicle*, April 18, 1970: 33.
27. "1st Complete Game for Jets," *Rochester Democrat and Chronicle*, May 4, 1970: 39.
28. Bill Christine, "GM Brown Goes to Bat for Danny as Top Pilot," *Pittsburgh Press*, August 28, 1970: 29.
29. "Pirates Welcome Blass Back, Lose Dock Ellis," *Tyrone (Pennsylvania) Daily Herald*, August 15, 1970: 8.
30. "Pirates Buy Fred Cambria, Release Pena," *Pittsburgh Post-Gazette*, August 20, 1970: 30; Cambria, telephone interview.
31. "Cambria Sparkles in 2-1 Loss: San Diego Stalls Pirates Again," *Pittsburgh Press*, August 27, 1970: 45.
32. Chass, "A Former Mets Fan Returns as a Foe."
33. "Banks to Miss Cubs' Opener, Expos Give Up on Phillies," *Philadelphia Inquirer*, April 2, 1971: 25.
34. "Deleted, Tired Caps," *Charleston (West Virginia) Daily Mail*, July 7, 1971: 19.
35. "Underhanded Experiment," *Charleston Daily Mail*, May 17, 1972: 18.
36. Cambria, telephone interview.
37. Bill Christine, "Playing Games – Back to the Bushes," *Pittsburgh Post Gazette*, August 15, 1973: 27.
38. Cambria, telephone interview

39 Christine, "Playing Games."

40 Eric Pate, "Seeking Stability, Monarchs Open '90, *Tampa Bay Times*, February 3, 1990: 80.

41 Steve Persall, "St. Leo Hires Coach, Third in Three Years," *Tampa Bay Times*, July 12, 1989: 67.

42 "Highlights in History: The Many Names of St. Leo," https://www.saintleo.edu/about/stories/blog/highlights-in-history-the-many-names-of-saint-leo (accessed April 2023).

43 "Baseball Records," https://saintleolions.com/sports/2017/8/1/baseball-records.aspx (accessed February 2023).

44 "Cambria Named HCBL Commissioner," https://pointstreak.com/news_story.html?id=72187 (accessed February 2023).

45 Weiss, "Saint Leo Baseball to Retire Jersey of Its First MLB Draftee"; Cambria, Fred," https://www.suffolksportshof.com/fred-cambria/ (accessed April 2023).

46 "Baseball Still the Life for Former MLB Pitcher."

47 Cambria, telephone interview; Agnello, "Major League Lessons."

JIM CLINTON

BY MARK PESTANA

Nineteenth-century journeyman Jim Clinton logged 400-plus games in baseball's three major professional leagues between 1872 and 1886 and, in the midst of that (1877-1881), probably an equal number in various leagues and associations we would now categorize as "minor." He served with seven different clubs over the course of 10 seasons in the National Association, the National League, and the American Association, and with several more in the minor leagues. While the bulk of his diamond time was spent in the outfield, he played at every position. He made 19 major-league appearances as a pitcher, winning a single game. Remembered best for his fielding skills as an outfielder, he was popular wherever he went, well-respected as a gentleman and an honest player.

James Lawrence Clinton was born on August 10, 1850, in New York City, the second child of 31-year-old Lawrence Joseph Clinton and 20-year-old Mary (McLaughlin) Clinton. Both parents emigrated to the United States from Ireland, and at the time of James's birth, Mary's 60-year-old mother, Ann McLaughlin, also lived with the family at their home in New York's 17th Ward. The elder Clinton was a butcher, and census reports for at least the next 20 years listed his occupation as such. When he was born, James had a 1-year-old sister, Margaret, and Lawrence and Mary would eventually give him an additional seven siblings, the last being born in 1872.

Jim Clinton's earliest forays into the New York baseball scene came in the summer and fall of 1869, his first known appearance being on August 19, when he subbed for the Mutuals' regular right fielder in a game against Ross, a Harlem-based club, and made four safe hits and scored six runs in a lopsided 49-5 Mutuals victory.[1]

When the Mutuals opened their 1870 season on April 19, Clinton was at third base for an opposing picked nine.[2] He showed up with the Oriental Club on April 27, when, it was reported, he "handsomely whitewashed the Eckfords by the good stops he made at short field, and his accurate throwing."[3] His first known pitching effort came on May 3, in the Orientals' 29-5 loss to the Mutuals. Despite the overwhelming deficit, he was singled out as a "young player pitching with considerable judgement."[4] By September, he had upgraded to Brooklyn's Eckfords, taking turns in both infield and outfield.

Clinton was with the Eckfords again at the beginning of the 1871 season, but by June 7 had taken up with another venerable Brooklyn club, the Atlantics, playing second, third, and the outfield in a dozen or so games through late September.

Clinton's "big league" debut came in 1872. He was back with the Eckfords, who, along with the Atlantics, had paid the nominal $10 entry fee and officially joined the National Association. Clinton quickly became an Eckford regular, hitting safely in his first five games and demonstrating his versatility, appearing at second base, shortstop, third, catcher, and outfield.

His best offensive day came on June 21, versus the Mansfields of Middletown, Connecticut, when he stroked three hits in five trips to the plate, scored three runs, and knocked in one run. The next day, against these same Mansfields, Clinton made his first pitching start, going the full nine innings and suffering a 36-6 loss in which only seven of the Mansfield runs were earned. He spent most of the season at third base, playing in 25 games overall, the most on the club. The Eckfords had a miserable year, finishing 3-26, but, unlike five other weak NA franchises, they at least completed their schedule.

In 1873 Clinton departed Brooklyn and joined the Resolutes of Elizabeth, New Jersey, a new co-op club in the National Association, making his first appearance on May 6. Referring to him as "Clinton of the old Eckfords," the *New York Clipper* noted the improvement he provided at third base, praising his "sharp fielding."[5] The Resolutes never made it to the 1873 finish line, folding in early August with a 2-21 record. Clinton played in nine games, all at third base, including the August 7 finale in Brooklyn against the Mutuals. In its review of National Association third basemen, the *Clipper* stated, "Clinton did some good third-base play for the Resolute Club, but he was not kept in the position long enough. He is a very good and quite reliable player."[6]

With the Resolutes out of the NA, Clinton returned to the Atlantics for 1874. In their first official contest of the season, on May 5, Clinton played second base and notched two hits, two RBIs, and three runs as the Brooklynites crushed Baltimore, 24-3. Despite the impressive start, Clinton played only one more game with the Atlantics, on June 1, and then spent the remainder of 1874 with Reliance, a strong Brooklyn amateur club, playing mostly at shortstop but also appearing behind the plate and in the outfield.

The Atlantics brought Clinton back into the fold at the start of the 1875 season, and on May 11 he made his first pitching appearance in nearly three years, facing the Athletics of Philadelphia on Brooklyn's Union Grounds, the result being a 5-0 Atlantics loss, though only one of the five Athletic runs was earned. "Clinton threw the ball in by a plain underhand throw," said the *New York Clipper*, and "he had speed and tolerable command of the ball; but he should avoid all the preliminary motions in delivery that he can; for the moment he makes one of these movements, and fails to follow it up by delivering the ball, he commits a balk."[7] The *New York World* noted that he pitched "very swiftly" and that his "pace bothered the Athletics so much that they appealed as to its legality and it was tested, and the delivery being found to be below the hip the umpire very properly ruled it as legal."[8]

The next to last in a string of nine consecutive pitching starts by Clinton resulted in the single win of his big-league career. On May 26, before a crowd of only about 100 at the Union Grounds, he faced off against Harry Luff of the New Haven club and, in what turned out to be the longest Atlantics game of the season (3 hours and 10 minutes), came out on the winning end of a 14-4 score. The two teams combined for 30 errors, and the *Brooklyn Times Union* drily summarized: "[T]he game was not over brilliantly played," but also said that Clinton "pitched well."[9]

On August 6, Clinton made his final start for the Atlantics, losing 13-0 to Hartford's Tommy Bond. It was his worst defeat of the season, though only three of his opponents' runs were earned. At this point, the Atlantics were 2-30, and would eventually finish 2-42. In light of the team's performance, Clinton's 1-13 record seems not so much an embarrassment as an inevitability. His 104 runs allowed in 123 innings look incongruous alongside his 2.41 ERA, but this was an era when gloveless fielders were still the norm and earned runs were typically outnumbered by unearned ones. He did complete nine of his 14 starts, and allowed no home runs.

Shortly after his final start, Clinton was released by the Atlantics,[10] but was quickly picked up by the semipro Eagle Club of Louisville, Kentucky, debuting at third base in the club's game of August 16. Two days later, the Eagles tested his pitching skills, sending him in to hurl the final three innings against the NA champion Boston Reds. "The Eagles would improve their nine by putting Clinton as regular pitcher," opined the *Clipper*,[11] and the team did just that. Clinton pitched consistently for the Eagles into early October, notching several wins.

On the day after Christmas, 1875, 25-year-old James Clinton married Lillian A. McKay, age 19. Lillie was born in New Jersey, to Richard and Frances McKay, the third youngest of their 10 children. Jim and Lillie eventually had three sons and one daughter of their own: James, Francis, Joseph, and Mary, born between 1877 and 1889.

In March 1876 Clinton returned south, signing with a Memphis semipro team. He was named captain of the club. "In Jimmy Clinton the Olympic Club has secured the services of an excellent pitcher and as nice a gentleman, quiet and unobtrusive in his manners, as ever stepped on the ball field," a newspaper observed.[12]

The National League opened play in April 1876, and one of its eight entries was a club in Louisville, known as the Grays. The Grays visited Memphis the first week of April for a series of practice games with the Memphis club and must have been impressed by what they saw in Clinton, for they signed him to a contract later in the season.[13] Although Clinton was tapped for pitching duty in a few exhibition games against amateurs and semipros, he quickly became the Grays' regular right fielder. He made his only pitching start on the last day of Louisville's season, October 5, an 11-2 complete-game loss to Candy Cummings and the Hartfords.

His 16 games with Louisville would prove to be Clinton's last major-league work for five years. In 1877 he landed with the Syracuse Stars, a club in the League Alliance.[14] The Stars featured once and

Jim Clinton, front and center, with the Syracuse Stars.

future major-league notables such as Pete Hotaling, Hick Carpenter, and Dick Higham. Frequently playing NL teams, they proved they could hold their own against the big leaguers. On May 4 they lost a 1-0 contest to the Anson- and Spalding-led Chicago White Stockings. Only three days earlier, they had participated in one of the most astonishing matches of the era: a 15-inning scoreless tie with the St. Louis Brown Stockings.[15] On July 2 they shut out the Bostons 2-0, and they took revenge on Chicago with a 5-2 victory on August 31. Clinton played mostly outfield with the Stars but was occasionally used as the change pitcher, including on August 28, when he notched a 4-1 win against fellow Alliance club Indianapolis.

The 1878 season was a busy one for Clinton. His first engagement was with the New Haven club, a member of the International Association. The IA at the time was a sprawling organization that welcomed any and all professional teams, covering a wide swath of geography from Pennsylvania and upstate New York to New England and even into Canada. With the NL fielding a mere half-dozen teams in 1878, the IA was a force to be reckoned with, both in drawing power and on-field talent.

Clinton played a handful of games with New Haven but was released in early May, then quickly hooked up with another IA club, the Alleghenys of Pittsburgh. Playing mostly outfield, but with a couple of relief pitching appearances, he was a regular with Allegheny until the team disbanded on June 8. He latched on with the Erie IA club shortly thereafter but it disbanded as well, in early July.

After umpiring a game between IA Hartford and the Brooklyn Witokas on July 9, Clinton was engaged as first baseman by Hartford, but made only three games with them before the club was expelled from the Association for failing to pay guaranteed gate receipts to a visiting team. He continued to umpire Brooklyn area games through mid-September, and then joined the co-op New York Club of the seven-team Metropolitan organization. His first game with the New Yorks was September 28. In his next outing, September 30, he racked up 10 putouts in left field. The *Clipper* said, "Clinton's play in left field was the chief charm of the contest."[16] In all, he was with the New Yorks for probably fewer than 10 games, with a couple of pitching turns, before landing in late October on another local co-op, the Flyaways, with whom he finished the season.

In the early weeks of play in 1879, Clinton showed up in various picked nines and as a substitute for missing or injured players. He played one game for the reorganized Atlantics (still professional but no longer "major league") in May, and then signed on as left fielder for the Jersey City Browns of the National Association (as the IA was now known after the disbandment of the Tecumsehs of Ontario). The Browns fielded a strong team that featured future big leaguers Dude Esterbrook, Dasher Troy, and Tom Poorman. One of Clinton's best games came on August 19, when he connected for two triples in a 6-0 win over Springfield. In mid-October the Browns split a pair of games with the NL champion Providence Grays.

The *Clipper* lauded Clinton's outfield work: "Clinton, who ... played left field last season for the Jersey City Browns, had about the best fielding record in that position of all the professional players in the country, having missed but three catches, and those difficult ones, in seventy games; while he assisted the unusually large number of twenty-five times in retiring players on good throws from the outfield."[17]

Clinton's first action in 1880 was in early May with the Albany NA club, which also included Lip Pike and Tim Keefe. After being released by the Albanys, he moved on to a new Brooklyn professional nine but he, along with the team, seemed to disappear from the arena after a May 31 game against Clinton's ex-mates, the Jersey Citys. In August he played outfield on an ad hoc nine of local pros organized to participate in a three-team tourney with two top NA clubs, Washington and

Rochester. Clinton made five hits in the series and drew praise for his fielding.

The *Clipper* honored Clinton with a short bio and woodcut portrait in the edition of September 11, 1880, saying he was "at one time well known as a pitcher" and calling him "a faithful and earnest worker ... quiet and gentlemanly."[18]

September and October proved to be the busiest months of the baseball season for Clinton, as he rejoined the Jersey City Browns for a half-dozen games and then moved on to the newly formed Metropolitan club of New York. On September 29 the Mets opened up New York's first professional ball field, the Polo Grounds. Two days later, Clinton powered the Mets to a 7-3 victory over the Washington Nationals, blasting a two-run triple in the Mets' four-run ninth inning.

In October the Mets played several exhibition games against NL teams. In a series with the Worcesters, Clinton hit a home run off one of the League's top pitchers, Lee Richmond. The Mets dropped the first three of a series with Troy, but won the final three, with Clinton tagging future Hall of Famer Mickey Welch for two hits, including a triple in the closer.

Clinton was back with the Metropolitans as regular center fielder in 1881. Among his teammates were Dude Esterbrook, Mike Dorgan, and the "one-armed" pitcher, Hugh Daily. Over the course of their April-to-October schedule, the Mets surpassed all previous marks by playing 151 games. Clinton participated in nearly 100 games, the most by far for him in any season. After a loss to the Atlantic club on September 5, however, Clinton disappeared from the Mets lineup, Tom Mansell replacing him in center field for the remainder of the month. Clinton briefly renewed his membership with the Atlantics, joining the club on a Western tour to St. Louis and Louisville.

In early October, the Mets called him back to sub at first base for Esterbrook for four games, all against League clubs, but by the 11th, Esterbrook had returned and Clinton was relegated to umpiring duties for a Mets match with Troy. He bounced back to the Atlantics in mid-October, just in time for a series of games against the Mets, ostensibly for the "local championship."[19] His final appearances of the season came in the last week of October, playing center field for the Olympic Club of Paterson, New Jersey, in a couple of matches with – once again – the Metropolitans. The *Clipper*'s year-end review of the outfielding of 1881 hailed Clinton, Kennedy, and Roseman (all of the Mets), saying they had "borne off the palm by the splendid running catches each of them made."[20]

Clinton began the 1882 season at first base for the Atlantics, but when NL Worcester lost its first baseman to injury[21] and moved left fielder Harry Stovey in to fill that position, Clinton was signed to fill the outfield vacancy. He joined the Central Massachusetts club in time for a series with the Chicago White Stockings, making three hits and scoring three runs to help the Worcesters take the first two games of the series. From there, however, the team nosedived, winning only one of their next 20 games. After a long rough patch – only 10 hits in 17 games through July 4 – Clinton went missing from the Worcester lineup for most of July. He finally returned in games versus Providence and Boston in the final week of the month, his season highlight coming July 28 with two hits and two runs in a wild 12-11 win over Boston. After playing left field in a loss to the Detroit Wolverines on August 7, Clinton was released by Worcester. Within a week, he was back with the Metropolitans as they began a series of exhibition games with visiting NL teams that included wins over Detroit, Buffalo, Troy, and Providence.

In 1883 the sophomore campaign of the American Association, Clinton signed with the Baltimore Orioles, and it turned out to be his career year – the best he ever enjoyed at the plate. He led the Orioles in nearly every offensive category, and finished in the AA's top 10 in batting average, on-base percentage, slugging average, hits, singles, and walks. He played in 94 of the Orioles' 96 games, almost all in left field.

The month of July was especially hot for Clinton, including a 4-for-4 day against Columbus and 4-for-6 with three runs against Pittsburgh. In a July 19 tilt with the Athletics, he went 4-for-5 with five runs, including a single to start a three-run ninth-inning rally that gave the Baltimores a 10-9 victory. The highlight of the Orioles' season was a four-game sweep of Louisville in late August. After drawing a blank in the first match, Clinton went 8-for-15 the rest of the way, with three doubles, a triple, and seven runs scored.

Clinton's numbers fell off in 1884, but he remained one of the Orioles' best hitters, leading the regulars with a .270 batting average and a .334 on-base percentage, and hitting the only four home runs of his career. Alternating between left field and center field, he appeared in 104 of 108 games. His five double plays ranked second among AA outfielders.

By early November 1884, word was out that Clinton's days in Baltimore were numbered. In a letter dated November 3 and printed in the *Clipper*, he set the record straight about his move:

> "Dear Sir: Please allow me to contradict through your paper a statement regarding myself, made by the Baltimore correspondent of a Philadelphia paper, in which he assigns my main object in choosing Cincinnati in preference to Baltimore as a city to play in to be the size of the salary. It has never been a question of money between Manager Barnie and myself. I asked for my release simply on account of the continued ill-health of my wife, for whom a change of air was recommended as being highly beneficial. But some people seem to know more about my business than I do myself."[22]

The pundits in Porkopolis approved, writing, "In Clinton the home nine have secured a daisy"[23] and "In Clinton and Baldwin the club have two good batters, the former being the equal of such men as Carpenter, McPhee and Corkhill."[24]

While Clinton struggled at the plate for the first month of 1885, his fielding prowess left an immediate mark, as in the Reds' 2-1 win over St. Louis on April 21:

> "The king of the occasion, however, was Clinton. His center field work today has never been excelled even by Corkhill. Such fly catches as he made off three balls are seldom seen in a season. ... In the ninth inning their first two batters hit safe; the next flied out to Jones. Then Clinton made the greatest fly catch of the day, two inches from the ground on the dead run. A double play was easy, as both base runners were almost home."[25]

Sadly, 1885 was to bring personal tragedy to Jim Clinton, and the first hint of something amiss came in early July when he missed four consecutive games. The *Cincinnati Commercial Gazette* explained: "Clinton's wife and children are sick at their home in Baltimore. He left last night for that place on a leave of absence."[26] Within a month, he fell ill himself, but continued playing, the *Gazette* noting: "Clinton and McPhee have been suffering from malaria for three weeks past, yet both manage to play excellent ball."[27]

Two weeks later, the Reds hosted league-leading St. Louis for a three-game series. Clinton played the opener on August 22, but the next day "was at home anxiously watching by the bedside of a very sick child."[28] Four-year-old Frankie Clinton died on the evening of August 25. In the series finale, "in token of their sorrow for their comrade's loss the Cincinnati players wore crape on their left arms."[29] Clinton returned to the diamond on August 28. The *Gazette* said: "Jimmy showed that he was not feeling well, but he did the best he could. The warm sympathy of the crowd was expressed for him by a general yet quiet applause, which arose when he went to bat for the first time."[30]

Released at his own request[31] at the end of October, Clinton was a 35-year-old free agent as the 1886 season opened. He was appointed in early May to replace a resigning Association umpire, and through the third week of the month worked almost daily. But a match at Washington Park, Brooklyn, between visiting St. Louis and the Dodgers may well have been the low point of Clinton's career on the diamond. Making a bad call or two early in the game, he became so rattled by the crowd's backlash that he allowed his judgment to be clouded, leading to further mistakes.[32] The local gamblers, seeing their team jump to an early lead, had "invested at odds on the success of the Brooklyns" but then grew ever more agitated as the bad play of the Dodgers and Clinton's shaky work doomed their chances.[33] As the last out of the 7-4 St. Louis victory was tallied, the mob was ready to pounce. The Brooklyn players, along with club President Byrne and a contingent of police, shielded Clinton and escorted him to safety.[34] After umpiring games in Philadelphia and New York the next two days, Clinton tendered his resignation and returned home to Baltimore.[35]

Two weeks after doffing his arbiter's attire, Clinton was patrolling center field again in an Orioles uniform. He made a good start, with a couple of multihit games in his first few outings, but a return to 1883 batting form was not in the offing. In mid-July, after a disastrous 3-13 Western road trip, manager Billy Barnie released three players, including Clinton. He had fielded reputably, as always, but batted a mere .181. Even on a team with a collective .204 batting average, it had been a disappointing 23-game stint. He finished the season with another of his former teams, the Jersey Citys of the Eastern League.[36]

Though he had taken his final bow as a major leaguer, Clinton was not yet finished in professional ball. He was engaged by Nashville of the Southern League in early 1887 as its left fielder[37] and, beginning in May, added managerial duties.[38] Before financial instability forced the club to disband on August 2, Clinton played 49 games with Nashville, topping all regulars with a .389 batting average and stealing 25 bases. He went home to Brooklyn at this point,[39] but before month's end was headed back to the Southern League, engaged this time by the Birmingham Club.[40] Once again he was called upon to carry out dual duties as manager and outfielder. Still performing at a high level with the bat, he completed the season with Birmingham batting .336.

Signing on as player-manager of the Manchester (New Hampshire) Club of the New England League, Clinton had high hopes for 1888. At a benefit for the club in March, he proclaimed: "We don't want the earth; only a small portion of it; we want the championship of the New England League."[41] Calling Clinton "one of the very old-timers," the *Boston Globe* noted that he "can still hit the ball and field with the best of them."[42]

The good feelings were not to last, however, and Clinton batting .315 was not enough to lift his team out of its doldrums. By late June, the Manchesters' record was 18-21 and the club was at the bottom of the NEL standings. An uncharacteristically angry Clinton even drew a $10 fine for using bad language to an umpire.[43] He was released by the Manchesters in early July. The *Boston Globe* opined that he had "made a bad mistake" going to the team in the first place.[44]

Although rumors of offers from Charleston and Atlanta of the Southern League floated about in early 1889,[45] there would be no return trip south. Instead, on March 19, Clinton was appointed an umpire in the Atlantic Association, one of the minor leagues governed by the National Agreement.[46] This stint lasted only about two months and ended with Clinton being "removed" from the Atlantic Association's umpiring crew in mid-June. The exact cause of removal is not known, but the report of an early season Boston-Jersey City match hints at problems: "Jim Clinton, formerly of the Manchesters, umpired, and his work, in the main, was pretty bad. He made some very telling decisions and the clubs suffered about alike. ... Kelly was hit by a pitched ball, but the umpire did not see it. ... Clinton made an outrageous decision in calling Kelly out at second. ..."[47]

The *Clipper* reported in July, "The veteran James L. Clinton says that he has given up umpiring, and wants to get an engagement again as a player with one of the minor league teams."[48] There is no evidence he ever made any inroads on this wish, though speculation persisted as late as 1896 that he could return to the umpiring ranks.[49]

Though no longer directly involved in organized ball, Clinton kept up with current happenings. He was among the "prominent persons" at the February 1894 NL-AA meeting,[50] one of the "interested persons" at the Eastern League meeting in December 1895,[51] and among "the baseball men seen around the corridors" at the annual NL spring meeting in February 1896.[52]

Clinton's eldest son, James Jr., for a time sought to follow in his father's footsteps. He had a tryout with New Haven of the Connecticut State League in 1899, then moved on to Norwich, also of the Connecticut league, and Newark of the Atlantic League, playing a total of about 30 games for the season.[53] The next year he joined Petersburg of the Virginia League, batting .259 in 36 games, until the team disbanded in June. His baseball career was brief and, more sadly, so was his life. James Jr. became the second of Jim and Lillie's children to predecease his parents, dying on May 6, 1901, of scarlet fever, at the age of 23. His obituary referred to his father as "one of the best known old-time ball players in this section of the country."[54]

A December 1896 notice in the *Brooklyn Times Union* proclaimed: "Good News For Mr. Clinton," explaining that Clinton, "who is identified with the management of a Thirteenth ward hotel," had just received word from a law firm in Oakland that land he and a fellow Atlantics player bought on a Western tour in 1874 had increased in value to $20,000. The surprised Clinton asserted that either he or his friend would "go on to Oakland to investigate," hoping that an even "better price might be secured."[55] It is not known what came of this venture.

Clinton was a bartender in multiple New York establishments from at least 1900 onward. A brief note in the *Daily Eagle* said he was "in business in the Eastern District" in 1897.[56] A 1907 newspaper blurb about a friend of Clinton's, a welterweight boxer named Kid Williams, discloses that Clinton was then bartending at J.P. Stanton's Cafe at the Lincoln Hotel in Queens.[57]

At the time of the 1905 New York State Census, the two youngest Clinton children, Joseph and Mary, were still living with their parents in Brooklyn. By 1910, Mary was the last child still at home, age 20, employed as a stenographer. Wife Lillian died on January 16, 1914, at the age of 57.

Finally, the Brooklyn *Standard Union* of Tuesday, September 6, 1921, carried the following obituary notice for the old-time ballplayer who had died the preceding Saturday, September 3, at the age of 71:

"Funeral services are being held today for James L. Clinton, former member of the Baltimore Orioles, who died Saturday at his home, 768 Grand street. Interment will be made this afternoon at Calvary Cemetery."[58]

Jim Clinton's obituary oddly singled out his time with the Baltimore club, to the exclusion even of the many Brooklyn teams for whom he toiled. His connection to the City of Monuments was also evident in the wistful poetic exercise of a *Baltimore Sun* reader who, in 1912, versified a vision of his youth in Baltimore, surveying a myriad of people and places he remembered there from the "eighties":

I tell you, folks, this dream took me to every part of town.
I even saw a baseball game out on the York road lot –
Bob Emslie in the pitcher's box, with Henderson and Trott.
I saw old Traffley, Fulmer, York and Jimmy Clinton, too;
This bunch looked good to all the fans 'round eighteen eighty-two.[59]

SOURCES

In addition to the sources cited in the Notes, the author consulted

Baseball-Reference.com

Retrosheet.org

Familysearch.org

StatsCrew.com/minorbaseball

Nemec, David. *Major League Baseball Profiles: 1871-1900, Volume 1* (Lincoln, Nebraska: Bison Books, 2011).

NOTES

1. He is also very likely the third baseman identified as "Clayton" and "Cloton" «playing for the amateur Orientals of New York on September 30 and October 16.
2. *New York Clipper*, April 30, 1870: 29.
3. *New York Clipper*, May 7, 1870: 36.
4. *New York Clipper*, May 14, 1870: 45.
5. *New York Clipper*, May 17, 1873: 53.
6. *New York Clipper*, March 14, 1874: 397.
7. *New York Clipper*, May 22, 1875: 61.
8. *New York World*, May 12, 1875: 8.
9. *Brooklyn Times Union*, May 27, 1875: 3.
10. *New York Clipper*, August 28, 1875: 170.
11. *New York Clipper*, August 28, 1875: 173.
12. *Louisville Courier-Journal*, March 17, 1876: 4.
13. *St. Louis Globe-Democrat*, August 26, 1876: 8.
14. *New York Clipper*, November 10, 1883: 559, and *Chicago Daily Tribune*, March 4, 1877: 8. The League Alliance consisted of about a dozen "minor" professional and semipro clubs in different sections of the country, affiliated through an agreement with the NL meant to protect players (and teams) from contract raiding.
15. *New York Clipper*, May 12, 1877: 50. "For the first time in the history of the national game fifteen innings had been played without a run being credited to either side."
16. *New York Clipper*, October 12, 1878: 229.
17. *New York Clipper*, November 29, 1879: 282.
18. *New York Clipper*, September 11, 1880: 197.
19. *New York Herald*, October 17, 1881: 11.
20. *New York Clipper*, December 31, 1881: 676.
21. *New York Clipper*, June 10, 1882: 191.
22. *New York Clipper*, November 8, 1884: 540.
23. *Cincinnati Post*, November 13, 1884: 3.
24. *Cincinnati Commercial Gazette*, April 13, 1885: 8.
25. *Cincinnati Commercial Gazette*, April 22, 1885: 6.
26. *Cincinnati Commercial Gazette*, July 8, 1885: 3.
27. *Cincinnati Commercial Gazette*, August 11, 1885 3.
28. *Cincinnati Commercial Gazette*, August 24, 1885: 2.
29. *Cincinnati Commercial Gazette*, August 27, 1885: 3.
30. *Cincinnati Commercial Gazette*, August 29, 1885: 6.
31. *New York Clipper*, October 31, 1885: 522.
32. *Sporting Life*, May 26, 1886: 5; *New York Clipper*, May 29, 1886: 164.
33. *Brooklyn Daily Eagle*, May 20, 1886: 2.
34. *New York Tribune*, May 20, 1886: 2.
35. *Baltimore Sun*, May 28, 1886: 2, Supplement.
36. *Cleveland Plain Dealer*, August 14, 1886: 5.
37. *Brooklyn Daily Eagle*, February 20, 1887: 7.
38. *The Sporting News*, May 21, 1887: 4.
39. *The Sporting News*, August 13, 1887: 1.
40. *The Sporting News*, August 27, 1887: 4.
41. *Brooklyn Daily Eagle*, March 18, 1888: 6.
42. *Boston Globe*, May 11, 1888: 11.
43. *Brooklyn Daily Eagle*, May 27, 1888: 6.
44. *Boston Globe*, July 10, 1888: 5.
45. *Philadelphia Times*, March 17, 1889: 16; *The Sporting News*, March 30, 1889: 5.
46. *Brooklyn Daily Eagle*, March 20, 1889: 4, and April 19, 1889: 1.
47. *Boston Herald*, April 19, 1889: 4.
48. *New York Clipper*, July 6, 1889: 277.
49. *St. Louis Republic*, December 18, 1889: 6; *Kentucky Post*, December 20, 1895: 7; *New York Clipper*, January 4, 1896: 699.
50. *New York Clipper*, March 10, 1894: 9.
51. *New York Clipper*, December 21, 1895: 668.
52. *Boston Globe*, February 25, 1896: 2.
53. His obituary in the *Brooklyn Times Union* says he played in the Virginia League in 1900 and with Newark the year before (1899). StatsCrew.com lists "James Clinton" with New Haven in 1899 and with Petersburg, Virginia, in 1900. But it also lists a "Henry Clinton" with Norwich and Newark in 1899. It would appear that he played under the second name for parts of 1899, and that James and Henry must be the same person.
54. *Brooklyn Times Union*, May 7, 1901: 8.
55. *Brooklyn Times Union*, December 11, 1896: 1.
56. *Brooklyn Daily Eagle*, December 12, 1897: 9.
57. *Middletown Orange County Times Press*, July 19, 1907: 2.
58. *Brooklyn Standard Union*, September 6, 1921: 4.
59. *Baltimore Sun*, February 25, 1912: 26. The poem, "A Child Just for a Night," was signed "Peter A. Fahey, Cleveland, Ohio, 1912." The author was slightly off in assigning the date of 1882 to the players named in the poem. Clinton, Henderson, and Emslie didn't join the Orioles until 1883; Trott, York, and Traffley, not until 1884; Fulmer, not until 1886 All but Fulmer did play together in Baltimore in 1884.

ED COLE

BY GREGORY H. WOLF

After spring training tryouts with the Philadelphia Athletics and Phillies and seven years in the minors, Ed Cole caught on with the St. Louis Browns in 1938. Pitching primarily in relief, Cole won his only big-league game that season in a grueling start against the Boston Red Sox at Fenway Park. The rubber-armed pitcher, however, had a long career in Organized Baseball, toiling for 16 seasons and retiring at the age of 42 with more than 2,700 innings to his credit.

Ed Cole was the simplified, Americanized name the child of immigrants began using at around the age of 20. His exact name and birth date raise some questions. According to his birth certificate, he was born on March 22, 1909, in Wilkes-Barre, Pennsylvania; however, his World War II military draft card dates his birth as April 25, and his application for military benefits dates it as March 31. His parents were Stanislaw Kiselauckas and Marion Romaukas, both born in Lithuania, then part of the Russian Empire. They married in Lithuania in about 1891, had their first child, Joseph, and then immigrated to the United States. By 1895 they had settled in Wilkes-Barre, a booming industrial city of 40,000 residents located in the heart of northeastern Pennsylvania's coal region. Stanley, as he was known in the US, quickly found employment in the anthracite coal mines, notorious for their dangerous working conditions. Census and naturalization records provide a number of different spellings for the family's surname (Kisielauckas, Kisoloskie, for example); however, Kisloski became the norm. Edward William Kisloski was the family's ninth of 10 children born between approximately 1892 and 1913 (six boys and four girls). The family resided in the Georgetown neighborhood of south Wilkes-Barre.

Little is known about young Ed's introduction to baseball. It's likely he learned to play ball on local sandlots and then graduated to a mill team. Like his brothers, he had little formal education and completed just one year of high school. By 1930 he was working in a silk mill, as his brothers did. Silk and textiles were thriving industries in Luzerne County, in the Wyoming Valley, formed by the Pocono Mountains to the east, the Endless Mountains to the north and west, and the Lehigh Valley to the south.

Cole's professional career began with a brief stint with the Johnstown Johnnies in the Class-C Middle Atlantic League in 1931. The following season he hurled for the Stroudsburg Poconos in the Class-D Interstate League and won seven games before the league disbanded after about 26 games on June 20.[1] Cole remained with the club, which was converted into a semipro team skippered by former big leaguer Eddie Murphy, who had started in right field on Connie Mack's pennant-winning Philadelphia A's in 1913 and 1914. On September 7, 1931, Cole took the mound against the A's in an exhibition in

Stroudsburg. Described by the *Philadelphia Inquirer* as a "star ... with 23 wins and only 1 defeat," Cole held the A's scoreless through four innings and emerged victorious, 8-7 in a 10-inning tilt.[2] Mack apparently signed Cole on the spot.[3]

Coming off a second-place finish (94-60), Mack invited Cole to the A's spring training at Fort Myers, Florida, in 1933, but little was expected of the 24-year-old, 5-foot-11, 170-pound green recruit. Near the end of camp, Cole was assigned to the Wilkes-Barre Barons in the Class-A New York-Penn League. After logging 23 innings, Cole was released early in the season, and resumed playing semipro ball for Stroudsburg,[4] as well as the Philadelphia All-Stars, managed by former big-league hurler Joe Bush.[5]

Cole's wait for another shot on the big stage did not last long. Philadelphia native Jimmie Wilson, who returned to the Phillies as player-manager after six seasons with the St. Louis Cardinals, signed the 25-year-old right-hander and invited him to spring training in Winter Haven, Florida, in 1934.[6]

Ultimately assigned to Hazleton, located only 25 south miles from his hometown, Cole emerged as one of the New York-Penn League's top hurlers in 1934. While the Mountaineers finished a half-game out of the cellar of the eight-team league, Cole won 18 games and logged 250 innings (the circuit's fourth best totals in each category). In mid-August he was traded along with Don Maynard to the Galveston Buccaneers in the Class-A Texas League for Jim Bivin and Orville Jorgens, for delivery the next season. The popular pitcher was feted by friends and family on September 23 beginning with an impressive caravan of 50 automobiles departing Wilkes-Barre en route to the ballpark in Hazleton, where Cole tossed a four-hitter to beat Harrisburg, 2-1, on a two-run ninth-inning rally.[7]

Cole spent the next three seasons (1935-1937) with Galveston developing a reputation as a hard-throwing, innings-eating workhorse. On July 10, 1935, he made national headlines. With a "hopping fast ball and a curve that was breaking," Cole tossed what was acknowledged as the first perfect game in Texas League history, fanning eight to beat Tulsa, 1-0, on Maggie McGee's ninth-inning inside-the-park home run.[8] That accomplishment provided Cole enough notoriety to serve as a pitchman for Huskies cereal, appearing in advertisements with nationally known figures like Ohio State University football coach Francis Schmidt and golfer Johnny Revolta, who had won the 1935 PGA championship.[9] Cole finished the season with 15 wins and a league-most 19 defeats, and logged 264 innings with a 3.20 ERA.

Described as a "speedballer,"[10] Cole was off to a fast start in 1936 and was leading the circuit in innings pitched by mid-July.[11] He was selected to the league all-star game, but came down with arm pain ("nursing injuries," reported *The Sporting News*) and did not play.[12] He was shut down soon after the

Ed Cole. Courtesy St. Louis Browns Historical Society Archives.

game with a season record of 9-11 and a 3.33 ERA in 165 innings.

In 1937 Cole put together the finest season in his 16-year career in Organized Baseball. He led the eight-team Texas League (which had been elevated to A1 status a year earlier) in innings pitched (313) and strikeouts (205) while posting a misleading 18-18 slate and 2.85 ERA for a sixth-place club (73-86), and earned another all-star berth.[13]

In a whirlwind series of transactions, Cole was the property of four different teams in less than six months. Galveston sold him to the St. Paul Saints of the American Association in September 1937.[14] A month later, the Cleveland Indians chose him in the Rule 5 draft, but before the 1938 season began, he was traded along with Roy Hughes and Billy Sullivan to the St. Louis Browns on February 10, 1938, for their disgruntled All-Star catcher Rollie Hemsley.

Cole joined the Browns in spring training in San Antonio. Coming off a miserable season with the major leagues' worst record (46-108), the Browns were in desperate of need of pitching, a seemingly annual conundrum. The staff's ERA (6.00) was the majors' highest for the third consecutive season. New manager Gabby Street, who had replaced Sunny Jim Bottomley, promised to instill discipline and teach fundamentally sound baseball. Demanding high expectations, Old Sarge, as Street was known, had skippered the Cardinals, the Browns' tenants at Sportsman's Park, to two pennants and a World Series title (1931) earlier in the decade.

Few expected Cole to make the Browns' roster, but the 29-year-old right-hander proved to be a surprise. The *St. Louis Post-Dispatch* raved about his "snapping curve" and "breezing" heater.[15] Street declared that he was "wholeheartedly sold on Cole's style of delivery and rubber arm" and his willingness to pitch "low and inside."[16] By the end of camp, Gateway City sportswriter Sid Keener praised Cole as one of the nine best prospects on both the Browns and Cardinals, an impressive group that included future Redbird All-Stars Max Lanier and Enos Slaughter.[17] On the Browns' trip north to St. Louis, they stopped in Kansas City to play an exhibition against the Chicago Cubs on April 12. Cole tossed what beat reporter Ray J. Gillespie described as "by far the best pitching exhibition" during the Browns' spring training, holding the Cubs hitless through five innings.[18] Despite that outing, Cole was slated to start the season in the bullpen.

After toiling for seven seasons in the minors (1931-1937), Cole finally made his major-league debut on April 22 against the Chicago White Sox at Sportsman's Park. Cole relieved starter Oral Hildebrand to start the eighth inning and tossed four scoreless frames, surrendering two hits and walking three in the Browns eventual 4-3 loss in 13 innings. Sportswriter W. Vernon Tietjen of the *St. Louis Star and Times* praised the debut as a "sleek" performance;[19] while beat reporter Robert L. Burnes of the *St. Louis Globe-Democrat* declared it "brilliant relief hurling" and predicted that "Cole won himself a starting assignment."[20] It was Cole's best outing as a big leaguer.

In his next appearance, Cole was clobbered as a starter, yielding eight hits and six runs to the Detroit Tigers on April 25 at Sportsman's Park. Shuffled back to the bullpen, Cole spent the remainder of the season primarily hurling in mop-up, low-leverage situations. His 36 appearances trailed only starter Bobo Newsom's 44. Cole pitched well in relief (3.62 ERA in 30 games), but struggled in his six starting assignments (8.47 ERA).

Cole picked up his first and only big-league win in a start against the Red Sox at Fenway Park on August 30. He labored through 6⅔ innings, surrendering 10 hits and walking five in the Browns' 9-5 victory. Cole was relieved by 44-year-old Fred Johnson, a minor-league legend whom the Browns had purchased in late July. Johnson was in the midst of a brief return to the majors since last playing for the New York Giants in 1923. In his next start, Cole went the distance for the first and only time in his career, losing to the White Sox, 8-2, at Comiskey Park.

It was another dismal season for the Browns (55-97), who replaced Old Sarge with Ski Melillo with nine games remaining, but squeaked out of the cellar by two games over the Athletics. The club batted a robust .281 (tied for the AL's third best mark), but was once again doomed by a revolving carousel of scuffling hurlers, 10 of whom started at least four games, and who posted the majors' highest team ERA (5.80). Cole finished the season with a 1-5 record and 5.18 ERA in 88⅔ innings. The Browns lost 29 of the 35 games in which he appeared.

Back with the Browns in 1939, Cole slogged through a rough spring training for new skipper Fred Haney, who had piloted the Browns' affiliate in the American Association the previous four years. Haney's biggest challenge was finding capable pitchers. After an especially atrocious performance by Cole in San Antonio, sportswriter W. Vernon Tietjen asserted that it "simply emphasized the Browns crying need for moundsmen."[21] Help would not come from Cole, who landed the last spot on the staff. Just days after a blockbuster 10-player trade with the Detroit Tigers, in which the Browns acquired three pitchers (George Gill, Vern Kennedy, and Roxie Lawson) among six total players on May 13, Cole was optioned to the San Antonio Missions in the Texas League. His demotion was no surprise: in four relief appearances, he had yielded five earned runs in 4⅔ innings and lost twice.

Flashing his heater and curve, Cole was one of the Texas circuit's best hurlers. He posted a 16-10 slate with a 2.70 ERA in 257 innings, helping the Missions to a tie for second place. He earned a call-up to the Browns in late September. In his final two big-league appearances, Cole was charged with no runs in 1⅔ innings, but walked four, yielded two hits, and let three inherited runners score. The Browns, whose 52-year history (1902-1953) in St. Louis was filled with nadirs, finished with the majors' worst record (43-111) and the worst winning percentage in franchise history (.279). [The 2018 Baltimore Orioles gave that team a run for that dubious mark, finishing with a 47-115 record and the second-lowest winning percentage (.290).]

Cole never made it back to the majors, either in spring training or the regular season. Over the course of his next nine seasons in Organized Baseball (1940-1941; 1946-1951), interrupted by four years during World War II, Cole gradually worked his way down the minors, playing for eight different teams in seven leagues.

In January 1940, Cole and several other Browns players (notably Johnny Berardino and Joe Glenn) as well as other major leaguers, were involved in a controversy when it was revealed that they had applied for and received unemployment benefits amounting to $15 per week during the offseason.[22] "The law was never meant to include baseball players," said Donald Barnes, president of the Browns. "They may receive their compensation during only the active months of the baseball season, but they actually are not unemployed."[23] Nonetheless, Missouri state Attorney General E.C. Crowe upheld the players' right to the benefit.

After splitting his time with Toledo and San Antonio and posting a combined 8-17 record in 1940, Cole was sold to the Seattle Rainiers (Pacific Coast League) for the 1941 season. A broken foot limited him to 123 innings, but he proved otherwise effective (11-6, 3.00 ERA).[24]

A bachelor with no dependents, Cole, by then in his 30s, enlisted in the US Army on March 31, 1942, at Fort Meade, Maryland.[25] He was later stationed at Fort Riley in Kansas, where he hurled for the base team.[26] He rose to the rank of tech 4. According to his application for World War II compensation, he saw action in the European Theater from April 1943 to September 1945, and was discharged from the Army in October 1945.

Almost four years removed from his previous appearance in Organized Baseball, the 37-year-old Cole returned to the Missions in 1946. He notched a robust 13-9 slate in 189 innings in the Texas League, which had been elevated to Double A in that season's reorganization of minor league classifications with the introduction of Triple A. Cole enjoyed his biggest success with the Wichita Falls (Texas) Spudders in the Class-B Big State League in 1948 and 1949, winning 18 and 16 games, respectively. He concluded his 16-year professional career with the Port Arthur (Texas) Seahawks in the Class-B Gulf Coast League, retiring at the age of 42.

In parts of two seasons with the Browns, Cole went 1-7 with a 5.31 ERA in 95 innings. Though his minor-league records are not complete, the rubber-armed right-hander logged in excess of 2,600 innings and won at least 164 games.

Cole worked as a carpenter in his post-baseball life, eventually settling in Nashville, Tennessee. He died at the age of 90 on July 28, 1999, at the Windsor House nursing home. He had no survivors.[27] There was no memorial service and he was buried at the Nashville National Cemetery, administered by the US Department of Veterans Affairs.

SOURCES

In addition to the sources cited in the Notes, the author accessed Retrosheet.org; Baseball-Reference.com; the SABR Minor Leagues Database, accessed online at Baseball-Reference.com; SABR.org; *The Sporting News* archive via Paper of Record; newspapers via Newspaper.com; and Ancestry.com.

NOTES

1. Lloyd Johnson and Miles Wolff, *The Encyclopedia of Minor League Baseball*, 2nd edition (Durham, North Carolina: Baseball America, 1997), 274.
2. James C. Isaminger, "Stroudsburg Tops Mackmen in Tenth," *Philadelphia Inquirer*, September 8, 1932: 16.
3. Isaminger.
4. "Northampton Books Stroudsburg Poconos," *Allentown* (Pennsylvania), *Morning Call*, June 2, 1933: 24.
5. "Inside Stuff," *Morning Call*, May 18, 1933: 16.
6. "Ed Cole Signed by Philadelphia Nats," *Altoona* (Pennsylvania) *Tribune*, February 20, 1934: 10.
7. "Georgetown Fans to Honor Cole Tomorrow Afternoon," *Wilkes-Barre* (Pennsylvania) *Record*, August 22, 1934: 15; "Hazleton Slugger Bats in Victory as Georgetown Homers Hurler," *Wilkes-Barre Record*, August 24, 1934: 17.
8. "First Perfect Game of Ball in Texas League History Is Hurled by Ed Cole Wednesday," *Tyler* (Texas) *Morning Telegraph*, July 11, 1935: 8.
9. An example of the printed advertisement is in the *Longview* (Texas) *News Journal*, March 13, 1936: 9.
10. Lorin McMullen, "Cats Have to Contend with That Stingy Cole Tonight," *Fort Worth Star-Telegram*, July 18, 1936: 13.
11. "Texas League Leaders," *Fort Worth Star-Telegram*, July 9, 1936: 17.
12. Jimmy Byron, "Southern Stars of Texas League Eclipse Constellation of North," *The Sporting News*, July 30, 1936: 2.
13. "Texas All-Stars Announced; Keesey, Severeid Rival Pilots," *The Sporting News*, July 15, 1937: 3.
14. Associated Press, "Galveston Ace Sold," *Abilene* (Texas) *Register News*, September 9, 1937: 14.
15. "Van Atta and Cole in Form as Browns Win in 11th," *St. Louis Post-Dispatch*, March 27, 1938: 11.
16. Maurice O. Shevlin," Gabby Street Calls Off Catcher's Battery Drill," *St. Louis Globe-Democrat*, March 12, 1938: 6.
17. Sid Keener, "Sid Keener's Column," *St. Louis Star and Times*, April 11, 1938: 20.
18. Ray J. Gillespie, "Browns' Rookie Pitcher Hurls Five Hitless Innings Against Cubs," *St. Louis Star and Times*, April 13, 1938: 21.
19. W. Vernon Tietjen, "Jack Knott Forgets Runner Moving to Third, Browns Lose," *St. Louis Star and Times*, April 23, 1938: 6.
20. Robert L. Burnes, "6 Fielding Marks Fall as Browns Bow to Chisox in 13, 4-3," *St. Louis Globe-Democrat*, April 23, 1938: 6-7.
21. W. Vernon Tietjen, "Ralph Kress Signs Contract with Browns After Long Holdout Siege; Don Heffner Fails to Reach Terms," *St. Louis Star and Times*, April 5, 1939: 22.
22. "Breadon, Barnes Look to Legislature," *St. Louis Post-Dispatch*, January 29, 1940: 17; Sid Keener, "Sid Keener's Column," *St. Louis Star and Times*, January 31, 1940: 20.
23. "Browns Players Cut In on Unemployment Fund," *St. Louis Post-Dispatch*, January 28, 1948: 41.
24. Gail Fowler, "Down Ye Old Sports Trail," *Oil City* (Pennsylvania) *Derrick*, July 8, 1941: 8.
25. US Military Draft Card, Ancestry.com.
26. "Cole Is Pitching for Uncle Sam's Team This Season," *Wilkes-Barre Times Leader*, May 8, 1942: 23.
27. "Local News: Deaths," (Nashville) *Tennessean*, July 29, 1999: 18.

BOB COONEY

BY MIKE COONEY

Bob Cooney pitched 110⅓ innings during a major-league career that included appearances in 28 games. He won one game.

The game he won was scheduled to be played the day after he was given credit for the win.

Robert Daniel Cooney was born in Glens Falls, New York, on July 12, 1907. He was the oldest of three children born to Francis "Frank" and Nan Cooney. Bob was 11 years old when his father, a hotel clerk, died.[1] His mother, Nan, worked as an operator in a shirt factory.[2]

At the age of 14, Cooney was pitching for the Mohican Street Sluggers in Glens Falls. The Sluggers' players and opponents had to weigh between 90 and 110 pounds.[3] Two years later, Cooney's pitching prowess resulted in his being recruited by St. Mary's Academy High School, for whom he became a starting pitcher as a freshman.[4]

During his high-school years Cooney continued to progress, and impress, with his pitching skills while still finding time to excel in bowling.[5] He also joined the track team, tackling the broad jump and the high jump.[6] In baseball, as a senior Cooney pitched shutouts in both games of the Glens Falls Championship.[7]

During the summer of 1925, after graduating from St. Mary's, Cooney joined the semipro Glens Falls Community team. He made his debut on June 21, when he was inserted into the lineup in center field.[8] He first pitched on June 30 against a strong Schenectady (New York) team. He struck out 10 batters, including six in a row, in a 3-0 victory.[9] In spite of several successful outings, many baseball skeptics felt Cooney had not really been tested. That test would come against Ticonderoga. One skeptic commented: "If he emerges from that game in the ninth inning still in the pitcher's box, and the game has not been altogether a rout for Cooney's team then ... [Cooney] will have proven that he has ability well beyond the ordinary." Cooney allowed two singles in winning the game 2-0.[10]

Shortly after the Ticonderoga game, Cooney agreed to pitch for the semipro Warrensburg team on Sundays after Warrensburg offered him more money than he was getting from Glens Falls. In what would prove prophetic, the *Glens Falls Post-Star* sports editor commented that he was concerned that Cooney would hurt his future in baseball if he pitched too many games too often.[11] Cooney finished out the 1925 season pitching for Warrensburg, Glens Falls, and, late in the year, Port Henry, for whom he pitched both games of a doubleheader against Ticonderoga.[12]

Having accepted a full-ride scholarship offer from Fordham University in New York City, Cooney joined the Fordham Rams varsity team as the number-three starting pitcher for the 1926 college season.[13] During his four years at Fordham, Cooney had a 64-18 record with six shutouts. Perhaps his highlight came in 1926 when he struck out 18 batters in a 14-inning game. In 1927 he set the Fordham record with a 0.85 earned-run average.[14]

During the summer of 1926, after his first season with Fordham, Cooney joined several semipro teams. In early June he pitched two games in three days; first for the YMHA (Glens Falls) and then for the D and H Generals (New York) for a game scheduled against the Boston Black Sox.[15] Later, pitching for Hudson Falls (New York), Cooney struck out 16 in a game against Western A.C. of Albany.[16] The following week Cooney was pitching for W.K.Y. of Glens Falls.[17] On July 3 he pitched for D and H against the Boston Black Sox, shutting them out 1-0.[18] On July 6 Cooney pitched a complete game for the Kingston (New York) Colonials.[19] While primarily used as a pitcher, Cooney played center field for the Colonials in an August 1 game.[20] Two days later he left the Colonials and returned to W.K.Y.[21] Then a week later he agreed to pitch for Fair Haven (Vermont) for the balance of the season in addition to continuing to pitch for W.K.Y.[22] Instead, he pitched for both Warrensburg[23] and Whitehall (New York), throwing two complete games in two days.[24]

Going into the 1927 Fordham season, a *New York Evening Graphic* sportswriter wrote: "[Cooney has] a low fastball and a deceptive curve." The writer went on to write that Cooney had stated he wanted to become a New York Yankee.[25] With the finish of the college season, Cooney was expected to join YMHA for the season.[26] Instead, he decided to play for Massillon (Ohio),[27] where he won his first seven games before losing his last game.[28] Once he returned to Glens Falls, the Kingston Colonials requested permission to use Cooney in its game against the Boston Braves.[29] In September he joined a local all-star team that was scheduled to play the Braves. While he didn't start against the Braves, he did pitch seven scoreless innings in relief.[30] Then, the day before he was scheduled to return to Fordham, Cooney pitched a game for the semipro Schenectady Police club.[31]

Cooney was elected captain of the Fordham Rams for his junior season. After again starring for the Rams, in 1928 he joined Otsego Lake (Cooperstown, New York) of the semipro Mohawk Valley League.[32] Several teams sought permission to use Cooney in games against major-league teams. Only the D and H Generals were able to obtain his service for a game against the Braves.[33] Cooney was the winning pitcher as the Generals beat the Braves 5-3.[34] After the game, Braves manager Rogers Hornsby questioned Cooney's weight and stature but thought that he could make the big leagues "if he set out earnestly to do so."[35]

As the 1928 season progressed, Johnny Evers decided to form a strong semipro team in Saratoga, New York with Cooney being the pitcher he wanted.[36] However, Evers did not think he could afford the $50 a game Cooney was making with Otsego.[37] However, Evers reported shortly that Cooney had agreed to join his Saratoga team.[38] There is no evidence that he played for Saratoga. Instead, he stayed with Otsego Lake and led it to the Mohawk Valley League championship.[39]

Early in 1929, the Cincinnati Reds offered Cooney a contract. He turned it down in favor of completing his senior year at Fordham.[40] Immediately after graduation, Cooney signed a contract with the St. Louis Browns. He was assigned to the Class-A Western League Tulsa Oilers.[41] In his first appearance for the Oilers, he struck out four in two innings of work.[42] Cooney won four games before his first defeat in a July 25 game against the Des Moines Demons.[43] He finished the season with an 11-5 record despite missing several games with an injury caused when he was hit while at bat.[44] His victories included the game that gave the Oilers their third straight Western League title.[45] His losses included what was probably 1929's weirdest inning. In the second inning of an August 15 game against Des Moines, Cooney gave up two doubles and a triple and hit a batter. The Demons scored one run.[46]

The Browns transferred Cooney to the Western League Topeka Senators for the 1930 season. He was lauded for both his fielding[47] and his pitching after a May 29 game against the St. Joseph Saints in which Saints starting pitcher Dizzy Dean was ejected for getting into a fist fight with two Senators players. Cooney won the game 4-1.[48] While not noted for his hitting, Cooney was the offensive star of a September 1 game against St. Joseph when his squeeze bunt drove in the first run. He then scored the winning run in a 2-1 game, and was the winning pitcher.[49] Cooney had an 8-4 record after eight weeks.[50] He finished the season with a 16-13 record.

The Wichita Falls Spudders of the Texas League became the Browns Class-A affiliate in 1931. In January the Spudders announced the purchase of Cooney's contract from Topeka.[51] By July 1 he had an 11-3 record. His .786 won-lost percentage was tied for league best with the Fort Worth Panthers' Dick McCabe.[52] Compared with modern-day games, Cooney's August 8 1-0 shutout win against the Panthers was unique. The seven-inning game was played in 59 minutes.[53]

On September 1 Cooney won his 17th game, against the San Antonio Indians. After the game, Spudders President William E. Hunt announced that Cooney had been sold outright to the St. Louis Browns.[54] He made his major-league debut against the Cleveland Indians on September 6. In a 7-5 loss, he gave up 13 hits and walked 7 in seven innings. With the game tied 4-4, he was relieved in the eighth inning after giving up three more runs. A sportswriter observed: "Although he failed to win, he made a more credible showing than some of the Brownie veterans did in the second game."[55] After a September 10 game, the *St. Louis Post-Dispatch* headlined: "Cooney, Rookie, Stars as Relief Pitcher; Goslin Hits Homer." In a game against the Philadelphia Athletics, Cooney had relieved in the first inning with the Browns down 4-0. Cooney pitched the final 7⅓ innings for the Browns, giving up two runs on seven hits.[56] (The Athletics won, 6-3.)

Perhaps Cooney's highlight came in a September 19 game against the Yankees. Though he was the losing pitcher in a 3-0 game, he held Babe Ruth to one single in two official at-bats while Lou Gehrig

Bob Cooney

went 0-for-4.[57] Cooney finished the season with an 0-3 record after four starts and one relief appearance.

After the season ended, Cooney was invited to join several major-league players in a barnstorming tour. However, he had to return to Glens Falls due to a family illness.[58] Shortly after his return home, Cooney was named to the Glens Falls all-star bowling team.[59]

After his September 1931 audition, the Browns offered Cooney a contract, albeit at a reduced salary, for the 1932 season. He had a successful spring training. At bat, he had a grand slam in one game[60] and three hits in another.[61] As for his pitching, *St. Louis Star and Times* writer Sid Keener wrote: "[Cooney] weighs 175 pounds, stands 5 feet 10 inches and is

Bob Cooney at Fordham.

smaller than the average pitcher in the big leagues. However, he zips a wicked curve and has a 'jump' to his fast ball." Keener went on to write that several Browns players, after facing Cooney's pitches, told manager Bill Killefer that he should "[k]eep your eyes on Cooney."[62] Another writer, Maurice Shevlin of the *St. Louis Globe-Democrat*, after an April 1 spring-training game, wrote: "[Cooney had] a fast ball that slipped across the corners and a tantalizing slow one that drifted across like a summer zephyr."[63]

While it was anticipated that Cooney would be one of the Browns' starting pitchers,[64] he opened the 1932 season as a reliever. In a 14-3 loss to the Cleveland Indians on April 24, he pitched 5⅓ innings, giving up just one hit and no runs.[65] Four days later, manager Killefer planned to use Cooney as his starter so as not "to take a chance on hurting [Lefty] Stewart's arm" in the cold weather.[66]

Cooney did not get a "cold weather" start. Instead, he continued to work out of the bullpen. While generally successful, Cooney's efforts in a July 2 game against the Chicago White Sox were disastrous when he allowed four runs in two-thirds of an inning.[67] As the season progressed, Cooney was frustrated that he wasn't given a chance to start.[68] Finally, after pitching 33⅔ innings in 13 appearances,[69] Cooney was called on to start a game originally scheduled for August 1, but rescheduled as the second game of a July 31 doubleheader against the Boston Red Sox. While Killefer had been hesitant to use him as a starter, Cooney took the mound and pitched a 7-3 complete-game win.

It was his only major-league victory.

After the game, *St. Louis Star and Times* writer Charles "Kid" Regan wrote that Killefer, after carefully watching, felt that Cooney "has promise they little suspected."[70] His promise was tested when he started an August 9 game against the Yankees. Cooney didn't fare near as well as he had against the Red Sox. In 5⅓ innings, he gave up 10 hits, 7 walks, and 5 runs. He was removed after giving up Babe Ruth's 32nd home run of the season and walking Lou Gehrig[71]

After finishing the 1932 season with a 1-2 record, Cooney signed a Browns contract for 1933.[72] At the end of spring training, Cooney, slated to be a reliever, headed to St. Louis for the Browns' opening game, on April 12 against the White Sox. He did not appear in either of the first two games. Then, on April 14, the Browns purchased Ed Wells from the Yankees and optioned Cooney to the Texas League San Antonio Missions.[73]

Through May 23, Cooney, after 36 innings, had a 1-3 record with a 6.31 ERA for the Missions.[74] On June 1 the Texas League Dallas Steers obtained Cooney on option from San Antonio.[75] While nursing a "tricky elbow," Cooney got off to a rough start with the Steers.[76] On June 21 Dallas released him.[77] He then moved to the Southern Association New Orleans Pelicans.[78] After starting a June 25 game against the Atlanta Crackers,[79] Cooney was released by the Pelicans on June 30.[80] After his release, Cooney went to Rochester, New York, for treatment for his "dead arm."[81]

As the 1934 season approached, with his arm feeling good, Cooney was recruited by Boston Braves scout Johnny Evers to pitch for the Harrisburg Senators. The Senators were the Braves' affiliate in the Class-A New York-Pennsylvania League.[82] On June 28 Cooney was the winning pitcher in a 7-6 exhibition win over Boston.[83] On July 10, with a record of six wins, including three shutouts, and seven losses, he was released by Harrisburg. He immediately joined the Hazelton Mountaineers of the same league.[84] Cooney's first game with the Mountaineers came on July 11. It also came with pain when the first batter he faced hit a line drive off his knee.[85] On July 23 he was released by Hazleton.[86] A week later, Cooney was signed by the Wilkes-Barre Barons of the New York-Pennsylvania League.[87] Wilkes-Barre used him primarily as a "relief artist and warm-up pitcher" before using him as a starter toward the end of the year.[88]

Robert Daniel Cooney married Anna Mae Ferguson on October 29, 1934.[89] They had no children. Both Cooneys went into the real estate business and continued until their respective deaths.[90]

Cooney returned to Wilkes-Barre for the 1935 season.[91] After a quick start (3-0), he left the Barons due to "financial troubles with management."[92] A week later he signed a contract with the Elmira Pioneers.[93] According to the Howe News Bureau, Cooney finished the season going 13-8 with a 4.24 ERA for the Pioneers.[94]

At the close of a successful 1935 season, Cooney told *Post-Star* sports editor Don Cunnion that "he hadn't used for several years the knuckle-ball with which he baffled many a batter back in his youth." Cunnion commented: "When Bob's arm developed a kink back in 1932, he tried to pitch it out, with almost fatal results."[95]

When Elmira offered Cooney a 1936 contract with a slight reduction in pay, he decided to return the contract unsigned.[96] After a brief holdout, he agreed to return to the Pioneers.[97] He won his first game, May 2, against the Binghamton Triplets, 4-2,[98] despite having to leave the game with an injured finger.[99] Elmira released Cooney on May 10,[100] and he signed a contract to return to Wilkes-Barre the same day.[101] The following day, Cooney pitched a complete game but lost 1-0 to Binghamton.[102] In a surprise move eight days later, May 19, he was released by Wilkes-Barre.[103] Cooney then signed a contract with the league's Scranton Miners on May 30.[104] He was released by the Miners on June 15.[105] Miners manager Elmer Yoter said that Cooney, after his release, went home "because he has a sore arm."[106]

With this release, Cooney's professional baseball career was over. A sore arm, probably caused by overwork in his early years, kept him from an extended major-league career.

Cooney joined his wife, Anna, in working for the real estate company they owned.[107] While his sore arm resulted in ending his baseball career, it was good enough to allow him to bowl at a high level.[108]

With the start of World War II, Cooney registered for the military draft on October 16, 1940.[109] He was inducted into the Army on January 9, 1943.[110] While on active duty he served in the Pacific.[111] He was discharged on October 20, 1945,[112] with the rank of sergeant.[113]

Cooney died on May 4, 1976, following a long illness. He is buried in St. Mary's Cemetery in South Glens Falls, New York.[114]

In 2007 Cooney was inducted as an honorary member of the Glens Falls Area Baseball Hall of Fame.[115] In 2012 he was inducted into the Fordham University Athletics Hall of Fame.[116]

SOURCES

In addition to the sources cited in the Notes, the author consulted Baseball-Reference.com and Johnson, Lloyd, and Miles Wolff, eds., *Encyclopedia of Minor League Baseball* (Durham, North Carolina: Baseball America, 2007).

The author is not related to Bob Cooney.

NOTES

1. See New York, US, State Census, 1915, and Obituary – Frank B. Cooney, *Glens Falls (New York) Post-Star*, January 28, 1919: 5.
2. New York, US, State Census, 1925.
3. "Mohican St. Sluggers Want Baseball Games," *Glens Falls Post-Star*, March 17, 1921: 6.
4. "St. Mary's Lose to Whitehall in Diamond Battle," *Glens Falls Post-Star*, May 7, 1923: 6.
5. "Lively Week Is Opening on Park Alley Tonight," *Glens Falls Post-Star*, February 24, 1925: 7.
6. "Mohican Track Team Is Looking for Some Meets During Spring," *Glens Falls Post-Star*, May 9, 1925: 7.
7. H.S. Did not Score a Run in Series of 1925," *Glens Falls Post-Star*, June 9, 1936: 6.
8. "Baseball Comment," *Glens Falls Post-Star*, June 22, 1925: 6.
9. "St. Mary's Star Shuts Out DORP in First Test," *Glens Falls Post-Star*, July 1, 1925: 6.
10. "Yielding 2 Hits and Walking Nobody, Rising Boxman Gets Shut-Out Victory by 2 to 0," *Glens Falls Post-Star*, July 20, 1925: 6.
11. "The Observatory," *Glens Falls Post-Star*, July 27, 1925: 6.
12. "Port Henry vs. TI," *Glens Falls Post-Star*, September 8, 1925: 6.
13. "Cooney Is Starring," *Glens Falls Post-Star*, June 1, 1926: 7.
14. https://fordhamsports.com/honors/hall-of-fame/bob-cooney/63.
15. "Cooney Pitches Two Games Here in Three Days," *Glens Falls Post-Star*, June 1, 1926: 6.
16. "Cooney Whiffs 16 as Hudsons Defeat Albany," *Glens Falls Post-Star*, June 21, 1926: 6.
17. "Cooney Pitches W.K.Y. to Win Over Foreigners," *Glens Falls Post-Star*, June 28, 1926: 2.
18. "Year's Home Star Helps Generals Win," *Glens Falls Post-Star*, July 6, 1926: 6.
19. "Cooney Is Sent to Box for Visitors and Wins Job for Himself by Fine Performance," *Glens Falls Post-Star*, July 7, 1926: 6.
20. "Shields Bests Atiyeh 2 to 1 at the 'Burg,'" *Glens Falls Post-Star*, August 2, 1926: 6.
21. "Post-Star Tries to Bring Chaps Here on Friday," *Glens Falls Post-Star*, August 4, 1926: 6.
22. "Cooney May Pitch for Fair Haven Against Chappies Today," *Glens Falls Post-Star*, August 10, 1926: 6.
23. "Burg Invades Corinth Sunday in Grudge Game," *Glens Falls Post-Star*, September 4, 1926: 6.
24. "Cooney, Pitching for Whitehall, Beaten by Fair Haven, 10 to 5," *Glens Falls Post-Star*, September 13, 1926: 6.
25. "Laudation for Bob Cooney, Local College Mound Star, in Interview by Graphic," *Glens Falls Post-Star*, April 22, 1927: 8.
26. "Smart Local Nine Is Aim of Group Now Organizing," *Glens Falls Post-Star*, June 23, 1927: 8.
27. "Hudson Falls Community Nine Appears at Rec Field – Cooney Lost to Local Ball Teams for the Summer," *Glens Falls Post-Star*, July 2, 1927: 8.
28. "Bob Cooney, Crack Local Pitcher, Is Back From the West," *Glens Falls Post-Star*, August 22, 1927: 8.
29. "Stone and Cooney Both Named for Pitching Labor," *Glens Falls Post-Star*, August 25, 1927: 8.
30. "Bob Cooney Stars as Boston Braves Beaten," *Glens Falls Post-Star*, September 8, 1927: 10.
31. "DORP Cops Win Behind Cooney," *Glens Falls Post-Star*, September 12, 1927: 8.
32. "Cooney and Stone Doing League Work," *Glens Falls Post-Star*, June 23, 1928: 8.
33. "Following the Ball with the Sports Editor," *Glens Falls Post-Star*, June 26, 1928: 8.
34. "Big Leaguers Hit Chutes in View of Record Crowd," *Glens Falls Post-Star*, June 28, 1928: 8.
35. "Following the Ball, *Glens Falls Post-Star*, June 28, 1928: 8.
36. "Something New in Baseball World," *Glens Falls Post-Star*, July 12, 1928: 8.
37. "Following the Ball," *Glens Falls Post-Star*, June 29, 1928: 8.
38. "Following the Ball," *Glens Falls Post-Star*, July 20, 1928: 8.
39. "Following the Ball," *Glens Falls Post-Star*, August 14, 1928: 8.
40. "Bob Cooney Heads Fordham Pitchers," *Glens Falls Post-Star*, March 16, 1929: 8.
41. George R. Loveys, "The Sports Periscope," *Glens Falls Post-Star*, June 24, 1929: 8.
42. "Wichita Crew Has the Lead in 3 Battle," *Wichita (Kansas) Evening News*, July 12, 1929: 5.
43. "Western League," *Wichita Eagle*, July 26, 1929: 15.
44. George R. Loveys, "The Sports Periscope," *Glens Falls Post-Star*, September 10, 1929: 8.
45. "Cooney Hurls Tulsa to Third Straight Western Loop Title," *Glens Falls Post-Star*, September 13, 1929: 9.
46. Sec Taylor, "Demons Wallop Oilers, 10 to 1," *Des Moines Register*, August 16, 1929: 11.
47. "Senators Take Game in Eighth," *St. Joseph (Missouri) Gazette*, May 30, 1930: 5.
48. "Cooney Pitches Invincible Ball as Kaws Win from St. Joseph by 4 to 1 Score," *Des Moines Register*, May 30, 1930: 14.
49. "Saint Errors Cost 2 Games," *St. Joseph Gazette*, September 2, 1930: 6.
50. "Bob Cooney Has Won 8 of 12 with Western Loop Team," *Glens Falls Post-Star*, June 14, 1930: 8.

51. "9 Athletes Obtained Within Week," *Fort Worth Star-Telegram*, January 4, 1931: 16.
52. "Buck Stanton Goes into Second Half as Batting Leader," *Fort Worth Star-Telegram*, July 5, 1934: 13.
53. "Panthers and Spudders Split Double Bill," *Fort Worth Star-Telegram*, August 9, 1931: 15.
54. "Spudders Triumph 15-11," *Fort Worth Star-Telegram*, September 2, 1931: 11.
55. "Indians Annex Two," *Cincinnati Enquirer*, September 7, 1931: 35.
56. "Cooney, Rookie, Stars as Relief Pitcher; Goslin Hits Homer," *St. Louis Post-Dispatch*, September 10, 1931: 13. Though not confirmed by other accounts, the *Post-Dispatch* reported that Cooney was even called on to pinch-hit for the Browns in a September 16 17-0 loss to the New York Yankees. "Play by Play of Browns First Game," *St. Louis Post-Dispatch*, September 17, 1931: 15.
57. "Browns, Baffled by Pipgras, Lose Another to Yankees, 3 to 0," *St. Louis Post-Dispatch*, September 20, 1931: 50.
58. "Bob Cooney Arrives Home as Season Ends," *Glens Falls Post-Star*, October 2, 1931: 8.
59. Local Pinners Meet Schenectady Saturday," *Glens Falls Post-Star*, October 30, 1931: 9.
60. "Browns get 14 Hits to Trounce Buffalo in Exhibition, 15 to 12," *St. Louis Globe-Democrat*, March 22, 1932: 8.
61. "Cooney Checks Bush's Sluggers with Seven Hits in 6-to-1 Victory," *St. Louis Globe-Democrat*, April 2, 1932: 8.
62. "Sid Keener's Column," *St. Louis Star and Times*, March 23, 1932: 18.
63. "Cooney Checks Bush's Sluggers with Seven Hits in 6-to-1 Victory," *St. Louis Globe-Democrat*, April 2, 1932: 8.
64. "Kress Will Be at Third Base, Bettencourt in Right Field," *St. Louis Post-Dispatch*, April 8. 1932: 46.
65. "Indians Pound Quartet of Hurlers for 14 Hits and Rout Browns, 14-3," *St. Louis Globe-Democrat*, April 25, 1932: 6.
66. "Browns Hurt by Erratic Work Afield," *St. Louis Globe-Democrat*, April 27, 1932: 9.
67. "Gray, Cooney and Kimsey Pummeled as Foe Gains First Victory in St. Louis," *St. Louis Globe-Democrat*, July 3, 1932: 21.
68. Charles "Kid" Regan, "Cooney Comes to Browns' Rescue in Hill Shortage," *St. Louis Star and Times*, August 1, 1932: 16.
69. "Browns Resume Yankees Series in Game Today," *St. Louis Star and Times*, August 9, 1932: 12.
70. Charles "Kid" Regan, "Cooney Comes to Browns' Rescue in Hill Shortage," *St. Louis Star and Times*, August 1, 1932: 16.
71. Martin J. Haley, "Ruth Clouts 32d Homer with Two on Base and Yanks Best Browns, 5-3," *St. Louis Globe-Democrat*, August 10, 1932: 8.
72. "Bob Cooney of Browns Signs 1933 Contract," *St. Louis Post-Dispatch*, February 20, 1933: 19.
73. "Browns Buy Wells from Yanks, Sending Bob Cooney to Texas," *St. Louis Globe-Democrat*, April 15, 1933: 17.
74. "Texas League Averages," *Fort Worth Star-Telegram*, June 3, 1933: 9.
75. "Steers Get Outfielder Brickell from Phils," *Fort Worth Star-Telegram*, June 4, 1933: 17.
76. Don Cunnion, "The Sports Periscope," *Glens Falls Post-Star*, June 17, 1933: 8.
77. "Herd Releases Cooney," *Fort Worth Star-Telegram*, June 22, 1933: 12.
78. Don Cunnion, "The Sports Periscope," *Glens Falls Post-Star*, July 1, 1933: 8.
79. "Atlanta Wins Two," *Shreveport* (Louisiana) *Times*. June 26, 1933: 7.
80. "Pels Release Cooney," *Fort Worth Star-Telegram*, July 1, 1933.
81. Don Cunnion, "The Sports Periscope," *Glens Falls Post-Star*, July 8, 1933: 8.
82. "Cooney Signs with N.Y.-P. Club," *Glens Falls Post-Star*, April 20, 1934: 8.
83. "Cooney Hurls Win Over Braves, 7-6," *Glens Falls Post-Star*, June 29, 1934: 8.
84. "Cooney Is Signed: Wydallis Released," *Hazelton* (Pennsylvania) *Plain Speaker*, July 12, 1934: 15.
85. "Scranton Slugs Ball to Give Hazelton Defeat," *Hazelton Plain Speaker*, July 12, 1934: 14.
86. "Simmons Joins Hazelton Club," *Hazelton Plain Speaker*, July 24, 1934: 12.
87. "The Talk," *Harrisburg Evening News*, July 27, 1934: 11.
88. "Cooney Turns in Fine Job to Trounce Miners," *Wilkes-Barre* (Pennsylvania) *Record*, September 3, 1934: 10.
89. "Miss Ferguson Becomes Bride," *Glens Falls Post-Star*, October 30, 1934: 14.
90. Obituary of Robert D. Cooney, *Glens Falls Post-Star*, May 5, 1976: 16.
91. "Cooney Signs Contract with N.Y.-Penn. Outfit," *Glens Falls Post-Star*, April 20, 1934: 20.
92. "Cooney May Join Elmira Team in NY-P Ball Loop," *Glens Falls Post-Star*, June 11, 1935: 12.
93. "Bob Cooney Signs with Elmira Club," *Post-Star*, June 12, 1935: 6.
94. Don Cunnion, "The Sports Periscope," *Glens Falls Post-Star*, December 6, 1935: 18. The 13-8 record appears to include Cooney's Wilkes-Barre wins. Various Baseball-Reference sites incorrectly give the entire 13-8 record to Wilkes-Barre.
95. Don Cunnion, "The Sports Periscope," *Glens Falls Post-Star*, September 18, 1935: 9.
96. "Bob Cooney to Return Elmira Club Contract, *Glens Falls Post-Star*, March 5, 1938: 8.
97. "Pioneers Obtain Infielder Coyle; Cooney Signed," *Elmira* (New York) *Star-Gazette*, March 21, 1936: 11.

98 Don Cunnion, "The Sports Periscope," *Glens Falls Post-Star*, May 5, 1936: 6.

99 "Pioneers Return From Road Trip to Face Barons," *Star-Gazette*, May 8, 1936: 24.

100 "Kimball to Make His First Start; Cooney Released," *Elmira Star-Gazette*, May 11, 1936: 12.

101 "Jake Pitler Is Feted and Gets Wrist Watch," *Wilkes-Barre Record*, May 11, 1936: 16.

102 "Barons Garner 4 Hits from 'Red' LaFlamme," *Wilkes-Barre Evening News*, May 12, 1936: 35.

103 "Pitler Gets Murphy and 3 Men on Option," *Wilkes-Barre Record*, May 20, 1936: 19.

104 "Bob Cooney Signs on Scranton Club," *Glens Falls Post-Star*, June 1, 1936: 8.

105 "Baseball News," *Wilkes-Barre Evening News*, June 16, 1936: 23.

106 Harry O'Donnell, "Sports Shorts from Around and Here," *Elmira Star-Gazette*, July 9, 1936: 23.

107 Obituary of Robert D. Cooney, *Glens Falls Post-Star*, May 5, 1976, 16.

108 "Norman Hits 259 Single; Cooney Chalks Up 651," *Glens Falls Post-Star*, December 21, 1938: 12.

109 US, World War II Draft Cards Young Men, 1940-1947.

110 US, Department of Veteran Affairs BIRLS Death File, 1850-2010.

111 Obituary of Robert D. Cooney, *Glens Falls Post-Star*, May 5, 1976, 16.

112 US, Department of Veteran Affairs BIRLS Death File, 1850-2010.

113 "Attends Funeral Services," *Glens Falls Post-Star*, August 8, 1944: 6.

114 Obituary of Robert D. Cooney, *Glens Falls Post-Star*, May 5, 1976, 16.

115 "Five Players Headed to Local Hall," *Glens Falls Post-Star*, September 7, 2007: 15.

116 https://fordhamsports.com/honors/hall-of-fame.

REESE DIGGS

BY ERIC VICKREY

The 1934 Washington Senators, defending American League champions, were out of the playoff race by August after being decimated by injuries. Thus, team owner Clark Griffith was willing to take a chance on Reese Diggs, a hard-throwing 18-year-old who caught the eye of one of his scouts while pitching on the sandlots of Baltimore. Starved for pitching, the team immediately tossed Diggs into action. The young hurler appeared in four games, three of them starts, and faced the likes of Hank Greenberg, Earl Averill, Jimmie Foxx, and Lou Gehrig. On September 17, 1934, Diggs received 13 runs of support and threw a complete game versus the Cleveland Indians for his only career victory.

Reese Wilson Diggs was born on September 22, 1915, in Mathews, Virginia. He was the youngest of nine children born to James Garrett and Mary Ellen (Adams) Diggs. The family lived on Gwynn Island, a small body of land on Virginia's Middle Peninsula where the Piankatank River flows into Chesapeake Bay. James Garrett Diggs worked as a fisherman.[1]

By age 16, the right-handed Reese was pitching for Edgecombe Athletic Club, an amateur team in Baltimore. He hurled for Edgecombe during the summers of 1932-34 and for a time attended Baltimore City College. Washington Senators scout Joe Cambria saw him pitch, and in late August of 1934 Diggs worked out in front of the team's brass at Griffith Stadium. Griffith signed Diggs to a contract and added him to the team as a batting practice pitcher. Before long, the pitching-thin Senators, with 40-year-old Alex McColl as their only available bullpen arm, added Diggs to the active roster.[2]

Al Schacht, filling in as Washington's skipper in place of player-manager Joe Cronin, who was away from the team because of a fractured wrist, shared his assessment of Diggs: "That kid has the fastest ball on the squad. No foolin'. He can burn 'em over. We've had him work on his curve, too, and it ain't bad, ain't bad. The main trouble with Diggs is that he is a little wild. Anyway, he is in batting practice. But he claims he can do better with a catcher behind him and I guess he can. He's gonna get a chance soon, anyway. I think he's got the stuff."[3]

Indeed, Diggs got his chance, making his major-league debut on September 15 in Detroit. The first-place Tigers feasted on Washington starter Jack Russell. With the Senators down 8-2 in the fifth inning, Diggs was called upon with two outs and runners on first and third. The rookie was put to the test immediately as two future Hall of Famers were next up in the Tigers lineup. Charlie Gehringer singled to score a run and Hank Greenberg walked to load the bases. Marv Owen then singled to center field, and the ball went through the legs of John Stone to clear the bases and make it a 12-2 game.[4] Diggs recorded his first out by inducing a fly out off the bat of Goose Goslin, another player who would be enshrined in Cooperstown, to end the inning.

Diggs held the dangerous Detroit lineup scoreless through the final three innings, allowing only two hits and a walk. He retired Greenberg the next time up. One reporter wrote that Diggs' windup resembled "that of a fan dancer without fans."[5] Another later compared his delivery to that of Dizzy Dean: "He is loose-jointed and snaps his wrist as he winds up. Then, just as he lets the ball go, he snaps an ankle of his highly raised left foot right in the batter's face."[6] Tall and wiry, Diggs stood 6-feet-2 and weighed 180 pounds.

Cronin, back with the team, was impressed by Diggs and named him his starting pitcher just two days later versus the Cleveland Indians. Diggs was opposed by Oral Hildebrand in the opening tilt of a five-game series. A paltry crowd of 298 gathered at League Park to see the Monday afternoon affair.[7] The Senators' bats were alive early, aided by two errors, and Diggs was given a five-run cushion before he threw his first pitch. Washington added another run in the second inning to knock out Hildebrand.

Diggs, described in Washington's *Evening Star* as "raw as they come and utterly lacking in slab form," held Cleveland scoreless through the first two innings.[8] The Indians plated their first run of the game in the third inning. Relief pitcher Bob Weiland hit a line drive over the shortstop that plugged the gap of League Park's spacious outfield for an inside-the-park home run. The Senators continued their hit parade and added five more runs of support for Diggs. Protecting an 11-1 lead, the rookie gave up a three-run home run to Earl Averill in the fifth inning. All three runs were unearned, however, after a catcher's-interference call had extended the inning. Diggs, who walked seven in the game, pitched around bases on balls in the next two innings and managed to escape without further damage.

At bat, Diggs was 1-for-4 in the game. He singled off Cleveland reliever Clint Brown in the eighth inning. In the ninth inning, Averill tripled off the right-field wall – just 290 feet from home plate and 40-feet tall – to drive in Milt Galatzer.[9] Averill then scored on a double by Joe Vosmik. Diggs closed out the inning to earn the complete-game 13-6 vic-

Reese Diggs. Courtesy of Rick Diggs.

tory. "Why, I didn't even have my fast ball," he said. "Anyway, look at the way our team batted in runs. I guess I could win in this league if they'd always hit that way."[10]

Diggs got another starting assignment a week later in the first game of a doubleheader against the Philadelphia Athletics. He exhibited better control and picked up his only two career strikeouts. The game was tied 4-4 in the eighth inning when Jimmie Foxx took Diggs deep for the game-deciding run. Diggs pitched his second complete game but took the loss.

Diggs's final start came in the next to last game of the season, the second game of a twin bill versus the New York Yankees. Babe Ruth, 39 years old and in his waning days as a Yankee, was on the bench after playing in the first game. As if facing the Yankees wasn't enough of a challenge, even without Ruth, Diggs did not arrive at Griffith Stadium until game time due to a flat tire.[11] He retired Frankie Crosetti to start the game but then allowed singles to Red Rolfe and George Selkirk and a walk to Lou Gehrig to load the bases. Two more walks and an error gave the Yankees a three-run lead. Diggs was pulled after allowing a leadoff hit in the second inning and took the loss to give him a record of 1-2. In 21⅓ innings pitched, he had an ERA of 6.75.

At the Senators' spring training camp in Biloxi, Mississippi, in 1935, Diggs impressed new manager Bucky Harris early on. "Griffith told me this Diggs had a whale of an arm, and I find the boss was right," said Harris.[12] The skipper compared Diggs's fastball to that of former Senators hurler Firpo Marberry.[13] The young pitcher started Washington's first exhibition game, against Albany. Diggs struggled and allowed seven runs in three innings.[14] He displayed "no fast one and lacked control," wrote one reporter, who also said Harris had changed his tune and was now convinced Diggs "never will make the grade."[15] On March 19, Diggs was sent to the Chattanooga Lookouts, a minor-league affiliate of the Senators.

The quick decision to farm out Diggs flummoxed the youngster. Said Diggs, who was quoted in his dialect: "Good gosh, wha's the matter wi' the guy? Didn't I guarantee t' win at least ten games fer the Washington bunch, and here I am foolin' around with a second-rate outfit. Gee – I don't get it!"[16] He initially said he would not report to Chattanooga but relented after the veteran McColl gave him some words of advice.[17] He barged into Clark Griffith's hotel room, interrupting his card game, and struck the owner on the chest with the back of his hand while declaring: "Well Griff, I've decided to go to Chattanooga."[18]

After failing to impress with the Lookouts, Diggs was cut by Chattanooga in early April and sent to Harrisburg of the New York-Pennsylvania League. Diggs reported to Harrisburg and barely a week later was traded to the Albany Senators for catcher Ray Starr. Diggs made a start for Albany on May 9 against Montreal. He allowed five runs in 1⅔ innings and took the loss.[19]

A few weeks later Diggs landed back in Harrisburg. He made a start on June 1 and allowed three runs but got no run support and took the loss. After two more losses in which he allowed a total of 13 runs, Harrisburg released Diggs. He next surfaced back in Baltimore in August pitching for the Bethlehem Shipbuilders in the Interclub League. His pitching career was over almost as quickly as it began. According to a son, an injury to his pitching arm was a factor in his having to give up the game.[20]

Diggs married Helen Cicero, and the couple had four children: Barbara, Carol, James, and Reese Jr. He served in the Army in World War II and fought in the campaign in Europe in 1944 and 1945. After his military service, he lived in Baltimore and worked in the seafood business with his brothers. Though he had a gregarious personality, he did not talk much about his brief baseball career and did not follow the game. Diggs battled alcoholism, the effects of which contributed to health problems, and he spent his final years in and out of Veterans Administration hospitals.[21]

Reese Diggs died in his sleep on October 30, 1978, at the age of 63. He is buried at Gwynn's Island Cemetery in Mathews, Virginia.

Acknowledgments

Special thanks to Reese "Rick" Diggs Jr. for sharing information about his father's childhood and life after baseball.

SOURCES

In addition to the sources shown in the notes, the author used Baseball-Reference.com.

NOTES

1. Virginia Department of Health; Richmond, Virginia; *Virginia, Births, 1864-2016*.
2. Francis E. Stann, "Diggs May Share M'Coll's Burden," *Evening Star* (Washington DC), September 7, 1934: 39.
3. Stann, "Diggs May Share M'Coll's Burden."
4. Francis E. Stann, "Champions' Slips Aid Pace-Makers," *Evening Star*, September 16, 1934: 31.
5. Stann, "Champions' Slip Aid Pace-Makers."

6. Wirt Gammon, "Just Between Us Fans," *Chattanooga Daily Times*, March 27, 1935: 8.
7. "All Is Forgiven When Diggs, After $4.68 Meal on Nationals, Trounces Tribe in First Start," *Evening Star*, September 18, 1934: 13.
8. Stann, "Rook Slabs Well in Tribe's Defeat," *Evening Star*, September 18, 1934: 11.
9. Bill Johnson. "League Park (Cleveland, Ohio)," SABR BioProject, https://sabr.org/bioproj/park/league-park-cleveland/. Accessed December 28, 2020.
10. "All Is Forgiven When Diggs, After $4.68 Meal on Nationals, Trounces Tribe in First Start."
11. Stann, "Sington, Powell, Cohen Sting Pill," *Evening Star*, September 30, 1934: 35.
12. John B. Keller, "Four Youngsters Make Impression," *Evening Star*, March 2, 1935: 10.
13. Keller, "Four Youngsters Make Impression."
14. John B. Keller, "Coppola Is Best in Practice Tilt," *Evening Star*, March 16, 1935: 11.
15. Keller, "Pettit, Coppola, Cohen in Battle," *Evening Star*, March 19, 1935: 15.
16. Jim Berryman, "Hurlers at Panama City Can't See How Griff Can Get Along Without 'Em, Nor Can Writer," *Washington Evening Star*, March 29, 1935: 51.
17. Gammon, "Just Between Us Fans."
18. Wilbur Kinley, "Today's Sports World," *Chattanooga News*, March 30, 1935: 12.
19. "Royals Defeat Albany 9-2," *Baltimore Sun*, May 10, 1935: 16.
20. Email communication between the author and Reese Diggs Jr., February 11, 2021.
21. Email correspondence with Reese Diggs Jr.

TOM "SUGAR BOY" DOUGHERTY

BY TIM NEWBY

Baseball players dream of being perfect. The perfect hit, the perfect pitch, going 4-for-4, but in a game where doing something right 3 out of 10 times makes you an all-star, perfection is hard to achieve. For pitcher Tom Dougherty, he was perfect throughout his major-league career, albeit his major-league career amounted to only one appearance. In his one appearance, on April 24, 1904, he pitched a perfect two innings, retiring all six batters he faced, and sparked the Chicago White Sox to a 5-4 come-from-behind win over the Cleveland Naps.

For Dougherty, whose nickname, Sugar Boy, came from his diabetes, it was a circuitous route that took him from his hometown of Chicago and around the country before he made his return back to the Windy City for his one and only major-league appearance. His path on the diamond was just as circuitous. The 5-foot-11, 195-pound Dougherty, who threw right-handed and batted left, started his career at first base and shuffled around the diamond with each stop of his career, moving to second, back to first, and then to the outfield before finally finding his place as a pitcher.

Thomas James Dougherty was born on May 30, 1881, in Chicago to Patrick and Ellen Dougherty, the youngest of eight children (four boys and four girls). His parents had immigrated from Ireland and settled in Chicago, where his father became a policeman. He discovered baseball as a youngster and began his professional career in his late teens in Manistee, Michigan, as a first baseman. In August of 1900 he signed with Manchester, Iowa, making his debut on the 5th at second base. Ten days later he made a solid if unspectacular debut as a pitcher in a 6-2 loss in which he gave up five hits, struck out five, and walked three. Over his season and a half with Manchester, he proved to be a solid and popular player.

In 1902 Dougherty made the jump to the Chattanooga Lookouts of the Southern League. He moved back to first base and while playing good defense struggled at the plate against the improved competition, hitting .226 in 17 games before being released. Dougherty's struggles at the plate would be a recurring theme for the rest of his career. He ended up with Crookston, Minnesota, of the Northern League at the end of June. He found his form and hit .328 in 41 games. When the season ended at the beginning of August, Dougherty signed with the St. Paul Saints of the newly formed American Association for the rest of the 1902 season. Again, against improved competition he struggled at the plate, hitting a weak .154 in 18 games.

Dougherty spent his entire career up to that point bouncing around the field trying to find a suitable position. He was noted for his speed and usually acquitted himself well defensively but was always a liability at the plate. His struggles at bat led to his never being able to find a steady spot, and after his miserable showing with St. Paul he was again looking for a new team. He eventually signed with the

Monroe Hill (Louisiana) Citys of the Cotton States League for the 1903 season. While waiting for the train to take him south to join the team, Dougherty was lamenting his hitting woes and struggles to a friend and bemoaning his future in baseball if his production at the plate did not improve. As he dejectedly discussed his prospects a local boy saw Dougherty's glove and asked if he would like to have a catch. The boy coaxed Dougherty into pitching a few to him. The boy was impressed with Dougherty's speed and control and said he must be a pitcher. Dougherty insisted he was not, but a seed was planted.[1] Over the ensuing days, Dougherty continued to work on his pitching, developing a small repertoire of pitches. Shortly after the start of the season, Monroe Hill was struggling and manager Harry Hunt was short of pitchers. Dougherty volunteered to pitch and impressed Hunt. Given the team's struggles, Dougherty soon became its top starter. Over the remainder of the season, he proved to be a workhorse. Multiple times throughout the season he pitched both ends of a doubleheader, including tossing complete-game 18-inning and 11-inning ties.[2] After years of struggling to find his place in baseball, Dougherty finally found it as a pitcher. On a terrible team that finished 36-75, 35½ games out of first, he won nearly a third of its games, going 11-3-2. His hitting was still dismal (he batted .232), but no longer mattered as he had established himself as one of the Cotton States League's top pitchers.

Dougherty's pitching drew the attention of several clubs that wanted to secure his services for the remainder of the season. Atlanta Crackers manager Ab Powell was especially interested in signing him. Atlanta was sitting fourth in the Southern League and Powell vowed to make a run at the league title.[3] He offered financial incentives to his team based on where they finished the season to improve their play and hoped to strengthen his pitching staff by signing Dougherty. He traveled to Monroe with "wads of dough stuffed in his inside pocket" in hopes of luring the pitcher into signing with Atlanta.[4] Powell was successful. Dougherty shined for Atlanta

Tom Dougherty with the 1905 Milwaukee Brewers. Dougherty is second from left in the middle row.

over the remainder of the season in the increased competition of the Southern League, going 9-1. His standout work on the mound did not translate into a championship for the Atlanta team, which finished the season where it was when it signed him, in fourth place. Dougherty still struggled at the plate, hitting .184, but was now firmly ensconced as a pitcher and starting to draw the interest of major-league teams, one of which, the White Sox, signed him.

Heading into the 1904 season, Dougherty struggled in preseason exhibitions, showing a "little raggedness in delivery," but White Sox owner Charles Comiskey thought he possessed potential and planned to develop him throughout the season.[5] Comiskey believed Dougherty would be a "good emergency twirler."[6] It appeared that Dougherty would get a chance to prove himself early in the year when manager Jimmy Callahan announced he would start the final game of the opening series against Cleveland. He did not; instead Doc White started, losing 5-0. Dougherty waited a few more weeks to get a chance to play in what proved to be his one and only game.

On April 24, a cold, wet day, in the third game of a four-game series with Cleveland, Chicago was down 4-1 heading into the eighth inning. Callahan called on Dougherty to replace starter Patsy Flaherty, who had given up all four runs in a disastrous seventh inning. Dougherty started the eighth inning and faced the heart of Cleveland's lineup. With his fastball working, he retired Cleveland's three, four, and five hitters, including future Hall of Famer Napoleon Lajoie. Chicago clawed back one run in the bottom of the eighth when center fielder Fielder Jones scored on a double by shortstop George Davis.

Dougherty again shut down Cleveland one-two-three in the top of the ninth. Chicago started the bottom half of the inning with third baseman Lee Tannehill reaching on an error. Catcher Billy Sullivan was retired, bringing up Dougherty for his one and only plate appearance in a major-league game. Proving that even though his pitching had improved, his hitting had not, Dougherty appeared to stall out the comeback with a weak fly out for the second out, threatening to end Chicago's hopes for a last-at-bat rally. Cleveland pitcher Otto Hess helped keep the rally alive by hitting the next batter, left fielder Ducky Holmes, and walking Jones to load the bases. Up next came Callahan, who delivered a three-run double to tie the game. Callahan scored the winning run and completed the comeback when Danny Green brought him home on a line shot to right field. In his one and only appearance in a major-league game he picked up a win while working two perfect innings in which he retired all six batters he faced and gave up neither hits, walks, nor runs. The next day the headline in the *Chicago Tribune* blared, "Sox Pull Game Out of the Fire."[7]

It was Dougherty's only big-league game played. While his career batting average was .000, he had handled two chances in the field, with a putout and assist to his credit for a career fielding percentage of 1.000.

A few weeks after his appearance, Dougherty was sent to Kenosha for a month before being sold to the Milwaukee Brewers of the minor-league American Association. The sale of Dougherty was not without controversy. The Atlanta Crackers believed he should have gone back to them, citing Article VI, section 9, of the National Agreement, which read: "If a selected player is released within the year of, or the next year after, his selection by a Major League club, and no other Major League club claims him prior to the expiration of his notice of release, the minor league club which lost him by selection shall have the priority of right to him over all clubs."[8] The National Commission ruled that the rule cited by Atlanta applied only if the player was given his unconditional release. The Commission determined that Dougherty was an asset of Chicago, so the club had a clear right to dispose of him by selling him outright.

At the end of the 1904 season instead of returning to Chicago, Dougherty returned to Milwaukee. Over the next few years there were rumors of a return to the majors, and Dougherty was even drafted by Cincinnati in 1910, but he never appeared in majors again, spending the remainder of his career with Milwaukee. In Milwaukee he had a solid 12-year career, compiling a 174-140 record, three times eclipsing the 20-win mark (22 in 1905, 20 in 1907, and 21 in 1909), and in 1910 putting together a 14-1 season. Dougherty, 34 years old, retired in 1915 after posting a disappointing 8-15 mark.

After retiring Dougherty worked as a foreman at the local branch of the Ford Company. He did not give up baseball completely. Over the next few years, he was the player-manager of the semipro Milwaukee White Sox of the Wisconsin State League. As he was at every stop in his career, he was always a fan favorite because of his friendly disposition, his willingness to work hard, and the success he had on the field.[9] Dougherty also briefly umpired in the Florida State League in 1920.

One sees no clear reason why Dougherty never played in the majors again. He was a good, not great talent who was weak with the bat, but was a solid pitcher and could have been a productive addition to any roster. Over the years he was often rumored to be signing with a major-league team, but after joining Milwaukee he married his wife, Emma, and was content to stay close to home for the remainder of his life. He died on November 6, 1953, in Milwaukee.

SOURCES

In addition to the sources cited in the Notes, the author used Baseball-Reference.com, Newspapers.com, manchesteria.advantage-preservation.com, Retrosheet.com, StatsCrew.com, Ancestry.com, and the 1902-1919 Milwaukee Brewers research files by Dennis Pajot.

NOTES

1. "Chicago Gleanings," *Sporting Life*, November 21, 1903: 5.
2. "Cotton States League," *Shreveport Times*, July 30, 1903: 3. "Demand for Dougherty." *Pine Bluff* (Arkansas) *Daily Graphic*, August 7, 1903: 5.
3. "Rich Rewards to Players if Atlanta Wins Pennant," *Atlanta Constitution*, August 9, 1903: 9.
4. "Rich Rewards to Players if Atlanta Wins Pennant."
5. "Sox Beat Blues in Fierce Rally," *Chicago Inter Ocean,* April 25, 1904: 6.
6. "Play Ball the Cry Once More," *Chicago Tribune*, April 14, 1904: 6.
7. "Sox Pull Game out of Fire," *Chicago Tribune*, April 25, 1904: 8.
8. "Court Cases," *Sporting Life*, July 23, 1904: 5.
9. "Johnny Hughes, Veteran Catcher, Quits the Game," *Milwaukee Sentinel*, February 27, 1916.

DICK EGAN

BY GLEN SPARKS

Willie Mays ripped Dick Egan's "best spitter"[1] out of blustery Candlestick Park on August 29, 1967. That solo home run in the seventh inning gave the San Francisco Giants a 7-1 advantage over the visiting Los Angeles Dodgers. (The Giants went on to win 11-1.)

Baseball's legendary "Say Hey Kid" knew all about Egan's habit of tossing wet pitches. Mays shouted as he rounded the bases that he hit the ball "on the dry side."[2]

Egan told that story to a newspaper reporter in 1991. By then, his playing career was long over, and he was working in the Florida Marlins front office. Later, he worked for the Detroit Tigers, the team that signed him decades earlier as a 6-foot-4-inch left-hander out of Northern California.

Yes, Egan confessed, he sometimes threw spitballs. "I had a good one until they changed the rule and disallowed going to your mouth," he said. "I never did learn to throw a Vaseline ball."[3]

Egan appeared in 74 games with three teams over parts of four seasons and won just one time, in a mop-up role in his final campaign. He lost two games and had a 5.15 ERA in 101⅓ career innings. Egan made all of his appearances in relief. Looking back, with a nod to his modest stats and to an instance of bad luck against maybe the greatest player ever, he said, "The one time I got Willie Mays out, I struck him out, but the catcher missed the ball."[4]

Richard Wallis Egan was born on March 24, 1937, in Berkeley, California, near Oakland. His parents were Massachusetts native David J. Egan and Barbara (Kierulff) Egan of California. In 1939, a daughter, Patricia Egan, was added to the family. According to the 1950 US census, David Egan worked as a wire threader in the steel industry, while Barbara was a housekeeper. The family lived in Contra Costa County, California.[5]

Young Richard earned plenty of headlines as an all-around star athlete at Pleasant Hill (California) High School. In May 1954 he threw a no-hitter against the Alhambra High School Bulldogs from nearby Martinez, a city best known as the birthplace of New York Yankees great Joe DiMaggio. Egan "baffled, bewildered, and bamboozled the Bulldogs for seven straight stanzas,"[6] according to a local newspaper. Later that season, he took home a trophy as the team's most valuable player.[7] He also played basketball and started at quarterback for the Pleasant Hill Rams football team.

After high school, Egan enrolled at nearby East Contra Costa Junior College. As a sophomore first baseman, he led the Vikings with a .357 batting average and 17 runs scored in 26 games. On the mound, he went 3-2 with 50 strikeouts in 41⅔ innings. The team finished 15-11.

Egan signed a professional contract in June 1957 with the Stockton Ports of the Class-C California League. "I decided to get into professional ball now, make the most of this chance and hope for the best," he said.[8]

Egan struggled in his 15 appearances and 60 innings, in large part due to the 53 walks he allowed. He posted a 1-3 record with a sky-high 8.25 ERA. The club released him soon after the season ended.

The Tigers signed Egan to a minor-league deal in February 1958 and sent him to the Erie (Pennsylvania) Sailors of the Class-D New York-Pennsylvania League. He had a 10-14 record and a 3.68 ERA. The following season, this time with the Montgomery (Alabama) Rebels of the Class-D Alabama-Florida League, Egan went 14-8 with a 2.70 ERA. He topped the league with 201 strikeouts.

And what did Egan recall decades later about his time with the Rebels, besides all the heat and humidity? "We had an old bus with room for three-four guys to sleep in back," he said. "Just a flat area for a bed but the starting pitcher the next day got a spot!" Also, "Fort Walton Beach (Florida) had a family-style all-you-can-eat restaurant. We would stop to eat and wipe them out of food."[9]

In evaluating his pitching style, Egan said, "I threw left-handed and had plus velocity and a sweepy curveball. I probably exceeded today's pitch counts often. Never hurt – we threw a lot – no weights, no drugs. Just baseball."[10]

Egan spent 1960 with the Knoxville Smokies of the Class-A South Atlantic League and the Portland Beavers of the Triple-A Pacific Coast League. He went 6-5 as both a starter and reliever and posted a 3.63 ERA. Egan pitched in 1961 for the Birmingham Barons of the Southern Association and the Denver Bears of the American Association, where he won a combined five games, mostly as a reliever, with a 4.19 ERA.

(In a questionnaire given to players in the PCL and other leagues out west and stamped May 6, 1961, Egan wrote that he had two children, Corinne Anne, 3 years old, and Richard Lee, 21 months. He listed his offseason occupation as "salesman" and his hobbies as fishing and golf.[11] Egan had married Lois Lieber on October 25, 1957.[12])

Egan's minor-league journey took him to Hawaii in 1962, and he put together a splendid season with the Islanders, a Los Angeles Angels affiliate in the Pacific Coast League. The team finished a middling 77-76, but Egan won a team-high 17 games against 11 losses. He had a 3.45 ERA and led the league in strikeouts, once again punching out 201 batters. PCL baseball writers voted him the league's Pitcher of the Year. During an interview in late May, Egan said he had made a few changes in his delivery, "but," he added, "basically I'm the same guy who's been trying to make the big time before." He said, "I think I've just gotten to the point of where it is now or never. If not this year, I may shop around for another job or go back to college. I know I've got the stuff to make the majors and I just want the chance to prove it to myself."[13]

The Tigers, coming off an 85-76 season, took a close look at Egan during spring training in 1963, and the pitcher enjoyed a solid few weeks. Over his first six appearances, he gave up just nine hits, two

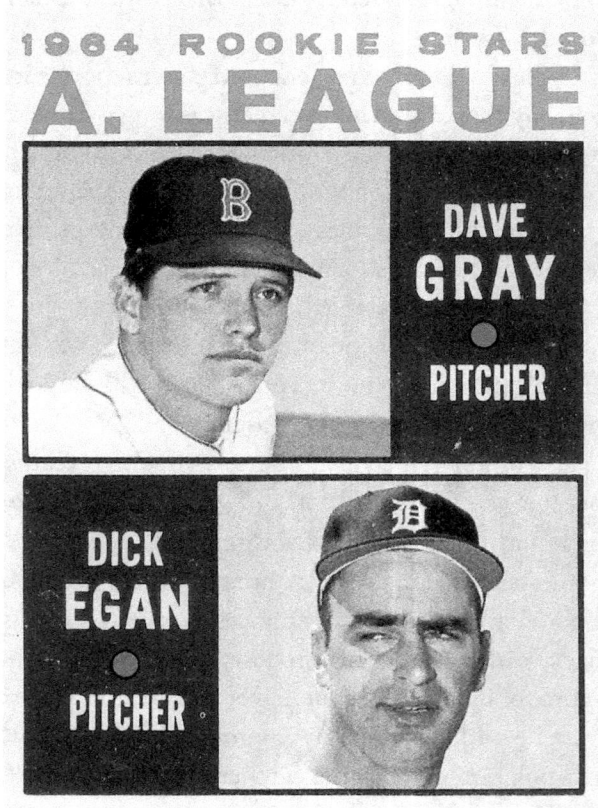

Dick Egan, rookie star. Courtesy The Topps Company, Inc.

walks, and four runs in 16 innings. "That's enough for me," Detroit manager Bob Scheffing said. "We're keeping him to be a short reliever, one that I can bring in early or in the middle of a game."[14]

Scheffing called Egan one of the team's two surprises. The skipper also liked a talented young catcher named Bill Freehan, who went on to a sensational 15-year career in Detroit. Freehan played on 11 All-Star teams and earned five Gold Gloves. "They really came along fast for us," Scheffing said. "Frankly, I had my doubts about both of them, but now I'd have to say that they look like they're ready."[15] Scheffing added, "This kid (Egan) knows how to pitch. I don't mean the stuff he has, but the way he uses it. He knows what it's all about."[16]

Egan sounded confident that he could do the job, in part because he gained 15 pounds over the offseason. He ate avocados and bananas and helped himself to double scoops of ice cream after meals. "I've never felt stronger in my life," he said. "I haven't gotten tired once this spring."[17]

He also added a changeup to his repertoire. Egan picked up the pitch during winter ball in Venezuela. George Brunet from the Houston Colt .45s offered a few pointers one warm afternoon. "I've been using it ever since," Egan said.[18]

Of note, Egan did not seem as angry as in past years. Tigers pitching coach Tom Ferrick said, "Before a pitcher can control the ball, he must learn to control himself. Egan has done both. He's matured."[19] Egan was ready for any role the Tigers had in mind. Scheffing said, "He told me this spring, 'I want to pitch in the big leagues, and I don't care how, start or relief.'"[20]

The 1963 Tigers pitching staff featured 19-game winner and future Hall of Famer Jim Bunning and 16-game winner Hank Aguirre (2.21 ERA). Terry Fox (3-1, 16 saves) anchored the bullpen. Detroit also had high hopes for a 23-year-old left-hander named Mickey Lolich. A trio of heavy hitters led the offense. First baseman Norm Cash belted 39 home runs the previous season, one year after hitting 41 and leading the American League with a .361 batting average (.487 on-base percentage) and driving home 132 runs. Rocky Colavito, the former Cleveland Indians star, hit 37 home runs and had 112 RBIs, while right fielder Al Kaline ripped 29 homers and led Detroit with a .304 batting average and a .593 slugging percentage.

Egan made his big-league debut on Opening Day, April 9, against the Chicago White Sox at Tiger Stadium. The White Sox won, 7-5, thanks in large part to a four-run seventh inning. Scheffing sent Egan into the game in relief of Bunning with two outs in the top of the eighth and runners on first and second. Egan struck out the only batter he faced, Nellie Fox, an infielder famous for the plug of tobacco that he kept firmly in his check. "They got me up, brought me in, and I struck out Nellie Fox with three straight sliders," said Egan. "Bob Scheffing, our manager, told me he's never seen Fox look that bad. Unfortunately, it didn't carry over to the rest of my career."[21] Bob Dustal pitched a scoreless ninth inning for Detroit.

Despite Scheffing's high hopes, Egan never settled into his role as a short reliever. He took the loss April 22 against the Kansas City Athletics after entering the game in the ninth inning with the score tied, 5-5. He retired the first two batters but then surrendered back-to-back singles. Scheffing brought in Ed Charles, who allowed the Athletics' third straight base hit, this one a game-winner. Egan had a 10.13 ERA over his first four appearances.

The Tigers demoted him to Triple-A Syracuse in mid-June. The *Detroit Free Press* lamented, "Egan was still another player who disappointed the Tigers."[22] Egan started and relieved for Syracuse. He posted a 5-8 won-lost record with a 3.53 ERA.

The next spring Egan brought another new pitch to Florida. Charlie Dressen, who took over as Tigers manager on June 18, had asked Egan to add a screwball "because I thought he needed another pitch. Every time he threw it – I guess he tried it about a half-dozen times – no one even came close to it."[23]

Once again Egan won a spot in the Detroit bullpen. This time he was mostly effective. He appeared in 23 games and had an ERA of 4.46, which is a bit deceptive. He gave up 17 earned runs in 34⅓ innings, but 10 of those runs came in two outings. Other than those, his ERA was 1.89.

On June 16 of that year, the Athletics' Jim Gentile crushed a home run off Egan in the eighth inning. The ball slammed onto the roof at Tiger Stadium, bounced back toward the field and headed straight to Kaline, who brought it back to the dugout. He later slipped the ball into Egan's hand. "You might want to keep this as a souvenir," Kaline said. "It's flat on one side."[24]

The Tigers demoted Egan in late July to make room for 25-year-old right-handed pitcher Jack Hamilton. Egan struggled in his return trip to Syracuse. He had a 4-4 won-lost record but with a 6.19 ERA in 48 innings.

In mid-September, with the Tigers stuck in fourth place, an Associated Press writer asked Dressen about the Tigers' plans for 1965. "A left-handed pitcher for the bullpen – and another left-handed starter if we can find one." Detroit had two lefties on the big-league squad, Aguirre and Lolich. Might Egan be a candidate for one of the roles, at least in the bullpen? The reporter, citing the pitcher's struggles in Syracuse, doubted it. "Egan's value is questionable," the scribe decided.[25]

Detroit traded Egan to the St. Louis Cardinals on January 2, 1965, for pitcher Glen Hobbie and catcher Bob Lipski. St. Louis assigned him to the team's Jacksonville affiliate in the International League, where he made 15 appearances, all but one in relief, with a 2-2 won-lost record and a 2.63 ERA.

The Cincinnati Reds purchased Egan's contract in June and sent him to the San Diego Padres of the Pacific Coast League. There, he won seven games, lost nine and had a 3.14 ERA in 129 innings. On June 27 the *Chula Vista* (California) *Star-News* praised Egan for "firing a brilliant two-hit shutout" against the Vancouver Mounties, a Kansas City Athletics affiliate.[26] Cincinnati sold Egan's rights to the California Angels on October 15.

His career with the Angels lasted 11 games and 14⅓ innings. On May 27 he was dealt to the Los Angeles Dodgers for pitcher Howie Reed and a player to be named later. (California completed the trade in December by sending infielder John Butler to Los Angeles.)

Now 29 years old, Egan reported to the Spokane Indians, the Dodgers' Triple-A farm team in the Pacific Coast League, and put up impressive numbers. In 35 games, he had an 8-1 record and a 1.92 ERA. Even so, he sounded discouraged about his big-league future. "Heck, when you're cut from the Angel roster, you've got to feel you're in trouble," he said. "I didn't like my chances in the Dodgers organization, either."[27]

That pessimism notwithstanding, Dodgers general manager Buzzie Bavasi said "[A]ll (Egan) has to do is work hard." He added, "Egan has a good chance to make this club. We're looking for another lefthander in the bullpen and Egan is the type that can help us." Manager Walter Aston complimented the pitcher's side-arm sinker. "He's been around a little and has a pretty good idea of what he's doing," Alston said. "It looks like he has good control, and the ball moves pretty well. I like what I've seen so far."[28]

Over the winter, Egan had once again pitched in Venezuela. That was one reason for the early zip on his fastball. "Normally, I don't believe in winter ball, but this year it was a financial necessity," Egan said. "I'm usually a fast starter, maybe more so this year because this is do or die. I don't figure to have many more chances."[29]

As he did so often, Egan impressed observers during spring training. Maxwell Stiles from the *Valley Times* wrote in mid-March that "Egan delivers the ball with one of the smoothest sweeping swings of his left arm you're likely to see. His easy grace in delivery reminds me of the golf swings of Sam Snead and Julius Boros."[30] Maybe to Egan's surprise, Alston named him to the Dodgers' staff.

He joined a ballclub that was minus a superstar. Future Hall of Famer Sandy Koufax, the winner of three Cy Young Awards and the 1963 National League Most Valuable Player, retired after the 1966 season due to an arthritic left elbow. The author of four no-hitters, including a perfect game, was just 30 years old. The Dodgers still boasted a strong starting staff with Don Drysdale, Claude Osteen, Don Sutton, and promising prospect Bill Singer, plus a bullpen that featured Ron Perranoski, Jim Brewer, and Phil Regan.

Egan won his only big-league game on April 24. The Dodgers, off to just a 3-6 start, were playing at home against the St. Louis Cardinals, who had a 7-2 mark. LA took an early 4-2 lead but gave it back and the game went into extra innings. St. Louis jumped ahead 5-4 on a Curt Flood RBI single with one out in the top of the 13th. Dodgers skipper Walter Alston lifted Joe Moeller and replaced him with Egan, who was making his second appearance that season. Baserunners took their leads off second and third.

Roger Maris popped out, and Egan gave Orlando Cepeda a free pass. The next batter, Phil Gagliano, grounded out to end the inning. The Dodgers scored twice in the bottom half of the frame, thus giving Egan a victory. In the *Long Beach Press-Telegram*, writer Jack Lederer joked that Egan "got a large charge" out of his first big-league win. It seems that when Egan tried to start his car afterward, the battery was dead, and he was forced to call for help.[31]

As in other years, Egan searched to find any consistency in 1967. He pitched several scoreless outings but got hit hard in others. In that final big-league season, Egan appeared in 20 games and threw 31⅔ innings. He had a 1-1 record and a career-high 6.25 ERA. (Egan took the loss on May 4 against the Pirates when he allowed three earned runs and did not record an out. The Dodgers lost 9-3.) In his last appearance, on September 4, against the Cubs at Wrigley Field, he gave up an earned run in two-thirds of an inning. That ended Egan's playing career. He retired with 85 wins in professional baseball, 84 as a minor leaguer.

In need of work, Egan spent a few years dealing craps at Harrah's casino in Lake Tahoe and later switched to blackjack. Egan saw little future, though, in the late-night hours and neon-lit world of professional gambling. "Too boring," he said. He already had spent a few offseasons as a security guard at Harrah's. That job required some heavy lifting. "They told us the doors were unbreakable glass," he explained. "Sometimes, you get your point across by opening the door with a guy's head. The first time I tried it, the guy went right through the door."[32]

Egan left Harrah's and took a job with the Major League Scouting Bureau. He wrote reports on, among other players, a young pitcher named Jack Morris. "He was just like he is now," Egan said in 1991. "Same bulldog make-up. Grunt and groan."[33] The right-hander went on to win 254 games, with the Tigers and other teams. Writers voted Morris into the National Baseball Hall of Fame in 2018.

After 14 years at the Scouting Bureau, Egan joined the Texas Rangers organization. In 1991 he managed the Rangers' team in the rookie-level Pioneer League, the Butte Copper Kings, who finished in third place (out of four teams) with a 29-41 record. "Never had so much fun in my life," Egan said. "Kids were eager to learn."[34]

Egan spent five years with Texas and later filled scouting roles with the Marlins. He revealed one of the truisms of scouting. "Sign a kid to pro ball, and some fold like a wet pile in the rain. Others are so hungry, and they get better and better."[35]

Dave Dombrowski offered high praise for Egan in an article from 2021. At that time, Dombrowski was leading the baseball operations department with the Philadelphia Phillies and looking back on a World Series championship run in 1997 when he ran the Florida Marlins front office.

On July 27 of that year, Dombroski traded for Craig Counsell of the Colorado Rockies in exchange for relief pitcher Mark Hutton. Counsell, who was 26, replaced Luis Castillo and hit .299 with a .376 on-base percentage in 51 games for the Marlins and .293 with a .423 on-base percentage in the postseason. Dombrowski acquired Counsell on Egan's recommendation. "(Egan) calls me and says, 'I think we have the answer for our second-base situation. This guy is really good and fundamentally sound.'" Dombrowski said, "I don't think we win without Craig Counsell because he did so much. ... He recommends Craig Counsell out of Triple A for a world championship club. What kind of scouting is that?"[36]

Egan joined the Tigers in 2002 as a major-league scout and was named a special assistant to general manager Dombrowski in 2007.[37] Egan offered pointers to Detroit pitchers, of course, but also to Texas Rangers left-hander Kenny Rogers, who knew Egan from his time years earlier in the instructional league. "I get information from everybody, and I use everybody," Rogers said in 2005. "(Egan's) got a history with me that other people don't have. He has a way of getting through to me. He's had that from Day 1."[38] Rogers joined the Detroit staff in 2006 and made the last of his four All-Star appearances. He won 219 career games.

The Professional Baseball Scouting Foundation honored Egan in 2016 with a Legend in Scouting Award, presented at the In Spirit of the Game gala in Beverly Hills, California. The annual event attracts some of the sport's best-known figures. Dennis Gilbert, a businessman and former player agent, created the gala as a way to help scouts in financial need. "Over the 15 years, we've helped more than 100 scouts and their families," Gilbert said in an mlb.com article in 2018. "That's what this dinner is about."[39]

In December 2020, the Tigers let go of Egan and several other "outstanding scouts." An article on mlb.com gave a review of Egan's lengthy career. "I knew I wanted to play baseball forever," he once said.[40] He could never do that, of course. Even so, he made baseball his life.

As of 2023, Egan lived in Garland, Texas, outside Dallas.

SOURCES

In addition to the sources listed in the Notes, the author also consulted baseball-reference.com.

NOTES

1. Gordon Edes, "Egan Has Eye for Talent – And Stories," *South Florida Sun-Sentinel* (Fort Lauderdale), November 7, 1991.
2. Edes.
3. Edes.
4. Edes.
5. 1950 US Census https://www.ancestrylibrary.com/discoveryui-content/view/268853070:62308.
6. Clif Moore, "The Scoreboard," *Concord* (California) *Transcript*, May 11, 1954: 6.
7. "Pleasant Hill High School Athletes Honored at Spring Banquet by Parents," *Concord Transcript*, June 8, 1954.
8. Jerry Gandy, "A Gander at Sports," *Contra Costa* (California) *Gazette*, June 5, 1967: 12.
9. "An Interview with Montgomery's All-Time Strikeout Leader," drmiraculousblogspot.com, January 13, 2017.
10. "An Interview with Montgomery's All-Time Strikeout Leader."
11. https://www.ancestrylibrary.com/discoveryui-content/view/7988:61599.
12. California, US, Marriage Index, 1949-1959, https://www.ancestrylibrary.com/discoveryui-content/view/526460:5186.
13. United Press International, "Tigers Need Pitchers? Dick Egan May Be Real Find," *Traverse City* (Michigan) *Eagle*, May 31, 1962.
14. Jerry Green (Associated Press), "Dick Egan Wins Job in Detroit Club's Bullpen," *Ironwood* (Michigan) *Daily Globe*, April 1, 1963: 9.
15. Joe Falls, "Egan and Freehan Are Big Surprises," *Detroit Free Press*, April 6, 1963:13.
16. Falls, "Egan and Freehan Are Big Surprises."
17. Falls, "Egan and Freehan Are Big Surprises."
18. Falls, "Egan and Freehan Are Big Surprises."
19. Green, "Dick Egan Wins Job in Detroit Club's Bullpen."
20. "Fans Keep Eyes on Dick Egan," *Pleasant Hill* (California) *News*, April 11, 1963: 11.
21. David Laurila, FanGraphs Sunday Notes, March 20, 2016. https://blogs.fangraphs.com/sunday-notes-dick-egan-heyward-buxton-padres-indians-more/.
22. Joe Falls, "Tigers Re-Acquire Thomas," *Detroit Free Press*, June 17, 1963: 33.
23. Bernie Kennedy, "Hurler Egan Impresses Dressen," *Lansing* (Michigan) *State Journal*, March 7, 1964: 9.
24. Edes, "Egan Has Eye for Talent – And Stories."
25. Bernie Kennedy, "Dressen Starts Making Plans for Next Year," *Ironwood Daily Globe*, September 18, 1964.
26. "Tompkins Dealt 2-0 Setback," *Chula Vista* (California) *Star-News*, June 27, 1965.

27 George Lederer, "Ex-Angel Egan Dodger Delight," *Long Beach (California) Independent*, March 6, 1967: 19.
28 Lederer, "Ex-Angel Egan Dodger Delight."
29 Lederer, "Ex-Angel Egan Dodger Delight."
30 Maxwell Stiles, "Stiles in Sports," *Valley Times* (North Hollywood, California), March 16, 1967: 14.
31 George Lederer, "Egan Gives Dodgers Charge, Then Left Dry," *Long Beach Press Telegram*, April 25, 1967: 19.
32 Edes, "Egan Has Eye for Talent – And Stories."
33 Edes.
34 Edes.
35 Edes.
36 Bob Brookover, "Deal for Dalton Was one of His Best," *Philadelphia Inquirer*, June 13, 2021.
37 Anthony Fenech, "Tigers' Dick Egan Honored for Many Years as a Pro Scout," *Detroit Free Press*, January 17, 2016.
38 "Time for Phils to Step Up to the Plate," *Philadelphia Daily News*, May 13, 2005: 129.
39 Ken Gurnick, "Scouts Foundation to Host Star-Studded Dinner," mlb.com, January 11, 2018.
40 Jason Beck, "What Is Tigers' Mindset for Winter Meetings," mlb.com, December 4, 2020.

STEVE ELLSWORTH

BY DAVID LAURILA

Two weeks after being shelled in his debut, Steve Ellsworth was credited with his first big-league win. The 27-year-old right-hander was on the mound for the Boston Red Sox, and the team he bested was the same one that had sent him to the showers after just two-plus innings. Going seven strong at Tiger Stadium, on April 21, 1988, Ellsworth allowed three runs as the team his father once pitched for cruised past Detroit by a count of 12-3.

It turned out to be his only big-league win.

Steven Clark Ellsworth was born in Chicago on July 30, 1960, to Dick and Jean Ellsworth, the former of whom was then a 20-year-old rookie left-hander with the Cubs. Dick Ellsworth would go on to play for four other teams – including the Red Sox – in a career that spanned 13 seasons. The family remained in Chicago until the father was traded to the Philadelphia Phillies in December 1966, then moved to Dick and Jean's hometown of Fresno. It was there that the second-generation hurler became a two-sport star, excelling in both baseball and basketball. The latter was his primary passion.

"Basketball was by far my favorite sport," explained Ellsworth, who eventually grew to be 6-feet-8. "I wanted to play college basketball, and I had a few offers, but then during baseball season I pitched a no-hitter and people started paying attention. Next time out, I pitched a one-hitter. I knew that I wasn't going to play in the NBA, and people were saying I could play professional baseball, so that's what I did."[1]

His early memories of watching his father face big-league hitters are cloudy. Ellsworth knows that he attended games at Wrigley Field, and he assumes that he did so in Philadelphia. But it wasn't until the family patriarch was dealt to Boston prior to the 1968 season – and later to Cleveland and Milwaukee – that the memories are clear. Ellsworth recalled how his father would occasionally take him to the ballpark, and how he would get to stand in the outfield and shag fly balls during batting practice. Come game time, he would join his mother and sister in the stands.

Being the son of a big leaguer had its perks. Ellsworth remembered his father introducing him to Elston Howard, who gave him a catcher's mitt, and to Frank Howard, an experience that was "for a kid, a little bit scary." Howard was a gentle giant, but at 6-feet-7 and built like a mountain, he was intimidating for an impressionable youngster.

Meeting Carl Yastrzemski and Ken Harrelson was a different story. At the time of the 2021 interview, Ellsworth still had signed pictures of both, and it was Boston's all-time leader in hits and games played that made him the envy of his peers.

"Yaz pretty much owned the town at that time – he was everybody's hero – so I remember meeting him and thinking it was pretty cool," recalled Ellsworth. "At the same time, it was my normal life. It was a bigger deal to the neighborhood kids in

Boston. They'd be like, 'Wow. You know Yaz!?' I was like, 'Yeah, my dad plays on the same team as him.'"

The son went on to have legendary teammates of his own. The tall right-hander's lone big-league season was in 1988, a year that the Red Sox roster included, among others, Wade Boggs, Roger Clemens, and Jim Rice.

Ellsworth attended Fresno City College and Cal State Northridge. He was drafted three times while a collegian. In 1980 the Minnesota Twins selected him in the seventh round of the January draft, and in 1981 the Cleveland Indians took him in the third round of the secondary-phase June draft. Wanting to continue his education, he bypassed both opportunities to sign. When the Red Sox subsequently selected him in the June 1981 draft, he decided the time was ripe to go pro. Joe Stephenson, who scouted for the Red Sox for close to five decades, signed the promising young pitcher.

Finishing school remained a priority. For each of the next four years, Ellsworth returned to the classroom for the fall semester upon the completion of the minor-league season. In 1985 he graduated from Cal State Northridge with a degree in business administration.

Ellsworth's professional baseball career got off a bumpy start. He was assigned to the Elmira Pioneers in the Class-A New York-Penn League, and a handful of batters into his first appearance he experienced pain in his pitching elbow. His 1981 season was over after just one inning.

Ellsworth went into the offseason with a doctor having found no meaningful structural damage, but something was clearly amiss. Come spring training, his arm began barking again. It then got worse in extended spring training, where his teammates included Mark Fidrych, who was trying to make a comeback with the Red Sox. Six years earlier, Fidrych had been a national sensation with the Tigers, only to have an arm injury torpedo what might have been a brilliant career.

Ellsworth's own career was put on hold. Surgery was in order, causing him to miss the entire 1982 season. What followed wasn't much better. He spent much of the 1983 campaign pitching through discomfort, and at times, through pain, at low-A Winter Haven. Moreover, the results were ugly. Working as a starter, and on a pitch count that rarely gave him an opportunity to qualify for a win, Ellsworth finished 1-11 with a 7.56 ERA over 83⅓ innings. In his own words, "It was a nightmare. I hated every minute of it."

To some degree, he expected it. Knowing that a full recovery from elbow surgery takes time, Red Sox team physician Arthur Pappas told Ellsworth in spring training that he should expect a disastrous season.[2] That Pappas's prediction came to fruition didn't deter the determined hurler from moving forward. Ellsworth later told the *Hartford Courant*'s Steve Fainaru, "The last thing I wanted to do was end my career 1-11 in Class A ball."[3]

Things improved markedly in 1984. Not only was his arm feeling better, his manager, a former pitcher named Bill Slack, had his back.

"I think he saved my career," explained Ellsworth. "He told me to tell him how I felt, and how often I could pitch. I did really well and they ended up moving me up to Double A. He treated me with respect. Not that the other guys didn't, but he gave me confidence."

Ellsworth went 13-8 with a 3.29 ERA for Slack at Winston-Salem, then split two decisions while logging a 2.95 ERA in three starts with New Britain.

His 1985 season was relatively nondescript – returning to New Britain, he went 7-8 with a 4.26 ERA over 20 starts – but that was followed by a 1986 breakthrough in which he emerged as a potential big-league performer. Ellsworth dominated Double A to the tune of a 1.97 ERA over nine starts, earning a promotion to Triple-A Pawtucket. There he fashioned a 3.36 ERA while winning six of eight decisions.

In 1987 Ellsworth's performance was more workmanlike than noteworthy. Taking the mound 27 times, all but once as a starter, he went 11-8 with a 4.29 ERA for the Pawtucket Red Sox. Then came the most meaningful year of his life in baseball. Buoyed by a strong spring, he began the 1988 season in Boston. On April 7, 1988, he made his big-league debut.

He wasn't expecting to be on the mound that day.

"We had just gotten into town," explained Ellsworth. "Todd Benzinger and I were going to be roommates and had basically stayed up all night, getting moved into an apartment. When you're a starting pitcher, you're on a five-day life – you pitch every fifth day – and it was my day-three, which would have been my day to throw on the side. I figured that not getting much sleep wouldn't matter. All I'd have to do is throw in the bullpen."

Ellsworth's role wasn't entirely clear at the start of the season. Boston manager John McNamara had recently told reporters that he wasn't sure if the rookie right-hander would be utilized as a starter or as a reliever.[4]

Upon arriving at Fenway Park, Ellsworth was told that Oil Can Boyd wasn't going to be able to pitch as planned. Instead, Ellsworth would be getting the start. Things didn't go well. Taking the mound on little sleep and short rest, Ellsworth lasted just two-plus innings, giving up eight hits, including a pair of home runs to Matt Nokes, and five earned runs. One of the few highlights was his first career strikeout, which came against future Hall of Fame shortstop Alan Trammell. The final score was Detroit 11, Boston 6. Ellsworth was tagged with the loss. "I just gave them too many good pitches to hit," he said afterward. "I have no excuses. I just got hit today. My arm felt fine but I just couldn't get going."[5]

Ellsworth's second outing was a loss in which he pitched well. On April 16, the right-hander held the Texas Rangers to just one run over seven innings, but his teammates couldn't dent the scoreboard. One of the four hits Ellsworth surrendered was a home run into the Fenway Park bullpen by Larry Parrish, who finished the season in a Red Sox uniform. The final score was 2-0.

Ellsworth's lone win came in his third-ever outing, on April 21. As was the case when he made

Steve Ellsworth. Courtesy The Topps Company, Inc.

his debut, he wasn't expecting to be on the mound. It wasn't until that morning that he learned he would once again be facing the Tigers. The second time proved to be the charm. Ellsworth recalls not having his best stuff that afternoon, but it didn't matter. Making good pitches when he needed to, he scattered six hits over seven innings as the Red Sox rolled to a 12-3 win. He told the *Boston Globe*, "I'm glad I finally got this game, especially against this team. You could say they owned me the last two times out. This will help me confidence-wise."[6]

Notable among the six hits surrendered by Ellsworth was a home run off the bat of Matt Nokes, who had twice victimized the rookie in his debut. The left-handed-hitting Detroit catcher went deep three times in five career at-bats against him. "For whatever reason, some guys just have your number," Ellsworth mused three decades later.

That he finished with just the lone victory wasn't indicative of how well he pitched during his brief Boston tenure. His fourth outing was a case in point. For the second time in two weeks, he was on the wrong end of a 2-0 score. The Kansas City Royals dented the rookie right-hander for just one earned run in 6⅔ innings.

Ellsworth's eight outings in a Boston uniform were split between two stints. Having had mixed results, and with Bob Stanley coming off the disabled list, Ellsworth was demoted to Pawtucket on May 20. The following spring, he would tell a reporter for United Press International that he'd expected to be sent back down, adding that Dwight Evans had told him, "Making it here is the easy part. Staying here, that's the hard part."[7]

Ellsworth was called back up to the big leagues six weeks after the demotion and made his next to last Red Sox appearance. On July 1 – three days after being summoned as a precautionary measure, lest Roger Clemens couldn't make a scheduled start – he entered the game in the second inning after the Kansas City Royals had scored six times off Bruce Hurst.[8]

His lone relief appearance also resulted in a tough-luck loss. Ellsworth allowed a pair of runs, one scoring on a groundout, over 4⅓ solid innings. Seven games into his big-league career, Ellsworth had a 1-5 record, and it easily could have been 3-3. Looking back, he couldn't help but wonder what might have happened had he been on the winning end a few more times.

"I've thought about that a lot over the years," acknowledged Ellsworth. "There were a couple of games where I had no business winning, but there were a couple of others that could have gone my way. I remember pitching a pretty good game against Texas where we ended up losing. From a mental standpoint, when you start out the year 3-1 or 4-2, you feel more confident each time you go out there. When you start out 0-3 or 0-4, you're thinking, 'Can we erase that and have a do-over?'"

There are no do-overs in baseball, nor was there another opportunity for Ellsworth with a big-league club. Demoted right before the All-Star break, the tall right-hander spent the rest of the season in the minors.

Being back in Pawtucket meant that he missed out on Morgan Magic. Right around the time he was sent back to Triple A, the Red Sox fired manager John McNamara and replaced him with Joe Morgan. What followed was 19 Boston wins in 20 games, and ultimately a playoff berth. Ellsworth could only enjoy it from a distance.

One of Ellsworth's best outings of the season came after his late-May demotion. His first outing after returning to the PawSox was memorable, yet at the same time disappointing.

"We were in Oklahoma City and I had a no-hitter until two outs in the ninth inning," recalled Ellsworth. "Tom O'Malley, a left-handed hitter that always seemed to get the best of me, hit a home run. The next guy struck out."

Ellsworth was named the International League's Pitcher of the Week for May 22-28 following his near-no-hitter. After the outing, the *Los Angeles Times* wrote of the former Cal State Northridge hurler, "If Steve Ellsworth had pitched for the Boston Red Sox the way he did for their Triple-A affiliate, he might be still be in the major leagues."[9]

Ellsworth's 1988 season also included the onset of a shoulder ailment. He felt something after delivering a pitch – he didn't recall exactly when it happened – and the discomfort lingered for the rest of the year. Hoping to return to the big leagues, he opted to "not make a big deal out of it." He simply continued to pitch.

Ellsworth's arm felt good when he reported to spring training in 1989. He pitched often that spring, possibly because he was being showcased. The righty recalled rumors that the Red Sox were trying to include him in a trade, and how a couple of teams were looking at him. No deal came to fruition, and he began the season back in Pawtucket. Then the shoulder issue returned.

"A few games into that year, what I'd felt the summer before came back," said Ellsworth. "My shoulder started hurting, and then hurting quite a bit. At that point I was 28 years old, turning 29, and the only way I was possibly going to make it back was to pitch. So I went out there and was in pain every time I took the mound."

The writing was on the wall. Ellsworth realized that his career was on borrowed time. Later that season, the fears came to fruition.

"I was pitching in Pawtucket and my arm was absolutely killing me," recalled Ellsworth. "When the manager came out to get me, I told him, 'I've got nothing left. I can't throw another pitch.' I went into the clubhouse, and when the trainer came over, I told him, 'That was probably the last game I will ever pitch in.'"

When Ellsworth went to see the team doctor a few days later, his shoulder was so inflamed that they couldn't even do a full exam. Surgery followed, but not the hoped-for recovery. Ellsworth tried to come back, but his velocity – up to 90 MPH per a May 1988 Peter Gammons article – had dropped to the low 80s.[10] His playing days were over.

"The day you get released is rough," said Ellsworth. "Even if you're expecting it, it's a rough day. You've pretty much dedicated your whole life to something, and now it's over. You drive away from the ballpark, realizing that you're no longer part of that team. You see the guys out on the field and think, 'I'm no longer welcome. It's over.'"

Recently married with a college degree in his back pocket, he was ready for the next chapter in his life. Released in April 1990, Ellsworth was back in California by that June, with he and his wife, Molly, both gainfully employed. After leaving baseball, Ellsworth joined a real estate brokerage, and as of 2023 had been at the same brokerage firm for 33 years. He and his wife raised three sons, all of whom have college degrees. His mother died in 2019, while his father died in October 2022.

That Ellsworth followed in his father's footsteps remains a point of pride. At the same time, it's not lost on the second-generation hurler that his career was comparably unremarkable. Dick Ellsworth pitched in 407 games from 1958 to 1971 and was credited with 115 wins. Steve appeared in eight games and had just the one win.

"A few years ago I was at a gathering and someone brought up that my dad and I were the first father-son duo to win games for the Red Sox," Ellsworth recalled. "I was like, 'Yeah, but I mean, I only won one game.' Not that it wasn't meaningful to me. The veteran guys got the ball and wrote, 'First major league win' on it. I still have the ball. At the time, I wasn't expecting it to be my only win."

SOURCES

In addition to the sources cited in the Notes, the author consulted Baseball-Reference.com and Retrosheet.org. Thanks to Rod Nelson of SABR's Scouts and Scouting Research Committee.

NOTES

1. Author interview with Steve Ellsworth on April 27, 2021. Unless otherwise indicated, all direct quotations come from this interview.
2. *Lewiston* (Maine) *Sun-Journal*, April 10, 1988.
3. Steve Fainaru, "Ellsworth Follows Dad's Footsteps to Mound," *Hartford Courant*, April 1, 1988: D4.
4. Fainaru.
5. Rich Thompson, "Rookie Rough-Up for Ellsworth," *Boston Herald*. April 8, 1988: 126.
6. Dan Shaughnessy, "Burks' Fine Start Is Worth the Weights," *Boston Globe*, April 22, 1988: 48.
7. United Press International March 1, 1989. https://www.upi.com/Archives/1989/03/01/Steve-Ellsworth-has-made-a-short-trip-back-to/3560604731600/. Accessed November 22, 2022.
8. "Baseball Central," UPI Archives, June 28, 1988. https://www.upi.com/Archives/1988/06/28/Baseball-Central/6450583473600/. Accessed December 12, 2022.
9. "Ellsworth Builds Case for Recall," *Los Angeles Times*, May 28, 1988: BV21.
10. "Baseball," Peter Gammons, *Sports Illustrated*, May 2, 1988.

EDWIN ESCOBAR

BY TONY S. OLIVER

Escobar family reunions could pass for baseball clinics. Since patriarch Oscar Santiago Escobar founded a team in 1963, seven descendants have reached the major leagues: José Escobar, Ángel Escobar, Vicente Campos, Alcides Escobar, Kelvim Escobar, Ronald Acuña Jr., and Edwin José Escobar. Others, like Oscar Jr. and Elvis Escobar, enjoyed long careers in the Venezuelan Winter League and the American minor leagues but did not reach "The Show."

José Elias Escobar Sánchez had a cup of coffee with the Cleveland Indians in 1991. As a 30-year-old rookie, the 5-foot-10, 140-pound infielder went 3-for-15 in 10 games, mostly as a late-inning defensive replacement. However, his limited experience in the big leagues was but a small chapter of his baseball life. He played 14 seasons in the Venezuelan Winter League, intertwined with 13 others in the American minor leagues. He had two sons with his wife, Oneida: Edwin José and Elvis José.

Edwin was born on April 22, 1992, in La Boyera, Estado de Miranda, Venezuela, and sibling Elvis followed two years later. José soon realized his children would continue the family tradition: "Edwin was always the best pitcher on his team and Elvis was also quite good."[1]

Edwin grew to an imposing 6-foot-2, 225-pound left-handed pitcher. He was signed by the Texas Rangers as an amateur free agent on July 2, 2008, and began his professional career in the Arizona Fall League in 2009. At 17, he was 3½ years younger than the league average, and he struggled in 13 games (12 starts). He gave up 10.6 hits and 5 runs per nine innings, but demonstrated promise with his 48 strikeouts and only one home run allowed in 45 innings. Nevertheless, the Rangers traded him to San Francisco on April 1, 2010, for fellow minor leaguer Brad Snyder.

The Giants sent him to the Salem-Keizer Volcanos of the short-season Class-A Northwest League, managed by former big-league skipper Tom Trebelhorn. Escobar started 14 games and posted a 4.86 ERA with 69 strikeouts in 63 innings. During the offseason, he played in Venezuela with the Lara Cardenales, pitching 22⅓ innings (1-0, 2.82).

Escobar split time in 2011 between the Augusta GreenJackets of the low Class-A South Atlantic League, where he performed poorly in four appearances (12 earned runs in six innings), and the Arizona Fall League (5.09 ERA in 46 innings). He again played in Venezuela during the winter, but was ineffective (14 earned runs in 22 innings).

Despite the rough year, the Giants saw potential and Escobar returned to Augusta for the 2012 season. He sharply lowered his ERA to 2.96 in 22 starts and displayed superb command, walking only 32 batters in 130⅔ innings. The pitching-rich GreenJackets led the league in ERA, with Escobar among the top 10 qualifiers. His 7-8 record underscored the lack of consistent run support, as he got no-decisions in many of his quality starts. He was named the league's pitcher of the week on August 27 during a stretch of 17 consecutive innings.[2] After a 1-0 win over the Greensboro Grasshoppers, he remarked, "My confidence is better, and I've been able to stay focused even before the game. I'm just doing what I'm supposed to be doing."[3] Manager Lipso Nava praised his effort: "He was the story tonight, and he's been the story of the last month. He's been tremendous with the command over all his pitches and changing speeds."[4]

Escobar credited his success to his cousin Kelvim, whom he regarded as "almost a pitching coach." He added, "I ask him after every start, 'What should I improve? What did you do when you were in the minors?'"[5] About his repertoire, he added, "[M]y fastball is lively, with a lot of movement, but my curve and my changeup have helped me a lot this year," and said he appreciated his Venezuelan Winter League experience for "facing hitters already in Double A, Triple A, and the major leagues. That's helped me a lot to understand how to throw."[6]

Thanks to his breakthrough campaign, *Baseball America* ranked Escobar as the Giants' 14th best prospect before the 2013 season. He began the season with San Jose (Class A advanced), where his solid 2.89 ERA and 92 strikeouts in 74⅔ innings produced three wins and four losses, again due to poor run support. He was selected to the California League All-Star team and was soon promoted to Richmond of the Double-A Eastern League and started 10 games, improved his ERA to 2.67, and struck out 54 opponents in 54 innings.

Escobar returned to California in 2014, this time with Fresno Grizzlies of the Triple-A PCL as the Giants' second-best organizational prospect, but his ERA almost doubled to 5.11 in 20 starts.[7] Nevertheless, Escobar was selected to the 2014 MLB Futures game. In one inning, he allowed three hits and one run in the World team's 3-2 loss to the US squad.[8] He acknowledged that adjusting to Triple A "(has) been real(ly) different. It's tough because

Edwin Escobar on July 15, 2016. Photograph by Sarah Sachs/Arizona Diamondbacks.

you have to face a lot of guys who are major league ready."[9] He acknowledged his struggles against right-handers and added, "I feel pretty good throwing to a right-handed hitter. My thing is I get a little bit unlucky. … A lot of hits against right handers are bloopers, singles, a lot of groundballs, and stuff getting through the field."[10]

Escobar hoped to join the Giants, who featured fellow Venezuelans Pablo Sandoval and Marco Scutaro. However, the contending Giants, worried about the health of workhorse Matt Cain, traded Escobar and Heath Embree to the Boston Red Sox for All-Star Jake Peavy. The transaction paid off for San Francisco as Peavy stabilized the rotation during Cain's absence and helped the franchise to its third World Series title in five years.

Boston assigned Escobar to Pawtucket, where he would spend the bulk of his time with the franchise. He threw 27⅓ innings, struck out 20 batters, and posted a 4.28 ERA in five starts in 2014. The rebuilding Red Sox promoted Escobar in late summer, and he debuted on August 27 in Toronto. He threw a scoreless eighth inning and retired all three batters he faced. Boston lost the game, 5-2. Despite the result, Escobar was thrilled to have reached the major leagues: "It's an honor to be in the same role as my father back in the day … not just for me, for the entire family, and the region of La Sabana. We're always in touch, whether I'm doing well or poorly. They've always been supportive."[11] The Escobars became the third father/son duo from Venezuela to play in the big leagues, after the Armas (Tony and Tony Jr.) and the Torrealbas (Pablo and Steve) duos. José Escobar was able to catch the magical moment: "I was at home, switching channels and stumbled upon a Dominican station that only reaches La Sabana. It was showing the Boston-Blue Jays game. We started watching and to our great surprise, Edwin took the mound in the eighth inning. Now everyone in town says, 'Of course, he's from the Escobars' or 'The dynasty continues.'"[12]

Escobar returned to Triple A and waited almost a month for his next opportunity, an 11-3 victory over Tampa Bay on September 24. He entered in the ninth inning and hit the first batter, Brandon Guyer. He regained his poise and struck out Sean Rodríguez and José Molina, but Ben Zobrist's double to deep left-center field drove in Guyer. Escobar retired Kevin Kiermaier on a fly ball to center to end the game.

Less than a week later, almost 60 family and friends gave Escobar a warm welcome upon his return to Venezuela. Not content to rest on his laurels, he shared his plans "to keep working hard to return next year and establish myself in 'The Show.' There is, without a doubt, a world of difference between the minors and the majors. In the minors you have a lot of youngsters but in the majors, the competition is more intense, there's more talent with superstar players. I sensed the change, but I adapted and did rather well."[13]

Named as Boston's 18th best prospect,[14] Escobar he returned to the minors in 2015 and struggled with Triple-A Pawtucket (3-3, 5.07 ERA, 25 walks, and 24 strikeouts in 49⅔ innings) and a perfect one-inning appearance with Class-A Greenville. He returned to Venezuela, but the 2015-2016 season would be Escobar's last playing winter ball. In seven starts, he uncharacteristically struggled with his control (19 walks in 27 innings). Overall, Escobar played five seasons and compiled a 1-6 record with a 4.07 EA in 117⅓ innings.[15]

Although he played spring-training games with the Red Sox, Escobar began 2016 with Pawtucket (three games, seven innings, no earned runs allowed). A flurry of moves made him the odd man out on the 40-man roster, and he was designated for assignment. He was selected by the Arizona Diamondbacks off waivers on April 29 and soon thrust into the starting rotation.

On May 30 Escobar gave up eight runs (seven earned) against the Astros in 3⅓ innings. Though the Astros had not yet ascended to the top of the American League, their young nucleus of Carlos Correa, George Springer, and José Altuve had already become bothersome for opposing hurlers.

Escobar was reflective in a postgame interview: "I broke some bats, and they still got some base hits. I just think it wasn't my day."[16] Manager Chip Hale offered a balanced assessment: "We saw some good things. There's some stuff that needs to be refined and (pitching coach Mike Butcher) likes the arm. We get four days of work before he starts again, so we'll see what we can do to tighten it up a little bit. I think he's going to help us."[17] Catcher Welington Castillo opined that "Escobar was inconsistent with fastball command and the slider, too, was moving a lot. So he didn't have really good command today, but I think the stuff is pretty good."[18]

Escobar faced the Chicago Cubs on June 4, and the eventual 2016 World Series champions gave him no quarter. Though staked to a 2-0 lead on Jake Lamb's home run, he allowed a leadoff home run to Dexter Fowler. He kept the Cubs off the scoreboard in the next two innings before Jorge Soler hit a ground-rule double, driving in Ben Zobrist, and opposing pitcher Jason Hammel singled in two runs. After four runs and 3⅔ innings, he was replaced by Randall Delgado, who retired Fowler to close the frame. This time, Hale was less sanguine about Escobar's role: "We think this (relieving) is more his niche, too, to be a reliever so we're interested to see it."[19]

Escobar was demoted to Triple-A Reno, where he spent the bulk of the summer (6-3, 4.25 ERA in 16 starts). Recalled to the majors, he turned the corner as a left-handed specialist, or Left-handed One-Out Guy (LOOGY). In 16⅔ innings of relief, he allowed eight earned runs, registered four holds, blew one save, and won his first major-league game on August 26.

Down 2-1 with two outs and two strikes in the ninth, Cincinnati tied the Diamondbacks to force extra innings. After the teams each scored a run in the 10th, Escobar took the mound in the 11th. Although he allowed two baserunners, he kept the Reds from scoring. In the bottom of the inning, Arizona's Brandon Drury scored the winning run on a mad dash to the plate on Blake Wood's wild pitch to finish a thrilling game and give Escobar the victory.

Escobar did not allow a run in his last seven appearances for the Diamondbacks, seemingly securing a spot in the 2017 roster. However, he was left off the offseason 40-man roster and was claimed by the Cleveland Indians on November 18, 2016.

Without assurance that he would be on the big-league roster, Escobar asked Cleveland for his release so he could play baseball in Japan. The team granted his wish, and he became a free agent on January 10, 2017. He pitched for the Nippon Ham Fighters in 2017 and appeared in 14 games (5.64 ERA, 1-2) before a midseason trade to the Yokohama Baystars (27 games, 3.44 ERA, 1-3). The adjustment was not easy; he readily admitted that "the smallest things can become big details so now I'm much more careful about them. Here a walk can become a double after a bunt and lots of other things follow. You don't see that in the United States. There, a batter who gets a base on balls will stay on the base and wait for a big hit to advance. Runners rarely advance on the bases so with a double play you can get out of the jam. Not here: A small detail can quickly become a large detail. I think it's the most important thing I've learned."[20]

Yokohama made it to the Japan Series but lost to the Fukuoka Softbank Hawks. Escobar said, "It was a wonderful experience since it was my first year in Japan; to play through November was very emotional. I was never able to play in the postseason in the United States, so I'm proud of having accomplished it in my first year in Japan. I'm very happy with the success I've had with my breaking ball, it has helped me a lot thus far."[21]

Early in the 2019 season, Escobar said, "My goals are the same each year: Finish strong, stay healthy, pitch in 60 games, and help the team to win, above everything else."[22] As of 2023 Escobar was still pitching in Japan. He became a very effective left-handed specialist out of the bullpen, the role the Diamondbacks hoped he would play. From 2017 to 2022, he won 20 games, lost 22 others, saved 5, and held 136 leads.²³

Escobar started an athletic clothing company, "Everyday Edwin," a nod to his durable arm and willingness to take the mound every day.²⁴ Though some players head to Japan to earn a second chance at the major leagues, Escobar has found a home in Nippon Professional Baseball. Despite the language barrier, he became a fan favorite and earned his teammates' trust. The bond helped Escobar deal with anonymous, racist posts in the social media platform X that threatened his family. Teammate Yasuaki Yamasaki replied to the posts and reiterated the team's support for Escobar.

Though he was named to Venezuela's 30-man roster for the 2017 and 2023 editions of the World Baseball Classic, Escobar did not see action in the tournament. Through 2023, his major-league register stands at one win, two losses, 27 games, and a 7.01 ERA.

Escobar, a devout Christian, is married and has three children. In his early 30s he expressed optimism about playing several more years in Japan: "It's like a gift from God. I just say keep working, get better, get stronger, and the outcome is going to come."²⁵

SOURCES

In addition to the sources listed in the Notes, the author consulted Baseball-Reference, Pelota Binaria, and the Nippon Professional Baseball Organization (NPB) website.

NOTES

1. Alexander Mendoza, "Edwin Escobar de continuidad a la tradición familiar," *Béisbol 007*, August 31, 2014, https://beisbolnew.wordpress.com/2014/08/31/edwin-escobar-da-con-tinuidad-a-la-tradic-ion-familiar/.
2. Billy Blyer, "GreenJackets Lefty Edwin Escobar Earns South Atlantic League Pitcher of the Week Award," *Augusta Chronicle*, August 27, 2012.
3. Billy Blyer, "GreenJackets Beat Greensboro with Another Gem from Edwin Escobar," *Augusta Chronicle*, August 26, 2012.
4. "GreenJackets beat Greensboro with another gem from Edwin Escobar."
5. Angel Cuevas, "Edwin Escobar: 'Kelvim para mí ha sido como un coach de pitcheo," *Porelcentro*, August 24, 2012, https://porelcentro.wordpress.com/2012/08/24/edwin-escobarkelvim-para-mi-ha-sido-como-un-coach-de-pitcheo/.
6. "Edwin Escobar: 'Kelvim para mí ha sido como un coach de pitcheo."
7. https://www.thebaseballcube.com/content/player/152910/prospects/.
8. https://bleacherreport.com/articles/2128837-mlb-futures-game-2014-results-box-score-top-performers-from-target-field.
9. Conner Penfold, "Q&A with Giants No. 2 Prospect Edwin Escobar," *The McCovey Chronicles/SBNation*, April 21, 2014, https://www.mccoveychronicles.com/2014/4/21/5631504/edwin-escobar-giants-prospect-scouting-video-interview.
10. "Q&A with Giants No. 2 Prospect Edwin Escobar."
11. Alexander Mendoza, "Edwin Escobar de continuidad a la tradición familiar."
12. "Edwin Escobar de continuidad a la tradición familiar."
13. Galvis Guzmán, "La Sabana recibió a su quinto grandeliga: Edwin Escobar," *Diario La Verdad de Vargas*, September 30, 2014, https://laverdaddevargas.com/la-sabana-recibio-a-su-quinto-grandeliga-edwin-escobar/
14. https://www.thebaseballcube.com/content/player/152910/prospects/.
15. Edwin Escobar player profile, *Pelota Binaria*, https://www.pelotabinaria.com.ve/beisbol/mostrar.php?ID=escoedw001.
16. Nick Piecoro, "Diamondbacks, Edwin Escobar See Positives in Debut Loss," AZ Central Sports, May 30, 2016, https://www.azcentral.com/story/sports/mlb/diamondbacks/2016/05/30/diamondbacks-edwin-escobar-see-positives-debut-loss/85175796/.
17. "Diamondbacks, Edwin Escobar See Positives in Debut Loss."
18. "Diamondbacks, Edwin Escobar See Positives in Debut Loss."
19. Scott Bordow, "Diamondbacks Sending Edwin Escobar to Bullpen," AZ Central Sports, June 6, 2016, https://www.azcentral.com/story/sports/mlb/diamondbacks/2016/06/06/dbacks-corbin-miller/85532454/.
20. Claudio Rodríguez Otero, "Escobar: 'Aquí los pequeños detalles se hacen grandes,'" *Béisbol Japonés.com*, August 2, 2017, https://beisboljapones.com/noticias/entrevistas/1281-escobar-%E2%80%9Caqu%C3%AD-los-peque%C3%B1os-detalles-se-hacen-grandes%E2%80%9D.
21. Claudio Rodríguez Otero, "Escobar: 'Mis lanzamientos han mejorado mucho aquí," *Béisbol Japonés.com*, June 28, 2018, https://beisboljapones.com/noticias/entrevistas/1703-escobar-%E2%80%9Cmis-lanzamientos-han-mejorado-mucho-aqu%C3%AD%E2%80%9D.

22 Claudio Rodríguez Otero, "Escobar: 'He trabajado duro para lograr este éxito,'" *Béisbol Japonés.com*, May 10, 2019, https://beisboljapones.com/noticias/entrevistas/1939-escobar-%E2%80%9Che-trabajado-duro-para-lograr-este-%C3%A9xito%E2%80%9D.

23 Nippon Baseball League, Edwin Escobar Player Page, https://npb.jp/bis/eng/players/63365134.html.

24 Everyday by Edwin Escobar, https://everyday62.base.shop/.

25 Jason Coskrey, "Hard-Throwing Edwin Escobar Keeping Things Simple with the BayStars."

CLAY FAUVER

BY MARK HODERMARSKY

One of the most unlikely pitchers in baseball history among the "One-Win Wonders" must be Clayton King Fauver of the National League Louisville Colonels. On September 7, 1899, at Pittsburgh's Exposition Park, Fauver, appearing in his only game as a major leaguer, flustered the Pirates by giving up 11 hits and 4 runs (none of them earned) and tossing a complete game that ended with a 7-4 win for the Colonels. Perhaps more remarkable than the major-league career stat line which reads 1 win, 0 losses, and a 0.00 earned-run average is that at the time of his debut, Fauver was attending Western Reserve Law School in Cleveland.

Clay Fauver was born on August 1, 1872, in North Eaton, Ohio, about 30 miles southeast of Cleveland, the son of Alfred and Elizabeth King Fauver. He had four brothers, Lester, Louis, and twins Edward and Edgar, and a sister, Mabel. Clay, or C.K., as he was often called, and his family moved to nearby Oberlin (13 miles west) in 1892, where he attended Oberlin Academy, a private preparatory school. The following year, Clay entered Oberlin College and began an illustrious collegiate career as a student and athlete.[1] His father, Alfred, a onetime Lorain County commissioner and mayor of Oberlin, modeled examples of public and community service that his children would emulate. Alfred and Elizabeth also raised "scholar-athletes" long before the term existed.

Lester, the eldest child, became president of the Ohio Engineering Company. Edwin Fauver was director of athletics at the University of Rochester from 1916 to 1945 as well as a professor of hygiene/physical education and a college physician. The university's acclaimed 5,000-seat athletic facility, Edwin Fauver Stadium, was built in his honor in 1930.[2] Edgar, like his twin, a renowned football and baseball player at Oberlin College, also accomplished much, earning a medical degree from Columbia University in 1909 and an assistant professorship position at the school. In 1913 he left Columbia for Wesleyan University, serving as a coach in several sports and director of athletics while maintaining his roles as a professor and college physician. Interestingly, Edgar also had an athletic field and two undergraduate housing projects named in his honor – Fauver Field (1959) and Fauver Field Residence Halls (2005).[3] Continuing the Fauver chronicle of service, sister Mabel became an admired high-school teacher.

On the Oberlin campus, Clay, a Phi Beta Kappa graduate in 1897, was manager of the yearbook, assistant editor of the student newspaper, and a member of the debate team, experiences that would portend a law career. Although he was popular among fellow students and instructors, Fauver's fame derived chiefly from his success on the baseball diamond and, especially, on the football gridiron. An outstanding athlete and leader, C.K. captained the Yeomen baseball team in 1896 and the football team in 1893 and 1894. Still a player, Fauver nonetheless took on more responsibilities as Oberlin's head football coach in 1896.[4]

Between 1892 and 1896 Oberlin was a football powerhouse, claiming victories over the likes of Ohio State and Michigan with Clay Fauver as a star tackle and halfback. Louis, his 24-year-old brother, was a teammate when he and C.K. were coached by the legendary John W. Heisman in two of those years. (Louis also achieved much success after his Oberlin years, establishing a law firm in Elyria, Ohio, after graduating from Dartmouth College and earning a law degree from Harvard Law School.) Interestingly, before graduating in 1895, Clay Fauver took over football head coaching duties for three weeks at Miami University in Oxford, Ohio, becoming the first paid coach in school history while leading the Redskins to a 3-0 record. He also played in those wins over Wittenberg, Butler, and Cincinnati.

After graduating from Oberlin College in 1897, Clay Fauver began pursuing a law career, enrolling at Western Reserve Law School in Cleveland. At the time he could never have imagined getting a chance to appear in a National League baseball game. In one of the rarest of opportunities ever granted a former collegiate pitcher, particularly someone who had not played competitive baseball in a couple of years, Harry Pulliam, president of the Louisville Colonels, invited C.K. to be his starting pitcher for a road game against the Pittsburgh Pirates on Thursday, September 7, 1899.

Going into the September 7 contest, the Colonels found themselves in ninth place, 29 games behind the Brooklyn Superbas, the eventual National League champions that year. Despite filling the 1899 roster with future Hall of Famers – Honus Wagner, Fred Clarke, and Rube Waddell – Louisville, for the eighth and final year as a major-league franchise, wound up near the bottom of the standings by finishing ninth. (The Colonels never placed higher than ninth among the 12 NL teams and ended up 11th or 12th in five of those eight years.)

Entering the September 7 game against Louisville, the 1899 Pittsburgh Pirates' record stood at 61 wins and 59 losses, 22 games out of first place. Some of the more impactful players on the Pittsburgh roster,

Clay Fauver.

including first baseman Willie Clark and outfielders Jack McCarthy and player-manager Patsy Donovan, must have salivated at facing the unknown rookie. Adding a greater threat to Clay Fauver's challenge, however, was his pitching rival that day. On the mound for the Pirates was one of the best pitchers of his era, Jesse "Powder" Tannehill, who that year posted a 24-14 record along with a 2.82 ERA. Tannehill would end his 15-year career with 197 wins, 117 losses, a 2.80 ERA, and clearly in the discussion for Hall of Fame consideration. He was also a fair hitter as his .255 lifetime batting average testifies.

The headline above the recap in the next day's issue of the *Louisville Courier-Journal* read: "New Pitcher Was on Deck, His Identity Not Known, but He Is Not Peck," followed by the drop head: "Clarke and Pulliam Refuse to Tell Who the New

Twirler Is – He Is Not Waddell." The reporter in his opening paragraph explains:

> "A mysterious twirler won for Louisville to-day. On the score card he passed as Peck, but Pulliam was authority for the statement that the name is an assumed one and is worn to disguise one much better known in baseball business circles. Pulliam asserted that he was bound to protect the new twirler's secret, and as Manager Fred Clarke was also uncommunicative the mystery remains unsolved."[5]

The circumstances surrounding Clay Fauver's summons to the mound remain murky. The 27-year-old was studying law at Western Reserve and would not receive his law degree until 1900. That Clay was asked to join the club for only one game is intriguing. How did the Colonels learn about his availability, interest, and, importantly, ability to pitch against a major-league team? Was the Louisville pitching staff depleted? Did the short train ride from Cleveland to Pittsburgh enter into the decision? The precise factors putting Fauver on the hill at Exposition Park may never come to light, but his extraordinary performance can at least be documented.

What was slated to be a doubleheader became one game because the train bringing the Pirates back home from Chicago experienced a three-hour delay. According to an account, "the local players did not wait for lunch, but were hauled to the park as soon as the train arrived."[6] Perhaps the completion of a late-season, long (four games) series on the road against the Orphans, the subsequent train snafu, and the missed lunch contributed to their poor play that day. However, as suggested by the *Pittsburgh Post-Gazette* scribe's sardonic recap, titled "Too Tired to Play," the home team did not deserve much sympathy:

> "It was probably just as well that Patsy Donovan and his Pirates did encounter a wreck on the Lake Shore road which delayed their arrival for a couple of hours, and therefore prevented a double header with the Louisville team. The Pirates had barely time to play one game, and goodness knows that one was enough for the 1,500 spectators. A second dose of the same kind of play would probably have driven the entire crowd to drink."[7]

The Colonels, conversely, were a fresher adversary, not having taken the field the day before. The *Courier-Journal* reporter summarized the contest as follows:

> Manager Donovan showed eagerness to get a victory by sending Tannehill in to do the pitching, but the star failed to stop the slugging of the visitors. Fred Clarke and [Chief] Zimmer led the attack upon the southpaw's benders with four hits each, but [Mike] Kelly was not far behind, [Tommy] Leach, Clarke and [Billy] Clingman carried off the honors in the field."[8]

The Pirates scored four runs in the first four innings on eight hits and two errors. After that, the Colonels improved their fielding and the pitching advanced, too, the consequence being that the locals failed to score again.[9] But it was the 5-foot-10, right-handed "mystery" pitcher who grabbed, by far, the most attention. At game's end, the name "Fauver" landed in the box score, revealing the Louisville pitcher's true identity and his stunning performance – 9 innings, 0 earned runs, and a win. The *Post-Gazette*'s writer praised the performance by the Louisville pitcher, describing him as "a well-built young fellow, and he is going to make a reputation in the big league, because he knows something about the art of twirling. He has lots of speed, a good change of pace, and, better than all, a good head."[10]

That reporter's prediction for Fauver's stardom would not come to fruition, of course. When the game ended, so did Clay Fauver's career. Clay boarded a train bound for Cleveland to resume his law studies.

In the long run, however, it was the Pittsburgh franchise coming out on top. Mediocre play, poor attendance, and a fire that burned down the grandstand at Eclipse Park on August 12, 1899, contributed to the collapse of the Louisville NL franchise at the end of the year. And the immediate beneficiaries were the Pirates. Barney Dreyfuss, team owner of both the Pirates and Colonels, with Louisville President Harry Pulliam's assistance, fashioned a trade with Pittsburgh by moving the team's best players to Pittsburgh, including three future Hall of Famers – Rube Waddell, Fred Clarke, and Honus Wagner. In all, 12 players were sent to the Pirates while, in exchange, the Colonels received $25,000 and four players. Fred Clarke went on to player-manage and bench-manage (1914, 1915) the Pirates for the next 16 seasons, winning four pennants and a 1909 World Series championship over Detroit.[11]

Clay Fauver's eventful pitching debut in the big leagues apparently motivated him to not step away completely from baseball. A year later, 1900, while keeping up with his law-school obligations, Fauver joined the American League Cleveland Lake Shores (officially Blues), formerly the Grand Rapids Rustlers, a minor-league franchise in the Western League. (In 1900 the league was renamed the American League.) In 1901 American League President Ban Johnson declared the league a major league.

Managed by Jimmy McAleer, a Youngstown, Ohio, native and 13-year professional ballplayer, including nine years as a NL Cleveland Spider outfielder, the 1900 Blues, whose home ballpark was League Park, finished in sixth place out of eight teams with a 63-73 record. Clay Fauver played in exactly 10 games, winning four and losing six as a pitcher (no official record of his ERA exists), and in 34 plate appearances he had 7 hits for a .206 batting average. Judging from these stats, we might assume that Fauver appeared only in home games to balance the rigors of finishing his studies with his pitching performances.

Fauver's limited professional baseball career may have ended in 1900 but not so his love of the game. After earning his degree from Western Reserve Law School that year, he began to practice law in Cleveland with two firms while teaching law at Western Reserve. In 1902 he coached the Western Reserve baseball team to a 5-6 record.

Fauver remained in Cleveland until 1916, when he moved to New York City, where he practiced import and export trade law and became vice president and general counsel of a renowned import-export company, Gaston, Williams, & Wigmore, and "an authority on legal matters concerning foreign trade."[12] He also formed the law office of Fauver, Albertson and Schoble before returning to his beloved Oberlin in 1933.[13]

Upon his return to Oberlin, Fauver, reflecting the commitment to service so much a part of the Fauver family DNA, seized one opportunity after another to better his community as Oberlin College's investment executive and president of a local bank, Oberlin Savings Bank. The list also includes his role as trustee of both the First Church and Phillis Wheatley Community Center, plus a membership in the Exchange Club and Chamber of Commerce.

Reported in the March 5, 1942, issue of the *Oberlin News-Tribune*, the sudden death at age 69 of Clayton K. Fauver from coronary thrombosis in Chatsworth, Georgia, where he and his sister, Mabel, had stopped on their way to Sebring, Florida, must have shocked and saddened readers, despite Fauver's being in poor health for some time. Following the front-page headline, they learn that

> "Storm bound, Mr. Fauver and his sister had stopped Monday afternoon in Chatsworth and had stayed overnight at the hotel there. They had just eaten breakfast and were descending the stairs at the hotel, preparatory to continuing their journey, when

Mr. Fauver was stricken. He died almost instantly."[14]

On page two of the newspaper, Louis E. Lord, a close friend and college classmate, offered this reflection: "In the few hours that had since passed since I heard of his death, I have been constantly thinking that no one, literally no one, could be taken from this town who would be missed in so many ways. It will not be hard, it will be impossible, to fill his space."[15]

SOURCES

Career statistics and player information from baseball-reference.com.

Thanks to Mike Risley and Wendell Jones from the Pee Wee Reese SABR Chapter in Louisville for finding the *Courier-Journal* recap and box score of the September 7, 1899, game between the Louisville Colonels and the Pittsburgh Pirates, and to Allie Petonic from the Forbes Field SABR Chapter in Pittsburgh for the *Post-Gazette*.

NOTES

1 "C.K. Fauver Stricken in Georgia," *Oberlin News-Tribune*, March 5, 1942, accessed March 13, 2021, http://dcollections.oberlin.edu/digital/collection/newstribune/id/872.

2 "Edwin Fauver Stadium," *University of Rochester Yellow Jackets*, accessed March 10, 2021, https://uofrathletics.com/facilities/edwin-fauver-stadium/6.

3 Sarah Lippincott, "Retrospective on Fauver Field," *Wesleyan Argus*, accessed March 10, 2021, http://wesleyanargus.com/2004/04/27/retrospective-on-fauver-field/.

4 "C.K. Fauver Stricken in Georgia."

5 "New Pitcher Was on Deck," *Louisville Courier-Journal*, September 8, 1899, accessed March 12, 2021, https://courier-journal.newspapers.com/clip/73766869/mark-here-is-the-report-in-the/.

6 . "Too Tired to Play," *Pittsburgh Commercial Gazette*, September 8, 1899, accessed March 12, 2021, http://www.newspapers.com/image/85602358.

7 "Too Tired to Play."

8 "New Pitcher Was on Deck."

9 "New Pitcher Was on Deck."

10 "Too Tired to Play."

11 David Hill, "Pittsburgh Pirates History: Stars Transferred to Team from Louisville," calltothepen.com. Accessed March 17, 2022, https//calltothepen.com/2016/12/08/.

12 "C.K. Fauver Stricken in Georgia."

13 "C.K. Fauver Stricken in Georgia."

14 "C.K. Fauver Stricken in Georgia."

15 Louis E. Lord, "A Tribute to Clayton Fauver," *Oberlin News-Tribune*, March 5, 1942, accessed March 8, 2021, http://dcollections.oberlin.edu/digital/collection/newstribune/id/873.

MIGUEL FUENTES

BY TONY S. OLIVER

What if? Are there any more tragic words in the English language?

Helen of Troy's face is reputed to have launched a thousand ships. Miguel Fuentes' story may have launched fewer conversations, but the former is a myth while the latter is reality. Or in Shakespearean terms, a tragedy.

For the Seattle Pilots' fans, whose team was seized by a literal used-car salesman and later commissioner of baseball – Bud Selig – the what-if questions are endless. What if Sick's Stadium had been adequately prepared before the 1969 season, as promised by the city? What if William Daley, who owned more of the club than anyone else, had been willing to provide more financing? What if the other American League owners had not been nervous about the Pilots' misfortunes putting their own investments in peril?

As those quandaries were being considered, a promising 23-year-old pitcher, seemingly at the cusp of living up to his potential, lay dying in a dark alley in Loíza, Puerto Rico, on January 29, 1970. The Seattle press was not immediately aware of the importance of his demise, though his death presaged the end of major-league baseball in Seattle until the arrival of the Mariners in 1977.

Not much is recorded about Miguel's youth. He was born in Loíza, a town to the east of San Juan, on May 10, 1946. Only two Puerto Ricans, Hiram Bithorn and Luis Rodríguez Olmo, had played in the major leagues by then. Their Caucasian features enabled them to bypass the "unofficial" color rule, which was broken by Jackie Robinson barely a year after Fuentes was born.

Fuentes' father, Miguel Fuentes Ortiz, was previously married before exchanging vows with Nery Pinet Pizarro. As a youth, the baseball-mad Miguel Jr. attended Jesusa Vizcarrondo Middle School, though it is unclear whether he graduated from high school. At 18, he starred with the Río Piedras *Cardenales* (Cardinals) under skipper Ramón "Monche" Román. Two years later, his contract was transferred to Río Grande, a town next to Loíza; he led the *Guerrilleros* (Warriors) to the national title, defeating the Aibonito *Polluelos* (Chicks) 7-1 on September 8, 1968. His personal statistics (17-12, 236⅓ innings, 192 strikeouts, 2.70 ERA) were among the league's best.

Former Negro League player Félix "Felle" Delgado, who once hit a home run against Satchel Paige in the Puerto Rican Winter League, noticed the youngster. Although Delgado played only one season for the New York Cubans, he wore the San Juan Senators uniform for 27 years as a player and three more as a manager. He scouted for the Kansas City Monarchs and later became the Latin American supervisor for the Seattle Pilots/Milwaukee Brewers franchise, signing 31 players who reached the majors, with Fuentes being the first.[1]

More than 2,000 miles separate Iowa from Puerto Rico, but as the spring of 1969 began, five islanders were on the Clinton Pilots roster. Outfielder

Miguel Fuentes with the Seattle Pilots. Courtesy National Baseball Hall of Fame.

Domingo Apellaniz did not advance beyond Double A. Infielders Pedro García and Fernando González would appear in hundreds of major-league games. Carlos Velázquez, himself also a pitcher from Loíza, lasted only one season in the majors. But it was Fuentes who reached the promised land first, even if his stay was all too brief. The club, previously a Pirates affiliate, won 72 games against 51 defeats, good for second place in the circuit behind the Appleton Foxes, who were declared the champions after winning both halves of the season.

Fuentes produced superb numbers, including a 1.46 ERA in 74 innings pitched. He was careful to keep the ball within the ballpark, as evidenced by his two home runs allowed, and was stingy with walks (22, against 62 strikeouts). The team employed a dozen other hurlers as starters, wanting to give everyone a chance to display his talents. Half of Fuentes' six starts were complete games, two of them shutouts. Overall, his 8-2 mark, along with two saves, was enabled by a .932 WHIP, the best in the league (minimum 25 innings pitched). The *Cedar Rapids Gazette* noted that "Fuentes, the winner, stopped the Cards without a hit in the last three innings" during the Pilots' June 16 win over the Cedar Rapids Cardinals.[2] On July 5, 1969, as the Angels affiliate swept a doubleheader from the Pilots, the *Quad City Times* noted, "Miguel Fuentes pitched the last four innings for the Pilots, giving only two hits and an unearned run."[3]

The Pilots called up the promising young hurler to the majors when rosters expanded in September. Fuentes was given uniform number 14, the third Pilot to don it. (Jim Gosger had earlier been traded to the Mets while Gordy Lund returned to the minors after a swap with the Angels.) He was thrust into service on September 1 at Yankee Stadium, tossing a scoreless ninth inning with two strikeouts and a groundout. The Pilots, however, lost, 6-1. His second appearance was five days later, again closing the game in another Seattle loss, this time against their expansion siblings the Kansas City Royals. Fuentes faced the minimum as a batter he walked was caught stealing.

Satisfied by the right-hander's performance, the Pilots handed him the ball on September 8 against the White Sox. The clubs played a day-night doubleheader and the Pilots won the first contest, 2-1. Seattle fans were treated to his home debut, and Fuentes did not disappoint. A crowd of 10,831 witnessed three first-inning Pilot runs, the only run support he would need. The White Sox, ahead of only Seattle in the American League Western Division standings, were far from a dangerous team, finishing in the bottom third of the league's offensive categories, but Fuentes showed remarkable poise while facing, for the first time, an entire lineup of big leaguers. Fuentes handcuffed Chicago until the eighth inning, when Angel Bravo tripled to lead off the frame and scored on a single by Walt Williams. Fuentes helped himself at the plate, delivering a single, advancing to third on a wild pitch and groundout, and scoring a run. He went the distance, allowing only Bravo's run, seven hits, and two walks for his only major-league win.

The United Press noted "slender Miguel Fuentes pitched a seven-hitter in his first major-league start…Fuentes was in complete control."[4] Chicago manager Don Gutteridge reckoned, "It's too early to know for sure, but it looks like that youngster is going to be one fine pitcher. He had lots of poise and was throwing good stuff."[5]

Five days later Fuentes faced the Angels. He yielded a first-inning run, retired the side in order in the next two innings, and allowed a single in the fourth. The fifth inning began with promise as he induced a fly out and a pop fly before he walked Sandy Alomar Sr. His countryman ran wild on the bases, stealing second and third before scoring on a triple by Jim Spencer. The next frame brought another run across the plate as Aurelio Rodríguez drove in Bill Voss, prompting Pilots manager Joe Schultz to lift Fuentes with one out. His opponent, Eddie Fisher, kept the Pilots scoreless through eight-plus innings for the 4-2 victory.

The White Sox figured out the right-hander and their next meeting, on September 17, was rough for the pitcher. Marty Pattin opened for Seattle and allowed three runs in five innings; Fuentes, in relief, faced nine batters and retired four, allowing four hits, a walk, and three runs. California may have also studied their scouting reports and they reached Fuentes for five runs in 5⅔ frames, tagging him with his second loss on September 23. His final start of the season was against Minnesota on September 28 and he quickly ran into trouble, yielding a leadoff home run to Ted Uhlaender. Two more runs crossed the plate in the second inning before Fuentes was lifted for John O'Donoghue. The loss dropped his register to 1-3 and swelled his ERA to 5.40.

The Pilots' lone regular season in Seattle ended on October 2, 1969, in front of 5,473 fans. Starter Steve Barber allowed three runs (two earned) in two innings; subsequent relievers kept Oakland scoreless. The Pilots could muster only one run against Jim Roland and fell, 3-1. Taking the mound in the ninth inning, Fuentes retired Phil Roof via groundout and struck out Roland. Bert Campaneris singled and stole second. With a runner in scoring position, Fuentes walked Danny Cater before inducing Reggie Jackson to line out to center field. The ledger showed no runs, one hit, no errors, and two men stranded on base, but a lot more was left on the field of Sick's Stadium. The crowd had unknowingly witnessed the last pitch not just in Pilots history but also of Fuentes' big-league career.

A few months later, after the end of the semifinals of the Puerto Rican Winter League, Fuentes went to a bar in his hometown. A plumbing issue rendered the bathroom unusable, prompting a trip outside to relieve himself. Another patron, perhaps believing Fuentes was purposely urinating on his car, shot him three times, in the right hand, left

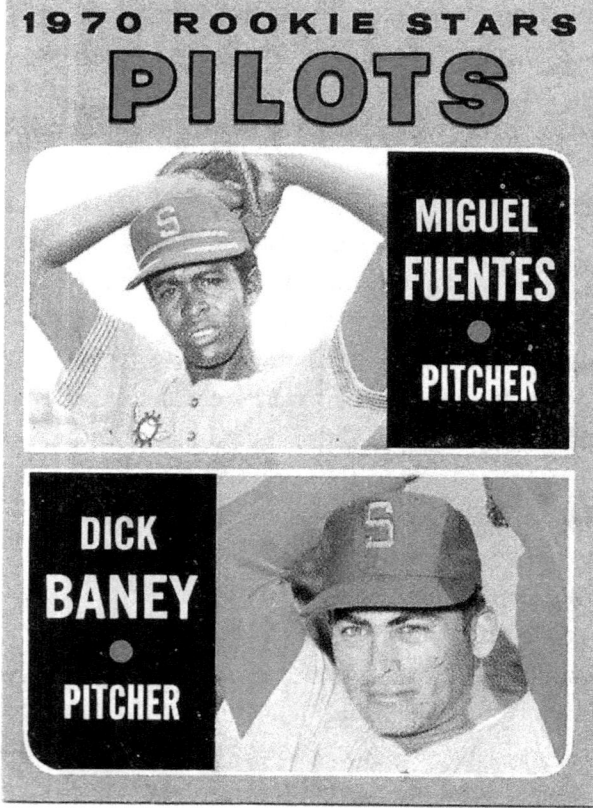

Miguel Fuentes and Dick Baney with the Pilots.
Courtesy The Topps Company, Inc.

thigh, and abdomen. Although Fuentes received medical care at a nearby hospital, his body had gone into shock and the doctors could not save his life during the surgery. The police detained a suspect, but he was not charged with a crime. In a bittersweet twist, Fuentes' brief major-league career is captured in only one baseball card, number 88 in the 1970 Topps set. He shares the honor with Dick Baney, under the optimistic title "Pilots Rookie Stars." Baney would later fondly recall him as the "nicest kid you'll ever meet."[6]

Despite its rich baseball tradition and hundreds of major leaguers, Puerto Rico has not produced many high-caliber hurlers. Javier Vázquez, with a 3:1 strikeout-to-walk ratio and 165 victories, is arguably the first face on Mount Rushmore. Juan Pizarro, who tossed 17 shutouts during his 18 years (both highs among natives), can claim second place. Jaime Navarro and Joel Piñeiro, the only others to reach triple-digit victories; Willie Hernández, the 1984 American League MVP and Cy Young Award winner; Luis Arroyo, All-Star Yankees closer for the 1961 World Series team; and Roberto Hernández, 19th on the all-time save list, can argue for the other two spots.[7] (Brooklyn-born John Candelaria, whose parents were born on the island, earned 177 big-league wins.)

Would Fuentes have reached such heights? It's hard to tell. His professional baseball career was very short. Perhaps the best comparison is Juan Nieves, whose career was cut short by an arm injury at the tender age of 23. Nieves' 94 games in the majors included not just 32 victories but also the only (as of 2022) no-hitter tossed by a Puerto Rican-born pitcher, also the first no-hitter in Milwaukee Brewers history.[8] Rangers prospect Ed Correa, who led 1986 rookies with 189 strikeouts at 20 years old, serves as a fair comparison, as his career-ending injury in 1987 produced eerie similarities.

Fuentes' story is far from rare among Puerto Rican players. Bithorn, the first native to play in the major leagues, was killed by a police officer under mysterious and controversial circumstances while playing in Mexico in 1952. Luis "Canena" Márquez, the third islander to reach the majors, was murdered by his son-in-law in 1988. The perpetrator was never convicted of the crime. In 2003 Iván Calderón, a one-time All-Star with the Montréal Expos who spent a decade in the big leagues, was also murdered in Loíza, a victim of rival gangs and his own willingness to lend money to people involved in underground betting.

Sadly, younger generations of Puerto Ricans are unaware of Fuentes' legacy. Ironically, Hurricane María, which devastated the island in 2017, may have broadened the scope of his story. Miguel Fuentes Pinet Stadium, home to the Double-A *Cocoteros* de Loíza, was severely damaged. As residents seized the opportunity to rebuild, its walls were decorated by defiant silhouettes of Afro-Puerto Rican pride. The murals captured the fighting spirt of the northeastern town, long celebrated as the birthplace of *bomba* music. African traditions remain strong in the town, with *vejigante* festivals, where local artisans craft elaborate masks from coconut husks, adorn storefronts. Among those works of art adorning the field, only one depicts an athlete. Against a backdrop of red, much like the three crimson stripes of the Puerto Rican flag, is the visage of Fuentes, composed of mostly gray and white mosaics with a cap showcasing his hometown "L." The hundreds of pieces aptly represent the shattered potential taken by the assassin. The work, titled "Between Dreams Achieved and Dreams Still to Be Achieved," by local artisan Celso González and the Monument Art initiative, proves that the eternal promise of Fuentes has not been forgotten by its hometown.[9]

The Milwaukee Brewers did not enjoy a winning season until 1978, when they began a streak of six consecutive years above .500, marked by the 1982 American League pennant. The franchise has been unable to develop strong pitching; its WAR leader, Teddy Higuera (30.3, 1985-1991, 1993-1994) was a one-time All-Star eclipsed by contemporaries like Roger Clemens, Dave Stewart, Dave Stieb, and Bret Saberhagen. The mediocre early 1970s Brewers may have been helped by a developing Fuentes, though his trajectory was far from guaranteed. A team official, lamenting his death, noted that "he was extremely poised" despite his youth.[10] Another news report confirmed that the Pilots had added Fuentes to the 40-man roster, remarking, "[H]e was a fine prospect with a major-league arm. ... [A]ll he needed was the experience so he could learn how to pitch."[11]

Fuentes' star may have shined brightly in the otherwise dark skies of 1970s Brewers baseball. His dominant performance in the Midwest League augured a promising future. Perhaps if he had been called up to the big leagues earlier, his story might have had a different ending. None of the eight pitchers who started 10 or more games for the 1969 Pilots enjoyed a winning record; only John Gelnar had an ERA below 4.00. Clearly the club needed the pitching Fuentes could have provided. Had his workload gone beyond the 26 innings tossed in September, would the franchise had allowed him to pitch in the Puerto Rico Winter League? Back in the 1960s and 1970s, the circuit was a breeding ground for young talent who sought to prove their worth against established big leaguers, so his workload might have not been restricted.

Fuentes remains forever entrenched in Pilots lore not just for that magical September night, but also for throwing the last pitch of the franchise's stay in Seattle on October 2, 1969, before its sudden move to Milwaukee in the spring of 1970 after being purchased by future Commissioner Selig. Much like the Pilots, Fuentes represents what could have been.

Acknowledgments

The Loíza *Cocoteros* for providing details on Miguel Fuentes (accessible via https://www.loizacocoteros.com/miguelfuentespinet).

Héctor "Titito" Rosa for providing information about Miguel Fuentes' youth and amateur career.

Retrosheet.org and Baseball-reference.com for Fuentes's statistics and game logs.

NOTES

1. Negro Leagues Baseball Museum, eMuseum Electronic Resources for Teachers, Profile on Félix Delgado, https://nlbemuseum.com/history/players/delgado.html.
2. Gus Schrader, "C.R. Cards Lose, End Home Stay," *Cedar Rapids* (Iowa) *Gazette*, June 16, 1969: 15
3. Jerry Jurgens, "Riggins Sets Off Fireworks as Q-C Angels Sweep," *Quad City Times* (Davenport, Iowa), July 5, 1969: 13.
4. United Press, "Pilots Deal Two Defeats to White Sox." *Washington Post*, September 9, 1969: D2.
5. Associated Press, "Seattle Battles for Cellar Spot in West," *Albany* (Oregon) *Democrat Herald*, September 9, 1969: 11.
6. Larry Stone, "Greg Halman's Death Reminds of Other Major Leaguers Killed," *Seattle Times*, November 22, 2011, https://www.seattletimes.com/sports/mariners/greg-halmans-death-reminds-of-other-major-leaguers-killed/.
7. Hernández and his 326 saves ranked 19th in the all-time list as of the conclusion of the 2022 season.
8. Nieves's no-hitter was also the only one in the Brewer franchise history through 2021, when Corbin Burnes and Josh Hader combined to no-hit the Cleveland Indians on September 11.
9. The mural can be seen on this Website: https://repeatingislands.com/2020/09/03/explore-local-puerto-rican-art-in-this-urban-route/. It is a reproduction of the Fuentes image used in the 1983 Renatta Galasso trading card set of the 1969 Seattle Pilots (https://www.tcdb.com/ViewSet.cfm/sid/80771/1983-Galasso-1969-Seattle-Pilots).
10. Associated Press, "Young Pilot Pitcher Is Shot, Dies," *Johnson City* (Tennessee) *Press-Chronicle*, January 30, 1970: 39.
11. United Press International, "Pilot Rookie Dies After Bar Shooting," *Honolulu Advertiser*, January 30, 1970: 34.

RYAN GARTON

BY BILL HICKMAN

Ryan Garton is an example of a boy who grows up rooting for his hometown big-league team and dreaming of one day playing for it, and then, with the benefit of hard work, talent, and some good fortune, sees that dream come to fruition.

Ryan Patrick Garton was born on December 5, 1989, in Clearwater, Florida to parents Ed and Lori Garton. Ed Garton had played minor-league baseball for one year as a third baseman for the Little Falls Mets in the New York-Pennsylvania League. After Ed's playing career was over, he continued in baseball as a Little League coach, and coached his own two sons. Lori had played field hockey. Ryan's aunt, Flo Massero, Lori's sister, was the women's tennis and weightlifting coach at Ryan's high school his freshman year.[1] Flo had helped raise Ryan while his mother was working. Eddie, Ryan's older brother, played baseball in high school.[2] When Ryan was little, he always had to come along when his parents took Eddie to the ballpark.[3] It came as no surprise that Ryan joined the rest of the family in participating in sports.

Ryan's baseball playing began at the T-ball stage. As he grew, he became a Little League player. In those days, he was a catcher, though he played several other positions as well, including pitching. One year his team came close to capturing the local championship but was thwarted by a bungled play in the ninth inning. Later he played on numerous teams that took championships.

To aid in his baseball development, Ryan also played in American Athletic Union (AAU) baseball and travel ball. And then it was on to high school, where he began to make his mark.

At J.W. Mitchell High School in New Port Richey, Florida, Ryan played soccer, football, and baseball. He made the varsity football team as a wide receiver. "I could take a hit," he said, "but I didn't particularly like hitting the other guy."[4] So baseball was his destiny, and he was on the Mitchell varsity team all four years. Under coach Phil Bell in his freshman year, he made the all-conference team as a third baseman and pitched as well.[5] He was also honorable mention all-county.[6] In his sophomore year, he became a steady starting pitcher under coach Scott Williams and pitched to a 3.36 ERA. The team had moved into a more competitive district and its won-lost record worsened. Garton's batting average dropped off that year. Before his junior year of baseball, he suffered a torn labrum in his right shoulder and had arthroscopic surgery. As a consequence, he started only one game that season. Nevertheless, Garton managed to play the infield and batted .289 with 9 doubles and 13 RBIs. In his senior year, a new coach, Scot Wilcox, succeeded Scott Williams. Wilcox was younger than Williams and seemed to mesh well with the players. The team came together well and had a winning season. Garton pitched to a sensational 1.55 ERA and set the stage for his advancement to the college level.[7] He had a teammate, Patrick Schuster, who also eventually became a major-league pitcher. Ryan met up with Patrick again in the minor leagues and remained friends with him back home, joining him on outings in the offseason.[8]

An interview with a Mitchell High School teammate revealed some of Garton's characteristics as a high-school player. Scott Lane, who had also been a pitcher, indicated that Ryan was probably the most competitive person he had ever encountered. No matter what the sport or game, Garton was always determined to win. If he noticed that a teammate was not giving his full effort, he would get on the player and insist that he do his best.[9]

In considering where he wanted to attend college, Garton had set his sights on a Division I school in Florida. He attended a college showcase where he met Brad Frick, the assistant baseball coach at Florida Atlantic University. Frick urged Ryan to attend a second showcase, hosted by FAU. There Garton met the FAU head coach, John "Mac" McCormick. By the end of the showcase, McCormick had indicated that a pitching slot would be available on the FAU baseball team for Garton.[10] However, Garton still had thoughts of becoming a position player. McCormick said, "We liked him as a pitcher, not as a position player. He was good." With some stubbornness, Garton became a walk-on as a position player without a baseball scholarship. "We kept telling him he has to pitch," McCormick emphasized.[11]

Garton's freshman year of baseball with FAU was a struggle. His record was 0-1 with a 6.95 ERA. He attributed it to the huge transition of being away from home and adjusting to college life. After that 2009 season, he played summer college ball with the Maryland Redbirds of the Cal Ripken Collegiate Baseball League. The tug-of-war between position playing and pitching continued that summer. Coach Mac was in communication with the Redbirds and insisted that Garton be given more mound experience, and he did well at it.[12] As a position player, Garton hit .273 (3-for-11). As a hurler, he went 2-2 with a 1.95 ERA and one save in 10 games, two as

Ryan Garton. Courtesy of the Seattle Mariners.

a starter.[13] Back at FAU as a sophomore in 2010, he went 7-3 with a 4.87 ERA.[14] By the end of the season, he had become the ace of the staff. How did he get to that level? Coach Mac explained: "He had an above-average breaking ball and a certain toughness. He had a good relationship with his pitching coach."[15] Clearly, Garton was learning and improving.

In the summer after his sophomore year, Garton played for the Columbia Blowfish of the collegiate Coastal Plain League. He was 0-2 with a 1.85 ERA in six games, all as a starter.[16] Shortly before Garton's junior season (2011) began, his aunt Flo died from a heart attack. This left him shaken and distracted. He was still the leading FAU hurler, but his record took a downturn to 5-4 with a 5.17 ERA.[17]

After that season, Garton pitched summer ball once again, this time with the Bethesda Big Train (named after Walter Johnson) of the Cal Ripken Collegiate Baseball League. He was housed with his college roommate, Hugh Adams, and Hugh's parents, Bruce Adams and Peggy Engel. Ryan credited Bruce and Peggy with putting him at ease and helping him to have a fine summer of baseball, restoring his prowess on the mound. His Big Train manager, Sal Colangelo, said Garton was blessed with a power arm and came in with great potential, but that his pitching wasn't as polished as it could be. Garton worked with Big Train pitching coach Bill Sizemore, but Colangelo gave great credit to Garton himself.[18] He pitched in five games, all as a starter, and posted a 1.90 ERA. He struck out 20 in 19 innings pitched while walking only five.[19] Big Train team founder Bruce Adams remarked: "Ryan isn't your prototype 6-foot-5, 230-pound major-league pitcher. He got there with grit and hard work."[20]

The Big Train team was ranked number one in the nation among summer collegiate baseball teams by Perfect Game USA.[21] Among Garton's Big Train teammates were future major leaguers Hunter Renfroe and Matt Bowman. In discussing Ryan's summer with Big Train, Coach Mac commented: "It was an important step and really good atmosphere for him. He was surrounded by good players. The more he was on the mound, the more confidence he gained as a pitcher."[22]

In his senior year at FAU, Garton caught fire. He became the dominant ace of the staff and registered a 9-3 mark with a 3.09 ERA.[23] He helped lead the Owls to the Sun Belt Conference regular-season title.[24] He was named the league's pitcher of the year.[25]

The three days of the major-league draft were agonizing for Garton. He had spent a lifetime working toward a career in baseball and began wondering, "What do I do if it doesn't happen and I don't get drafted?" When the phone call finally came after he was selected by his favorite team, Tampa Bay Rays, in the 34th round, it was a feeling of absolute relief. Garton was signed by scout Evan Brannon, another Florida Atlantic alumnus.[26]

Garton said at the time, "It's still kind of crazy to me. For the past 22 years, it seemed like all I've done is play baseball for AAU or Little League or high school or college. Now I'm going to play baseball as a job. It's crazy to think that, and it's still sinking in a bit, but I can't wait." Of his selection by the Rays, he said, "I definitely wished upon it. I grew up watching the Rays and going to games and it's always been my favorite team to watch. It's a dream come true."[27]

Garton's high-school coach Scot Wilcox commented on his selection by the Rays, "He deserves it. He had a live arm and worked harder than anyone else on the team."[28]

Garton had been a starting pitcher throughout his high-school and college careers. As soon as he entered the Rays' minor-league system, he was transformed into a reliever, because he was now facing a new level of competition and the Rays had an ample supply of starters. "As a 34th-round draft pick, I'm behind a lot of good arms," he noted. "I came to realize that I was a roster filler."[29]

Garton made the most of his opportunity. He started with the Hudson Valley Renegades in the Low Class-A New York-Pennsylvania League. His record that year was 4-0 with seven saves and a 2.00 ERA. He pitched in the playoffs that year, hurling 2⅓ innings with a 0.00 ERA. His team won the playoffs. His record earned him a promotion to the next level.

In 2013, Garton pitched for the Bowling Green Hot Rods in the Class-A Midwest League. He racked up another impressive record. This time it was 4-3 with eight saves and a 2.44 ERA.

In 2014 he was with the Charlotte Stone Crabs of the Class-A Florida State League. Here he pitched to a 6-2 record with four saves and a 3.07 ERA.

In 2015, Garton joined the Montgomery Biscuits of the Triple-A Southern League, and was 6-1 with a 2.95 ERA. His strikeout rate increased, with 70 K's in 61 innings pitched. There was no accident to this improvement. When he was at Charlotte, his velocity had dropped off into the high 80s. The

Rays placed him in their arm-strength program. The program involved throwing weighted balls at varying distances. "That turned around my career," he said.[30] After he finished the program, his velocity was back in the 90s. He was promoted again for the following season, to the Durham Bulls of the Triple-A International League. His full-year record for the Bulls was 4-0 with two saves and a 3.09 ERA in 22 appearances. He struck out 39 batters in 32 innings pitched. In late May Garton got the call to the majors. He was in Toledo when he received the news from Durham manager Jared Sandberg. "It was crazy," he said. "I was feeling well. And then it was a dream come true. I was just a guy that did my job."[31] His opportunity had come because Steve Pearce needed to go onto the disabled list and the Rays wanted another arm in an overtaxed bullpen.[32] Garton joined the Rays on May 25 and made his major-league debut the following day, May 26.[33] At Tropicana Field in St. Petersburg against the Miami Marlins, the Rays had fallen behind 5-1 over the first six innings, tossed by Drew Smyly. Garton's debut was not stellar. He gave up six hits and three earned runs, but he hung on for two innings and could now identify as being a major leaguer. His family and friends rejoiced along with him. About 20 to 30 had attended the game and gathered afterward with Ryan to celebrate.[34]

Tyler Clippard, the first Mitchell High graduate to make the big leagues, posted on the Twitter page of Coach Scot Wilcox that he was happy to see that Garton had made it to the major leagues. Garton's brother Eddie was Clippard's classmate. (Garton and Clippard became major-league teammates in the Minnesota Twins' training camp in 2020.)

For the remainder of 2016, Garton shuttled between the Rays and Durham. When he was called back to the Rays in September, it was his fourth stint of the year with them.[35] His record with Tampa Bay for the year was 1-2 with one save and a 4.35 ERA in 37 appearances. He pitched in 39⅓ innings, which proved the season high for his major-league career.

The jitters of his debut on May 26 had left Garton with an ERA of 13.50. With resolve, he returned to the mound on May 30 against the Kansas City Royals, allowed no earned runs, and began to drive his ERA on a steadily downward path until it reached a season's low of 2.53 on June 27 against the Boston Red Sox. The ERA blew up a bit once again on June 30 when he faced the Detroit Tigers, but he had it under reasonable control for the remainder of the season.

On June 14 Garton earned his one major-league win. The game was at Tropicana Field against Seattle. The Mariners led 5-4 after six innings. Dana Eveland started the seventh hurling for the Rays. The Mariners padded their lead in the top of the seventh. Robinson Canó and Nelson Cruz led off with singles. Kyle Seager walked, loading the bases. The Mariners got a run when first baseman Adam Lind hit a sacrifice fly to right, scoring Canó and advancing Cruz to third. Manager Kevin Cash brought in Garton to relieve Eveland. Seager stole second and Chris Iannetta walked, and the bases were loaded again. Nori Aoki grounded to shortstop and Cruz scored. (The run was charged to Eveland.) Ketel Marte's groundout ended the inning. The Rays were behind 7-4.

In the bottom of the inning, Rays center fielder Desmond Jennings led off against Nick Vincent and flied out to right. Catcher Curt Casali singled to left. Second baseman Logan Forsythe struck out for the second out. The situation still didn't look promising for the Rays. Shortstop Brad Miller walked, and with two runners on base, Evan Longoria drove a pitch from Vincent out of the park, tying the game. Mike Montgomery replaced Vincent on the mound and walked Logan Morrison and Steve Pearce. Corey Dickerson drove in a run with a single but was thrown out trying to stretch his hit into a double. The inning ended with the Rays leading 8-7.

From there on the bullpens traded scoreless innings and Garton had his first and only major-league win. He looks back at it with mixed emotions: "I was hard on myself. It had been my job to go in there and get a groundball double play, and that didn't happen. When I got out of the inning, I wasn't happy. But afterward it was cool. Longo bailed us out. I got a beer shower. It's crazy what the game can do to you."[36]

Two days later, Garton made the second longest appearance of his major-league career. Still facing Seattle, he pitched 2⅔ innings, striking out five batters. He gave up two hits, a single and a double. He had entered in the fourth inning with the bases loaded and one out. He struck out the first batter, Nelson Cruz. Dae-ho Lee doubled, driving in two inherited runners. Kyle Seager was given an intentional walk. Garton finished off the inning by striking out Chris Iannetta with the bases loaded. He had a little trouble in the fifth inning, committing a fielding error, but he induced a double play to end the inning. He yielded a single to Cano to start the sixth inning but knuckled down and retired three straight batters after that.

"Ryan Garton, closer."[37] That's the way a Tampa reporter introduced his account of the game on July 4 when Garton recorded his only major-league save. Garton said that game remained the most memorable for him. He retains the game ball, lineup card, and jersey from it.[38] It was on the Fourth of July holiday at Tropicana Field against the Los Angeles Angels. He entered the game with one out in the ninth, none on, and the Rays ahead 4-2. He walked Yunel Escobar but struck out Mike Trout looking for the second out. Albert Pujols smacked the ball hard and got a single, but it could have been worse. It hit third-base umpire Mike Estabrook. That prevented it from rolling down the left-field line and possibly driving in a run. The next batter, Chris Cron, popped up to first baseman Logan Morrison. The game was over, and the save was in the books.

Kevin Cash commented: "Hopefully, Ryan Garton has a smile ear to ear and doesn't wipe it off all night." Garton's comment at the time: "I was super-excited I did my job. As long as we're getting the win. That it happened to be a save, too, is awesome."[39] It was a great day, and he went out with his family afterward to celebrate in his hometown.[40]

On August 3 Garton set down six batters in a row at Tropicana Field against the Kansas City Royals. On August 12, he played a part in the closing of the noteworthy career of Álex Rodríguez. The game was at Yankee Stadium. A-Rod's retirement had been announced a few days in advance and 46,500 fans turned out for the occasion. The star responded by hitting a double in the first inning. Ryan had been brought in to pitch the seventh and eighth innings for the Rays. When A-Rod came to bat, there were two out in the seventh and none on. The Rays trailed 6-3. "I didn't know it was his last at-bat," Garton said. "I threw a cutter and it hit the bottom of the barrel. If I had thrown a fastball, he would have hit it a mile."[41] The cutter led to a groundout from deep short in the final at-bat of A-Rod's career.

For the first time in Garton's career, he was placed on a major-league spring roster for 2017.[42] Once the regular season began, however, it was another back-and-forth between the Rays and Durham. He started the season with Durham but was recalled by the Rays on April 22.[43] He made only three appearances and was returned to Durham around May 2.[44] He came back to the Rays around May 25,[45] pitched on May 28, yielding three runs, and was returned to Durham the next day.[46] He bounced back quickly to the Rays, pitched in three games, and it was back to Durham on approximately June 11.[47] There was one notable game while he was with the Rays that season.

On June 2, Garton pitched in the longest outing of his career with the Rays – 3⅔ innings. Against the Mariners at Safeco Field in Seattle, Jake Odorizzi had started the game for the Rays and had fallen behind 8-0. Garton entered the game in the third inning with one out and none on. He got two groundouts to end the inning. In the fourth, he hurled a one-two-three inning, and then pitched two more scoreless innings. In reflecting on the game, he commented: "You almost don't want to be part of [that kind of blow-out game]. I had been struggling, which is probably why I was assigned that day. But I came to realize that I saved other pitchers on the team by doing what I did. After the game, Logan Morrison came up to me and said some things that made me feel better."[48]

Then, on August 6, came a big surprise. The Rays traded Garton and Mike Marjama to the Mariners for two minor-league prospects and a player to be named later. He had no hint that this trade was coming, saying, "I was doing a good job, but just not at the right time. I thought of trades happening with the big players, so yes, I was surprised."[49] It meant picking up and relocating to a major-league city that couldn't be any farther away from Florida than Seattle is. It also meant starting all over again in building the kinds of relationships he had established throughout the Rays' system. But there was no choice other than to continue working hard and demonstrate that he could do the job.

With the Rays' AAA team, Durham, Ryan had posted a 2-0 mark with four saves and a 1.64 ERA for the 2017 season. Garton reported to Seattle's Triple-A team, the Tacoma Rainiers, in the Pacific Coast League. The PCL is known as a hitter's haven and it's usually tough on pitchers. That proved to be the case with Garton in 2017. He went 0-2 with a 6.00 ERA in seven appearances with Tacoma. Nevertheless, when rosters expanded in September, he got the call to join the Mariners. He responded well, appearing in 13 games and pitching to a 1.54 ERA at the major-league level.

On September 21 Garton had a particularly fine outing for the Mariners. He hurled two innings and retired six straight batters. He had had an impressive September with the Mariners, but pitched in pain. Not long after the season ended, he underwent hip surgery. There was a period when he wasn't throwing at all, and then he had to go through rehab. So instead of being back with the big-league club in 2018, he was returned to Tacoma, where he went 1-0 with four saves and a 3.16 ERA in 35 appearances.

Garton began 2019 as a nonroster invitee to the Mariners' spring camp.[50] It didn't take him long to see that he was destined for another summer at Tacoma. About March 10, he was reassigned to minor-league camp.[51] He was called back to the Mariners on May 17.[52] He had outings on May 18 and 20 against the Twins and Rangers respectively, both of which proved to be difficult. The May 20 game turned out to be his final major-league game, and he finished the year with a 12.00 ERA for three innings pitched.

Garton had made 59 appearances in the big leagues using an arsenal consisting of a fastball, curve, and cutter. He completed the season at Tacoma.[53] His record with the Rainiers for 2019 was 4-2 with one save and a 3.99 ERA. On October 8, the Mariners cut him loose and he was a free agent. On November 27, he signed with the Minnesota Twins.

Heading into 2020, Garton was facing a period of uncertainty. The country had begun to lock down because of the onset of the worldwide coronavirus pandemic. Soon the major-league baseball season was postponed, and there was no minor-league season at all. So the major-league teams would have a stock of available players to bring up if needed, a number of alternate training sites were established.

Garton was a nonroster invitee to the Twins' July training camp, which substituted for what otherwise would have been spring training. He was given a reasonable opportunity to make the big-league club, but he kept issuing too many walks.[54] When the season began later in July, Garton was sent to the alternate training site. The Twins released him on September 4.

In 2021 Garton had pain in his right forearm, his pitching hand. He wasn't sure that he could pitch adequately, but he was still practicing – and coaching – at the Heisler Heat Baseball Academy in Mobile, Alabama. In July an opportunity arose in the Mexican League with the Monclova club. A couple of their players were going to be away for two weeks to play in the Olympics, so some roster spots needed to be filled temporarily. This enabled Garton to test his arm at the Triple-A level. He pitched in nine innings over eight appearances and registered an ERA of 7.00. He satisfied himself that the arm problem was too severe and it was time to make the difficult decision to call it a career.[55]

It takes more than one player to spur a team to a championship, but it is worthwhile to note the number of Garton's teams that earned pennants.

- •His 2010 FAU team won the Sun Belt Conference championship.
- •His 2011 Big Train team won the Ripken Collegiate League championship and was ranked number-one summer team in the nation.
- •His 2012 FAU team again won the Sun Belt Conference championship.
- •His 2012 Hudson Valley Renegades won the New York-Pennsylvania League playoff.
- •His 2013 Bowling Green Hot Rods won the Eastern Division championship of the Midwest League.
- •His 2015 Montgomery Biscuits won the second-half title for the Northern Division of the Southern League.
- •His 2017 Durham Bulls won the South Division of the International League and the Triple-A championship.

Sal Colangelo, Garton's Big Train coach, said of him, "He was a quiet, hard-working guy who was fun to be around."[56] John "Mac" McCormick, his FAU coach, said: "Ryan was extremely loyal to his teammates. He believes in himself, yet he is extremely grateful for everything he has gotten."[57]

As of 2022, Garton lived in Oxford, Mississippi, with his wife, Christina, a strength and conditioning coach at Ole Miss. He works at the Southern Performance Institute, where he gives pitching lessons to youngsters.[58]

What he had said about his experience in football has been true in his baseball career and life. He could take a hit, rise up, and get back into the game. Resilient, hard-working, and determined. That's Ryan Garton.

SOURCES

In addition to the sources cited in the Notes, the author consulted Baseball-Reference.com and Retroshseet.org.

NOTES

1. Frank Pastor, "Hudson Hires Massaro," *Tampa Bay Times* (St. Petersburg, Florida), August 4, 2005: 4.
2. Author interview with Ryan Garton, December 7, 2021, hereafter Ryan Garton interview.
3. Author interview with Lori Garton, Ryan's mother, December 12, 2021.
4. Ryan Garton interview.
5. Joey Knight, "Not First – But Best," *Tampa Tribune*, May 4, 2005: 12.
6. "2005 Times Pasco All-County Baseball Team," *Tampa Bay Times*, June 12, 2005: Pasco 4.
7. www.maxpreps.com/high-schools/mitchell-mustangs-(new-port-richey,fl)/baseball/previous_seasons.htm.
8. Ryan Garton interview. Schuster had one season in the major leagues, 2016, when he pitched for the Oakland Athletics and Philadelphia Phillies.
9. Author interview with Scott Lane (fishing boat captain), January 20, 2022.
10. Ryan Garton interview.
11. Author interview with John "Mac" McCormack, FAU baseball coach, December 10, 2021.
12. "Mac" McCormack interview.
13. Email to author on December 10, 2021, from Alex Thompson, independent director, Cal Ripken Collegiate Baseball League.
14. https://www.fausports.com/sports/baseball/stats; https://fausports.com/sports/baseball/stats/2010
15. "Mac" McCormack interview.
16. https://www.thebaseballcube.com/college/summer/stats.asp?Y=2010&T=Columbia_Blowfish.
17. https://fausports.com/sports/baseball/stats/2010.
18. Author interview with Sal Colangelo, Bethesda Big Train manager, December 11, 2021.
19. Author's records as Big Train team historian.
20. Email from Bruce Adams, president and co-founder of Bethesda Big Train, to author on November 29, 2021.
21. *Bethesda Big Train 2012 Souvenir Program*: 3.
22. "Mac" McCormack interview.
23. https://fausports.com/sports/baseball/stats/2012.
24. Chad Bishop, "Hilltoppers Meet Owls in Round 1 Tonight," *Park City Daily News* (Bowling Green, Kentucky), May 23, 2012: C1.

25 Chad Bishop, "Error Costs WKU in Tournament," *Park City Daily News*, May 24, 2012: C3.
26 http://www.thebaseballcube.com/players/profile.asp?ID=150535&View=Awards.
27 Mike Camunas, "Baseball Dream Comes True," *Tampa Tribune*, June 8, 2012: Pasco 6.
28 "Baseball Dream Comes True."
29 Ryan Garton interview.
30 Mark Topkin, "Garton Poster Child for Unusual Program," *Tampa Bay Times*, May 29, 2016: C8.
31 Ryan Garton interview.
32 Marc Topkin, "Slumping Rays Need Some Help," *Sarasota Herald-Tribune*, June 24, 2016: C4.
33 Roger Mooney, "Mitchell's Garton Joins Hometown Club," *Tampa Bay Times*, May 26, 2016: C4.
34 Lori Garton interview.
35 Marc Topkin, "Gamboa, Specialty Pitch Ready to Debut," *Tampa Bay Times*, September 2, 2016: C4.
36 Ryan Garton interview.
37 Martin Fennelly, "When Your Commute to Work Is a Dream Come True," *Tampa Bay Times*, July 5, 2016: 31.
38 Ryan Garton interview.
39 Fennelly, "When Your Commute to Work Is a Dream Come True."
40 Ryan Garton interview.
41 Ryan Garton interview.
42 *Athlon Sports Baseball 2017*: 83.
43 Roger Mooney, "Cedeno Looking at Long Absence," *Tampa Bay Times*. April 23, 2017: C7.
44 "Slide Continues," *Palm Beach Post*, May 2, 2017: C2.
45 Dick Scanlon, "Angels Fall Against Rays, Souza," *Palm Springs* (California) *Desert Sun*, May 25, 2017: C6.
46 'DeLeon Bolsters Pen," *Tampa Bay Times*, May 30, 2017: T22.
47 "Transactions," *Indianapolis Star*, June 12, 2017: C7.
48 Ryan Garton interview.
49 Ryan Garton interview.
50 Who's in Camp?," *Tacoma News Tribune*, February 11, 2019: B3.
51 "King Felix Won't Be Opening Day Starter," *Helena* (Montana) *Independent Record*, March 11, 2019: B2.
52 "Perez Silences M's to Join Two Twins with Six Wins," *Spokane Spokesman Review*, May 18, 2019: B2.
53 "Transactions," *Salem* (Oregon) *Statesman Journal*, May 22, 2019: B3.
54 Ryan Garton interview.
55 Ryan Garton interview.
56 Sal Colangelo interview.
57 "Mac" McCormack interview.
58 Ryan Garton interview.

TOM GILLES

BY TOM HAWTHORN

Cito Gaston had seen enough of Duane Ward. The Toronto Blue Jays manager had replaced starter John Cerutti with Ward to open the seventh inning with the visitors nursing a 4-2 lead over the Milwaukee Brewers at County Stadium.

Four singles, two sacrifice flies, and an intentional walk later, Toronto was trailing 5-4. The Brewers had runners at first and second with Glenn Braggs coming to the plate.

Ward was out. Tom Gilles was in.

It was June 8, 1990. The 27-year-old rookie right-hander had made his major-league debut the previous day against Minnesota in Toronto.

"I was called up on June 7 and we were in Skydome," he later said. "We were up 10-2 and they put me in the last inning to get my feet wet. We were playing the Twins and the first two guys I faced got hits, but I broke both of their bats. So I had second and third and nobody out."

"Then I struck out Al Newman. The next guy grounds out to short [with a run scoring], the next guy flies out, and I was out of the inning. I threw 12 pitches, 10 of them strikes."[1]

On his second day of work in a Blue Jays uniform, he threw only two pitches.

Braggs ignored the first offering he faced from Gilles, a called strike on the outside corner to the right-handed batter.

He swung at the second pitch.

It bounced high off the dirt just in front of the plate and then bounced off the grass before Gilles, who had waved off catcher Greg Myers, gloved the ball halfway to home plate, spinning to throw to Fred McGriff at first base and end the inning.[2]

In the top of the eighth inning, George Bell hit a three-run homer for the Blue Jays.

Gaston then called on closer Tom Henke, who had a one-two-three inning.

In the top of the ninth, the Jays added another four runs on four singles and an error by Milwaukee shortstop Bill Spiers.

Henke got out of the ninth without surrendering any runs.

With his two pitches, Gilles secured his first major-league win. And his last.

Days later, he was returned to the minors to make way for a fifth outfielder in Ken Williams, picked up on waivers from Detroit. The Blue Jays, who had been carrying 11 pitchers on a road trip, replaced a hurler with a position player. Despite the demotion, Gaston had words of praise for Gilles: "This last road trip has given us a chance to do this. Our starters have been going longer. I like Gilles. I think he's going to be okay."[3]

As it turned out, Gilles's major-league career was at an end.

His two-pitch victory proved to be the only decision in a two-game, 14-pitch major-league career.

He kicked around the minors for a few seasons, tried a comeback with an independent team at age

32, then replaced the baseball uniform with regular workday clothes.

The baseball dream Gilles pursued was his from his earliest memory. It was also his father's, whose own brief minor-league foray fed the ambitions of his two sons.

Thomas Bradford Gilles was born in Peoria, Illinois, on July 2, 1962, to Thomas Eugene and Norma Mae (Muzzarelli) Gilles. He was the firstborn son of the couple's four children, including Tonya, Mark, and Brenda.

Norma played drums in her high-school marching band, while also taking part in choir and theater, where she performed in the senior class production of *Our Town*.[4] She was named Miss Farmington in her Illinois hometown. On February 20, 1960, six days after Valentine's Day, she married Tom, who had served in the Korean War as a US Army sergeant. He had been a pitcher in the Philadelphia Phillies system, throwing for the Bradford (Pennsylvania) Phillies of the PONY League in 1954. He had at least one pinch-hit appearance the following season for the renamed Bradford Beagles of the also renamed New York-Pennsylvania League, a Class-D circuit. The growing family lived in a house across from the outfield of a neighborhood baseball diamond in Kickapoo, Illinois. Gilles worked on the line at the local Hiram Walker and Sons distillery for more than a quarter-century, and, after his parents died, owned Gilles Tavern, which was on the home-plate side of the same diamond.

The senior Gilles coached all four of his children in baseball and softball, and all four received Division 1 scholarships in those sports.[5] In 1979 he coached the Peoria Karmelcorn softball team to a state and regional championship before finishing fifth in the nation. Illinois Central College later hired him as a hitting coach.

His eldest son was a standout athlete at Bergan High School, a Catholic school where Tom was named all-state in both baseball and basketball. In 1980, as a senior, Tom led the hoops Trojans to the state finals with a steal and a layup with seven

Tom Gilles. Courtesy Toronto Blue Jays.

seconds remaining for a 56-55 victory over rival Sterling-Newman.[6]

"Tom was a great all-round athlete," said Jim Carlson, who was an assistant coach for the Bergan squad. "And he was like having another coach on the floor."[7]

The guard was named to United Press International's All-State team.[8] The basketball coaches at Illinois Wesleyan University hoped to recruit him by suggesting the 6-foot-1, 185-pound athlete could be a two-sport star.[9]

In the end, Gilles accepted a baseball scholarship from Indiana State, though the basketball coaches there also urged him to join the team at the end of baseball season. The program was just two years removed from the Larry Bird years.

"I practiced with the basketball team for about three weeks," Gilles later said. "But I felt a little uncomfortable because they had already been practicing while I was playing baseball. I had to make a decision where my future was. So I decided to focus on baseball."[10]

Bone spurs developed in his pitching elbow, so the recruit was moved to shortstop. He pitched in relief a bit in his sophomore season but elbow pain forced a permanent move to the infield, where he played third base as a senior. In his final two campaigns, his Sycamores won the Missouri Valley Conference tournament.

Gilles passed the first cut in tryouts for the US Olympic team in 1984 only to have the lingering elbow injury end his attempt.

The same issue left him in the 1984 draft until the New York Yankees picked him in the 47th round. His bonus: A measly $1,000.[11]

Gilles played first and third base in in the New York farm system with the Sarasota (Florida) Yankees and the Oneonta (New York) Yankees, under manager Buck Showalter, over two seasons before being released.

"After that, I went to seven tryout camps and nobody signed me," he said.[12]

After surgery on his elbow, which caused him to miss the 1986 season, Gilles decided to return to pitching. He was signed as a free agent by the Kansas City Royals. He pitched just three innings in one game for the Appleton (Wisconsin) Foxes before being released.

Minnesota picked him for the 1988 season, which he spent with the Kenosha (Wisconsin) Twins before being promoted to Double-A Orlando. Despite going 9-3 that season with two complete games in 14 starts, he was released.

Toronto signed the then 26-year-old as a free agent and assigned him to the Knoxville (Tennessee) Blue Jays, where his 5-1 mark over 12 games (just four starts) earned him a promotion to Triple-A Syracuse.

By then, his repertoire included a slider, a change-up, and a knuckleball he called a "knuckle Johnson."[13]

On June 3, 1990, Gilles pitched for the Chiefs in an exhibition game in Syracuse against the parent club. The manager clearly liked what he saw,[14] as Gilles switched places on the Blue Jays roster with demoted right-hander Steve Cummings.[15] At the time of his promotion, Gilles was 2-1 with a 1.95 earned-run average.

To recap:

On Monday Gilles had pitched in an exhibition game.

On Thursday he made his major-league debut.

On Friday he got his first major-league victory.

Twelve days after his promotion, he was returned to Syracuse.

The Blue Jays organization released him at the end of the season.

Gilles attempted a comeback with the unaffiliated Reno (Nevada) Silver Sox in 1991, but he went 1-5 as he surrendered nine home runs in just 46⅔ innings.

His major-league career consisted of 14 pitches to six batters in 1⅓ innings over two games.

He surrendered one earned run. He struck out one and walked none.

In the minors over five seasons, he went 22-16 with a 3.46 earned-run average. In 372 innings, he walked 101 and struck out 189.

Three years later, in 1994, Gilles tried one final time, pitching in Minnesota for the independent Duluth-Superior Dukes of the Northern League. His only decision in six appearances was a loss, as he gave up five earned runs in his only start after fielding a bunt and throwing wildly to third base.[16]

A younger brother, Mark Elliott Gilles, also pitched professional baseball for four seasons in the low minors for Cleveland. He went 39-26 without ever playing above Double A. His final season was 1989.

After his baseball career ended, Tom Gilles returned to the Peoria area, where he was a baseball and softball instructor for 16 years before becoming a vitamin supplements distributor.[17]

In 2018 he was inducted into the Greater Peoria Sports Hall of Fame.

"How many guys get drafted in the 47th round as an infielder and ended up pitching in the big leagues?" he once asked. "I doubt you'll find anybody."[18]

How did he regard his brief foray in the majors?

"It was like getting to the top of the mountain," he said in 1997, "and someone pushes you off."[19]

NOTES

1. Dave Reynolds, "GPSHOF: Tom Gilles Still Savors His Most Memorable Cup of Coffee," *Peoria (Illinois) Journal Star*, March 24, 2018. www.pjstar.com/story/sports/2018/03/24/gpshof-tom-gilles-still-savors/12913119007/. Accessed December 23, 2022.
2. Tom Gilles: The Road to Success. [April 29, 2020] *Facebook* [fan page]. Accessed December 31, 2022, from www.facebook.com/profile.php?id=100035569916347.
3. Larry Millson, "Williams Has No Illusions About Role with Blue Jays." *Toronto Globe and Mail*, June 20, 1990: C14.
4. "Farmington Seniors Will Give 'Our Town,'" *Galesburg (Illinois) Register-Mail*, March 17, 1954: 8.
5. Thomas Gilles [paid obituary], *Peoria Journal Star*. www.legacy.com/us/obituaries/pjstar/name/thomas-gilles-obituary?id=26071411. Accessed December 24, 2022.
6. Associated Press, "Bergan edges Sterling Newman," *Bloomington (Illinois) Pantagraph*, March 12, 1980: 37.
7. Reynolds.
8. "UPI All-state," *Moline (Illinois) Dispatch*, March 4, 1980: 10.
9. Jim Barnhart, "Big Men at a Premium in State – or Anywhere," *Bloomington Pantagraph*, March 16, 1980: 21.
10. Reynolds.
11. Reynolds.
12. Reynolds.
13. Phil Luciano, "Kickapoo Family Shared Dreams of Baseball Fields," *St. Louis Post-Dispatch*, November 24, 1997: 98.
14. Tom Slater, "Jays Shuffle Pitching Corps," *Toronto Star*, June 7, 1990: E3.
15. Larry Millson, "Twins a Big Hit, Crush Blue Jays with Puckett Power," *Toronto Globe and Mail*, June 7, 1990: A21.
16. "Explorers Get Tie for First with 8-7 Win Over Dukes," *Sioux City (Iowa) Journal*, June 22, 1994: 15.
17. Reynolds.
18. Reynolds.
19. Luciano.

BILL GING

BY WILLIAM H. BREWSTER

In the New York State League, he came to be known as "Bill Ging with the Wonderful Wing." William Joseph "Bill" Ging was born in Elmira, New York, on November 7, 1872, the second son of Lawrence and Mary Ging. Lawrence was born in Ireland and immigrated to the United States in 1860 before marrying Mary, an immigrant from Canada, and settling first in Southport, New York, and then in adjacent Elmira. According to local census records and city directories, Lawrence ran a successful blacksmith shop at 603 South Main Street for over 25 years, roughly a mile from the local baseball park.

Baseball was popular in Elmira, and the Ging brothers likely played with and learned from older future professionals in the city like Danny Richardson, Jack Barnett, and Bill Heine. When not playing ball or attending school, the Ging brothers also likely helped out at their father's blacksmith shop. By 1892, according to city directories, Bill was a laborer and big brother John a clerk, both still living at their parents' house.

The author found no record of Ging's baseball work prior to 1897, by which time he had grown into a lean 5-foot-10 right-handed pitcher known for his intelligence and finesse. In 1897 he pitched for a semipro team in New London, Connecticut, alongside fellow Elmiran Ralph Hutchinson. Ging and Hutchinson were both known for being smart players. According to the *Elmira Daily Gazette and Free Press*, "Either is capable of the best kind of work with head as well as arm."[1]

During the war-dominated 1898 season, Ging pitched for New London in the Connecticut State League and finished with a promising 22-10 record. "In Ging and [Ike] Van Zant, New London has without a doubt two of the best twirlers in the League," *Sporting Life* reported on July 2. "They are cool and calculating, never 'go up in the air,' as the saying is."[2]

Ging started the 1899 season with Montreal in the Eastern League, but was back with New London by May 20.[3] On August 16 he traveled to Boston to watch the Brooklyn-Boston National League contest, where Brooklyn manager Ned Hanlon greeted him and asked him to join the Brooklyn team after the Connecticut League season.[4] The attention bode extremely well for Ging's chances to earn a major-league trial.

Ging pitched well through the end of 1899, leading New London in wins for the second straight year, but his 16-17 record was not quite as stellar as 1898's had been. Nevertheless, as September rolled around, he joined numerous other minor-league and college prospects in hoping for a late-season call-up.

For whatever reason, the Brooklyn transaction did not materialize. Instead, Ging and teammate Pete Woodruff, the league home-run leader, were among the fortunate few to receive major-league call-ups or "trials" – Woodruff going to New York and Ging going to Frank Selee's defending champion Boston Beaneaters club.[5]

Soon after his arrival with Boston, Ging made his major-league mound debut on September 25, 1899, earning a 2-1 complete-game victory over the New York Giants at the Polo Grounds.

Speculation as to Ging's next step began in earnest in the sports media, and on October 7 *Sporting Life* reported, "Boston had an option on this man but failed to avail itself of it, and it looks as if Brooklyn would get him. There are few opportunities offered nowadays to get such men as Ging for the modest price of $200. If he enters fast company and does not do well it will be a great surprise to many."[6]

On December 9 *Sporting Life* reported that "Pitcher Ging, who was dropped by Boston after winning one game for the Beaneaters, has been secured by Brooklyn." *Sporting Life* went on to explain that Ging "wanted more than a Class Z salary from the Boston Club, and so they allowed him to go."[7]

Unfortunately for Ging, however, heading into the 1900 season, the National League contracted from 12 teams to eight. The reduction in teams cost at least 60 major-league player jobs in addition to the jobs of all those who supported each team, which did not sit well with players.

As a result, Ging started the 1900 season back in the minor leagues, not far from his Elmira hometown. He had signed with Brooklyn, which farmed him to Syracuse in the Eastern League in early March.[8] (That was the National League's way of reserving Brooklyn's right to retain him.)

On April 26 Ging pitched in relief for Syracuse against Worcester and made a "good showing" despite losing 8-6. He gave up none of the runs, but walked five and struck out only two. He made his first start for Syracuse on May 1, while on the road against Providence, facing 27-year-old major-league veteran Danny Friend.

Friend had no problem with the Syracuse hitters at first, shutting them down for the first four innings. The same could not be said for Ging, however, as he gave up two runs in the first inning and three movre in the second. His control was better than in his previous appearance on the pitcher's mound, but those five runs were enough for him to absorb the loss.

It was an adequate performance that should have earned Ging another start. However, Willie Brandt came in to relieve Ging and promptly gave up 15 runs. In the end, Syracuse lost 20-4. It was an ugly loss.

"Providence hammered both Ging and Brandt all over the lot and piled up twenty runs on Syracuse," said *Sporting Life*. Afterward both Ging and Brandt were released and "sent home by Manager [Arthur] Irwin."[9] Had it been a simple 5-4 loss, the story might have been different.

Ging still had options, but his odds of getting back to the majors in 1900 had worsened considerably. "Oswego [in the New York State League] is after Ging," the *Elmira Daily Gazette* reported on May 10. "The Oswego team has wired Ging for terms, but as yet has heard nothing from him."[10]

While waiting for other potential offers, Ging joined the semipro team in Waverly, New York, 16 miles east of Elmira. A salacious local murder in early April earned the small town unflattering headlines throughout the region, and Waverly was eager to build a powerful semipro team that would enable it to compete against Elmira and Binghamton for attention and business. Ging was a perfect addition.

Ging's work for semipro Waverly included not only pitching for the team but occasionally pitching for the opposition. This included several town teams throughout the region as well as traveling teams. It was ideal for both Waverly and for Ging, since it

Bill Ging.

contributed to competitive games and allowed him to pitch multiple innings to keep his arm in shape. Before the late spring was out, however, Ging made the mistake of accepting an offer from Jersey City in the Atlantic League just before that team folded. As a result, instead of rejoining the professional ranks that summer, he stuck with semipro Waverly.

Among the strong semipro teams Waverly played in 1900 was the shoe factory team from Lestershire, New York, featuring future major-league stars Frank "Wildfire" Schulte and Harry Lumley. During one popular series of games between the teams, Ging had no problem handling the Lestershire lineup when his turn on the mound came up, defeating them 7-2 before a large crowd.[11]

Waverly next welcomed one of the era's legendary barnstorming teams – the "much heralded" Nebraska Indians – to a morning-afternoon doubleheader on Labor Day Monday, September 3, at the Howard Street Grounds in Waverly. The Indians, led by lawyer and promoter Guy Wilder Green, had been touring the Upper Midwest each year since 1897, and in the previous two years expanded the trip East to include Pennsylvania and New York. The team was primarily composed of indigenous Americans from Nebraska and Kansas tribes, with a few nonnatives sprinkled through their lineup. In addition to playing excellent baseball – their reported 1899 record was 108-35[12] – the Indians were known to entertain spectators with baseball gags, as well as Native and clown costumes, "Indian village" encampments, mock war chants, and the like.

Reliable Ging pitched the first game of the doubleheader against the tall, dark-haired 26-year-old Danny "The Terrible Swede" Salene for Nebraska. Salene and Ging each held most of their opposing batting orders in check through the first few innings. Unfortunately for Salene, Waverly smacked three home runs leading to nine runs. Ging, meanwhile, seemed to lull the Indians hitters to sleep by scattering eight hits and giving up only four runs, resulting in a 9-4 Waverly victory.

The second game was more exciting, with Waverly winning 6-5, sweeping the doubleheader before a raucous crowd of nearly 2,000 that included the town band.

Subsequently Waverly and Ging played several town teams and then wound up the season losing a two-game series on September 24-25 to the Cuban X Giants, an African American barnstorming club led by Clarence Williams that had been playing almost daily since early February. The X Giants' season started with a tour of Cuba, and continued through the Midwest and Northeast straight through September.

Ging failed again to secure a professional spot during the offseason, and remained with Waverly in 1901, earning a 28-8 Opening Day win against the Syracuse Shamrocks. Roughly 1,500 fans crowded into the Howard Street Grounds to witness the festivities.[13] A few weeks later, Waverly played a three-game series against future Hall of Famer Frank Grant and the Cuban Giants (a different team from the Cuban X Giants), with Ging defeating the Giants 10-1 in his turn in the rotation.[14]

In July Waverly's semipro days were over, as the town assumed a New York State League franchise from Cortland. This brought Ging and his teammates more consistent competition and media attention. With this in mind, Waverly began a homestand on July 29 with a two-game series against first-place Albany. Ging started on the mound for Waverly, but had trouble handling Albany's top four batters, especially veteran left fielder Hank Simon. Dell Hughes relieved Ging in the late innings, but did not have much better luck. Simon and the other top four Albany hitters combined for 10 of the team's 13 hits, three of them triples, and seven runs in defeating Ging and Waverly 11-6. The *Waverly Free Press* reported that Albany was "more than we could handle," and *Sporting Life* called the game "slow and uninteresting."[15]

Ging did not do well against the NYSL competition immediately after the shift from semipro, struggling through July and early August with a 0-7 record. At this point a most unusual series of events occurred that brought Ging's prospects renewed publicity.

Mickey Mullin, Ging's roommate on the road, had been Waverly's most effective pitcher, and he was frustrated when a scheduled pitching start against Binghamton was rained out. The team remained in Binghamton on Tuesday, August 6, in anticipation of traveling to Troy the next day. The team slept at the Lewis House, near the Erie Railroad station.

Like baseball players today, players in 1901 tended to be very superstitious, and few objects were more associated with superstition than the number 13. Waverly was traveling with 13 players, and Ging and Mullin were roommates in the Lewis House, assigned to room 13 on the fourth floor. According to multiple news accounts, that night's events were ascribed to "unlucky 13."

Very early Wednesday morning, while sleeping, Mullin dreamt he was playing in a big game. Around 2:30, Mullin yelled out, "Thirteen, my God!" as if celebrating a victory, which awoke Ging. Ging shouted his roommate's name and watched helplessly as Mullin jumped out of bed and started to act out a slide into home, diving head-first straight over a chair and out through their fourth-floor window. Mullin plunged onto a veranda below, and then dropped in a clump onto Prospect Avenue.

J.W. Stevens, the baggagemaster of Erie train number 13, was the first to find Mullin in the street, his head in a ditch, blood everywhere. Ging and a local barber staying in the neighboring room soon joined them on the street. Mullin groaning and moving very slowly, was found to have "three deep gashes on his left leg, some bad bruises on the head and body and a broken collar bone."[16] Fortunately for Mullin, his internal injuries were found to be insufficiently severe to threaten his survival, but he remained too banged up to pitch again in 1901.

Grateful for Mullin's likely eventual recovery, Waverly resumed its schedule, traveling that Wednesday afternoon to Troy and losing 11-1, with Jack Lee taking the loss. Thursday's game with Troy was rained out.[17]

The team headed to Albany for a Friday doubleheader. Mullin was out, and Lee had just pitched. This meant that, despite having just witnessed his roommate's four-story tumble and carrying a 0-7 record, Ging had to pitch the first game of the doubleheader against Albany, the NYSL's first-place team. And given the lack of any other available pitchers, he likely had to pitch the second game as well.

Waverly arrived at Riverside Park on Friday morning well aware of the odds against them for the day's doubleheader. Riverside Park was located in Rensselaer, directly across the Hudson River from the capital city, and a crowd of 1,200 gradually streamed into the park from all directions, including many in boats. They were eager for two easy wins that would increase the daylight between them and second-place Schenectady, with third-place Utica close behind. They had little respect for the visitors, whom the local press dubbed "babies" and "orphans" on account of their newly found league status.

While Bill Heine and the other Waverly old-timers on the team took the disrespect in stride, Ging warmed up before the hostile crowd. The Albany hitters had just lit up Ging 10 days earlier, and they must have been extremely eager to get into the batter's box against him again.

Game one began with the two starters picking carefully through the lineups. Ging gave up early hits, just as he had in his last appearance against Albany. Only this time in the early going, the hits were scattered, not bunched, and they were mainly singles, not triples. He walked four batters, including Simon, in an effort to keep his pitches from being too hittable. Meanwhile, Albany's Bill Cristall kept the Waverly hitters off-balance as well, and the two remained scoreless through five innings. Cristall's luck ran out in the sixth, when he gave up one run. This was followed by two more in the seventh for a 3-0 Waverly lead. Ging gave up one run in the eighth, and then shut Albany down in the ninth, quieting the crowd, and earning a 3-1 win.[18]

In the second game, Waverly jumped on Albany starter Charles Baker right away, bunching hits and stolen bases to score two runs in the first inning and take a 2-0 lead. Pitching with a lead, Ging went right back to work on the Albany hitters, strategically scattering hits so as to keep the baserunners away from the plate. His control was better as well, and he whitewashed the Senators through all nine innings, earning a 2-0 shutout victory and a doubleheader sweep, sending the crowd home disappointed.[19]

Ging "pitched great ball and was given fine support," noted the Cortland Evening Standard.[20] "We still lead," reported Sporting News Albany correspondent H.L. Fry, "although our margin has been materially reduced mainly through the great pitching feat accomplished by Ging of Waverly on Friday last. In a doubleheader, this tireless gentleman allowed the usually hard-hitting Senators exactly one run and 14 hits. Ging, who seemed to grow stronger as the afternoon waned, was invincible, and our five scattered hits resulted in a symmetrical row of ciphers."[21]

Ging and teammates celebrated the doubleheader win that night in Albany, but they may have imbibed too much or too late, as the very next day they returned to Riverside Park and were listless in a 2-0 loss. They then returned home to lose to last-place Ilion, 8-4, on August 12.[22] Rather than change the team's momentum, Ging's doubleheader victories appeared to merely represent a joyful blip in an otherwise rough stretch of August's dog days.

The long 1901 season was finally winding down, and Waverly's last four games were at home. Ging's last pitching appearance for Waverly was a 4-3 loss to Schenectady. In 1902 the Waverly franchise moved to Johnstown-Amsterdam-Gloversville. Several Waverly players continued to play for the team, settling in with the "JAGs" and enjoying a measure of success. Among these were Ging and fellow pitcher John "Sandy" McDougal. Ging and McDougal stood out for the length of time and number of games they pitched for both Waverly and the JAGs. Each had a brief stint in the National League before joining Waverly, and each also had stints in the high minors before, during, and after their time in Waverly, thus demonstrating their ability to be noticed and recalled.

In 1902 they both started with the JAGs and faced plenty of good competitive hitters in the NYSL. One such competitor was Syracuse's Wildfire Schulte, formerly with Lestershire (and briefly with Waverly). Another was Troy's Johnny "Crab" Evers. Both Ging and McDougal faced Schulte and Evers multiple times with mixed success.

Ging at 29 was a crafty baseball veteran. "To see 'Bill' mix 'em up and toss 'em over, one would imagine he was playing ping-pong at a swell evening party," the Gloversville Daily Leader wrote. "His smile was childlike and bland, but he was a gay deceiver with the sphere."[23]

Ging faced Syracuse on July 8, and held Schulte hitless in earning a 9-2 victory.[24] Ging would meet Schulte many more times before their minor-league careers were over. In 1903 Ging started against Schulte in at least three games, and Schulte gradually caught up to him, going 5-for-13. By 1904, Schulte had the fifth-highest batting average in the league, at .307, and was sent to the major leagues for outfield duty with the Chicago Cubs in time to help propel them to World Series championships in 1907 and 1908.

One of Schulte's teammates for those Cubs teams, Johnny Evers, played for Troy in 1902 and finished his season with them with a .285 batting average. A talented infielder, Evers reached the Cubs after just one season in the NYSL. This was plenty of time for him to get a good taste of Ging. Unlike the hard-swinging, right-handed Schulte, Evers was an excellent bunter and a "pesky left-handed hitter"[25] with a good batting eye, which made him less likely to be fooled by "crafty" pitches.

In his first game against Ging, on June 25, 1902, Evers tagged him for a double and two singles, but Ging held on for an 11-10 victory.[26] Evers feasted on Ging's pitching again at their next meeting, on August 8, cracking a triple and two singles.[27]

Ging and McDougal had a number of opportunities to face each other during their years in the NYSL. On August 18, 1903, for instance, Ging pitched for the JAGs and faced McDougal, pitching for Schenectady.

The umpire that day was 29-year-old Bill Klem, who was in the midst of a miserable year for umpires in the NYSL. Umpires were so routinely harassed by players and fans that most left the league before the season was over. In Klem's case, he was in perpetual battle with fans and players, resorting to whatever means he could to keep the peace. On June 25, for example, he fined Binghamton outfielder Harry Croft $5 for laughing at one of his decisions. On July 10 Binghamton fans were so annoyed by his calls that they locked him out of the ballpark. His biographer wrote, "His tenacity and courage were tested on an almost daily basis in a league [that] refused to hire more than one umpire for a game."[28]

On August 18, both Ging and McDougal "pitched fine ball" against one another, and Schenectady won 3-0. McDougal had five strikeouts to Ging's two, and McDougal helped himself to a single and scored a run. The game lasted just 1 hour and 20 minutes, and appeared to be free of incident, which must have suited the young Klem just fine.[29]

"Bill Ging with the Wonderful Wing," as local crowds knew him, never did return to the major leagues, but continued to pitch in the minors until his arm stopped "working properly" while he pitched for Scranton in 1905.[30] In the meantime, he "had all the curves in the book and remarkable control."[31] After a successful outing against Ilion in '03, the *Gloversville Leader* remarked, "The way [Ging] treated the Ilion crowd was like refusing children a ride on a merry-go-round. They wanted to hit the ball and William knew it. He had all the change in his pocket – and kept it there."[32]

Ging was a fan favorite and an effective mentor to many teammates, including George "Farmer" Bell, who went on to pitch several years for Brooklyn.

After baseball, Ging was an active Democrat in Elmira politics, serving as city sealer in 1906, the position in charge of the city's weights and measures. He worked in Elmira for the next 44 years as a bartender, clerk, and watchman. He remained active in local sports and politics, serving as an umpire in the Southern Tier League and as an officer with local civic groups. He never married or had children. His grandnephew, Jerry Coffey, recalled that Ging was an invalid and chain smoker in his later years who, contrary to his pitching reputation, always gave his nephews pocket change to use to buy candy.[33] Upon Ging's death in Elmira in 1950, multiple newspapers in the state mentioned both his five-hit victory against New York and his "iron man stint" against Albany.[34]

Ging happily attended Elmira baseball games throughout his life and enjoyed greeting old friends at the ballpark. He passed his love of baseball onto his niece, Gladys. Gladys in turn shared this love of baseball with her husband, John. They frequently attended minor-league games at Elmira's Dunn Field, the same Maple Avenue location where "Uncle Will" once pitched, and traveled to New York City several times to watch the World Series. By the late 1940s, the two were Brooklyn Dodgers fans.

In 1951, a little over a year after Ging died, Gladys and John left their five children with a sitter and took the train to New York City to catch the World Series. The Yankees had already clinched the American League pennant, and the National League pennant was up for grabs between the Dodgers and Giants.

On October 3 the two teams played the deciding game of a best-of-three playoff series between the two pennant contenders. It was held at the Polo Grounds, the same spot where "Uncle Will" had spun his complete-game victory over the Giants 52 years and 8 days earlier.

Not to miss such an occasion, Gladys and John were there at the Polo Grounds that auspicious day to witness the Giants' revenge. It was the first-ever nationally televised baseball contest and arguably the century's most dramatic game, as the Giants defeated the Dodgers 5-4 on Bobby Thomson's ninth inning walk-off home run, known by fans as baseball's "Shot Heard 'Round the World"[35] – a suitable Polo Grounds connection for a family proud of its wonderful baseball lineage, even if the major-league portion lasted just one game.

SOURCES

Portions excerpted from:

Brewster, William H. *That Lively Railroad Town: Waverly, New York and the Making of Modern Baseball, 1899-1901* (Eugene, Oregon: Luminare Press, 2020).

In addition to the sources cited in the Notes, the author consulted US census records and other public records via Ancestry.com and Baseball-Reference.com. Thanks to the Chemung Valley Historical Society (Elmira, New York), the Waverly Free Library, the Waverly Historical Society, and the National Baseball Hall of Fame and Library.

Bevis, Charlie. *Jimmy Collins: A Baseball Biography* (Jefferson, North Carolina: McFarland, 2012).

Brands, H.W. *The Reckless Decade: America in the 1890s* (Chicago: University of Chicago Press, 1995).

Brewster, William H. *The Workingman's Game: Waverly, New York, the Twin Tiers and the Making of Modern Baseball, 1887-1898* (Eugene, Oregon: Luminare Press, 2019)

Green, Guy W. (Jeff P. Beck, ed.) *The Nebraska Indians and Fun and Frolic with an Indian Ball Team*. (Jefferson, North Carolina: McFarland, 2010).

Lomax, Michael E., *Black Baseball Entrepreneurs, 1860-1901* (Syracuse, New York: Syracuse University Press, 2003).

Riess, Steven A. *Sport in Industrial America, 1850-1920* (Arlington Heights, Illinois: Harland Davidson, 1995).

White, Sol. *Sol White's History of Colored Baseball* (Lincoln: University of Nebraska Press, 1995).

NOTES

1. "The Coming Season," *Elmira Daily Gazette and Free Press*, July 29, 1897: 8.
2. "Kinney's Kids," *Sporting Life*, July 2, 1898: 6.
3. "Connecticut Lease," *Sporting Life*, May 20, 1899: 7.
4. "Notes of the Game," *Hartford Courant*, August 23, 1899: 2.
5. "Out of the Grater," *Sporting Life*, September 23, 1899: 9.
6. "Hub Happenings," *Sporting Life*, October 7, 1899: 4.
7. "The Great Failing," *Sporting Life*, December 9, 1899: 4. The reference to "Class Z" was likely a tongue-in-cheek reference to a very low (i.e. the lowest) salary available in the National League's classification system.
8. "Hub Happenings," *Sporting Life*, March 3, 1900: 6.
9. "Items of Interest," *Sporting Life*, May 12, 1900: 6; "Syracuse Stars," *Sporting Life*, May 12, 1900: 7.
10. "Oswego After Ging," *Elmira Daily Gazette and Free Press*, May 10, 1900: 6.
11. "Ging Pitched Well," *Elmira Daily Gazette and Free Press*, September 1, 1900: 6.
12. "News and Comment," *Sporting Life*, February 17, 1900: 4.
13. "The Opening Game," *Waverly* (New York) *Advocate*, April 30, 1901: 1.
14. "The Waverly Baseball Team Trims the Dark Nine," *Waverly Advocate*, June 21 1901: 1.
15. "Games Played July 29," *Sporting Life*, August 10, 1901: 11; "Base Ball," *Waverly Free Press*, August 3, 1901: 1.
16. "Mullen Got a Fall," *Waverly Advocate*, August 9, 1901: 1.
17. "Base Hits," *Waverly Free Press*, August 10, 1901: 1.
18. "Albany Lost Two to Waverly," *Albany Evening Journal*, August 10, 1901: 6.
19. "Albany Lost Two to Waverly."
20. "Waverly Wallops the Senators," *Cortland* (New York) *Evening Standard*, August 10, 1901: 7.
21. "Wilson Is a Wonder," *The Sporting News*, August 17, 1901: 1.
22. "No More Baseball," *Waverly Free Press*, August 17, 1901: 1.
23. "A.-J.-G. 10, Ilion 3," *Gloversville Evening Leader*, July 16, 1902: 5.
24. "Games Played July 8," *Sporting Life*, July 19, 1902: 21.
25. David Shiner, "Johnny Evers," SABR BioProject.
26. "Games Played June 25," *Sporting Life*, July 5, 1902: 21.
27. "Games Played Aug. 8," *Sporting Life*, August 23, 1902: 6.
28. David W. Anderson, "Bill Klem," SABR BioProject.
29. "Games Played Aug. 18," *Sporting Life*, September 5, 1903: 12.
30. "News Notes," *Sporting Life*, June 17, 1905: 21.
31. "Death Serves to Recall Ging and His Work," *Gloversville and Johnstown Morning Herald*, September 16, 1950: 9.
32. "Tall Typewriters Trimmed Twice," *Gloversville Daily Leader*, July 24, 1903: 3.
33. Author interview with Jerry Coffey, February 22, 2018.
34. "Ex-Ball Player Billy Ging Dies," *Elmira Star Gazette*, September 15, 1950: 14.
35. Author interview with Jerry Coffey, February 22, 2018.

GEORGE GOETZ

BY RICHARD BOGOVICH

George Goetz is among those rare pitchers who won his only major-league game. It was in 1889 for Baltimore of the American Association, which existed from 1882 to 1891. In contrast to so many other major leaguers over the decades who played very few games at that level, Goetz had a very short career in the minor leagues as well.

Important details of Goetz's life remain obscure, despite the efforts of several researchers of his family tree. He was often called Bert (or Bert), and occasionally George B. or George Burt Goetz, though more than one family tree online shows his middle name as Albert (without citation). He was apparently called Albert in his mother's obituary.[1] He was born in Greencastle, Pennsylvania, in or around 1865 – the year based mainly on his age of 5 in the 1870 census.[2] His parents were Philip and Ann (Rhoadarmer) Goetz, who were married on September 30, 1856.[3] He was the oldest boy and among the couple's 11 children, seven of whom were still living at the time of the 1900 census (which he himself might not actually be in, anywhere).

Greencastle is a small community about 10 miles north of Hagerstown, Maryland. In the 1870 and 1880 censuses, Philip Goetz was identified as a shoemaker. At least one son, Frank, had been "educated in the Greencastle public schools," though that likely applied to the other Goetz children as well.[4] However, at the time of the 1880 census (which somehow omitted Frank), only 13-year-old Ross was identified as a student. "Bert," age 15, worked in a machine shop. Their sister Mollie graduated from Greencastle High School in mid-1891.[5]

Two Goetz children died prior to the 1880 census, and two more by the one in 1900. First was an unnamed baby boy in 1875. The other three were Edith in 1878, Ruth in 1884, and Emma in 1895.[6]

In September of 1883, Greencastle's "association team" played a baseball game in Hagerstown against a nine of that city's Iolanthe Club, and at the bottom of the visitors' lineup in a Hagerstown newspaper's primitive box score was a player named Goetz. Positions weren't identified, but the description of the game noted that Greencastle's pitcher was named Flack.[7] Whether or not that Goetz was George, he soon demonstrated promise as a ballplayer around age 19. By mid-1884, he and two teammates agreed to travel west more than 300 miles to play ball in a big city: "Bert Goetz, Clarence Murray and Philip Baer have accepted positions on an ameteur [sic] base ball club in Columbus Ohio; Goetz as pitcher, Murray catcher, Baer short stop – will start next Tuesday," an area newspaper reported. "The Greencastle club will miss these boys."[8] Shortly before the trio left, Goetz struck out eight visiting Hagerstown batters in a 23-6 romp over that Maryland club.[9]

It's unknown if Goetz played ball during 1885, but in 1886 he pitched for a club in Bedford, Pennsylvania, about 60 miles northwest of his hometown. He did likewise the following summer, at least briefly.[10] In 1888 he played for a team in Roanoke,

Virginia, 230 miles to the southwest of Greencastle. "The club is composed entirely of workmen in one of the manufactories there," a paper in his home county noted while mentioning that the distant team included "Goetz, the well-known pitcher of the old Greencastle club."[11] That Roanoke club didn't simply play locally. For example, for a game in mid-July it traveled about 150 miles to the twin cities of Bristol in Tennessee and Virginia. Goetz, described in a Knoxville newspaper as "a fine pitcher," was the starter but had to be relieved as the home team rallied late to tie the score, and the game was thus called at 9-9.[12]

By the end of July, Goetz was back in his home county and pitched one inning in a local game, "but the catcher was too weak for him and he gracefully withdrew," an area paper reported. However, the next day another paper there listed "Bert Goetz of Roanoke" among Greenfield natives who were visiting "their old homes the past week," perhaps implying his return was temporary. It appears he actually stuck around. A few days into August, he played for a Greencastle club against Hagerstown's, and by mid-September he agreed to pitch a few games for a team in Hollidaysburg, Pennsylvania, about 75 miles to the northwest of his hometown and not in the direction of Roanoke.[13]

Goetz didn't seem especially close to entering any of the minor leagues that were springing up across the Eastern United States, but his baseball career took a sudden lunge forward in April of 1889. A traveling salesman named J.M. Ritter was so impressed with how Goetz pitched while observing him in Virginia previously that he took the young man to Baltimore, and on April 5 Goetz approached the American Association's Orioles as they prepared at home for the regular season. Soon enough, he was pitching to big leaguers. "The ball-players laughed at first, but soon found that they could not hit the stranger," reported a Baltimore daily. "He placed the ball in every conceivable position, and his curve, and in-and-out shoots were remarkable." He also tried batting, and smacked a ball to the center-field fence.[14]

Goetz's height was reported inconsistently in newspapers that month, probably most commonly as 6-feet-2 but also as 6-feet-4 and just 6-feet. One newspaper that reported him as 6-feet-2 gave his weight as 175 pounds. It also said he "pitched a peculiar zig zag ball," which Goetz dubbed a "whipporwill [sic] swoop."[15] That served as the basis for one nickname for him.

Another paper paraphrased Baltimore manager Billy Barnie's assessment that Goetz had "greater speed than any pitcher he ever saw. The trouble now is where to get a catcher to hold his cyclonic curves." Goetz soon had the nickname "Cyclone" as well.[16]

Four days after his tryout, Goetz pitched the first five innings of a game against the University of Pennsylvania's team. He gave up just two hits and no runs while striking out four batters. He and one teammate led the Orioles' very potent offense that day with four hits each.[17]

A few days later, Goetz had apparently picked up the nickname "Snipes," for no stated reason. That was alluded to in the *Philadelphia Times*, which referred vaguely to a second exhibition game for him that week. Though other papers had emphasized his fastness, the *Times* focused on a different pitching strength: "He generally pitches a slow ball, but it has a curve and drop about it that is very mysterious."[18]

On April 15, 1889, Goetz had a very different experience when Baltimore hosted Boston's National League team. After three innings, the home team gave Goetz a lead of 6-1, but over the middle three innings Boston plated six unanswered runs. A five-run eighth sealed a 12-8 win for the visitors. Goetz gave up 16 hits for 22 total bases in his eight innings of work.[19] Be that as it may, by April 18, the American Association had "promulgated" Baltimore's contract with George B. Goetz, according to the *Washington Post*.[20]

At the end of April, Goetz was suffering from a bout of malaria, but that wasn't mentioned on May 12, when the *Philadelphia Times* reported that he and another young Orioles hurler, Pat Whitaker, were "becoming tired doing nothing but practicing at home."[21] The latter didn't pitch his lone regular-season game for Baltimore that season until July 25. Goetz did wait two full months, but not quite as long as Whitaker.

In the meantime, Goetz did get to pitch in an important home exhibition game on June 7. The Orioles split their roster in half to raise funds for victims of the Johnstown flood, and the proceeds totaled $130.65. Though Goetz gave up five runs across the first two innings and nine overall, he reportedly gave up just four hits. Meanwhile, Whitaker was pounded for 17 runs on 17 hits for the other half of the roster.[22] If the two were auditioning for a start in a regular-season game, Goetz seemingly got the part.

On June 17, 1889, the front page of the *Baltimore Sun* included a small ad of sorts about that day's doubleheader at home vs. the Louisville Colonels, and it announced the "First Appearance of Goetz in a Championship Game." (In this context, "championship" meant a league game.) A few pages inside, the paper said he was scheduled to pitch in the first of the two games.[23] The *Baltimore American* wrote that there was "some talk of saving him for the second game."[24]

The first game it was. Catching for Goetz was backup Bart Cantz, who had a 62-game major-league career from 1888 through 1890. Cantz had played for Chambersburg's team in the Keystone Association in 1884. This battery faced visitors who started play having lost an astounding 20 games in a row. As a result, not only had Louisville already lost more games than any other American Association team previously, no team in the contemporary National League had lost that many consecutive games, either.[25]

Though the Orioles were the home team, they batted first. They didn't score in the opening inning off 24-year-old lefty Toad Ramsey, who won an impressive 75 games for Louisville in 1886 and 1887 against only 54 losses. Captain-manager Chicken Wolf was the first batter Goetz faced. The count reached three balls and two strikes, and then Wolf grounded out to Goetz. Next up was center fielder Farmer Weaver, who was also known as "Buck" (as were several other pros through 1930). The count also went full on him, and he likewise grounded back to the pitcher. Soon enough, Goetz completed his first inning unscathed.[26]

Goetz did yield the day's first run, an unearned one in the second frame. Three Baltimore dailies and the *Louisville Courier-Journal* all agreed on the innings in which runs were scored. However, three of these papers credited Baltimore with scoring four earned runs and Louisville with just two, whereas the *Sun* instead reported Baltimore with a fifth earned run and the visitors with four instead of a pair.[27] Goetz's baseball-reference.com entry uses the *Sun*'s higher total of four earned runs.

Baltimore took the lead in the third inning by scoring three runs. The Colonels responded to the Orioles' outburst with a run in the bottom of the third and tied the game at 3-3 with one more in the fifth. The earlier run resulted when Goetz allowed a triple and then a double. The tying run simply resulted from a single followed by a double. Newspaper reports were a bit vague about how the visitors broke this tie off Goetz in the bottom of the eighth inning. Apparently the visitors' one big inning started with an infielder's error. After that, Goetz allowed two singles, followed by a successful sacrifice. Ramsey himself singled to complete the three-run rally.[28]

Was Louisville suddenly about to end its horrible losing streak? "Six to three was the gloomy outlook when Baltimore faced Ramsey in the ninth inning," the *Sun* wrote. Amazingly, the Orioles responded with three runs of their own to tie the game. Goetz kept the Colonels from scoring in the bottom of the ninth, so an extra inning was required. Baltimore promptly added four more runs, to demonstrate a clear shift in momentum.[29]

Bert Cunningham, who had a record of 22-29 for Baltimore the previous season, relieved Goetz for the bottom of the 10th. When fans noticed the switch, "a shout of protest went up from the open stand," the *Sun* reported. Dissenters presumably wanted Goetz to pitch a complete game. The *Sun* countered:

> The protest was based on sentiment, not on judgment. The management acted wisely. There has been two [sic] much sentiment in running the club in the past. From this time out it should be run on business principles.[30]

Goetz was still the pitcher of record when his teammates made the score 10-6, so he was the winning pitcher after Cunningham ended the game with relative ease. Assessments of the rookie's nine-inning debut varied. A harsh viewpoint was printed back in his home county. "Goetz pitched for Baltimore yesterday and his team would have been snowed under had Cunningham not come to his rescue," wrote the *Franklin Repository*. "Another exploded phenomenon." The *Baltimore Morning Herald* called him "a dangerous experiment." That daily's negativity was lengthier than the *Repository*'s, and read, in part: "He was weak just at the time when he should have been strong, and the Baltimores were so afraid that he would go to pieces in the tenth inning that Cunningham was sent in to finish the game. Goetz seemed very nervous."[31]

Another Baltimore daily, the *American*, expressed a very different viewpoint of Goetz: "He pitched a very creditable game, and fielded his position well." Similarly, a report in *The Sporting News* said Goetz did "good work," and added that he could "with a little practice, become a success in the association." A third Baltimore daily was more neutral about Goetz: "With hard, steady work and a display of intelligence he may become a success," the *Sun* said. "At times he would fire the ball over the plate with a speed like a rifle shot, but when men were on bases he was nervous."[32]

The baseball-reference.com entry for Goetz shows him yielding 12 hits, with four of the six runs off him earned. Among the 39 batters he faced, he struck out two and walked none. He was charged with one wild pitch. As a fielder, he logged four assists and an error. As already noted, the newspapers disagreed on Louisville's earned runs. Daily papers and the sports weeklies had some other totals that differed, such as for hits he allowed and his assists.[33] The *Sun*'s box score specified that all four of the outs Goetz made as a batter were strikeouts.[34]

Baltimore began a weeklong road trip two days later and was back home for a game on June 27. Goetz and Whitaker were the only two players who didn't travel with the team. Baltimore released Goetz on July 3.[35] That outing on June 17 turned out to be the only major-league game of his career. A *Sporting Life* columnist almost predicted as much after Goetz's game against Louisville, writing that "it is certain he will never do the Baltimore Club much good, and you need not be surprised if he is dropped altogether."[36]

Four days later the *Philadelphia Times* printed an anonymous commentary about Goetz: "A good, hustling captain could have made something out of the long, lanky Pennsylvanian, but he was allowed to loaf, never compelled to practice, and in consequence never developed into anything else but a disappointment," a special correspondent wrote. "Some good manager will take hold of Goetz and make a player out of him."[37] Back in his home county, the *Public Weekly Opinion* of Chambersburg reported on his reaction to the decision to release him. "Bert is certainly a phenomenal pitcher, and says he is glad to be released, as he was given no chance whatever by Manager Barnie to show the club or people what he could do," the paper wrote.[38]

Goetz joined another pro team by midmonth, York of the Middle States League. On July 17 he started a home game of historical significance, against one of the two all-Black teams in that league, the New York Gorhams. At second base for the latter nine was future Hall of Famer Sol White, whom Goetz struck out in the first inning. Goetz lasted only two innings, leaving with cramps in his arm. During his short stint he threw three wild pitches, but allowed only one run. York won, 9-6.[39]

On July 20 Goetz pitched two innings in Hagerstown, close to home, for a temporary team with players from six Pennsylvania cities.[40] Still, he was on York's roster for the remainder of July at a minimum, because manager William Whorl received a letter from Goetz on the 30th in which the hurler said his arm was improving quickly and he would return to the team in a few days. He may have been far too optimistic, because he apparently disappeared from York and other Pennsylvania newspapers in August plus the first half of the following month. On September 16 Goetz was presumably the catcher, not the pitcher, for the Greencastle Clippers in an 11-4 loss at home to the Hagerstown Unions.[41] After his two innings on July 20, he might not have pitched in a game until September 27. On that occasion, he pitched for a Chambersburg team against the Harrisburg Ponies, champions of the Middle States League. Before 400 fans on what a Harrisburg daily condemned as a very rocky field, the visitors beat Goetz and Chambersburg, 15 or 16 to 7. Goetz exited the game after allowing 13 runs in six innings, according to a local paper. Nevertheless, his single and double reportedly led the home team's offense and thus earned him a diamond scarf pin.[42]

The "new twirler" — George Goetz — as depicted in the April 10, 1889 *Baltimore American*.

All told, apparently George Goetz pitched in only two regular-season pro games during 1889. Still, barely two months into 1890, a Chambersburg paper said he was "again in good shape," fit enough to pitch "for an American association team this season if he wants to."[43] A freak injury about a month later prevented that for a long time, likely for the remainder of that year at a minimum. Goetz had just moved to Altoona, Pennsylvania, 80 miles to the northwest. On April 6, while descending some stairs near a bridge, he lost his footing and an upright prong of an iron fence penetrated a few inches into one of his arms. Newspapers disagreed on which arm, but two of three said it was his left (and the one that said it was the other incorrectly said he was a catcher for Baltimore in 1889). Goetz was a right-handed pitcher, but an injury to his left arm could have limited his ability to catch a hit or thrown ball.[44]

One day after initial the reports of this calamity, it was deemed more serious than initially thought. One Altoona daily said an artery had been severed, "causing a very serious, and it may turn out to be a fatal, injury." Another paper only disagreed on that last prognosis but added that Goetz had become "irrational" at times. When he visited his parents early that summer, he still hadn't recovered fully, so he recuperated there for a time.[45]

During the spring of 1891, Goetz provided a little evidence that he had recovered, by pitching a Greencastle team to a 19-1 victory over Hagerstown on May 18. Four days later, watching a game between a Chambersburg team and a collegiate squad, he told a local paper about his health. "Goetz, of Greencastle, says his arm is again in good condition and he can now pitch better ball than he could ... for the Baltimore Association team," the *Franklin Repository* reported.[46] Then he again seemingly disappeared from Pennsylvania newspapers from June through the remainder of baseball season.

In late May of 1891, a catcher arrived in Greencastle who would form a battery with Goetz during subsequent seasons in at least three other states, two a considerable distance from Pennsylvania. He was M.K. Osborn, whose surname was spelled a few different ways. On May 26 the *Baltimore Sun* reported that "Osbourn, of the Marylands, will leave for Greencastle tomorrow to play with the Pennsylvania Club. For the past two years he has played with the Charlotte and Norfolk Clubs. On the Greencastle Club he will probably be Goetz's catcher. Goetz is the man who pitched several games for Baltimore last year and was nicknamed 'Whip-Poor-Will.'"[47] If Osborn did join Greencastle's team, he also didn't draw attention there for the rest of 1891.

In the spring of 1892, Goetz was pitching very far from home, for a team in Hayward, Wisconsin. In June a paper back in his home county reported that in one recent game he had struck out 14 batters and yielded only four hits. In August the *Sun* received a report on Goetz from his catcher, "M.K. Osbourn," about their experiences in the Wisconsin and Minnesota League. First, though, the *Sun* said it was led to believe "that Goetz was drowned in the Johnstown flood, but he seems to have turned up again." In a game between Hayward and the West Superior team, Goetz struck out 19 of the latter's batters.[48]

The duo played in the same area in 1893, except for a team in Little Falls, Minnesota. A reporter for the *Brainerd* (Minnesota) *Journal* complained that Little Falls had recruited a few players who were so new that they hadn't become voting residents of that city, and pointed first to their pitching ace: "His nibs, Mr. Goetz, we have seen before in our travels among salaried teams around the Forks," the Brainerd reporter grumbled. Conversely, he asserted that Brainerd's team comprised solely local residents, and all were amateurs.[49]

Goetz saw considerable action with the Little Falls club through August, and reportedly did some moonlighting at least once, with a club in St. Cloud. However, toward the end of August, the *Brainerd Dispatch* hinted that Goetz may have been experiencing some arm trouble. In fact, during a game against Brainerd on September 7, in which Little Falls was pummeled 18-5, Goetz started in center field but switched to pitcher in midgame and may have been responsible for 15 of those runs. One newspaper said the Little Falls team might have disbanded after that game.[50]

In October Goetz was pitching for a team in Chambersburg, back near his hometown. On the 9th he defeated Harrisburg of the Pennsylvania State League, 10-7. He scattered eight hits while striking out five, walking five, and tossing one wild pitch. Goetz pitched in a rematch the next day, but was on the losing end of an 8-7 score.[51]

Early in 1894, the *Baltimore Sun* said "Osburn" was hoping to get Goetz and himself onto a Southern League team for the coming season. In April the duo joined Lynchburg of the Virginia State League. That is Goetz's only other professional team in his baseball-reference.com entry besides the pair in 1889.[52]

In Lynchburg's first game, against Norfolk, Goetz and "Osburn" played left field and center field, respectively, in a 9-0 loss. They were the battery in the team's second game, and were trounced, 18-2. Goetz gave up 13 hits and walked five, but was charged with only five earned runs. Goetz lost the next day as well, 13-2 to Petersburg. Two days later, he relieved in another loss to Petersburg "and was hit hard," according to the *Norfolk Virginian*. Two more days later Goetz started against Richmond but exited due to a sore arm, apparently after just one inning. Richmond scored five times, but Lynchburg countered immediately with eight runs. That was all the scoring Lynchburg could manage, and it suffered a truly astonishing drubbing, 45-8 in eight innings.[53] Osborn continued to appear in Lynchburg lineups for a few weeks, if only as the center fielder,[54] but Goetz seems to have vanished after all that agony in April.

Goetz resurfaced in Greencastle by mid-June. He pitched for his hometown team in a 16-12 loss that received minimal coverage. In July, the *Baltimore Sun* reported that he pitched a complete game for the Chambersburg Country Club in Hagerstown and won it. The detailed account in the *Hagerstown Herald and Torch Light* showed Chambersburg ahead 6-5 after eight innings, though the final score was 12-9. The paper said Goetz had "splendid command of the ball."[55]

Goetz won again about a month later, pitching for Hagerstown against a Chambersburg team. He reportedly pitched well until he was removed in the seventh inning after being hit on the arm by a pitch. By August 25 he was reunited with Osborn on a Shenandoah club in a 16-11 victory in Luray, Virginia.[56] The victors presumably represented the town of Shenandoah, less than 20 miles to the southwest of Luray.

In April of 1895, Goetz had a tryout with Hagerstown's "Association" team in preparation for a season scheduled to begin on May 1. He started a game against a Lancaster team on April 18 but was replaced after six innings because he'd given up 15 runs on the way to an 18-1 clobbering. The opposing pitcher was Frank West, who had pitched three innings in a game for Boston's NL team in 1894.[57]

Before April was over, Goetz jumped to the Luray Browns. He was with that team longer than he'd been with many others over his career. In June he was named first by Luray's weekly among players given the most credit for the team's first two victories ever over its rivals from its sister city, Front Royal.[58] By mid-July he'd apparently become his club's pitching ace, and a rumor surfaced that the rival Harrisonburg club had lured him away. To the contrary, he was Luray's losing pitcher in a game on August 4 that was reported in the *Baltimore Sun*. After "pitching great ball at Luray" on September 6, the *Franklin Repository* in his home county reported that he'd returned to Greencastle.[59]

Then Goetz largely disappeared from the public record, as noted by historian Jackie Howell, known as "The Baseball Bloggess." As she pointed out, one of the few significant mentions of him in a newspaper ever again was in his father's obituary, in 1913, among the surviving offspring.[60] However, one clue was printed in a Greencastle newspaper shortly after his return from Luray. On September 9 "Cyclone Goetz" and a man named George Eachus began a "drive" to Ohio, presumably in an automobile. Eachus was expected to settle in Ohio, but Goetz planned to continue on to Chicago.[61] The name Goetz turns up on Chicago-area baseball teams in 1896, including as the winning pitcher in a game between two Chicago Telephone Company ballclubs in late April, but there may be no additional possibilities more substantial than that example.[62] Of course, George Goetz may have given up baseball after 1895.

In early 1898 Goetz probably visited his family back in Greencastle. "Mr. Bert Goetz is visiting his parents on south Carlisle street," the *Franklin Repository* reported. In the 1900 census, his parents, three sisters, and nephew Clement Gordon lived together in a house on Carlisle Street.

On August 22, 1905, a festival in Greencastle included a baseball game between "old boys" and the current local team. The elder players included a Goetz in the outfield. George's brother Ross was among the residents who returned for the festival, but George very likely wasn't the "G.A. Goetz" attending from Hagerstown. The latter was a married shopkeeper there in 1899.[63]

In the spring of 1906, Goetz presumably was out near San Francisco, at the time of the historic earthquake in that area on April 18. "Clay Hawbecker [*sic*] and Bert Goetz, formerly of Greencastle, both went through the California earthquake safely but lost all they had," the *Franklin Repository* wrote. That terse report left it unclear whether Hawbaker and Goetz had some connection out near San Francisco, or had each ended up in that area separately. Perhaps only by coincidence, in early 1904, Clay H. Hawbaker was elected to the board of directors of the newly incorporated Oakland Association baseball team.[64] There's no indication that anyone named Goetz was associated with that club.

Goetz was reportedly out in California (still, or again) at the time his brother Fred was struck and killed by a train in early 1913. The surviving siblings included "Bert, California." "Bert" was again included among the survivors when their father died late that same year. One newspaper didn't identify where any of them were residing, but another identified five relatives named Goetz who attended the funeral from out of town, two of whom were presumably George's two surviving brothers. Also listed was a "George Goetz, Altoona" (where brother Ross still lived),[65] but there were at least two other men named George Goetz with roots in or other strong connections to Greencastle, with whom the ballplayer could easily be confused.

For example, engaged to be married in early 1900 were a "George F. Goetz and Rilla C. McKelvey, both of Greencastle, Pa." However, most likely to cause confusion was the George B. Goetz of approximately the same age who is buried in the same cemetery as much of the ballplayer's nuclear family. He was among five top Army officers tried for profiteering during World War I who were acquitted in early 1924.[66]

When the ballplayer's brother Frank died in early 1929, George wasn't listed among the surviving siblings. It's possible he was still alive, but relatives had no idea.[67] An unpublished 1984 paper held by Greencastle's public library might explain why. Author W.P. Conrad, who called Goetz a "free spirit" with "eccentricities," wrote: "His last known residence was said to have been in Australia and he was never heard of again."[68] As of this writing, when and where pitcher George Goetz died remains unknown.

NOTES

1. "Mrs. Philip Goetz," *Franklin Repository* (Chambersburg, Pennsylvania), August 23, 1905: 3. Her seven surviving offspring who were living at the time of the 1900 census were all listed, including sons Frank, Ross, Albert, and Fred. In the 1880 census, younger brothers Ross and Frederick were listed after "Bert." The 1880 census taker may simply have omitted the fourth brother, Frank, whose full name was Benjamin Franklin Goetz, according to online genealogical records. Frank, age 1, was indeed in the 1870 census with his older siblings, including George B., age 5.

2. His birthplace might be assumed, based on his parents' long residency in Greencastle, and genealogical records identifying that community as the birthplace of several siblings, but it was specified that he was born there in "A Base-Ball Deal," *Baltimore Sun*, April 6, 1889: 4. The 1970 census page listing his family was dated July 19.

3. "Married," *Franklin Repository and Transcript*, October 8, 1856: 5.

4. "Deaths," Chambersburg (Pennsylvania) *Public Opinion*, February 4, 1929: 2. The obituary gave his name as B. Frank Goetz. As of this writing, one Ancestry.com family tree has January 31, 1929, as the date of George's death, without citation, but that was the date of Frank's death.

5. "All About Home," *Chambersburg Valley Spirit*, June 10, 1891: 7. Based on censuses and her death certificate, Mollie may have been 20 years old at the time of her high-school graduation.

6. A photo of a gravestone in the local Cedar Hill Cemetery, accessible via findagrave.com, shows an infant boy who was born in 1875 and died that year shares it with Edith and Ruth. Each of the daughters received a death notice in newspapers: "Died," *Chambersburg Saturday Local*, October 5, 1878: 3. "Died," *Public Weekly Opinion* (Chambersburg, Pennsylvania), February 16, 1884: 2. "Obituary," *Franklin Repository*, February 1, 1895: 1.

7. "At the Bat," Hagerstown (Maryland) *Herald and Torch Light*, September 6, 1883: 3. In 1927 and 1928, the Hagerstown Hubs of the Class-D Blue Ridge League had a player named John Edward Goetz, but he was apparently no close relative of George Goetz. That much younger Goetz, who grew up in Washington, D.C., wasn't born in either Pennsylvania or Maryland.

8. "From Greencastle," *Franklin Repository*, July 25, 1884: 1. A search of the *Columbus Dispatch* from mid-July to October turned up no mentions of the three players. Most coverage of the base ball in that city during 1884 focused on its American Association team, which finished second that season.

9. "Base Ball at Greencastle on Saturday," *Franklin Repository*, July 29, 1884: 4. The line score indicated that Goetz limited his opponents to five hits for eight total bases. Murray was mentioned as his catcher that day.

10. "Fireman's Day," Everett (Pennsylvania) *Press*, August 24, 1887: 3. It's unclear when this article first mentioned "Goetz, now of Altoona," whether that meant he'd moved to that city or had been on that city's baseball team. However, see mention of Altoona herein during April of 1890.

11. "A Chambersburg Ball Player Goes South," *Valley Spirit*, July 5, 1888: 4.

12. "Bristol on the Border," Knoxville (Tennessee) *Journal*, July 15, 1888: 1. A line score with additional information was printed on the same page, under the headline, "Bristol Vs. Roanoke."

13. "The National Game," *Franklin Repository*, July 26, 1888: 1; "All About Home," *Valley Spirit*, July 27, 1988: 3; "Men and Affairs," *Valley Spirit*, August 4, 1888: 3; "Affairs Around Home," *Valley Spirit*, September 19, 1888: 3.

14 "A Base-Ball Deal," *Baltimore Sun,* April 6, 1889: 4. This paper said he was 6 feet tall.

15 "A Real Phenom," *Pittsburgh Dispatch*, April 7, 1889: 6.

16 "A Phenomenal Pitcher," *Philadelphia Times*, April 7, 1889: 3.

17 "Burt Goetz Is All Right," *Baltimore Sun*, April 10, 1889: 5.

18 "Barnie's New Wonder," *Philadelphia Times*, April 14, 1889: 16.

19 T.H. Murnane, "Poor Prodigy," *Boston Globe*, April 16, 1889: 5.

20 "Behind the Bat," *Washington Post*, April 18, 1889: 2.

21 "Base-Ball Notes," *Baltimore Sun*, April 29, 1889: 6; "The Orioles Jubilant," *Philadelphia Times*, May 12, 1889: 16.

22 "Couldn't Hit Goetz," *Baltimore Sun*, June 8, 1889: 6.

23 "Base-Ball Gossip and Games," *Baltimore Sun*, June 17, 1889: 5. See also the announcement in the first column of the front page, near the top.

24 "Gossip of the Diamond," *Baltimore American*, June 17, 1889: 5.

25 See https://www.baseball-almanac.com/recbooks/games_lost_records.shtml for all teams to have lost 20 more games consecutively. The 1876 Cincinnati Reds lost 18 consecutive games, as shown at https://www.baseball-reference.com/teams/CIN/1876-schedule-scores.shtml. Information on Cantz is from his baseball-reference.com entry.

26 "Hard on Old Kentuck," *Baltimore American*, June 18, 1889: 5. See also the box score on that same page. . Information on Ramsey is from his baseball-reference.com entry. Baseball-reference.com identifies one other major leaguer and seven minor leaguers named Buck Weaver, though six of the latter were reportedly named Buck at birth.

27 "Two More Games Won," *Baltimore Morning Herald*, June 18, 1889: 1; "Hard on Old Kentuck," *Baltimore American*, June 18, 1889: 5; "Almost Won It," *Louisville Courier-Journal*, June 18, 1889: 2; "Two Games in a Day," *Baltimore Sun*, June 18, 1889: 6. The box scores in the *American* and the *Courier-Journal* included columns for times at bat.

28 See the first two articles identified in the previous note.

29 See the articles in Baltimore newspapers identified in Note 27.

30 "Base-Ball Notes," *Baltimore Sun*, June 18, 1889: 6. Here the *Sun* said, "Cunningham took Goetz's place in the ninth inning" but Goetz was the winning pitcher and thus remained the pitcher of record into the extra inning. Cunningham's record in 1888 is from his baseball-reference.com entry.

31 *Franklin Repository*, June 18, 1889: 3; "Two More Games Won," *Baltimore Morning Herald*, June 18, 1889: 1. The former news item had no headline.

32 "Hard on Old Kentuck," *Baltimore American*, June 18, 1889: 5; Job Lots, "Baltimore Briefs," *The Sporting News*, June 22, 1889: 1; "Two Games in a Day," *Baltimore Sun*, June 18, 1889: 6.

33 See https://www.baseball-reference.com/players/g/goetzge01.shtml. *The Sporting News* reported that Louisville had "only eleven hits" off Goetz, which could've implied that Cunningham yielded the 12th, but the box score printed six pages later showed Louisville with 11 hits total. See Job Lots, "Baltimore Briefs," *The Sporting News*, June 22, 1889: 1; "Game Played June 17," *The Sporting News*, June 22, 1889: 7. The box scores in two Baltimore dailies credited Goetz with six assists, not four, while a third box score showed him with five assists. Respectively, see "Two Games in a Day," *Baltimore Sun*, June 18, 1889: 6. "Two More Games Won," *Baltimore Morning Herald*, June 18, 1889: 1; "Hard on Old Kentuck," *Baltimore American*, June 18, 1889: 5.

34 "Two Games in a Day," *Baltimore Sun*, June 18, 1889: 6. Also, the two batters Goetz struck out were identified, Guy Hecker and Bill Gleason.

35 "Base-Ball Notes," *Baltimore Sun*, June 19, 1889: 6. "Not Up to the Work – Pitcher Goetz Is Broken," *Chambersburg Valley Spirit*, July 5, 1889: 3. The latter said he was signed on April 7. In addition to the June 17 game, it summarized his preseason outings against the Pennsylvania collegians and Boston.

36 T.T.T., "Baltimore Bulletin," *Sporting Life*, June 26, 1889: 6. It was common practice for this national weekly to identify writers only by their initials.

37 "Among Barnie's Men," *Philadelphia Times*, July 7, 1889: 9.

38 "Pitcher Goetz Released," *Chambersburg Public Weekly Opinion*, July 12, 1889: 3. This paper printed an item that originated in the *Everett Press*.

39 "Middle States League," *Philadelphia Inquirer*, July 18, 1889: 6.

40 "Base Ball," *Hagerstown Herald and Torch Light*, July 25, 1889: 3.

41 "The Champions on Friday," *Franklin Repository*, September 18, 1889: 3.

42 "Base Ball," *Harrisburg Daily Patriot*, September 28, 1889: 1. "Done Up," *Chambersburg Valley Spirit*, September 28, 1889: 3. "Has Not Yet Received the Pin," *Franklin Repository*, October 3, 1889: 3. "Newsy Paragraphs," *Franklin Repository*, October 4, 1889: 3. The latter confirmed that Goetz did receive the prize.

43 "Newsy Paragraphs," *Franklin Repository*, March 3, 1890: 3.

44 "A Very Serious Accident," *Altoona* (Pennsylvania) *Times*, April 7, 1890: 1. "At the Hospital," *Altoona Tribune*, April 7, 1890: 4. The latter said the injury was to his right arm, but it also identified him as having been a catcher for Baltimore in 1889. Years later, another paper noted that he was a righty and a few years earlier it was "an injury to his left arm that rendered it useless." See "It Was a Lively Game," *Hagerstown Herald and Torch Light*, July 10, 1894: 4. The first of these articles specified that Goetz lived at 1402 Seventh Avenue in Altoona, and the local city directory that year listed laborer John E. Goetz as boarding at that address. George's brother Ross, a longtime Altoona resident, was presumably the Ross L. Goetz in Altoona's 1888 directory.

45 "At the Hospital," *Altoona Tribune*, April 8, 1890: 4. "Hospital Notes," *Altoona Times*, April 8, 1890: 4. "Newsy Paragraphs," *Franklin Repository*, June 26, 1890: 3. "All About Home," *Chambersburg Valley Spirit*, July 2, 1890: 3.

46 "Base Ball Notes," *Franklin Repository*, May 20, 1891: 3; "Stopped by the Rain," *Franklin Repository*, May 23, 1891: 3.

47 "The National Game," *Baltimore Sun*, May 26, 1891: 4.

48 "Personal Points," *Franklin Repository*, June 11, 1892: 2; "Success of Pitcher Goetz," *Baltimore Sun*, August 16, 1892: 8.

49 "Base Ball," *Little Falls* (Minnesota) *Transcript*, June 9, 1893: 1; "Brainerd Registers a Kick," *Little Falls Transcript*, June 23, 1893: 1. It was the earlier of these two articles that quoted the *Brainerd Journal*.

50 "Base Ball Notes," *Little Falls Transcript*, August 4, 1893: 3; "Won Two Games," *Brainerd* (Minnesota) *Dispatch*, August 25, 1893: 8; "Base Ball," *Little Falls Transcript*, September 8, 1893: 1.

51 "The Professionals Lose," *Franklin Repository*, October 10, 1893: 3; "The Tables Turned," *Franklin Repository*, October 11, 1893: 2.

52 "Base-Ball Gossip," *Baltimore Sun*, February 13, 1894: 8; "Diamond Flashes," *Baltimore Sun*, April 23, 1894: 7.

53 "We Can Play Baseball," *Norfolk Virginian*, April 25, 1894: 2; "The Second Waterloo," *Norfolk Virginian*, April 26, 1894: 2; "Norfolk Defeated," *Norfolk Landmark*, April 27, 1894: 1; "Lynchburg Weak," *Norfolk Virginian*, April 29, 1894; "Victory Number Seven," *Richmond* (Virginia) *Times*, May 1, 1894: 1; "Norfolks Win Again," *Norfolk Landmark*, May 1, 1894: 1. The latter, which specified arm soreness as the reason for Goetz leaving, reported the score as only 42-8.

54 For example, see "A Day of Heavy Batting," *Norfolk Virginian*, May 18, 1894: 1.

55 "Notes," *Franklin Repository*, June 16, 1894: 1; "Chambersburg Defeats Hagerstown," *Baltimore Sun*, July 10, 1894: 6; "Base Ball Notes," *Franklin Repository*, July 10, 1894: 2; "It Was a Lively Game," *Hagerstown Herald and Torch Light*, July 10, 1894: 4. The second of these *Franklin Repository* articles specified that Chambersburg had two other strong ballclubs besides the Country Club's.

56 "Hagerstown at Home," *Franklin Repository*, August 9, 1894: 1; "Local Matters," *Hagerstown Herald and Torch Light*, August 9, 1894: 18. "Base Ball," *Luray* (Virginia) *Page Courier*, August 30, 1894: 3.

57 "Notes of the Diamond," *Hagerstown Herald and Torch Light*, April 9, 1895: 4; "The Murray Hills Are Here," *Hagerstown Herald and Torch Light*, April 12, 1895: 4; "Lancaster Wins Easily," *Hagerstown Herald and Torch Light*, April 19, 1895: 4.

58 "Diamond Tips," *Hagerstown Herald and Torch Light*, April 23, 1895: 4; "Luray vs. Front Royal," *Luray Page Courier*, June 20, 1895: 3. This weekly noted that the team was named the Browns in honor of its manager. Goetz apparently pitched a complete game to win one game, 22-4, but the naming of the battery for the other win, which ended 17-9, implied he was the catcher. Similarly, he was listed last in the three-player battery of a win on June 27 over Harrisonburg, 31-10, in "Luray vs. Harrisonburg," *Luray Page Courier*, July 4, 1895: 3. This weekly noted that a rematch started at 9:30 the next morning, and Goetz apparently hurled a complete game on the way to another victory for Luray, 16-4.

59 "Penciligraphs," *Luray Page Courier*, July 18, 1895: 3; "Other Games," *Baltimore Sun*, August 5, 1895: 6. The latter reported on a doubleheader in Berryville, Virginia, in which Goetz and Luray lost the second game, 12-8. See also "The Local Base Ball News," *Franklin Repository*, September 6, 1895: 3.

60 Jackie Howell has made available a collection of newspaper snippets relating to his lone American Association game at https://thebaseballbloggess.com/2020/06/17/june-17-1889-george-goetz-the-fallen-phenom/. She also posted the Orioles' team photo taken that month, and speculated that Goetz is in it.

61 "Personal Mention," *Hagerstown Herald and Torch Light*, September 13, 1895: 4. This paper quoted a paper in Greencastle, the *Press*. In mid-1893, Goetz had mailed newspaper accounts of his performance for his team in Little Falls, Minnesota, to a J.H. Eachus back in Greencastle, according to "Gathered within the County Line," *Hagerstown Valley Spirit*, June 28, 1893: 3. This paper quoted a different paper in Greencastle, the *Echo*.

62 "Amateur Baseball Notes," *Chicago Record*, April 29, 1896: 6.

63 "Old Home Week in Greencastle," *Franklin Repository*, August 23, 1905: 3; "Exciting Burglar Chase," *Franklin Repository*, July 20, 1899: 3.

64 "About People," *Franklin Repository*, May 23, 1906: 3; "Oakland Club Is Incorporated," *Oakland* (California) *Tribune*, January 13, 1904. The Clayton Henry Hawbaker associated with the Pacific Coast League was born in "Green Castle, Pa., in 1856," according to "C.H. Hawbaker of Pythian Home Claimed by Death," *Santa Rosa* (California) *Republican*, August 21, 1937: 3.

65 "Greencastle Native Killed by Train," *Franklin Repository*, February 26, 1913: 1; "Philip Goetz," *Chambersburg Public Opinion*, December 3, 1913: 5; "Greencastle's Days Doings," *Franklin Repository*, December 4, 1913: 4.

66 "Marriage Licenses," *Hagerstown Morning Herald*, February 20, 1900: 3; "Army Officers Freed in Harness Conspiracy," *Philadelphia Inquirer*, January 25, 1924: 1; "Col. Goetz Is Dead at Charles Town," *Washington Post*, November 10, 1937: 4. See also https://www.findagrave.com/memorial/177152549/george-b-goetz.

67 "Deaths," *Chambersburg Public Opinion*, February 4, 1929: 2. One family tree made public on Ancestry.com has a 1929 death date for George Goetz, but that presumably was mixed up with Frank's. Their brother Ross apparently provided an example of the family losing touch with one another over the years. When their sister Alice passed away in 1942, she was survived by several nephews and nieces but otherwise was reportedly "the last of her family." However, their brother Ross didn't die until May of 1945, according to the Certificate of Death accessible online, yet he hadn't

even moved out of Pennsylvania. See "Miss Alice M. Goetz," *Chambersburg Public Opinion*, March 16, 1942: 2.

68 W.P. Conrad, "Franklin County's Oldest Team Sport: Baseball," 1984: 5. This is an unpublished 11-page paper in the history file of the Lilian S. Besore Memorial Library in Greencastle, Pennsylvania, very kindly supplied in 2022 by the director, Kiely A. Fisher. Special thanks also to SABR members in Australia who likewise tried to solve the mystery of his death, particularly Tanith Harley, Eddy Campbell, and Robert Laidlaw. Conrad's paper contains several entertaining anecdotes about Goetz but none are included here because of the possibility of inaccuracy; on the same page he incorrectly stated that Goetz pitched had two victories in the major leagues and both "were shutouts, 4-0 and 7-0, against Boston."

KENNY GREER

BY RORY COSTELLO

Righty reliever Kenny Greer's 10-year career in pro ball featured two stints in the majors, in 1993 and 1995. In his big-league debut, he pitched a perfect 17th inning and got the win as the New York Mets scored the game's lone run in the bottom half. His only other big-league decisions were both losses, which came in eight outings with the San Francisco Giants.

That one win at the top level proved memorable to Mets fans. Greg Prince – whose book *Faith and Fear in Flushing* is subtitled "An Intense Personal History of the New York Mets" – made good use of it in his afterword. Prince's interview with longtime Mets broadcaster Gary Cohen is called "From Greer to Eternity."

Kenneth William Greer was born on May 12, 1967, in Boston. He has called the Bay State home for his entire life. His father, James Greer, was a firefighter, mailman, and bus driver.[1] His mother, Pauline (née MacDonald), had two other sons, James and Kevin, and a daughter named Kathy.[2] All of the children were good athletes – "the whole family is competitive," said Kenny Greer in 1993.[3]

Young Kenny was greatly influenced by his older brother Kevin. After Kevin died suddenly at age 51 in 2016, Kenny said that there were multiple teams he probably made because of Kevin, starting with Little League – "The reason I played in the major leagues is because I was chasing him." Kevin had pro potential too, according to Kenny, but he hurt his shoulder in a skiing accident during his senior year at Westfield State University in Massachusetts.[4]

Kenny Greer attended Hull High School in the Boston suburb of Hull. He played football in addition to baseball. He became a member of Hull High's Athletic Hall of Fame in 2012.

Greer then went on to the University of Massachusetts at Amherst. The Minutemen had two other future big leaguers during his time there. Fellow pitcher Dave Telgheder was also later Greer's teammate with the 1993 Mets – they were roommates in both places.[5] Their shortstop was Gary DiSarcina.

One might have expected Greer to play in one of the nation's premier summer collegiate baseball circuits, the Cape Cod Baseball League. It was close to home, and brother Kevin had previously pitched there.[6] Kenny Greer was supposed to play on the Cape after his junior year – but instead, he was drafted and turned professional.[7]

The New York Yankees selected Greer in the 10th round of the June 1988 amateur draft. In a 1998 interview with David Wolcott of a Boston-area local newspaper, the *Cohasset Mariner*, he said he'd expected to be drafted, but not as high as he was. Greer was a lifelong Red Sox fan, as one would expect, and "becoming a Yankee led to the requisite amount of razzing from friends and family." Yet he was still happy to be in the archrival organization. "It was exciting just to be in a professional baseball uniform," he said.[8]

The new pro's first assignment was Oneonta in the New York-Penn League. His manager there was former Red Sox catcher Gary Allenson, of whom he said, "We took some friendly abuse and had a lot of things to talk about."[9] In 15 games – all starts – Greer posted a sharp ERA of 2.40 and displayed excellent control, walking just 18 men in 112⅓ innings.

In the championship game of that season, however, his career was jeopardized by a shoulder injury. With one out remaining and Oneonta leading 2-1, Greer made a pickoff throw to second base. He recalled, "I felt excruciating pain in my shoulder and fell to the ground."[10] Fortunately, "winter rehab on a slightly torn rotator cuff took care of it."[11] The problem did not recur.

Greer graduated from UMass in 1989 with a bachelor's degree in sports management. He came to view it as a vital achievement. "Right after my first season I went back to Amherst and got my degree. I didn't realize it was that important then. My family and coaches advised me to do it. Now I'm glad I did," he said in 1993. "Most of the guys in my situation say they want to wait a few years before going back. However, when you are 26 or 27 it is a lot tougher to go back to college and get a degree. Most of them don't."[12]

With Prince William of the Class-A Carolina League in 1989, Greer started 13 times while coming out of the bullpen in 16 other games. Over the remainder of his career, he pitched almost exclusively in relief.

In February 1993 the *Boston Globe* ran a feature on Greer, focusing on his travails as a minor leaguer. He told the feature's author, Paul Harber, that during his first two years in the minors, he worried incessantly about other pitchers in the system and where he ranked among them. "Doing that is crazy," Greer said. "You can't think about that all the time or it will drive you crazy. It doesn't bother me anymore. Call it mental maturity. All I can worry about are things I control. All I can do is go out there and pitch. Worrying won't make it any better and can make it a lot worse."[13]

Over the course of the 1990-93 seasons, Greer climbed up the organizational ladder. He was on the verge of quitting before the '92 season, but it was a turning point for him, as he developed a forkball that helped him get lefty hitters out.[14] He later told David Wolcott that whereas he'd been a pure power pitcher in high school, he had to change through college and the minor leagues. "Everyone can throw 90 mph once you go professional, so you need to have something that makes you special," he said.[15]

Greer worked multiple jobs in the Boston area during the 1992-93 offseason. On weekends, he was at the South Shore Baseball Club, teaching high-school and youth players in the pitchers and catchers clinic. During the Christmas season, he was a sommelier for Boston Pops orchestra shows. Weekdays, he worked at the Bay State Bodybuilders Gymnasium, and when he wasn't there, he served as a substitute teacher for the Hull public school system.[16]

"Sometimes I wonder why I'm doing this," Greer muttered to himself during the *Globe* interview. But as Paul Harber noted, the answer didn't take long. "It's a once-in-a-lifetime opportunity."[17]

That opportunity arose several months later – with a new team. Greer was with the Yankees' top farm club, Columbus, for most of the season. He pitched reasonably well (9-4, 4.42 ERA), although reportedly the organization thought that manager Stump Merrill overused the righty after he came off the disabled list.[18]

On September 17, 1993, Greer was dealt across town to the Mets in one of the rare transactions between the two teams. The Yankees – then still in contention in the AL East race – acquired 40-year-old veteran Frank Tanana, whose 21-year career in the majors was drawing to a close. The *New York Times* observed that the Yankees rotation had included three struggling rookie starters in the previous three weeks. The club was "just hoping that [Tanana's] tired left arm can crank out six or seven capable innings a start for the next two weeks because hardly anyone one else's can."[19] As it turned out, Tanana did go six to seven innings in each of his remaining three starts, though he lost both of his decisions. The Yankees finished a distant second to Toronto, which went on to repeat as World Series champion.

As for Greer, then aged 26, the *Hartford Courant* noted that "he was not expected to be kept on the 40-man roster by the Yankees this winter and could have become a six-year, minor league free agent."[20]

Greer's new club was limping toward the finish of a dismal 59-win season. The rookie did not get into a game until September 29. Manager Dallas Green (who'd replaced Jeff Torborg earlier that season) said, "I'd been saving [Greer] for a spot free of pressure. I guess the 17th inning of a scoreless game doesn't have much pressure."[21]

Greer needed just 13 pitches as he set the St. Louis Cardinals down in order. After Erik Pappas lined to left, Greer struck out Gerónimo Peña and opposing pitcher Les Lancaster. "I hadn't pitched in a month," said Greer. (The Columbus season had ended on September 4.) "I was trying to get pitches over the plate."[22]

In the home half of the 17th, Jeff Kent's two-out double brought home Eddie Murray and the game was over at last.

Fellow Mets pitcher Eric Hillman had a wry remark about Greer's win. "He just tied me and A.Y. for victories in 1993," said Hillman, who was then 1-9.[23] Anthony Young, whose record-setting 27-game losing streak had ended earlier that season, was 1-16.

The Mets won their remaining four games, finishing with a winning streak of six. Greer did not make any further appearances that season.

Greer went to spring training with the Mets in 1994 but was optioned to Triple-A Norfolk at the end of March. Early that season, he held the "stopper" role in the Norfolk bullpen but went on the disabled list in April.[24] He appeared four times for the Mets' team in the Gulf Coast Rookie League while rehabbing from the elbow problem. Overall,

A rare photo of Greer in Mets uniform, probably from spring training 1994. Courtesy of John Galluzzo, Committee for the Preservation of Hull's History. Originally published in the book *Hull and Nantasket Beach* (2001).

he got into 25 games with the Tides, pitching 31 innings. In August he passed through waivers and was taken off the Mets' 40-man roster, though he remained with Norfolk.

Near the end of November 1994, Greer signed as a free agent with San Francisco. The following February, with the major leagues' crippling strike still in effect, he found himself walking a fine line. Technically, he wasn't on strike, because he was in camp on a minor-league contract – but he felt very strongly about the issue because his father was a union man. "I never gave a thought to being a replacement player," Greer said. "It's been my dream all my life to play in the major leagues, but I don't want to have to tell my son someday that I made the major leagues as a scab." Yet he also said, "I need to be in camp to get my arm back in shape if I'm going to make it to the majors this year. I've been scraping by for seven years. If I don't get to the major leagues, it'll be like I wasted seven years of my life."[25]

Greer began the 1995 season with the Giants' top farm club, Phoenix in the Pacific Coast League. The big club called him up in June after Trevor Wilson went on the DL. The veteran had adjusted as a pitcher after surgery on his elbow the previous year to remove six bone chips and a bone spur. Greer later said, "After the surgery I actually picked up a little bit of velocity. I got to be a little more of a power pitcher."[26]

Greer got into eight games in long and middle relief for San Francisco from June 21 through July 17. He posted an ERA of 5.25 while going 0-2. The Giants then returned him to Phoenix and called up Carlos Valdéz.

Greer became a free agent again after the 1995 season. The Chicago Cubs invited him to spring training in 1996, but he was unsuccessful in his bid to make the club. However, he joined the Pittsburgh Pirates organization that May.[27] He spent the rest of the year pitching for their top affiliate, Calgary in the Pacific Coast League.

Greer's final season as a pro, 1997, began with Calgary. He was released in May after making 15 appearances. Later that month, he caught on with the Baltimore Orioles, who signed him to a minor-league deal and assigned him to Triple-A Rochester. He got into 15 games for the Red Wings – a stint that he later called "simply horrible"[28] – and was bumped down to Double-A Bowie. The 11 appearances he made for the Baysox were his last in pro ball.

After his release by the Orioles, Greer still held hopes of getting a nonroster invitation in 1998 from his lifelong favorites, the Red Sox. He contacted the team himself to tell them "I really do think that I could pitch at Fenway Park." He called it the only thing that could stand between him and starting a new life after baseball. He still wanted to be involved with the game in some fashion, though, so he took a job as pitching instructor at a newly opened facility, the Bases Loaded Training Center in Hingham. One of his colleagues was his brother Kevin.[29]

In 2021 Greer recounted his final decision to retire. "At the end of my career, I had an invite to big-league camp with the Diamondbacks that I walked away from. I promised Abby [his wife] when I turned 30 I would make a decision. I had not been back to the big leagues in two-plus years and it was time."[30]

For 10 years after leaving baseball, Greer worked for several leading home construction materials companies. His focus areas were sales, marketing, and management.

Greer became an executive recruiter in 2008, joining the firm of Executive Search Partners and becoming a partner the following year. His new career path was a good segue in view of his industry experience, people skills, and team orientation. He places high-level candidates in executive positions, as well as front- and back-office roles, within the nation's leaders in the energy industry. Clients include investment banks, hedge funds, merchant/utility companies, and consulting firms.[31]

Greer is a longtime resident of Cohasset, which adjoins Hull to the south. Executive Search Partners is based there and it's where his wife comes from. He and Abigail (née Adams) had three children: son Will and daughters Molly and Kate. Will, who became a pitcher like his father, was a member of the Bucknell University team in 2020 and 2021. As of 2021, Molly was playing lacrosse at Wesleyan University in Connecticut, and Kate was a seventh-grader in the Cohasset school system.[32]

In 2021 Greer continued to participate in public and media events promoting baseball. He was involved as a consultant/speaker for youth baseball and proper coaching techniques. In his leisure time, Greer enjoyed coaching youth sports, golfing, fishing, family events, and country music. He and Abby were very active in their local church and community.[33]

Looking back on his time in pro baseball in 1998, Kenny Greer was realistic and content. He told David Wolcott, "As you get older, if you don't perform you go out the door. That's just business, but you have to go out there and enjoy it as long as you can.

"I had a great career. I got to play with the Giants and the Mets and was traded straight up for Frank Tanana. I have no regrets."[34]

Acknowledgments

Special thanks to Kenny Greer for his input (email to Rory Costello, May 21, 2021).

SOURCES

Kenny Greer's page on LinkedIn.com (https://www.linkedin.com/in/kenny-greer-3ba8455/)

Kenny Greer's page at Executive Search Partners website (https://www.ex-sp.com/team-member/kenneth-w-greer/)

Prince, Greg W. *Faith and Fear in Flushing* (New York: Skyhorse Publishing, 2009).

NOTES

1. Kenny Greer, email to Rory Costello, May 21, 2021 (hereafter Greer email).
2. Kevin Greer obituary, *Boston Globe*, January 21, 2016: B7.
3. Paul Harber, "For Minor Leaguer, Pitching Never Ends," *Boston Globe*, February 7, 1993: 35.
4. Ruth Thompson and Will Wassersug, "Scituate Mourns Kevin Greer, Coach and Teacher," *Quincy* (Massachusetts) *Patriot Ledger*, January 21, 2016. https://scituate.wickedlocal.com/article/20160121/NEWS/160129198. Accessed May 22, 2021.
5. Greer email.
6. Harber, "For Minor Leaguer, Pitching Never Ends."
7. Greer email.
8. David Wolcott, "Free Agent Has Dreams of Pulling on Red Sox," *Cohasset* (Massachusetts) *Mariner*, January 15, 1998: 13.
9. Wolcott, "Free Agent Has Dreams of Pulling on Red Sox."
10. Harber.
11. Greer email.
12. Harber.
13. Harber.
14. Harber.
15. Wolcott.
16. Harber.
17. Harber.
18. Michael Kay, "Stump Still Bitter?" *New York Daily News*, September 3, 1993: 76.
19. Jack Curry, "Last Gasp: Yanks Get Tanana From the Mets," *New York Times*, September 18, 1993: 29.
20. Jack O'Connell and Sean Horgan, "Tanana Goes Crosstown and Uptown Just Like That," *Hartford Courant*, September 18, 1993: D5.
21. Joe Sexton, "And So, After 17 Innings, the Mets Finally Rest," *New York Times*, September 30, 1993: B13.
22. Sexton, "And So, After 17 Innings, the Mets Finally Rest."
23. Sexton. Hillman got one more win that season. Young's last appearance of the year came on September 11.
24. Mike Holtzclaw, "Hitting, Relief Pitching Lead Tides to 6-3 Victory," *Newport News* (Virginia) *Daily Press*, April 20, 1994: 6.
25. John Harper, "At Least His Role Is Major," *New York Daily News*, February 26, 1995: 46.
26. Wolcott, "Free Agent Has Dreams of Pulling on Red Sox."
27. "PCL Postponement," *Calgary Herald*, May 2, 1996: 61.
28. Wolcott.
29. Wolcott.
30. Greer email.
31. Kenny Greer's page at Executive Search Partners website (https://www.ex-sp.com/team-member/kenneth-w-greer/).
32. Greer email.
33. Kenny Greer's page at Executive Search Partners website.
34. Wolcott.

CHARLIE GUTH

BY JEFF FINDLEY

On September 30, 1880, in his only appearance in a professional base ball game, a 24-year-old Chicagoan whose previous athletic accomplishments occurred in performances in local amateur base ball contests took the mound for the professional Chicago White Stockings in a game that had little relevance to anyone or anything beyond delivering a favor to a local sporting-goods company owner.

Offering a work history as an engraver's apprentice and shirt cutter, he tossed a complete-game victory, ensuring that the locals finished the 1880 season of the National League with a 15-game margin.

His name was Charlie Guth.

Framing the background of a nineteenth-century individual isn't an easy task, but there exists limited news coverage of the time that illustrates Guth's talents. In 1879 a recap of an amateur game in Chicago noted that the "Dreadnaughts and Athletes played as fine a game of base ball yesterday as has been seen between amateur clubs this season. The game was remarkable for the heavy battling of the Athletes."[1]

In that game, the Athletes featured a pitcher named Guth, who posted an 18-5 win, striking out seven. Offensively, he had three hits and scored four runs, batting in the cleanup spot. It was one of his earliest documented appearances among local teams of the time.

A man in his early 20s, Charlie Guth was employed by the A.G. Spalding & Brothers Company, a Chicago sporting-goods company that would develop the first major-league baseball which became the official baseball for the National League (1876-1976) and American League (1889-1973).[2]

The Spalding company was founded by Albert Goodwill Spalding, a native of Byron, Illinois, who was a dominant pitcher for the Boston Red Stockings, leading the National Association in victories in every full season he participated for Boston (1871-1875). As a pitcher and manager, Spalding also led the National League in victories during its inaugural season in 1876, winning 47 games for the first-place Chicago White Stockings (52-14).

In 1877 Spalding relinquished the primary pitching duties, appearing in just four games as a hurler and winning his only start. Instead, he played first base in 45 games, second base in 13 games, and third base in 4. Offensively, he produced a less than stellar .256 batting average. Spalding played in only one game in 1878, his final major-league appearance, and had a 2-for-4 performance on August 31. He was off to bigger things, including a future Hall of Fame induction as a baseball executive. In addition to managing his sporting-goods business, Spalding became secretary of the White Stockings, which eventually led to the club president's role in 1882.

As an amateur and an employee of Spalding's company as a uniform manager, Guth did not achieve his livelihood through his baseball talents. For the 1880 season, he joined the semipro Chicago Lake Views; Guth was the only personnel change from the prior season and was listed as the team's

Lake Front Park, Chicago, 1880.

primary hurler. The Lake Views were one of the prominent amateur teams in the Chicago area, evidenced by an August 1, 1880, entry in the *Chicago Tribune* that noted a matchup with the Franklins "for the amateur championship at White-Stocking Park[,]" where "neither club has thus far lost a game this season."[3] The Lake Views won the game 9-8, but it did not bring a title to Guth's nine. A meeting of the Board of Directors of the Amateur Base-Ball Assocation of Chicago determined that the local Dreadnaughts would be awarded the city championship with 17 victories. Guth's Lake Views club, after several unsuccessful protests about games awarded and umpire decisions, finished in second place with 16 wins. The Franklins finished third.[4]

In 1880 the White Stockings had distanced themselves from all other teams in the National League. Entering the final day of the season with a 14½-game lead over the second-place Providence Grays, they would contest a meaningless Thursday afternoon home game against the floundering seventh-place Buffalo Bisons without the availability of Larry Corcoran or Fred Goldsmith, their primary pitchers of record during the season.

Enter Al Spalding. As the game had no real significance, Spalding, an officer and owner of the White Stockings, persuaded manager Cap Anson to allow Guth to pitch the game. Guth didn't disappoint.

After giving up a run in the first inning on a two-out hit by Buffalo's Jack Rowe and subsequent errors by Tom Burns, George Gore, and King Kelly, Guth held the Bisons scoreless for the next six innings. The game account of the early innings described him as having "all the elements of a first-class pitcher, unless it be experience, coolness, and nerve, which only comes with time. His variations of curve and speed are extremely puzzling."[5]

Chicago posted three runs in each of the first, fifth, and seventh innings, and a single counter in the eighth that gave the White Stockings a commanding 10-1 lead. It was then that Buffalo mounted a challenge.

One game summary said: "If [Guth] had maintained his pace throughout the game he would have proved a phenomenal success, but he weakened visibly in the eighth inning and became unsteady."[6] Guth relinquished three earned runs on five hits and three wild pitches in the inning.

The ninth saw more struggles, as Guth allowed five hits and gave up four runs. An error by Joe Quest made the final three tallies unearned. Corcoran "made a high jump for [Davy] Force's bounder and threw him out at first"[7] to secure the victory. In his first and only major-league appearance, Charlie collected a win, striking out seven with one walk and four wild pitches. The *Chicago Tribune* game account estimated 400 in attendance.

Guth remained with the White Stockings for two additional exhibition games at season's end with Buffalo. The games were scheduled to test a new style of ball made of cork wound by string, rubber, and yarn, and the use of a square bat developed by George Wright, a future Hall of Famer who opened Wright & Ditson Sporting Goods in partnership with Boston businessman Henry Ditson. The game recap indicated that neither innovation improved the game, and beyond the 12-10 score in favor of Chicago, there was no mention of individual accolades. Guth's major-league career was over, although his name continued to appear in occasional game coverage as he continued his amateur career.

On January 1, 1881, a base ball game of local professional and amateur players was organized and played on ice skates. Al Spalding was one of the captains and organizers, and Charlie Guth was the pitcher for the Spalding nine. However, the side managed by White Stockings slugger Ed Williamson was victorious, 22-21.[8]

In late March of 1881, the Lake View Base-Ball Club announced the elected officers and players who would constitute that season's team. Guth remained prominent on the player roster, again listed as the pitcher. The announcement in the *Chicago Tribune* hints at the team's competitive desires, stating that the "Lake Views have decided not to enter the Amateur League, preferring to forfeit their membership than be compelled to play on Sunday. They intend visiting larger cities the coming season, and with that end in view have organized an unusually strong nine."[9]

Future coverage saw the Lake Views competing against teams from Dubuque, Iowa, and Goshen, Indiana, among others.

An exhibition in April 1882 was contested between the White Stockings and a local amateur team called the Spaldings. By this time, Al Spalding had retired as a player to become president of the White Stockings, succeeding William Hulbert, who died that same month. Charlie Guth was one of two pitchers used by the Spaldings, who endured a 21-0 shellacking at the hands of the professional club. (The White Stockings sported the "new regulation league uniform: each member wore a badge of crape on the arm out of respect to the memory of the late President Hurlbert.")[10]

A later mention in 1882 showed Guth pitching for Tuscola, Illinois, a presumed "ringer" in a rematch against Urbana, which had previously downed Tuscola 12-2 on August 10. A game recap, referencing that first loss, noted that "the favorable termination of this game brought forward plenty of backers for our boys, and as the Tuscola sport's confidence was materially increased by the addition of Guth, pitcher of the Spalding's, of Chicago, the best amateur club in the city, plenty of money was put up on the game, about $400."[11]

A colorful recap in the *Champaign County Herald* describes the contest, emphasizing "a line catch" in the ninth inning which prevented what could have been the winning run.

"As the score shows the game resulted in a tie at the end of the ninth inning," the newspaper said. "After a consultation between the captains and umpire, it was decided to call the game a draw, and to be played off in this city at some future date. All bets were declared off."[12]

It was the final playing reference the author could verify.

Beyond baseball, an accounting of Guth's life exists in bits in pieces.

Charlie was the fifth child of foreign-born parents. His father, John B. Guth, a barber, was born in Alsace, France, in or around 1829. Guth's mother, Anna R. (Murphy) Guth, was born in about 1833 in Ireland, and listed dressmaking and "keeping house" as her primary occupations in various US Federal Census reporting.

Guth was an employee of A.G. Spalding & Brothers during most of his playing days in Chicago, and for several years served as a uniform manager.

Photograph of what is believed to be Charlie Guth's unmarked grave, Graceland Cemetery.
Photograph courtesy of Sam Gazdziak.

(Earlier job references include shirt cutter.) At some point in late 1882 or early 1883, Guth joined the Wright & Ditson Company.

Charlie married Mary Lizzie Rowlands, who was born in Chicago, on March 7, 1883. The couple relocated to Boston, where Wright & Ditson's primary operations were centered. Four months later, he was dead.

The cause of death was listed as asthenia, which was described as a general weakness or loss of strength. The date was July 5, 1883, in Cambridge, Massachusetts. He was 27.

Despite his being a newcomer to the area, the *Boston Globe* gave fitting notice of Charlie's demise:

"Charles J. Guth, for several years in charge of the uniform department of Al Spalding & Brothers, Chicago, and afterwards with Wright & Ditson of this city in the same capacity, recently died in Boston. He was well known in the leading amateur base ball circles of Chicago as a fine pitcher. He was of a very sunny and genial disposition, and his death will be regretted by his many friends in the West."[13]

Just as his fleeting notoriety in life centered on a single game in the major leagues, Guth's death resulted in similar future anonymity. He is buried in Graceland Cemetery in Chicago, near the graves of several of his wife's relatives.[14]

His grave is unmarked.

SOURCES

In addition to the sources cited in the Notes, the author consulted Ancestry.com, Baseball-Reference.com, Retrosheet.org, and SABR.org.

NOTES

1. "Dreadnaughts vs Athletes," *Chicago Inter Ocean*, September 23, 1879.
2. https://www.spalding.com/about-spalding.html, December 17, 2021.
3. "Ball Gossip," *Chicago Tribune*, August 1, 1880: 8.
4. "Winter Notes About the Game," *Chicago Tribune*, December 5, 1880: 7.
5. "The Chicagos Finish the League Season with a Victory over Buffalo," *Chicago Tribune*, October 1, 1880: 8.
6. "The Chicagos Finish the League Season with a Victory over Buffalo."
7. "The Chicagos Finish the League Season with a Victory over Buffalo."
8. "Sporting Matters. Ball on Ice," *Chicago Inter Ocean*, January 3, 1881: 2.
9. "Not Good Weather for the Game," *Chicago Tribune*, March 20, 1881: 12.
10. "A Practice Game," *Chicago Inter Ocean*, April 17, 1882: 5.
11. "Match Game Between the Tuscola and Urbana Club," *Champaign County Herald*, August 30, 1882: 1.
12. "Match Game Between the Tuscola and Urbana Club."
13. "Spheric Sitings," *Boston Globe*, July 15, 1883: 6.
14. "Grave Story: Charlie Guth (1856-1883)," https://ripbaseball.com/2019/06/25/grave-story-charlie-guth/.

JORDAN JANKOWSKI

BY JOHN FREDLAND

Jordan Jankowski was a record-setting high-school power hitter in Western Pennsylvania, but a full-time turn to pitching in college opened his path to the pros. Taken by the Houston Astros in the 34th round of the June 2012 draft out of Catawba College, an NCAA Division II school in Salisbury, North Carolina, Jankowski reached the majors in 2017, appearing in three games with the Astros, notching his only major-league win in relief on a wild Sunday in Minneapolis, and earning a World Series ring.

Jankowski, the son of Ronald and Lisa Jankowski, was born on May 17, 1989.[1] His father owned a bar in Pittsburgh, and his mother worked there as a bartender.[2] Jordan Jankowski grew up in Pittsburgh's Carrick neighborhood and started playing baseball at age 5.[3] By age 12, he was a member of two Little League teams and an American Athletic League team, playing in what he estimated as 120 games that spring and summer.[4]

"My dad would take me to the field probably six days a week to make sure that I was putting the work in," Jankowski remembered in 2020.[5] In the winter, Jankowski practiced his swing on a soft-toss station in the basement of his family's home.[6]

"Before I was allowed to play any video games or hang out with my friends, I would take like 250 swings per day in my basement," he said.[7] "My dad's attitude was, 'If you want to be good at anything, you have to put your work in first.'"[8]

Jankowski's biggest headlines at Peters Township High School came from his bat; a catcher, he hit 36 home runs over four seasons and drove in 132 runs.[9] In one game as a junior, he hit four home runs – with a potential fifth homer clearing the fence but going foul.[10]

He also drew acclaim as a pitcher, racking up a 15-4 record in his sophomore through senior seasons.[11] At Peters Township, Jankowski played on a state runner-up team in 2005, a team that finished its regular season undefeated in 2006, and back-to-back Western Pennsylvania-wide championship teams in 2007 and 2008.[12]

The *Pittsburgh Post-Gazette* selected him as its high-school baseball Player of the Year after his senior season in 2008 and concluded that his lifetime homer total was the Western Pennsylvania Interscholastic Athletic League's (WPIAL) all-time record.[13]

"He just loved to swing the bat," Joe Maize, Jankowski's high-school coach, remembered.[14] "Unbelievable bat speed. I haven't seen too many high school kids who had bat speed like he had."

Schools from the Big Ten, Big East, and Southeastern Conferences were interested in Jankowski, but many wanted him as a pitcher only.[15] Jankowski was not ready to give up catching, and he signed with Miami University in Oxford, Ohio, a member of the Mid-America Conference.[16] He kept his college commitment after the Astros selected him as a catcher in the 34th round of the June draft in 2008.

With future major leaguer Adam Eaton as a teammate at Miami University, Jankowski split time between pitching and catching during his freshman year. He distinguished himself most as a pitcher, finishing with a 6-1 record and a team-high five saves.[17]

Jankowski remained Miami's closer in 2010 and became the team's main designated hitter.[18] He recorded 10 saves, good for second in the Mid-America Conference, and hit eight home runs.

"As a hitter I think like a pitcher," Jankowski said in May 2010. "And as a pitcher I think like a hitter."[19]

After the 2010 season, Jankowski transferred to Catawba. As of 2023, he was one of only two Catawba alumni to reach the majors in the twenty-first century.[20]

"I was playing in a summer league ... and one of my teammates went to Catawba," Jankowski recounted in a 2015 interview. "I felt that if I was going to become a pitcher I wanted to go south to get more work in and to take better care of my arm. I talked to the coach there and I didn't have to sit out a year, so I decided to transfer."[21]

At this point a starting pitcher, he led the South Atlantic Conference in strikeouts per nine innings with 11.12 and earned first-team all-conference honors in 2011.[22]

"You develop at different times in your life as an athlete," Jankowski said in 2020. "I think I plateaued as a hitter and I kind of took off as a pitcher at a weird time. Most people do that when they're younger. It happened to me when I was in college, really."[23]

During Jankowski's time at Catawba, a family member introduced him to his future wife – a Pittsburgh-area native also named Jordan.[24]

"Most of my family call me 'J.J.' and call her 'Jordan,'" Jankowski said in a 2023 interview.[25] As of 2023, they had three sons and a daughter.[26]

Jankowski went undrafted and returned to Catawba in 2012 for his final season of college eligibility. Catawba had an outstanding team, eventually finishing fourth in the NCAA Division II College World Series.[27] Pitching mostly as a starter, Jankowski had a 9-2 record, a 3.79 ERA, and 126 strikeouts in 90⅓ innings.[28] He was named the South Atlantic Conference's co-Pitcher of the Year and selected to the all-conference first team as a starting pitcher.[29]

The Astros were the only team to invite Jankowski to a predraft workout in 2012, four years after selecting him out of high school,[30] but their nearest tryout – in Atlanta – was at the same time as Catawba's conference tournament.[31] With time running out before the June draft, one of Houston's area scouts suggested that Jankowski come to another Astros tryout in the Los Angeles area to throw a bullpen session.[32]

Jankowski told Catawba coach Jim Gantt he was going to make the trip to California[33] on a travel day for Catawba before the tournament.[34] Two hours later, as Jankowski recounted in a 2023 interview, Gantt kicked him off the team.[35]

"His attitude was 'If you're not all-in, you're off the team,'" Jankowski said.[36]

Jankowski's college career was over, but he had made an impression on the Astros, who selected him in the 34th round – the same as in 2008 – that June. In 2017 Bobby Heck, who was Houston's scouting director from 2007 through 2012,[37] told the *Houston Chronicle* that Jankowski most likely would have been drafted without going to the workout, but that flying to California significantly boosted his chances with the Astros.[38]

"You could see he was passionate," Heck remembered. "The guy wants to play. You go across the country and put his eligibility with his team in peril, I think that says a little bit about how much he wanted to play professional baseball."[39]

Jankowski signed with the Astros for $2,000: the typical $1,000 offered to seniors selected in the later rounds, plus another $1,000 for travel expenses.[40] He reported to Greenville of the short-season Appalachian League, where his teammates included

Jordan Jankowski began his college career at Miami University before transferring to Catawba College. Courtesy of Miami University Athletic Communications.

the Astros' two first-round draft selections, shortstop Carlos Correa and pitcher Lance McCullers.

Pitching in relief in Greenville, Jankowski led the team with 23 appearances; his four saves tied for the team lead. He praised Greenville pitching coach Héctor Mercado, who had pitched in the major leagues for the Cincinnati Reds and Philadelphia Phillies, for "putting in my head that I have to pitch inside."[41]

Jankowski moved up to Quad Cities River Bandits and the Class-A Midwest League in 2013. As a River Bandit, he started in about half of his 26 appearances as part of a tandem pitching system and recorded a 2.61 ERA in 89⅔ innings. His performance earned him a spot in the Midwest League All-Star Game, alongside teammates Correa and McCullers.[42]

"He took it by the horns and made himself better," said Quad Cities pitching coach Dave Borkowski, who had a seven-season big-league career.[43]

"All my pitching coaches going up were awesome," Jankowski said. "Before Dave Borkowski, I had shied away from contact, but he was the one who taught me to pitch to contact."[44]

A *Houston Chronicle* profile of the Astros' farm system in June 2013 listed Jankowski with Correa, McCullers, and Teoscar Hernández – all future major-league All-Stars – as top players on the team.[45]

After reaching the High-A California League during the 2013 season, Jankowski – who completed his college degree in health administration with Pittsburgh's Robert Morris University during the 2013-14 offseason[46] – continued to advance through the Astros system. He spent 2014 in Double A with Corpus Christi of the Texas League, where his pitching coach was longtime major-league reliever Doug Brocail.[47]

"I made my biggest leap in the minors with Doug Brocail," Jankowski remembered. "He pushed me to my limits and instilled in me that I was better than the competition. More than a coach, he was a good friend."[48]

The Astros made Jankowski a nonroster invitee to spring training in 2015, then again in 2016.[49] He pitched in Triple A with Fresno of the Pacific Coast League in both seasons, working almost exclusively in relief. In 2015 Jankowski did not allow a single home run in 62⅓ innings pitched; he was the only reliever in the PCL who pitched more than 50 innings or made more than 40 appearances without yielding a homer.[50]

His pitching coach in Fresno was Dyar Miller, who was at the end of a five-decade career in professional baseball.

"Dyar Miller was cool," Jankowski said. "When you're in Triple A, you can get a little bit frustrated [being so close to the majors]. He made it more fun and got rid of all the stress."[51]

While in Fresno in 2016, Jankowski taught teammate Brad Peacock how to throw a sweeping slider, a pitch that Peacock deployed prominently during his 2017 big-league breakthrough with the Astros.[52]

"I had a slider going into [2016], but it was getting crushed," Peacock said in 2017. "I'd just try to throw it hard, but it really wasn't moving much. I kind of just said, 'I need something new,' and I asked one of my buddies who had a good slider on the team."[53]

"Peacock was one of my best friends," Jankowski recounted in 2023. "We got to talking and messing around with grips. "One thing I loved doing was messing with people's grips and helping my teammates. It was more the hard work that he put in, rather than what I taught him."[54]

Again a nonroster invitee to Astros spring training in 2017, Jankowski was, as the *Houston Chronicle* noted, "a dark-horse candidate for a September promotion last year but never got the call. He projects to return to Class AAA."[55] He was back in Fresno's bullpen when the 2017 season started.

"I knew I had some pretty good years, and I was wondering what I needed to do to get to the next step," Jankowski remembered. "Everyone said just to be patient."[56]

With a 1.42 ERA through his first 19 innings pitched at Fresno, Jankowski received the call to the majors on May 22, 2017.[57] The Astros were running away with the American League West, but they needed another pitcher with starter Dallas Keuchel sidelined with a pinched nerve in his neck and Ashur Tolliver having gone four innings in relief a day earlier.[58]

Jankowski learned about his promotion in the aftermath of a poor performance for the Fresno club. After Grizzlies manager Tony DeFrancesco finished chewing out his team, he informed them that Jankowski was going to the majors.

"They all mobbed me at my locker," Jankowski said. "I couldn't even breathe. They were all jumping on top of me. It was pretty cool."[59]

"It was a lot of guys on the team who I had played with for three years. I think they realized that I needed a shot."[60]

Jankowski made his big-league debut at Houston's Minute Maid Park on May 24, 2017, a week after his 28th birthday. He entered in the ninth inning, with the Astros trailing the Detroit Tigers, 4-2. He fanned the first two batters he faced, Mikie Mahtook and Andrew Romine, but allowed a triple to Tyler Collins, then a home run to José Iglesias on a full-count pitch, a homer that barely reached the close-target Crawford Boxes in left field.

"I remember the real tough at-bat I had with Iglesias," Jankowski remembered in 2023. "I got back to my room and saw it on SportsCenter. They called it up on Statcast and said there was a 99.7 percent chance it would not have been a home run anywhere else – and that this was the 0.3 percent!"[61]

Jankowski regrouped to strike out Ian Kinsler for the third out. Television cameras found his wife in the stands and broadcast images of her emotive responses to Jankowski's pitching.[62]

Before Jankowski appeared in another game, the Astros informed him on May 26 that he was returning to Fresno, in anticipation of Keuchel returning from the disabled list.[63] But another injury to a Houston starter – this time, Charlie Morton – led to Jankowski's rapid recall on May 28.[64]

"I landed in Fresno – and then had to catch a flight to Minneapolis," Jankowski said. "I missed the first flight to Minneapolis, so I got in late at night."[65]

A day later, on Memorial Day, he was in the bullpen at Minneapolis's Target Field as Peacock, who had joined the rotation after Keuchel's injury, faced the Twins. Peacock started strongly, shutting out the Twins on one hit through four innings, but Minnesota rallied for three runs in the fifth to take a 3-2 lead. With one on and two outs, Houston manager A.J. Hinch summoned Jankowski from the bullpen. "I had to eat as many innings as I could at that point, just to help the team."[66]

Jankowski faced 13 batters over the next 2⅓ innings. By the time he had thrown his final pitch of the afternoon, he had allowed five hits, including home runs to Miguel Sano and former Fresno teammate Robbie Grossman, and the Twins had a seemingly commanding 8-2 lead after seven innings.

Houston's offense then flashed the firepower that led the majors in runs scored, battering three Twins pitchers for 11 runs in the eighth, then tacking on three more in the ninth. When the dust had cleared, the Astros had a 16-8 victory, their fifth in a row, and Jankowski, as pitcher of record for the 11-run outburst, was credited with the win.

"It was definitely crazy," Jankowski said after getting the win. "It was a cool experience. I'm just glad we won."[67]

The Astros, seeking a fresh arm after Jankowski's 46 pitches, optioned him to Fresno after the game.[68] He returned to the majors on June 24 when Peacock went on the paternity list.[69] Once the weekend was over, Jankowski was back in Triple A without making a major-league appearance.[70]

He made it back to Houston one last time, when the Astros put relievers Tony Sipp and Michael Feliz on the disabled list on August 1. He pitched a scoreless ninth inning a day later in the Astros' 3-0 loss to the Tampa Bay Rays, catching Logan Morrison looking for the third out.

On August 14, the Astros faced a catching crisis with Brian McCann and Evan Gattis on the disabled list. They added Max Stassi to their 40-man roster, which meant having to clear a spot. Jankowski was designated for assignment.

The Los Angeles Dodgers claimed Jankowski on waivers on August 20 and assigned him to Triple-A Oklahoma City.

But on September 3, Los Angeles designated him for assignment. Jankowski was on the sidelines in October when his two professional organizations played in the World Series. The Astros' seven-game win gave him a World Series ring.

Jankowski went to spring training with the Dodgers in 2018 but was released in March. The Los Angeles Angels signed him as a free agent, then released him in May after 15 appearances with an 8.68 ERA at Triple-A Salt Lake.

Jankowski retired from affiliated baseball at that point, returning to Pittsburgh to work as a realtor.

"I'm still competitive," Jankowski said in 2020. "When I got out of baseball I came home and wasn't sure what was next for me. So I got my real estate license and everything just took off. I really like real estate. It's different than sports, but it's still very competitive. I don't know which one is more stressful."[71]

He returned to action in 2020 in an independent league near Pittsburgh, hosted by the Frontier League's Washington Wild Things during the COVID pandemic, before ending his professional career for good.[72]

"They called me and asked if I wanted to close," Jankowski remembered in 2023. "My son was 3, and he had never seen me play. I hurt my arm in the first game and tried to pitch through it. It was still cool, playing against some guys who had been in the minors."[73]

As of 2023, Jankowski's 36 high-school home runs remain an unofficial Western Pennsylvania record, even more than notable players like Donora High School's Stan Musial and Ken Griffey, Wampum High School's Dick Allen, Upper St. Clair High School's Sean Casey, and Pittsburgh Central Catholic's Dan Marino, who was drafted by the Kansas City Royals out of high school before devoting himself to football full-time.[74]

"I didn't even know it was a thing [when I was in high school], but it's definitely cool to know that," Jankowski said. "It's funny that the most prolific home run hitter in the WPIAL didn't even take one at-bat professionally."[75]

SOURCES

The author thanks Jordan Jankowski for discussing his life and baseball career in a telephone interview on June 19, 2023. In addition to the sources cited in the Notes, the author consulted Baseball-Reference.com and Retrosheet.org for pertinent information.

NOTES

1. "Jordan Jankowski," MiamiRedhawks.com, accessed March 10, 2023, https://miamiredhawks.com/sports/baseball/roster/jordan-jankowski/121.

2. Telephone interview with Jordan Jankowski, June 19, 2023.

3. Steve Rotstein, "Unofficial Home Run Champion," *Pittsburgh Post-Gazette*, May 15, 2020: LX-5.

4. Rotstein.

5. Rotstein.

6. Telephone interview with Jordan Jankowski, June 19, 2023, hereafter Jankowski interview.

7. Rotstein.

8. Jankowski interview.

9. Rotstein.

10. Mike White, "Peters Twp. Junior Missed 5-Homer Record by a Foot," *Pittsburgh Post-Gazette*, April 29, 2007: C-12.

11. Jankowski was 6-0 as a sophomore in 2006, 4-3 as a junior in 2007, and 6-1 as a senior in 2008. Chris Adamski, "Division I Colleges Taking a Look at Peters Junior," *Pittsburgh Post-Gazette*, March 29, 2007: S-8; "All-Stars: Washington," *Pittsburgh Post-Gazette*, June 24, 2007: W-5; "All-Area: The Best in High School Baseball and Softball for the 2008 Season," *Pittsburgh Post-Gazette*, June 22, 2008: D-8.

12. Mike White, "Different Year, Same Ending in Title Game: Peters Township Falls for Second Year in a Row," *Pittsburgh Post-Gazette*, June 18, 2005: C-9: David Assad, "Peters' Perfect Season Pops: Top Seed Stumbles, But '07 Hopes High," *Pittsburgh Post-Gazette*, May 28, 2006: W-6; Chris Adamski, "WPIAL Champion Peters Simply Has No Regrets," *Pittsburgh Post-Gazette*, June 14, 2007: S-9; Chris Adamski, "Peters Bids Adieu to Excellent Senior Class," *Pittsburgh Post-Gazette*, June 15, 2008: W-6.

13. "All-Area: The Best in High School Baseball and Softball for the 2008 Season"; Mike White, "JJ = HR: With a Record-Shattering 36 Career Home Runs, Peters Township's Jordan Jankowski Is the WPIAL's Sultan of Swat," *Pittsburgh Post-Gazette*, May 18, 2008: D-10.

14. Rotstein.

15. Pete Conrad, "Bullpen Ace a Big Hit at Plate, Too," *Hamilton* (Ohio) *Journal News*, May 7, 2010: B1.

16. Conrad.

17. Jordan Jankowski, The Baseball Cube, accessed July 12, 2023, https://www.thebaseballcube.com/content/player/143072/.

18. Conrad.

19. Conrad.

20. Jerry Sands, who appeared in 156 games with four teams from 2011 through 2016, is the other. Nine other players from Catawba, most notably six-time All-Star Johnny Temple, have also reached the majors.

21. "Jordan Jankowski: Story and Interview," ChasingMLBDreams.com, January 26, 2015, https://chasingmlbdreams.com/2015/01/26/jordan-jankowski-story-and-interview/.

22. "2011 SAC Baseball All-Conference Team, Award Winners Announced," TheSAC.com, April 19, 2011, https://www.thesac.com/sports/bsb/2010-11/releases/a2571.html.

23. Rotstein.

24. Jankowski interview.

25. Jankowski interview.

26. Jankowski interview.

27. "Jim Gantt: Head Baseball Coach," *2013 Catawba College Baseball Media Guide*: 2.

28. "2012 Statistics," *2013 Catawba College Baseball Media Guide*: 21.

29. "College NCAA Division II All SAC Teams," *Knoxville News-Sentinel*, April 19, 2012: 2C.

30. Jake Kaplan, "Pitcher Jordan Jankowski Took Unique Path to Astros," *Houston Chronicle*, May 26, 2017: C2.

31. Jankowski interview.

32. Jankowski interview.

33. Jankowski interview.

34. Kaplan, "Pitcher Jordan Jankowski Took Unique Path to Astros."

35. Jankowski interview.

36. Jankowski interview. In 2017 the *Houston Chronicle* reported that Gantt said the decision to kick Jankowski off the team was made "because NCAA rules at the time stipulated a college player lost his eligibility if he worked out for a professional team before his college season ended." Kaplan, "Pitcher Jordan Jankowski Took Unique Path to Astros."

37. Jose de Jesus Ortiz, "Astros Report," *Houston Chronicle*, August 12, 2012: C6.

38. Kaplan, "Pitcher Jordan Jankowski Took Unique Path to Astros."

39. Kaplan, "Pitcher Jordan Jankowski Took Unique Path to Astros."

40. Kaplan, "Pitcher Jordan Jankowski Took Unique Path to Astros."

41. Jankowski interview. Mercado appeared in 112 games with the Reds and Phillies from 2000 through 2003.

42. Daniel Makarewicz, "Bandits' Jankowski Finds All-Star Touch," *Rock Island* (Illinois) *Argus*, June 17, 2013: D1.

43. Makarewicz, "Bandits' Jankowski Finds All-Star Touch."

44. Jankowski interview.

45. Brian T. Smith, "Stockpile of Seeds Bearing Fruit on the Farm," *Houston Chronicle*, June 23, 2013: C1.

46. Daniel Makarewicz, "Back to School for River Bandits' Hurlers," *Rock Island Argus*, July 8, 2013: D1.

47 Brocail appeared in 626 major-league games – all but 42 in relief – with the San Diego Padres, Detroit Tigers, Texas Rangers, and Astros from 1992 through 2009.

48 Jankowski interview.

49 Jose de Jesus Ortiz, "Correa '100 Percent' Ready," *Houston Chronicle*, January 14, 2015: C3; "Bregman Invited to Astros' Camp," *Houston Chronicle*, January 2, 2016: C9.

50 Angel Moreno, "Bullpen Key to PCL Title Run," *Fresno Bee*, August 23, 2015: 5C.

51 Jankowski interview.

52 Jake Kaplan, "Health, Slider Key to Peacock's Emergence," *Houston Chronicle*, July 25, 2017: C1.

53 Kevin Santo, "Astros Pitchers Are the Kings of Ks, But Can They Avoid Dangerous Curves in October," *USA Today*, July 25, 2017, https://www.usatoday.com/story/sports/mlb/2017/07/25/astros-fastballs-mlb-strikeout-leaders-brad-peacock-slider/508813001/.

54 Jankowski interview.

55 "Non-Roster Invitees," *Houston Chronicle*, February 10, 2017: TEXAS SPORTS NATION, 31.

56 Jankowski interview.

57 Jake Kaplan, "Jankowski Called to Majors," *Houston Chronicle*, May 23, 2017: C5.

58 Kaplan, "Jankowski Called to Majors."

59 Rotstein.

60 Jankowski interview.

61 Jankowski interview.

62 Matt Young, "Jordan Jankowski's #1 Fan? Jordan Jankowski: Astros Pitcher's Wife Shows a Wave of Emotions as He Makes His Debut," *Houston Chronicle*, May 26, 2017: A2.

63 Jake Kaplan, "Anticipate Keuchel, McCann Playing Today," *Houston Chronicle*, May 27, 2017: C3.

64 Hunter Atkins, "Right Lat Strain Sends Morton to Disabled List," *Houston Chronicle*, May 29, 2017: C3.

65 Jankowski interview.

66 Jankowski interview.

67 Jake Kaplan and Hunter Atkins, "Astros Report: Gonzalez Extends His Very Merry May," *Houston Chronicle*, May 30, 2017: C5.

68 Jake Kaplan, "8 Years After Signing, Guduan Makes Debut," *Houston Chronicle*, June 1, 2017: C2.

69 Jake Kaplan, "Peacock Goes on Paternity Leave List, Martes to Start Series Finale," *Houston Chronicle*, June 25, 2017: C5.

70 Jake Kaplan, "Keuchel's Return Likely to Come After Break," *Houston Chronicle*, June 26, 2017: C3.

71 "Dugan, "Numbers Game."

72 Jankowski appeared in six games for the Steel City Slammin' Sammies, who competed in a four-team league with the Wild Things, Baseball Brilliance Sox, and Road Warrior Black Sox. Chris Dugan, "Numbers Game: Jankowski Making More Pitches to Home," *Observer-Reporter* (Pennsylvania), July 14, 2020, https://observer-reporter.com/sports/pro_sports/wild_things/numbers-game-jankowski-making-more-pitches-to-home/article_8ea4cc9c-c610-11ea-8ece-b7142e8f1e8a.html.

73 Jankowski interview.

74 Steve Hecht, "Royals to Share Marino with Pitt," *Pittsburgh Post-Gazette*, June 6, 1979: 30; Steve Hecht, "NCAA Ruling Spurs Marino to Choose Pitt over Pros," *Pittsburgh Post-Gazette*, June 28, 1979: 10.

75 Rotstein.

JIM JOHNSON

BY JIM MOYES

Jim Johnson may have second thoughts if he grew up in today's era of millionaire ball players. However, the southpaw who pitched for one season with the 1970 San Francisco Giants, valued family and a desire to become an educator as more important values than remaining in the big leagues.

Just as he did by reaching the top rung of the ladder in baseball, Johnson did the same in the field of education. Before succumbing to cancer at the much too young age of 42 in December of 1987, Johnson reached the top of his profession as Superintendent of Schools at North Muskegon, Michigan High School.

Born on November 3, 1945 Jim Johnson was the son of Ed and Dorothy Johnson, the second of two children raised by his parents. Father Ed Johnson was born December 16, 1903 and graduated from Otisville, Michigan High, and later attended Western Michigan. Ed was a standout catcher for the Broncos, leading the team in hitting in 1930, a feat accomplished twice by his son Jim in the 1960s. While attending Western, Ed married Dorothy Watson on November 19, 1929 and both became school educators, Dorothy as a teacher while Ed served as a teacher, coach, and administrator.[1]

Jim was a 7-year-old in elementary school in Muskegon, Michigan in 1953, when an armistice was reached in the Korean War in August. This was more than welcome news for the Johnsons: Jim's brother Bill, who was a prisoner of war, was freed by North Korea and reunited with his family.

Jim Johnson was big winner, all throughout his amateur years. He played on three division winners in Little League, won titles in all three of his years in Pony League, and during the summer he led his Connie Mack teams to wins in every regular season contest.[2]

Pitching for the Kiwanis team in the Pony League as a 13-year-old, Johnson struck out 20 of the 21 batters he faced in a 2-0 victory.[3] Unfortunately, tragedy struck late in the season when his father, the team manager, passed away suddenly from a massive heart attack. Just days following his father's death, a grieving Jim Johnson struck out 15 batters in the championship game. Despite the three-hitter pitched by Johnson, an unearned run in the last inning led to a 1-0 loss.[4]

As a senior at Muskegon High in 1963, Jim was selected the MVP in leading the team to a 21-1 record. Johnson wasn't the only player on this team to make to the major leagues. Jim Johnson and Ray Newman were part of a rare fraternity of high school pitchers that graduated from the same high school class and also pitched in the major leagues. (Newman pitched for the Cubs in 1971 and the Brewers in 1972-73.) Early in the season, they each pitched three innings for a combined no-hitter in the season opening 16-0 thrashing of Muskegon Christian.[5]

After graduating, Johnson joined an independent team, the Muskegon Pepsis of the highly competitive United Baseball League. The step up in talent posed no problem. Playing for the Pepsis, Johnson had a 4-1 pitching record and batted a lofty .421.

It was now on to Western Michigan University for the talented left-handed thrower and batter where he received a scholarship – not for baseball, but for his academic achievements at Muskegon High.

After biding his time playing for the freshman team, (freshmen were not eligible for varsity competition at the Division 1 level until 1970) Johnson had an immediate impact when he joined the varsity squad. In addition to patrolling center field for the Broncos, Johnson began his record-setting career by compiling a perfect 6-0 record and a team-low ERA of 1.98 in 1965, while also handing Ohio University its only defeat on the season. (Ohio University finished with an all-time best mark of 26-1.) Johnson not only went the distance in the 2-1 win, he also scored the winning run by being on the front end of a double steal.

"Western Michigan's baseball record of 16-6 and 9-1 in the league play was somewhat unexpected this year. And most of the credit belongs to a sophomore southpaw, Jim Johnson of Muskegon," wrote Jerry Hagan of the *Kalamazoo Gazette*. Johnson ended his first year as a Bronco by beating Michigan State on a two hitter. Jim was one of four Broncos selected to the Mid-American Conference first team.[6] Among his six victories was a one-hitter with 13 strikeouts in a conference matchup with Marshall University. Only a "seeing-eye" single in the second inning deprived Johnson of a perfect game. Johnson was none too shabby as a hitter, batting a healthy .325.[7]

Johnson may have been even more dominant that summer while pitching for the Pepsis. In a game called after five innings due to a "mercy" rule, Johnson faced 15 batters and fanned 14. The only batter who put the ball in play was out attempting to bunt.[8]

Johnson shined at the NBC (National Baseball Congress) regional playoffs. He began the tournament by pitching a 6-0 shutout and then later in the playoffs he won both games of a doubleheader with some stellar relief work. He was not only selected to the all-tournament team, but was named tournament MVP. Joining Johnson on this all-star team was a former Detroit Tiger slugger from nearby Paw Paw, Charlie Maxwell, who amassed three homers.[9]

There was no letup from Jim in 1966, his second season with Western Michigan. Sportswriter Hagan tabbed Johnson as its best pitcher, best outfielder, and best hitter. Johnson was also the team's leading base stealer.[10] The team was 21-5 in 1966 but deprived of a trip to Omaha as they lost to Ohio State in the district's NCAA playoffs. Ohio State won the championship.[11]

Adding salt to the wounds, during the regular season WMU defeated OSU three times. The Broncos played the Buckeyes early in the season in Columbus and swept the three-game series. The highlight of the sweep was Johnson hurling a one-hitter against the Buckeyes to hand his veteran coach Charlie Maher his 400th victory as the Broncos head coach.

Jim preferred to play the outfield, but would "help out" if asked to pitch. As a junior, he hit .415 with a .500 average during conference play. How often does a pitcher lead his team in stolen bases? Jim did it twice – in 1966 and 1967.[12]

Although he was coveted by many teams following his junior season, Jim had made it clear that he was intent on finishing his schooling at Western and would not enter the draft. "The offer would have to be awful tempting before I'd ever leave school," said Jim in an interview with Mart Tardani of the *Muskegon Chronicle*.[13] The Detroit Tigers did take a flyer on Jim and made him their last player to be drafted (36th round) in the June 1966 draft and Houston selected him in the 3rd round of the January secondary draft in 1967 but Jim declined both offers.

Johnson played his summer ball in 1966 in Rapid City, South Dakota in the Basin League. The team had five players who made it to the majors.[14] After hitting over .400 at WMU, Johnson was recruited to play center field for Rapid City. Scouts told him to concentrate on playing the field, but when asked to work one inning in relief, he complied by striking out the side.[15]

Just as Charley Maher quickly discovered his pitching talent at WMU, Rapid City manager Floyd Temple did as well following his impressive one-inning pitching debut. In his first start on July 9, Jim pitched a two-hit 8-0 shutout over Mobridge.[16]

Midway through his senior season at WMU, Johnson posted six straight victories, five of them shutouts. In 53 1/3 innings of work, Johnson allowed but one earned run.

There were two unanimous choices on the 1967 All Mid-American Conference team, Johnson and Kent State's sophomore hitting sensation Thurman Munson. Jim ended the season with a perfect 7-0 record while hitting .339 and leading the team in RBIs with 16.[17]

The case could be made for Jim Johnson as the best overall player in WMU's storied history. He was inducted into the WMU Athletic Hall of Fame in 1997.

After inking a contract that included a sizable bonus with the San Francisco Giants, Johnson wasted little time in making his presence known in the pro ranks. He made his professional appearance in relief for the 1967 Salt Lake City Giants against the Tommy Lasorda-managed Ogden Dodgers. He retired all 11 Ogden batters he faced in order while striking out seven.[18]

Pitching stats posted in *The Sporting News* showed Johnson leading all pitchers in the Pioneer League with a 3-2 mark with a remarkably low ERA of 0.75. He was promoted to Fresno for the final month of the season, where he was 2-0.[19]

On the same day that the 1967-68 school year drew to a close on Friday, June 7, Johnson married his childhood sweetheart, Mary Ruth Wagner. No exotic honeymoon travels were on the newlyweds' docket as they departed for Jim to join the Decatur (Illinois) Commodores shortly after the wedding.[20]

Jim Johnson, with the 1970 Giants. Courtesy of Jim C. Johnson.

Johnson was first thrust into action on July 19 at Clinton and quickly displayed his fitness by pitching a complete-game victory. He allowed a pair of first-inning runs before hurling six shutout innings to notch his first win in Midwest League action.

In his final start to wrap up the season for the league-leading Decatur Commodores, Jim hiked his final regular season record to 6-4. After a shaky start in the first inning, he found his pitching groove and at one span retired 14 men in a row, striking out nine. He also helped his team at the plate as he had a pair of hits and three RBIs in a 7-3 win over runner-up Quad City.[21]

In a best-of- three game series to decide the playoff championship, Johnson won a 7-1 decision over Quad City to tie the series at 1-1. He allowed six hits and struck out eight while also going 1-3 at the plate. Quad City won the deciding game 3-1 to capture the title.[22]

Including the playoffs, Johnson finished with an impressive ERA of 2.06 with 97 strikeouts before heading back home to Muskegon, Michigan to return to his job as a schoolteacher at Muskegon High.

Johnson reported for his first spring training with the Giants organization in 1969 and was promoted to Amarillo of the Texas League. He started with a perfect 4-0 record including a complete-game 6-1 win over Arkansas in which he fanned 10 and walked just one batter.[23]

With a 7-2 record and a low ERA that ranked in the top five in the Texas League, Johnson was called up to AAA Phoenix in mid-June 1969. His first start was a no-decision. His first victory in Pacific Coast League action came on August 6 when he pitched his Giants to a complete-game 5-2 victory in a road win against Vancouver and went 3-for-4. (In his two years in Phoenix, Johnson posted an impressive .341 batting average.)

Johnson pitched much better than his 1-3 record during his first stint in Phoenix. He posted a 3.56 ERA before the Giants brass approved his early departure from the club so he could pursue a master's degree at Michigan State University.[24]

The following March, Johnson joined the San Francisco Giants at their training site in Scottsdale, Arizona. He quickly made a positive impression with Giants manager Clyde King.[25]

During his stint in spring training, which included a controversial nine-game series of games in chilly Japan, Johnson allowed but four hits and two runs in nine innings. At 24 years of age, with a degree in mathematics and one semester shy of earning his master's degree, Jim Johnson made the Giants roster.

After two early-season road appearances, Johnson earned his first major-league victory in Cincinnati on April 18, 1970. It was an improbable victory to be sure.

Playing in front of a crowd that included his in-laws from Muskegon, Johnson replaced starter Frank Reberger in the fourth inning. When he arrived on the mound to take the ball from Clyde King, he was not looking at a pretty scene. Three runners had already crossed the plate, Cincinnati led 4-3 and the bases were full of Reds.

To make matters even worse, he had inherited 2-0 count on the first batter he faced, Bobby Tolan. He proceeded to walk Tolan, the walk was credited to Reberger. and Bernie Carbo scored. Johnson uncorked a wild pitch that scored Pete Rose. Before the dust had settled and he had retired Lee May for the final out of the inning, the Reds had seven runs cross the plate, giving Cincinnati a commanding 8-3 lead. None of the runs were charged to Johnson; they were all charged to Reberger.

Johnson had an efficient fifth inning, retiring the side with only one walk allowed. When the Giants came to bat, Cincinnati pitcher Ray Washburn couldn't find the plate and walked the first four batters he faced. Tony Cloninger replaced Washburn and had seemingly got the Reds out of trouble with a made-to-order 1-2-3 double play on a comebacker.

Bob Heise kept the two-out rally going, though, with a two-run single that narrowed the gap to 8-6. Johnson's day was done when Steve Whitaker, batting for him, drew a walk. So did Bobby Bonds. Ron Hunt stepped in with the bases loaded. Hunt made Johnson a winner with a grand slam which gave the Giants a 10-8 lead they did not relinquish as Mike McCormick pitched the final four innings and allowed only one run.

Even though Jim Johnson was the winning pitcher – with no earned runs allowed – it was the last game he pitched in the major leagues. Shortly thereafter, he was sent to Phoenix to pitch for his "old friend" Charlie Fox.

Perhaps still seething over Johnson's early departure to pursue a graduate degree in 1969, Fox seldom called upon Johnson before May 28 when the manager was elevated to replace Clyde King as San Francisco manager.

After pitching but 15 innings following his departure from the majors, Johnson got his first starting assignment in over a year on June 23. He responded by pitching a complete game victory over Tacoma, allowing but five hits, no walks, while striking out 10, which may have prompted local fans to inquire as to why was he languishing on the bench.

New Phoenix manager Hank Sauer said, "He was something else out there. All he needed was a shot and he certainly earned a spot in the starting rotation."[26]

Johnson went the distance for the second time in three starts in a 4-3 win over Tucson on July 3, spacing out seven hits, all singles, walking just two, and striking out six. All runs charged to him were unearned.

He had more on his mind than trying to tame Tacoma in his next outing. "I was nervous in the first inning," said Johnson, who issued three walks, permitted one hit and allowed a run in the first frame. "My wife is due to have our first baby any time now, and I couldn't keep my mind on the game for the first few minutes. Once I settled down, I was OK." He was more than OK, however, as he pitched hitless ball for the next six innings before giving way to the bullpen. It was his fourth victory in five decisions, and third without a loss, since he was inserted into the starting rotation.[27]

Johnson was scheduled to pitch one game of a doubleheader at Tucson on July 28 but was removed from the start due to what was described as a "stiff arm."[28]

A very nervous Johnson was more than 100 miles from Phoenix when his son, Jimmy, was born on July 30. Clubs in this era allowed no time off for expectant fathers. After the Phoenix club returned home on August 1, Johnson, stiff arm and all, was thrust into action in a 1-0 game with Hawaii and he responded with a shutout inning.

He picked up the win in what proved to be the penultimate outing in his professional career, just nine days after becoming a father. He worked 6 2/3 innings in Honolulu, a 2-1 win over the PCL leaders. When asked by *Arizona Republic* sportswriter Bob Eger about his sore arm of late, Johnson replied: "It still hurts. I noticed the pain more on breaking balls then on the fast balls, but it's not bad enough to keep me from pitching. I have all winter to rest it."[29] He clearly didn't have retirement in mind.

On August 14, pitching with a lame arm for a depleted Phoenix pitching staff, he gave up four runs on six hits but struck out eight in a 4-2 loss in Hawaii. Although unbeknownst at the time, it was his last appearance in organized ball.

After earning his graduate degree during the offseason, Johnson had a major decision to make. Should he continue his career while still in the prime of his career, or pursue another long-term goal of a career in education?

Instead of heading for the bright lights of San Francisco, Jim Johnson had made the decision to retire from the game of baseball. The Johnson family left for a remote town in Central Michigan where Jim served as a schoolteacher and principal while his wife Mary taught sixth grade in Evart, Michigan.

Over the ensuing years Johnson took on similar administrative positions at Kent City High and South Haven High, both in Michigan. In 1983, at the age of 38, Jim reached the pinnacle of his educational career by returning to his hometown of Muskegon to become Superintendent of North Muskegon High School.

Although he had retired from the game, Johnson never lost his love for the game of baseball. His extensive duties in education limited his active baseball participation, but he often took his family, which now included a second son Joel, the short two-hour drive to take in games at Comiskey Park in Chicago.

Johnson often returned to Western Michigan to play in the university's annual old-timers/varsity exhibition game in late fall. His son Jimmy recalled one time: "It was interesting – because he was the most popular of all the guys there…Everyone wanted to talk to him – old timers and the current players and coaches. I found that odd. I remember Mike Squires being at one of the games and at the time he was a starter with the White Sox, and I wondered why they didn't want to talk to (Squires) more. I actually asked Mr. Squires this question and he said: 'Because your dad was the best to play here.'"

Son Jim remembered his father as rarely talking about his baseball accomplishments. "When I was a little older and just entering high school, my dad was asked by Walt Gawkowski if he would play for his City League team one game as his team was short of players. My dad was probably 36 or 37… right before he got sick …. and to my knowledge had not lifted a bat competitively in years and definitely had not pitched.

"I remember for the first time in my life I really understood that my dad could 'really play.' He pitched/threw strikes/threw hard/dominated in the couple innings he pitched. He went 3-for-3 at the plate and they were just BB's up the middle. He stole bases and looked fast."

"After the game we went home, had dinner, did the dishes, homework, never discussed the game. That was how he was… he just wanted to be Jim Johnson, the father/husband/superintendent. But I got clues every now and then that he was that 'plus,' a pretty good ball player. I always respected that humility," reflected a proud son.[30]

Jim Johnson passed away from pancreatic cancer on December 6, 1987 at 42. Shortly thereafter the baseball field at North Muskegon High was renamed: James B. Johnson Baseball Field. He was inducted into the Greater Muskegon Hall of Fame in 1992; his acceptance speech was eloquently given by his son Jimmy. He was inducted into the WMU Athletic Hall of Fame in 1997.

Author's note

Your author would be remiss if I didn't point out that I married Jim Johnson's widow Mary in October of 1991. I am honored to make known that Jim retired from baseball well before his prime with a 1-0 record, but batted 1.000 as a great teammate, father, husband, and educator, and one well remembered and respected by this author.

SOURCES

Much of the info used in this biography were actual newspaper clippings from three scrapbooks that were kept by his late mother Dorothy during Jim Johnson's baseball career, from Little League to major-league baseball. The actual dates for these clippings were not noted by his mother. Stats for Jim Johnson were accessed through the Minor League Players Encyclopedia at Baseball Reference.com, *The Sporting News*, Retrosheet.org, and the Western Michigan Baseball Media Guide. The following newspapers were used during research for this biography to include *the Muskegon Chronicle, Kalamazoo Gazette, Grand Rapids Press, Western Herald, Rapid City Journal, Rapid City Yearbook of 1966, Deseret News, Amarillo Globe, Arizona Gazette, San Francisco Examiner,* and *Arizona Republic*. Personal information related to this bio were obtained through numerous interviews with Jim's wife Mary, and sons Jim and Joel Johnson.

NOTES

1. Verified by John Winchell, Curator University Archives, Western Michigan University, and in interviews with player's widow Mary in 2021.
2. Mart Tardani, "'Can't Miss' Tag Pinned on Jimmy Johnson," *Muskegon Chronicle,* August 24, 1963.
3. "Johnson Gives One Hit in Win," *Muskegon Chronicle,* July 1960, Johnson Scrapbook.
4. "Wins 1-0 over Kiwanis Nine," *Muskegon Chronicle,* August 13, 1960.
5. "Two Muskegon Hurlers Combine for No-Hitter," *Muskegon Chronicle*, April 12, 1963.
6. Jerry Hagan, Sportitorial, "Muskegon Southpaw Helped Keep Western in Baseball Limelight," *Kalamazoo Gazette*: June 1965.
7. "Johnson Yields One Hit, Broncos Romp," *Kalamazoo Gazette,* April 1965, Johnson Scrapbook.
8. : "Johnson Fans 14 in 8-0 Win," *Muskegon Chronicle,* July 1965 Johnson Scrapbook.
9. Mart Tardani, "Top Award goes to Jim Johnson," *Muskegon Chronicle*, August 17, 1965. Also see Clark Stoppels, "Co-Champs Top All-NBC Club." *Grand Rapids Press*: August 16, 1965
10. Jerry Hagan, Sportitorial, "Jim Johnson: Top Pitcher, Hitter, Outfielder for WMU." *Kalamazoo Gazette,* June 3, 1966.
11. WMU had defeated OSU three times during the regular season, sweeping a three-game series in Columbus. The highlight of the sweep was Johnson hurling a one-hitter against the Buckeyes to hand his veteran coach Charlie Maher his 400th victory as the Broncos' head coach. Bob Wagner, "Broncs Win Pair from OSU – Johnson's One-Hitter Ends Sweep," *Kalamazoo Gazette*, April 3, 1966. Johnson hit .463 that year.

12 Despite his numbers as a pitcher and hitter, Johnson, who led the entire MAC in hitting, was relegated to the 2nd team All-MAC team, depriving him of first team All- MAC in all three seasons as a collegian. See *Western Michigan University Baseball Media Guide*.

13 Tardani, "Top Award goes to Jim Johnson."

14 Retrosheet.org. The five players were Lou Camilli, Danny Thompson, Gary Neibauer, Gary Moore, and Jim Johnson. His 14 stolen bases set a Rapid City franchise record for thefts. See Jerry Hagen, Sportitorial, "Bronco Pitching Ace Now Top Outfielder in Basin League," *Kalamazoo Gazette*, July 11, 1966.

15 Jerry Hagan, Sportitorial, "Bronco Pitching Ace Now Top Outfielder in Basin League," *Kalamazoo Gazette*, July 11, 1966.

16 Roger Towland, "Chiefs Bump Lakers 8-0," *Rapid City Journal*, July 9, 1966: 8.

17 "Johnson Named to All-League Baseball Team," *Muskegon Chronicle*, May 25, 1967.

18 Norm Sheya, "Giants Find Bats; Gloves Still Missing," *Deseret News* (Salt Lake City), June 24, 1967: A5.

19 When he left Salt Lake City, he was not only leading his team in wins and ERA, but his .389 batting average also led the team in hitting.

20 Interview with Jim's wife Mary.

21 "Johnson Beats Angels 7-3, Commodores Win, Lead by 5," *Decatur Herald*, August 27, 1968. 13.

22 Joe Cook, "Commodores Even Playoff Series With 7-1 Victory Over Angels," *Decatur Herald*, September 5, 1968: 15.

23 Len Giles, "Johnson Goes Route In A-Giant Victory," *Amarillo Newspaper*, May 1, 1969, 15.

24 The front office approval was likely not greeted with as much enthusiasm from manager Charlie Fox.

25 Jim McGee, "Reberger's Baffling Pitches," *San Francisco Examiner* March 8, 1970: 2C.

26 "Johnson's Gem Halts Tacomans," *Phoenix Gazette*, June 24, 1970.

27 Bob Eger, "Johnson gets Phoenix Win," *Arizona Republic*, July 4, 1970: 57.

28 Bob Eger, "Giants, Tucson divide 2 games," *Arizona Republic*, July 29, 1970: 71.

29 Bob Eger, "Giants notch 2-1 triumph over Hawaii," *Arizona Republic*, August 11, 1970: 33.

30 Interviews with Johnson immediate family.

JOSH KINNEY

BY JOSH KAISER

Josh Kinney was an unlikely candidate to become a major-league ballplayer. He grew up in rural Pennsylvania and spent most of his time dreaming not of baseball, but of hunting turkeys and deer. He attended a high school that lacked a baseball program, forcing him to commute each afternoon to a neighboring school to play. He might just as easily have entered the family logging business after high school if not for several serendipitous events that led to a baseball career at Quincy University. Even then, when college was finished, he was ready to forgo any future in baseball in order to take a job as a fly-fishing guide. It was only as a favor to his college coach that he tried out for an independent league team at the exact moment that a local scout for the St. Louis Cardinals was desperate to sign capable pitchers to fill roster spots in the low minor leagues. There are other professional players with stories marked by greater obstacles and more unlikely events, but it is hard to argue that Kinney's baseball journey from small-town Little League player to standout reliever for a World Series champion does not make for a compelling narrative.

Joshua Thomas Kinney was born on March 31, 1979 to Tom and Debbie Kinney in Coudersport, Pennsylvania, a small town just south of the New York border. As Kinney would later quip, both Coudersport and nearby Roulette, where he spent his childhood, were located in a part of the country "with more turkeys than people."[1] It was the kind of rural setting that gave plenty of opportunities for outdoor adventure. Kinney loved to hunt and fish and developed an aptitude for working with wood, a knack instilled in him by his father, a logger.[2] It was the beginning of a lifelong love affair with outdoor pursuits, which would later inspire manager Tony La Russa to refer to Kinney as "Daniel Boone."[3]

Along with hunting and fishing, there was also baseball to play. By age 7, Kinney was riding his bike to a friend's house and recruiting him to play catch at the local T-ball field, basking in the carefree joy of throwing a baseball, but also strengthening a pitching arm that would serve him well in later years.[4] After T-ball, it was on to Little League, where Kinney collected a number of trophies, including the Don Hoak Award.[5] He was a fitting recipient: Just as Hoak, who grew up in Potter County, Pennsylvania (of which Coudersport is the county seat), won World Series championships with the 1955 Brooklyn Dodgers and the 1960 Pittsburgh Pirates, so too would Kinney one day serve on a World Series-winning team as a pitcher for the St. Louis Cardinals.

At nearby Port Allegany High School, Kinney played basketball and baseball. His commitment to baseball was especially impressive given that his school lacked a team. Along with a handful of other students, Kinney had to commute 30 minutes each afternoon to a second high school, Oswayo Valley, in order to compete. The commute was worth the trouble: Kinney excelled as a player and won conference co-MVP honors in his senior season.[6]

Kinney threw hard on the mound with good downward movement on his pitches, a fact not lost on a local high-school umpire named Carl Atwell. Atwell moonlighted as an informal scout for his son, Pat Atwell, who led the baseball program at Quincy University in Quincy, Illinois. Carl told Pat about the talented young pitcher he had seen and Pat, trusting his father's judgment, set out to recruit Kinney to play for him at Quincy.[7]

The recruitment process, however, posed challenges. For one thing, it was not clear that Kinney envisioned himself as a college baseball player. Many of his classmates were considering the military or entering the work force directly after high school; attending college was certainly not a given.[8] There was also a second problem: Quincy University, an NCAA Division II school far from Pennsylvania, was completely unknown to Kinney; in fact, he could not even locate Quincy on a map.[9] Pat Atwell worked to overcome these obstacles by connecting personally with Kinney and helping him imagine what a college baseball career might entail.[10] Still, what clinched the deal was something else altogether.

Kinney discovered that Adams County, Illinois, part of a region known as the Golden Triangle, was a mecca for those in pursuit of white-tailed deer. And Quincy, the county seat, was generally regarded as one of the best hunting towns in Illinois – if not the entire country – both for its local amenities and its prodigious population of large whitetails, not to mention its abundance of turkeys and waterfowl.[11] For an avid hunter like Kinney, it was too tempting to resist.[12] "I didn't even go visit Quincy," Kinney remembered, "I enrolled and just winged it. ... I don't think my parents were real happy I made my decision based on deer antlers."[13]

Kinney's talent was evident as a freshman, although his college career got off to an inauspicious start. In his first game, appearing in relief with men on base, he hit the only batter he faced. Upon being removed from the game, Kinney could only watch in dismay as the hit batter came around to score, representing the winning run and making Kinney the losing pitcher of record (as one of his teammates helpfully pointed out).[14]

Despite this rough start and a significant bout of homesickness, Kinney began learning how to control his pitches and to believe in himself on the mound. He could already throw in the 90s with exceptional movement and once he tightened up his volatile windup, his sinker/slider combination became especially deadly. The slider, in particular, was "legendarily nasty," according to Atwell.[15] It was already clear that when Kinney was healthy and focused, he could dominate at any level.

Kinney won three games as a freshman and beginning with his sophomore season he became hard to beat on the mound. All told, he finished his

Josh Kinney. Digital image enhancement by Bob Plant, based on Kinney's 2006 Topps rookie card.

Quincy career with a 22-12 record, leaving school as the leader in innings pitched (291⅓) and strikeouts (229) and contributing mightily to the success of the Hawks in both 1999 and 2000 when they went a combined 85-30.[16]

At the end of his Quincy career, Kinney found himself at a crossroads. Although he had the talent to continue in baseball, he also had a strong desire to return home and take up a position as a fly-fishing guide, a job he had greatly enjoyed during his college summers. As Atwell remembered it, Kinney arrived at his office at the end of the year, packed up and ready to leave for home. Atwell had never asked Kinney for a favor, but on this occasion, he persuaded him to try out for the River City Rascals, an independent Frontier League team in O'Fallon, Missouri.[17] Kinney initially dismissed the suggestion: "I told him I really didn't want to do it."[18] Atwell, however, was insistent: "Try out for me," he implored, to which Kinney finally acquiesced: "I couldn't tell him no."[19]

It was no surprise to Atwell when Kinney proceeded to make the Rascals squad as a 22-year-old starting pitcher. His time there was brief, but not due to underperformance. In three games, he went 1-0 with a 1.71 ERA and 18 strikeouts in 21 innings pitched. As it happened, Scott Melvin, a scout for the St. Louis Cardinals, lived in Quincy and had seen Kinney pitch on several occasions. He asked Atwell if Kinney would consider signing with the Cardinals; Atwell answered affirmatively. Melvin next called Kinney directly and in short order signed him as an undrafted free agent. As Kinney remembered it, his signing bonus amounted to a prime rib sandwich and a plane ticket.[20] Nevertheless, it was a dream come true. Kinney had made it into a major-league organization, and not just any organization, but the one his family had rooted for during his childhood.[21]

As with many young players, Kinney's signing marked the beginning of a peripatetic and perennially uncertain minor-league existence. He was signed to fill a roster spot for the summer, beyond which nothing was guaranteed. However, Kinney did well in his first assignment with the New Jersey Cardinals in the New York–Penn League in the summer of 2001. After only three games (5⅔ innings pitched, five strikeouts, zero runs) he was promoted to Class-A Peoria, for whom he accumulated a 4.39 ERA over 41 innings to finish the season.

Kinney showed even more promise in 2002 as a 23-year-old, pitching for the high Class-A Potomac (Virginia) Cannons (2.29 ERA and 42 strikeouts in 55 innings), before blossoming further in a 2003 season split between the high Class-A Palm Beach Cardinals and the Double-A Tennessee Smokies (Knoxville). In 81 innings for the two teams, he went 5-1 with a 1.11 ERA and 83 strikeouts against only 22 walks. His success not only put him firmly on the Cardinals' internal radar, but earned him recognition in the larger baseball community as he appeared for the first time in the 2004 *Baseball America* preseason rankings of the Cardinals' top prospects.

Kinney's time in the minors was a process of development and maturation, both professionally and personally. He willingly accepted instruction at each step of his journey and relied on a strong work ethic, instilled by his parents, to maximize his talent.[22] He took a relentless approach to his pitching craft, even seeing it as a kind of selfish pursuit, albeit a necessary one in order to play baseball at a high level. "I don't know how to describe it other than that," he said. "You've got to be committed to the game – the work … and I've always been good with that."[23]

After a subpar 2004 season (64 innings, 5.34 ERA) pitching for Palm Beach and Tennessee, Kinney rebounded in 2005. Pitching now for the Double-A Springfield Cardinals, he put up exceptional numbers (42 innings pitched, 1.29 ERA, 11 saves, and 42 strikeouts) and had an equally outstanding visit to the local Bass Pro Shop one day where he met his future wife, Jorni. Although he left Springfield behind after a promotion to Triple-A Memphis by season's end, he would eventually return to settle there with his family at the conclusion of his career.[24]

The 2006 season was surely the pinnacle of Kinney's career, although at the time it seemed to be just the beginning of a steady ascent. He started the year in Memphis, accumulating a 1.52 ERA and 76 strikeouts in 71 innings, which was good enough to earn him a place as a Triple-A All-Star. His pitching coach claimed at the time that Kinney's breaking pitches gave him "the best stuff in our league."[25] The question, however, was how that "stuff" would play at the next level. Kinney would find out in early July. In an interview that year, his father, Tom, recounted the early morning call, around 2:00 a.m., when his son informed him of the good news. The elder Kinney did not sleep the rest of the night. How could he? His son was headed to the majors.[26]

Officially called up on July 2, 2006, Kinney entered his first game the next day for a division-leading Cardinals club playing the Atlanta Braves on the road. He threw his first pitch in the bottom of the seventh inning, trailing 5-3, and avoided the ignominy of hitting the first batter, as he had done in college. Still, the result was no better: Braves left fielder Ryan Langerhans deposited the ball over the right-field fence for a home run.

It was a tough way to begin a major-league career, but there was a certain justice to the proceedings. After all, as Kinney scrambled to arrange a game ticket for his sister on short notice, it was Langerhans, of all people, who offered one of his own through their mutual agent.[27] Having repaid his debt to Langerhans, Kinney rebounded in the inning, retiring the side, and pitched a second scoreless inning which included his first major-league strikeout.[28]

Kinney pitched in nine more games that July, allowing runs in four of them, and was optioned back to Memphis on August 1. Crucially, however, the Cardinals recalled him on September 5 to bolster the bullpen for the stretch run. This time, Kinney's success in Triple A carried over to the big-league club. He appeared in 11 games (several in high-leverage situations) and surrendered only two earned runs while striking out 10. His performance not only earned him a place on the playoff roster, but a favored position in Tony La Russa's bullpen hierarchy during the postseason.

In the National League Division Series, against the San Diego Padres, Kinney appeared in high-leverage situations in Games Two and Four, surrendering zero hits and earning two holds. In the National League Championship Series against the New York Mets, he appeared in Games Two, Three, and Five, pitching 3⅓ innings and earning a win (Game Two) and a hold (Game Five) without allowing a run. In Game Two, in particular, Kinney showed his poise, entering a 6–6 game in the bottom of the eighth and working around a single and walk before inducing a double-play groundball from Carlos Beltrán. Thanks to an improbable home run from So Taguchi off dominant Mets closer Billy Wagner, Kinney earned the sole postseason win of his career.

Kinney's season culminated with two more appearances in the World Series against the Detroit Tigers. His work in Game Four helped preserve a narrow Cardinals lead in the seventh inning, a game they won 5-4. All told, Kinney pitched 6⅓ innings in the postseason, allowing no runs and striking out six.

The future looked bright for Kinney in the afterglow of his World Series success. Derrick Goold of the *St. Louis Post-Dispatch* remarked on Kinney's "durable arm" and "electric breaking stuff" and said he had "the makeup of a setup man."[29] It was not just the St. Louis journalists who were high on Kinney's future with the Cardinals. The 2007 *Baseball America Prospect Handbook* ranked Kinney the ninth best prospect in the Cardinals system, mentioning his "fearless approach and his ability to generate strikeouts and grounders" and viewing him as a "key cog" in the bullpen going forward.[30]

In an alternative reality, Kinney became a shutdown setup man – perhaps even the closer – for the defending champion Cardinals; as it happened, such possibilities never materialized as Kinney injured his arm in the run-up to the 2007 season and had Tommy John surgery in March. He celebrated the Cardinals' 2006 World Series championship with his teammates on Opening Day 2007, but it was bittersweet: he knew he would be unavailable for the entire season. "It was a disappointment," he said. "I felt like a bum. Here I was riding around in a convertible … with my arm brace on, just a week out of surgery and miserable. You're not a part of the team and it wasn't a glamorous first Opening Day for me."[31]

In typical Kinney fashion, he diligently worked his way through rehab during the 2007 season and looked to be on the path to full health when he fractured his elbow in August during a routine throwing session. This second injury meant that not only would he miss the 2007 season, but almost the entire 2008 season as well. There was doubt about whether he would make it back at all.[32]

Kinney managed to return briefly in September 2008, pitching seven innings, and he attended spring training in 2009 competing for a spot in the Cardinals bullpen. Pitching coach Dave Duncan commented on the "remarkable" nature of Kinney's career up to that point. "Stop and think where he was in 2005. And before that, independent league. Throw-away pitcher. He persevered."[33] "I'm not a quitter," Kinney remarked. "I was bound and determined that no matter what, I was going to prove to myself and my family that I could get back on the field."[34]

Kinney fulfilled his vow to return by making the big-league club out of spring training in 2009, although he was unable to solidify a spot in the bullpen. He appeared in only 17 games for the Cardinals, spending considerable time at Triple-A Memphis. Nevertheless, he did achieve a career milestone in 2009: his first regular-season victory.

The victory occurred on June 27 just after Kinney had been recalled. The Cardinals faced the Minnesota Twins on a hot day at Busch Stadium and called upon Kinney in the top of the third inning, trailing 3-2. Kinney dutifully recorded two outs to finish the inning and then watched from the dugout as Albert Pujols, at the height of his powers, blasted a two-run homer to make the score 4-3 Cardinals.

After another run scored later in the inning, Kinney found himself pitching the top of the fourth with a 5-3 lead; he got two more outs before leaving the game. His final line was not overly impressive – 1⅓ innings, two hits – but he earned his first and what would be his only regular-season major-league victory to complement his single postseason victory.[35]

Kinney would remain an effective reliever into his 30s, despite battling further injuries (a shoulder impingement in 2010 and a stress fracture in 2013). In 2010, pitching for Triple-A Memphis, Kinney recorded a 1.80 ERA in 60 innings with 17 saves, helping the Redbirds advance to the Pacific Coast League championship. In 2011, having signed as a free agent with the Chicago White Sox, he pitched for the Triple-A Charlotte Knights (61⅔ innings, 2.77 ERA, 66 strikeouts, 17 walks) for much of the season, and earned an August call-up to the White Sox, for whom he pitched 17⅔ innings. "It's been a long road for me in my career," Kinney commented wryly.[36] In fact, at the finish of the 2011 season Kinney had tallied 21 innings in independent ball and over 550 innings in the minor leagues. He had missed almost two complete seasons due to injury. His 65 innings in the major leagues were a testament to his can-do attitude. "My dad always told me I could do anything I wanted to if I put my mind to it," Kinney said in an interview. "He was right."[37]

Then 33 years old, Kinney signed a one-year contract with the Seattle Mariners for the 2012 season, pitching first for Triple-A Tacoma and then for the Mariners, where he displayed a strong 10-to-1 strikeout-to-walk ratio in 32 innings. He also earned his first career save, which came after a three-inning outing against (once again) the Twins. Seattle manager Eric Wedge asked Kinney after the game whether it really was his first career save. "I was like, 'First what?,'" Kinney said, "I really didn't have any idea it was a save, so it was pretty cool."[38] As of 2022 Kinney still held the distinction of being the only major-league player to earn, in order, a postseason win, a regular-season win, and a regular-season save.

Kinney's injury-marred 2013 season saw him pitching only 33 innings for Tacoma. In 2014 he joined the Pittsburgh Pirates organization, but never earned a promotion from the Triple-A Indianapolis Indians. With no one expressing interest in Kinney's services after the 2014 season, he retired at age 35, content with his accomplishments and excited about the life ahead of him.[39] He finished his 93-game major-league career with a 1-3 record, a 4.73 ERA, 94 strikeouts in 97 innings pitched, one save, and a magical 6⅓ innings of scoreless ball in the 2006 postseason when he helped the St. Louis Cardinals become World Series champions.

Whatever regret Kinney has from a playing career marked by injury is difficult to discern. He told a sportswriter he missed the camaraderie of the clubhouse. But he added that he relished his role as a husband and father to four children and enjoyed the variety of life in Springfield, Missouri. He owns Cardinal Country Logging & Sawmill, following in the tradition of his father. He spends time doing the things he has loved since childhood: hunting and fishing, working with wood, and enjoying friends and family.

SOURCES

In addition to the sources cited in the Notes, the author consulted Baseball-Reference.com for statistical data and game notes and YouTube.com for game footage.

NOTES

1. David Adam, "Sunday Conversation with Josh Kinney," *Quincy* (Illinois) *Herald-Whig*, May 22, 2016, https://www.whig.com/archive/article/sunday-conversation-with-josh-kinney/article_2092d491-038e-5fc3-b3f6-43684477c0b7.html, accessed January 12, 2022.
2. Adam.
3. Pat Atwell, telephone interview, November 18, 2021.
4. Lori Chase, "Kinney Still Has Passion for the Game," *Potter Leader-Enterprise* (Coudersport, Pennsylvania), August 15, 2014, https://www.tiogapublishing.com/potter_leader_enterprise/sports/kinney-still-has-passion-for-the-game/article_32c691b4-2431-11e4-aece-0014bcf887a.html#tncms-source=signup, accessed January 12, 2022.
5. Chase.
6. Port Allegany High School, *Tiger Lilly 98* (Port Allegany, Pennsylvania: 1998), 129.
7. Atwell interview.
8. Atwell interview.
9. Adam.
10. Atwell interview.
11. Jeffrey Dorsey, "Quincy Area in Top Ten for Best Places to Hunt," *100.9 The Eagle*, June 10, 2015, https://10.theeagle.com/quincy-area-in-top-ten-for-best-places-to-hunt/, accessed January 12, 2022.
12. Adam.
13. Adam.
14. Atwell interview.
15. Atwell interview.
16. Atwell interview. Riley Martin eclipsed Kinney's career strikeout total in 2021. See Will Conerly, "Martin Becomes QU's Strikeout King, Hawks Top USI 3-2," Quincy University Hawks Baseball Webpage, March 19, 2021, https://quhawks.com/news/2021/3/19/baseball-martin-becomes-strikeout-king-hawks-top-usi.aspx, accessed January 12, 2021.
17. Atwell interview.
18. Adam.
19. Adam.
20. Adam.
21. Although Kinney's affections tended toward the Pittsburgh Pirates – he often imagined himself in a Pirates uniform during backyard Wiffle Ball games – the Cardinals were in the Kinney family blood ever since his great-grandfather spent time in St. Louis as a bottle maker before returning to Pennsylvania. See Kary Booher, "Kinney Not About to Hang It Up," *Springfield* (Missouri) *News-Leader*, February 3, 2014, https://www.news-leader.com/story/sports/baseball/Springfield-Cardinals/2014/02/04/kinney-not-about-to-hang-it-up/5197395/, accessed January 12, 2022.
22. "Catching Up with Josh Kinney," March 11, 2007, https://www.milb.com/news/gcs-190115, accessed January 12, 2022.
23. Lori Chase, "Kinney Gets the Call from ChiSox," *Port Sports* (Port Allegany, Pennsylvania), August 25, 2011, https://portsports.wordpress.com/category/pahs-sports/baseball/, accessed January 12, 2022.
24. Atwell interview.
25. Derrick Goold, "Going Looper: Seeking an Alternative Starter," *St. Louis Post-Dispatch*, December 6, 2006, https://www.stltoday.com/sports/baseball/professional/birdland/going-looper-seeking-an-alternative-starter/article_cea1fb57-2c25-5c9d-b350-6a31a598f9ac.html, accessed January 12, 2022.
26. Neil Linderman, "Port Allegany's Kinney in World Series," *Potter Leader-Enterprise*, October 25, 2006, https://www.tiogapublishing.com/potter_leader_enterprise/sports/

27 Atwell interview.

28 After Kinney struck out Andruw Jones on a ball in the dirt, the ball was flipped into the Braves dugout where a batboy retrieved it and subsequently threw it into the crowd as a souvenir. Kinney's roommate, attending the game, immediately left his seat, talked his way through security, and found the boy who had caught the souvenir ball. After a brief negotiation involving a $50 bill, Kinney's roommate returned to his seat, triumphant, with ball in hand. Atwell interview.

29 Goold.

30 Jim Callis, Will Lingo, John Manuel, eds., *Baseball America Prospect Handbook* (Durham, North Carolina: Baseball America, 2007), 373.

31 Rick Hummel, "Kinney Relishes Opening Day," *St. Louis Post-Dispatch*, April 3, 2009, https://www.stltoday.com/sports/kinney-relishes-opening-day-a-postseason-hero-for-the-cardinals-in-2006-championship-run-reliever/article_513bc08f-f24d-566e-9532-1ee8900cd978.html, accessed January 18, 2022.

32 Hummel.

33 Hummel.

34 Hummel.

35 Kinney also recorded his first (and only) major-league at-bat, striking out on three pitches.

36 Sahadev Sharma, "Sox's Kinney Thrown into the Fire." ESPN.com: Chicago White Sox Report, August 20, 2011, https://www.espn.com/blog/chicago/white-sox/post/_/id/7068/soxs-kinney-thrown-into-the-fire, accessed January 18, 2022.

37 Adam.

38 Geoff Baker, "Josh Kinney Works Late for First Career Save," *Seattle Times*, August 19, 2012, https://www.seattletimes.com/sports/mariners/josh-kinney-works-late-for-first-career-save-mariners-notebook/, accessed January 28, 2022.

39 Adam.

BRANDON KNIGHT

BY STEVE SISTO

Brandon Knight is on the list of major-league pitchers who have just one career win, but his life and career go far beyond that unique distinction. In addition to being a major leaguer, he was an Olympic athlete who represented the United States, and he also enjoyed a successful baseball career overseas in both Japan and South Korea.

Knight was born in Oxnard, California, on October 1, 1975, to Michael Knight, a Navy equipment buyer, and Tahnee Knight, a trust officer. A brother, Trevor, was born in 1978.[1]

Baseball became a passion for Knight early on: "The only organized sport I played was baseball," he said. "I played all the other sports with the neighborhood kids but stuck to baseball. Wanted to play football in high school but my dad talked me out of it."[2] Those he counted among his favorite athletes as a kid were "Steve Sax, Magic Johnson, Don Mattingly, Will Clark, and Roger Craig. … I liked guys who had reputations as hard workers and great competitors."[3]

He attended Buena High School in Ventura and won the junior-varsity league batting title his sophomore year. He was promoted to the varsity in his junior year and was the starting second baseman.[4] He posted a team-leading .391 batting average and also pitched, putting up a 0.96 ERA over 31 innings, which earned him a selection to the All-Ventura County Team.[5] As a senior he went 6-2 with a 2.05 ERA.[6] That summer (1993), he was drafted as a second baseman by the Colorado Rockies in the 55th round of the Amateur Draft, but did not sign.

Instead, Knight attended nearby Ventura College, where he remained a two-way player. In his freshman year, he hit .343 with 24 RBIs and went 4-3 with a 3.48 ERA and a team-leading two complete games from the mound.[7] He was again selected by the Rockies, in the 51st round of the June 1994 Amateur Draft, again as a second baseman, but he did not sign this time either. In December 1994, he signed a letter of intent to play baseball at the University of Southern California starting in 1996.[8]

In 1995, his sophomore year, Knight quickly emerged as Ventura College's ace pitcher, going 14-3 and setting a school record with 10 complete games.[9] "It's not so much of a surprise," Knight said of his success on the mound. "I worked real hard. I've been hitting spots and changing speeds. My change has been really effective. Before this year, I didn't throw much of a change."[10]

"He's your typical power pitcher," said coach Don Adams. "He has a live arm and he has control. He worked hard in the offseason to make it stronger."[11]

Knight was also Ventura College's best offensive player, leading the team with a .446 batting average, 24 RBIs, and 10 doubles.[12] At the end of the season, he was named Western State Conference Player of the Year.[13]

In June 1995 Knight was drafted for the third consecutive year, this time by the Texas Rangers in the 14th round, No. 374 overall. This time he signed a contract, passing up USC. The Rangers decided to make Knight a full-time pitcher, and it was not easy for him to give up hitting: "I remember sitting in dugouts between starts, knowing there were guys I could hit better than. … It took a while to accept 'You're a pitcher.'"[14] His first year, he went 6-3 with a 3.51 ERA and 63 strikeouts in 66⅔ innings with the Class-A Charleston RiverDogs and the Rookie League Gulf Coast Rangers. He started 1996 with the Class-A Advanced Port Charlotte Rangers, but after losing his first six decisions was sent down to the Hudson Valley Renegades, the Rangers' Class-A short-season team.[15] "My fastball was up in the zone, my curveball was nonexistent, I was behind in the count and I didn't have much of a changeup," Knight said. "Overall, it was horrible. After the first couple games I kept thinking it would get better, but it kept not getting better."[16]

He managed to get things back on track a bit, going 4-4 in his last eight decisions, and in 1997 he was back with Class-A Port Charlotte. That spring, he began developing a new slider and even got advice from Rangers closer John Wetteland. "Wetteland changed my grip for the slider the way he's thrown it and that's made it more effective for me," Knight said in a 1997 newspaper interview. "Now I can throw it more like a fastball."[17]

The new changes seemed to help him; he went 7-4 with a 2.23 ERA and 91 strikeouts in 92⅔ innings with Port Charlotte before being promoted to the Double-A Tulsa Drillers in June.[18] "Basically I'm just happy that it's all kind of come together," Knight said in the 1997 interview. "Last year was a big struggle for me. I just all of a sudden lost everything that I had ever learned."[19] He went 6-4 with a 4.50 ERA over the rest of the season in Tulsa. In November, he was one of six players added to the Rangers' major-league roster.[20] Two months later, he and the Rangers agreed on another one-year contract.[21]

Knight began 1998 with Tulsa and was promoted to the Triple-A Oklahoma RedHawks in June after going 6-6 with a 5.11 ERA, but then things took a turn for the worse.[22] He went 0-6 with a 10.01 ERA as a starter for the RedHawks and was moved to the bullpen for the remainder of the season, finishing 0-7 with a 9.74 ERA. His struggles were attributed to his upright pitching motion, which made it difficult to keep the ball down in the zone.[23] "He reached the conclusion that he was going to have to make a dramatic change in his delivery to have command down in the strike zone," said Rangers assistant general manager Dan O'Brien. "It's one thing to say you're going to change your delivery. It's another thing to be committed to changing your delivery."[24]

That offseason, Knight and the Rangers again agreed on a one-year deal.[25] His new pitching motion seemed to help him in 1999; he posted a 9-8 record with a 4.91 ERA while playing for Oklahoma. His strikeout rate dropped from 7.2 per nine innings to 5.4, but his walk rate improved significantly, falling from 4.0 to 2.6.

In December 1999 Knight and fellow minor-league pitcher Sam Marsonek were traded to the New York Yankees in exchange for outfielder Chad Curtis.[26] Part of the reason Knight was included in the deal was so the Rangers wouldn't lose him for $50,000 in the coming Rule 5 draft, for which he was eligible.[27] He started 2000 with the Yankees' Triple-A Columbus Clippers and went 10-12 with a 4.44 ERA. Knight led the International League with 184⅔ innings pitched and led all the minor leagues with eight complete games. He came close to making his first major-league start on July 8 against the New York Mets, but was passed up in favor of former Cy Young Award winner Dwight Gooden, then 35, who had signed with the Yankees a month earlier.[28] That December, Knight was selected by the Minnesota Twins with the second pick in the Rule 5 draft, but was returned to the Yankees before the 2001 season began.[29]

Knight started 2001 with Columbus but was called up to the Yankees in early June with plans for him to serve in long relief.[30] "We just flew right in and it seemed like I was almost eye level with the World Trade Center and the Empire State Building," Knight told a local sportswriter about his first time arriving in New York. "I saw all the high rises. It hit me then. ... I'm staying in a hotel in Manhattan and I'm taking my first subway trip. I'm getting the whole experience in one day so far. I walked into the stadium today. I'm not a really excitable guy, but I'm about to jump out of my shoes right now."[31]

Knight made his major-league debut on June 5, 2001, against the Baltimore Orioles. He struck out the first batter he faced, Jerry Hairston, but then gave up back-to-back homers to Brady Anderson and Mike Bordick. Over four innings, he gave up four earned runs and eight hits while striking out four in the Yankees' 10-3 loss. "I remember jogging to the mound at a sold-out Yankee Stadium. I made sure to take it all in. I didn't keep my head down and try to block it out, I wanted to absorb the whole experience. As I was throwing my warm-up pitches the crowd started cheering really loud. I turned and looked at the scoreboard and it said I was making my debut. That was really cool."[32]

"He got his feet wet," Yankees manager Joe Torre said of Knight's outing.[33]

Knight's next appearance came four days later, on June 9. He entered in the top of the ninth inning with the Yankees trailing the Atlanta Braves 8-6. He gave up two home runs in the inning and the Yankees lost 10-6. After five innings of work in the major leagues, Knight had allowed four home runs and his ERA was 10.80. "This is a chance for me to show what I can do," Knight said. "The home runs have got to stop. I need to get groundballs. This isn't a team that can wait for you to develop. It wants results now."[34]

Five days later, Knight was back in Columbus.[35] He continued to put up impressive numbers in the minors, going 12-7 with a 3.66 ERA and 173 strikeouts, which led the International League. In September, he was called back up to the Yankees.[36] He came in as a reliever in the third inning on September 22 against the Orioles and allowed three earned runs in 1⅓ innings. A week later, again facing the Orioles, he gave up three earned runs, including a home run, over 4⅓ innings. After four major-league outings totaling 10⅔ innings, Knight had a 10.13 ERA and no decisions. When the regular season ended, he was not put on the Yankees' postseason roster.[37]

Knight got an invitation to spring training in 2002 but was cut on March 11 and sent to the Yankees' minor-league camp.[38] "The inevitable came a little earlier than I expected," he said. "But I understand. If you don't, you're a moron. I'm not upset at them for doing what baseball teams have been doing for years. All you can do is play hard and give them a reason to bring you up. ... They know I'm going to work my butt off, no matter what. Last year, when I got my cup of coffee, it was a big deal. I was just happy to be there. But when I came back in September, that feeling kind of left me. I wanted to pitch. I was done with, 'Oh, it's great to be here. "I wanted the damn ball."[39]

Knight was back in Columbus to start the 2002 season, and the Yankees decided to convert him into

Brandon Knight. Courtesy of The Topps Company.

a closer. "He's got a very good arm," Mark Newman, the Yankees vice president of baseball operations, said in May. "He throws 97, he's got a slider, and he's athletic and competitive. ... We'll see, maybe it's a new life for him. He never could get over the hump as a starter. We don't want to get too geeked about it yet, but it's been good so far."[40]

"This is kind of fun," Knight said about his new role. "You get to play every day and I always liked that."[41] The move worked out for Knight, who collected 12 saves while compiling a 3.90 ERA with Columbus. His newfound success earned him a call-up to the Yankees in early July.[42] He pitched eight innings over six relief appearances for the Yankees, giving up six earned runs, walking four and striking out six. He held his opponents to a .207 batting average and a .483 slugging percentage.

Knight was sent back down to Columbus on August 8 but was back with the Yankees less than a month later when rosters expanded.[43] In his lone appearance in September, he gave up five runs on five hits and a walk to the Chicago White Sox, recording only two outs. The outing raised his ERA to 11.42. The Yankees made the playoffs again in 2002, but once again, Knight was not on the postseason roster. After 11 appearances over two years in the major leagues, he had yet to get a decision as a pitcher.

In January 2003, the Yankees sold Knight's contract to the Fukuoka Daiei Hawks of the Japan Pacific League.[44] "First year in Japan," Knight said, "I thought to myself, 'Oh, my God. What did I do? I shouldn't be here.'"[45] He went 6-4 with a 4.86 ERA in 16 starts for the first-place Hawks. He pitched in Game Four of the 2003 Japan Series against the Hanshin Tigers, giving up three runs in five innings and ending with a no-decision in the Hawks' loss. (The Hawks won the Series in seven games.) The next season Knight became a reliever for the Hawks, compiling a 12.00 ERA in six appearances. After the season he signed a one-year contract with the Hokkaido Nippon-Ham Fighters, also of the Pacific League, for 2005.[46] The deal was worth 40 million yen, plus a 10 million yen signing bonus, equivalent to approximately $450,000. He pitched to an 0-2 record and 11.12 ERA in two starts and six relief appearances.

In 2006 Knight was back in the United States after signing a minor-league deal with the Pittsburgh Pirates.[47] He started the season with the Double-A Altoona Curve and quickly became the team's go-to closer, at one point pitching 20⅓ innings over 12 outings without giving up a run.[48] He finished the season with an Eastern League-leading and franchise record 27 saves, in addition to a 2-7 record and 2.25 ERA.

After not getting any major-league interest before the 2007 season, Knight considered retiring from baseball, until he got a call from Brett Jodie, director of player procurement for the Somerset Patriots of the independent Atlantic League.[49] "He asked if I was still interested in playing," Knight said. "I said I was thinking about it. I wouldn't mind. I certainly didn't think that at 31 years old I was done."[50]

Founded in 1998, the Atlantic League has eight teams and is viewed as a steppingstone to the major leagues or, in the case of players like Knight, a path to getting back to the majors. "All the times when guys say they would play for free, that's what you're doing here," Knight said. (Players in the Atlantic League typically earn between $800 and $3,000 a month.) "It's almost like some kind of baseball camp where you're paying to play. But it certainly isn't all about money. We're all here playing and trying to move on and play someplace else."[51]

Knight ended up joining Somerset and made his mark immediately. In his first appearance, he was told he was going to be the starter just three hours before the game. In his second appearance, he was brought in during the sixth inning with the bases loaded and no outs with his team down 7-3. He escaped the inning unscathed, and the Patriots ultimately won the game. "He won us that game in Lancaster," Patriots manager Sparky Lyle said. "He got us out of that bases-loaded jam when nobody else could throw the ball over the plate. When he came out of the bullpen, I said, 'This is what you do.' And he said, 'You're right.'"[52]

"Surprise doesn't suit me well because I've been starting for 11 years," Knight said, "but if you can't get up for a situation like the other night, there's something wrong."[53]

Knight was initially brought on to the Patriots as a reliever, but within a month he was moved to the starting rotation.[54] "I like him on the mound all the time," said second baseman Danny Garcia. "In the beginning of the game, the end of the game, it doesn't matter. He's got good stuff."[55]

The Patriots made it to the Atlantic League championship in 2007, losing to the Newark Bears.[56] Knight finished the year with a 12-5 record and a 4.03 ERA in 91⅔ innings pitched. "Baseball is a whole heck of a lot better than I expected," he said at the time. "I knew this was basically the best league as far as talent-wise, but I really did not realize how well some of the competition was going to be."[57]

The 2008 season was one of the most successful years of Knight's career in terms of activity and achievements. He re-signed with the Patriots in March and started the season 0-2 with a 2.56 ERA over six starts but led the league with 50 strikeouts.[58] In May, Knight returned to major-league baseball after signing a contract with the New York Mets.[59] "I'm glad I stuck it out because it obviously paid off," Knight said of his time in the Atlantic League. "Going to Triple A makes the decision real easy. Of course, they already have their guys who are pitching well, and I'm going to have to work hard."[60]

The Mets sent Knight to the Triple-A New Orleans Zephyrs, where he was 5-1 with a 2.28 ERA and 55 strikeouts in 43⅓ innings. Then in July, he was named to the 2008 US Olympic Baseball team.[61] A week later, he was called up to the Mets, putting his spot on the Olympic team in jeopardy, as Olympians were not allowed to be on major-league rosters.[62] "They're going to do whatever they want in the next couple of weeks," Knight said. "I'm just going to have to let that go. This is the chance of a lifetime. I've already been to the big leagues. From a career standpoint, playing in the big leagues is probably better, but I can't imagine playing in the Olympics is going to hurt my career."[63]

"Major league baseball takes precedence over the Olympics," Mets manager Jerry Manuel said. "He's got some nice options, though."[64]

Knight was given the ball on July 26 against the St. Louis Cardinals, his first start ever in the majors and his first major-league appearance in six years. He lasted five innings, giving up four earned runs with four strikeouts and two walks. He got no decision in the Mets' 10-8 loss to the Cardinals. Two days later, he was designated for assignment, clearing the way for him to join the Olympic team.[65]

At 32, Knight was the oldest player on Team USA, a roster that included future major leaguers like Jake Arrieta, Stephen Strasburg, and Dexter Fowler. He started against South Korea during the group stage, allowing six runs on eight hits, two strikeouts, and two walks in 4⅓ innings, and got no decision as Team USA lost to South Korea, 8-7. His second and final start of the Olympics came on August 19 against Taiwan. Team USA entered the game with a 3-2 record and a spot in the medal round on the line. Knight went 6⅓ innings, giving up two runs on five hits, struck out five, walked two, and got the win as Team USA defeated Taiwan, 4-2, to advance to the medal round. Team USA lost to Cuba in the semifinals but beat Japan to win the bronze medal. "The Olympics were pretty unbelievable," he said. "It was such an unexpected honor for me. I never thought I would have the chance to be on the team at my age. ... Something I'll take with me for the rest of my life."[66]

Knight returned to New Orleans after the Olympics, then was called back up to the Mets in September. After a pair of one-inning relief appearances, it was announced that he would get the start on September 17 on the road against the Washington Nationals. If not for a rainout on the preceding Friday, September 12, Knight likely never would have gotten the nod. That postponement pushed Johan Santana's start to the first game of the doubleheader on Saturday, and Manuel chose to give Jonathan Niese the ball for game two instead of Pedro Martínez, who was the original scheduled starter. Oliver Pérez pitched Sunday, followed by Martínez on Monday, bumping Mike Pelfrey to Tuesday. That created a hole in the rotation for Wednesday, which is how Knight ended up getting the call.[67] Without the rain on Friday, Santana would have been on the mound that night and then again on Wednesday, meaning there would have been no need for Knight to pitch.

September 17 was perhaps the most crucial game of the Mets season up to that point. They entered riding a three-game losing streak and were a half-game behind the Philadelphia Phillies in the NL East, their first time in second place in three weeks. With just 12 games left to play, this was a must-win for the Mets. "At this point, right now, every game counts," Knight said before the game. "That's the way it is in the Olympics. You lose one or two games and you're done. I love it. This is where you want to be."[68]

"I think he's going to do well because I don't think he will be intimidated by any means," said Sparky Lyle. "He's got enough self-control to know what he has to do. This is a big shot for him, but he doesn't have anything to lose. I think he's hungry for it."[69]

Before the game, manager Jerry Manuel joked about what he was expecting from Knight: "Shutout – Nine innings of shutout ball and I won't take anything less."[70] Knight may not have lived up to that lofty goal, but he still delivered a solid outing, allowing two earned runs on six hits, five strikeouts, and four walks in five innings. When he left the game, the Mets were up 7-2. Seven Mets pitchers followed Knight over the next four innings, only two of whom recorded three outs. Another run in the sixth and Carlos Beltrán's solo home run in the eighth provided much-needed insurance runs, and the Mets escaped with a 9-7 victory. Seven years after his major-league debut, Knight had his first major-league win.

"I came out in the fifth inning, I went to the clubhouse and watched the rest of the game from the clubhouse," Knight said. "I don't remember being that nervous, but it wasn't lost on me that it was my first MLB win."[71]

After that game, the Mets went 5-6 in their final 11, finishing the season three games behind the Phillies and missing the playoffs. Knight's win on September 17 proved to be his final major-league appearance. His career statistics were a 1-0 record, 8.62 ERA, 24 strikeouts, and 15 walks in 31⅓ innings across two starts and 13 relief appearances.

"I wasn't even sure if I was going to play that year," Knight said about his 2008 season. "But my wife said, 'Just play one more year. You're going to be mad at yourself if you don't play one more year.' So I play independent ball, then I get picked up by the Mets after a month or two. I was having a good season in Triple A, and that's right around the time that I found out the Olympic team was interested in me. And then I got called up back to the big leagues before heading off to the Olympics. It catapulted me into playing baseball for six more years, after I thought I was going to be done forever."[72]

Knight signed a one-year deal with the Mets in March 2009 but was sent down to the Triple-A Buffalo Bisons during spring training.[73][74] He went 4-9 with a 5.06 ERA in 20 appearances with Buffalo. In July he was released from the Bisons and signed with the Samsung Lions of the Korean Baseball Organization.[75]

"Playing [in Korea] was the best opportunity to provide for my family," Knight said. "Being Triple A, you never know when you might get released for being too old or in the wrong position. When you play in Asia, if you are conducting yourself with class and playing well, you will have a job. That is comforting for someone who has been playing as long as I have."[76]

Over 10 starts with the Lions in 2009, Knight was 6-2 with a 3.56 ERA and 51 strikeouts in 60⅔ innings. In 2010, his first full season in the KBO, he went 6-5 with a 4.54 ERA in 14 starts and seven relief outings. Before the 2011 season, Knight left the Lions and signed with the Nexen Heroes. That season he led the team in nearly every pitching category, including wins (7), losses (15), games started (30), innings pitched (172⅓), and strikeouts (115).

The 2012 season was the best of Knight's career from a statistical standpoint. He had a career-best 16 wins (four losses) and a 2.20 ERA, and he also pitched over 200 innings for the first time. He was selected to the KBO All Star team and he was also a finalist for the MVP award, ultimately losing to teammate ByungHo Park.[77]

In 2013, at the age of 37, Knight started 30 games for the third year in a row, posting a 12-10 record, tied for the team lead in wins, with a 4.43 ERA and a team-high 172⅔ innings pitched. The following year, 2014, was his last: He was released by the Heroes after going 1-2 with a 5.52 ERA in six starts to begin the season.[78] Knight's time in the KBO was the best stretch of his career; he compiled a 48-38 record with a 3.84 ERA in six seasons.

With his playing career over, Knight said, he didn't have any regrets over how it unfolded, but added: "If I could do it again, I would focus more on preparation, more so mental focus, in those first years. I would've focused a little bit on making sure I was the best pitcher I could be. … I was too content with throwing hard. I fell into the trap of being a 'thrower,' which you don't want to be. I wish I would've focused on actually being a good pitcher."[79]

In 2014 Knight worked as a scout for the KBO's SK Wyverns before being hired back by the Nexen Heroes to be the pitching coordinator for their Futures League affiliate. "I'm super excited and eager to get back to Korea and start working," he said.[80] Two years later, he was promoted to pitching coach for the Heroes.[81] Between 2018 and 2020, the team, now known as the Kiwoom Heroes, finished in the top four or better in ERA and WHIP with Knight as pitching coach. "At the end of the day, all the analytics are a supplement. The bottom line: You have to be able to pitch," Knight said about his pitching philosophy. "If you have good vertical movements but if you can't throw strikes, it doesn't matter. So my main focus is making sure these guys know how to pitch, and then use analytics and data to make their pitches even better."[82]

In 2021 Knight was hired as a pitching coach for the SSG Landers, the team that was previously called the SK Wyverns before they were purchased by the Shinsegae Group. "It'll be fun. It'll give me an opportunity to coach and teach," he said.[83] "Luckily, from a coaching standpoint, I've been in control of the pitching staff from the moment I started."[84]

Knight has been married to his wife, Brooke (Archer), since 2004. They have four children: Brandon Jr., Bastien, Benjamin, and Brinley.[85]

Knight may never have put up huge numbers or received lots of accolades, but he still got to experience things in his baseball career that not many people do: winning a major-league game, winning an Olympic game and a medal, and playing in multiple countries. Ultimately, that's a successful life spent in baseball.

"I never thought this was realistic," Knight said of his baseball career. "It's amazing how this game is, how life is, and how it can all change just like that."[86]

NOTES

1 Author interview of Brandon Knight, October 23, 2021, referred to hereafter as Knight interview.
2 "MyKBO.net Interviews Brandon Knight," MyKBO, August 22, 2012. https://sites.google.com/site/mykbonet/interviews/mykbonetinterviewsbrandonknight
3 MyKBO, 2012.
4 "High School Baseball," *Los Angeles Times*, March 7, 1992: C17.
5 "Valley Sports," *Los Angeles Times*, June 11, 1992: C11.
6 "Junior College Baseball," *Los Angeles Times*, February 3, 1994: C9.
7 "Final Area Junior College Baseball Statistics," *Los Angeles Times*, July 14, 1994: C15.
8 "College Signings," *Los Angeles Times*, December 4, 1994: C11.
9 "College Roundup," *Los Angeles Times*, April 9, 1995: C13.
10 Fernando Dominguez, "Knight Has Two-Edged Sword," *Los Angeles Times*, April 20, 1995: C8-10.
11 Dominguez.

12 Dominguez.
13 "Valley Sports," *Los Angeles Times*, February 2, 1996: C11.
14 Knight interview.
15 "Knight Gets Everything Together," *Los Angeles Times*, May 22, 1997: C10.
16 "Knight Gets Everything Together."
17 "Knight Gets Everything Together."
18 Johnny Paul, "Around the Farm," *Fort Worth Star-Telegram*, June 20, 1997: D5.
19 "Knight Gets Everything Together."
20 "Rangers Increase Roster," *Fort Worth Star-Telegram*, November 21, 1997: C5.
21 "Transactions," *Los Angeles Times*, January 10, 1998: C10.
22 Johnny Paul, "Rangers report," *Fort Worth Star-Telegram*, June 20, 1998: D4.
23 Johnny Paul, "Knight Changes Ways – and Gets Better," *Fort Worth Star-Telegram*, May 2, 1999: C4.
24 Paul.
25 "Transactions," *Austin American-Statesman*, January 20, 1999: D4.
26 T.R. Sullivan, "Ranghers Acquire Curtis," *Fort Worth Star-Telegram*, December 14, 1999: D1.
27 Sullivan.
28 Anthony McCarron, "Doctor Feel Good," *New York Daily News*, August 6, 2000: 86.
29 "Baseball," *Los Angeles Times*, December 12, 2000: D10.
30 Peter Botte, "Mendoza Gets Nod, Knight Receives Call," *New York Daily News*, June 3, 2001: 64.
31 Brian Heyman, "Knight Wants to Enjoy Time with Yankees," *White Plains* (New York) *Journal News*, June 4, 2001: C5.
32 MyKBO.
33 Associated Press, "Orioles Bomb Yankees," *Glens Falls* (New York) *Post-Star*, June 6, 2001.
34 John Delcos, "Yanks' Pen Running Dry," *White Plains* (New York) *Journal News*, June 10, 2001: C5.
35 Associated Press, "Yankees Rough Up Ex-Mate Irabu," *Binghamton New York) Press and Sun Bulletin*, June 14, 2001.
36 "Deals," *Elmira* (New York) *Star-Gazette*, September 5, 2001: B2.
37 "Former 'Gade Left Off Roster," *Poughkeepsie Journal*, October 11, 2001: E4.
38 Anthony McCarron, "For Sterling, There's a Hitch," *New York Daily News*, March 11, 2002: 71.
39 Vic Ziegel, "The Cheers Begin Here," *New York Daily News*, March 31, 2002: 58.
40 "Pen Makes for Good Knight," *New York Daily News*, May 5, 2002: 90.
41 "Pen Makes for Good Knight."
42 Associated Press, "Thome Homers; Yanks Win," *Glens Falls* (New York) *Post-Star*, July 4, 2002.
43 "Clemens Looks Sharp," *Orlando Sentinel*, August 8, 2002: D4.
44 "Transactions," *Los Angeles Times*, January 3, 2003: D18.
45 Knight interview.
46 "Fighters Finalize New Contracts," *Japan Times*, January 18, 2005.
47 "Curve Opens 2006 Season Tonight," *Tyrone* (Pennsylvania) *Daily Herald*, April 6, 2006: 5.
48 "Curve Lose Two to Cats," *Indiana* (Pennsylvania) *Gazette*, June 4, 2006: C4.
49 Melissa Chodan, "Different Talent Pools, Different Rules Mark Independent Leagues," *Bridgewater* (New Jersey) *Courier-News*, August 26, 2007: C4.
50 Chodan.
51 Chodan.
52 Ryan Dunleavy, "Knight Could Help Patriots Bullpen," *Bridgewater* (New Jersey) *Courier-News*, June 12, 2007: C1.
53 Dunleavy, "Knight Could Help."
54 Dunleavy, "Pats Spot Knight Big Early Lead," *Bridgewater Courier-News*, July 18, 2007: C1.
55 Dunleavy, "Pats Spot Knight Big Early Lead."
56 Dunleavy, "Patriots Focused on Season's Successes," *Bridgewater Courier-News*, September 26, 2007: C1.
57 Chodan.
58 "Pats Re-Sign Former Yankee Knight," *Bridgewater Courier-News*, March 12, 2008: C2.
59 Ryan Dunleavy, "Knight, Minix Leaving," *Bridgewater Courier-News*, May 28, 2008: C7.
60 "Knight, Minix Leaving."
61 "Around the Horn," *Bridgewater Courier-News*, July 18, 2008: C3.
62 Ryan Dunleavy, "Knight to Pitch for Mets," *Bridgewater Courier-News*, July 25, 2008: C4.
63 "Knight to Pitch for Mets."
64 Stefan Bondy, "Enjoying a Minor Miracle," *Passaic* (New Jersey) *Herald-News*, July 26, 2008: E5.
65 Ryan Dunleavy, "Knight Designated for Assignment," *Bridgewater Courier-News*, July 28, 2008: C4.
66 MyKBO, 2012.
67 Steve Popper, "Extra rest," *Hackensack* (New Jersey) *Record*, September 14, 2008: S5.
68 David Lennon, "Much Power, but Little to Spare," *Long Island Newsday*, September 18, 2008: A66.
69 Ryan Dunleavy, "It's Knight's Time," *Bridgewater Courier-News*, July 26, 2008: D1.
70 Steve Popper, "Mets Keep Eyes on Prize with Victory," *Hackensack Record*, September 18, 2008: S1.

71. Knight interview.
72. Ben Tully, "BrandonKnight: A One of a Kind Hero," *A Frozen Rope to the Hot Corner*, August 9, 2020. https://frozenropeblog.wordpress.com/.
73. "Transactions," *Hackensack Record,* March 2, 2009: S10.
74. "Transactions," *Rochester Democrat & Chronicle*, March 23, 2009: D2.
75. "Knight Flight," *New York Daily News*, July 27, 2009: 51.
76. MyKBO, 2012.
77. Moon Gwang-lip, "Despite Tough Season, Nexen Has Its Heroes," *Korea JoongAng Daily*, October 3, 2012.
78. Yoo Jee-ho, "Nexen Heroes Bring Back Ex-Pitcher Knight as Minor League Coach," Yonhap News Agency, November 3, 2015. https://en.yna.co.kr/view/AEN20151103005400315.
79. Knight interview.
80. "Nexen Heroes Bring Back Ex-Pitcher Knight as Minor League Coach."
81. Yonhap News Agency, "Ex-U.S. Pitcher Promoted as Pitching Coach for Former KBO Club," *Korea Herald*, July 31, 2017.
82. Yoo Jee-ho, "Armed with Strong Bullpen, American Pitching Coach Confident His KBO Club Will Contend Again," Yonhap News Agency, April 24, 2020. https://en.yna.co.kr/view/AEN20200424002200315.
83. Yoo Jee-ho, "New Coach for Newly Named KBO Team Embraces Opportunity to Teach," Yonhap News Agency, March 17, 2021. https://en.yna.co.kr/view/AEN20210317005200315.
84. Knight interview.
85. Knight interview.
86. "Enjoying a Minor Miracle."

GEORGE KORINCE

BY JERRY NECHAL

There are many stories of famous pitchers, like Satchel Paige or Bob Feller, who began in their youth by throwing rocks or other objects at targets. George Korince's path to becoming a big-league baseball pitcher began the same way. "I was about 9 or 10 years old. I happened to be throwing stones in a pond. My mother saw me and suggested that I go out for baseball. So I did. …"[1] With early success in his native Canada, he became a much acclaimed professional prospect. Korince's major-league career lasted only parts of two seasons with just 11 appearances. Nevertheless, he came away with one big-league victory, success in the minors, and some great memories of playing professional baseball. Years later he reminisced, "[T]hose were probably the best five years of my life, the camaraderie between the guys and the people that I met."[2]

George Korince, the son of George Sr. and Simone Korince, was born on January 10, 1946, in Ottawa, Ontario, one of five children. His father was an autoworker. He moved at an early age with his family to St. Catharines, Ontario. In his formative years Korince became a much-heralded local athlete, except in hockey. "I tried to skate a couple of times. I didn't care for it much, weak ankles."[3]

In youth sports there is often someone who dominates because he is bigger than the rest of the kids. In baseball, that person is frequently the pitcher, who throws harder than his peers. Parents of opposing players may question his age. George Korince was likely that person. He became known as Moose. His hometown paper labeled him as "husky."[4] By the age of 18 Korince was an imposing athlete at 6-feet-2 and 200 pounds. His pitching helped his youth teams win four provincial baseball championships between 1958 and 1962. Former batboy Pat Leahy recalled "[H]e would strike out 11-14 without even thinking about it."[5] At Merritton High School, George was also on the track and basketball teams. He held district records in shot put and javelin.

Korince's moment of outside discovery came in the summer of 1964. Bob Prentice, a Detroit Tigers scout, was in the stands at a tournament game in Toronto between the Merritton Juniors and the Toronto Columbus Boys Club. Korince hurled a no-hitter for Merritton. Impressed, Prentice began to follow him. Within a few months, Korince signed with the Tigers for a $1,500 bonus.

In 1965, when Korince reported to the Tigers for spring training, professional baseball players from Canada were still somewhat of a novelty. Korince's beginning journey generated a lot of attention in his home country. A Canadian Broadcasting Company TV special that followed his first steps in professional baseball, titled *The Tigers That Bloom in the Spring*, was broadcast in April of that year.[6] The Tigers assigned Korince to Jamestown in the Class-A New York-Pennsylvania League. He struggled at the start of the season, going 0-5. Then on May 25 he earned his first professional win, pitching a four-hitter against Geneva. That season Korince worked as both a starter and a reliever. He appeared in 35 games with 13 starts, finishing the season with a 7-11 record and a 3.38 ERA. Most impressive were his 151 strikeouts in 133 innings pitched. At the same time, he exhibited control issues with 96 walks and 13 wild pitches.

One of Korince's catchers that season was future major-league manager Jim Leyland. The two became friends and were known for their playful antics off the field. In the 1960s the path from Canada to the major leagues was challenging. It was generally acknowledged that Canadian prospects were about two years behind their US counterparts, in terms of coaching and skill development. Korince and future Tigers star pitcher John Hiller, a fellow Canadian, discussed the disadvantage in a 1967 *Calgary Herald* interview. Korince confirmed, "I always thought I could throw a curve when I was at home. Hell I didn't even know how to hold the ball."[7] Hiller added, "I remember my coaches … always somebody's father, a nice guy. … But all they could tell you, really, was to pick up the ball and throw it. … The first time I pitched on a mound was after I turned pro. We had no mound in our park at home."[8]

Given these handicaps, the progress of the 20-year-old Korince was remarkable. In the spring of 1966, Tigers manager Charlie Dressen was already interested in him.[9] At the end of spring training Korince was moved up to Double-A Montgomery. There he again dominated batters, leading the Southern League with 183 strikeouts in 182 innings pitched. He also improved his control, issuing fewer bases on balls, 69. By midseason he had already been given a "can't miss" label. Detroit chief scout Ed Katalinas said, "Korince is one of those guys who can make it all the way overnight. He's just a big boy who can throw hard."[10] By September of 1966 Korince was in the big leagues. As a late-season call-up, he made his first major-league appearance pitching the eighth inning on September 10 in a 5-0 loss to the Kansas City Athletics. He struck out the first batter he faced, Phil Roof. After retiring the next batter on a groundout, he hit Bert Campaneris, who then stole second and third. Korince then retired Jim Gosger on a fly ball for a scoreless inning. He made one more appearance on September 24, pitching two scoreless innings in a 12-4 loss to the Twins. He gave up only one hit but walked three batters.

After the season Korince pitched in the Florida Instructional League. There his 3-3 record included a no-hitter. He finished with an ERA of 2.90 while striking out 57 in 59 innings. At same time, he was tutored on throwing the slider. Tigers pitching coach Johnny Sain commented, "He picked up a breaking ball pretty fast. … I was impressed the way Korince put spin on the ball."[11]

In the spring of 1967 Detroit was looking to improve its bullpen. Manager Mayo Smith told reporters, "I have good reports on a number of young pitchers in our farm system and I am eager to look at them, particularly George Korince and Pat Dobson."[12] The *Detroit Free Press* referred to Korince as "the golden boy of the organization."[13] Korince did not disappoint. He put together multiple strings of scoreless relief appearances while finishing spring training with a 1.21 ERA.

That performance vaulted Korince onto the Opening Day major-league roster. At the start of the 1967 season, the 21-year-old Korince was the youngest player on the Tigers team. He was thrilled to be in the majors. "I just can't believe that I am here pitching now," he said. "There's a lot of tension, but I just try to pitch."[14]

A parallel thrill for a young rookie is to appear on a baseball card. In Korince's case this did not happen as expected. He initially appeared on a 1967 Topps Tigers Rookie Stars card with Tommy Matchick. But Topps erroneously put a photo of another Tiger, Ike Brown, on the card instead of Korince. The difference received additional attention in that Korince was Caucasian and Brown was African American. Topps corrected this error by issuing another Tigers Rookie Stars card with Korince's correct picture alongside a different player, Pat Dobson.

Korince started the 1967 season strong. In his first two appearances, he yielded no runs and no

George Korince. Courtesy of the Detroit Tigers.

hits with four strikeouts over three innings. Then on May 13 at Fenway Park, with the Tigers trailing the Red Sox, 5-4, Korince was called upon to pitch the eighth inning. "We were losing at the time so I knew they were going to bring me in to get more experience," he said in a 2012 interview.[15] He issued a walk but held Boston scoreless. Then in the top of the ninth, Detroit rallied to score six runs. The Red Sox retaliated with three runs against Dave Wickersham in the bottom of the inning, but the Tigers held on to post a 10-8 victory. Korince was the winning pitcher in what would be his only big-league decision. No one thought of giving him a game ball. In 2012 Korince recalled, "There was nothing like that then."[16]

The next day, May 14, the teams played a doubleheader and Korince was called from the bullpen in each game. In the opener he retired one batter in an 8-5 loss. This appearance stretched his hitless and scoreless streak to four games and 4⅓ innings. But in the second game, summoned from the bullpen in the second inning, he pitched into the fifth, leaving the game after yielding five hits, five runs, and three walks in a 13-9 loss to the Red Sox.

After this setback, Korince pitched in four more games with mixed results. There were two scoreless appearances. Then, in his last two games he gave up three runs, three hits, and three walks in 2⅓ innings.

On May 28, the day after his last appearance, Korince was optioned to Triple-A Toledo. The second-place Tigers were in a tight pennant race that was not decided until the last game of the season. In 14 innings Korince had an ERA of 5.14, and Detroit did not have the luxury of being patient with a young pitcher who, with a 1.50 WHIP (walks plus hits per innings pitched), was struggling with his control.

At Toledo, Korince reverted to being a starter. He won his first game, allowing two runs in six innings, with six walks and six strikeouts. In his next 10 games, Korince went 1-5. With continued control issues, he was demoted to Montgomery. He finished the season there, improving his control and posting a 2.41 ERA in 41 innings with 39 strikeouts.

But Korince's own season was not finished. He again played in the Florida Instructional League, and there he seemed to find himself. He finished with a 5-0 record, a 1.62 ERA, and 55 strikeouts in 50 innings. Toledo manager Jack Tighe observed that Korince had "improved his curve 100 percent."[17] The Florida Tigers roster included 15 players who would later reach the majors. They captured the Florida Instructional League championship.

At the beginning of 1968, Korince found himself on the Detroit 40-man roster and was given a good chance to make the team. A poor bullpen in 1967 was seen as one of the chief culprits in the team's failure to win the pennant that year. The competition among several young prospects to fill open bullpen slots for 1968 was intense. In the end, Korince did not go north with the team, but was assigned to Toledo. But after appearing in only four games as a reliever while posting a 9.00 ERA with three walks and four strikeouts in two innings, it was again back to Montgomery.

Within a few hours of reporting to the team, Korince picked up a win after 1⅔ innings of scoreless relief. He once more found Double-A ball to his liking. He had another stellar season, primarily as a starter, posting a 13-7 record with a 3.18 ERA. He captured his second Southern League strikeout crown (146 K's in 161 innings) and also was the league leader in complete games. Korince's control also improved; he walked only 58 batters.

Korince also managed a two-day honeymoon after marrying his wife, Gail, with Jim Leyland as his best man. On his return to the team, he threw a 6-0 shutout.

Entering the 1969 season, Korince was still on the 40-man major-league roster. However, he did not last long in spring training; in fact, he was the first player cut. He began the year back at Toledo, and this time he stayed for the season. Used mostly as a reliever, he went 1-4 with a 4.74 ERA. His control remained an issue, with 57 walks in 57 innings.

The 1970 season was Korince's last as a professional. He began once again with Toledo. He started well, with three scoreless appearances, but then arm problems struck. His ERA skyrocketed to 10.80 after five more outings. He was then picked up by the Montreal-affiliated last-place Buffalo Bisons. There Korince pitched in only three games to end his time as a professional player. At the young age of 24, his career was finished. Years later he said, "I had chips in my elbow and my arm was hurting really bad."[18]

Korince's career was brief but not without its accomplishments. Only 10 percent of all who play in the minors ultimately make it to the big leagues. He recorded a major-league victory. He had the opportunity to face future Hall of Famers Mickey Mantle and Carl Yastrzemski. He was a strikeout phenom who led his league twice in that category. Across all levels of play, he averaged an impressive 8.7 strikeouts per nine innings. Finally, as noted earlier, Korince would look back at this time as "probably the best five years of my life."[19]

After baseball, Korince worked in the professional cleaning business and for General Motors. In 2012 he was inducted into the St. Catharines Sports Hall of Fame. As of 2022 he was retired and living in North Fort Myers, Florida.

SOURCES

In addition to the sources cited in the Notes, the author used Baseball-Reference.com.

NOTES

1. "Korince Is Happy to Be in Majors," *Beckley* (West Virginia) *Post-Herald*, May 4, 1967: 2.
2. Bernie Puchalski, "Merritton's Moose Joins St. Catharine's Sport Hall," *St. Catharine's Standard*, May 4, 2012: B2.
3. George Cantor, "Baseball Gold Up in Canada," *Detroit Free Press*, February 20, 1966: Section E.
4. Puchalski.
5. Pat Leahy, telephone interview, February 7, 2022.
6. "The TV Journal," *Ottawa Journal*, April 17, 1965: 15.
7. Paul Rimstead, "In Big League Ball, the American Kid Has a Two-Year Break," *Calgary Herald*, April 29, 1967: 27.
8. Rimstead.
9. "Tigers Open Training Camp," *Sault Sainte Marie* (Michigan) *Evening News*, February 16, 1966: 3.
10. George Cantor, "Crop Is Thin on Tiger Farms," *Detroit Free Press*, July 1, 1966: 36.
11. Watson Spoelstra, "Tigers Turn to Home Remedies to Obtain Some Bull-Pen Relief," *The Sporting News*, December 31, 1966: 33.
12. "95 Victories Enough for Mayo Kayo," *Oneonta* (New York) *Star*, March 30, 1967: 15.
13. "4 Rookie Hurlers Rate Tiger Shot," *Detroit Free Press*, February 22, 1967: 3-D.
14. "Korince Hopes He Can Stick," *Port Huron* (Michigan) *Herald*, May 2, 1967: B-6.
15. Puchalski, "Merritton's Moose Joins St. Catharine's Sport Hall."
16. Puchalski.
17. Watson Spoelstra, "Gladding's Departure Saddens Lolich," *The Sporting News*, December 9, 1967: 36.
18. Puchalski.
19. Puchalski.

JACK KULL

BY JACK V. MORRIS

What do you do, when at the age of 26, you discover you can throw a baseball harder than most professionals? If you're Jack Kull and it's 1908, you go to the local minor-league ballpark, climb a tree and wait until an opposing manager comes out of the ballpark after the game. You then offer your services for free to him. Three times Kull was taken up on his offer. Three times he was auditioned in a regular-season game. And three times he was cut after the game.[1] While this questionable strategy didn't initially work, Kull nonetheless found himself pitching a game for the 1909 Philadelphia Athletics a little more than a year later. Not only was he pitching for the Athletics, he was in a battle against Walter Johnson.

Kull was a large man, standing 6-feet-2 inches and weighing 190 pounds. With a "particularly husky" build, he was a "veritable giant" among his pitching peers.[2] It was easy to see why managers would offer Kull a game-day audition. And why after less than a year of minor-league experience, Connie Mack took a chance on him, even going so far as to say he had a "million dollar arm."[3] He was blessed with "awful speed"[4] but had control issues early on. He conquered those issues as the 1909 season wore on.

Kull's major-league debut was a resounding success, a win in relief against the Big Train. Not only that, he singled off Johnson, driving in two runs and tying the game that the Athletics eventually won. It was also his last game as a major leaguer, giving him a perfect 1-0 pitching record along with a 1.000 batting average and a fielding percentage of 1.000 (when he handled his only chance in the field successfully).

Despite his major-league success, the rest of Kull's baseball career was marked by short stints with ballclubs where he had varying degrees of success, most of it unsuccessful. The few places he did have success, he still found himself being let go. It may have been that Kull had an alcohol problem. In one of the few times in his career when he had sustained success, he was let go for breaking training.[5] Another time he was let go by a team because "he broke the discipline by drink."[6] Ironically, when he was first being noticed, he was compared to Rube Waddell, another power pitcher with a drinking problem.[7] Both pitchers died relatively young of tuberculosis. Kull was penniless at death.

John A. Kull was born on June 24, 1882, in Shenandoah, Pennsylvania, a coal-mining community 108 miles northwest of Philadelphia. The only "official" document that is currently available is his death certificate. It's clear that Kull was an abbreviation for a longer ethnic name despite the fact that his death certificate listed him as John Kull.[8] A newspaper story on his death claimed his last name was Kolonauski, while during his career it was claimed he was born Kolenski.[9] There are no ideal matches for John/Jack Kull/Kolonauski/Kolenski in the various censuses during Kull's life. His father is listed as Andrew Kull on his death certificate.

Jack Kull, as shown in the May 18, 1911 *Trenton Evening Times*.

No ideal matches for Andrew Kolonauski/Kull are found in the censuses as well.[10]

Kull, like most of his neighbors in Shenandoah, worked in the coal mines when he came of age.[11] His name doesn't appear in local newspapers until his tryout with Mount Carmel of the 1908 Atlantic League when he was 26 years old. He didn't make the Mount Carmel team but did pitch in single games with Shamokin, Hazelton, and Pittston, all Atlantic League teams, during the season when he used his unusual approach to be noticed. He was a raw talent – "wild and untamed."[12] He eventually caught on with a semipro team in Shenandoah called the West End Browns.[13]

Based on Kull's arm, in 1909 Pottsville of the Atlantic League gave him a tryout in the spring. Frank Eustace, a veteran ballplayer who had played part of a season with the 1896 Louisville Colonels of the National League, was Pottsville's manager. He gave Kull a tryout when all the other clubs had turned him down.[14] Still there were doubts whether Kull could harness his fastball. One paper remarked that he "has not been developed sufficiently to be used safely on the slab."[15] Another wrote that he "will prove a wonder if he can get any kind of control."[16] He was "by far the speediest twirler who ever played ball in Pottsville."[17]

The Atlantic League season began on May 6. It was a full week before Kull was used by Eustace. He started the game but was knocked out of the box and took the loss. The next two times he got into games, it was in relief, one of which he lost. Finally on May 18, Eustace put Kull in the regular pitching rotation. He responded with a win.

Kull then went on a tear. His next two starts, he pitched back-to-back two-hitters. On June 5 Sam Kennedy, a Philadelphia Athletics scout, was so impressed he signed Kull to a contract with the understanding that he would join the Athletics at season's end. Kennedy called Kull "a dead ringer for 'Rube' Waddell."[18]

Kull continued to pile up wins throughout the season. From June 20 through June 30, he started five games, going 5-0 in 43 innings pitched. He gave up a total of 11 runs during that stretch. When the Atlantic League collapsed on July 21, Kull's record stood at 15-7 in 26 appearances, 23 of them starts. His strikeout-to-walk ratio was approximately 2:1, showing that he was finding the plate in most of his games.[19] As the season wore on, Eustace had increased his workload. From July 4 through July 9, he pitched every day except one. Two of the games were complete-game wins.

Kull was sent to the Fayetteville Highlanders of the Class-D Eastern Carolina League. He continued his torrid pitching. He went 7-2 down the stretch, doing "magnificent work" for Fayetteville.[20] With Fayetteville's season over, he headed to Philadelphia to join the A's.

He reported to the Athletics on September 15 with Philadelphia in a pennant race with the Detroit Tigers. The Athletics pulled within two games of the league-leading Tigers but faded in the last week. On October 2, with the Athletics mathematically eliminated and playing a doubleheader against the Washington Senators, Connie Mack played players he had sitting on his bench who had been signed during the season. Tommy Atkins, the A's starting pitcher, made his debut against Walter Johnson in game one. Also making his debut was Jim Curry at second base, with future Hall of Famer Eddie Collins moving to shortstop for the game. Atkins pitched six innings, giving up four runs before Mack sent in Kull to start the seventh inning with the Senators up, 4-1. After pitching a scoreless top of the seventh, the Athletics started a rally with Kull finding himself in the middle of it. With the bases loaded and one run already in, Kull flared a single to right off Johnson, scoring two runs, tying the game. Morrie Rath followed with a sacrifice fly, giving the A's the lead. Both teams scored single runs in the eighth, then Kull shut down the Senators in the ninth for the win, 6-5.

The future looked bright for Kull. He had beaten Walter Johnson and acquitted himself well not only on the mound but at the bat. But Mack decided Kull needed more seasoning and in February 1910 Kull was released by purchase to Trenton of the Class-B Tri-State League. According to reports, Mack could recall Kull whenever he wanted to.[21] Kull pitched one game before he was released by the pitching-rich Trenton Tigers. So began a cycle of being picked up and then cut in short order for most of the rest of his career. It was reported that he caught on with Scranton of the Class-B New York State League. If he did, he didn't get into a game. On June 28 old friend Frank Eustace, who was coaching Youngstown of the Class-C Ohio-Pennsylvania League, tried to rekindle the magic with Kull the previous season. Instead, Kull went 2-7 and was released in early August. With his release it was reported that he was catching on with a semipro team in Maysville, Kentucky. By September he was pitching for the Alcos, a semipro team from Dunkirk, New York.

In 1911 Kull started spring training initially with Newark (New Jersey) of the Class-A Eastern League. It appears he had also taken residency in Newark at this time.[22] By May he was back in the Tri-State League with Trenton. He went 1-3 with Trenton before being released. He stayed in the league with Reading in June but was soon released. In July, Anderson of the Class-D Carolina Association picked Kull up. He stayed with Anderson for the rest of the season, going 3-7 for the season. While his record didn't indicate it, he "pitched great ball" for Anderson and the club reserved him for 1912.[23]

That next season, Kull reported late to Anderson. He made the squad but was injured near the end of spring training. Kull headed back home and in May wrote Anderson manager Buck Ramsey that he had his arm x-rayed. The x-ray found a fractured bone and a twisted ligament.[24] At the same time, stories appeared saying that the Philadelphia Phillies had signed Kull.[25] The stories all seem to originate with Kull. There is no other evidence that the Phillies signed an injured minor-league pitcher who hadn't had a winning record in three years. He didn't pitch in 1912.

In 1913 Kull regained some of his former form but not until he had been picked up and released by three teams. He started the year with Newport News of the Class-C Virginia League, going 2-5 before being released for drinking on a Friday night after a game.[26] He was picked up by Troy of the Class-B New York State League, pitched one game which he lost, and was cut. Poughkeepsie of the Class-D New York–New Jersey League was next. They held onto him for three weeks until they cut him loose on July 12. Danbury, which was in the same league, picked Kull up. The Poughkeepsie newspaper wrote upon notice of his release, "If Kull buckles down and makes a serious business of the game he should make Danbury a good pitcher." The sportswriter was prophetic. Kull pitched excellent ball, culminating on August 21, when he pitched a no-hitter against his old team, Poughkeepsie. Kull's final record was 11-7 in the league.

He was back with Danbury,[27] now in the Class-D Atlantic League, in 1914 but then his demons got the better of him. He was Danbury's Opening Day pitcher and had a record of 9-4 on July 28. He had the fourth-best record of any pitcher in the league with more than 10 decisions, yet on July 31, Danbury released him because "he had a tendency to break the training rules."[28] With Kull promising to "keep in form," Poughkeepsie picked him up.[29] He pitched a couple of games and was released by Poughkeepsie.

Kull remained in Newark for the 1915 season, pitching for the Oxweld Acetylene Company in the Manufacturers' League. He also pitched for the Montclair, New Jersey, town team. The 1916 season was Kull's last as a pitcher at any level. He started with Paterson, New Jersey, of the Atlantic League, pitching the second game of the season and lasting four innings.[30] He was cut shortly after. In early June, he pitched for the Newark Athletic Club.

Little is known about Kull's life from 1917 to 1936. In 1935 he returned to Shenandoah[31] and asked the chief burgess to "secure a berth for him in the [Schuylkill County] Almshouse."[32] He was ill and died of tuberculosis at the almshouse's hospital in North Manheim Township, Pennsylvania, on March 20, 1936, at the age of 53. He had no known survivors in the area at the time of his death. His body was taken to Union, New Jersey, where he is buried in the Hollywood Memorial Park.

SOURCES

In addition to the sources cited in the Notes, the author relied on Ancestry.com, Baseball-reference.com, LA84 *The Sporting News* contract cards database via SABR.org, and Retrosheet.org.

NOTES

1 "Games Played in the Atlantic League," *Mount Carmel* (Pennsylvania) *Item*, July 31, 1908: 4.

2 "The Man in the Grand Stand," *Trenton Evening Times*, April 5, 1910: 8; "Pitcher Kull, Veritable Giant, Arrives in Camp, Big Jobson Is Signed Up," *Newport News Daily Press*, March 26, 1913: 5.

3 "Dots and Dashes," *Pottsville Republican & Herald*, April 3, 1936: 18.

4 "Banner Crowds for Pottsville Players," *Philadelphia Inquirer*, May 9, 1909: 18.

5 "Kull Signed Here," *Poughkeepsie Eagle-News*, August 1, 1914: 2.

6 "Sporting Comment," *Newport News Daily Press*, June 1, 1913: 5.

7 "Interesting Ball Notes," *Mount Carmel Item*, April 30, 1908: 4.

8 "Games played in Atlantic League."

9 "'Big Jack Kull' Dies in County Almshouse," *Pottsville Republican*, March 31, 1936: 2; "Diamond Dust," *Wilkes-Barre Evening News*, September 13, 1909: 9.

10 There are Jack Kulls and Andrew Kulls in the censuses but none are ideal matches for the son or father. The "informant" for his death certificate is listed as "record," presumably meaning the doctor's records. The only other contemporaneous document, his *Sporting News* contract card, lists his home as 50 Napoleon Street in Newark, New Jersey. It's clear he moved to Newark sometime after playing for the Philadelphia Athletics. He is buried in North Jersey so he had family there. One newspaper claimed his wife lived there while another paper said he lived with his sister there. Again, no Kull/Kolonauski/Kolenski that matched Jack Kull was found in the censuses.

11 "Pottsville Going at a Phenomenal Pace," *Philadelphia Inquirer*, July 4, 1909: 18.

12 "Games Played in Atlantic League."

13 "Base Ball Bunts Some Live Games," *Pottsville Republican & Herald*, July 20, 1908; "Clippers, Browns, Atlantics Won," *Pottsville Republican & Herald*, July 20, 1908; "Sport Shorts," *Pottsville Republican*, July 9, 1931.

14 "Pottsville May Join Tri-State," *Philadelphia Inquirer*, August 8, 1908: 2.

15 "Pottsville Team Is Hustling Bunch," *Philadelphia Inquirer*, May 16, 1909: 17.

16 "Pottsville Has Surfeit of Starts," *Philadelphia Inquirer*, May 2, 1909: 28.

17 "Pottsville Has Surfeit of Starts."

18 "Kull to Pitch for Athletics," *Philadelphia Inquirer*, June 6, 1909: 27.

19 Strikeout and walk data were found for 21 of his 26 games. He struck out 91 and walked 55 in those 21 games.

20 "Minor Stars Go Higher," *Richmond Times-Dispatch*, August 31, 1909: 7.

21 "Pitcher Kull Farmed Out," *Pottsville Republican & Herald*, February 9, 1910: 1.

22 "White Sox Owners Buy Anderson Club," *Newark Evening Star*, May 20, 1912: 8.

23 "Pitcher Kull Located by Anderson Management," *Winston-Salem Twin-City Daily Sentinel*, April 1, 1912: 6.

24 "Three New Pitchers," *Greenville* (South Carolina) *News*, May 22, 1912: 2.

25 "Former Steelman with Philadelphia Nationals," *Erie Times-News*, September 12, 1912: 4; "Dooin Signs Johnny Kull," *Pottsville Republican & Herald*, May 10, 1912: 2. Kull's *TSN* contract card does not indicate that he was signed by the Phils.

26 "Sporting Comment," *Newport News Daily Press*, June 1, 1913: 5.

27 There were two players named John/Jack Kull in the Atlantic League in 1914. Paterson signed infielder Jack Kull, who had played with the Morristown (New Jersey) Athletic Club in 1913. He played the entire season for Paterson. He also went to camp with Lewiston in 1915 but appears not to have made the team. He returned to New Jersey to play for a semipro team called the Silk Sox.

28 "Kull Signed Here," *Poughkeepsie Eagle-News*, August 1, 1914: 2.

29 "Kull Signed Here."

30 "Local Team Won 2nd Game From Easton," *Paterson News*, May 12, 1916: 16.

31 "Dots and Dashes," *Pottsville Republican & Herald*, April 3, 1936: 18.

32 "'Big Jack Kull' Dies in County Almshouse," *Pottsville Republican*, March 31, 1936: 2.

LARRY LANDRETH

BY GARY BELLEVILLE

On September 16, 1976, Larry Landreth made his major-league debut with the Montreal Expos. In doing so, he became the first homegrown Canadian to play for a big-league team based in Canada.[1] The 21-year-old hurler had quickly advanced through the Expos' farm system, compiling a 44-32 record and a 3.10 ERA in his first four minor-league seasons.[2]

Landreth won four league championships in a professional career that spanned seven seasons. The hard-throwing right-hander was a key contributor to West Palm Beach's Florida State League title in 1974 and the Denver Bears' back-to-back American Association championships in 1976-77.[3]

Landreth's major-league career was limited to a pair of September call-ups with the Expos immediately after Denver's postseason triumphs. After becoming disillusioned with life in the minor leagues, he decided to retire from professional baseball shortly after his 25th birthday. It was time to embark upon the next stage of his life.

Larry Robert Landreth was born on March 11, 1955, in Stratford, a small city on the banks of the Avon River in southwestern Ontario. He was the youngest of two children born to Donald John and Florence Mary (née Calvert). Don worked as a welder for the Dominion Chain Company, a large manufacturer of chains and related products.[4] The Landreths raised Larry and their older son, Doug, in a home that they built in the early 1950s at 5 Burritt Street in Stratford.[5]

As a youngster, Larry participated in just about every sport possible. He began playing organized baseball as a pitcher at age 8.[6] Larry's baseball skills blossomed in Stratford's outstanding minor baseball system, and between the ages of 11 and 17, he helped their teams win five provincial championships.[7]

Although Canada didn't get its first major-league team until the expansion Expos joined the National League in 1969, young Larry still had the opportunity to see big leaguers up close. At least once a year, the Landreth family would drive the 165 miles to Tiger Stadium to catch a major-league game.[8]

Landreth's biggest baseball influence was his brother Doug,[9] who was six years his senior. Doug pitched for the Stratford entry in the Intercounty Baseball League (IBL) from 1967 until 1983. The IBL, which has featured future and former major leaguers like Ferguson Jenkins, Chris Speier, Jesse Orosco, and Denny McLain, is generally regarded as the best amateur baseball circuit in Canada. In 2018 the league celebrated its 100th anniversary by selecting the top 100 players in its history, and Doug Landreth was named to that prestigious list.[10]

Two of Larry's coaches in Stratford minor baseball, Barry Jesson and Denis "Dinny" Flanagan, also made significant contributions to his development as a ballplayer. Jesson coached him from tyke until bantam, while Flanagan guided his team at the junior level.[11] "I was very fortunate to have Barry and Dinny from the get-go," Landreth said in 2011. "They molded us into winners."[12]

Like many Canadian kids, Larry enjoyed playing hockey. However, when his hockey and high-school basketball schedules conflicted at age 14, he decided to give up the national sport. The decision paid dividends, as Larry helped Stratford Central Secondary School win two Huron-Perth regional basketball championships. He also participated in track and field in high school, specializing in the high jump.[13] In 1971 he was named Stratford's outstanding male athlete.[14]

Larry's stellar pitching started to attract the attention of professional scouts at age 14.[15] By the time he was playing for the Stratford Optimists in the Junior Intercounty Baseball League (1971-72), scouts were regularly in attendance when he was on the mound.[16]

In the summer of 1971, Larry attended an Expos tryout camp in Kitchener, Ontario. The 16-year-old threw batting practice and pitched in a simulated game, making a big enough impression to earn one of two invitations to a second-tier tryout camp later that year in Montreal.[17] When he showed up to the second evaluation camp, the Expos brass knew everything about him.[18] They continued to monitor his development closely from that point on.

A few weeks after leading the Optimists to Stratford's first Junior Intercounty Baseball League championship in the summer of 1972, the Expos invited Larry and his family to Montreal to get acquainted.[19] They were introduced to various front-office staff and taken out for a nice dinner in Old Montreal.[20] The next night, they attended a doubleheader between the Mets and Expos at Jarry Park, and, as luck would have it, Bill Stoneman threw his second career no-hitter.[21] It was the first major-league no-hitter tossed outside of the United States.

The Expos made it clear to Landreth during the Montreal rendezvous that they wanted him to be a part of their organization.[22] At the time, Canadians weren't eligible for the major-league draft, although they could be signed as amateur free agents once they turned 18.[23]

Larry Landreth. Courtesy of Canadian Baseball Hall of Fame.

Less than three weeks after Larry's 18th birthday, Expos scout Bill Schudlich was in Stratford with a contract in hand. A family friend came to the Landreth home to look over the pact and provide legal counsel during the negotiations. Larry signed for an $8,500 bonus, provided he could join the Expos' other top prospects in the Florida Instructional League after the 1973 season. Moments after the Landreths agreed to the deal, the Baltimore Orioles called in the hopes of signing Larry. His father, Don, answered the phone. "You're too late," he told them.[24]

After finishing high school, Landreth reported to the Jamestown Expos in the short-season A New York-Penn League. Jamestown was managed by 30-year-old Walt Hriniak, who was in his second year of managing in the minor leagues. Landreth enjoyed playing for the fiery Hriniak. He remembered learning a lot from the former major leaguer during several sitdown talks they had that summer. "You played hard for him," Landreth recalled. "If you didn't, look out."[25]

After holding his own against older competition in the New York-Penn League, Landreth took a big step forward in the fall of 1973, pitching for the Expos' entry in the Florida Instructional League. In one particularly eye-catching start, he tossed a seven-inning one-hitter against St. Louis Cardinals prospects.[26] Despite missing a week to attend his high-school graduation ceremony in Stratford, Landreth finished the fall season with a 5-0 record and 2.33 ERA.[27] His performance caught the attention of *The Sporting News*, which referred to him as an "18-year-old phenom."[28] The Expos earned the league's "Most Improved" honors largely because of Landreth and a pair of 19-year-old prospects, Gary Carter and Bill Atkinson. Carter led the squad with a .315 batting average, while Atkinson, a relief pitcher from Chatham, Ontario, posted a 0.91 ERA.[29]

Landreth enjoyed an outstanding season in 1974, recording a 2.54 ERA for West Palm Beach in the High-A Florida State League. His 15 wins were one off the league lead, and he put up similar numbers to Dennis Martínez despite being a year younger than the Baltimore prospect. Landreth's season highlights included a 15-strikeout performance against the Miami Orioles on June 1 and an outing against Key West on June 18 in which he retired the first 17 batters in order and finished with a two-hit shutout.[30]

In early July, the *Miami Herald* wrote a feature article on Landreth. The story, which ran under the headline, "The Prospect: 19, Energetic, All Business," showed the young hurler to be serious, hard-working, and mature beyond his years. It was also clear that Landreth was already thinking ahead to life after baseball. "I'll go as far as I can," he said. "Until I know myself that I can't go any further. Believe me, I'll know."[31]

Landreth and his roommate, reliever Len Yonkman from Punnichy, Saskatchewan, showed their Canadian pride after a doubleheader against Miami on July 22. Landreth outpitched Martínez in the first game to earn the victory, with his roomie chipping in with the save. Yonkman also picked up the win in relief in the nightcap.[32] "It was a sweep for Team Canada," proclaimed Yonkman. "We've been waiting a long time for this to happen, and it finally did."[33]

West Palm Beach went on to win the FSL championship series two games to one over Fort Lauderdale. Landreth was in a reflective mood in the locker room after the final game. "It's hard to imagine that most of us will probably never see each other again after tonight," he told reporters.[34] The next day, he was on his way to Quebec City of the Eastern League, where he made one relief appearance and got his first taste of Double-A baseball.

In August of 1974, Expos GM Jim Fanning had predicted that Landreth would be the team's first homegrown Canadian player.[35] "The way things are going now," wrote *Toronto Star* reporter Milt Dunnell, "Landreth might even arrive before the (domed) stadium."[36] His rapid advancement was great news for the Expos, who had signed 18 Canadians in their first six years of existence.[37] Not only were they hoping for a lucrative gate attraction, but as Canada's sole major-league team, they were under increasing pressure to have at least one Canuck in their lineup. The fans and media took note of the big-league success enjoyed by Canadians like Jenkins, John Hiller, and Reggie Cleveland in 1974, and many expected the Expos to feature similar players.[38]

Landreth's repertoire consisted mainly of a fastball and a slider, with an occasional curveball and changeup mixed in.[39] He returned to the Florida Instructional League in the fall with the goal of improving his curveball.[40] The extra work paid off, and he led the circuit with a 0.61 ERA. His Instructional League manager, Karl Kuehl, was so impressed that he lobbied the organization (unsuccessfully) to move Landreth all the way up to Kuehl's Triple-A Memphis squad.[41]

Montreal named Landreth its top prospect early in 1975.[42] He was rewarded with an invitation to spring training as a nonroster invitee, making him the youngest player in camp. The just-turned-20-year-old impressed Expos manager Gene Mauch before he was reassigned to the minor-league camp on March 20.[43]

Landreth spent all of 1975 with the Quebec City Carnavals, leading the fifth-place team with 10 wins and a 2.69 ERA. He finished second in the league in complete games (17) and tied Len Barker for second in strikeouts (133). Player development director Mel Didier, one of the architects of the great Expos teams of the late 1970s and early 1980s, assessed Landreth in early July.[44] "He's at the same stage right now that Steve Rogers was when we called him up in 1973. We would like to have him pitch a little longer in the minor leagues," Didier revealed. "We can afford to do that now because our own pitching staff is stronger."[45] Landreth was named the Expos' 1975 Minor-League Pitcher-of-the-Year, and in late October he was added to Montreal's 40-man roster, along with his countryman, Bill Atkinson.[46]

Landreth also had a great year off the field in 1975. While shopping at a Stratford department store, he recognized one of the staff members who was working there part-time during high school.[47] It turned out to be his future wife, Jane Finch. Larry knew of her through one of his high-school friends, so he went up and introduced himself to her in the store, and they started dating shortly afterward.[48]

Landreth held a variety of offseason jobs during his professional baseball career. He worked at a government-run liquor store for two winters; another year he was employed as a salesman at a high-end clothing store in downtown London, Ontario.[49]

Kuehl was hired as the Expos' new manager for the 1976 season.[50] That spring, major-league owners were upset at the prospect of free agency, and so they locked out the players for three weeks. As a result, the Expos camp didn't get underway until March 18. Landreth, still the youngest player on the roster, was late reporting because of the difficulty in getting a last-minute flight from Toronto to Florida during spring break.[51] With only 13 spring games scheduled,[52] he had few opportunities to show what he could do against big-league hitters.

Landreth began the season at Triple A. Since Montreal had just switched its top affiliate from Memphis to Denver in 1976, Landreth had to pitch home games in the mountain air of Mile High Stadium. Despite being the third-youngest pitcher in the American Association, the 21-year-old posted a solid 3.72 ERA that season, and his 13 wins were only one off the league lead.[53]

The 1976 Denver Bears, featuring top hitting prospects like Andre Dawson, Warren Cromartie, and Ellis Valentine, were stacked with young talent. They easily won the Western Division by 13½ games. In Game One of the league championship series, Landreth picked up the victory by limiting the Omaha Royals to three hits in eight shutout innings.[54] He also won Game Five in Denver to grab a 3-2 series lead.[55] As soon as the Bears won Game Six to claim the American Association championship, the Expos called up nine Denver players, including Landreth, Atkinson, and Dawson.[56]

Landreth made his major-league debut on September 16, 1976, in a start against the Chicago Cubs at Jarry Park. He had tried to relax the evening before by watching Team Canada play Czechoslovakia in the thrilling finale of the Canada Cup hockey tournament.[57] It didn't help. "I might as well have not gone to bed," he said. "I was tossing and turning all night."[58]

With his parents in attendance, Landreth tossed six shutout innings and earned the victory.[59] The nervous rookie walked six batters, although he limited the Cubs to only four hits. Most impressively, he held the dangerous Bill Madlock hitless in three at-bats, which helped snap the defending batting champion's 10-game hitting streak.[60]

Landreth's debut resulted in several firsts. He became the first homegrown Canadian to play for the Expos,[61] the first pitcher from Canada to start a game for Nos Amours,[62] and the first Stratford native to appear in a big-league game. Landreth also became the first Canadian-born hurler to start and win his major-league debut since Dick Fowler turned the trick for the Philadelphia Athletics in 1941.[63]

Landreth's other two outings in September were against the red-hot New York Mets, who were on their way to leading the majors with a 20-9 record that month. He was thrilled to find out that his boyhood idol, Tom Seaver, was his scheduled mound opponent for his second start.[64] But the Expos wanted him to pitch in the nationally televised home game on September 22, and so they juggled their rotation.[65] The plan backfired when Landreth was knocked out of that game in the second inning after giving up three earned runs. His September 27 start at Shea Stadium wasn't much better, as he gave up six hits and two earned runs in 3⅓ innings. In both games against the Mets, Jon Matlack earned the victory and Landreth took the loss.[66]

In an eventful offseason, Larry and Jane were engaged to be married. The *Montreal Gazette* reported in January 1977 that the Stratford couple were planning to wed in the fall.[67]

Dick Williams took over as the Expos' manager in 1977, giving Landreth his third different skipper in three major-league camps.[68] With 27 of the 40 players on the roster 25 or younger, Williams focused heavily on the fundamentals during spring training.[69] Pitchers and catchers worked out for two full weeks before their first intrasquad game.[70] In early March, Landreth won $25 in a bunting competition among the Expos pitchers. "If he makes the team and misses his first bunt, he'll have to give the money back," quipped Williams.[71]

With 16 hurlers in camp fighting over six available roster spots, Landreth had a reasonable shot at making the big club that spring.[72] However, a couple of subpar outings against the Phillies and Dodgers proved costly. He was reassigned to the minor-league camp on March 23.[73]

Landreth returned to Triple-A Denver, and after struggling through much of the season, he turned it on down the stretch. He persevered through three consecutive hard-luck defeats in a 10-day period, losing by scores of 1-0, 2-1, and 1-0.[74] The only run Denver scored during those three frustrating outings was knocked in by Landreth himself.[75]

On the next to last day of the season, he tossed a clutch four-hit, complete-game shutout against Wichita to eliminate the Aeros and clinch the division.[76] His strong finish earned him the Expos' minor-league Pitcher-of-the-Month award in August.

Landreth finished the season with the most strikeouts in the American Association (134), and he tied for the league lead in starts (29). He paced the Bears with 10 wins, 195 innings pitched, 9 complete games, and 2 shutouts.

After Denver dropped the first two games of their best-of-seven series to Omaha at home, Landreth got the start in a must-win game at Mile High Stadium. He responded by tossing an eight-hit, complete-game victory, with the final two outs coming on strikeouts with the bases loaded and the potential tying run on first base.[77] Landreth's clutch performance was the pivotal event of the series. The Bears won the next three games and claimed their second consecutive American Association championship.

Landreth was called up by Montreal immediately after Denver's postseason. He made a pair of September appearances against the Phillies and Pirates, teams that finished with 101 and 96 wins respectively. His only start was on September 17 against Pittsburgh on a damp Montreal evening. With the rain stopping and starting multiple times during a 2-hour 10-minute delay, both starting pitchers were forced to warm up three times.[78] Veteran Pirates hurler Jerry Reuss stiffened up on his third attempt to get ready and was replaced by rookie Ed Whitson.[79] Landreth, on the other hand, soldiered on. He gave up five earned runs in 4⅔ innings, and the Expos lost, 6-3.

His best outing during his second stint with Montreal was against the Phillies on September 30; he limited Philadelphia to a single and a walk in two innings of relief. It was the final appearance of his major-league career.

Larry and Jane were married on October 8, 1977, at St. James Anglican Church in Stratford.[80] Jane had completed her first year of nursing studies at Fanshawe College earlier that year. Since Larry had been invited to pitch in the Puerto Rican Winter League and would have to leave shortly after their wedding day, Jane took a year off from college to give the newlyweds more time together. They enjoyed a brief honeymoon at Niagara-on-the-Lake, Ontario, before setting off for Puerto Rico a few weeks later.[81] Landreth pitched out of the bullpen, helping the Caguas Criollos win their fourth consecutive regular-season crown.[82]

Before the start of the 1978 season, Montreal greatly improved its starting pitching by acquiring proven left-handers Ross Grimsley and Rudy May.[83] As a result, competition to make the Expos starting rotation was fierce during spring training. Landreth found himself battling five other pitchers for the fifth starter/long-relief role.[84] He pitched decently in the spring, but one poor outing against Boston on March 15 landed him in Williams's "early doghouse," along with Will McEnaney, Santo Alcalá, and Rick Sawyer.[85] He was reassigned to the minor-league camp later that month.

After five Triple-A starts with Denver, Landreth was blindsided by a trade on May 20. Montreal desperately needed to improve its bullpen,[86] and so they packaged two young starters, Landreth and Gerald Hannahs, in a swap with the Dodgers for reliever Mike Garman. Los Angeles assigned Landreth to its Triple-A affiliate in Albuquerque. He went from one high-altitude environment to another, except that Albuquerque was even drier than Denver. "There was a trough in Albuquerque that ran from right-center to left-center, and if a fly ball got in the trough, you could kiss it goodbye," Landreth recalled.[87] He posted a 6.28 ERA in 22 appearances with the Dukes.

Landreth was not happy with the trade, mainly because of the pitching depth in the Dodgers organization.[88] "It was a dead end (for me) there," he said.[89] He decided that he wouldn't report to spring training in 1979, and in early February he asked the Dodgers for his release.[90] Los Angeles finally granted him his wish on March 27. He immediately went down to Florida to try to catch on with the Expos. However, Fanning was hesitant to sign him after hearing rumors at the Winter Meetings that he had arm troubles.[91] Landreth returned a couple of days later and threw about 20 pitches for Fanning, and he was quickly signed to a minor-league deal.[92]

For the fourth year in a row, Landreth started the season in Denver. After several inconsistent starts, the Bears' new manager, Jack McKeon, could no longer guarantee him a regular spot in the rotation, much to Landreth's displeasure.[93] The breaking point came when he was charting a game the day before a scheduled start, and then, out of the blue, he was sent in to pitch in relief.[94] Disillusioned with minor-league life and unhappy with his role on the Bears, Landreth decided to pack it in.[95] "It's tough … there's not a lot of money, for one thing," he told a reporter after returning to Stratford. "The first year I signed for $500 a month, and that's hard to live on."[96] He was placed on Denver's suspended list on June 14.

The Brewers contacted Landreth later that summer. He signed with Milwaukee and was assigned to their Double-A affiliate in Holyoke, Massachusetts, where he compiled a 5.76 ERA in five late-season starts.

Landreth attended Milwaukee's minor-league camp in the spring of 1980. But the Brewers released him on April 1, less than three weeks after his 25th birthday. Although he had a couple of other teams interested in his services, he asked Milwaukee for a plane ticket home.[97] "I just grew tired of it (the minor leagues)," he explained. "So instead of waiting until I was 28 and having to face starting all over again, I just quit. I didn't want to have to start looking for a job when I was that old."[98]

In seven minor-league seasons, Landreth amassed a 62-56 record and a 3.89 ERA despite spending almost half of that time pitching home games in the hitter-friendly environments of Denver and

Albuquerque. In four starts and three relief appearances at the major-league level, he compiled a 1-4 record and a 6.64 ERA.

Larry returned to Stratford and took a job as a hydro lineworker. His brother Doug and several friends were playing in the IBL, and so he decided to have some fun and join them on the Stratford Hillers. With both Landreth brothers on their pitching staff, the Hillers won the IBL championship in 1980 and represented Ontario in the senior men's national championship in 1981.[99]

Larry joined the Stratford Fire Department as a firefighter in 1981, eventually rising to the rank of captain. In 2002 and 2011, he was awarded the Governor General's Fire Services Exemplary Service Medal.[100] He retired in 2015 after serving more than 33 years as a firefighter. Jane worked as a registered nurse for 30 years, and, later in life, as a real estate sales representative. Together they raised three children, Sean, Kate, and Scott.[101]

The Landreths spent their early retirement years living in the Town of the Blue Mountains (Ontario) to be closer to their three grandchildren. They returned to Stratford in 2020, to a home just a four-minute walk from the golf course. In addition to golfing as much as possible, Larry enjoys pickleball and five-pin bowling.[102] He is also a regular participant in the Celebrity Golf Classic, an annual tournament to raise funds for the Canadian Baseball Hall of Fame in nearby St. Marys, Ontario.

In 2011 Landreth was inducted into the Stratford Wall of Fame as part of an inaugural class that included his former coach, Dinny Flanagan, and the "Stratford Streak," Howie Morenz.[103]

Acknowledgments

The author wishes to thank Larry Landreth for graciously answering questions via phone and email. Thanks also to Cassidy Lent of the Giamatti Research Center at the National Baseball Hall of Fame in Cooperstown for providing a copy of Landreth's Hall of Fame file.

SOURCES

In addition to the sources cited in the Notes, the author consulted Baseball-Reference.com, Retrosheet.org, *The Sporting News* Player Contract Cards, and Ancestry.com.

NOTES

1. Landreth was the second Canadian to play for the Montreal Expos, but he was the first Canadian produced by their farm system. On August 19, 1969, Montreal purchased the contract of 32-year-old reliever Claude Raymond from the Atlanta Braves, and he pitched for the Expos during the franchise's first three seasons (1969-71). Raymond, a native of Saint-Jean-sur-Richelieu, Québec, was a National League All-Star with the Houston Astros in 1966. He went 8-16 with a 4.47 ERA in 111 relief appearances with Montreal, and he led the team with 23 saves in 1970. Thirty-five-year-old pitcher Ron Piché was activated by the Expos in September 1970, although he never saw any game action. Piché was born in Verdun, Québec.

2. Landreth also posted a WHIP (walks plus hits per innings pitched) of 1.243 in his first four professional seasons. Those statistics were especially impressive considering that one of those seasons was spent pitching in the thin air of Denver's Mile High Stadium. It was not the only season that Landreth spent pitching in an extreme hitters' park. He played home games in Denver and Albuquerque for close to half of his seven-year professional career.

3. Landreth was also a member of the Albuquerque Dukes in 1978. The Dukes and the Tacoma Yankees were named co-champions of the Pacific Coast League that season because of continuous rain in the playoffs.

4. Email from Larry Landreth to author, February 8, 2021.

5. "Florence Landreth," *Stratford Beacon Herald*, https://stratfordbeaconherald.remembering.ca/obituary/florence-landreth-1077022662, accessed February 3, 2021.

6. Larry Landreth, telephone interview with author, January 27, 2021.

7. "Larry Landreth First Canadian Starter for Expos," *Toronto Star*, September 17, 1976: C-1.

8. Email from Larry Landreth to author, February 8, 2021. Tiger Stadium in Detroit (165 miles) was significantly closer to Stratford than Jarry Park in Montreal (420 miles). Historically, there has been a large contingent of Detroit Tigers fans in southwestern Ontario. As of 2021, many fans in southwestern Ontario still cheered for the Tigers, although most baseball fans in the area supported the Toronto Blue Jays.

9. Kevin Glew, "Ex-Expos: Whatever Happened To? ... Larry Landreth," Cooperstowners in Canada, July 30, 2020, https://cooperstownersincanada.com/2020/07/30/

9. ex-expos-whatever-happened-to-larry-landreth/, accessed February 3, 2021.

10. Bob Elliott, "Stead Headlines IBL's All-Time Top 100 Players," Canadian Baseball Network, February 7, 2018, https://www.canadianbaseballnetwork.com/canadian-baseball-network-articles/stead-headlines-ibls-all-time-top-100, accessed March 9, 2021.

11. Larry Landreth, telephone interview with author, January 27, 2021. Flanagan was an accomplished amateur hockey player in his younger days. He played on the Canadian team that won the 1951 Ice Hockey World Championship before going on to manage the Stratford Junior B Hockey Club for 21 years.

12. Mike Savage, "Landreth Role Model for Many," *Beacon Herald* (Stratford, Ontario), April 16, 2011: B-1.

13. Larry Landreth, telephone interview with author, January 27, 2021.

14. "Larry Landreth First Canadian Starter for Expos."

15. Larry Landreth, telephone interview with author, January 27, 2021. There had also been a minimal amount of contact with professional scouts at the bantam level.

16. Larry Landreth, telephone interview with author, January 27, 2021; Glew, "Ex-Expos: Whatever Happened To? ... Larry Landreth."

17. The other invitation went to Mike Teahen, a catcher from St. Marys, Ontario. Teahen went on to play for Canada's national team. A few years later he had a son, Mark Teahen, who played in the American League for seven seasons with the Kansas City Royals, Chicago White Sox, and Toronto Blue Jays. Cory Smith, "'No one can take it away from me:' After 45 years, Larry Landreth remains Stratford's only big leaguer," *Stratford Beacon Herald*, December 1, 2021; Bob Duff, "Teahen Drawn to Canada," *Windsor Star*, September 24, 2007: 9.

18. Larry Landreth, telephone interview with author, January 27, 2021.

19. "Larry Landreth First Canadian Starter for Expos."

20. Email from Larry Landreth to author, February 27, 2021. Old Montreal is the city's historic district known for its charming architecture and cobblestone streets. European settlers arrived in the area in 1642.

21. Larry Landreth, telephone interview with author, January 27, 2021. The doubleheader was played on October 2, 1972.

22. Larry Landreth, telephone interview with author, January 27, 2021.

23. Canadians attending college in the United States have been eligible for the major-league draft since 1985. Starting in 1991, Canadians could be drafted out of high school.

24. Larry Landreth, telephone interview with author, January 27, 2021.

25. Larry Landreth, telephone interview with author, January 27, 2021.

26. Jack Ellison, "Montreal Youngsters Are 'Most Improved,'" *The Sporting News*, November 24, 1973: 47.

27. Ian MacDonald, "Foote Candidate to Start for Expos; 'He Can Catch for Us,' Says Fanning," *Montreal Gazette*, November 15, 1973: 34.

28. Ellison, "Montreal Youngsters Are 'Most Improved.'"

29. MacDonald, "Foote Candidate to Start for Expos; 'He Can Catch for Us,' Says Fanning."

30. John Kelso, "Expos End Slump, 3-2; Landreth Strikes Out 15 Orioles," *Palm Beach Post*, June 2, 1974: 72; "West Palm Rolls, 2-0," *Miami Herald*, June 19, 1974: 2-E.

31. Skip Bayless, "The Prospect: 19, Energetic, All Business," *Miami Herald*, July 3, 1974: 2-B.

32. This was not the first time that a pair of Canadians had won both ends of a doubleheader for the same professional team. The most high-profile example of this occurred on August 17, 1947, when Dick Fowler of the Philadelphia Athletics earned the victory in the first game of a doubleheader against the Washington Senators, and his teammate Phil Marchildon picked up the win in the second game.

33. Larry Mlynczak, "Sweep Puts Expos in 1st," *Palm Beach Post*, July 23, 1974: 16.

34. Skip Bayless, "In Class A, Champs Get Beer," *Miami Herald*, September 4, 1974: 2-B.

35. Milt Dunnell, "Homebrew Looms in Expos' Future," *Toronto Star*, August 27, 1974: C-1.

36. Dunnell, "Homebrew Looms in Expos' Future." To help secure Montreal's major-league franchise in 1968, Mayor Jean Drapeau had promised the National League a domed stadium in time for the start of the 1971 season. The Expos did not play their first game in Olympic Stadium until April 15, 1977. Dunnell's prediction came true, as Landreth made his major-league debut on September 16, 1976.

37. Bob Dunn, "Expo Homebred Search Turns to Finlayson," *The Sporting News*, January 25, 1975: 41.

38. Older Canadian fans were used to seeing native sons on their Triple-A teams as well. In the 1950s and 1960s, it was not out of the ordinary for the rosters of the Montreal Royals, Toronto Maple Leafs, and Vancouver Mounties to feature multiple Canadians.

39. Smith, "'No one can take it away from me:' After 45 years, Larry Landreth remains Stratford's only big leaguer."

40. Ian MacDonald, "Expos May Just Have 'Future' in Canadian Rookie," *Montreal Gazette*, November 28, 1974: 34.

41. MacDonald, "Expos May Just Have 'Future' in Canadian Rookie"; Larry Landreth, telephone interview with author, March 13, 2021. Landreth also lobbied the Montreal front office to start the 1975 season with Triple-A Memphis.

42. Canadian Press, "Expos Keep Eye on Hurler from Stratford," *Globe and Mail* (Toronto), March 4, 1975: 37. Gary Carter and Warren Cromartie had made their major-league debuts in September 1974. Andre Dawson wasn't drafted by the Expos until June 1975.

43 "Expos Trim Seven from Camp Roster," *Montreal Gazette*, March 21, 1975: 27.

44 The Expos had the best winning percentage in the National League (.548) in the five-year period from 1979 to 1983. Their Pythagorean won-lost percentage in that period was .552, which was also tops in the National League.

45 Ian MacDonald, "Expos Struggle, but Farmhands Plow Straight Lines," *Montreal Gazette*, July 3, 1975: 37.

46 Ian MacDonald, "Expos Show Faith in Canadian Talent," *Montreal Gazette*, October 30, 1975: 32.

47 Email from Larry Landreth to author, February 1, 2021.

48 Larry Landreth, telephone interview with author, January 27, 2021.

49 Larry Landreth, telephone interview with author, January 27, 2021.

50 Gene Mauch was fired at the end of the 1975 season, in part because of his reluctance to use young players. Thirty-eight-year-old Karl Kuehl, who had worked with many of Montreal's prospects, was named as his replacement. The 1976 season was a complete disaster for the Expos. Injuries, clubhouse dissension, and disappointing performances from several players led to Montreal's worst season since its inaugural 1969 campaign, and Kuehl paid the price when he was fired on September 3, 1976. Consequently, Landreth lost perhaps his biggest champion in the organization.

51 Ian MacDonald, "Lather up … Expos Open Training," *Montreal Gazette*, March 19, 1976: 19.

52 MacDonald, "Lather up … Expos Open Training."

53 In 1976 Landreth was the youngest pitcher in the American Association not named Manny. The only two hurlers in the league younger than him were Manny Sarmiento and Manny Seoane.

54 "A.A. Day by Day," *The Sporting News*, September 25, 1976: 31.

55 "American Association," *The Sporting News*, September 25, 1976: 38.

56 Associated Press, "Expos Call Up Nine off Farm," *Monroe (Louisiana) News-Star*, September 7, 1976: 9. Cromartie and Valentine had been called up to the Expos earlier in the 1976 season.

57 Canada beat Czechoslovakia 5-4 in overtime to win the 1976 Canada Cup. At the time, it was the most watched television broadcast in Canadian history.

58 Glenn Cole, "Canadian Rookie Wins for Expos," *Ottawa Journal*, September 17, 1976: 20.

59 Ian MacDonald, "Morales Sets Record with 25th Pinch Hit," *Montreal Gazette*, September 17, 1976: 19.

60 Madlock won his second consecutive batting title with a .339 batting average in 1976. He finished his career with four batting titles. After Madlock grounded into a double play against Landreth in the first inning, he flied out to center field in the third and lined out to center field in the sixth. Madlock was walked by Joe Kerrigan in the eighth inning in his only other plate appearance of the game.

61 Reliever Bill Atkinson made his major-league debut two days after Landreth. Atkinson went on to post an 11-4 record and 3.42 ERA in 98 relief appearances during his four-year major-league career. All 98 appearances were with the Expos. The only Canadian to play for the Expos before Landreth was relief pitcher Claude Raymond.

62 "Nos Amours" is the nickname given to the Expos by their French-speaking fans. The nickname's English translation is "Our Loves."

63 Ferguson Jenkins won his major-league debut in 1965 pitching in relief. Four Canadian-born pitchers in a starting role won their major-league debut in the American, National, or Federal League between 1901 and 1976: Alex Hardy of the Chicago Orphans on September 4, 1902, Ernie Ross of the Baltimore Orioles in the second game of a doubleheader on September 17, 1902, Dick Fowler of the Philadelphia Athletics on September 13, 1941, and Landreth. As of the end of the 2020 season, the feat had been accomplished five more times since Landreth's victory: Rhéal Cormier of the St. Louis Cardinals on August 15, 1991, Jason Dickson of the California Angels on August 21, 1996, Andrew Albers of the Minnesota Twins on August 6, 2013, James Paxton of the Seattle Mariners on September 7, 2013, and Mike Soroka of the Atlanta Braves on May 1, 2018.

64 Larry Landreth, telephone interview with author, January 27, 2021.

65 Bob Dunn, "Injuries Ruin Soph Season for Expos' Carter," *The Sporting News*, October 9, 1976: 15. The September 22, 1976, game between the Expos and Mets was televised nationally by the Canadian Broadcasting Corporation (CBC). The CBC televised approximately one Expos game per week during the 1976 season.

66 The two victories for Matlack against Montreal raised his record to 17-9. His 17 wins in 1976 were the most victories in his 13-year major-league career.

67 "Sports Shorts," *Montreal Gazette*, January 14, 1977: 26.

68 Williams had been fired as manager of the California Angels on July 23, 1976. While he was at the helm, the Angels compiled a record of 147-194 (.431) over parts of three seasons. In contrast to Kuehl, who had been hired for his experience within the Montreal organization, Williams was brought in because of his reputation as a hard-nosed winner with Boston (1967-69) and Oakland (1971-73).

69 Chuck Otterson, "Williams Expects Expos to Climb," *Palm Beach Post-Times*, March 13, 1977: E-7.

70 "Expos' Tickets Are $1 to $6.50," *Montreal Gazette*, March 5, 1977: 40.

71 "Charlie O. Keeps Lines Open with Expos but Demands Dim Hopes of Deal for Blue," *Montreal Gazette*, March 4, 1977: 23.

72 Ian MacDonald, "Carrithers Keyed for 'Mop-Up' Role," *Montreal Gazette*, March 10, 1977: 26. Starter Steve Rogers, swingman Don Stanhouse and reliever Will McEnaney

73 Ian MacDonald, "Bad News for Blair as Expos Make Cuts," *Montreal Gazette*, March 24, 1977: 28.

74 "American Association; Monday, August 8," *The Sporting News*, August 27, 1977: 34; "American Association; Saturday, August 13," *The Sporting News*, September 3, 1977: 36; "American Association; Thursday, August 18," *The Sporting News*, September 3, 1977: 36.

75 Larry Landreth, telephone interview with author, March 13, 2021.

76 Associated Press, "Bears Take It All in Western Division," *Colorado Springs Gazette-Telegraph*, September 1, 1977: 33. Wichita came into the game one game behind Denver with two games to play.

77 Frank Haraway, "Bears Demonstrate Heavy Hitting to Gain A.A. Title," *The Sporting News*, September 24, 1977: 31.

78 Larry Landreth, telephone interview with author, January 27, 2021.

79 Bob Smizik, "Taveras Steals 64th as Pirates Win, 6-3," *Pittsburgh Press*, September 18, 1977: 65. This game was Whitson's first major-league start. He gave up three earned runs in five innings on the hill and earned his first career win. Goose Gossage picked up a four-inning save.

80 The Landreths were married a mere six days after the end of Montreal's regular season.

81 Email from Larry Landreth to author, February 16, 2021.

82 "Expos Faring Well in Winter Ball," *Montreal Gazette*, January 18, 1978: 22; Ian MacDonald, "Expos' Staff Could Include Pair of Canadians," *The Sporting News*, March 25, 1978: 50. Caguas was upset in the semifinals by Mayagüez.

83 Rudy May, Bryn Smith, and Randy Miller were acquired in a trade with the Baltimore Orioles in return for Joe Kerrigan, Gary Roenicke, and Don Stanhouse on December 7, 1977. Ross Grimsley was signed by Montreal as a free agent on December 21, 1977. Grimsley and May had combined to win 32 games for Baltimore in 1977. Grimsley went 20-11 for the Expos in 1978. He was the only 20-game winner in the 36-year history of the Montreal Expos.

84 MacDonald, "Expos' Staff Could Include Pair of Canadians."

85 Ian MacDonald, "Cutting Job Looks Easier," *Montreal Gazette*, March 18, 1978: 42. Rudy May and Stan Bahnsen also struggled in the March 15, 1978, game against Boston; it was just one of those days. Boston scored 8 runs on 13 hits against May, Landreth, and Bahnsen. Carl Yastrzemski had three hits; Jerry Remy, Rick Burleson, Bernie Carbo, and Butch Hobson had two hits each.

86 Ian MacDonald, "Critics Get Eyeful from Expo Relievers," *The Sporting News*, May 13, 1978: 9. The Montreal scribes were correct in their preseason criticism of the Expos bullpen. Montreal relievers went 14-25 with 15 blown saves in 47 opportunities in 1978.

87 Glew, "Ex-Expos: Whatever Happened To? … Larry Landreth."

88 Montreal's pitching staff led the major leagues with a 3.14 ERA in 1979. However, Landreth was correct in his assessment of the Dodgers' pitching. Between 1980 and 1986, Los Angeles led the major leagues with a 3.24 ERA. Montreal was third in the big leagues with a 3.48 ERA during that period.

89 "American Association," *The Sporting News*, June 2, 1979: 38.

90 Larry Landreth, telephone interview with author, January 27, 2021.

91 Larry Landreth, telephone interview with author, January 27, 2021. Landreth never had any arm or shoulder injuries during his professional career.

92 Larry Landreth, telephone interview with author, January 27, 2021.

93 Canadian Press, "Landreth's Dream Comes to an End," *Regina Leader-Post*, August 29, 1979: 29. Jack McKeon was a member of the Expos organization for only one season. He piloted the Bears to a 62-73 record in 1979. Four days after Denver's season ended, he was named assistant general manager of the San Diego Padres.

94 Larry Landreth, telephone interview with author, January 27, 2021.

95 Canadian Press, "Landreth's Dream Comes to an End"; Larry Landreth, telephone interview with author, January 27, 2021.

96 Canadian Press, "Landreth's Dream Comes to an End."

97 Larry Landreth, telephone interview with author, January 27, 2021.

98 Terry England, "Chiefs Learn Co-operation Returns Heftiest Dividends," *Windsor* (Ontario) *Star*, August 29, 1980: 37.

99 In addition to pitching, Larry also played first base.

100 The Fire Services Exemplary Service Medal honors members of a recognized Canadian fire service who have completed 20 years of service, 10 years of which have been served in the performance of duties involving potential risks. A Bar may be added to the recipient's Medal for each additional 10-year period of service. "Fire Services Exemplary Service Medal," The Governor General of Canada, gg.ca/en/honours/canadian-honours/directory-honours/exemplary-service-medals/fire-services-exemplary-service-medal, accessed February 25, 2021.

101 Larry Landreth, telephone interview with author, January 27, 2021.

102 Larry Landreth, telephone interview with author, January 27, 2021. Five-pin bowling is a Canadian version of ten-pin bowling. A smaller, lighter ball without any finger holes is used. Each pin is approximately 25 percent smaller than those in ten-pin bowling.

103 Savage, "Landreth Role Model for Many." Howie Morenz is widely considered to be professional hockey's first superstar. In 1950 he was voted the top hockey player of the first half of the twentieth century by the Canadian Press.

WILLIAM J. MADIGAN

BY RICHARD RIIS

To Washington Nationals fans, he was "Pony" for his youth and diminutive size. In his post-major-league playing days, he was "Kid." To some in Washington's first and second Irish-American community, he was "Tice," from the Old English for "kid goat." Everywhere else he was simply William J. Madigan. Madigan made the major leagues in 1886 as a 17-year-old phenomenon, a hopeful midseason pickup for the otherwise hopeless first-year Washington Nationals, and retired from the professional ranks as a 20-year-old former major leaguer with a career won-lost record of 1-13.

William J. Madigan was born on July 18, 1868, in the District of Columbia's predominantly middle-class Fourth Ward. He was one of nine children of Patrick, a shoemaker, and Bridget Madigan, immigrants from Ireland. Little is known of Madigan's childhood or when he started playing baseball, but at a tender age he had developed into a pretty fair pitcher on the amateur sandlots of Washington. In 1885, playing for a "crack amateur team" known as the English Hills, Madigan, all of 16 years old at the start of the season, won 19 of his club's 22 games.[1] The following year, playing for the Merchants, D.C.'s leading amateur nine, the 17-year-old Madigan struck out 19 batters in one game and 23 in another.[2] Despite such success against amateur batsmen, Madigan seemed an unlikely prospect as a major-league hurler – in addition to his youth, he stood just 5-feet-5 and weighed but 118 pounds.[3]

The Nationals, however, were floundering. Despite the presence of two-time NL batting champion and first-ever Triple Crown winner Paul Hines and a rookie catcher named Connie Mack, the team had managed to win only nine of its first 47 decisions, and was buried in last place, 28½ games behind the league-leading Detroit Wolverines. With little to lose, the bereft Nationals signed the homegrown Madigan to pitch.

The right-handed Madigan made his first start on July 10 against Boston at Washington's Swampoodle Grounds. Although the Beaneaters took the game, 6-1, their captain, John Morrill, was impressed enough with Madigan's pitching to remark that the Nationals would have had no trouble winning the game "had they been able to bat at all."[4] "His slow ball," Morrill said of the youngster, "is different from any now pitched in the league, and all the teams will have difficulty batting it, at least until they get used to it."[5]

The *Washington Post* reported that Madigan, "who made his first appearance yesterday, impressed … as a plucky one in the box and, as he expressed himself after the game, 'I expected to be hit, but they could not scare me.'"[6]

Pluck wasn't enough for Madigan, who pitched well in his second start, again at Washington, against New York on July 15, "completely puzzl[ing] the Gothamites"[7] until the eighth inning, when the Giants scored three runs on five hits to win, 5-2.

The Philadelphia Quakers came to Washington on July 16 for a three-game stand against the Nationals. Relieving a sore-handed Bob Barr with three runs across and none out in the first, Madigan squandered a seven-run comeback by Washington in the sixth by giving up four in the seventh to lose, 9-8. Philadelphia found it easier going the next day, winning 8-1.

For the third and final game of the series, on July 19, Nationals manager Mike Scanlon pitched Madigan with two days' rest. Washington, losers of its last 11 games and 26 of its last 29, was at the bottom of the league standings with a record of 9 wins and 44 losses. The fourth-place Quakers, by contrast, had won six in a row and 13 of their last 15 for an overall record of 34-20. To take on Madigan and the Nationals, Quakers manager Harry Wright chose hard-throwing 19-year-old rookie left-hander Ledell Titcomb (0-3).

The Nationals took the lead on hustle in the second inning when third baseman Hines and shortstop Davy Force singled on either side of a walk to second sacker Jimmy Knowles to load the bases, and successive sacrifices by catcher Barney Gilligan, center fielder Ed Crane (safe on an error by Titcomb), and Madigan pushed two runs across the plate.

Washington tallied an additional run in the third, but the Quakers put up single runs in the third, fourth, and sixth innings to tie the game, 3-3.

Hines opened the eighth inning for Washington with a single. A base hit by Knowles and a sacrifice by Force put runners on second and third, and Gilligan walked to load the bases. Crane followed with a single to left field, scoring Hines and Knowles. Madigan slapped a grounder between second and short for a single, his first major-league hit, scoring Gilligan. When left fielder George Wood fumbled recovering the ball, Crane scooted home for the fourth and final run of the inning.

Pitching now with a 7-3 lead, Madigan retired Wood and right fielder Ed Daily before Hines's fumble of center fielder Jim Fogarty's grounder and subsequent wild throw to first put Fogarty on base. Shortstop Arthur Irwin tripled over the head of Crane in center field, scoring Fogarty, then scored himself when Hines booted a grounder off the bat of third baseman Joe Mulvey. Mulvey was put out trying for second, ending the inning.

Both teams were retired scoreless in the ninth to clinch the 7-5 victory for Washington. One day after his 18th birthday, the Nationals' Pony had his first major-league victory and driven in the game-winning run, and "the enthusiasm of the fifteen hundred people who saw the home club break a monotonous series of defeats was unbounded."[8]

Madigan pitched his finest game in his next start, on July 23 in Boston, despite winding up on the losing end of a 3-2 score. "There was a general smile among the spectators of yesterday's ball game when Scanlon's feather-weight twirler stepped into the box. He is short in stature ... and looks so slender that one could easily imagine that a hot ball would take him clean off his pins. His boyish face formed a strong contrast to those of the bronzed veterans he had the temerity to face. ... But the big fellows went out one after the other. ... [Madigan] throws a straight ball most of the time and has very few curves, or if he has, he did not use them yesterday. He has a slow drop that fooled the heavy men frequently. In fact, his effectiveness may be said to lie in his slowness, and it was not apparent that he relies much on speed."[9]

The loss in Boston was the first in a string of 10 in a row for Madigan. In two more July starts, he was tagged for 22 hits in an 18-1 rout by the Giants and contributed five walks and a wild pitch to an 11-run, third-inning outburst in a 13-1 loss to the Wolverines. Madigan let victory slip away on August 7 when he allowed the St. Louis Maroons to tie the game on two runs in the ninth inning and win 6-5 in the 10th. Subsequent starts and losses by the scores 9-1, 8-1, and 8-0 made it clear that young Madigan had little left to offer even the lowly Nationals. His final start of the season, September 4 at Washington, resulted in a 20-hit, 13-6 loss to Chicago.

In a syndicated review of NL pitchers that originated in the *New York World*, Madigan was described as "the featherweight of the League corps of pitchers … earning his first laurels as a professional with the Capital City team, and [giving] evidence of making an excellent player when a year or so shall have added to his weight and strength. … Madigan's work in the box is as yet very ungraceful and boyish, but practice is lending finish to his delivery. He will no doubt make a name for himself in the near future."[10]

There was no future, however, for Madigan in the major leagues. His release by the Nationals was reported on September 16.[11] Eleven days later, Madigan, "late of the Nationals," was once again pitching for the amateur Merchant club of Washington.[12]

Despite his youth, Madigan never made it back to the big leagues. He closed out his major-league career on a 10-game losing streak, with a 1-13 won-lost record and an ERA of 4.87. He pitched in 14 games, starting 13 and completing 12, for 114⅔ innings (the most for a major-league pitcher whose career ended before he turned 19[13]), giving up 154 hits, walking 44 and striking out 29. Opposing batters raked him for a .313 batting average.[14] In addition to his pitching, Madigan played three games in right field and batted .083 in 49 plate appearances. The Nationals finished the season deep in the cellar with a dismal record of 28 wins against 92 losses, 60 games behind the pennant-winning Chicago White Stockings.

Madigan signed with the Binghamton Crickets of the International League for 1887, starting and winning the season opener against Utica, 8-2. His pitching was only sporadically effective and after being "knocked silly"[15] by Toronto, 15-2, on August 4, Madigan was released with a won-lost record of 6-12.[16]

William J. Madigan, from the *Kalamazoo Daily Telegraph*, February 25, 1888.

Madigan started the 1888 season with the Kalamazoo Kazoos of the Tri-State League but pitched ineffectively and was released in June.[17] In his final start for the Kazoos, Madigan was knocked out of the box in the eighth inning of a 19-2 rout at the hands of the last-place Jackson Jaxons.

Speaking to a Kalamazoo sportswriter, the frustrated 19-year-old placed the blame for his pitching woes on the league's umpires. "Am I in trim? Well, I thought so, but you can't do much with the Ohio umpires unless you put the ball square over the plate. My effective point is on the corner of the plate, and when I saw that they were all called balls, I pitched to the center of the plate, where they could hit me."[18]

Madigan shows up later in 1888 and in 1889 pitching and playing right field for an amateur club, the Alerts, which featured his older brother Jack at second base and future major-league pitcher Harry Mace.[19] After this, the thread gets lost on Madigan's ballplaying days.

After leaving the ranks of professional ballplayers, Madigan clerked for a D.C. law firm,[20] then operated a saloon, "popular among sports personalities, especially baseball players,"[21] in Washington from 1890 to 1914. On June 3, 1896, he married Margaret "Maggie" Riordan at St. Aloysius Church in Washington,[22] and a son, Francis Raymond, was born in October 1898. Maggie died in 1904 at the age of 31 or 32.[23] Madigan never remarried.

July 20, 1912, was celebrated as Amateur Day at American League Park in Washington, with a parade of 39 old-time amateur nines and a "platoon" of former professionals that included Madigan and a few of his teammates, including Hines and Scanlon, from the 1886 Nationals. All were guests at the game that followed between the AL's Washington Nationals and St. Louis Browns.[24]

In 1914 Madigan, "widely known in baseball circles in the Capital,"[25] made a brief return to the game as a scout for the Federal League. Despite his "hopes to pick up several promising young players from colleges in this locality and from the sandlot brigade of the District,"[26] no notable signings appear to be attributed to him.

Madigan was a salesman for the Pabst Brewing Company until 1920, when he began working for the US Government Printing Office.[27] He retired in 1933 at the age of 65.[28]

After an illness of six weeks, Madigan died on December 4, 1954, at Providence Hospital in Washington. He was 86 years old. He is buried alongside his wife, Maggie, in Washington's Mount Olivet Cemetery.[29]

NOTES

1 "Baseball Matters," *San Francisco Examiner*, September 5, 1886: 1.
2 "Several Fairy Tales," *The Sporting News*, July 19, 1886: 1.
3 "Base Ball," *New Orleans Times-Picayune*, July 28, 1886: 2.
4 "Another Defeat for the Nationals – Sunday Games," *Evening Star* (Washington DC), July 12, 1886: 1.
5 "Another Defeat for the Nationals – Sunday Games."
6 David Nemec, *Major League Baseball Profiles, 1871–1900, Volume 1: The Ballplayers Who Built the Game* (Lincoln, Nebraska: Bison Books, 2011), 118.
7 "Nationals Defeated by the Giants," *New York Tribune*, July 16, 1886: 2.
8 "Washington and Philadelphia," *Philadelphia Inquirer*, July 20, 1886: 3.
9 "Great Work in the Box," *Boston Globe*, July 24, 1886: 5.
10 "Baseball Matters," *San Francisco Examiner*, September 5, 1886: 1.
11 "Base Ball Notes," *Morning Call* (Paterson, New Jersey), September 16, 1886: 8.
12 "Base Ball Notes," *News* (Frederick, Maryland), September 22, 1886: 3.
13 Nemec, 118.
14 "Anson at the Top," *St. Louis Post-Dispatch*, September 25, 1886: 9.
15 "Newark No Longer Leads," *Rochester Democrat and Chronicle*, August 5, 1887: 7.
16 Nemec, 118.
17 "Base Ball Briefs," *Wheeling* (West Virginia) *Daily Intelligencer*, June 7, 1888: 4.
18 "Notes from the Diamond," *Wheeling Daily Intelligencer*, May 5, 1888: 4.
19 Nemec, 118.
20 Nemec, 118.
21 "W.J. Madigan, 86, Ex-Baseball Player," *Evening Star*, December 6, 1964: 14.
22 "Marriage Licenses," *Washington Morning Times*, June 4, 1896: 6.
23 "Died," *Washington Evening Star*, May 13, 1904: 5.
24 Alfred L. Stern, "Amateur Day Outlook Good," *Washington Post*, July 19, 1912: 19.
25 "Tice Madigan, Fed Scout, Seeks to Sign Billy Martin," *Washington Times*, April 29, 1914: 15.
26 "Tice Madigan, Fed Scout, Seeks to Sign Billy Martin."
27 "Madigan, William J.," *Evening Star*, December 6, 1954: 15.
28 "Madigan, William J."
29 "Madigan, William J."

RALPH MAURIELLO

BY ALAN COHEN

"The best birthday present I ever got."
– Ralph Mauriello, September 6, 1958[1]

Ralph Mauriello had been born on August 25, 1934, in Brooklyn, New York, and less than two weeks after his 24th birthday, after six minor-league seasons, he joined the Los Angeles Dodgers. Within two weeks of joining the club, he had his first major-league win. It was his only major-league win. Although he won only one big-league game and was out of Organized Baseball shortly after his 26th birthday, Mauriello, for the balance of his life has regaled those wanting to listen – and seemingly everyone does – to stories of his time in baseball and the people with whom he interacted.

His parents were Salvatore and Rachel Mauriello. Ralph's older sister, Gina Mauriello Garcia, was born in 1931. Younger sisters Mary Mauriello Taylor (born in 1941; died in 1986) and Marjorie Mauriello Baker (born in 1949) completed the family. Ralph's father was a barber who had been born in Port-de-Bouc, France, and raised on the Italian island of Ischia. He came to the United States at the age of 14. Salvatore Mauriello achieved a degree of fame in Brooklyn in 1945 when he rescued a 2-year-old boy, Marvin Goldstein, who had fallen from the fifth-floor ledge of an apartment building in Brooklyn.[2] Ralph's sister Marjorie, an accomplished chef, authored a cookbook featuring four generations of her family's recipes, taught Italian cooking, and served as guest chef at small dinner parties in the Los Angeles area.[3] She was married for 45 years to journalist Robert Baker, who died in 2015.[4]

Singing has always been a big part of Ralph's life, and he recollected that "one of my earliest memories as a child was singing in the 'Amateur Hour' contests at my grandmother's house every Sunday. My Aunt Mary always organized it. All the cousins (and there were many) had to perform in some way; sing, dance, recite a poem, etc. And I've been singing ever since … in church, in choirs, in choruses, and, while I was still working, even while walking down the hall to a meeting."[5]

Ralph started playing baseball at a young age and was encouraged by his father. He remembered attending games at Ebbets Field and one was particularly memorable. Dolph Camilli and Dixie Walker were Ralph's favorite players. Camilli, in his MVP year, led the league in homers and RBIs in 1941, when Ralph turned 7. Late in the season, Ralph and his dad took in a game. His father said that Camilli would not be with the Dodgers much longer. Ralph asked why and his father explained that Dolph was 34, which was old for a ballplayer. Ralph then realized that even if he played pro ball, he would have to find another career after his playing days.

He would play catch with his dad, but the catches ended when Ralph was 12. One day, one of his fastballs hit his father on the hand and jammed his thumb. Even then, Ralph was big and playing with the older kids.[6] The right-hander got his start playing sandlot ball at McCarron Park in the Greenpoint section of Brooklyn, playing against older boys in the Police Athletic League during the summer of 1948.

Ralph's family moved to California shortly after he turned 14. They arrived in Los Angeles on September 1, 1948, in 100-degree heat. He attended North Hollywood High School in Los Angeles, graduated in 1952, and received a scholarship to USC.

As a 14-year-old he showed promise while pitching for the Sherman Way Merchants in the North Hollywood Playground League. In a mound duel on August 5, 1949, he allowed no hits until there were two outs in the ninth inning. He struck out 19 batters but was on the losing end when a Texas League double brought across the winning run in the ninth inning.[7] As a high-school sophomore in 1950, he went 8-0 and was named to the All-Valley League team. On April 30, 1951, he hurled a no-hitter as his North Hollywood team defeated Verdugo Hills, 13-0. Teammate Bert Convy led the offense with five hits, two of which were triples.[8]

After graduating from high school, Mauriello participated in the annual All-City vs. CIF game at Gilmore Field in Los Angeles, sponsored by the *Los Angeles Herald-Express*. He hurled five shutout innings for the All-City team, allowing two hits and striking out 11 batters, as his team won, 6-4.[9] Off this performance, he was selected to represent Los Angeles in the annual Hearst Sandlot Classic in New York, where he was named the starting pitcher. In the game at New York's Polo Grounds on August 20, he hurled two shutout innings, allowing one hit and striking out three batters. He did not figure in the decision. His team, the US All-Stars, lost in 11 innings to the New York All-Stars, 5-4.

While in New York, Mauriello took time to visit his aunt in Brooklyn and pal around with teammate Bobby Locke. He also remembered one night back in his room at the Hotel New Yorker with roommate Bob Borovicka (the other Los Angeles representative). Bob had gone 0-for-2 in the Hearst Sandlot Classic and was taking some vicious swings with his bat. The bat flew out of his hands through the open window and sailed down to the street. Thankfully, nobody was injured. Borovicka, an outfielder, signed with Cleveland but made it only as far as Class B.

The folks back home got to see a pregame picture of Ralph, Bob, and Joe DiMaggio in the *Los Angeles Herald-Express*.[10]

Before heading back to Los Angeles, Mauriello worked out with the Yankees and the Dodgers, and he went home with a professional contract. The signing with the Dodgers was announced on August 30.

Mauriello was evaluated by Dodgers scout Matt Burns and signed by Fresco Thompson, the club's vice president of player personnel. His bonus was estimated to be in the $35,000 range ($25,000 at signing and another $10,000 when he made the majors). He also received a stipend of $300 a month. The bonus went for a new home for his parents, a new barbershop for his father, and an Oldsmobile for himself.[11] The bonus, at the time, was the largest ever given to a pitcher by the Dodgers, eclipsing the estimated $21,000 that had been given to Billy Loes in 1948.

USC, at the insistence of baseball coach Rod Dedeaux, did not renege on the scholarship offer, and Ralph began classes there in the fall of 1952.

After playing semipro ball in the Los Angeles area in the 1952-1953 offseason, Mauriello's professional travels began at Vero Beach when he went to spring training with the Dodgers, appearing in several games with their minor-league affiliates. Opening Day found him hurling for Newport News in the Class-B Piedmont League. His first performance was a bit of a disappointment. He was removed with one out in the fourth inning after allowing five hits and walking seven batters and yielding seven runs, with a wild pitch and a hit batter, as Richmond defeated Newport News, 10-5 in front of a record 4,392 onlookers.[12] Two days later Mauriello redeemed himself, pitching a hitless 3⅓ innings in relief as the Baby Dodgers broke open a tie game in the late innings, giving Mauriello his first professional win, 8-5.[13]

Ralph Mauriello, at the Hearst Game. Courtesy of Ralph Mauriello.

After going 3-8 with Newport News (his last win coming on June 15), Mauriello was sent to Class-C Santa Barbara on July 23. In one of his more memorable outings in Virginia, on May 23, he lost a 16-inning game at Norfolk, 5-4, when infielder Charlie Neal made two errors in the final inning. In the game, Mauriello allowed 14 hits, walked 16 batters, and had a wild pitch.[14] His wildness, a career-long problem, was the key factor in his being sent down. He had walked 88 batters in 90 innings. With Santa Barbara, Mauriello was 6-4 with a 2.49 ERA and walked 55 batters in 83 innings.

One of Mauriello's teammates with Santa Barbara was first-year pro George Anderson, whom Mauriello called Georgie. In Tales Beyond the Dugout, Mauriello devoted a chapter to Anderson, who later acquired his more familiar nickname, Sparky. They, along with four other players, shared a home in Santa Barbara in 1953. On one occasion, the young teammates were in a hotel in San Jose. In their youthful enthusiasm, Georgie and his road roommate, Dale Johnson, took to throwing balloons filled with water at unsuspecting passers-by on the street below their rooms. One balloon found the head of team manager George Scherger, who was peering out from a window on the floor below. Scherger wound up fining all of the players on the floor above, including Mauriello.[15]

In the offseason, while continuing his studies at USC, Mauriello turned to the hardwood, playing semipro basketball with Shortie's Café in the Los Angeles area Valley Municipal League.

The next year, Mauriello started his season with Pueblo in the Class-A Western League. He was with them through June 18, posting a 1-2 record in nine games. While he was there, on May 15 to be precise, he acquired a new roommate, with whom he roomed for much of his time in the minors. Jim Gentile was a hard-hitting first baseman in an organization with an abundance of hard-hitting first basemen. Their adventures from Pueblo to Mobile to Fort Worth, and eventually the Los Angeles Dodgers were outlined in Tales Beyond the Dugout. Jim was Ralph's best friend in baseball and served as best man at Ralph's wedding.

Mauriello was demoted to Asheville in the Class-B Tri-State League, where he was mentored by team manager Ray Hathaway. After winning his first game with Asheville, a complete-game 5-3 victory,[16] he went on to register an 8-4 record with a league-leading and career-best 2.45 ERA, and he mastered the changeup. For the Tourists, a 2-0, 11-inning, four-hit whitewashing of Rock Hill on July 26 was Mauriello's best outing of the season.[17] He capped his season with a 12-strikeout performance in an 11-2 win on August 23 that put the Tourists within a game of clinching the league pennant.[18] Control, however, continued to be an issue. He walked eight in each of his wins on July 26 and August 23, and, with Asheville, had 101 walks in 136 innings. But his 6.2 hits allowed per nine innings led the league and secured his promotion to Double A the following season.

The 1955 season proved to be the best of Mauriello's career in terms of games won. He put up an 18-8 record with the Mobile Bears in the Southern Association, and he led the league with a 2.76 ERA. But the walk bugaboo accompanied him to Mobile and almost derailed his season before it began. In his first start, on April 14, he walked three batters and gave up a hit in the first inning before he was removed from the game by manager Clay Bryant. He rebounded in his second start, a 12-inning 2-1 win over Little Rock.[19] In June he pitched three consecutive shutouts.

Although Mobile had the fourth best record (79-75) during the regular season, the Bears advanced to the playoffs and eliminated Memphis and Birmingham to win the league championship. In the league playoffs, Mauriello won three games, including the decisive seventh game in the opening series against Memphis on September 13. In the opener of the Dixie Series against Texas League champion Shreveport, Mauriello pitched an 8-0 shutout.[20] Mobile went on to sweep the best-of-seven series. Mauriello was named to the season-end Southern Association's All-Star team. He finished in second place in the MVP balloting and won the league's Rookie of the Year award.

In 1956 Mauriello got his first taste of Triple-A ball, starting the season with St. Paul. In 10 games (seven starts) with the Saints, he was 1-1 before being sent to the Fort Worth Cats in the Double-A Texas League at the end of May. It was a reunion of sorts as the Dodgers had moved their affiliation from Mobile to Fort Worth at the beginning of the 1956 season. In his first game with the Cats, he defeated Shreveport 4-1 on May 31.[21] His season in Texas was plagued, once again, by walks and his record was only 7-10. Mauriello did, however, post a team-best ERA of 3.22 and led his squad's staff with 107 strikeouts. His best effort of the season was a three-hit shutout of San Antonio on August 19. Backed by five home runs, he defeated the Spurs, 9-0.[22]

Mauriello spent all of 1957 at the top rung of minor-league baseball. With the Los Angeles Angels of the Open Classification Pacific Coast League, he went 11-5 in front of the home folks. But early that season, he received a notice from his local draft board to report for induction on May 20. During the pre-induction physical he was ruled medically ineligible because of a perforated eardrum. He returned to action after a 21-day layoff and pitched his first complete game of the season on May 31, striking out 11 batters in a 5-2 win over San Diego.[23] He followed that up on June 6 with the first of his two shutouts in the season, defeating Seattle 1-0 with nine strikeouts.[24] His second shutout was a seven-inning performance in the second game of a doubleheader against Sacramento on July 28. He became the team's first and only 10-game winner when he defeated Portland 7-1 on September 4. The Angels, in their last Pacific Coast League season, finished in sixth place with an 80-88 record.

In 1958 Mauriello began the season with Spokane, the Los Angeles Dodgers' new Triple-A team. Mauriello got off to a rocky start. In his first appearance of the season, he lasted only four innings and was charged with the loss as Spokane lost to Seattle, 3-2.[25] In 10 games (seven starts) with Spokane, Mauriello went 2-3 and was sent down to Victoria of the Double-A Texas League on June 3. His lack of control once again was the issue as he issued a league-leading 36 walks in 37 innings at Spokane. With Victoria he had his first successful outing of 1958, on June 19, pitching a complete game and defeating Corpus Christi, 6-3.[26] He registered a 6-8 record with Victoria and was called up to the Dodgers on September 6.

A week after reporting to the Dodgers, on September 13, Mauriello made his big-league debut, starting against the Pirates at Pittsburgh. After walking Bill Virdon, he gave up a single to Roberto Clemente. He then recorded his first big-league strikeout, getting Dick Stuart to swing in vain at a

3-and-2 pitch. Consecutive run-scoring singles by Bob Skinner and Frank Thomas ended Mauriello's day. He was charged with the loss as Pittsburgh went on to win, 9-4.

Mauriello's next start was the realization of the dream that began when he was a child in Brooklyn. On September 19 Mauriello took his 81.00 ERA to the mound at Chicago's Wrigley Field and pitched a masterpiece. He shut out the Cubs for seven innings on three hits and took a 3-0 lead into the bottom of the eighth inning. After Jerry Kindall became his sixth strikeout victim of the afternoon, singles by Al Dark and Ernie Banks put runners on first and second. Mauriello seemed poised to get out of the inning unscathed when he got Walt Moryn to fly out for the second out of the inning.

Then Mauriello began to stumble. He dropped the ball while throwing his first pitch to Dale Long, balking the runners to second and third.[27] After he hurled a wild pitch that allowed Dark to score from third, manager Walt Alston brought in Johnny Podres, who secured the last four outs for Los Angeles, giving Mauriello his first and what was to be his only big-league win.

"And I'll swear that Alston (our manager) was out on the mound to take the ball out of my hand before the guy (Long) reached first base." – Ralph Mauriello's memory of leaving the game on September 27.[28]

Mauriello's next, and last, major-league appearance came against the Cubs at Los Angeles on September 27. He entered the game in the third inning with the score tied, 1-1. Nine outs later, his teammates had given him a three-run lead. The score was 4-1 going into the top of the sixth inning. After getting two quick outs, Mauriello walked Walt Moryn, bringing up Bobby Thomson, who homered to bring the score to 4-3. When he walked Dale Long, putting the potential tying run on base, manager Alston summoned Roger Craig to get the Dodgers out of the inning. Mauriello's hopes for a second win evaporated when the Cubs scored four ninth-inning runs to win the game, 7-4.

The season over, Mauriello resumed his studies in electrical engineering at USC. On January 31, 1959, he married Caroline June Paulenko, known to the world by her middle name. She is a graduate of Franklin High School and was valedictorian of the Class of 1956. When they were wed, she was a mathematics major at UCLA.[29] They had met during the 1957 season when Mauriello was playing with the Angels. She and her sister were outside the ballpark in Los Angeles after a game between the Angels and the San Francisco Seals on June 29. Ralph introduced himself to June, and their romance flowered.

In the spring of 1959, Mauriello was assigned to the Dodgers' farm club at Spokane. He was the Opening Day pitcher but did not factor in the decision as Spokane lost at Phoenix, 6-5. His stay with Spokane was brief. After six appearances, he was 0-2 and had an ERA of 7.20. Clearly, a change of scenery was in order. On May 13 he was sent down to Victoria for the second time in as many years. He got off to a rocky start in Texas, losing his first four decisions, but showed good form in defeating Corpus Christi, 6-1, on June 21. His complete-game outing featured 10 strikeouts. He won four of his last five decisions to bring his record to 4-5 with a 3.31 ERA. Mauriello moved on to the Triple-A Montreal Royals on July 23 after winning his last outing with Victoria, striking out 10 in defeating Amarillo, 3-2. In his first game with the Royals, on July 31, he defeated the Havana Cubans, 6-2, then lost his next three decisions.

"Way back, I always figured it this way: If I stick around in the minors, I'll get my college degree in the off-season and quit; if I make it to the majors, I'll go ahead and get my Master's Degree. I didn't want to start my career at 35. I felt I had a better future as an engineer starting at 26." – Ralph Mauriello, August 20, 1961.[30]

Although still relatively young, having turned 25 during the 1959 season, Mauriello felt that it was time to consider a career change. To move on, he had to complete his education. He completed his college work by staying in school for the entire 1959-1960 school year and getting his bachelor's degree. He then reported to Montreal for his last season of professional baseball. He went 7-5 for the Royals and called it a career. As a minor-league pitcher, Mauriello had gone 75-68 in eight seasons.

In the offseason, Mauriello took a position with Litton Industries, a major defense contractor. He was with Litton for 30 years and earned his master's degree from UCLA before starting his own computer design company, Mauriello and Associates. It was a small firm with only six employees, including Mauriello. Ralph and June had the first of their three daughters, Tami, in 1960. They later welcomed Gina and Michelle to the family and, as of October 2021, they have been married for 63 years, with six grandchildren and two great-grandchildren.

The professional baseball part of his life over, Mauriello turned to other pursuits, principally singing. He had often sung during the time he played ball but in the 1960s, outside of work and taking an occasional turn in the mound in semipro ball, singing became his primary focus. He became a featured soloist for the San Fernando Valley Male Chorus and Shepherd of the Valley Lutheran Church choir. He performed with community theater productions and was in the chorus for two operas performed by the West Coast Opera company. He also did 30-minute shows for various organizations near his home. He has sung the National Anthem at Los Angeles Lakers basketball games and Los Angeles Kings hockey games. Since 2008, he has performed the anthem at least once a season at Dodger Stadium.

As for those turns on the mound, they continued for many years. In the spring of 1989, at the age of 54 and more than three decades removed from his only big-league win, Mauriello was in uniform for the Outlaws in a Los Angeles area Municipal League.

SOURCES

In addition to the sources shown in the Notes, the author used Baseball-Reference.com, *The Sporting News*, and author interviews with Ralph Mauriello on January 8, 2015, and September 29, 2021.

NOTES

1. Frank Finch, "Podres to Duel Cardinals' Jackson," *Los Angeles Times*, September 7, 1958: 3-2.
2. Salvatore Mauriello Obituary, *Los Angeles Times*, January 11, 1992: B-4.
3. Marjorie Mauriello Baker, "Just Like Nonna Used to Make," *Los Angeles Times*, October 10, 2004: L-11.
4. Jean Merl, "Bob Baker 1947-2015: Times Journalist Fulfilled Music Dream," *Los Angeles Times*, July 18, 2015: 3-B.
5. Correspondence between author and Ralph Mauriello, March 15, 2021.
6. Mauriello grew to become 6-feet-3 and is listed at 195 pounds.
7. "Hot Shots Win Extra-Innings Pitching Duel," *Van Nuys (California) News*, August 8, 1950: Part 2, 3.
8. "Ralph Mauriello Hurls No-Hitter," *North Hollywood Valley Times*, May 1, 1951: 6. High School teammate Bert Convy, after a short minor-league career, became an entertainer and was successful, for three decades, as an actor and television game show host.
9. "City Diamond All-Stars Top Ace CIF Squad by 6-4," *Los Angeles Times*, June 28, 1952: Part 2, 10.
10. *Los Angeles Herald-Express*, August 21, 1952.
11. Jeff Meyers, "Stardust Memories: 31 Years After Failing to Stick with the Dodgers Ralph Mauriello Is Still Pitching – and Pondering What Might Have Been," *Los Angeles Times*, April 23, 1989: F-18.
12. "Crowd of 4,392 for Opening Game at Newport News," *Hagerstown (Maryland) Daily Mail*, April 24, 1953: 14.
13. Charles Karmosky, "Neal Hurt as Dodgers Cash In on Portsmouth Error for 8-5 Win," *Newport News (Virginia) Daily Press*, April 26, 1953: C-1.
14. "Miscue Ruins Sterling Effort for Mauriello," *Newport News Daily Press*, May 24, 1953: C-1.
15. Ralph Mauriello, *Tales Beyond the Dugout: The Zany Antics of Baseball Players of the Fifties* (Los Angeles: Mauriello Publishing, 2017), 28.
16. Bob Terrell, "Mauriello Stops Rock Hill in Asheville Debut, 5 to 3," *Asheville (North Carolina) Citizen*, June 21, 1954: 11.
17. "Tourists Defeat Rock Hill Twice; Fessette Gets 19th," *Asheville Citizen*, July 27, 1954: 13.
18. Bob Terrell, "Reid and Mauriello Pace Tourists Win," *Asheville Citizen*, August 24, 1954: 13.
19. Vernon Butler, "Mobile Rookie Wins in 12, 2 to 1," *Birmingham News*, April 16, 1955: 9.
20. "Mauriello, Bears Blank Sports, 8-0," *Birmingham News*, September 25, 1955: C-8.
21. Lorin McMullen, "Mauriello Halts Sport Attack, 4-1," *Fort Worth Star-Telegram*, June 1, 1956: 17.

22 McMullen, "Cats Try Again for Infielder," *Fort Worth Star-Telegram*, August 20, 1956: 20.

23 Frank Finch, "Angels Score 5-2 Win Over Padres," *Los Angeles Times*, June 1, 1957: 2-1.

24 "Angels Win in 9th, 1-0, Over Suds," *Los Angeles Times*, June 7, 1957: 4-2.

25 Bob Johnson, "Hurlers Star for Spokane; Twin Bill Divided," *Spokane Chronicle*, April 17, 1958: 37.

26 John Lyons, "Mauriello Snaps Corpus Christi Win Streak," *Victoria* (Texas) *Advocate*, June 20, 1958: 8.

27 Richard Dozer, "Dodger Rookies Humble Cubs, 5-1," *Chicago Tribune*, September 20, 1958: Section 2, 3.

28 Mauriello, 194.

29 "Franklin Ephebian to Wed Dodger Baseball Player," *(Los Angeles) Eagle Rock Sentinel*, October 9, 1958: 6.

30 Jack McCurdy, "Ex-Dodger Goes into Electronics," *Los Angeles Times*, August 20, 1961: F-10.

BRENT MAYNE

BY PAUL HOFMANN

A well-traveled catcher, Brent Mayne played with the Kansas City Royals, New York Mets, Oakland Athletics, San Francisco Giants, Colorado Rockies, Arizona Diamondbacks, and Los Angeles Dodgers. Used primarily in a platooning role against right-handed pitchers or as a late-inning defensive replacement, Mayne was remembered more for his defense than his offense. A strong-armed catcher who wasn't afraid to block the plate and who had a reputation for handling a pitching staff, Mayne played in 1,279 games during his 15-year major-league career and finished with a career batting average of .263 with 38 home runs, 403 RBIs, and a single victory as a pitcher.

Brent Danem Mayne was born on April 19, 1968, in Loma Linda, California, the oldest of the two sons of Michael and Patricia Mayne. Mike Mayne was a high-school and college baseball coach. After a successful coaching stint at Eisenhower High School in Rialto, California, the senior Mayne coached baseball at Orange Coast College for 15 years, compiling a career record of 400-188-6. His teams won five South Coast Conference championships, two Orange Empire Conference championships, and the 1980 California State Community College Championship. He later was the pitching coach at Fresno State, where he helped the Bulldogs to the 2008 NCAA championship before joining the coaching staff at California State University Bakersfield. In 1993 Mike Mayne was inducted into the California College Baseball Association Coaches' Hall of Fame.

Having a successful baseball coach for a father had a profound impact on the development of Brent as a baseball player. Brent characterized his father as a no-nonsense, demanding, taskmaster type of coach. He described his father as "like a Bobby Knight kind of coach … very tough, work-oriented, the full regimen. 'If you can›t do it right, don't do it at all!' That sort of thing."¹ Brent, who had a more carefree approach to life, often struggled with his father's overbearing nature. Instead of being committed to putting in the time and effort to becoming a polished ballplayer, he gravitated to the world of surfing.

At the same time, Mayne said he understood just how lucky he was to have a father as a baseball coach. "Personally, I lucked into [baseball]. … since we had only one car, I had to go the field every day after school till practice was over to go home – whether I liked it or not. As a result, I played and watched a lot of baseball."²

Brent attended Costa Mesa High School. He was a slow, undersized second baseman in high school who was forced to sit out his senior year at Costa Mesa High School due to tendinitis in his shoulder. When he graduated, he was just 5-feet-6 and 135 pounds. There was no indication that he was a major-league, or even a Division I college, prospect at that time. He understood he was at a crossroads as far as baseball was concerned. He had to make a decision whether to continue to pursue baseball or find something outside of sports. It was at this point that Brent's father told him that his only chance of continuing as a ballplayer involved strapping on the tools of ignorance.

Mayne recounted his transition from second base to catcher as follows:

"At the same time I was changing positions, my father, Cal State Fullerton coach Larry Corrigan, and big-league receiver Jamie Nelson were involved in the process of breaking down the mechanics of catching and more or less reinventing it ... and they needed a guinea pig for this experiment. They needed someone (preferably with no catching experience because there would be no bad habits to break) to see whether the 'Bench style' could be improved upon with their innovative ideas about athletic foundation, stances, and receiving and blocking techniques. With my options severely limited, I jumped at the opportunity and quickly embodied their vision of a modern catcher."[3]

The transition to catcher continued when Mayne enrolled at Orange Coast College, where he played baseball for his father. After his freshman year, he transferred to California State University Fullerton. He was the Titans' starting catcher in 1988 and 1989. He earned first-team All-Big West Conference honors both seasons and earned American Baseball Coaches Association (ABCA) second-team All-American honors in 1988, when he batted a team-high .393 with 22 doubles, 1 home run, and 31 RBIs. He batted .350 with 5 home runs and 34 RBIs in 1989 and as of 2022 held the school record with a 38-game hitting streak in 1988.[4]

Mayne was selected in the first round (13th overall) in the 1989 amateur draft by the Kansas City Royals. He was the third catcher taken overall, behind Tyler Houston, who was selected second by the Atlanta Braves, and Charles Johnson, who was selected 10th by the Montreal Expos. He signed on June 16 and began his professional baseball career with the Baseball City Royals of the Florida State League in 1989. He caught seven games and hit .542 (13-for-24) with 8 RBIs.

Despite the limited number of games played at the Class-A level the previous season, Mayne began 1990 with the Memphis Chicks of the Double-A Southern League. He played in 115 games, 92 as a catcher, and hit .267 with 2 home runs and 61 RBIs. When major-league rosters expanded in September, the 22-year-old catcher was brought up to Kansas City.

Mayne made his major-league debut on September 18, 1990, in the Hubert H. Humphrey Metrodome in Minneapolis. Starting at catcher and batting eighth in the Royals lineup, Mayne wasted no time collecting his first major-league hit when he singled off Twins starter Scott Erickson in the top of the third inning to drive in Sean Berry and tie the score, 1-1. Mayne ranked his first major-league hit as his favorite memory of playing baseball.[5] The Twins rallied for six runs in the fifth and two runs in the eighth to best the Royals, 10-4. Mayne appeared in five games for the Royals that fall, hitting .231 (3-for-13).

The Royals broke spring training in 1991 with Mayne as the backup catcher. By the second half of the season, Mayne became the starting catcher when Mike Macfarlane suffered torn knee ligaments. While he struggled with throwing would-be basestealers out (23 of 76, or 30 percent), he did handle the pitching staff well and was particularly impressive in the clutch, hitting .349 with runners in scoring position. He finished the season batting .251 with 3 home runs and 31 RBIs.

Mayne hit his first major-league home run on August 1 at County Stadium in Milwaukee. The Royals were trailing the Brewers 4-2 with one out in the top of the eighth when Kurt Stillwell doubled. Manager Hal McRae then called on Mayne to pinch-hit for Tim Spehr. With the count at 2-and-2, the left-handed-hitting Mayne launched a two-run home run to deep right field off right-hander Julio Machado to tie the game, 4-4. He later drove in a much-needed insurance run in the top of the 11th inning when he grounded out to second to drive in Todd Benzinger and put the Royals up 6-4. Mayne had three RBIs as the Royals hung on for a 6-5 victory.

On August 26 the rookie catcher experienced baseball immortality when he was the starting batterymate for Bret Saberhagen. That night, Saberhagen no-hit the Chicago White Sox in a 7-0 Royals victory. Years later, Mayne recalled how that evening felt like no other. "It was a unique experience, I don't know how to explain it other than it was really intense and pins and needles, but it was also very enjoyable because coming out of the bullpen that particular game (after the 10-15-minute warm-up session) I said he's going to throw a no hitter today, because it just felt like it was that kind of stuff."[6]

Mayne was the subject of trade rumors during the winter of 1991. It was reported that the Houston Astros were interested in him and were willing to deal fleet-footed outfielder Kenny Lofton for Mayne. The trade fell through when the Royals also asked for left-handed reliever Al Osuna.

With Macfarlane recovered from the knee injury he suffered the previous season, Mayne resumed his duties as the Royals backup catcher in 1992. He experienced a bit of a sophomore slump, batting .225 and driving in 18 runs. That year Mayne became a father. He had a daughter, Dylan, from a relationship that never led to marriage.[7] A year later, Mayne was introduced to a waitress named Hillary by a high-school teammate. A year later the couple were married. They have two children, a son (Noah) and daughter (Jaia).

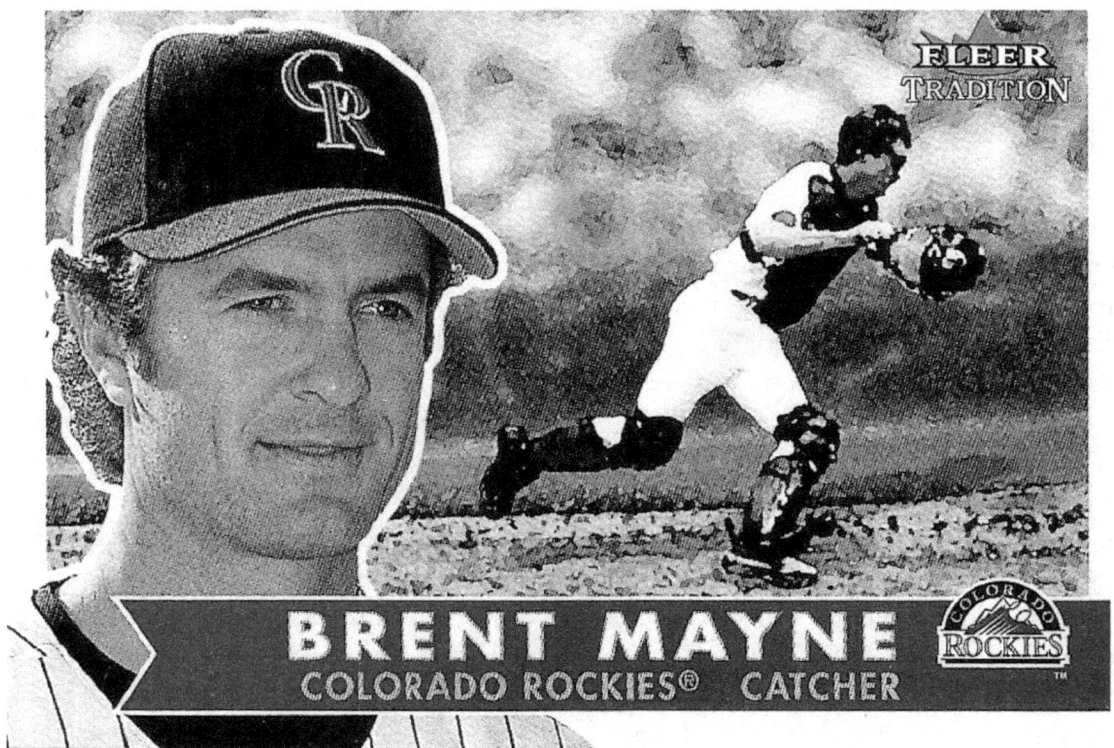

Brent Mayne with the Rockies. Courtesy The Topps Company, Inc.

Mayne again backed up Macfarlane during the 1993 and 1994 seasons. In 1993 he played in 71 games and hit .254 with 2 home runs and 22 RBIs. Limited to 46 games because of the players strike in 1994, Mayne batted .257, hit 2 home runs, and drove in 20 runs.

In 1995 Mayne finally became the Royals starting catcher when Macfarlane signed with the Boston Red Sox at the end of the strike in April 1995. Now 27 years old, Mayne played in 110 games and hit .251 with 1 home run and 27 RBIs.

On December 19, 1995, the Royals traded Mayne to the New York Mets for minor-league outfielder Al Shirley.[8] Mayne had become expendable when a few days earlier the Royals reacquired Macfarlane through free agency.

In New York Mayne saw limited action behind the plate. He was the backup catcher to Todd Hundley, who was enjoying a career year that included 41 home runs and 112 RBIs. Mayne appeared in only 21 games as a catcher and 70 overall. In 113 plate appearances he hit .263 with 1 home run and 6 RBIs.

Mayne became a free agent in December 1996. A month later he signed with the Seattle Mariners. The Mariners signed Mayne as a third catcher who would compete for the backup catching job. At the end of spring training, he was released in favor of veteran John Marzano, who continued to back up Dan Wilson. However, Mayne's baseball career was far from over. On April 8 he signed with the Oakland Athletics.

An avid surfer, Mayne welcomed the return to his home state. He split the A's catching duties with switch-hitting George Williams. The pair were backed up by Izzy Molina. In 85 games Mayne batted .289, a career high to that point, and hit 6 home runs with 22 RBIs. That fall he was rewarded on the free-agent market, signing a two-year, $1.45 million contract with the San Francisco Giants to back up catcher Brian Johnson.

Mayne enjoyed two productive seasons in San Francisco. In 1998 he played in 94 games, only five fewer than Johnson, and batted .273 with 3 home runs and 32 RBIs. This may have factored into the Giants' decision to not re-sign Johnson after the season. In 1999 Mayne was the Giants' starting catcher, appearing in 117 games, and batted .301 with 2 home runs and 39 RBIs. He was also a reliable bat off the bench. In his two seasons in San Francisco, Mayne was 11-for-28 (.393) as a pinch-hitter.

During his time in the Bay Area, Mayne compared his approaches toward baseball and surfing. "I'm always fighting this battle about performance in baseball, like trying to duplicate a great game I had, when I'd rather just stay in the moment, trust myself and everything will be all right," he told an interviewer. "And that's surfing. I mean, there's never the same wave twice. You might be out there trying to work on something, but the wave may not allow it (laughter). It commands spontaneity, the ability to just react and flow with the dynamics of the situation. I'm so drawn to all of that."[9]

That December, Mayne signed a two-year contract with the Colorado Rockies worth $3.9 million. He played in 117 games for the Rockies in 2000, none more memorable than the one on August 22 at Coors Field against the Atlanta Braves.

On that night Mayne joined the small fraternity of position players who have earned a victory as a pitcher. Not in the starting lineup because of a sore wrist, he was given the opportunity out of necessity. The story begins with two outs in the top of the 11th inning.

The Braves and Rockies were tied 6-6 when Rockies manager Buddy Bell called on his last available reliever, right-hander John Wasdin, to presumably pitch the rest of the way. On a 3-and-2 pitch, Wasdin hit Andrés Galarraga with an off-speed pitch that was up and in. Galarraga, who made no attempt to get out of the way of the pitch, began making his way toward first base before charging the mound and inciting a bench-clearing brawl (despite the hit batter being the first of the game … in extra innings … on a full count … with two outs).[10]

Bell called on the previous night's starter, Brian Bohanon, to get them through the 10th inning. The left-handed Bohanon, who had thrown 99 pitches the night before, walked Brian Jordan before retiring Javy López on a fly ball to deep left. Despite throwing only 10 pitches, Bohanon had nothing more to give.

While Scott Kamieniecki was retiring the Rockies in the bottom of the 11th, Bell, managing from the clubhouse, had no idea which of his position players could pitch. Mayne recalled his conversation with Bell as follows:

"I was up in the clubhouse after the fight, and I walked by Buddy's office," Mayne recalled. "He called me and said, 'What are we gonna do? We're out of pitchers. Who can pitch?' He said, 'Can Juan (Pierre) pitch?' I said, 'Yeah, I guess he can pitch.' Then he said, 'Can you pitch?' And I said, 'Yeah, I can pitch.' He said, 'OK, you're pitching.'"[11]

Mayne speculated that perhaps Bell was thinking, "Catchers usually have strong arms, or whatever, hell, I don't know."[12] He later admitted he had never pitched at any level, not even in Little League.[13]

Entering the game in the top of the 12th inning with the score tied at 6-6, Mayne stood on the mound, fulfilling a lifelong dream.[14] First up was Tom Glavine, the Braves' All-Star starting pitcher, who was called on to pinch-hit for Kamieniecki. After getting ahead with a 1-and-2 count, Mayne sailed an off-speed pitch five feet behind the left-handed-hitting Glavine. Two pitches later, Glavine hit a little nubber between the mound and first base, which Mayne fielded cleanly and tossed to first for the inning's first out. Walt Weiss flied out to center for the second out. Things then turned a bit tense when Rafael Furcal singled and moved to second on a wild pitch. Mayne then walked Andruw Jones on five pitches to set the stage for Chipper Jones, who chopped a weak, checked-swing grounder to third to end the Braves' half of the inning.

Controversial left-handed reliever John Rocker started the 12th inning for the Braves. Perez singled to center and raced to third when Todd Helton singled to right. When Jeffrey Hammonds lined out to center, Perez played it safe and stayed at third. Braves manager Bobby Cox called on right-hander Stan Belinda to extinguish the fire and keep the game tied. After striking out Terry Shumpert, Belinda intentionally walked Jeff Cirillo to pitch to Mayne. However, Mayne was lifted for pinch-hitter Adam Melhuse. On Belinda's first pitch, Melhuse made catcher-turned-pitcher Mayne the winning pitcher with a line-drive single to left that scored Perez. Rocker was tagged with the loss.

Mayne's victory marked the first time a position player had picked up a win since Rocky Colavito relieved Steve Barber and pitched 2⅔ shutout innings in the first game of doubleheader against the Detroit Tigers at Yankee Stadium on August 25, 1968.[15] As of 2022, Mayne was one of only eight position players who earned a win in their only pitching appearance.[16]

In a 2009 interview with David Allan, Mayne reflected on his single victory. "You know the funny thing about baseball, the way baseball is, it's so upside down, I spent my whole life trying to be a great catcher but the thing I'll probably be recognized most for when I die is that I won a game as a pitcher, that's so like baseball."[17]

Mayne matched his career-high 117 games played the year earlier and finished 2000 with a .301 batting average, 6 home runs, and a career-high 64 RBIs. Before 2000 he had never driven in more than 39 runs in a season. It appeared the 32-year-old left-handed-hitting Mayne had found a home behind the plate with the Rockies. However, this proved to not be the case.

After the emergence of rookie catcher Ben Petrick as the Rockies' catcher of the future, Mayne was traded to the Royals for right-handed pitcher Mac Suzuki and catcher Sal Fasano. Mayne, who was hitting .331 at the time of the trade, hit only .241 after his return to Kansas City. He finished the year with a .285 average, 2 home runs, and 40 RBIs. At the time of the trade, Royals general manager Allard Baird spoke highly of Mayne and his ability to impact the team's future: "He is an above-average receiver. ... He has the experience we need at the major-league level to continue the development of our pitchers here as well as the guys we will bring up."[18]

Mayne was the Royals' regular catcher in 2002 and 2003, backed up by A.J. Hinch and Mike Difelice, respectively. However, his offensive production never rebounded to the level of his previous five seasons. In 2002 he hit .236 with 4 home runs and 30 RBIs. He followed this with a .245 average, 6 home runs, and 36 RBIs in 2003. He finished his Royals career with the third most games caught in team history, behind Macfarlane and John Wathan.

After the 2003 season, Mayne was granted free agency. On December 18 he signed a one-year, $800,000 contract with the Arizona Diamondbacks. The Diamondbacks were coming off a third-place finish, after a World Series championship in 2001 and back-to-back AL West Division championships in 2001 and 2002. The 2004 Diamondbacks, however, failed to follow up on their success of the previous seasons and were quickly out of pennant race. The team was 28½ games off the pace (on its way to a 51-111 record) when it traded Mayne and outfielder Steve Finley to the Los Angeles Dodgers on July 31. In return the Diamondbacks received minor-league outfielder Reggie Abercrombie, catcher Koyie Hill, and left-handed pitcher Bill Murphy. At the time of the trade, Mayne had played in 36 games and was batting .255 and had driven in 10 runs.

The trade took Mayne back to his boyhood home in Southern California and from the last-place Diamondbacks to the first-place Dodgers. With the departure of Paul Lo Duca, Mayne was the Dodgers' regular catcher down the stretch. In 47 games he hit .188 with 5 RBIs as the Dodgers hung on to win the NL West by two games over the San Francisco Giants, giving Mayne his first chance to play in the postseason.

Mayne appeared in all four games of the National League Division Series matchup against the St. Louis Cardinals. The Cardinals finished with a NL-best record of 105-57 and won the NL Central handily. Starting three games behind the plate, Mayne went 2-for-6, scoring a run in Game Three. In his final plate appearance of the series, he hit a comebacker to pitcher Jeff Suppan before being replaced as part of a double switch. The Cardinals won the series in four games.

The Dodgers and Mayne failed to reach an agreement before the January 8, 2005, deadline, signaling an end to Mayne's career. While Mayne's agent, Barry Meister, stopped short of officially announcing the catcher's retirement, he did say, "Los Angeles is home for him. He really only wanted one of two things. He either wanted to play for the Los Angeles Dodgers or retire."[19]

Mayne didn't hit for much of an average, display a great deal of power, miraculously turn around pitching staffs, or even throw out would-be basestealers at a very high rate. Yet, when his 15-year career was done, Mayne had played in 1,279 games (1,143 as a catcher) and finished with a career batting average of .263 with 38 home runs and 403 RBIs. This is testament to his collective catching abilities and understanding of the game.

In 2008, Mayne wrote *The Art of Catching: The Secrets and Techniques of Baseball's Most Demanding Position*. He authored the book in part because he believed there was a lack of quality information available to those interested in catching.[20] The book provides readers with a comprehensive overview of the art of catching.

As of early 2022, Mayne resided in Southern California with his wife and two children, and remained an avid surfer.

SOURCES

In addition to the sources cited in the Notes, the author also relied on Baseball-reference.com and Retrosheet.org.

NOTES

1. Bruce Jenkins, "Mayne's the Giant Who Really Knows How to Swing," March 21, 1998, www.sfgate.com/sports/jenkins/article/Mayne-s-the-Giant-Who-Really-Knows-How-to-Swing-3330135.php

2. Brent Mayne, *The Art of Catching: The Secrets and Techniques of Baseball's Most Demanding Position* (Costa Mesa, California: Cleanline Books): 86.

3. Mayne, 15-16.

4. "Brent Mayne," Retrieved from https://www.fullertontitans.com/athletics/Hall_of_Fame/HOF_Bios/HOF_Mayne

5. "Bent Mayne," June 4, 2021, Letters from Home Plate, https://lettersfromhomeplate.com/2021/06/01/brent-mayne/

6. David Allan, "Interview with Former MLB Catcher Brent Mayne," June 23, 2009, baseballreflections.com/2009/06/23/interview-with-former-mlb-catcher-brent-mayne/.

7. Jenkins.

8. Shirley was also a first-round draft pick, 18th overall in 1991. Just 21 years old at the time of the trade, Shirley struggled to make contact at the plate and never progressed beyond the Double-A level. He finished his nine-year minor/independent-league career with a .213 average.

9. Jenkins.

10. Kevin Henry, "Colorado Rockies History: Brent Mayne Makes History on the Mound," *Fansided*, August 22, 2017,roxpile.com/2017/08/22/colorado-rockies-history-brent-mayne-makes-history-mound/.

11. Jayson Stark, "The Catcher and 'The Shade Man' Toe the Rubber," ESPN.com, August 30, 2017. https:// www.espn.com/mlb/columns/stark_jayson/703979.html.

12. Grant Brisbee, "The Time a Catcher Pitched at Coors Field and Won," SBNation.com, August 21, 2015. sbnation.com/2015/8/21/9188267/brent-mayne-pitching-rockies-braves.

13. Brisbee.

14. Brisbee.

15. Brisbee.

16. Zachary Rymer, "Chris Davis and Top 10 Position-Player Pitching Performances of All-Time," BleacherReport.com, May 7, 2012, https://bleacherreport.com/articles/1175094-chris-davis-and-top-10-position-player-pitching-performances-of-all-time.

17. David Allan, "Interview with Former MLB Catcher Brent Mayne."

18. Max Rieper, "The 100 Greatest Royals of All-Time – #56 Brent Mayne," royalsreview.com, May 9, 2008, https://royalsreview.com/2008/5/8/482638/the-100-greatest-royals-of ???? -all-time ???

19. Tony Jackson, "Mayne Not Re-Signed by Dodgers; Agent Says He Most Likely Will Retire," *Palm Springs* (California) *Desert Sun,* January 9, 2005: 43.

20. Mayne, 8.

ED MCCREERY

BY CHAD MOODY

"Errors of the hands, mind, feet and errors of omission followed one another in such rapid succession that only a mental genius could keep a record of them," reported the *Detroit Free Press* of the Cleveland Naps' exceedingly poor play in their blowout loss to the Detroit Tigers on August 16, 1914.[1] Making the most of his major-league debut in the contest, Tigers starting pitcher Ed McCreery rode the Naps' ineptness to his lone career victory. Despite appearing in only two other big-league games, the "one-win wonder" nonetheless became a dubious entry in the annals of baseball because of his own dreadful performance in his one and only win.

Esley Porterfield McCreery was born on December 24, 1889, in Florence, Colorado, a railroad town 40 miles southwest of Colorado Springs that was in a boom period as a result of oil discovery there in 1881.[2] His mother, Elizabeth (née Gardiner), was a homemaker, and his father, John, was a druggist. Elizabeth's parents both hailed from Scotland, while at least some of John's ancestors trace their heritage to Ireland. The couple had one other child, Dale, who was six years his brother's junior. While McCreery was an adolescent, his family moved 150 miles due north within the Centennial State to Loveland. Reports indicate that he had likely honed his craft on the mound for the semipro Loveland Grays in his late teens.[3]

After serious legal troubles befell McCreery's father stemming from the illegal sale of alcohol, the clan relocated in early 1909 to Filer, Idaho, a small town just west of Twin Falls.[4] In addition to becoming the proprietor of a drugstore there, the family patriarch quickly became one of the founders of Filer's baseball association.[5] Local baseball enthusiasts expected the embattled druggist's eldest son to also have an impact on the game upon his arrival. "[McCreery] is a crack baseball pitcher, and expects to join the league," wrote the *Twin Falls Times*.[6] Indeed, the 19-year-old played semipro ball throughout the '09 campaign, first with the Twin Falls team before joining the Idaho Falls Sunnylanders. "When big Mack gets on the slab and swings his mighty right he makes them all go way back and sit down," wrote the *Twin Falls News* of the popular hurler who had been "pitching winning ball."[7] The 6-foot, 190-pounder was "stingy with hits" during a season in which he tossed a no-hitter against a strong Salt Lake team; his success garnered him a roster spot on the San Diego club of the California Winter League.[8]

The 1910 season began with both promise and tumult for McCreery. Despite being reportedly signed in February by the Montgomery Climbers of the Class-A Southern Association, numerous stories circulated that the big right-hander had instead joined the Spokane Indians of the Class-B Northwestern League. "Somebody is on a wrong steer," quipped the *Montgomery Advertiser* of the mix-up.[9] Once the roster confusion was resolved, McCreery received a tryout with the Climbers, but was released during spring training. Returning home to Idaho, he spent the remainder of the campaign toeing the slab back in the independent ranks for Twin Falls.[10] McCreery wintered in Southern California as he had done the year before, this time keeping sharp as a member of the independent San Bernardino club.[11]

Early in 1911, reports surfaced that McCreery had signed with the Vernon Tigers of the Class-A Pacific Coast League and would be summoned by manager Wallace "Happy" Hogan in March; however, for unknown reasons there is no record of his joining the club.[12] Instead, McCreery spent the spring battling for a roster spot in Victoria, British Columbia, with the Northwestern League's expansion Islanders (as the club was locally known). "McCreery did some good work, confirming the opinion of [teammate Ed] Householder that he is improving every day, and is likely to make good," reported the *Victoria Daily Times* during spring camp.[13] Indeed, "Mac" not only made the team, but became the staff's workhorse ace. Although posting a substandard 11-23 record in 37 games largely due to poor support from the league's worst team, McCreery was nonetheless named to the all-star team despite battling poor eyesight and fatigue from overwork.[14] Recognizing his talent, the American League's Cleveland Naps drafted the 21-year-old in September. Because the big-league club had drafted a glut of recruits, McCreery was sent in the offseason to the Toledo Mud Hens of the Double-A American Association.[15] Nevertheless, it was quickly "arranged that he wear a Victoria uniform in the pitcher's box" once again for the following campaign.[16]

"McCreery will be the leading [Victoria] pitcher, undoubtedly," proclaimed former minor leaguer and Pacific Coast baseball pundit Elmer Emerson during spring training in 1912.[17] Despite the lofty expectations and being labeled the "first pitcher" of the team (now known as the Bees) heading into the season, McCreery suffered control problems – and a sophomore slump.[18] Although tossing 249 innings in 37 games as a mainstay within Victoria's rotation, he finished the "disappointing" year with an 11-14 record, a league second-worst RA9[19] among regular starters, and a league-most 95 walks.[20] Reportedly due in part to the "cold reception on the home grounds" given to the floundering hurler by the fans, the services of the "big, husky fellow" were offered for cash to Spokane in September.[21] After that deal fell through, he was traded during the offseason to the league-rival Vancouver Beavers for former big-league moundsman Eli Cates.

Early in the 1913 regular season, McCreery took a leave of absence from the Beavers to return to Idaho upon his father's passing. Despite the difficult circumstances, he attempted to remain in "midseason form" during his time away by taking the mound for the local Buhl-Filer semipro team.[22] In a start against his former Twin Falls team, McCreery was embarrassingly tagged for four runs by the de facto amateurs and picked up the loss; this seemingly foreshadowed his poor pitching after returning to Vancouver.[23] In fact, after taking a drubbing in early June, McCreery suffered another thrashing the following week by his old Bees club which turned him into fodder for the media.[24] "As per usual, as in the days of yore, our old team-mate McCreery, now of [team owner] Bob Brown's Beavers, blew up in the sixth inning and the Bees simply romped home with the second game of the series by hitting the ball on the nose for six runs," wrote the *Victoria Daily Times*.[25] And with Brown boasting a team full of strong arms and "too many men on his payroll," McCreery was released in early July.[26] He completed his stint in Vancouver with a 3-2 record and very subpar 5.25 RA9 in nine games. Demoted to the Butte Miners of the Class-D Union Association, where he finished out the year, McCreery became a rotation regular and appeared in 26 games. Despite posting an 8-7 record with statistics that were middling at best, he was nonetheless praised for his "speed" and called a "best buy" by local media.[27]

Prior to the 1914 campaign, McCreery indicated that his preference was to remain in the Golden State, where he had spent the offseason pitching for the Urbita Stars of the California Winter

League.²⁸ Although the 24-year-old reportedly had an opportunity to join the PCL's Oakland Oaks, the deal fell through by one account due to the contract not reaching the correct mailing address in a timely manner.²⁹ Despite lobbying the Miners for his release, he "evidently saw that he was to play in Butte or not at all and signed up."³⁰ Putting "his heart in the game" and the rocky business dealings behind him, McCreery quickly became the ace of the Miners' staff.³¹ "He is the only pitcher in the Union Association who can give three balls and then curve the next three strikes," wrote the *Anaconda (Montana) Standard*.³² Making a "big impression around the circuit," McCreery attracted the attention of clubs in the upstart Federal League, a maverick major league operating outside of Organized Baseball.³³ However, he spurned reported offers from the Indianapolis Hoosiers and Kansas City Packers, saying he would prefer to "remain in organized baseball, even if only in a class D circuit."³⁴ Finishing the campaign with a 14-10 record and ranking among the league leaders in nearly all major statistical categories, McCreery was named an all-star by circuit sportswriters.³⁵

During what turned out to be the final few remaining days of Butte's 1914 season, the American League's Detroit Tigers were seeking to shore up their "unreliable" pitching and build for the future.³⁶ As such, coach and scout Deacon McGuire was dispatched to Utah to see McCreery take on the Ogden Canners on July 27. McGuire "immediately found himself getting sweet" on "Big Ed," who held the strong Ogden club "at his mercy" in a 6-2 complete-game victory.³⁷ Immediately after the game, Detroit purchased McCreery's contract for $1,000 or $2,000 depending on the reports. These funds were viewed as a potential lifeline for the financially struggling Miners, whose players struck a week later for unpaid salaries. However, the money was too little, too late, leading to Butte's dropping out of the league – and causing the untimely demise of the Union Association itself in early August. This confluence of events nearly left McCreery stranded in Montana without the means to join his new team;

Some members of the 1912 Victoria Bees pitching staff, spring training, San Jose. L to R: Joe Berger, Young, "Rebel" Clark, "Kiddo" Wilson, Alfred Narveson, James Concannon, Ed McCreery, Olson, "Rube" Griffin. From the *Victoria Colonist*, March 27, 1912.

he called the difficult situation "the rawest experience he had ever met with in baseball."[38] Ultimately, McCreery was able to wire Tigers manager Hughie Jennings to cover his cross-country railroad expenses.

Described as tall and stout with brown eyes and hair, the youngster made his major-league debut in a road start against last-place Cleveland on August 16.[39] Aided by the Naps' sloppy fielding and mindless blunders in the top of the first, McCreery's teammates spotted him a four-run lead before he even took the mound. Despite getting off to a shaky start himself in the bottom half of the inning, the rookie Tiger limited the damage to one run on an RBI single by team namesake and future Hall of Famer Nap Lajoie. Cleveland's "comedy of misplays" in the field resumed in the top of the second, resulting in another four runs and gifting McCreery a comfortable 8-1 lead.[40] However, the Naps immediately rallied back in the bottom half of the frame. After allowing a leadoff single, McCreery retired the next two batters. But his debut quickly turned disastrous after the next five Clevelanders reached base safely. Before McCreery was finally able to stop the bleeding, four Naps had crossed home plate to trim Detroit's lead to 8-5. Although he managed to survive the calamitous second inning, McCreery was done for the day.[41] The Tigers ultimately cruised to a 13-6 victory in the error-filled "farce," with McCreery being credited with what resulted in his one and only career win – despite his "unsatisfactory" work.[42]

The Naps' defensive hijinks in the game obscured McCreery's historically bad outing. Although the official scoring rules of the day enabled him to pick up the victory, he allowed five earned runs, six hits, and three walks in only two innings pitched.[43] Since the onset of the Deadball Era (1901), McCreery's 22.50 ERA and 4.50 WHIP in the contest are both second worst of all time for a winning starting hurler.[44] And with only 12 victorious starters ever having tossed fewer innings in a game, McCreery holds the dubious distinction of arguably possessing the most suspect win ever for a pitcher in a starting role – and undeniably ranks as one of the least worthy of all the one-win wonders.

After his shellacking in Cleveland, McCreery tossed two scoreless relief innings over two appearances during the next couple weeks. He was also featured in an early September exhibition tilt against the Wilkes-Barre Barons of the Class-B New York State League, in which he pitched three shaky innings of mop-up duty and was himself interestingly relieved by future Hall of Fame outfielder Ty Cobb.[45] And despite pitching well a week later in a complete-game exhibition loss to the Grand Rapids Champs of the Class-B Central League, McCreery was released by Detroit shortly thereafter, ending his brief big-league career.[46] Slated to join the Chattanooga Lookouts of the Class-A Southern Association, McCreery was ultimately unable to agree on a contract with the club.[47] He spent the offseason playing winter ball in California for the independent Coalinga team.[48]

Signed for the 1915 campaign by the PCL's Salt Lake City Bees, McCreery was initially praised for his "tremendous speed and good curves," but was released during spring training by manager Cliff Blankenship due to his arm not being in proper shape.[49] Jumping to the newly launched Class-D Rio Grande Association, the 25-year-old became a rotation stalwart for the Phoenix Senators, finishing the season with a fine 11-5 record and ranking among the league leaders in most major statistical categories. However, McCreery's career in Organized Baseball came to a sudden and disappointing close on July 5 when, after he was shelled for 17 hits in a 13-5 complete-game loss to the Tucson Old Pueblos, "the Rio Grande Association blew into small fragments" and abruptly folded later in the day.[50] Although it was reported that McCreery had signed with the Sioux City Indians of the Class-A Western League shortly thereafter, no evidence exists indicating he ever played for the team.[51] Despite keeping his postseason promise to "shun professional ball for all time," he did continue to suit up for semipro teams for as many as a dozen years after leaving the pro ranks.[52]

Census and city directory information indicates that aside from a decade or so spent in Seattle, McCreery settled in the San Francisco Bay Area upon the conclusion of his professional baseball career. He and Emma (née Supple), his homemaker wife, whom he had married in 1911, had two children, Robert and Jane. From a professional perspective, McCreery spent many years working in engineering and management roles for industrial gas manufacturers before finishing his business career as a manufacturer's representative for electrical products.[53] Outside of work, he held memberships in the Old Timers Association of Oakland, the Elks Club, and the Holy Name Society of Castro Valley, California.[54]

After having suffered from lung cancer, McCreery died of congestive heart failure in Sacramento on October 19, 1960, at age 70.[55] Funeral services were held at the Chapel of the Valley Mortuary in Castro Valley. He was interred at Holy Sepulchre (Catholic) Cemetery in nearby Hayward.

SOURCES

In addition to the sources listed in the Notes, the author accessed McCreery's file from the library of the National Baseball Hall of Fame and Museum in Cooperstown, New York; McCreery's player contract card from *The Sporting News* collection; Ancestry.com; Baseball-Reference.com; Chronicling America; Fold3.com; GenealogyBank.com; NewspaperArchive.com; Newspapers.com; Paper of Record; Retrosheet.org; and Stathead.com.

NOTES

1. "Tigers Maul Naplanders with Gusto," *Detroit Free Press*, August 17, 1914: 8.
2. "Community History," Florence, Colorado, Chamber of Commerce, web.archive.org/web/20111107182105/http://www.florencecoloradochamber.com/community-history, archived from the original on November 7, 2011, accessed August 8, 2021.
3. "Ball Team Redeems Itself," *Poudre Valley* (New Windsor, Colorado), August 15, 1908: 12.
4. "Loveland Druggists Indicted by Jury," *Fort Collins* (Colorado) *Express*, September 18, 1907: 9.
5. "Drug Store Sold," *Twin Falls* (Idaho) *Times*, January 21, 1909: 8; "More Wells in Filer Vicinity," *Twin Falls News*, May 21, 1909: 6.
6. "Hotel Building for Filer," *Twin Falls Times*, February 11, 1909: 7.
7. "Filer and Buhl Fans to Play," *Twin Falls News*, September 24, 1909: 3.
8. "Big New Pitchers for the Indians," *Spokane Spokesman-Review*, February 18, 1910: 13; "Filerites Joining Apple Culturists," *Twin Falls News*, November 5, 1909: 9.
9. "Bliss to Be Climber Again," *Montgomery* (Alabama) *Advertiser*, March 2, 1910: 11.
10. "Lose Three Games – Tie One," *Twin Falls Times*, July 7, 1910: 1.
11. "Redlands After a Game with Red Sox," *San Bernardino* (California) *Daily Sun*, January 12, 1911: 10; "Red Sox Win from Redlands," *Los Angeles Daily Times*, March 7, 1911: Part III, 2.
12. "Redlands After a Game with Red Sox."
13. "About Baseball," *Victoria* (British Columbia) *Daily Times*, April 11, 1911: 7.
14. "McCreery Sold to Joe Cohn," *Nanaimo* (British Columbia) *Free Press*, September 9, 1912: 3; "About Baseball," *Victoria Daily Times*, October 2, 1911: 9; "About Baseball," *Victoria Daily Times*, July 29, 1911: 15; "About Baseball," *Victoria Daily Times*, August 17, 1911: 7.
15. "Lacrosse Game Was Disappointing," *Victoria Daily Times*, October 10, 1911: 6.
16. "McCreery to Victoria," *Vancouver* (British Columbia) *World*, November 30, 1911: 14.
17. "Veteran Picks Bees for 1912," *Victoria Daily Times*, March 30, 1912: 16.
18. "As Seen from the Press Box," *Victoria Daily Times*, April 29, 1913: 8; "McCreery to Victoria."
19. RA9 is similar to earned-run average except that it counts all runs, earned or not.
20. "Bees Exchange with Vancouver," *Victoria Daily Times*, October 2, 1912: 6.
21. "Pitcher McCreery Sold to Joe Cohn," *Nanaimo Free Press*, September 9, 1912: 3.
22. "Seven Home-Runs Feature Game; Brownies Again Defeat Indians," *Vancouver Sun*, May 12, 1913: 11.
23. "Twin Falls Hits League Pitcher," *Twin Falls Times*, May 23, 1913: 1.
24. "Beavers Break Even with Tigers on the Week's Series," *Vancouver Daily Province*, June 9, 1913: 10.
25. "M'Creery Does Not Disappoint Fans – Balloon Goes Up in Sixth," *Victoria Daily Times*, June 18, 1913: 8.
26. "Diamond Chatter," *Daily Province*, July 8, 1913: 14.

27 "Missoula and Butte Open Series Today," *Anaconda* (Montana) *Standard*, July 29, 1913: 3; "Holmes Is Manager Veteran of Game," *Anaconda Standard*, October 31, 1913: 2.

28 "Contest Results in Tie," *San Bernardino News*, December 8, 1913: 6.

29 "Sport Comment," *San Bernardino News*, March 2, 1914: 6; M'Creery Trying to Get Away from Butte," *Anaconda Standard*, February 25, 1914: 2.

30 "Ducky Goes South to Get Players," *Anaconda Standard*, March 1, 1914: 2.

31 "Gossip of Butte Sporting Circles," *Anaconda Standard*, May 11, 1914: 3.

32 "Gossip of Butte Sporting Circles."

33 "Baseball Opens in Butte at Two O'Clock," *Anaconda Standard*, May 26, 1914: 3.

34 "Two Players Are Purchased by Mr. Navin," *Detroit Free Press*, July 28, 1914: 12; "Two Butte Players Go to the Tigers," *Anaconda Standard*, July 27, 1914: 3; "Big League Scout Buys Pitcher M'Creery," *Salt Lake Evening Telegram*, July 27, 1914: 6.

35 "How Sport Writers Figure Stars of the Union Association of '14," *Butte Miner*, September 17, 1914: 9.

36 E.A. Batchelor, "May Pitch Coombs in Big Series," *Detroit Free Press*, August 13, 1914: 10.

37 "Big League Scout Buys Pitcher M'Creery"; "Scout's Presence Doesn't Bother Him," *Salt Lake Evening Telegram*, July 27, 1914: 6.

38 "Butte Ball Players Mobilize in Union Association and Declare War," *Missoulian* (Missoula, Montana), August 5, 1914: 6; "Union Association Is One Dead, Dead Corpse," *Anaconda Standard*, August 6, 1914: 2.

39 Information from McCreery's World War I Draft Registration Card.

40 "Tigers Maul Naplanders with Gusto."

41 "Tigers Maul Naplanders with Gusto."

42 "This Was a Farce," *Ann Arbor* (Michigan) *Daily Times News*, August 17, 1914: 6; "Aided by Naps, Tigers Grab a Weird Contest," *Detroit Times*, August 17, 1914: 6.

43 The modern rule requiring starting pitchers to pitch a minimum of five innings to qualify for a win (except in certain infrequent and unusual circumstances) was adopted before the start of the 1950 season.

44 The worst ERA in a game of all time by a winning starting pitcher was 36.00 posted by Duster Mails of the Cleveland Indians, who allowed four earned runs in one inning pitched on September 1, 1920, against the Washington Senators. The worst WHIP in a game of all time by a winning starting pitcher was 5.40 posted by Harry Courtney of the Washington Senators, who allowed four hits and five walks in 1⅔ innings pitched on May 3, 1920, against the Philadelphia Athletics.

45 "Tigers Wallop Minor Leaguers," *Detroit Free Press*, September 4, 1914: 12.

46 "Tiges Shut Out by Grand Rapids," *Lansing* (Michigan) *State Journal*, September 10, 1914: 8.

47 "Diamond Notes," *Billings* (Montana) *Daily Tribune*, November 19, 1914: 6; "Stove League Chatter," *Salt Lake City Evening Telegram*, February 3, 1915: 12.

48 "Coalinga Easy Victim of Porterville Nine," *Porterville* (California) *Daily Recorder*, November 23, 1914: 8.

49 "McCreery Coming," *Salt Lake Tribune*, February 4, 1915: 8; "McCreery Coming," *Salt Lake Tribune*, March 18, 1915: 8.

50 "Rio Grande League Dies in Phoenix," *Arizona Daily Star* (Tucson), July 6, 1915: 3.

51 "Diamond Dust," *Salt Lake Telegram*, July 6, 1915: 8.

52 "Amateur Baseball," *Oakland Tribune*, January 9, 1916: 23; "Baseball Gossip," *Oakland Tribune*, July 27, 1919: 29; "Eight Runs in 8th Frame Win for West Side," *Seattle Daily Times*, September 5, 1927: 17.

53 Jeff Littleboy, "Oxygen Plant Here Fills Gap in Trade," *Hanford* (California) *Daily Sentinel*, April 1, 1941: 5.

54 "Deaths," *Oakland Tribune*, October 21, 1960: 53.

55 State of California Department of Public Health Certificate of Death for Esley Porterfield McCreery.

TOM METCALF

BY MICHAEL TRZINSKI

Pitcher Tom Metcalf came from a small town in central Wisconsin but got to fulfill the dreams of his childhood when he spent two months in America's largest city as a member of the New York Yankees in 1963. The righty's major-league career was limited to eight appearances on the mound that season, in which the Yankees finished first in the American League but were swept in four games in the World Series by the Los Angeles Dodgers.

Metcalf was on the postseason roster but did not play in the Series and never appeared in another regular-season big-league game.

Thomas John Metcalf was born on July 16, 1940, to Rounds and Ruth Metcalf, who lived in tiny Amherst, Wisconsin, population 611 according to the 1940 census. Infant Thomas became child number three, following brothers Michael and James into the Metcalf clan. Brother Bill would be born a few years later to give the family a roster of four boys.

The Metcalf family moved to nearby Wisconsin Rapids in 1949, when Tom was 9 years old. He played baseball, basketball, and football at Lincoln High School and earned All-Wisconsin Valley Conference honors for all three sports his senior year, and for baseball and basketball in his junior year.

During his senior year (1957-58), playing as an offensive back, Metcalf led the Lincoln High Red Raiders football team to a 13-12 win over the P.J. Jacobs Panthers of Stevens Point in the annual battle for the Ol' River Jug. Lincoln had not won the trophy since 1948, but "took back the old crock in a momentous struggle on the Witter Field turf Friday night."[1] The Stevens Point quarterback was freshman Rick Reichardt, who went on to play for four teams in an 11-year big-league baseball career.

After the football season, Metcalf led the basketball team in scoring and was named by the Associated Press to the Wisconsin All-State Honorable Mention squad for the 1957-58 campaign.[2]

Then came the time for his best sport, baseball. In May, in perhaps two of his best performances, he first pitched a no-hitter against Stevens Point in May, striking out 12 batters,[3] then four days later took a tough-luck loss in the Wisconsin Valley Conference title game, dropping a 1-0 decision to the Merrill Bluejays. Metcalf struck out 10 and gave up an unearned run in the defeat. It was his only loss on his home field during his high-school career.[4]

Metcalf was honored during Lincoln High's Senior Recognition Night, and expressed to the audience his views on athletics and their value to participants. He received the Hagerstrom-Rude Post American Legion award for senior athletic excellence.[5]

After Lincoln's baseball season ended, Metcalf played for the National Guards in the Wood County Baseball League. He went 5-2 in seven games, including a 20-strikeout effort in one contest.[6]

In the fall of 1958, Metcalf made his way to Evanston, Illinois, to attend Northwestern University. Although he had a baseball scholarship,

233

he also played on the Wildcat freshman basketball team after varsity coach Bill Rohr saw him playing and asked him to play on the freshman team.[7]

Freshman basketball coach Harland Knosher called Metcalf "a pleasant surprise" and termed him one of the best natural athletes he had seen.[8] Metcalf, who stood 6-feet-2, impressed Knosher "with his fine natural ability."[9] At the time, freshmen were ineligible for varsity action, so they played mostly intramural games or scrimmaged with the varsity.

After the school year ended, Metcalf returned home and played amateur ball for another season (1959) in the Wood County Baseball League, this time as a member of the Wisconsin Rapids Lumberjacks. The team was sponsored by Rounds Metcalf's Rapids Lumber and Supply Company and ran through its opponents like a buzz saw, battling to a 13-1 season and a state tournament berth. The team won four games in the Class B Wisconsin Baseball Association tourney to take that title before Metcalf led the team to an 8-4 victory over Class A winner Soldiers Grove in mid-September.[10]

After returning to Northwestern for his sophomore year, Metcalf got into a few varsity basketball games as the Wildcats stumbled to a mark of 11 wins and 12 losses. That season was the last of Metcalf's collegiate hoops career.

"They had asked me back my sophomore year (but) I played sparingly," Metcalf recalled. "It got to be tough because in the winter the baseball team worked out in McGaw Hall just before basketball practice. Lots of hours between the two and I was wiped out. (I) kind of got tired of it."[11]

In the first few months of the fall semester, Metcalf had two sports and something else on his mind, at least for a while.

"There were two guys in our fraternity that were tremendous musicians, and they were practicing with this girl singer in our lounge where we had a grand piano," he recalled. "They played at various nightspots in the Chicago area, so they were practicing. Scott Smith, the piano player, came up and said, 'Ann-Margret wants to know if you would be interested in giving her a call.'"[12]

"My mother and dad came down to visit me that winter and my mother, who was a huge *Chicago Sun-Times* reader, asked me about this girl, Ann-Margret, that was being written up in the columns by Irv Kupcinet. She asked if that was the girl I was dating. I said yes. So, she said, 'I would like to go see her sing.'"[13]

"So we went out to this nightclub where she was entertaining and I was sitting at the table with my folks," recalled Metcalf. "And then she came and sat down at our table and started visiting with my mom and dad. In the meantime, I was kind of gawking around and my mom says, 'Tom, I'm trying to get your attention.'"

Without skipping a beat, Ann-Margret said, "Mrs. Metcalf, I've been trying to get his attention for weeks.'"

"Believe it or not, I kind of lost interest (in her)," said Metcalf later with a chuckle.[14] The Swedish stunner would go on to be a huge star in Hollywood.

A couple of months later, Metcalf turned in his shoes and sneakers for a pair of spikes and a glove.

The Northwestern varsity baseball coach was Freddie Lindstrom, a star player with the New York Giants and three other teams in the 1920s and 1930s, who was inducted into the Baseball Hall of Fame in 1976. "Lindstrom recruited me to come to Northwestern," recalled Metcalf. "And I still think it may have been that Lindstrom was a friend of Yankee scout Art Stewart, who maybe didn't want to sign me yet, but wanted to keep an eye on me (through Lindstrom)."[15]

The right-hander was off to a good start, fashioning a record of six wins and one loss, when disaster struck. Before a game at Indiana on May 27, Metcalf was struck in the right eye by a foul ball glancing off the batting cage during practice. He was kept in the Indiana infirmary overnight for observation.[16]

Metcalf's cheek had been split open – good for 12 stitches – and his eyeball was injured. He woke up with his eye completely bandaged. After a week in the hospital, John Alexander, a Wisconsin Rapids-area paper industry magnate, flew Metcalf's father to Indiana to pick him up.

"I never touched a book that summer, but took my finals and flunked a religion course, dropping my GPA to 1.99," said Metcalf. That made him scholastically ineligible and while he was sitting out the fall 1960 quarter, the pro scouts started calling.[17]

Fast forward to mid-March 1961.

While Metcalf was discussing bonus terms with a Cincinnati scout in his living room, a Chicago White Sox scout was waiting in the hall. Then the phone rang – it was Art Stewart from the Yankees.[18] Yes, the Yankees outbid the Reds and the White Sox, with what Metcalf call to this day, "a satisfactory five-figure bonus."[19]

After Stewart and Metcalf came to terms, he had a special request: Tell the press you signed for double the actual bonus. The rationale was, of course, to make it look as if the Yankees were very generous, or perhaps that they couldn't be outbid for players. Tom's mother, who was in the room at the time, firmly said, "Tell the papers it was a satisfactory five-figure bonus. We're not going to put anything false in the newspaper."[20]

"My biggest disappointment was that the Milwaukee Braves never contacted me," commented Metcalf, referring to the "hometown" big-league team. "I really wanted to play for them."[21]

Metcalf was told to report to the Yankees' Class-A camp in Bartow, Florida. He didn't have spikes or a glove because he had left them at Northwestern. Art Stewart said, "Don't worry about that, they'll take care of you."

When the rookie got to Florida, he found out that wasn't exactly true. Instead of having equipment on hand for him, camp director Jim Gleeson sent Metcalf to a hardware store in downtown Bartow.

"I ended up buying a Japanese glove and a cheap-ass pair of spikes," Metcalf recalled with a laugh. "I go back in the afternoon and boy, did I get a ribbing from the players."

After about a week, Metcalf was sent to St. Petersburg of the Class-D Florida State League. He was immediately inserted into the starting rotation and did not disappoint. He pitched a complete-game four-hitter but suffered a tough-luck 2-1 loss on April 21.[22]

Five days later, Metcalf picked up his first professional win, striking out eight and walking two as he evened his record at 1-1.[23] But then he ran into more tough luck in his next eight starts, losing five of them despite pitching to a 3.40 ERA during that span.

"He's one of our best prospects," said manager Bob Bauer. "He certainly has a future with the Yankees."[24]

Then, after splitting his next two decisions, Metcalf ran off six consecutive victories in eight starts, with two no-decisions. Not including two relief appearances that were mixed in, the lanky right-hander tossed 26 straight scoreless innings in a span of four starts from June 26 through July 12.

He didn't fare as well in August, winning two of three with a trio of no-decisions. Metcalf did pitch six no-hit innings on August 1 against Sarasota before getting roughed up in the seventh for five runs, but he did earn the win in that contest.[25]

Metcalf's final stats for the season showed a record of nine wins and eight losses, with an ERA of 3.26. He pitched 12 complete games, including four shutouts.

The former high-school basketball star stayed in shape over the winter, playing in a YMCA league in Wisconsin Rapids. He also attended UW-Stevens Point during the winter semester.

Much to Metcalf's surprise, the Yankees decided to switch his role to relief for the 1962 campaign and assigned him to Augusta (Georgia) of the Class-A South Atlantic League.

"I had a pretty good year in 'D' ball as a starter (in 1961)," said Metcalf later. "Manager Ernie White said the Yankees wanted me to be a reliever. I said okay, because I figured it would give me a quicker path to the big leagues."

Tom Metcalf, with the Yankees. Courtesy of Tom Metcalf.

Metcalf's best pitch was a big roundhouse curve, but then old Phillies reliever Jim Konstanty – who'd just returned to baseball as a minor-league pitching coach for the Yankees – visited the team.

Konstanty wanted Metcalf to throw a smaller curve while White wanted the big-breaking "hammer." One time in a game, Metcalf threw the smaller breaking pitch and White immediately called time and ran to the mound.

"You'll be riding the first train back to Whiskey Rapids or wherever the hell you're from if you don't go to the hammer on the next pitch," White told him. "I'll still be here managing this team, even if you're not on it."

Needless to say, Metcalf went back to the hammer.

Around midseason, Metcalf was getting noticed. A Charlotte sportswriter commented that "Tom Metcalf of Augusta has developed into one of the league's best relievers and appears to have made successful the jump from Class D to A."[26]

Although Augusta struggled, finishing with a record of 57-83, Metcalf led the team with 14 wins in 52 appearances, and posted the second-best ERA (2.56) with pitchers who threw 100 innings or more.

In the offseason, Metcalf enlisted in the Army's reserve program and did a six-month stint during which he was stationed at Fort Sam Houston near San Antonio, Texas.[27] On the surface, it seemed like that plan would jibe with his baseball career.

But then the Yankees invited Metcalf to the club's advanced training camp, scheduled to begin on February 11. The problem? Metcalf was not scheduled for discharge until March 15.

The commanding general at Fort Houston insisted that Metcalf would not have completed his basic training by February 11. Nonetheless, he gave tentative approval for discharge "on or about March 1."[28]

Metcalf did finagle the discharge in early March and reported to the Yankees camp, where he stayed for only a short time before being sent to New York's minor-league camp in Hollywood, Florida. There he joined his team for 1963, the Triple-A Richmond Virginians.[29]

Ernie White was by then the New York Mets' pitching coach and sang Metcalf's praises, telling a reporter, "He has a great overhand curve and he's quick."[30]

Metcalf pitched well in the spring exhibition games and Richmond manager Preston Gómez was keeping an eye on him. "He has a good arm," said Gómez.[31]

The 22-year-old started the season strong, allowing no earned runs in his first five outings, covering nine innings. In his first 34⅓ innings – through June 9 – he allowed only two earned runs in 22 appearances for a microscopic ERA of 0.52. He notched five wins and, unofficially, five saves during his team's first 48 games.[32]

Then the warm Richmond summer (average high 86 degrees Fahrenheit) might have gotten to Metcalf, who had said two months earlier: "I like to pitch in this cold weather. Wish we could have it all season."³³ Between June 10 and June 24, Metcalf gave up six earned runs in six outings. In the next 14 days, he got back into rhythm, keeping his opponents off the scoreboard in six of seven relief appearances.

After Independence Day, things got kind of ugly. Metcalf gave up 10 earned runs in 10 innings as July came to an end. At that point, his record was 9-5, and his ERA had increased to 2.69. But then the right-hander got some good news: He was being called up to the Yankees.

Not everyone thought it was a good idea. A Richmond columnist wondered why the Yankees would call up Metcalf "at a time when the early season 'Golden Boy' of the Virginians' bull pen was being hit hard every time he relieved a faltering Vee pitcher."³⁴

But up to New York he went. After getting his bearings for a few days in the bullpen, Metcalf got the call in the eighth inning on August 4 for his major-league debut in Yankee Stadium against the Baltimore Orioles. He entered the game with the Yankees trailing 4-2, and promptly allowed a leadoff double to Russ Snyder; after he got Boog Powell on a fly ball to center, John Orsino crushed a home run to left. Though shaken, the rookie still retired Jim Gentile and Brooks Robinson to end the inning.

In the ninth, Jerry Adair cracked a one-out double and was knocked in by pitcher Dick Hall before Snyder grounded into a double play. The Yankees lost 7-2.

Metcalf was getting antsy because he felt he would be sitting too much, so he went to manager Ralph Houk with a request. "I asked him to send me back to Triple A because I wanted to pitch," he recalled.

"I brought you up here and I want you on this roster," replied the hard-nosed Houk, known as The Major. "I'm going to work and try to get you out there. I'm not sending you down."³⁵

Metcalf sat in the bullpen for the next few days but got a chance in a blowout loss on August 14 when he came into a 14-5 game in Boston. He pitched a perfect eighth, giving him some confidence.

Three days later, Houk brought Metcalf into a game when the Yankees trailed to the White Sox, 2-0, in the eighth inning. Although Metcalf gave up two hits, he got a double play and a groundout to get out of the inning.

"You make mistakes, and guys turn them into a double play," noted Metcalf. "Especially that Yankees infield."³⁶

A few days later, Metcalf pitched two perfect innings against Cleveland in Yankee Stadium in a 7-4 loss.

Then, continuing his "good game, bad game" pattern, Metcalf got into trouble on September 1. Even so, he earned his first and only big-league win in a 5-4 decision in Baltimore. He pitched a scoreless sixth but was touched up for a run on two hits in the seventh. The Yankees then trailed, 4-1, but rallied with four runs in the top of the eighth.

Two days later in Detroit, the rookie right-hander held the Tigers at bay in the seventh and eighth innings, after which the Yankees scored twice to tie the contest, 2-2. But the Yankees came out on the short end of a 3-2 game that lasted 15 innings.

The next to last game of Metcalf's big-league career was a doozy. With the Yankees trailing Detroit 6-3, he entered the game in the top of the fifth inning. He allowed a walk and a hit but got out of the inning unscathed. The Yankees scored eight runs in the bottom half to take an 11-6 lead, which was the final score.

Wrote Joe Trimble in the New York Daily News, "Metcalf actually was the pitcher of record, when the big inning erased a 6-3 Detroit edge, but the official scorer gave credit to [Hal] Reniff. The scoring rules permit this elasticity of choice in a flappy game such as this."³⁷

The Wisconsin star sat nearly two weeks before getting his last outing. He finished his season with a pair of scoreless innings against the Kansas City Athletics on September 20, ending with a very respectable ERA of 2.77.

Tom Metcalf, 2023. Photograph by Michael Trzinski.

In eight relief appearances, Metcalf tossed 13 innings and allowed four earned runs, striking out three and walking three. His record was 1-0.

The 1963 World Series started four days after the regular season ended, and it took just four games for the Los Angeles Dodgers to claim the crown. Metcalf did not play in the Series – four other pitchers handled relief chores.

During the Series games in Los Angeles, Metcalf got in touch with Ann-Margret's agent and was able to get the star's phone number.

After a few minutes of small talk, the pitcher said, "I have some tickets if you want to go to a game; you can be my guest. And if we can get together, I'll have dinner with you."

"Well, I really can't," said Ann-Margret. "I'm dating someone."

"Who?" asked Metcalf.

"Elvis."

"Elvis who?" joked Metcalf.

Ann-Margret chuckled and said, "Okay, let's stop the joking."

That was the last time Metcalf had any interactions with the singer/actress.

A couple of weeks later, Metcalf, who had been brought up in early August, received a check for $3,149.72, two-fifths of the Yankee players' full shares.[38]

Metcalf was feted by his hometown with a Tom Metcalf Day program on January 16, 1964. The event was arranged by the Amherst Lions Club.[39]

Hopes were high that Metcalf would earn a spot on the Opening Day roster in 1964. New Yankees manager Yogi Berra (who'd retired as a player) even sent a letter to be read at the Tom Metcalf Day program, which in part said, "We look for big things from Tom, and he is one of the reasons the Yankees are optimistic about the future. This is the first of many thrills he will enjoy in 1964."[40]

Ralph Houk – who moved up to the front office as general manager in the offseason – also praised Metcalf in a telegram to the Lions: "We of the New York Yankees are proud he is with our organization. It is ball players of his high standards of living and ability that make the Yankees the successful team they are."[41]

Alas, Berra and Metcalf ran afoul of each other in the spring. Although the manager stated in early April that Metcalf was part of the bullpen plan, he sent the pitcher down to Richmond despite a 0.69 ERA in the exhibition season.[42]

Pete Mikkelsen and Metcalf were battling for the same spot in the bullpen. Berra chose Mikkelsen because he threw sinkers, while Metcalf was more of a fly-ball pitcher.

"Ralph Houk came up to me and said, 'Tom, I'm not in favor of this deal, but Yogi has the right to choose his players. Go down and do the best you can, and I'll try to get you back here.'"[43] So Metcalf reported to Richmond, albeit a couple of days late, and started working on a sinkerball.

"And that's when I ruined my arm," he recalled.[44]

Metcalf pitched into early August and then was put on the disabled list. He appeared in 50 games and had a record of 3-7 with six saves, along with a rather high ERA of 4.29. At the end of the month, it was announced that Metcalf "probably" would be pitching in a winter instructional league in Florida, but he never did.[45]

Instead, the pitcher married Crystal Winston, a former Miss Richmond (1962), in October 1964.

The two had met while working in Richmond the year before.

In 1965 spring training, Metcalf started one game against the Twins, allowing one hit and one earned run in three innings. "This is my first start in four years," he noted.[46] But after struggling in a relief outing a few days later, he was sent to the minor-league camp.[47]

Metcalf began the season with Toledo and had some good and bad appearances in April, ending the month with an 0-1 record, one save, and an ERA of 2.35.

May was a different story. Metcalf was lit up on May 2, allowing 11 hits and 8 earned runs in 2⅓ innings against Rochester. He struggled in his next three outings before righting the ship in the last half of May, allowing only three hits in 7⅔ innings.

In late May, Metcalf was sent to Syracuse in exchange for infielder Bill Roman, who wanted to play nearer to his hometown of Detroit.[48] In 13 appearances for the Mud Hens, Metcalf had an ERA in the high fours and a won-lost record of 1-1, with the one save.

He did okay with Syracuse in nine June outings, with one win and an ERA of 3.07. July was a different story, with an ERA of 5.14 in eight appearances and 14 innings, and a win and a save.

Metcalf pitched once more for Syracuse in early August before being sent back to Toledo. He ended the season with a record of 3-4, two saves, and an ERA of 5.61. He did not earn a big-league call-up but in September was ordered to report the following spring to the Yankees spring training camp in Fort Lauderdale.[49]

But in the same month the Yankees sold Metcalf's contract to Toledo. He said he did not know whether he would be invited to spring training with the Yankees until he received his 1966 contract.[50]

Metcalf opened spring training at the minor-league camp in mid-March, but then was acquired by Cleveland's affiliate in Indianapolis. He and Lou Vickery were supposed to report to the team in Sarasota, but Metcalf dropped Vickery off and drove back home to Wisconsin. Cleveland refused to complete the paperwork on the transaction, so Metcalf was technically still a Yankee farmhand.[51]

"I told Johnny Keane, 'I'm going back to my room and packing my bags and I'm heading back to Wisconsin,'" remembered Metcalf.[52] And just like that, his professional career was over.

"It was a tough decision," Metcalf said. "But I have no regrets. I have had experiences in baseball that will never be repeated as long as I live. I wouldn't trade those things for a million dollars."[53]

Metcalf joined his father in the lumberyard business in Wisconsin Rapids until retirement. As of 2022 he and Crystal lived in the village of Port Edwards, which is adjacent to Wisconsin Rapids. They have two sons, Thomas Andrew (Andy) and Rob, who played Division I basketball at Virginia and Minnesota. An avid golfer, Metcalf still shoots regular rounds in the 80s at a local country club.

Acknowledgments

This biography was reviewed by Rory Costello and Len Levin and fact-checked by Ray Danner.

SOURCES

In addition to the sources shown in the Notes, the author used Baseball-Reference.com.

NOTES

1. "Red Raiders Regain River Jug, 13-12," *Wisconsin Rapids (Wisconsin) Daily Tribune*, October 26, 1957: 3.
2. Chuck Capaldo, "Zweifel, Gharrity, Hughbanks, Kimble, Powers Make All-State," *Wisconsin Rapids Daily Tribune*, April 1, 1958: 6.
3. "Metcalf Hurls No-Hit Gem Against Point, 3-0," *Wisconsin Rapids Daily Tribune*, May 28, 1958: 7.
4. "Merrill Beats Raiders, 1-0," *Wisconsin Rapids Daily Tribune*, June 2, 1958: 6.
5. "Outstanding Lincoln High Seniors Get Recognition," *Wisconsin Rapids Daily Tribune*, May 28, 1958: 3.
6. "Metcalf Fans 20 as National Guards Blast Sherry-Blenker," *Wisconsin Rapids Daily Tribune*, August 11, 1958: 6.

7 Interview with Tom Metcalf, December 22, 2021 (hereafter Metcalf interview).
8 "Metcalf Earns Starting Spot on NU Frosh," *Wisconsin Rapids Daily Tribune,* January 27, 1959: 7.
9 "Frosh Cagers Bid for Stardom; Combine Speed, Good Shooting," *Daily Northwestern,* February 26, 1959: 1.
10 "Jacks Net '59 State Baseball Bunting," *Wisconsin Rapids Daily Tribune,* December 30, 1959: 8.
11 Metcalf interview.
12 Metcalf interview.
13 Metcalf interview.
14 Metcalf interview.
15 Metcalf interview.
16 "N.U. Wins, 10-6," *Chicago Tribune,* May 28, 1960: 39.
17 Metcalf interview.
18 Don Lindstrom, "Sports Lookout," *Wisconsin Rapids Daily Tribune,* March 27, 1961: 7.
19 Metcalf interview.
20 Metcalf interview.
21 Metcalf interview.
22 "Saints Lose Despite 4-Hit Pitching 2-1," *Tampa Bay Times,* April 22, 1961: 24.
23 "Saints Trim Leesburg 7-1 to Take Over First," *Tampa Bay Times,* April 27, 1961: 29.
24 "Wildcat Star Under Unlucky Star Here," *Tampa Bay Times,* June 1, 1961: 33.
25 "Saints Capture 3rd Straight; Home Tonight," *Tampa Bay Times,* August 2, 1961: 25.
26 Bob Myers, "Sally League Notebook," *Charlotte News,* June 27, 1962: 24.
27 Stan Isle, "Over My Shoulder," *Wisconsin Rapids Daily Tribune,* February 8, 1963: 6.
28 Isle, "Over My Shoulder."
29 Laurence Leonard, "Virginians Open Drills; 23 Candidates Report," *Richmond News Leader,* March 15, 1963: 1.
30 Laurence Leonard, "Sports," *Richmond News Leader,* March 27, 1963: 26.
31 Shelley Rolfe, "Crackers Take Pair from Vees," *Richmond Times-Dispatch,* March 31, 1963: 37.
32 Stan Isle, "Over My Shoulder," *Wisconsin Rapids Daily Tribune,* May 18, 1963: 6 details early-season success. Statistics for 1963 season compiled using box scores from the *Richmond Times-Dispatch* and *The Sporting News.*
33 Bill Deekins, "Foul Dulls Virginians Win, Gibbs' Best Showing of Year," *Richmond News Leader,* April 19, 1963: 26.
34 Chauncey Durden, "Sportview," *Richmond Times-Dispatch,* August 1, 1963: 18.
35 Metcalf interview.
36 Metcalf interview.
37 Joe Trimble, "Yanks' 8-Run Fifth Smothers Tigers, 11-6; Rog Connects," *New York Daily News,* September 8, 1963: 150.
38 "Series Takes Are Records," *Corpus Christi* (Texas) *Caller,* October 17, 1963: 29.
39 Stan Isle, "Over My Shoulder," *Wisconsin Rapids Daily Tribune,* November 1, 1963: 3.
40 "Amherst Star Honored," *Appleton Post-Crescent,* January 21, 1964: B6.
41 "Amherst Star Honored."
42 "Yanks Cut State Hurler Metcalf," *Oshkosh Daily Northwestern,* April 9, 1964: 32.
43 Metcalf interview.
44 Metcalf interview.
45 Ted Findlay, "Broward to Field 3 Winter League Teams," *Miami Herald,* August 29, 1964: 54.
46 Bob Bassine, "Top of the Morn," *Orlando Sentinel,* March 16, 1965: 19.
47 "11 Yanks Sent to Hollywood," *Fort Lauderdale News,* March 23, 1965: 8.
48 Bill Reddy, "Keeping Posted," *Syracuse Post-Standard,* June 9, 1965: 18.
49 Joe Trimble, "Shortstop, 19, Among 5 to Join Yankees Soon," *New York Daily News,* September 2, 1965: 351.
50 "Tom Metcalf's Contract Sold to Toledo Club," *Wisconsin Rapids Daily Tribune,* September 9, 1965: 7.
51 Max Greenwald, "Baseball Chatter," *Indianapolis Star,* April 6, 1966: 28.
52 Metcalf interview.
53 Metcalf interview.

CRAIG MINETTO

BY BOB WEBSTER

Craig Minetto was born in Stockton, in California's Central Valley, on April 25, 1954, to Armando and Lorene Azzaro Minetto. He had an older sister, Chris.

Minetto spent much of his childhood at two businesses founded by his grandfather and operated by Craig's mother, Lorene, the Alpine Nursery and the San Francisco Floral Company.[1] Lorene took over managing Alpine Nursery after a divorce from Craig's father.[2]

After attending the Cathedral of Annunciation School, Minetto lettered in baseball and basketball at Amos Alonzo Stagg High School in Stockton and was an All-City selection in both sports in his senior year of 1971-72. He set a record for assists on the basketball team that finished the season with a 25-0 record and went on to the Tournament of Champions. At the time, the Tournament of Champions were played regionally and was the only level of postseason tournament play. After his senior year, Minetto was drafted in the 35th round of the June 1972 amateur draft by the Los Angeles Dodgers, but he did not sign.[3]

Minetto attended San Joaquin Delta College in Stockton, where he played baseball in 1973 and '74. The Dodgers drafted him again in the third round of the January 1973 draft-secondary phase and again he did not sign.

Minetto signed a contract with the Montreal Expos on May 19, 1974, as an amateur free agent. He reported to the Expos Rookie League team in the Gulf Coast League where he started five games and surrendered 32 hits in 19 innings. He was promoted to the Kinston Expos of the Class-A Carolina League where he pitched five innings before being released by the Expos on September 18.

Luckily for Minetto, an Italian scout in the Bay Area had a passion for looking up family trees. He discovered that Minetto's grandfather had never become an American citizen, so Minetto was eligible to play in the Italian Baseball League. Another hurdle appeared. The league made Minetto agree that if Italy and the United States ever went to war, he would fight for the red, white, and green (Italy). Playing for Fortitudo Baseball Bologna in 1975, Minetto compiled an 18-3 record[4] and struck out 253 batters.[5]

Minetto returned to the United States and played in the semipro Cal-Mex League. Harry Allen, a scout for the Oakland A's, saw Minetto play and signed him to a minor-league contract in December 1976.[6] Minetto started the 1977 season with Modesto of the Class-A California League, where he compiled a 5-4 record. He started 14 games, threw five complete games, including one shutout, and struck out 85 batters in 89 innings. That earned him a promotion to Chattanooga of the Double-A Southern League, where he was also 5-4, but his ERA was 3.12 compared with 4.96 at Modesto. He finished the season at San Jose of the Pacific Coast League, appearing in two games, with one start, a complete-game loss with 10 strikeouts.

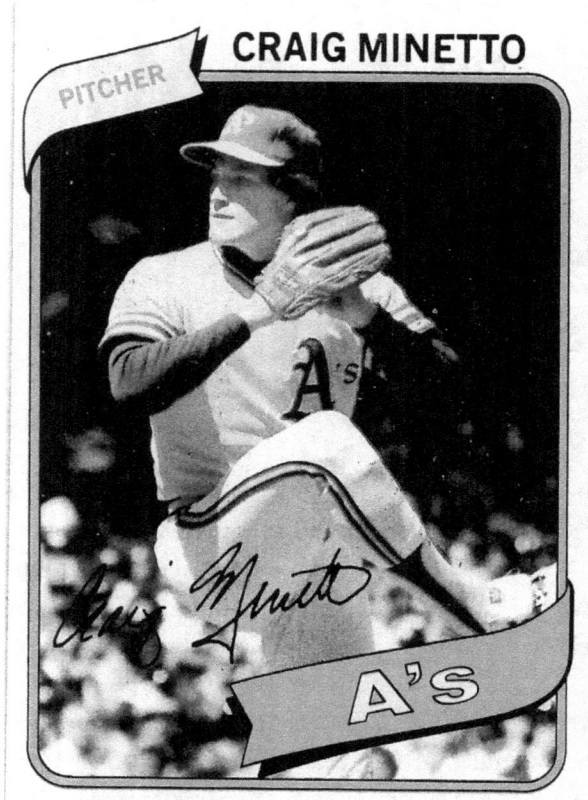

Craig Minetto, Oakland A's. Courtesy The Topps Company, Inc.

Minetto started the 1978 season with the Vancouver Canadians of the Pacific Coast League, where he pitched in 23 games, starting 19. He threw six complete games, including two shutouts. In 134 innings, he gave up 142 hits. He started the season with a 7-0 record and that earned him a promotion on July 1 to the Athletics, with whom he spent five weeks and pitched 12 innings over four appearances, starting one game.

The 24-year-old Minetto made his major-league debut in Seattle on July 4, pitching 3⅓ innings before being replaced on the mound by Elias Sosa with the A's leading 5-2. The 9-4 win went to Sosa. Four days later, on July 8, the Athletics hosted the Minnesota Twins. In the top of the 11th, the A's Dave Heaverlo surrendered a run to the Twins and Minetto came in down 9-8 with one out and runners on first and second. Minetto retired the side, but the A's couldn't score in the bottom of the 11th and the Twins won.

Minetto pitched again on August 3, in Anaheim. He pitched the seventh and eighth innings and gave up two runs (one earned) in the Angels' 8-1 win. On August 10, Minetto made his fourth and final appearance of the season for the A's, against the Angels at Oakland-Alameda County Stadium. With the Angels leading 10-1 in the top of the fourth, two runners on base and none out, Minetto came in and gave up a walk to load the bases. He escaped the inning on a line drive double play and a fly out. Minetto stayed in the game and gave up two runs in the ninth. Minetto ended up pitching six innings, giving up six runs (two earned), walked six and struck out a batter in the longest outing of his brief major-league career. Soon after, he was sent back down to Vancouver.

Minetto spent all of 1979 with Oakland. After two relief appearances totaling five innings, he got the call to take the mound against the Yankees in Oakland-Alameda County Stadium on April 25.

He pitched 6⅓ innings, giving up seven hits, and left the game with a 1-0 lead.

Making only his second career start, Minetto gave up a couple of two-out singles in the first inning for the Yankees, but they did not score. He got through the second and third innings three-up, three-down. In the fourth inning, Thurman Munson reached on an error, Lou Piniella flied out to left, and Reggie Jackson singled, sending Munson to second. Minetto retired Craig Nettles and Chris Chambliss to get out of the inning.

Mickey Rivers with a two-out single was as the only Yankee base runner in the fifth inning. And in the six he retired all three batters he faced. The game was scoreless.

Glenn Burke tripled to open the bottom of the sixth for the A's. After a walk to Joe Wallis, Mitchell Page grounded to second for a fielder's choice, scoring Burke and giving the A's a 1-0 lead.

After striking out Nettles in the top of the seventh, Minetto surrendered singles to Chambliss and Juan Beníquez and that ended his night. Jim Todd came in to pitch for the A's and got pinch-hitter Jim Spencer to hit into a 1-6-3 double play to get out of the inning. Todd retired the Yankees one-two-three in the eighth and ninth innings to earn the save and give Minetto his only major-league career victory.

Minetto's victory came on his 25th birthday. "I couldn't have asked for a better present," he said. "Right now I'm pretty celebrated out. I'm going to go home, relax, and tell everyone how I beat the world champions. I especially want to go over the game with my grandfather. He couldn't come out to see me because it was a little late for him. I hope he makes it next time. Just think, if he had bothered to become an American citizen, I wouldn't have been able to pitch in Italy and my career might have been over a long time ago."[7]

A's manager Jim Marshall said, "He wasn't afraid. He goes out and challenges. Once in a while he gets ripped, but he's not afraid."[8]

"The kid showed a lot of poise, Yankees manager Bob Lemon said. "He didn't walk anybody, did he?"[9]

For the next six weeks, Minetto was mainly in the starting rotation, with a couple of relief appearances mixed in. He pitched in 36 games, starting 13. He struck out 64 batters in 118⅓ innings. He finished the season with a 1-5 record and an ERA of 5.55. Minetto had plenty of opportunities to pick up another win, but couldn't do it. On August 14, 1979, Minetto pitched eight innings, giving up four runs on six hits, but the A's lost 6-2.

On July 24, 1979, Minetto caught Carl Yastrzemski's 400th homer. Minetto was in the bullpen beyond the right-field wall at Fenway Park when Yastrzemski cleared the fence. Minetto jumped out of his bullpen seat and caught the ball. He flipped the ball to Bill Campbell in the adjoining Red Sox bullpen to give to Yastrzemski for his trophy case.[10]

The 1980 season started in Ogden in the Pacific Coast League for Minetto. He was used mainly as a reliever, appearing in 22 games. In 41 innings, he gave up 50 hits while striking out 35 batters before being called up to the A's on July 12. A's manager Billy Martin gave the ball to Minetto to finish the game with a 5-1 lead over the Angels. Minetto had not pitched since an Ogden game on June 21. There were two outs with a man on first and Rod Carew at bat. Carew took a called third strike and the A's won.[11] Minetto was awarded a save.

On September 1, 1980, while warming up in the bullpen, Minetto strained some ligaments in his left knee and was lost for the season.[12]

Minetto started the 1981 season with the A's. He appeared in eight games for the A's, pitching 6⅔ innings, before heading back to Triple A, this time in Tacoma. (Tacoma was Oakland's fifth Triple-A affiliate in six years.) It was good for Minetto that he was sent down because major league players struck beginning June 12, and play did not resume until August 10. Minetto was able to keep pitching – and getting paid – while the major leaguers were on strike. "Pitching competitively is the only way to stay in shape," he said, "Even the [major leaguers] who are throwing at home on their own … it just isn't the same. I support the players totally in the strike. But it's nice to be pitching."[13]

The major reason for Minetto's lack of appearances early in the 1981 season was that A's manager Billy Martin had the starting rotation pitching complete games. In the prervious season, 1980, Oakland's starters threw 94 complete games, a modern-day record. This was with a rotation of Mike Norris, Matt Keough, Rick Langford, Steve McMatty, and Brian Kingman. "It's been a pattern around here and we learned to accept it," said Minetto. "Of course, we're all anxious to get in there when we can. We have a lot of time on our hands. But we spend that time talking about baseball. Jeff Jones and I are always helping each other out with different ways to improve."[14]

After pitching in relief on May 15 against Milwaukee, Minetto was sent down to Tacoma and never pitched in the majors again. He was traded to the Baltimore Orioles after the season for Allen Edwards. He spent the 1982 season with the Orioles' Triple-A affiliate, the Rochester Red Wings of the International League, where he appeared in 55 games, with 71⅔ innings pitched. He finished the season with a 4-5 record and an ERA of 3.27.

Minetto was back with Rochester in 1983. He recorded a 3-6 record with a 3.59 ERA in 95⅓ innings. After the season he was traded to the Houston Astros for Bobby Sprowl.

Minetto reported to the Tucson Toros of the Triple-A Pacific Coast League for the 1984 season. In 45 games and 58⅓ innings, he had a 5-5 record with an ERA of 4.47.

As a free agent after the 1984 season, Minetto was invited to spring training with the Giants in 1985. He did not make the cut and decided to retire from baseball.[15]

Minetto went back home to Stockton and joined the family business. His mother still owned Alpine Nursery, but Minetto managed it. After 75 years in business, the Minettos closed Alpine Nursery in 2012. "We've been here 75 years, and we decided that 75 was a good number to go out on," Minetto said. Craig was 58 and his mother was 87 when the business closed.[16]

As of 2023, Minetto was a scout for the San Francisco Giants and an instructor at the Baseball Factory.[17] Baseball Factory has worked with over 100,000 college players, 5,000 drafted players, and over 600 Baseball Factory alumni have played in the major leagues.[18]

Minetto resides in Lodi with his wife, Barbara. They have one daughter, Annalisa.[19]

NOTES

1. Reed Fujii, "Nursery Calls It Quits," Recordnet.com (*Stockton Record*) June 29, 2012. Retrieved July 17, 2023, from https://www.recordnet.com/story/lifestyle/home-garden/2012/06/29/nursery-calls-it-quits/49579007007/.

2. Lorene Azzaro Minetto obituary, https://www.recordnet.com/obituaries/pyrk0473983

3. Stockton Sports Hall of Fame. Retrieved August 2, 2023, from https://stocktonhalloffame.com/craig-minetto/.

4. Tom Weir, "Minetto Pours Out Winning Tonic for A's," *Oakland Tribune*, April 26, 1979: 45.

5. Stockton Hall of Fame

6. "Stockton Prep Standouts Will Play for Modesto A's," *Modesto Bee*, December 16, 1976: 15.

7. United Press International, "A's Minetto Gets Birthday Present," *Napa Valley Register* (Napa, California), April 26, 1979: 12.

8. "Minetto Pours Out Winning Tonic for A's."

9. Eric Prewitt, "A's Blank New York," *Merced* (California) *Sun-Star*, April 26, 1979: 17.

10. Associated Press, "400th Homer Troubled Yaz," *Springfield* (Ohio) *News-Sun*, July 25, 1979: 16.

11. John Hillyer, "Relivers, Armas Glitter in A's Victory," *San Francisco Examiner*, July 13, 1980: 36.

12. Bruce Jenkins, "Yanks Top A's; 6th Loss in Row," *San Francisco Chronicle*, September 3, 1980: 57.

13. Bob Slocum, "Minetto Craves Major Role," *Modesto Bee*, June 19, 1981: 43.

14. Terence Moore, "A's Bullpen: Time on Their Hands," *San Francisco Examiner*, April 19, 1981: 29.

15. Stockton Hall of Fame.

16. Reed Fujii, "Nursery Calls It Quits."

17. Retrieved August 13, 2023 from BaseballFactory.com: https://www.baseballfactory.com/training/spring-training-west-coast-hs/.

18. Retrieved August 13, 2023 from BaseballFactory.com: https://www.baseballfactory.com/our-alumni/.

19. Stockton Hall of Fame.

WILLIE MUELLER

BY DENNIS D. DEGENHARDT

In 1989, the Yankees closer got his big start as the late-inning specialist for the Holyoke Millers of the Eastern League. Not Mariano Rivera, but Duke, the closer in *Major League* portrayed by Milwaukee Brewers reliever Willie Mueller.

Willard Lawrence "Willie" Mueller Jr. was born in West Bend, Wisconsin, 35 miles north of Milwaukee, on August 30, 1956, the oldest of four children of Willie L. Mueller Sr. (1932-2010) and Patricia (Murphy) Mueller (1935-2005). He was followed by two sisters, Kelly and Abbe, and a brother Spencer. Willie Sr. loved baseball but never played in high school, leaving school after his mother died in childbirth when his father needed him on the family farm. He became a local legend as a hard-throwing right-hander for 27 years in the amateur Land O'Lakes League, mostly with the West Bend Lithias (a local brewery),[1] leading to enshrinement into the Land O'Lakes Hall of Fame. His love and passion for the game was passed on to the youth of West Bend. As Willie Jr. told West Bend's *Washington County Daily News* at the time of his father's death, "My father taught me, I would say 80 percent of the things I know." "[I] was just fortunate to have a father that pushed [me] to become not just a great baseball player but a great person."[2] Willie's mother, Pat, was an LPN and a good-hitting softball shortstop, occasionally pitching, and an accomplished bowler. Going to Willie Sr.'s games became family outings on most weekends and baseball was a big part of their family.

Willie Jr.'s sisters were good high-school softball players. His brother starred in baseball and basketball in high school. Willie Sr. and Pat's grandson (Kelly's son), Ryan Rohlinger, joined Willie Jr. as a major leaguer with San Francisco, and another, Mike Mueller (Spencer's son), spent three seasons in the Braves organization. Ryan's brother Adam was a baseball star and hall of famer at Concordia College of Wisconsin, while Spencer's daughter, also named Abbe, was an All-American volleyball player and UW-Whitewater hall of famer.

Willie Jr. attended Holy Trinity Grade School in Newburg, Wisconsin. Because he did not live in West Bend, he was not eligible for Little League, but Karl Kuss, heading the city's recreation baseball program, helped him enroll at age 6, a year under the minimum.[3] When he was 10 he was the batboy for the West Bend Lithias.[4] He also played in the Pony League for Newburg.

At West Bend West High School, Mueller participated in four sports from 1971 to 1974 – wrestling, track, baseball, and basketball. He was a hard-throwing pitcher like his father. When not on the mound, the righty played second base his first two years and then shortstop. As a sophomore, he helped win his school's first Wisconsin Interscholastic Athletic Association (WIAA) Summer Baseball Championship, besting the Plymouth Panthers 7-2.[5]

During his junior year, Mueller was 8-0 with a 0.40 ERA, surrendering only one extra-base hit, while fanning 61 and walking 17. At the plate, the right-handed swinger hit .308, smacking 20 hits.[6] The Spartans finished 18-4 but lost in the first round of the state regionals to hometown rival West Bend East. He started his senior season fanning 55 of the first 67 batters he faced.[7] Mueller pitched a seven-inning no-hitter that sealed the Spartans' 17th consecutive victory to end the season. Facing rival East in the regional finals again, the 6-foot-4 tosser allowed only six hits while fanning 13. But the defense faltered as the Suns prevailed, 6-2; the Spartans ended with a 17-2 record. Willie finished 8-2 with a 0.60 ERA, with 123 Ks and 16 walks. He batted .320 with half of his 16 hits for extra bases, swatting the team's only two homers.[8] He was voted West's MVP and named a second-team All-State pitcher, finishing his career 21-2.[9]

Mueller was not drafted but signed a free-agent contract with the Milwaukee Brewers on July 13, 1974. Most Wisconsin summer league players are not selected in the June amateur draft because practice cannot start until May 15 with games eight days later. Longtime scout Emil Belich, who inked Mueller, had only one mother – Willie's – in 50 years of scouting mail him a letter advising he needed to look at her son. He did and liked what he saw.[10] The 17-year-old started his professional career in Newark, New York, in the Low-A New York-Pennsylvania League. The Newark Co-Pilots' youngest player made seven appearances, hurling 15 innings and finishing with a 6.00 ERA.

Mueller spent most of the next three seasons with Burlington, Iowa, in the Class-A Midwest League. He began as a starter but struggled developing a changeup.[11] Seeing how hard he threw ("mid-to-low 90s – a hard slider"[12]) Bees manager Matt Galante moved Mueller to the bullpen to better use his speed an inning at a time. He finished with a winning record, 5-4 and a 3.12 ERA, earning a save, the first of 52 in the minors. At the plate, he had the bulk of his professional batting, 31 of 35 career at-bats,[13] smacking six hits, with three doubles and two RBIs.

In 1976 Mueller broke his right thumb during spring training, losing pitching time, and was assigned to the Midwest League's Clinton Pilots instead of Burlington because Milwaukee had other pitchers to develop. This upset the 19-year-old, who explained how it reignited his determination: "I wasn't in a good way after breaking the thumb and felt rejected by the Brewers. I was mad and it lit a fire under my ass."[14] After 12 games in Clinton, Mueller returned to the Bees, making 17 relief appearances with five saves. He had his best ERA, 1.75, going 5-4.

Needing more closing experience, Mueller returned to Burlington in 1977. After the June amateur draft, Mueller got a new roommate when the Brewers' first pick, future Hall of Famer Paul Molitor, asked Bees manager Denis Menke for a mature roomie. Menke suggested Mueller, the same age but with three years' minor-league experience; starting a lifetime friendship.[15] Burlington struggled early, finishing last in the Southern Division but put it together to win the second half. After defeating their first-half rival, Cedar Rapids, in the semifinals with Mueller closing the clincher, they faced the Northern Division winner, Waterloo. Burlington won the championship with Mueller wrapping up the 3-0 victory.[16] For the season, Mueller led the league in games (55) and was second in wins (15). He fanned a career-high 114 batters in 124 innings. After the season, he played for Milwaukee's Winter Instructional League team in Arizona; he topped Brewers pitchers with 20 appearances, finishing with a 3-4 record and a 4.38 ERA.

Moving up to Double-A Holyoke (Massachusetts), Mueller was the team's closer in 1978 and was leading the Eastern League with 53 games and 15 saves in August when the Brewers, struggling for pitching, became interested in him. GM Harry Dalton visited Holyoke to see Mueller throw. Liking what he saw, Dalton drove the young hurler to Boston (the Brewers were playing the Red Sox) so manager George Bamberger could see him work. Bamberger also liked what he saw, saying, "He probably throws harder than anyone in our bullpen. … [a]nd he throws as hard as or harder than anyone on our staff. He's got a chance to make it as a big

Willie Mueller, with the Brewers. Courtesy of Willie Mueller.

league relief pitcher"[17] Mueller was asked to stay overnight to work out again the next day. He was subsequently promoted to the Brewers.

Mueller did not wait long for his major-league debut, entering the fray at Fenway Park that evening, August 12, 1978, 18 days shy of his 22nd birthday. He became the fourth Brewer Wisconsinite.[18] Entering the contest in the fifth inning, he relieved starter Mike Caldwell, with runners at first and third, one out and the Brewers trailing 6-0. The first batter, Butch Hobson, struck out looking. Rick Burleson then tripled to right, plating both runners. Burleson scored on first baseman Ben Oglivie's error before future Hall of Famer Jim Rice flied out to end the inning. The rookie retired eight consecutive batters before running into trouble with one out in the eighth. After Mueller yielded a single, Rice slugged a homer over the right-field bullpen for Boston's final runs. In 3⅔ innings pitched, he surrendered three hits and two earned runs, fanning four. The four strikeouts established a Brewers' relief pitcher debut record that held until Jake Cousins whiffed five Diamondbacks on June 21, 2021.[19] Bamberger was "impressed very much," by Mueller, stating, "He handled himself like a veteran who has been around 10 years."[20]

The 220-pound reliever's next opportunity was on August 22, his first home game in County Stadium, with parents, family, and friends attending. Coming into game two of a twilight-night doubleheader in the sixth inning with Milwaukee trailing Cleveland, 4-2, he replaced starter Eduardo Rodriguez. With two outs and a runner on third, Mueller retired the side on a pop foul. He kept the Brewers close, holding the Indians scoreless, working out of a jam in the seventh frame with two runners on base. The only hit surrendered was to a fellow Wisconsinite, Sturtevant's Duane Kuiper, in the ninth. Mueller was rewarded with his first win when the Brewers rallied for three runs in the bottom of the ninth, capped by Cecil Cooper's bases-loaded single scoring Don Money, and sweeping the doubleheader. Excited after the victory, Mueller said, "I'll never forget it. I didn't have my best stuff. I was pitching wild."[21] His manager saw it differently, saying he was "fantastic."[22] It proved to be Mueller's only decision in the majors.

Pitching three more times for a total of 5⅔ innings, Mueller struggled with baserunners, allowing 12 hits and four walks for eight runs, seven earned. He whiffed only two after his debut. His 2.57 ERA ballooned to 6.39. But with Holyoke he had led the Eastern League in games pitched (53) and saves (15). And at age 22, he had debuted in the majors and earned a win. With the Brewers enjoying the franchise's first winning season, finishing third, he received a $175.26 partial share bonus; he saved it.

Reporting in 1979 to his first big-league spring training, in Sun City, Arizona, Mueller was one of four pitchers battling for two spots.[23] He didn't get much action and was disappointed with early demotion to Triple-A Vancouver.[24] Mueller was a starting pitcher early but didn't fare well, returning to the bullpen, where he thrived. He enjoyed playing for the 1979 Canadians. "It's very pretty up here – they have a nude beach – and the ballpark is beautiful," he told a Milwaukee sportswriter.[25] In May, when the home-plate umpire was hit on the elbow, leaving the game, Dennis Kinney of the Hawaiian Islanders manned first base and Mueller umped at third, both in uniform, until a local replacement arrived in the fourth. Mueller had a "tough call" on a caught-stealing.[26] In June he pitched "two perfect innings" against the Brewers in an exhibition game in Vancouver.[27] In his first Pacific Coast League campaign, Mueller was second in team appearances and fourth in victories, with another winning record of 7-3. That fall when the Brewers sold him to Vancouver to free up space on the 40-man roster, he responded positively: "I knew I had to keep working and glad to be able to so."[28]

As one of five nonroster invitees to spring training in 1980, Mueller thought he had an opportunity after an offseason of running and lifting weights,[29] aided by Bamberger saying at the end of the previous season that the 23-year-old would be one of his long relievers if he worked out.[30] But the manager retired during the offseason for health reasons following a heart attack the previous spring, and his replacement, Buck Rodgers, did not follow through, demoting Mueller in the second round of cuts. Mueller was angry, saying, "I just wish someone would give me a chance in the big leagues."[31] Returning to Vancouver, he was quite effective out of the pen, leading the Canadians in games pitched (57), and second by one in the league. Mueller also was third in innings pitched (112), and wins (8, against 6 losses).

Milwaukee's arms pursuit continued in 1981, with 25 pitchers invited to camp, but not including Mueller. He did throw occasional batting practice and twirled in their final Cactus League match, yielding three hits and two runs to Cleveland in two innings.[32] Returning to Vancouver, he posted

Willie Mueller, gripping the game ball from his victory. Courtesy of Dennis D. Degenhardt.

a 1.78 ERA, fourth in the PCL, and finished 21 of his 31 appearances for a 5-3 record with five saves. Late in the season, he was loaned to the Denver Bears of the American Association, Montreal's Triple-A affiliate, which needed pitching because of injuries. The Brewers thought a different league would be good experience. The righty was angry with the move, especially after three Vancouver teammates were recalled to Milwaukee. Unable to understand why another minor-league team was more important than the Brewers, he said, "All I know is if Milwaukee doesn't have any plans for me after the season I had this year ... I can't do better than that."[33] Pitching for Felipe Alou, the former Milwaukee Brave and Brewer, Mueller worked two regular-season innings, earning a save in his first outing, and then got a postseason win in 4⅓ innings of relief. Denver swept the Omaha Royals for the American Association championship.[34] Mueller was recalled to Milwaukee on September 15 and pitched in one game. Mueller entered the contest in the sixth inning with Milwaukee trailing Baltimore 7-2 at Baltimore. Pitching two innings, he gave up four hits and one earned run. Mueller did not pitch in the major leagues again. After the season he pitched in the Puerto Rican Winter League for the Santurce Crabbers (20⅔ innings pitched, 3-1, 1.71 ERA[35]).

The 1982 season is filled with fond memories for Brewers fans as their team made its only World Series appearance, losing in seven games to the St. Louis Cardinals. But it wasn't so good for the pitcher who grew up 35 miles away. Entering spring training, Mueller was hopeful. "Anybody in this camp has a shot at it," he said. "If you didn't you wouldn't be here."[36] Making the majors at age 21 may not have been the best for him, said. "When you get called up that young, some people might not be able to handle it. I guess I couldn't. Instead of keeping my nose to the grindstone like I did at Double A, I kind of let myself go a little bit."[37] But after a solid spring with a 2.25 ERA in four innings, he was optioned to the Expos' new Triple-A team, in Wichita, remaining Brewers property with 24-hour recall. Montreal expressed interest in Mueller after the previous year's playoffs but the teams failed to make a deal. The big reliever wasn't happy after learning of the move from manager Buck Rodgers and GM Harry Dalton and stormed out of the clubhouse.[38] Feeling he was being taken advantage of, he said, "Why optioned? Why not trade me for a player to be named later? Or why not sell me to them."[39] With Wichita, Mueller was the top righty out the bullpen,[40] tied for the club lead in games pitched (56) and second in the American Association in saves (12). He suffered his first losing season, 3-9. Although Wichita returned to the playoffs, Mueller didn't pitch for them; Milwaukee pulled him and stopped trade talks holding him in reserve in case Pete Ladd failed as replacement for injured closer, Rollie Fingers. Mueller never received that call. He was notified in November that he was being dropped from the 40-man roster.

For Mueller the start of the 1983 season was delayed because of knee ligament damage suffered playing basketball.[41] When he was able to resume throwing at Vancouver, he had arm troubles, his ERA surpassing 7.00 into July. Mueller's difficulty was surrendering too many hits and walking too many batters. When healthier, he started improving. By season's end, he had lowered his ERA to 6.87, pitching 74⅔ innings in 40 games. More telling were the 102 hits and 40 walks surrendered, leading to five saves and a 3-9 record. The disappointing year finished when Mueller was one of six Vancouver players released by the Brewers. Bruce Manno, Milwaukee's coordinator of minor league operations, told a sportswriter, "We just felt it would be more advantageous for them to go somewhere else and get another start."[42]

As a free agent at age 27, Mueller was invited to San Francisco's spring-training camp, but decided to retire when he was demoted to Triple A. "My arm was losing power and elasticity. I gave it 10 years, it was time to leave." The Brewers offered him some coaching opportunities but he wanted to return home and work with West Bend's youth.[43] His 10 minor-league seasons included 395 games with 809 innings pitched and a 52-41 won-lost record. As a major-leaguer he pitched 14⅔ innings in six games and had the one victory.

Willie married Ruth Ann Enright of Sheboygan, a water utility clerk with the city of West Bend on November 30, 1985. They had two children. Daughter Lindsey starred on West Bend West High School's volleyball team and played Division 1 volleyball at Binghamton University. Their son, Daniel, repeated Willie's feat of pitching West Bend West to the Summer Baseball Championship as a sophomore.[44] Dan was an infielder at Concordia College when his father was the pitching coach. The couple divorced in 2012; Mueller has not remarried.

In 1988 the movie *Major League* was filmed in Milwaukee. (Cleveland Stadium was unavailable because it was being used by the NFL Browns.) The movie was about the hapless Cleveland Indians, whose new owner wanted the team to lose so she could move it to Miami. Former Brewers starter Pete Vuckovich was originally cast as the Yankees' closer, Duke, but when director David Ward first saw him he thought Vuckovich would be perfect instead as the slugging first baseman they were struggling to cast.[45] Ward turned to Mueller to become Duke on Vuckovich's recommendation. Mueller was skeptical when contacted and asked how they obtained his phone number. He was told that Vuckovich had been asked "if he knew anybody who could play the part, someone who was big, kind of ugly and (could) throw the ball." The caller said Vuke didn't pause, responding, "Willie Mueller."[46] That convinced Willie that the call was legitimate. Ward and producer Chris Chesser in the extras included with the 2007 DVD release *Major League Wild Thing Edition* said that "Mueller really got the character."[47] Mueller spent three months on the set, even assisting former Dodgers catcher Steve Yeager, the film's technical adviser. Mueller said he had many great memories of the experience, and cherished two autographed baseballs, one signed by Tom Berenger, Corbin Bernsen, and Pete Vuckovich and the other by Charlie Sheen and Wesley Snipes. About 10 years after the movie was released, the family was watching it when 10-year-old Lindsey refused to accept that "Duke" was her father and young Dan broke out crying when the Yankees lost, feeling bad for daddy.[48]

Like his father, Mueller worked with West Bend's young people at all levels – Little League, high school, and college. He was a Little League umpire for seven years and coached youth football and basketball. In the late 1980s he began conducting baseball clinics year-round at the local indoor baseball facility and throughout southeast Wisconsin. He said his philosophy is simple and no-nonsense: "Respect the game, expect failure and learn how to deal with it."[49]

In the fall of 2003, Mueller and other former West Bend ballplayers and coaches organized the West Bend Baseball Association. The nonprofit foundation's mission states, "WBBA is committed to preserving West Bend's fine baseball tradition by promoting and supporting youth, high school, and adult baseball in our community." It has provided scholarships to baseball players in the city's two high schools and supported Little League field improvements and supplies. WBBA's greatest focus is Karl M. Kuss Memorial Field at Regner Park, where the high-school and adult teams play. Under Mueller's leadership as president, more than $1.4 million was raised for a new grandstand and turf field, completed in the summer of 2021, updating the Depression-era ballpark. The organization continues raising funds to replace the lighting and make other additions to the ballpark.

Mueller worked as the pitching coach for Concordia University in Mequon, Wisconsin, a Milwaukee suburb, from 2005 to 2012. The Division III school is a member of the Northern Athletic Conference. His son, Dan, received All-Conference Honorable Mention after leading the team in batting average (.354), at-bats, runs, hits, doubles, and RBIs as a senior.

Mueller has been recognized by two organizations. In June 2011 he and his father were included in the inaugural class of the WBBA's Diamond of Honor Wall of Fame. He told the *Washington County Daily News,* "I was quite humbled, there's a lot of emotion here. … I feel honored especially for my dad."[50] The following year, he was enshrined in the Old Time Ball Players Association of Wisconsin's Hall of Fame.

After baseball, Mueller had several jobs before joining the City of West Bend in 1989, for which he has held several positions, mostly for the Parks Division. He has worked doing maintenance and delivery for Furey Filter and Pump since retiring from the city in 2013 and retired again at the end of 2022.

In 2017 Mueller was invited to participate as a coach at the Brewers Fantasy Camp by camp director Bill Schroeder, a former Brewers catcher turned broadcaster. He went with three friends including Mike Gonring, former West Bend East baseball coach and fellow inaugural WBBA Wall of Fame inductee, who was a camper. The team coached by Willie and former Brewers outfielder Corey Hart went undefeated and won the camp championship.

SOURCES

In addition to the sources cited in the Notes, the author consulted Baseball-Reference.com, Retrosheet.org, and SABR.org.

The author met Willie Mueller at the RBI Baseball Academy in West Bend for an initial interview. All other telephone interviews and interactions were conducted around his camp schedules.

Special thanks to SABR member Bill Mortell of Maryland, whose knowledge of Ancestry.com and research skills have again proven to be invaluable.

NOTES

1 Similar to town ball, the Land O'Lakes League was founded in 1922, with teams throughout Southeast Wisconsin.

2 Pat Neumuth, "Life Long Mentor – Baseball Remembering Willie Mueller Sr.," *Washington County Daily News* (West Bend, Wisconsin), July 22, 2010: 9.

3 "Mueller Signs Brewers Pact, Reports to Newark Tuesday," *West Bend News*, July 15, 1974: 10.

4 Pat Neumuth, "Old Time Ballplayers Induct Mueller into the Hall of Fame," *West Bend News*, September 12, 2012: 9.

5 "First Championship for West Bend Since 1951," *West Bend News*, July 28, 1972: 7. The Wisconsin Athletic Association instituted two leagues in 1965 (through 2018), spring and summer. West Bend High split into two high schools in 1969, East and West (both in the same building).

6 Leif Eriksen, "Pitching Was West's forte," *West Bend News*, August 3, 1973: 7.

7 "Mueller Fans 20 as West Blanks Plymouth," *West Bend News*, June 12, 1974: 9.

8 "Pitching Was West's Strong Suit," *West Bend News*, July 23, 1974: 9.

9 West Bend Baseball Association 2012 Wall of Fame Induction.

10 "2000 Midwest Scout of the Year," Belich started scouting with the Milwaukee Braves in 1953. Besides the Brewers, he also scouted for the Phillies and San Diego as well as the Major League Scouting Bureau. He signed two stalwarts of the 1982 Brewers, Hall of Famer Paul Molitor and Jim Gantner.

11 Telephone interview with Willie Mueller on January 2, 2022, hereafter referred to as "Mueller interview."

12 "Four Men Born in West Bend Have Played in the Big Leagues. These Are Their Stories," *Washington County Daily News*, October 27, 2012: 1.

13 Mueller had four at-bats over the course of the 1979, 1981, and 1982 seasons to avoid using another reliever with three strikeouts.

14 Mueller interview.

15 Mueller interview.

16 "Bees Swarm to First Midwest Title Since '65," *The Sporting News*, September 27, 1977: 41.

17 "Brewers Test State Hurler," *Milwaukee Sentinel*, August 12, 1978: Part 2, 3.

18 Mueller was preceded by Gene Brabender of Black Earth, Wisconsin; Jerry Augustine of Kewaunee; and Jim Gantner of Eden.

19 Todd Rosiak, "Brewers Shuffle Roster as Anderson Goes on the Injured List," *Milwaukee Journal Sentinel*, June 23, 2021, C1. Mueller and most Brewer fans, including the author, were not aware of the record until Cousins broke it.

20 "Haas Will Make Brief Showings," *Milwaukee Sentinel*, August 14, 1978: Part 2, 4.

21 Lou Chapman, "Brewers Pull Off a Miracle," *Milwaukee Sentinel*, August 23, 1978: Part 2, 1.

22 Chapman, "Brewers Pull Off a Miracle."

23 Lou Chapman, "Smooth Camp Suits Dalton Just Fine," *Milwaukee Sentinel*, March 6, 1979: Part 2, 1.

24 Mike Gonring, "West Bend's Mueller Doing His Chores in Triple A," *Milwaukee Journal*, June 26, 1979: Part 2, 7.

25 Gonring.

26 "Pacific Coast League," *The Sporting News*, May 26, 1979: 39.

27 Gonring.

28 Mueller interview.

29 "Eight Seeking Pitching Berth," *Milwaukee Sentinel*, March 7, 1980: Part 2, 1.

30 Mueller interview.

31 George Sauerberg, "Rookie Outfielder, Replogle Sparks Brewers," *Milwaukee Sentinel*, March 22, 1980: Part 2, 2.

32 "Brewers Whip Indians in Exhibition Windup," *Milwaukee Sentinel*, April 9, 1981: Part 2, 3.

33 Steve Aschburner, "Mueller to Miss Bus for Brewers Stretch Drive," *Milwaukee Journal*, September 3, 1981: Part 3, 10.

34 "Mueller Wins for Denver," *Milwaukee Journal*, September 4, 1981: Part 2, 8.

35 Statistics furnished by Jorge Colon Delgado, official historian, Roberto Clemente Professional Baseball League.

36 Tom Flaherty, "Mueller Hopes He'll Beat the Odds," *Milwaukee Journal*, March 2, 1982: Part 2, 5.

37 "Mueller Hopes He'll Beat the Odds."

38 Vic Feuerherd, "Brewers Trim Porter, Mueller From Roster," *Milwaukee Sentinel*, April 1, 1982: Part 2, 1.

39 Tom Flaherty, "Spring Training," *Milwaukee Journal*, April 2, 1982: Part 2, 10.

40 Dale Willenbrink, "Update on State Players in the Minor Leagues," *Milwaukee Journal*, July 15, 1982: Part 3, 8.

41 Tom Flaherty, "Baseball Dances to the Tune of Musical Managers," *Milwaukee Journal*, February 13, 1983: Sports 3.

42 Tom Flaherty, "If Lachemann Answers, It's Not Your Lucky Day," *Milwaukee Journal*, November 13, 1983: Sports 11.

43 Mueller interview.

44 "Stevens Point – 'Yes He's Only a Junior,'" *Washington County Daily News*, July 27, 2007.

45 Director David Ward and producer Chris Chesser discussing the film on the 2007 DVD release *Major League Wild Thing Edition*.

46 Nicholas Dettmann, "'League' Still Resonates," *Washington County Daily News*, April 4, 2014: 7.

47 Ward and Chesser.

48 Nicholas Dettmann, "'League' Still Resonates," *Washington County Daily News*, April 4, 2014: 7.

49 Mueller interview.

50 Nicholas Dettmann, "For Love of the Game," *Washington County Daily News*, June 24, 2011: 1.

SHANE NANCE

BY ALAN COHEN

"I've been told as long as I can remember, 'You're too small. You'll never pitch in the big leagues. You're too short.' I've always used that to kind of fuel my fire"
– Shane Nance, June 12, 2002.[1]

"When you get sent down, your goal is to get back up. I got some things figured out down there. My confidence was the main thing. I felt good about the way I was throwing the ball again."
– Shane Nance, July 3, 2003, upon his recall to the big leagues[2]

"LHP Shane Nance was called up from Class AAA Indianapolis to replace RHP Curtis Leskanic, who was traded to the Royals for minor league RHP Wes Obermuller and IF Alejandro Machado. Nance will pitch mostly in the middle innings.
– *The Sporting News*, July 14, 2003[3]

The last of these quotes, a brief notice in *The Sporting News*, heralded the arrival of Shane Nance for his third shot in the big leagues, after a journey that had taken him from J. Frank Dobie High School in Pasadena, Texas (just outside of Houston), to the University of Houston and five minor-league stops. In those and subsequent minor-league stops, he compiled 36 wins against 22 losses. At the big-league level, in parts of three seasons, he had only four decisions, one of which was a win.

Joseph Shane Nance was born on September 7, 1977, in Pasadena. His parents were Joe Wayne Nance and Kimberly Denise Nance. The left-hander grew to be 5-feet-8-inches tall and weighed 180 pounds.

During his senior year of high school, things could not have been more promising. His performance in Galveston on March 4, 1996, drew a particularly favorable review. He pitched a one-hitter, striking out nine, as Dobie defeated Ball High School of Galveston, 4-0. He also homered in the game. Opposing coach Gary Key indicated that he would not have been surprised if Nance drove the team bus and said, "He probably teaches biology there, too."[4]

Nance appeared in the regional all-star game, where he came in to squelch an eighth-inning rally and pitched a perfect ninth to gain the save as his South team won the game, 8-6.[5] He was named to the Class-5A All-State team.

He went on to play at the University of Houston.

On May 1, 1998, in Hattiesburg, Mississippi, Nance hurled another one-hitter, this time victimizing Southern Mississippi on a diet of changeups mixed in with his 88-mph fastball. The 3-1 win brought his record to 8-4. The previous day, the sophomore had been told that he had been selected to try out for Team USA.[6]

On June 13 it was announced that Nance was selected to play on Team USA, and he picked up a win, in relief, as the US defeated the Dominican Republic, 4-3 (11 innings), in the World Championship qualifier tournament in Nicaragua.[7]

Nance's career highlight came on July 4, 1998. He pitched for Team USA against the Japan College Stars at Hi Corbett Field in Tucson. He pitched the first seven innings, allowing no runs, scattering seven hits, and striking out six batters, and was credited with the win as Team USA won, 6-0.[8]

It was the third of his four wins in the qualifying rounds. In all, Nance was 4-0 (0.93 ERA) as Team USA qualified for the World Cup tournament. The fourth win came on July 10, when he pitched five innings (the first four being perfect), allowing only one hit in an 11-0 win over Mexico at Tucson, bringing Team USA's record to 22-9.[9] Casey Fossum came on in relief to secure the win for Team USA.[10] Six years later, their paths would cross again.

Before Team USA headed to Italy for the 16-team World Cup championship round in Palermo, Italy, they had a tune-up game in Norwich, Connecticut, defeating Canada, 8-4. Nance hurled the first six innings, striking out 10, to gain the win.[11] In Italy, Team USA failed to make it to the quarterfinals. In a tough-luck loss, Nance struck out 12 as the Team USA lost to South Korea, 3-1, on July 23.[12]

After going 7-6 (5.00 ERA) as a junior in 1999, Nance was drafted in the 24th round by the Los Angeles Dodgers. He elected not to sign and returned to Houston for his senior year. When not pitching, Nance played in the outfield and on February 22, 2000, when it seemed that everyone except Nance pitched, he slugged two homers in a 14-12 win over Rice.[13] It was while playing the outfield on March 10 that he sprained his shoulder and missed the next month of games. When he returned, he showed good form and, on April 23, he posted his 28th collegiate win, setting the record at the University of Houston,[14] a record that had previously been held by Doug Drabek. Nance's final collegiate record included Houston career highs in wins (32) and strikeouts (388). After the season, in which he finished 8-1 (2.05 ERA), he was named to the all-tournament team in the Conference-USA tournament, which was won by Houston. He then went on to defeat Rice in the NCAA regional tournament, but Houston lost to San Jose State in the super-regional.

The Dodgers once again drafted Nance in 2000, this time in the 11th round. He was signed by scout Chris Smith, and the signing was announced on June 12.

Nance's first stop in the minor leagues was at Yakima in the Northwest League, where he went 2-4 with a 2.48 ERA in 12 games. He split 2001 between Class A Vero Beach (6-3) and Double-A Jacksonville (7-0), earning a promotion to Triple A for 2002. One of his more memorable appearances during his time at Vero Beach came on May 5. The Cinco de Mayo Classic went 19 innings (6:26), and Nance, who had pitched in the prior game, was not available, or so it seemed. A cell-phone call to the Dodgers organization resulted in authorization for Nance to enter the game in the 19th inning after Vero Beach had taken an 11-7 lead. He became the ninth player to pitch for Vero Beach, and he closed out the win with three strikeouts sandwiched around two walks. The last pitch was thrown at 1:35 A.M.[15]

With Jacksonville, Nance was on a team that finished the season with an 83-56 record. His 7-0 mark came in 28 relief appearances (45⅓) innings during which his ERA was 1.59. The team finished first in the East Division of the Southern League, but proceeded no further as the playoffs were canceled after the 9/11 attacks.

In 2002 Nance led the PCL with 10 wins at the All-Star break. He hurled the sixth inning in the Triple-A All-Star Game and received credit for the win as the PCL defeated the International League, 5-0. On July 23, 2002, he was traded, along with Ben Diggins, to the Milwaukee Brewers for Tyler Houston and Brian Mallette. He was sent

Shane Nance pitching against the Dodgers on June 4, 2004. Photograph by Norm Hall/Arizona Diamondbacks.

to Indianapolis where, in nine relief appearances, he pitched 16⅔ scoreless innings and was credited with three wins.

Nance was called up to the majors and made his debut with Milwaukee on August 24, 2002. By the time he entered the game, the Brewers trailed 14-3. He pitched a scoreless seventh inning and came up to bat in the bottom of the inning with runners on second and third base and the score 14-4. His single to the right side scored Eric Young, but it was a case of too little too late. With the score 14-6 and the bases loaded, Paul Bako lined into a double play, stranding Nance at third and ending the Brewers rally. With one out in the top of the eighth, Nance's ERA of 0.00 was jolted when Armando Rios hit a solo homer. In the bottom of the eighth, Nance was removed for a pinch-hitter and the Brewers lost 17-10.

A week later, Nance's dreams were put on hold. He entered a game at Cincinnati with the Brewers in front 11-2. The Reds had scored their second run, and there were runners at the corners with one out. Nance recorded two outs without further scoring and was allowed to bat in the top of the ninth. During that at-bat, he tore his right biceps swinging at a pitch and required season-ending surgery. In four appearances with the Brewers, Nance had no decisions and a 4.26 ERA in 6⅓ innings.

Nance began the 2003 season with the Brewers but was largely ineffective in his first nine appearances, with a loss, a blown save, and a 6.75 ERA. He was sent back to Indianapolis on May 2. He was with Indianapolis for three months during which he put together, from May 23 through June 26, a streak of 17⅓ scoreless innings.

Back with Milwaukee, Nance continued to have problems at the big-league level. He gave up home runs in each of his first two games against the Colorado Rockies. Although he came around and was not scored on in his last four July outings, he was once against sent back to Indianapolis. On July 31 at Indianapolis, he pitched 1⅓ inning of hitless relief after starter Derek Lee had allowed only one hit, as Indianapolis defeated Durham, 2-0.[16]

The performance on July 31 added to Nance's scoreless streak at Indianapolis, and it continued to grow. On August 8 he extended the streak to 29 innings, and on August 10 he tacked on two more zeros. On August 18 Nance received his first starting assignment since his first year in pro ball and allowed one run in 3⅔ innings. A first-inning home run by Cody Ross snapped the scoreless streak at 34⅔ innings.[17] On August 25 he struck out all four batters he faced as he closed out a 5-2 win over Louisville.[18] The next night it was more of the same as he recorded another save, pitching a scoreless ninth inning. It brought his ERA for the season to 1.38. Nance had allowed only one run in his last 42 innings of work.[19] His ERA was the lowest in the league for any pitcher with more than 50 innings.

With Milwaukee in September, Nance had a 3.00 ERA in nine innings. He was charged with one loss and credited with a hold.

After the season, Nance was traded to the Arizona Diamondbacks in a nine-player deal that sent Richie Sexson, minor leaguer Noochie Varner, and Nance to Arizona for six players. Nance battled a sore elbow in spring training and began the 2004 season on the disabled list.[20] He did a rehab assignment with Tucson of the Pacific Coast League, appearing in 22 games with the Sidewinders. He joined the Diamondbacks on June 2, but the stay was brief. After two appearances he was sent back to Tucson. He was in another 24 games with Tucson before returning to the Diamondbacks on August 8.

From August 8 through 23, Nance appeared in seven games (5⅓ innings) without yielding a run. He adapted well to his role of being brought in to face left-handed hitters.[21] His appearance at Pittsburgh August 23 resulted in his only big-league win. The starting pitcher for the Pirates that night was Casey Fossum, who had been a teammate of Nance's on Team USA in 1998. Fossum was out of the game by the time Nance entered the contest with one out in the eighth inning and the score tied 4-4. He was brought in to face José Bautista, but Pirates manager Lloyd McClendon sent up right-hand-hitting Rob Mackowiak to pinch-hit. Nance struck out Mackowiak for the second out of the inning but yielded singles to Tike Redman and José Castillo. Pinch-hitter Humberto Cota flied to center field to end the threat. The Diamondbacks took the lead in the top of the ninth inning after Nance, who was due to lead off the inning, came out of the game for a pinch-hitter. Greg Aquino pitched the bottom of the ninth inning for Arizona and saved the win for Nance.

Nance made 10 more appearances for the Diamondbacks in 2004 without a win. He finished the season 1-1 with a 5.84 ERA. He never pitched again in the majors. His major-league record in parts of three seasons (49 appearances) stands at 1-3 with a 5.02 ERA in 43 innings.

Nance began the 2005 season with Tucson and was released on June 15. Shortly thereafter, he signed with the Kansas City Royals and was placed with Omaha in the Pacific Coast League, for whom he went 3-2 in 23 appearances. After the season, he signed a minor-league contract with the Brewers, but chose to retire, announcing his retirement on March 12, 2006.[22]

As of 2023 Nance lived with his wife, Amy, and two daughters in the Houston area.

SOURCES

In addition to the sources shown in the Notes, the author used Ancestry.com, Newspaper Source Plus, Baseball-Reference.com, Retrosheet.org, and the following:

McManaman, Bob. "Cintron RBI Lifts D-Backs," *Arizona Republic* (Phoenix), August 24, 2004: C5.

NOTES

1 Mark Anderson, "51s' Nance Provides Relief with Unexpected Win Total," *Las Vegas Review-Journal*, June 13, 2002: 5C.

2 "Around the Horn," *Wisconsin State Journal* (Madison), July 4, 2003: C2.

3 "Milwaukee Brewers," *The Sporting News*, July 14, 2003: 37.

4 Manuel Moreno Jr., "Dobie's Nance Does In Ball High," *Galveston News*, March 5, 1956: 1B.

5 "De La Garza Helps South Triumph 8-6," *McAllen* (Texas) *Monitor*, June 18, 1996: 10.

6 Jim Mashek, "Pitcher Shuts Down USM," *Biloxi* (Mississippi) *Sun Herald*, May 2, 1998: C-1.

7 "UH Pitcher Gets First Win," *Fort Worth Star-Telegram*, June 20, 1998: D8.

8 Phil Villareal, "Ludwick Takes Brother's Cue to Success After Draft Snub," *Arizona Daily Star* (Tucson), July 5, 1998: C-6.

9 Phil Villareal, "U.S. Has Another Big Win," *Arizona Daily Star*, July 11, 1998: C7.

10 "Easy Win Puts Team USA on Verge of Sweep of Mexico," *Las Vegas Review Journal and Las Vegas Sun*, July 12, 1998: 11C.

11 "Italian Wins Stage, Aussie Still Leader," *Toronto Star*, July 17, 1998.

12 Howard Fendrich, "South Korea 3, United States 1," AP Online, July 23, 1998.
13 "Houston 14, Rice 12," *Waco Tribune-Herald*, February 23, 2000: 6D.
14 "Colleges," *Fort Worth Star-Telegram*, April 24, 2000: 2C.
15 Phil Denis, "Welcome to the Twilight Zone," *Venice (Florida) Herald-Tribune*, May 7, 2001: 1C-2C.
16 Sarah Trotto, "Indian Pitchers Hurt 1-Hitter," *Indianapolis Star*, August 1, 2003: D5.
17 Hank Lowenkron, "Luuloa Sparks Tribe to Sweep of Hens," *Indianapolis Star*, August 19, 2003: D4.
18 Lowenkron, "Louisville Hopes Take Another Jolt at Hands of Tribe," *Indianapolis Star*, August 26, 2003: D4.
19 Lowenkron, "Tribe Wins 5th in Row from Division Leader," *Indianapolis Star*, August 27, 2003: D5.
20 "Short Hops," *Arizona Republic*, April 6, 2004: C4.
21 "Nance Embraces Role," *Arizona Republic*, August 12, 2004.
22 "Notes," *Milwaukee Journal-Sentinel*, March 13, 2006: 10C.

EDDIE O'BRIEN

BY TIM HERLICH

In 1969 the expansion Seattle Pilots hired Eddie O'Brien as bullpen coach. His role was to assist manager Joe Schultz and pitching coach Sal Maglie. Asked at the start of the season to specifically describe his duties, O'Brien offered "Well, I look in to Sal or Joe, and they let me know when I'm supposed to get a pitcher ready." Asked how he would know if a pitcher was ready, he replied with a grin. "They tell me."[1]

Eddie O'Brien is immortalized as "Mr. Small Stuff" in *Ball Four*, the ground-breaking work by pitcher Jim Bouton recounting the travails of his 1969 season.[2] Bouton depicted O'Brien as a clueless minion who refuses to warm up the knuckleballing hurler and obsesses over trivialities. The appointment was a goodwill gesture and public-relations move by club management.[3] It also gave Eddie the necessary service time to qualify for a major-league pension.[4] At the time, a cumulative four years of major-league service (player, coach, manager) was required to qualify for a pension. Despite Bouton's unflattering portrait, O'Brien enjoyed iconic status in Seattle until his death in 2014. He and his identical twin brother, Johnny, were legendary collegiate athletes and coveted major-league prospects. After brief pro baseball careers, both returned to the Pacific Northwest and contributed to civic life.

Edward Joseph O'Brien and his brother were born on December 11, 1930, in South Amboy, New Jersey, the eldest of Edward James and Margaret (Smith) O'Brien's five children. Their father, a native of South Amboy, was employed as a deckhand by the Pennsylvania Railroad. The boys and their siblings grew up in a tiny, two-bedroom apartment. Neither parent lived past middle age. Their mother died in 1950; their father succumbed in 1955.

In 1948 the O'Briens graduated from St. Mary's High School in South Amboy, an Irish-Catholic enclave on the banks of Raritan Bay. Eddie was primarily a center fielder and exhibited a strong throwing arm. Johnny played the infield. Both were right-handed batsmen. The catcher on their high-school team was Jack McKeon, who would gain prominence as a big-league manager and general manager decades later. The school also produced Tom Kelly, manager of the Minnesota Twins from 1986 through 2001. An earlier alumnus of St. Mary's was Allie Clark, a major-league outfielder from 1947 to 1953.

"Wherever they went, they had a baseball glove on," Clark recalled about the 5-foot-9-inch twins. "If it was winter, they had a basketball."[5] Despite their modest size, they were two-sport stars. In March of their senior year, Eddie was chosen for second team and Johnny the first team on the Middlesex All-County basketball squad.[6] That summer, they helped lead the South Amboy All-Stars to the New Jersey state championship and a berth in the All-American Amateur Baseball Association tournament in Johnstown, Pennsylvania. Although South Amboy bowed out in five games, Eddie batted .500 and clubbed two home runs among 11 hits.

The twins needed scholarships to attend college, and were determined to enroll together. Tryouts at Seton Hall and Columbia Universities proved fruitless. The Brooklyn Dodgers, under general manager Branch Rickey, offered to pay their way to attend St. John's University if they signed with the Dodgers and forfeited their collegiate sports eligibility.[7] The O'Briens stayed in South Amboy that winter and played amateur baseball in 1949. While competing at the National Semi-Pro Baseball tournament in Wichita in August, they caught the eye of Al Brightman, the first baseman on a rival team from Washington State. Brightman was also the baseball and basketball coach at Seattle University, a small independent Division I school with an undistinguished athletic program. After the tournament, Brightman secured scholarships for the twins to attend the Jesuit institution and compete in both sports.

The freshmen made an immediate impact. "O'Brien Boys Are Pitchers' Scourge," wrote sportswriter Jack McLavey in 1950. "Seattle University's popular twin-brother act, John and Ed O'Brien, kept their basketball opponents in a dither last winter [and] are treating rival baseball pitchers in the same ungentlemanly fashion."[8] Eddie posted a .341 batting average that season. His sophomore and junior years were even better. In 1951 he compiled a .393 average and .607 slugging percentage. In a game against Seattle Pacific College, the center fielder hit two inside-the-park home runs and a triple, and drove in nine runs. In 1952 Eddie hit .431 and slugged .794. His nine round-trippers broke the single-season school record of eight set by his brother the previous year. The fleet-footed leadoff hitter stole 17 bases.[9] Johnny's production during this period was similarly robust. Over three seasons, the duo led the Chieftains'[10] baseball program to a 61-14 won-lost record and a berth in the 1952 National Collegiate Athletic Association tournament.

Their exploits on the basketball court were equally sensational. They adopted a fast-paced style of play to take advantage of their speed and neutralize their height disadvantage. "Eddie-O" was the playmaker, "Johnny-O" the prolific scorer. On December 22, 1952, Eddie uncharacteristically outscored his brother 33 to 29 in a 102-101 win over New York University at Madison Square Garden. In the era before a mandatory shot clock, it was the first collegiate game in which both teams scored over 100 points. Perhaps their most impressive performance came on January 21, 1952, when they led the Chieftains to an 84-81 upset victory over the much taller Harlem Globetrotters. The tandem led the varsity hoopsters to a 90-17 record and appearances in the 1952 National Invitational Tournament and 1953 NCAA Tournament.[11]

During this period, Branch Rickey's interest in the O'Briens intensified. The Mahatma had left Brooklyn and was general manager of the cellar-dwelling Pittsburgh Pirates. In May 1952 a sportswriter reported that the twins would likely pass up their senior year of collegiate baseball eligibility to sign with the Corsairs.[12] That summer, they worked out before Rickey at Forbes Field. Seven other major league clubs were also in pursuit. The

Pirates scout Ed McCarrick signs twin brothers on same day. L to R: Johnny O'Brien, McCarrick, Eddie O'Brien. Courtesy National Baseball Hall of Fame.

Seattle Rainiers of the Pacific Coast League saw the hometown heroes as a prime gate attraction and were serious bidders.

There was disagreement among scouts over which of the twins had more potential, and conjecture that some clubs wanted to sign only one, not both. "No, that isn't true," Eddie said later. "We both had offers from the same clubs. No one spoke to us about only one of us signing."[13] Rickey enlisted the help of minority club owner Bing Crosby to woo the O'Briens to Pittsburgh. "He'd send us Christmas gifts every year," Eddie remembered of the popular entertainer. "He was a close friend until the day he died."[14]

On March 19, 1953, Pittsburgh announced that scout Ed McCarrick had signed the brothers to contracts calling for bonuses of $40,000 each.[15] Other reports pegged the O'Brien bonuses at between $15,000[16] and $45,000.[17] The actual amount was $25,000 each, and included their first-year major-league salary of $6,000.[18] The twins used the funds to buy their father a house and a new car.

Under the major-league bonus rule in effect at the time, the O'Briens would have to be retained on the Pirates' active roster for at least two years.[19] The bonus rule, which was approved at the winter meetings during the first week of December 1952 and remained in effect through 1957, mandated that players signed for bonuses of more than $4,000 be kept in the major leagues for two years.

The bonus babies left Seattle immediately and reported to spring training in Havana. Rickey wanted to maximize the novelty of identical twins playing on the same team and informed Eddie that he was to become an infielder. "I have never played in the infield in my life," the center fielder confessed, "but Mr. Rickey wants Johnny and me to play together so I'll have to learn."[20] The rookies flew to the Bucs' minor-league camp at Brunswick, Georgia, to begin the conversion. Eddie was to play shortstop, Johnny second base.

The O'Briens were the first twins in major-league history to play for the same team since Red Shannon and Joe Shannon appeared in one game together in 1915. Manager Fred Haney brought the newbies along slowly. Eddie appeared as a pinch-runner in his first four major-league games, and finally saw action in the field and at the plate in a May 27 doubleheader. He collected his first hit and stolen base off Steve Ridzik, but also made two errors. The same day, he and his brother were ordered to take their US Army physical exams.[21] On June 7 the O'Briens appeared together in the starting lineup for the first time. From then until September 2, they were the Pirates' primary keystone tandem.

Haney was generous in his assessment of the youngsters. "The O'Brien kids have done a fine job defensively. In a couple of years, they should be finished ball players, but the Army probably will interrupt before that time."[22] As the season progressed, local sportswriters were not as kind. "The O'Briens were handling the key infield spots and the Pirates were going down with disgusting regularity," wrote one. "Both started kicking the ball around, couldn't hold throws and were out of position on numerous occasions."[23] All told, Eddie committed 23 errors at shortstop in 81 games. At the plate, he averaged .238 with five doubles, three triples, and an on-base plus slugging percentage (OPS) of .569 in his rookie year.

On September 10, 1953, the O'Briens were inducted into the Army and assigned to the Aberdeen Proving Ground in Maryland. "John and I didn't play [baseball] at all in the service," Eddie lamented. "They didn't have a team at Aberdeen [at least then[24]], and most of the time if we wanted to work out we had to do it ourselves."[25] The twins returned to the hardwood for competitive action. In March 1954, they led the Aberdeen base cagers to victory in the Second Army basketball tournament.[26] On June 26 of the same year, Eddie married Patricia McGough, a Seattle U. Homecoming Princess, to whom he had become engaged the previous Christmas.

Eddie and his brother were discharged from the Army on June 10, 1955. Since military service time was excluded from the bonus rule, they returned to the Pirates' active roster. Dick Groat, the former Duke basketball star, had firmly grasped the starting shortstop position that spring following two years of military service. After several weeks of utility play, manager Haney inserted Eddie into the starting lineup. From July 17 until the end of the season, he was the team's leadoff hitter and center fielder. The fly chaser fielded much better at his former collegiate position than he did at shortstop. In 56 games he made just one error and recorded nine assists. But his hitting was anemic. Eddie finished the 1955 season with a .233 batting average, three doubles, one triple, and a .544 OPS. This level of production was inadequate, especially at a position that featured Willie Mays, Duke Snider, and Richie Ashburn among the Bucs' National League rivals.

In the fall, the O'Briens returned to Seattle to complete their college degrees. In the wake of their father's death earlier in the year, the twins moved their young siblings from New Jersey to Washington State so the family could be together. Eddie also coached the Seattle University freshman basketball team.

On February 27, 1956, O'Brien departed for the Pirates spring-training camp. Fiery Bobby Bragan had replaced the congenial Haney as manager of the Pirates. At the conclusion of spring training, a reporter asked the skipper if he had any disappointments. "Yes," Bragan replied candidly. "I just wish that Eddie O'Brien had played the infield in college. He would be that much more advanced. He isn't big enough, nor does he have the power, to play in the outfield."[27] Unfortunately, the bonus rule prohibited the O'Briens from being sent to the minors to gain playing time until midseason. Pittsburgh solved its center-field problem in May by trading for 1955 Rookie of the Year Bill Virdon. The bonus designation for the O'Briens terminated on July 2, and the Pirates attempted to farm them out. The Braves, managed by Haney, put in a waiver claim, and the move was withdrawn.[28] Eddie appeared in only 63 games, mostly as a pinch-runner, and came to bat just 58 times. He played sparingly at six different positions in the field. On July 31 he made his mound debut. Eddie and his brother each pitched two scoreless innings of mop-up relief. "I am not so sure their future in the big leagues isn't on the mound," Bragan mused afterward.[29] Both were described as having a herky-jerky delivery and sharp control.[30]

Eddie and Patricia returned to Seattle after the season. The couple started building a house in the Seattle suburbs. By this time, they had started a family. Edward Joseph Jr. was born in July of 1955. Peggy came along the following year.

On January 19, 1957, the O'Briens signed new contracts with Pittsburgh, succeeding their initial bonus agreements from 1953. One month later, Eddie hitched a trailer to his station wagon and drove nine days with his wife and children from Seattle to the Pirates' spring training camp in Fort Myers, Florida. His status with the club was precarious. The 26-year-old was no longer guaranteed a major-league roster spot previously secured under the bonus rule. Furthermore, Pittsburgh signed a new bonus baby, USC shortstop Buddy Pritchard, to its big-league roster on February 7. In late March the Pirates again attempted to waive the O'Briens to the minor leagues. Eddie cleared waivers; Johnny did not. "John and I had an emotional parting in Fort Myers," the demoted utilityman confided. "In this business, there is no room for sentiment."[31] Eddie was assigned to Hollywood of the open-classification PCL on a 24-hour recall, necessitating a second transcontinental trip with his family. "This was a rugged grind," Eddie recalled. "Ever tour the country with two babies in a station wagon?" But the optimist was not complaining. "I would rather play in Hollywood than sit on the bench in Pittsburgh.[32]

His wish was granted immediately. The starting shortstop for the Stars, three-year incumbent Dick Smith, suffered a fractured jaw in the first game of the season.[33] O'Brien was given the everyday job, but could not hold it and was benched as soon as Smith became healthy. He played in 20 games at shortstop, pitched once, and batted a mere .158. On May 23 Pittsburgh reassigned him to its International League affiliate in Columbus, Ohio. For the third time in four months, the family piled into the station wagon to make the cross-country auto trek. Upon arrival, a sportswriter asked the versatile utilityman to name his favorite position on the diamond. "Wherever I can play every day," Eddie replied.[34]

A second chance for O'Brien to prove himself arose on June 2 in his first game with the Jets, Shortstop Dick Barone was hit by a pitch that broke his hand. Subbing for Barone, O'Brien made the most of his opportunity. In his first 100 at-bats as a Jet, the former bonus baby tallied 36 hits and was named Jet Player of the Month in June. He collected six hits vs. Toronto in a June 9 doubleheader, including his first home run in Organized Baseball, off Ross Grimsley Sr. One week later in a twin bill against Buffalo, he reprised the six-hit performance and hit his second home run, a grand slam off journeyman Glenn Cox. On June 20 O'Brien laid down a walk-off suicide-squeeze bunt in a win over Rochester. His offensive production cooled as the season wore on, but Eddie was still named to the league all-star team in August.[35] In a season-ending poll, league managers chose him as the infielder with the best throwing arm.[36] O'Brien appeared in 71 games at shortstop and six games at third base. He averaged .276 with 15 doubles, a triple, 3 home runs, and a .683 OPS.

O'Brien also pitched in nine games. The Pittsburgh organization apparently felt that he was no longer a major-league prospect in the field. "Eddie has great desire and fine aptitude," said Joe L. Brown, Rickey's successor as Pirates general manager. "He could develop into a fine shortstop. The trouble is that he probably wouldn't hit enough."[37] "Eddie isn't sold on that," countered one reporter, "but the Pirates are his employer, and he'll go along with their project, although admittedly against it."[38] O'Brien made his Jets mound debut on July 31, and followed with six more relief appearances. His first start came on August 31 in Havana. Eddie threw a complete-game 7-3 win over the Sugar Kings. The right-hander was described as "firing an explosive fast ball, effective sliders and occasional change-ups.[39] He was knocked out of his final start on September 7. His pitching line for Columbus was a 2-0 won-lost record and 3.97 earned-run average over 34 innings.

Eddie was recalled on September 9 and rejoined his brother on the Pirates' roster. Five days later, he hurled a complete-game 3-1 victory in the first game of a doubleheader at Wrigley Field, allowing six hits and fanning eight Cubs batters. Eddie earned the family bragging rights that day, as Johnny was the losing pitcher in the second game. Eddie pitched twice more in relief, finishing the season with a 2.19 ERA over 12⅓ innings, with 10 strikeouts.

Entering 1958, O'Brien was one of 20 pitchers on the Bucs' 40-man roster. In an intrasquad game on March 2, he surrendered 11 runs in just two innings.[40] Despite a lackluster spring training, O'Brien made the Opening Day roster. On April 19 he gave up three runs in two innings in relief against the Reds. Four days later, the Pirates optioned him to their Pacific Coast League club in Salt Lake City. O'Brien made his first appearance with the Bees on April 26 in his hometown of Seattle. He suffered a 4-1 defeat to the Rainiers. The right-hander picked up his first win on May 3 against Vancouver. He victimized the Mounties again on July 27 with a three-hit shutout, and whitewashed Seattle on August 6 to gain a measure of revenge. His final appearance, on September 3, was a near-perfect postscript to a once-promising career. The former bonus baby pitched seven innings to earn a 5-2 victory, and was a perfect 3-for-3 at the plate, with a stolen base and two runs scored. For the season, O'Brien fashioned a 9-11 won-lost record and 4.35 ERA. The versatile hurler started 15 games and relieved in 21 others, several of which were in high-leverage save-type situations. He pitched 147 innings for the Bees, second-most on the club, and posted a .305 average in 59 at-bats.

The Pirates intended to recall O'Brien after the end of the PCL season.[41] On September 4, word leaked out that he had accepted an offer to become athletic director at Seattle University. The appointment was confirmed the next day. His annual salary at Seattle U. was rumored to be $10,000, likely a significant increase over his pay in the minor leagues.[42] "The Pirates wanted me to pitch," the soon-to-be 28-year-old explained. "Old hands will tell you that when you're a pitcher, it may take two or three years to get back to the majors. I thought it was time to look around for something so my family could be together where we want to be, in Seattle. As things stand right now, I am through with baseball."[43] Later, Eddie demurred. "If I were to play for anybody, it would have to be for Seattle."[44]

Seattle Rainiers general manager Dewey Soriano coveted the O'Brien twins as a potential drawing card. He had tried to purchase their contracts from Pittsburgh for years, but was repeatedly rebuffed. On October 14, 1958, Soriano finally obtained Eddie in a trade for minor-league outfielder Edward Moore. He expressed confidence that he could reach an agreement with the university that would allow Eddie to play.[45] But reuniting the O'Briens in Seattle was not to be. "I talked it all out with the school and the club," Eddie concluded. "Being an athletic director is a full-time job. The Rainiers would want me to play shortstop. You can't play shortstop without spring training. I couldn't make that."[46]

O'Brien's final major-league stats include a .236 batting average in 605 plate appearances, 10 doubles, 4 triples, no home runs, and an OPS of .557. He won his only decision as a pitcher and posted a 3.31 ERA over 16⅓ innings.

O'Brien was the Seattle University athletic director from 1958 until 1980, except for a one-year sabbatical in 1969 to join the Seattle Pilots, whose president was none other than Dewey Soriano. Even before that season was over, and well before the club moved to Milwaukee, O'Brien announced that he would not return.[47] He coached varsity baseball at the institution for 14 years and compiled a 276-135 won-lost record. He departed when Seattle U. downgraded its programs and dropped out of Division I athletics.

O'Brien began his own public-relations and consulting business. From 1982 to 1984, he was president of Arctic Gulf Marine, an Alaska shipping company, but had no substantive operational tasks. He resigned when the owners of the company became embroiled in a corruption scandal.[48] Although O'Brien was never implicated in any malfeasance, the experience was an awkward transition from academia to the private sector.

Over the years, Eddie and his brother remained in the public eye. They were very involved in the Forgotten Children's Fund, a charity that delivers Christmas gifts to hundreds of families each year, and operated a baseball camp that served 6,000 youths. They hosted the O'Brien Open, an annual golf tournament benefiting athletics at Seattle University, which returned to Division I sports in 2012. In recognition of their contributions to the university, the athletic administration building on campus is named the Ed and John O'Brien Center.[49]

Eddie and Patricia raised six children. They divorced in 1978. Eddie married Terryl Hackett in 1990. She had three children from a previous marriage. O'Brien died on February 21, 2014, of complications related to Parkinson's disease. "He was literally the most generous, giving man I know," asserted stepdaughter Jill of O'Brien.[50] "He was five foot, eight and a half inches tall," brother Johnny eulogized at Eddie's funeral Mass, "but he lived a seven-foot-seven life."[51]

Acknowledgments

Thank you to SABR member Blake Sherry for providing access to the Columbus Metropolitan Library database. Thanks also to Dan Raley, who conducted extensive interviews of the O'Brien family, Kevin Ticen, and Dave Eskenazi.

This biography was reviewed by Rory Costello and Len Levin, and fact-checked by Bill Lamb.

SOURCES

In addition to the sources shown in the notes, the author used:

www.baseball-reference.com

www.newspapers.com

www.retrosheet.org

www.sabr.org

www.legacy.com/obituaries/seattletimes/obituary.aspx?n=eddie-obrien&pid=169880924

Columbus Metropolitan Library, Columbus www.columbuslibrary.org

Seattle Public Library, Seattle www.spl.org

Baseball guides (St. Louis: The Sporting News, 1954 through 1959).

NOTES

1   Georg N. Meyers, "The Sporting Thing," *Seattle Times*, April 21, 1969: 19.
2   Jim Bouton and Leonard Shecter (ed.), *Ball Four* (Cleveland: World Publishing Company, 1970), 143.
3   Bill Mullins, *Becoming Big League: Seattle, the Pilots, and Stadium Politics* (Seattle: University of Washington Press, 2013), 102.
4   Meyers.
5   Rick Malwitz, "South Amboy Twins to Be Honored," *Home News Tribune* (New Brunswick, New Jersey), February 2, 2003: B1.
6   Gil Geis, "All-County: Sica, Ballou, O'Donnell, O'Brien, Kaskiw," *Sunday Times* (New Brunswick, New Jersey), March 14, 1948: 20.
7   Malwitz, "South Amboy Twins to Be Honored": B5.
8   Jack McLavey, "The Terrible Twins," *Seattle Daily Times*, May 19, 1950: 28.
9   Ed Donohoe, "'Get O'Briens,' B.R. Told Scout Last Year," *The Sporting News*, April 1, 1953: 23.
10 Seattle University changed the name of its sports mascot from Chieftains to Redhawks in 2000.
11 Dave Eskenazi and Steve Rudman, "Wayback Machine: Seattle U. Shocks Globetrotters," http://sportspressnw.com/2124463/2011/wayback-machine-seattle-u-shocks-the-globetrotters.
12 Jack Hewins, "Rickey Keeping Close Eye on O'Brien Twins," *Seattle Sunday Times*, May 25, 1952: 39.
13 Jack Hernon, "Twins Rickey's Hope for New Gate Appeal," *The Sporting News*, July 1, 1953: 6.
14 Malwitz, "South Amboy Twins to Be Honored": B5.
15 Dan McGibbeny, "Bucs Pay $80,000 Bonus for O'Brien Twins," *Pittsburgh Post-Gazette*, March 20, 1953: 20.
16 Frank Eck, "Bonus Baby Parade to Bushes Due This Season," *The Sporting News*, April 13, 1955: 13.
17 Davis J. Walsh, "To Whom It May Concern," *Pittsburgh Sun-Telegraph*, April 21, 1953: 21.
18 Phone interview with Dan Raley, March 4, 2021.
19 Brent Kelley, *Baseball's Biggest Blunder: The Bonus Rule of 1953-1957* (Lanham, Maryland: Scarecrow Press, 1997), 19-20.
20 Richard Minor, "O'Briens, Janowicz Drill at Bucco Farm Base," *The Sporting News*, April 8, 1953: 17.
21 "Major League Flashes," *The Sporting News*, May 27, 1953: 21.
22 Hernon, "Four 'High Aptitude' Aces on Rickey U. Roster," *The Sporting News*, July 1, 1953: 5.
23 Hernon, "Roamin' Around," *Pittsburgh Post-Gazette*, August 17, 1953: 19.
24 Another future Seattle Pilot, Gene Brabender, pitched for Aberdeen's team while in the service in 1964 and 1965.
25 Hernon, "Roamin' Around," *Pittsburgh Post-Gazette*, March 29, 1956: 23.
26 "Aberdeen Cagers Win Second Army Basketball Title," *Baltimore Sun*, March 20, 1954: 11.
27 Hernon, "Roamin' Around," *Pittsburgh Post-Gazette*, April 14, 1956: 15.
28 Oscar Ruhl, "From the Ruhl Book," *The Sporting News*, August 1, 1956: 14.
29 George Kiseda, "Long on Bench as Bucs Nosedive," *Pittsburgh Sun-Telegraph*, August 1, 1956: 18.
30 *The Sporting News*, August 8, 1956: 24.
31 Meyers, "The Sporting Thing," *Seattle Daily Times*, April 4, 1957: 26.
32 Meyers, "The Sporting Thing," *Seattle Daily Times*, April 4, 1957: 26.
33 John B. Old, "Stars Keystone Combine Hurt in Coast Inaugural, *The Sporting News*, April 17, 1957: 41.
34 Eddie Fisher, "O'Brien Arrives Anxious to Play," *Columbus Dispatch*, June 2, 1957: 34B.
35 "Eddie O'Brien All-Star Pick," *Pittsburgh Press*, August 13, 1957: 30.
36 Neil MacCarl, "Richmond's Coates 3-Way Top Pitcher, Say Int. Managers," *The Sporting News*, September 11, 1957: 35.
37 Lenny Anderson, "An Old Refrain," *Seattle Daily Times*, June 22, 1958: 28.
38 Fisher, "Naranjo, Powers Lead 4-0 Victory," *Columbus Dispatch*, August 31, 1957: 8.
39 Fisher, "Homers by Jets Beat Havana," *Columbus Dispatch*, September 1, 1957: 21A.
40 Les Biederman, "Thomas Off to Booming Start in Camp Play," *Pittsburgh Press*, March 3, 1958: 21.

41 "Pirates Call Up Five Buzzers After PCL Play," *Salt Lake City Tribune*, September 3, 1958: 23.

42 John Lindtwed, "Ed O'Brien to Take S.U. Post," *Seattle Times*, September 4, 1958: 26; "3-Man Staff to Guide Chiefs," *Seattle Times*, September 5, 1958: 21.

43 Meyers, "The Sporting Thing," *Seattle Times*, September 11, 1958: 17.

44 "Reidenbaugh Roundup," *The Sporting News*, October 15, 1958: 12.

45 Anderson, "Rainiers Land Eddie O'Brien," *Seattle Times*, October 14, 1958: 26.

46 Meyers, "The Sporting Thing," *Seattle Times*, December 2, 1958: 26.

47 Hy Zimmerman, "Borrowed Shoes Revive Donaldson," *The Sporting News*, September 6, 1968: 20.

48 *Decisions of the Federal Maritime Commission, Volume 28, July 1985 to June 1987*, US Government Printing Office: 800.

49 https://www.legacy.com/obituaries/seattletimes/obituary.aspx?n=eddie-o-brien&pid=169880924.

50 Bud Withers, "Eddie O'Brien of Twins SU fame Dies at 83," *Seattle Times*, February 22, 2014: C11.

51 Withers, "Eddie O'Brien, Seattle U Icon, Remembered Fondly," *Seattle Times*, March 4, 2014: C4.

JOHNNY O'BRIEN

BY TIM HERLICH

"The bonus rule will ruin baseball if it isn't curtailed," proclaimed Branch Rickey, Pittsburgh Pirates general manager, in August 1952."[1] A revised rule was adopted by the major leagues that winter. Clubs were required to carry any player receiving a signing bonus of more than $4,000 on their major-league roster for a minimum of two years.[2] The rule aimed to discourage huge bonuses to high-school and collegiate prospects. It failed miserably. Spending on amateur talent continued unabated.

The bonus rule of December 1952, which went into effect during that year's winter meetings and continued through 1957, had unintended consequences: irreparable damage to most of the players it governed. Johnny O'Brien and his identical twin brother, Eddie, were archetypal victims. Prohibited from developing their skills at the start of their pro careers at lower levels, they achieved minimal success in the majors. "[They] would've been fine major league players had they started where they belonged," observed Joe L. Brown, Rickey's successor in Pittsburgh. "They were talented young men but they had to stay in the major leagues. They graduated from college at like 22 and they were over 24 by the time that they could go down. That's a little late to be learning."[3]

John Thomas O'Brien was born on December 11, 1930, a few minutes before Edward, in South Amboy, New Jersey. They were the eldest of Edward James and Margaret (Smith) O'Brien's four sons and one daughter. Their father was a laborer with the Pennsylvania Railroad. The boys shared bunk beds in one bedroom of the family apartment, their parents had the other, and their sister slept on the living-room sofa.[4] "Sports were our life," Johnny recalled of growing up in the Great Depression. "We made our own baseball and we got a brakeman stick (from the railroad). We played night and day because nobody had any money."[5]

The twins described their father as very loving, but also a taskmaster. "He never patted us on the back, no matter what we did," they said. "He was more likely to point out our mistakes, but we knew – and he knew we knew – he was always in our corner."[6] Johnny was an infielder and occasionally pitched. Eddie patrolled the outfield. Both batted and threw right-handed.

The O'Briens attended St. Mary's High School in South Amboy. They graduated in 1948, the same year that Allie Clark, an earlier alumnus of the school, helped the Cleveland Indians win a World Series championship. Future big-league Managers of the Year Tom Kelly and Jack McKeon are also St. Mary's graduates. McKeon was the catcher on the O'Briens' team. His father owned a garage that housed snowplows and other large vehicles. On cold winter nights, the three teenagers transformed the garage into an indoor batting facility. "We moved all the vehicles out, put screens on the windows and lights, and took batting practice for hours," McKeon recalled.[7]

Johnny O'Brien was both an infielder and pitcher for the Pittsburgh Pirates. Courtesy National Baseball Hall of Fame.

Despite their small height and slight build, the twins also excelled in basketball. Johnny was chosen to the first team and Eddie the second team on the Middlesex All-County basketball squad.[8] In the Catholic Schools Class B Championship game against Holy Family of Union City, Johnny was outstanding. "Racing underneath for twisting, underhanded lay-ups, he constantly outsmarted the Holy Family back line," wrote one reporter. Johnny scored 23 of the Eagles' 47 tallies in a heartbreaking one-point loss.[9]

According to Johnny, 14 major-league clubs wanted to sign the twins to minor-league contracts after high school. Their father, though, had attended school only through fifth grade and insisted that they get a college education.[10] Scholarships would be essential. A physician in South Amboy offered to pay their way at Mount Saint Mary's in Maryland if they promised to become doctors. They respectfully declined. "You can't believe how many lives that saved," Johnny wisecracked years later.[11] Seton Hall University, which had future bonus baby Ted Lepcio in its baseball program, rejected the undersized duo. The Brooklyn Dodgers proposed to pay their way to attend St. John's University. In exchange, they would have had to sign contracts with the Dodgers organization and forfeit their collegiate sports eligibility.[12] The twins turned down the offer, and spent the winter working in a local factory.

The following summer, they played semipro baseball for various teams. In August 1949, at the National Semi-Pro Baseball tournament in Wichita, Kansas, the teenagers grabbed the attention of a rival player, 26-year-old Al Brightman, who also happened to be the baseball and basketball coach at Seattle University. Brightman arranged for scholarships, and Johnny and Eddie headed west to play both sports for the Chieftains.[13]

"No one would take Ed and [me] for a basketball scholarship," Johnny recalled much later. "Who's going to go for two 5-foot-9 guys from New Jersey? Seattle U. took a chance on us."[14] The duo exceeded all expectations on the hardwood for the tiny Jesuit institution. "Johnny-O" was a scoring machine, "Eddie-O" the playmaker. Over four years, Johnny tallied 3,302 points, more than any other college player at the time, and was the first collegian to top 1,000 points in a season.[15] On February 15, 1953, he set a school record with 51 points in a game vs. Gonzaga University, a mark broken a few years later by future NBA star Elgin Baylor.[16] In his senior year Johnny was selected first-team All-American by both the Associated Press and United Press.[17]

His most celebrated game took place in Seattle on January 21, 1952, against the Harlem Globetrotters. The match was a fundraiser for the US Olympic Committee. Known for their entertaining antics on the court, the legendary Globetrotters were also very skilled cagers. They routinely dispatched collegiate foes on national barnstorming tours, and had beaten the Minneapolis Lakers, champions of the fledgling NBA, twice in serious exhibition games.[18] Founded in 1926, they arrived in Seattle seeking their 4,000th victory against just 253 losses.

Despite a six-inch height disadvantage, Johnny flummoxed his taller defenders, including the fabulous Reece "Goose" Tatum. "With my first three shots, I hit a right-handed hook, then a left-handed hook, and a jumper," Johnny said. "After that, they didn't know what I was going to do." In one of the biggest upsets in Seattle sports history, Johnny netted 43 points, Eddie chipped in 13, and the Chieftains posted a shocking 84-81 victory.[19] This David vs. Goliath-like triumph vaulted Seattle U. to national prominence and the O'Briens to local stardom. Johnny was voted "Man of the Year" at Seattle's prestigious sports banquet.[20] Over three years, the tandem led the Chieftains to a 90-17 record and appearances in the 1952 National Invitational Tournament and 1953 National Collegiate Athletic Association Tournament.[21]

Johnny-O was just as dazzling on the baseball diamond. As a freshman he hit .350; the following year, he averaged .566 with 22 of his 47 hits going for extra bases, and compiled an astounding slugging percentage of 1.110. The infielder also pitched twice in relief, striking out seven in three innings.[22] In his junior season, Johnny "cooled off" to a .433 batting average and .784 slugging mark. The cleanup hitter also stole 13 bases.[23] Eddie's production during this period was similarly impressive. Over three seasons, the duo led the Chieftains to a 61-14 record and a berth in the 1952 NCAA tournament.

They returned to South Amboy that summer to play for the "Brooklyn Against the World" team sponsored by the Dodgers organization. The program, initiated by then-Brooklyn GM Rickey in 1946, showcased amateur talent from the metropolitan New York area. In its formative years (1946-1947), Brooklyn Against the World, co-founded by Rickey and Lou Niss of the *Brooklyn Eagle,* pitted a team of Brooklyn youth (under age 19) against a group of star players from around the country. By 1952 the Brooklyn team, known as the "Dodger Rookies," dispensed with the age limit and became a barnstorming venture traveling to various locations in the Northeast. The 1952 team won eight of nine contests.[24]

Although Rickey left Flatbush in 1950 to take the reins of the moribund Pirates, he still kept tabs on the twin prodigies. Pittsburgh majority owner John Galbreath was not averse to spending big bucks for collegiate sports standouts. In June 1952 the Corsairs landed Duke basketball star and shortstop Dick Groat with a sizable bonus before changes to the bonus rules. On December 15, 1952, Heisman Trophy winner Vic Janowicz received a $25,000 bonus, the first contract signed under the new bonus rule.

Rickey hoped to lure the O'Briens to the Steel City as well, but he was not their only suitor. The Seattle Rainiers of the Open Classification Pacific Coast League valued the twins as a potential drawing card, and were willing to offer signing bonuses of up to $15,000 apiece. Several major-league clubs, including the Yankees, Dodgers, and Giants, were also in the hunt. With the help of the Pirates' minority owner, Bing Crosby, Rickey persuaded the O'Briens to pass up their final year of baseball eligibility. On March 19, 1953, in the Seattle U. gymnasium, scout Ed McCarrick signed the young men to a five-figure package deal. "We are mighty happy to have kids like this on our club," McCarrick enthused to the local press. He compared the O'Briens to Rickey's World Series champions from St. Louis two decades earlier. "They are the type of player Mr. Rickey likes – fast and aggressive. They've got the Gashouse Spirit."[25] The sizable bonus also dissuaded the twins from pursuing pro basketball, even though they were selected by the Milwaukee Hawks in the 1953 NBA draft.

The bonus babies left Seattle immediately and reported to Rickey at the Bucs' spring camp in Havana. The Mahatma wanted a quick return on the club's investment and decreed that the twins become the Pirates' new keystone combo. Johnny was moved from the left side of the infield, where he'd played in college, to second base. With Groat in military service, Eddie was groomed as a shortstop. "The idea of using the O'Briens at second and short was mine," Rickey declared.[26]

In a 2018 interview, Johnny humorously described their first workout in Havana:

"So, they start hitting balls (to Eddie), and Rickey's going, 'That's Pee Wee Reese. … Then, he says, let's have a double play. So, I come out and (Eddie) drills me. I said, Ed, you're not a center fielder anymore, you just get the ball (easy) to me. They hit another one, and again, boom, he drills me again. So, I say, 'Mr. Rickey, that might be Pee Wee Reese, but he's killing Jackie Robinson.'"[27]

The O'Briens were hyped as the Pirates' first brother act since Paul and Lloyd Waner. Manager Fred Haney brought his future double-play tandem along slowly, choosing not to play them together for the first two months of the season. Johnny appeared in several games at second with veteran Dick Cole at short; Eddie was paired with Danny O'Connell. Finally, on June 7, they started together for the first time. The O'Briens were the first twins in major-league history to play for the same team since Red Shannon and Joe Shannon appeared in one game together in 1915. From that day until September 2, they were the Bucs' primary middle infielders.

Haney defended his commitment to the greenhorns. "We have to find out what they can do. We're looking for the future, we are building for a winner," he said.[28] A few praised their defensive skills. "Those kids make the double play better than some veterans in the league," umpire Babe Pinelli assessed.[29] Others were not as kind. "There are no two players in the game that try harder than these youngsters," wrote one sportswriter after another Bucs loss, "but they repeated their Friday mistake of being in the wrong place, and their inability to get in front of bounding balls also proved costly."[30]

At second base, Johnny was officially charged with only seven errors for the season. At the plate, he averaged .247 with 13 doubles, 2 triples, 2 home runs, and an on-base plus slugging percentage (OPS) of .639. On August 23 at Forbes Field, the O'Briens put on a tantalizing offensive display in a doubleheader against Cincinnati. The pair scored six runs and drove in eight on seven hits, including Johnny's first big-league home run, off Harry Perkowski.

The twins' rookie season ended on September 10. They were inducted into the US Army and assigned to Aberdeen Proving Ground in Maryland. Despite missing the entire 1954 season, the twins were pictured together on a unique Topps baseball card. It has become one of the most desirable cards in the set.

The Aberdeen base did not have a baseball program at that time. It did have a basketball team, and Johnny excelled in competition against other Army bases. In March 1954 he was named to the Armed Forces Press Service all-star team. The following month, at the All-Army basketball tournament held at Fort Lewis, Washington, the scoring dynamo tallied 103 points in three games, including a tourney-record 41 for a single game.[31] Johnny was selected to the tournament's all-star first-team. Fellow All-American and future teammate Groat, stationed at Fort Belvoir, Virginia, was named second-team.[32]

On October 2 Johnny married Jeanne Kumhera, his college sweetheart and 1951 Homecoming Queen. They had become engaged the previous Christmas.[33] The wedding took place 14 weeks after Eddie and another Seattle U. grad were wed. Befitting the O'Briens' celebrity status, both nuptials received prominent coverage in the society pages of the *Seattle Sunday Times*.[34]

In 1955 the twins played some games with the Lancaster Red Roses of the Eastern Basketball League until their June discharge from the Army. Since military service time was excluded from the bonus rule, they returned to the Pirates' active roster. Haney inserted Johnny full-time at second base from late June until the end of the season. On July 2 he singled in the game-winning run against the Dodgers. The scrappy spray hitter went 4-for-4 against Brooklyn five days later, and drove in four runs vs. the Cubs on July 24. He batted well over .300 for most of the year before finishing with a .299 batting average, 15 doubles, 2 triples, 1 home run, and a .723 OPS. One of his most memorable hits occurred on July 1 at Ebbets Field. In the top of the second, he lined a double past Carl Furillo off the Abe Stark sign at the base of the right-field scoreboard and earned a free suit from the Brooklyn clothier.[35] O'Brien returned to Seattle University in the fall and earned a bachelor's degree in business administration.

"If running and hustle were the only credentials for the Hall of Fame, the O'Briens could dash right from Forbes Field to Cooperstown," opined one sportswriter. "Unfortunately, other essentials are needed."[36] Johnny opened 1956 as the starting second baseman, but slumped early at the plate. New Pirates manager Bobby Bragan wasn't as patient as Haney, his predecessor. O'Brien struggled to hit above .200 as Bragan shuffled him in and out of the lineup. When Bill Mazeroski was called up from Hollywood in July, any remaining hope Johnny had of reclaiming the starting job was over. In 104 at-bats for the season, he managed just 18 hits (.173).

Johnny had to remain on the major-league roster under the bonus rules, so Bragan got creative. On June 27, to save an overworked pitching staff in a lopsided loss, he summoned a shocked O'Brien to pitch the ninth inning against the Redlegs. The infielder had thrown some batting practice, but had not pitched competitively since his sophomore year at Seattle U. The first batter he faced was Frank Robinson. Using a fastball and knuckler, Johnny struck out the future Hall of Famer and retired the side unscathed. His next mound appearance was on July 3 vs. the Phillies. Behind 5-3, Bragan brought O'Brien in with two out and the bases loaded in the top of the seventh. The right-hander escaped the jam and shut out the Phils the rest of the way as the Pirates came back to win, 6-5. Johnny pitched six more games in relief and finished the 1956 season with a 1-0 record and a 2.84 earned-run average over 19 innings.

Pittsburgh sought waivers on the twins in late July in order to send them to the minors after their bonus designation expired. Milwaukee put in a claim and the request was withdrawn. The Braves were in pennant contention under former Pirates skipper Haney, who envisaged the O'Briens as pinch-runners and "cheer leaders on the bench."[37]

Pittsburgh again tried to farm out the twins in spring training 1957. This time, Eddie cleared waivers, but Johnny did not. He stayed on the Pirates roster the entire season as a utility infielder and relief pitcher and appeared in just 34 games. At the plate, he went 11-for-35. On the mound he served up seven home runs over 40 innings and finished 0-3 with a 6.08 ERA.

As the 1958 season began, the veteran (by then 27) was nearly a forgotten man. He appeared in just three of the Pirates' first 55 games, and even worked out as the team's emergency catcher.[38] At the June 15 trading deadline, Brown dealt O'Brien and Gene Freese to St. Louis for another former bonus baby, Dick Schofield. Cardinals manager Fred Hutchinson, also a Seattle sports hero, used O'Brien as a pinch-runner, defensive replacement, and mop-up reliever in a dozen games. On July 13 O'Brien was swapped to the Redbirds' Triple-A farm club in Rochester for Rubén Amaro Sr. "No player ever came out of the majors to display more spirit, hustle, fight and drive in his demotion," remarked one Red Wings reporter.[39]

The peppery middle infielder played errorless ball in 36 games and led the team with a .323 batting average. However, his prior inaction may have taken a toll. O'Brien played through a succession of pulled leg muscles before tearing knee ligaments in a take-out slide in the third game of the International League playoffs.

The St. Louis organization wanted Johnny to play winter ball, but he declined and was dropped from the Cardinals roster. The Rainiers club hoped to finally realize its dream to suit up the O'Brien twins. "I preferred to come back to Seattle," Johnny admitted.[40] It was not to be. Philadelphia unexpectedly claimed Johnny in the Rule 5 draft. He signed a five-figure contract, the largest of his career, and reported to the Phillies spring-training camp in Clearwater, Florida.[41]

Meanwhile, the Milwaukee Braves suffered a severe blow. Second baseman Red Schoendienst contracted tuberculosis, which sidelined the future Hall of Famer for nearly the entire 1959 season. The defending NL champions scrambled to fill the void. On March 31, in a six-player trade with the Phillies, they obtained O'Brien to join the competition. "He's a scrappy little hustler," his former manager Haney beamed. "I like his style of play very much." Braves GM John McHale vowed that "Johnny will be given every opportunity to play second. We think he'll go a long way in solving our infield problem."[42]

Coming off the bench, O'Brien got off to a good start with his new team. He drove in the game-winning run with an 11th-inning single on Opening Day, and socked a home run off soft-tossing Giants reliever Stu Miller on May 2. The next day, O'Brien joined the starting lineup; he remained the Braves' primary second baseman through mid-July, but struggled at the plate. His batting average stood at .198 on July 21 when McHale, desperate for more offense, claimed veteran Bobby Avila off waivers and returned O'Brien to Triple-A Rochester. Amid a variety of leg and hand injuries, he hit .208 in just 26 games for the Red Wings and finished the season on the disabled list.

Unexpectedly, Johnny's dismal year ended on a positive note. On September 7, Seattle announced that it had purchased O'Brien from Rochester for the 1960 season, ending its six-year quest. The Rainiers had a working agreement with the Cincinnati Reds and couldn't have made the deal without the help of Hutchinson, who had become the Reds manager, and general manager Gabe Paul.[43] Johnny welcomed the opportunity to play for Seattle, but apparently wasn't about to give the Rainiers a hometown discount. The Irish-American signed his contract on St. Patrick's Day, one day before spring training started. "I'm satisfied and I'm going to try to do a heck of a job," he declared.[44] Rainiers manager Dick Sisler named O'Brien team captain, citing his "ability, hustle, leadership and intelligence."[45]

Five days before the start of the Pacific Coast League season, the veteran severely sprained his right ankle. The injury kept him out of action for two months. On June 10 O'Brien finally made his Rainiers debut. He was the team's primary third baseman for the remainder of the season. The captain finished the year with a .309 batting average, including 12 doubles and 5 home runs, in 73 games. Nonetheless, O'Brien was not among the 10 players recalled to the Reds' major-league roster in September.

In October the locally owned Rainiers were purchased by the Boston Red Sox. O'Brien's contract was one of nine transferred to the Boston franchise for 1961.[46] The one-time bonus baby took stock of his life. He had bounced around six major-league organizations in less than three years. Meanwhile, Groat, Mazeroski, and many of his former Pirates teammates had won the 1960 World Series. During prior offseasons, O'Brien had been employed as a county coroner's deputy and a beverage company salesman. He also did color commentary with play-by-play announcer Keith Jackson on radio broadcasts of Seattle University basketball games. Twin brother Eddie had left professional baseball two years earlier to become athletic director at Seattle U. On February 13, 1961, the 30-year-old father of four children announced his retirement. "I've been thinking about it for quite a while," said Johnny. "Baseball has been very good to me and I've enjoyed it."[47] The Red Sox asked him to reconsider, promising a midseason call-up.[48] Despite the temptation of Fenway Park's friendly left-field wall, Johnny stood firm.

In the majors, he compiled a .250 batting average in 906 plate appearances, with 35 doubles, 5 triples, 4 home runs, and a .626 OPS. On the mound, he finished with a 1-3 won-lost record and 5.61 ERA in 61 innings.

O'Brien was a scout for the expansion Houston Colt .45s from July 1961 through November 1962. He entered Seattle politics and was elected King County commissioner and councilman, serving from 1962 to 1973. He was a strong advocate of public financing to build an indoor multipurpose facility to attract major-league sports to the Pacific Northwest. Voters approved funding in 1968, but site selection for the Kingdome took four years – too late to save the beleaguered Seattle Pilots from moving to Milwaukee. In 1974 O'Brien was appointed interim stadium manager while the domed ballpark was under construction. He applied for the position of permanent director, but lost out to former big-league pitcher and Anaheim Stadium executive Ted Bowsfield. O'Brien continued working in Kingdome security, sales, and promotion through 1993.

Johnny and his brother formed O'Brien Baseball Services and conducted instructional camps for 6,000 children over the years. The twins were involved in other philanthropic activities, delivering Christmas gifts to families in need through the Forgotten Children's Fund. The O'Briens are enshrined in the Seattle University Hall of Fame, and the athletics administration building is named the Ed and John O'Brien Center.[49] Eddie died in 2014.

Over the years, Johnny became a master storyteller who could regale an audience for hours. His quips and sharp wit endeared him to his adopted Seattle hometown. In 2020 the 89-year-old was bestowed the Sports Legend Award from the Seattle Sports Commission.[50] Johnny and Jeanne raised seven children and have 11 grandchildren. As of 2021 they were alive and well and resided in Seattle.

Acknowledgments

Thanks to Dan Raley, who conducted extensive interviews of the O'Brien family, Kevin Ticen, Dave Eskenazi, and Alan Cohen.

This biography was reviewed by Rory Costello and Len Levin and fact-checked by Bill Lamb.

SOURCES

In addition to the sources shown in the notes, the author used:

www.baseball-reference.com

www.newspapers.com

www.retrosheet.org

www.sabr.org

www.legacy.com/obituaries/seattletimes/obituary.aspx?n=eddie-obrien&pid=169880924

Seattle Public Library, Seattle www.spl.org

Baseball Guides (St. Louis: The Sporting News, 1954 through 1959).

Bouton, Jim, and Leonard Shecter (ed.). *Ball Four* (Cleveland: World Publishing Company, 1970).

Mullins, Bill. *Becoming Big League: Seattle, the Pilots, and Stadium Politics* (Seattle: University of Washington Press, 2013).

Raley, Dan. *Pitchers of Beer: The Story of the Seattle Rainiers* (Lincoln: University of Nebraska Press, 2011), 251-255.

NOTES

1. Les Biederman, "Rickey Heads Probers Into Bonus Curbs," *The Sporting News*, August 20, 1952: 1.
2. Brent Kelley, *Baseball's Biggest Blunder: The Bonus Rule of 1953-1957* (Lanham, Maryland: Scarecrow Press, 1997), ix.
3. Kelley, 25. In fact, Johnny was 27 years old in 1958 and Eddie was 26 years old in 1957 when they were first sent to the minor leagues.
4. Phone interview with Dan Raley, March 4, 2021.
5. Terry Mosher, "Two of a Kind – O'Brien Twins Put Seattle U. Basketball on the Map, Then Went On to Play in MLB," *Kitsap Sun* (Bremerton, Washington), February 7, 2017: B2.
6. Biederman, "Memory of 'Finest Father' Inspiration for O'Brien Twins," *The Sporting News*, March 21, 1956: 7.
7. Vincent M. Mallozzi, "One Small Town, Six Big-League Careers," *New York Times*, October 12, 2010: B4.
8. Gil Geis, "All-County: Sica, Ballou, O'Donnell, O'Brien, Kaskiw," *Sunday Times,* (New Brunswick, New Jersey), March 14, 1948: 20.
9. Les Shapiro, "St. Mary's Five Bows in Thriller, 48-47; Jackie O'Brien Stars," *Sunday Times*, March 21, 1948: 22.
10. Comments of Johnny O'Brien, Sports Star of the Year Banquet, February 6, 2020. https://onedrive.live.com/?authkey=%21ANDPTMwSF8GOyzs&cid=9591635355FDDC5D&id=9591635355FDDC5D%21197932&parId=root&o=OneUp.
11. Scott Hanson, "Little Giants," *Seattle Times*, February 13, 2018: C3.
12. Terry Mosher, "Two of a Kind."
13. Seattle University changed the name of its sports teams from Chieftains to Redhawks in 2000.

14. Mike Vorel, "Ruidiaz, Bates Win Sports Star of Year," *Seattle Times*, February 7, 2020: B3.
15. "O'Brien Adds to Seattle U. Scoring Marks," *Seattle Daily Times*, March 23, 1952: 47.
16. Bill Sears, "Johnny-O Hits 51; SU wins 109-68," *Seattle Post-Intelligencer*, February 16, 1953: 11. Dan Raley, "33-Day Countdown to New Division I Era: Story #3," July 18, 2012, https://goseattleu.com/news/2012/8/14/205584555.aspx
17. Ted Meier, "A.P. All-America Honors O'Brien, Houbregs," *Seattle Times*, March 1, 1953: 36. "O'Brien, Houbregs Named to U.P. Five," *Seattle Times*, March 4, 1953: 35.
18. Stew Thornley, "Minneapolis Lakers vs. Harlem Globetrotters," https://stewthornley.net/mplslakers_trotters.html
19. The Globetrotters chalked up their 4,000th victory two nights later in San Francisco. "Globetrotters Finally Score 4,000th Victory," *Seattle Times*, January 23, 1952: 28.
20. Mike Donohoe, "Johnny O'Brien Chosen Man of Year," *Seattle Post-Intelligencer* January 7, 1953: 20.
21. Dave Eskenazi and Steve Rudman, "Wayback Machine: Seattle U. Shocks Globetrotters," http://sportspressnw.com/2124463/2011/wayback-machine-seattle-u-shocks-the-globetrotters.
22. "Chieftain Nine Rewrites School's Baseball Records," *Seattle Times*, June 3, 1951: 42.
23. Ed Donohoe, "'Get O'Briens,' B.R. Told Scout Last Year," *The Sporting News*, April 1, 1953: 23.
24. "Major Flashes," *The Sporting News*, July 29, 1953, 21; Roscoe McGowen, "Out-of-Town Games Being Booked for All-Amateur 'Dodger Rookies,'" *The Sporting News*, February 29, 1956: 10.
25. Mike Donohoe, "Pirates Sign O'Brien Twins," *Seattle Post-Intelligencer*, March 20, 1953: 18. Various reports pegged the O'Brien bonuses at between $15,000 and $45,000 each. According to Dan Raley, who interviewed Johnny O'Brien, the bonuses were $19,000 each plus the $6,000 minimum major-league salary.
26. George Kiseda, "Rickey Moves Back His Timetable for Pirates," *The Sporting News*, July 29, 1953: 7.
27. Hanson, "Storytelling with Johnny: It Doesn't Get Much Better," *Seattle Times*, February 13, 2018: C2.
28. Jack Hernon, "Roamin' Around," *Pittsburgh Post-Gazette*, August 17, 1953: 19.
29. "Hat's Off …!," *The Sporting News*, September 16, 1953: 16.
30. Charles J. Doyle, "Braves Sink Bucs, 7-4; Mathews, Adcock Homer," *Pittsburgh Sun-Telegraph*, August 9, 1953: 31.
31. "Johnny O's 41 Points Sets Record, Aberdeen Bows Out of Army Meet," *Seattle Times*, April 8, 1954: 22.
32. "Major Flashes," *The Sporting News*, April 28, 1954: 37.
33. "John, Ed Reveal Engagements," *Seattle University Spectator*, January 8, 1954: 1.
34. "Jeanne Kumhera Is Wed to John O'Brien, Seattle University Basketball Star," *Seattle Sunday Times*, October 3, 1954: 6-2; "Seattle U. Has Feature Part in O'Brien-McGough Wedding," *Seattle Sunday Times*, June 27, 1954 6-3.
35. Hernon, "Law Tames Dodgers with Seven-Hitter, 3-2," *Pittsburgh Post-Gazette*, July 2, 1955: 10; Biederman, "Law Beats Dodgers (By Inches)," *Pittsburgh Press*, July 2, 1955: 6.
36. Biederman, "O'Briens Still in Thick of Pennant Race," *Pittsburgh Press*, August 19, 1955: 25.
37. Oscar Ruhl, "From the Ruhl Book," *The Sporting News*, August 1, 1956: 14.
38. Biederman, "21 Stitches in Foiles' Chin, but Hank Stands By to Catch," *The Sporting News*, June 4, 1958: 13.
39. George Beahon, "Browning Nips Herd; Bisons Rout Wings In 2d Game, 11 to 1," *Democrat and Chronicle* (Rochester, New York), July 21, 1958: 21.
40. Georg N. Meyers, "Rainier Twin Setback Foiled by Phillies," *Seattle Times*, December 2, 1958: 26.
41. John Lindtwed, "Phils to Give Johnny O Big Boost," *Seattle Times*, February 4, 1959: 15.
42. "Johnny O to Help Fill Infield Gap," *Seattle Times*, April 1, 1959: 30.
43. Lenny Anderson, "Rainiers Purchase Johnny O'Brien," *Seattle Times*, September 7, 1959: 22.
44. "Johnny O' Signs Contract," *Seattle Post-Intelligencer*, March 18, 1960: 24.
45. Hy Zimmerman, "O'Brien, on Crutches, Named Team Captain," *Seattle Times*, April 11, 1960: 18.
46. "Johnny O to Stay in Seattle," *Seattle Post-Intelligencer*, October 23, 1960: 18.
47. Paul Rossi, "John O'Brien Quits Baseball," *Seattle Post-Intelligencer*, February 14, 1961: 18.
48. Phone interview with Dan Raley, March 4, 2021.
49. https://goseattleu.com/news/2013/5/30/207997630.aspx.
50. Sports Star of the Year Banquet, February 6, 2020.

DON O'RILEY

BY PAUL WHITE

"It's really a dream come true – the happiest moment of my life. To get a chance to play before my home town." – Don O'Riley

The classic dream of kids who love baseball is that they will be good enough to play professionally and make the major leagues. If that can be done with their hometown team, in front of family and friends, that would be a particularly satisfying bonus. In a life that could otherwise be viewed as difficult and far too short, it's important to remember that Don O'Riley lived that boyhood dream, complete with the bonus so few major leaguers get.

Donald Lee O'Riley was born in Topeka, Kansas, on March 12, 1945, the youngest of five children of James P. and Laura Marie (Williams) O'Riley. Before Don was born, the first of many tragedies to strike the family had already occurred, when his brother, Thomas, died in late 1942 when he was just 2 years old.[1] Though Don was born in Topeka, the family's home was in Kansas City, Missouri, where James worked for the Kansas City Police Department[2] and Marie worked in cosmetic sales at a pharmacy.[3] Don and his siblings grew up in Kansas City and he spent almost his entire life there.

Don attended Northeast High School, where he lettered in three sports,[4] but not baseball. For that he played in a local amateur league called 3&2 Baseball, where he excelled,[5] regularly being named to its year-end all-star teams.[6] He continued in that league even after graduating from Northeast in 1963, and it was during the league's Senior division season of 1964 that he drew the attention of Kansas City Athletics scout and future Hall of Fame manager Whitey Herzog, who signed him as an amateur free agent.[7] It was a thrilling moment for O'Riley, not only because the Athletics were his hometown team, but also because, as he said, "the A's are going for youth. I figured it was my best bet, especially with my inexperience. I know you've got to bear down to make it in baseball. You've got to work. I'm ready to do that. Ever since I was old enough to play I've wanted to be a big leaguer."[8]

O'Riley's first season as a professional began with a happy family event, but ended with another family tragedy. In March 1965 he married his high-school sweetheart, Gail Nelson,[9] before reporting to the Burlington Bees of the Midwest League. O'Riley had a very good season for a strong Bees club that finished with a league-best 82-40 record and featured eight players who would eventually reach the major leagues, including future A's captain and third baseman Sal Bando. O'Riley appeared in 39 games, all but four of them in relief, posting a 7-1 record and a 2.01 ERA in 94 innings. Manager Gus Niarhos was very pleased with his young right-hander, saying, "Don has done a heck of a job for us. He has an outstanding curveball – and he knows how to get it

Don O'Riley, Courtesy of the Kansas City Royals.

over. He can throw every day. He does his best job in relief."[10] Don was happy with his performance as well, and enjoyed his role in the bullpen. "I like to come in from the bullpen," he said. "Right now, I don't think I have enough experience to start all the time. I like to go in with men on; you know you have to throw strikes."[11] Overall, it was an excellent debut, but it was sadly marred as the season was in its final days when Don's father, Jim, died from a heart attack at the age of just 50.[12]

The strong showing in 1965 wasn't enough to move Don along to the next level, and he started the 1966 season still in Burlington. He was one of only two players from the previous season to be assigned to the Bees again,[13] and he turned in a very similar performance, throwing 89 innings in 33 appearances, all but four still in relief, with a 6-9 record and a 3.34 ERA. This was enough to move him along to the Peninsula Grays of the Carolina League for the 1967 season. O'Riley was reunited with Niarhos, who was then managing the Grays, a strong club that finished 74-64 and featured 15 future big leaguers, including Jim Holt, Darrell Evans, and Gene Tenace. O'Riley pitched well, appearing in 42 games, all in relief, and posting a 2-3 record and a 2.13 ERA in 76 innings pitched. It earned him a promotion at the end of the season to the Birmingham A's of the Double-A Southern League, where he played for future major-league manager John McNamara and joined a championship team that featured many of the stalwarts of the A's three consecutive World Series-winning teams of the early 1970s, including Reggie Jackson, Rollie Fingers, and Joe Rudi. O'Riley pitched in only three games there before the season ended, but was on the roster for Birmingham's appearance in the 1967 Dixie Series against the Albuquerque Dodgers, the final time the long-running series was played between the winners of the Double-A Southern League and the Double-A Texas League.[14]

After the 1967 season ended, O'Riley learned that he was no longer working for his hometown franchise. After months of rumors, the American League allowed Athletics owner Charlie Finley to move the team from Kansas City to Oakland for the 1968 season.[15] A new franchise would eventually be placed in Kansas City, but at least for 1968, O'Riley would be working for the Oakland Athletics. He spent that winter preparing for the season by pitching in the Puerto Rican Winter League,[16] which was followed by a nonroster invitation to spring training with the A's.[17] His performance there was strong enough to allow him to be assigned to the Vancouver Mounties of the Triple-A Pacific Coast League.[18] O'Riley repeated his performances from his earlier minor-league stops, posting a record of 4-5 with a 3.26 ERA in 102 innings of almost entirely relief work. He was described as "a big righthander who they say doesn't give a damn about anything – except maybe getting the opposition out. … He's a bit of a comedian, as an afternoon paper writer from Vancouver found out the other day when O'Riley used the freeze gun that trainers find indispensable these days and put his left arm out of condition."[19]

Being a comedian with a good curveball and carefree attitude apparently wasn't enough for the deep Athletics to decide to protect him when the expansion draft was conducted at the end of the season. O'Riley was made available to the two new American League franchises, the Seattle Pilots and his hometown Kansas City Royals. In the fourth round of the draft, with the 38th overall pick, the Royals decided to bring O'Riley home and drafted him.[20] He was ecstatic with the news, going so far as to call the local paper to verify that it was true, and telling a sportswriter, "I've been over to my father-in-law's, then to my mother's. My mother was so happy, she's been crying and all that. I just can't believe it. I couldn't when I heard it. I had just got off work – I'm working construction in the offseason. I stopped by my mother's and she said she heard it on the radio. I didn't believe it, so I had to call up to find out for myself. It was the furthest thing from my mind. I didn't even give it a thought to going in the major league draft. I had thought maybe later in the minor league draft. It's really a dream come true – the happiest moment of my life. To get a chance to play before my home town."[21] He heard the news officially from the Royals after that, meeting with new manager Joe Gordon, and then traveling to Florida to work on his pitching.[22]

O'Riley further honed his skills in winter ball, playing for Acarigua in the Venezuelan Winter League.[23] Though he felt he improved his control and pitched well, he didn't enjoy the experience. "I'll never go back there," he said. "I was pitching against Rollie Fingers and the score was 0-0 going into the ninth. I was working on a three-hitter and Rollie had only given up five hits. The fans started throwing everything on the playing field. The plate umpire suffered a split finger when someone hit him with a rock or something and there was no way to quiet the fans so we lost the game on a forfeit. Those people like the game, but they don't know what's going on. It's not that way in Puerto Rico."[24]

When he returned from Venezuela, O'Riley decided to get a jump on spring training by arriving early, singularly focused on making the team. "I want to be there early," he said. "There's going to be many players in the camp and I want to be ready to throw. Winter ball has kept me in perfect condition and I'm ready right now."[25] He told another writer, "I'm going to spring training with one thing in mind – making the club. I'll worry about setting goals after that."[26] He did have at least one goal, though, beyond making the team: "I'm going after a starting job when we report to spring training."[27]

The Royals must have viewed O'Riley as a potential starter, too, because even though he was described as a potential piece of their bullpen early in spring training,[28] he was initially sent to Triple-A Omaha, where he worked primarily as a starting pitcher for the first time in his professional career. He made the conversion seamlessly and pitched well there, finishing the season with a 12-5 record and a 3.94 ERA in 137 innings pitched, tying Paul Splittorff for the team lead in victories for a strong club that won the league by six games. He received a solid report from his Triple-A manager, Jack McKeon, who advised Royals general manager Cedric Tallis that O'Riley had "an improved concept of pitching and definitely has a chance to become a major league pitcher."[29]

By mid-June, O'Riley was leading the American Association in victories with seven, while the first-year Royals had allowed the second-most runs in the American League. Feeling they needed an infusion of pitching help, the big-league club decided it was time to make O'Riley's dream come true, and called him up, along with veteran Galen Cisco, on June 19.[30] O'Riley was moved back to the bullpen for the major-league club, and no time was wasted getting him into a game. He debuted in Seattle against the Pilots the next day, entering the first game of a doubleheader to begin the seventh inning in relief of starter Bill Butler. O'Riley retired the heart of the Pilots' lineup in order, getting Rich Rollins and Tommy Davis on groundballs and Don Mincher on a lineout. He remained in the game for the eighth inning, walking John Donaldson but striking out

Jerry McNertney for his first major-league strikeout and completing a second scoreless inning.

Initial success notwithstanding, O'Riley was inconsistent in his first weeks in the major leagues. Three scoreless outings were followed by three in which he gave up multiple runs in each. He surrendered runs in 8 of 13 relief appearances and sometimes went a week between outings before being sent back down to Omaha at the end of July. Still, there were some highlights. He picked up his first and what turned out to be his only major-league save in front of his hometown fans on July 4, and got his only major-league victory in relief a week later. "It made me very happy to get my first save and victory in my hometown," O'Riley said. "It's almost unbelievable that I'm in the majors. I've looked forward to this for a long time."[31] O'Riley was called back up in September, making five more relief appearances and continuing to struggle. For the year, his Triple-A success as a starter didn't translate to big-league success as a reliever: He finished with a 1-1 record, just the one save, and a 6.94 ERA in 23⅓ innings of work.

O'Riley went into the winter more determined than ever to make the Royals' roster coming out of spring training.[32] He worked with the Royals trainers to get into playing shape as part of an offseason workout program started by new manager Charlie Metro.[33] During spring training, he opened up to a sportswriter about how much it meant to him to play in Kansas City, and how crushed he was when he didn't make the team the year before: "It was always baseball with me. I used to sit in the stands and say, 'I'll be out there some day.' I used to tell my parents, 'I'm going to play ball for Kansas City.' And nobody really knows what it means to finally make it. You can say it's a dream come true, but it's more than that. I tried to get there early; I entered every one of those batboy contests – and never came close to winning. ... I was disappointed, deeply disappointed, when I didn't stick last spring. I couldn't pitch better than I did down here last spring. I threw 13 innings, didn't allow an earned run. I thought I had it made. ... So I'm sent to Omaha. I didn't like it. I couldn't do anything about it. All I could do is tell them, 'I'll be back.' But I wasn't great when I did come up. There's something about pitching in your hometown, before all your friends and relatives. You get those butterflies; you try to be too good. It got to me. But I feel ready now. I feel like I'm going to get a fair deal. Charlie (Metro) treats everybody fair. And he's the one who picked me out of the draft. He knows what I can do. I haven't talked to anybody about my feelings. I'm keeping my eyes and ears open, my mouth closed. I know I'm going to have to pitch my way to Kansas City."[34]

In a repeat of the year before, O'Riley was sent to Omaha to start the season, a bitter disappointment. "I was ready to head back to Kansas City," he said. "What I would do I didn't know. I just wanted to get out of baseball. [My wife told me] baseball is your life. You would be miserable doing anything else. So you're not going to quit. Not now."[35] That pep talk, plus a discussion with McKeon, persuaded O'Riley to report to Omaha, where, other than his win total, he essentially repeated his performance from the year before. Used only as a starter again, he posted a 5-8 record and a 3.60 ERA in 110 innings. And just like the year before, his stay in Triple A was interrupted by a call-up to the Royals in June.[36] The results weren't much better than the year before. He did get to start two games, but had no record in nine appearances, posting a 5.40 ERA in 23⅓ innings, the exact total of major-league innings he'd managed in 1969. In his final big-league game, on August 1, 1970, he entered the game in the fifth inning in Baltimore with the Royals already trailing the Orioles 6-0. He held his own for three innings, keeping the eventual World Series champions scoreless, but in the final inning of his major-league career, the Orioles touched him up for three runs, including a two-run homer by Elrod Hendricks.

That spelled the end of O'Riley's time with his hometown Royals – and in the major leagues. He was traded on October 13, 1970, along with Pat Kelly, to the Chicago White Sox for Gail Hopkins and

John Matias.[37] White Sox manager Chuck Tanner didn't seem overly excited to have him. "We'll have to see how he does. He was just fair at Omaha this year with 5-8, but had a good season in 1969 with 12-5. I'm told he's a bulldog type, which means he's always got a chance."[38]

To say that O'Riley's life become a bit more unsettled after his final year in the major leagues would be an understatement. Ineffective in spring training with a sore elbow,[39] he was released by the White Sox before spring training ended, but didn't sign with another team and found himself back in Kansas City, serving as assistant coach on a Ban Johnson League team.[40] He managed to catch on with the Braves' Triple-A affiliate, the Richmond Braves, in 1972 and pitched well enough for them to return the following year, but couldn't earn a call-up to the big leagues, and then he struggled in 1973 before injuring his arm in a motorcycle accident,[41] ending his professional career. His marriage to Gail ended, and he would marry three more times while working as a truck driver for beer distributors,[42] keeping fit by golfing and playing fast-pitch softball,[43] and making occasional appearances for the Royals at alumni events.[44]

Eventually O'Riley went to work at the Fast Stop convenience store near his home, a job his family said he took to allow him free time during the day to golf.[45] On the night of May 2, 1997, 21-year-old Robert Muse entered the store and confronted O'Riley with a pistol, demanding the money from the store's cash register. O'Riley, the man described during his career as a "bulldog" who didn't "give a damn about anything – except maybe getting the opposition out," pulled out his own pistol rather than comply. Both men fired, O'Riley's shot hitting Muse in the back, while Muse's shot hit O'Riley in the head, killing him instantly.[46] He was found by police on the floor of the store, $136 from the cash register missing.[47] "I never did think he would die of old age," said his former wife, Gail.[48] Muse was arrested, convicted of second-degree murder, and sentenced to life in prison. O'Riley's daughter, Angela, who had become a sheriff's deputy, was able to witness Muse's sentencing.[49]

But that didn't bring back her father. Don O'Riley, the only Kansas City native from the original Royals expansion draft class, was dead at the age of 52. He left behind his fourth wife, Marquita, a son, a daughter, two stepsons, his mother, Marie,[50] and the memories of local Kansas City baseball fans, who at least got to witness one of their own live out the dream they shared with him.

SOURCES

In addition to the sources cited in the Notes, the author consulted Baseball-Reference.com for all statistics, transactions, and box score information.

NOTES

1 Find-A-Grave, https://www.findagrave.com/memorial/7285646/thomas-patrick-o'riley.

2 "James P. Riley Obituary," *Kansas City Times*, September 15, 1965: 21. The nature of his work is unclear. The obituary says he was a clerk in the department's detention bureau, but was also a member of the Missouri Peace Officers Association.

3 "Laura Marie O'Riley Moore Obituary," *Kansas City Star*, May 8, 2001: B5.

4 Dick Wade, "O'Riley Certain This Is His Year," *Kansas City Times*, March 1, 1970: 4S.

5 "Hurling Is Tough," *Kansas City Star*, June 19, 1961: 13.

6 "Folger's and Diesel Top Senior 3 and 2 All-Stars," *Kansas City Star*, July 13, 1964: 13.

7 Paul O'Boynick, "Kansas Citian Eyes Royal Hill Berth," *Kansas City Times*, January 25, 1969: 4D.

8 Sid Bordman, "Kansas City Hurlers on Beam for Burlington," *Kansas City Star*, August 27, 1965: 28.

9 Bordman, "Kansas City Hurlers on Beam for Burlington."

10 Bordman, "Kansas City Hurlers on Beam for Burlington."

11 Bordman, "Kansas City Hurlers on Beam for Burlington."

12 "James P. O'Riley Obituary."

13 Gus Schrader, "Red Peppers," *Cedar Rapids* (Iowa) *Gazette*, May 2, 1966: 17.

14 Jeb Stewart, "The 1967 Dixie Series," *Baseball Research Journal*, Spring 2020. SABR.org, https://sabr.org/journal/article/the-1967-dixie-series/.

15 Joe McGuff, "Long-Run Gain," *Kansas City Star*, October 19, 1967: 1.

16 Miguel Frau, "Bando's Bat Booming Despite Long Layoff," *The Sporting News*, January 20, 1968: 39.

17 "Slipping Vets Earn Another Shot at Majors," *The Sporting News*, March 2, 1968: 32.

18 Clancy Loranger, "Sports," *Vancouver* (British Columbia) *Province*, April 11, 1968: 14.

19 Loranger, "Sports."

20 Larry Claflin, "Pilots Select Vets, Royals Corral Kids," *The Sporting News*, October 26, 1968: 11.

21 Gib Twyman, "Dream Comes True for Don O'Riley," *Kansas City Times*, October 16, 1968: 2B.

22 Bill Ellingsworth, "Royals Give O'Riley Big Chance," *Kansas City Times*, October 24, 1968: 12A.

23 Eduardo Moncada, "Bob Lee's Hill Feats Pad Caracas' Lead," *The Sporting News*, December 21, 1968: 47.

24 Paul O'Boynick, "Save, Victory Surprise O'Riley," *Kansas City Star*, July 15, 1969: 15.

25 Paul O'Boynick, "Kansas Citian Eyes Royal Hill Berth," *Kansas City Times*, January 25, 1969: 4D.

26 Tom Murray, "Don O'Riley Awaits Chance to Make Hometown Debut," *Joplin* (Missouri) *Globe*, February 6, 1969: C1.

27 Murray, "Don O'Riley Awaits Chance to Make Hometown Debut."

28 Joe McGuff, "Royals Start Operation Shakedown," *The Sporting News*, March 1, 1969: 16.

29 Joe McGuff, "Home Park Is Royal Horror Chamber," *The Sporting News*, July 5, 1969: 21.

30 "Home Park Is Royal Horror Chamber."

31 Paul O'Boynick, "Save, Victory Surprise O'Riley," *Kansas City Star*, July 15, 1969: 15.

32 Sid Bordman, "Vacancy Sign in Royal Bullpen; Lefty Warden Says He'll Fill It," *The Sporting News*, January 17, 1970: 41.

33 Sid Bordman, "Metro the Captain Bligh of Baseball," *The Sporting News*, January 24, 1970: 40.

34 Dick Wade, "O'Riley Certain This Is His Year," *Kansas City Times*, March 1, 1970: 4S.

35 Dick Wade, "O'Riley Glad He Stayed in Game," *Kansas City Star*, July 2, 1970: 17.

36 Joe McGuff, "A New Pair of Shoes Robs Royals of Keough's Big Bat," *The Sporting News*, July 18, 1970: 34.

37 Joe McGuff, "Royal Fans Reserve Judgment on Trade," *The Sporting News*, October 31, 1970: 48.

38 Edgar Munzel, "Kelly Injects Speed Into Sluggish Pale Hose," *The Sporting News*, October 31, 1970: 46.

39 Richard Dozer, "Sox-Andrews Stalemate on Contract Looms," *Chicago Tribune*, February 27, 1971: 64.

40 "Back Home," *Kansas City Star*, May 21, 1971: 20.

41 Christine Vendel, "Former Royals Player Dies During Store Robbery," *Kansas City Star*, May 4, 1997: B1.

42 Matt Campbell, "Ex-Royals Player Donald O'Riley Is Buried," *Kansas City Star*, May 7, 1997: C-2.

43 "Farmland Wins City Fast-Pitch Title," *Kansas City Star*, September 1, 1977: 5 East.

44 Rich Sambol, "Around KC," *Kansas City Star*, December 1, 1995: D3.

45 Campbell, "Ex-Royals Player Donald O'Riley Is Buried."

46 Vendel, "Former Royals Player Dies During Store Robbery."

47 Joe Lambe, "Law Officer Sees Her Father's Killer Sent to Prison," *Kansas City Star*, January 13, 1999: B1-2.

48 "Ex-Royals Player Donald O'Riley Is Buried."

49 "Law Officer Sees Her Father's Killer Sent to Prison."

50 "Donald Lee O'Riley Obituary."

JOHN POLONI

BY JOHN WATKINS

On December 14, 1977, the Boston Red Sox traded pitcher Fergie Jenkins, who had clashed with manager Don Zimmer, to the Texas Rangers for 6-foot-5, 210-pound left-hander John Poloni and $25,000 cash.[1] Poloni had made his major-league debut with the Rangers in September after spending the season at Triple-A Tucson. "It's not that we wanted to give Fergie away," said Boston general manager Haywood Sullivan. "Far from it. But we need a left-handed starter and our scouts think [Poloni] has a chance."[2]

It didn't work out that way. Poloni hurt his arm at training camp the following spring and never pitched again in the major leagues. However, he fashioned a long career in professional baseball. Poloni was a minor-league pitching coach for 13 years, tutoring future All-Stars and a Cy Young Award winner, and a scout for two dozen more. Drawing on his experience as a coach, he developed "a reputation in the [scouting] business for finding pitchers where no one else does."[3]

John Paul Poloni was born on February 28, 1954, in Dearborn, Michigan, part of the Detroit metropolitan area. He was raised in nearby Allen Park by his adoptive parents, John Peter Poloni, an ironworker, and Margaret Moritz Poloni, a homemaker.[4] At Lutheran West High School in Detroit, Poloni compiled a 26-4 record over his last two years, leading the Leopards to the state Class-B championship in 1971. The team lost in the regional playoffs the next season, when Poloni was named to the all-state team. In June 1972 the Pittsburgh Pirates drafted him in the third round, but he opted to attend collegiate powerhouse Arizona State University.[5]

In his freshman year at ASU, Poloni divided his time between the junior-varsity squad and the varsity. He was 4-0 with a 0.40 ERA for the varsity Sun Devils, allowing one earned run in 22⅔ innings while striking out 15.[6] Arizona State was ranked first in the nation going into the 1973 College World Series but fell to Southern California in the championship round. In the summer Poloni played ball in Colorado, leading the Grand Junction Eagles with a 7-2 record, including two victories against the Fairbanks Goldpanners, winner of the National Baseball Congress World Series.[7] In December he was a member of the United States team that won the 1973 Amateur World Series in Nicaragua.[8]

Poloni joined Arizona State's starting rotation in 1974. Though the Sun Devils slumped to 39-24, he went 9-2 with a 2.89 ERA, led the team in strikeouts, and was the team's only pitcher named to the Western Athletic Conference's Southern Division all-star team.[9] His best game was perhaps a three-hit shutout of Texas-El Paso that earned him player-of-the-week recognition.[10] After the season he again played summer ball in Colorado, this time for the Boulder Collegians, runner-up to Fairbanks in the National Baseball Congress World Series.[11]

In 1975 Poloni had his best season at ASU, 10-1 with a 2.62 ERA,[12] as the team again advanced to the College World Series. In an elimination game against Oklahoma, Poloni pitched a "masterful" 11-inning, four-hit shutout a week after the Texas Rangers picked him in the sixth round of the June amateur draft.[13] The Sun Devils lost to South Carolina the next day and finished in third place.[14] To top off his season, Poloni was named to *The Sporting News* All-America team selected by major-league scouting directors.[15]

After Texas scout Harley Anderson signed Poloni to his first professional contract, the 21-year-old pitcher moved cross-country to Sarasota, Florida, to join the Rangers' rookie club in the Gulf Coast League. He made his debut on June 30 and in four starts went 2-1 with a 2.10 ERA. His last start was a 1-0 win over the Pirates on July 16,[16] and three days later he made his first appearance for the Pittsfield (Massachusetts) Rangers in the Double-A Eastern League, working two innings in relief.[17] On July 23 Poloni won his first start, going the distance and allowing two runs on four hits at Three Rivers, Quebec.[18] He finished with a 2-3 record for a Pittsfield team that was 32-41 in the season's second half, but his ERA jumped to 6.55 against the stiffer competition.

Poloni had his best season in Organized Baseball in 1976 at San Antonio in the Double-A Texas League. He started slowly for the Brewers, with an 0-2 record in his first three starts. But he then posted nine consecutive wins, breaking the franchise record set by Dennis Eckersley in 1974 and lowering his ERA to 2.11.[19] The ninth win, 1-0 over Lafayette, may have been his best outing of the season. Poloni was in trouble only in the first inning when the visiting Drillers got two of their six hits, and he allowed only two baserunners over the last six innings.[20]

With a 10-3 record and 2.45 ERA at the all-star break, Poloni was named the starting pitcher for the exhibition contest that pitted the Texas Leaguers against the Texas Rangers. "It's pretty exciting to show them what I can do," he said when chosen for the role.[21] He allowed one hit – a home run by Jeff Burroughs – and struck out two in two innings of work. Texas manager Frank Lucchesi was impressed.

"I liked what I saw from John," said Lucchesi, who said he would give Poloni a long look in spring training. "He knows how to pitch and stay out of trouble."[22]

For the rest of the season, the Brewers struggled to avoid finishing last in their division. Poloni, pitching with a lame arm, struggled as well; he went 1-4 in seven starts to end the season with an 11-7 record and a 3.40 earned-run average. "I got a really sore elbow," Poloni said later, "but the manager had me pitch anyway."[23] Nonetheless, he was one of the two pitchers named to the Texas League all-star team after the season ended.[24]

Poloni played in the Florida Instructional League in the fall[25] and went to spring training with the Rangers in February 1977. He was one of 21 pitchers in the Texas camp at Pompano Beach, all theoretically competing for 10 roster spots.[26] Four starters returned from the 1976 club – Gaylord Perry, Bert Blyleven, Nelson Briles and Jim Umbarger – and Doyle Alexander had been signed in the off-season. Three other new acquisitions were slotted for the bullpen: Darold Knowles, Paul Lindblad, and Adrian Devine. With Roger Moret and other veterans also in camp, the odds were long for Poloni and the other minor leaguers.

When he got the chance to pitch, Poloni acquitted himself well. On March 14, for example, he was one of a quintet of Texas pitchers who shut out the Atlanta Braves B team on six hits.[27] And in three innings against Atlanta regulars on March 24, he allowed one run on two hits with one strikeout and one walk.[28] Not surprisingly, however, the Rangers dispatched Poloni and the other minor-league pitchers to Plant City, site of the club's minor-league camp, when the spring's first cuts were made the next day. He was assigned to the Tucson Toros, the Rangers' affiliate in the Triple-A Pacific Coast League.[29]

Poloni was 8-13 with a 5.15 ERA for the Toros, who finished out of the PCL playoffs with a 65-73 record. He led the club in innings pitched with 187, fifth in the league, and in strikeouts with 101. His earned-run average was second among the Tucson starters to Bob Babcock's 4.57. No PCL starter who pitched at least 100 innings had an earned run average under 4.00. "It's a hitter's league, simple as that," one sportswriter observed. "Some of these umpires' strike zones are the size of a cigar box. Pitchers are constantly behind batters and are forced to throw the ball where it can be hit."[30]

The Toros starters were frustratingly inconsistent throughout the season, and Poloni was no exception. He got off to a shaky start. In the first inning of his first game, 20-year-old Pedro Guerrero of the visiting Albuquerque Dukes rocked him for a two-run triple, setting the tone in the 11-2 Toros' loss.[31] Over his first five starts, Poloni's record was 0-3 and his earned-run average a shade over 6.00.[32] But he went 3-1 in his next five starts with a 3.82 ERA and two complete games.[33]

After this stretch, however, Poloni went 0-3 with an ERA above 6.00 – almost a repeat of his first month's work. He again turned things around and, after a no-decision to end June and another to begin July, had his most effective period of the season, winning four of six starts and pitching well in a Toros win in which he did not figure in the decision. While he was hit hard in the two losses, his ERA was 3.56 overall and 1.78 in the four wins and the no-decision.[34]

The last of those seven games was perhaps Poloni's best of the season, a 3-2 win over Albuquerque in which he worked 7⅔ innings and allowed one earned run on four hits. He shut out the Dukes for seven innings, walked none, and struck out eight. The Toros got "splendid pitching from starter John Poloni," commented a Tucson sportswriter, adding that the left-hander had "pitched more innings than any other hurler on [the Toros'] staff" and "never missed a turn."[35]

At the end of August, the Rangers announced that Poloni was being called up when the rosters expanded in September, along with pitchers Tommy Boggs and Bobby Cuellar, first baseman Pat Putnam, and outfielders Lew Beasley and Keith Smith.[36]

Before departing for Texas, Poloni pitched his last game for the Toros on September 3 at Albuquerque, allowing one earned on five hits in seven innings. However, the Toros were shut out 2-0.[37]

Poloni made his major-league debut on September 16 at Arlington Stadium, allowing one run (earned) in two innings of relief as the Rangers lost 9-7 to the Minnesota Twins.[38] He did not figure in that decision but picked up a win on October 2, the last day of the season, against Oakland. Poloni started the afternoon game at Arlington Stadium and went five innings, allowed four runs, all earned, on six hits, and departed with an 8-4 lead. The Rangers held on to win 8-7, completing what was then the best season in franchise history with a 94-68 record. Predictably, Poloni was pleased with the win. "I wasn't all that sharp, but I'll take it," he said. "It's hard to be sharp when you've worked only two innings in a month."[39]

The trade to Boston came 2½ months later. "At the time it happened, I was kind of disappointed

John Poloni, preparing to deliver Courtesy ASU Sun Devil Athletics.

John Poloni in 1988, as pitching coach for Double-A Knoxville.

because I liked the Rangers and thought they had plans for me," Poloni said several years later. "I saw the people [the Red Sox] already had in the big leagues and didn't think there was any place for me."[40] To make matters worse, Poloni developed shoulder trouble during spring training, and Boston optioned him to Triple-A Pawtucket.[41] He spent considerable time on the disabled list, finished with a 1-6 record, and was released.[42]

Poloni was out of baseball the following year but signed a minor-league contract with Toronto in the spring of 1980. He spent the season at Double-A Knoxville, the first Blue Jays' affiliate at that level.[43] The team fared poorly, finishing last in its division both halves of the season with the worst overall record, 57-87, in the Southern League. Toronto President Peter Bavasi visited Knoxville in August and shouldered part of the blame for the poor record: "I believe we underestimated the strength of the Southern League," he said. "We now know that it takes a blend of youth and some veterans to win here."[44]

For his part, Poloni posted a 10-12 record with a 4.24 earned-run average. His 172 innings led the club, as did his nine complete games and 105 strikeouts. His best start of the season came against visiting Charlotte on May 26, a complete game in which he allowed one unearned run, struck out seven, and walked one. Yet Knoxville trailed 1-0 after eight innings before winning in the ninth, with Jesse Barfield and Ike Hampton igniting the rally.[45]

In 1981-1982, Poloni was again out of baseball, the Toronto organization having released him.[46] He was employed by a precious-metals broker in Scottsdale, Arizona, when on February 27, 1982, he married Lynn C. David, a New Jersey native then working for a computer company in Phoenix.[47] In college, Lynn had majored in psychology, and that background later helped her husband at what turned out to be pivotal point early in his scouting career.

A year after the wedding, Poloni began working as a pitching coach in the Seattle organization. He spent the 1983 season in Wausau, Wisconsin, in the Class-A Midwest League before moving the following year to Salinas in the Class-A California League. He also pitched in a few games at each stop as the managers sought to rest their tired hurlers.[48] At Salinas in 1986, he picked up his last professional win, a complete game against the visiting Modesto A's on August 18. Relying on a variety of off-speed pitches, he allowed seven hits (five of which didn't leave the infield), walked two, and struck out six. "Salinas Coach Teaches Modesto a Lesson," read the headline in the next day's Modesto newspaper.[49]

Poloni joined the Toronto organization in 1987, beginning at Myrtle Beach, South Carolina, in the Class-A South Atlantic League. Myrtle Beach won the pennant, defeating Asheville in the playoffs.[50] Doug Linton of Myrtle Beach was named the league's outstanding pitcher, and Poloni was chosen as the all-star team's coach alongside manager Keith Bodie of Asheville.[51]

For the next three seasons Poloni was back at Knoxville before joining the staff at Triple-A Syracuse in 1991. He finished his coaching career in 1995 with Toronto's Class-A team in Dunedin, Florida, where he tutored future Cy Young Award winner Chris Carpenter.[52] During his tenure with the Blue Jays, Poloni coached other pitchers who went on to the major leagues, including All-Stars Juan Guzmán, Pat Hentgen, Al Leiter, and Woody Williams. He also received a World Series ring after Toronto bested Atlanta in 1992.[53]

From 1996 through 2019, Poloni was a scout, starting at Oakland. He established his reputation for finding pitchers when he persuaded the Athletics to take Tim Hudson in the sixth round of the 1997 amateur draft. Hudson, a 6-foot, 165-pound right-hander for Auburn University, played center field on Friday and Saturday games when most scouts were watching. But Poloni stuck around on Sundays for Hudson's turn on the mound.

"He didn't have the prototypical body type you see in a pitcher," Poloni said later. "But what he had was moxie, intensity, competitiveness, a big heart and a good work ethic. I mean, he wasn't afraid of anything."[54] Poloni's wife, Lynn, accompanied him to Auburn on one trip and, drawing on her psychology background, told her husband that she noticed a swagger and confidence in Hudson, "an aura that set him apart from the rest of the other Auburn players."[55]

Hudson also had two outstanding pitches, a "turbo sinker" and a "wicked splitter,"[56] as well as an effective slider. "His stuff was so nasty," Poloni said.[57] On the scout's recommendation, Oakland's national cross-checker, Ron Hopkins, visited Auburn to see for himself. "There was nobody on [Hudson], other than us," Hopkins recalled. "I knew John's background [as a coach], that he'd probably seen 5,000 pitchers, and he's saying this guy's got the best sinker he'd ever seen."[58] Back in Oakland, Poloni pushed hard for Hudson at the draft meeting. "He was adamant about it," recalled Grady Fuson, then the club's scouting director. "John saw the athlete in him, and I give him a lot of credit not just for his evaluation but for his conviction."[59] The A's drafted Hudson in the sixth round, the 185th overall pick. He won 222 games in the major leagues.

With Oakland, Hudson teamed with Mark Mulder and Barry Zito in a dominant rotation, not that you would know much about them from reading *Moneyball* or watching the film based on the book. "*Moneyball* tells a fascinating story, but it is also misleading," wrote the baseball economist Andrew Zimbalist. "Clearly, the main explanation for the team's recent success [1999-2003] lies in its superlative starting pitching. How these remarkably proficient hurlers were identified, obtained, and developed ... remains largely untreated. Tim Hudson, the dominant right-handed starter, was identified by Oakland A's scout John Poloni, denigrated by author Michael Lewis in the book as the 'fat scout.'"[60]

Poloni left Oakland after the 2002 season, when he had scouted Florida for the club, to join the Texas Rangers. He was a cross-checker for the Milwaukee Brewers in 2004-2005, with an emphasis on pitching, and East Coast supervisor with the New York Mets in 2006-2007. Poloni returned to the Rangers the next two years and from 2010 to 2019 was with the Cincinnati Reds as scouting supervisor for Georgia and northwest Florida.[61] In addition to Hudson, Poloni signed other players who advanced to the major leagues, including pitchers Chad Harville, Robbie Ross, and Mike Wood, as well as catcher Tyler Stephenson and outfielder Taylor Trammell.[62] But as Poloni recognized, "there are no guarantees" in scouting, and every scout's résumé is full of draft choices that did not make the grade.[63] "A lot of times, it's pure luck," he said.[64]

As for the "fat scout" label, Poloni looked back on *Moneyball* with a sense of humor. "I've always been a little on the chunky side, [and] I'm 6-5," he told a reporter with a chuckle in 2013. "Other people in the room [at Oakland] had the same weight as mine but were half a foot shorter. I guess you've got to be known for something."[65] And when he opened a Twitter account the following year, he chose @fatscout as his handle.

SOURCES

In addition to the resources cited in the Notes, the author consulted Baseball-Reference.com and Retrosheet.org.

NOTES

1. "Sox Trade Jenkins to Rangers for Lefty," *Boston Globe*, December 15, 1977: 39; Randy Galloway, "Fergie Due Relief as Ranger Again," *Dallas Morning News*, December 15, 1977: 6B. Ironically, the Rangers hired Zimmer as manager in November 1980, thereby reuniting him with Jenkins for the 1981 season.

2. Larry Whiteside, "Sullivan Gets High Marks as Bosox' Chief Exec," *The Sporting News*, January 7, 1978: 45.

3. Gerry Fraley, "Rangers' Key Pickup Got His Start in 1977," *Dallas Morning News*, March 17, 2003: 1B.

4. Obituary, John P. Poloni, *St. Petersburg Times*, January 26, 2001: 8B; Obituary, Margaret M. Poloni, *St. Petersburg Times*, October 19, 2005: 7B; *Polk's 1956 Lincoln Park, Allen Park, and Melvindale Directory* (Detroit: R.L. Polk & Co., 1957), 337; *Polk's 1960 Lincoln Park, Allen Park, and Melvindale Directory* (Detroit: R.L. Polk & Co., 1960), 333; John Poloni player questionnaires, 1975 and 1984.

5. Hal Schram, "Three Titles for City," *Detroit Free Press*, June 20, 1971: 1C; Hal Schram, "It's Detroit Teams, 3-1, in 'A' Regionals," *Detroit Free Press*, June 11, 1972: 5D; "Two Strong Pitchers Head First UPI Baseball Team," *Ludington* (Michigan) *Daily News*, June 29, 1972: 7; "Pirates Draft Cal Shortstop, Two Locals," *Pittsburgh Post-Gazette*, June 7, 1972: 23; "Devils Sign Talented Trio," *Arizona Republic* (Phoenix), June 27, 1972: 59.

6. "Arizona State University 52 Game Baseball Statistics," *Arizona Republic*, May 3, 1973: 93. His best game for the varsity may have been his first start, a complete game against Michigan in which he struck out seven and did not allow an earned run. "Devils Rally To Win," *Arizona Republic*, March 8, 1973: 82.

7. "Eagles Edge Fairbanks 3-2," *Grand Junction* (Colorado) *Daily Sentinel*, June 26, 1973: 2A; "Eagles Trip Fairbanks in Ninth," *Grand Junction Daily Sentinel*, August 11, 1973: 8; *Grand Junction Eagles 1974 Yearbook*: 8, 10.

8. "Poloni Picked for U.S. Nine," *Arizona Republic*, November 8, 1973: E3; "U.S. Nine Wins Final in Nicaragua," *New York Times*, December 7, 1973: 53.

9. "Sun Devil Statistics," *Arizona Republic*, May 23, 1974: E6; "UA Places 7 on WAC All-Star," *Arizona Republic*, May 23, 1974: E3.

10. Jay Coleman, "ASU Sweeps Pair," *Arizona Republic*, April 28, 1974: D1; "Ute, Sun Devil Win WAC Baseball Honor," *Tucson Daily Citizen*, April 30, 1974: 33.

11. Gary Scharrer, "Eagles, Top-Rated Boulder Ready for Battle," *Grand Junction Daily Sentinel*, July 18, 1974: 1A; Russ Corbitt, "Panners End Long Day as Champs," *Wichita* (Kansas) *Eagle*, August 23, 1974: 1C.

12. "Sun Devil Statistics," *Arizona Republic*, June 26, 1975: D-5.

13. Bob Jacobsen, "Devils Win in 11th, 1-0, as Poloni Stops Sooners," *Arizona Republic*, June 13, 1975: D1.

14. Bob Jacobsen, "Sun Devils Derailed, 4-1, Wind Up Third in Series," *Arizona Republic*, June 14, 1975: E1.

15. "Campus Cream," *The Sporting News*, July 12, 1975: 20. Poloni was named to the second team.

16. "Rain Washes Out 2 GCL Contests," *Sarasota* (Florida) *Herald-Tribune*, July 17, 1975: 2D.

17. "Rangers Meet West Haven After Splitting Four Games," *Berkshire Eagle* (Pittsfield, Massachusetts), July 21, 1975: 26.

18. "Rangers Avenge Three Rivers Sweep," *Berkshire Eagle*, July 24, 1975: 22. The game, the second of a doubleheader, was a seven-inning affair.

19. Gary Gossett, "Poloni Captures Ninth Straight," *San Antonio Light*, July 17, 1976: 1B; Jeff Grossman, "Poloni Wins Record Ninth Straight, 1-0," *San Antonio Express-News*, July 17, 1976: 1C.

20. Gossett, "Poloni Captures Ninth Straight, 1-0."

21. Kevin O'Keefe, "Poloni Will Start for TL All-Stars," *San Antonio Express-News*, August 1, 1976: 4S.

22. Galen Wellnicki, "Rangers Demolish TL All-Stars, 18-4," *San Antonio Light*, August 3, 1974: 1D.

23. Steve Weston, "Poloni's Planning a Move," *Tucson Citizen*, April 9, 1977: 10A.

24. "Poloni Makes All-Star Team," *San Antonio Express*, September 22, 1976: 2D.

25. "Brewer Notes," *San Antonio Express*, October 19, 1976: 2C.

26. Jim Reeves, "Ranger Problem: Too Many Hurlers," *Fort Worth Star-Telegram*, February 28, 1977: 1D.

27. "Rangers Blank Braves' B Team," *Atlanta Constitution*, March 15, 1977: 5D.

28. Wayne Minshew, "Messersmith Sharp in Victory," *Atlanta Constitution*, March 25, 1977: 2D.

29. "Trade Winds Blow in Ranger Camp," *Fort Worth Star-Telegram*, March 26, 1977: 2D; "Toros Get Nine Players from Rangers," *Arizona Daily Star* (Tucson), March 25, 1977: 6F. Poloni pitched once more for the Rangers in the spring, brought in with David Clyde from the Tucson camp at Plant City for an exhibition game against the University of Texas Longhorns in Austin on April 5. Kirk Bohls, "Where Were the Rangers? 'Horns Lose to Scrubs, 9-4," *Austin American-Statesman*, April 6, 1977: D1. Poloni pitched 2 innings and gave up one run, earned, on 3 hits, walked 1, and struck out 2.

30. Steve Weston (untitled column), *Tucson Citizen*, June 15, 1977: 1D.

31. Dave Adam, "Albuquerque Batters Again Tee Off on Toro Pitching," *Arizona Daily Star*, April 16, 1977: 1F.

32. Steve Weston, "'New' Toros Getting Old Fast," *Tucson Citizen*, April 16, 1977: 10A; "Toros' Hurlers Shaky," *Tucson*

Citizen, April 21, 1977: 5D; "Toros' Pen Minus Bull," *Tucson Daily Citizen*, April 26, 1977: 3D; Dave Adam, "Phoenix Continues Mastery of Toros," *Arizona Daily Star*, May 2, 1977: E1; Steve Weston, "Lew Beasley' Trio of Threes Pushes Toros Past Salt Lake," *Tucson Citizen*, May 5, 1977: 2D.

33 "Toros Enjoy a Win Streak," *Tucson Citizen*, May 10, 1977: 1D; Steve Weston, "Bacsik Getting in on the Fun," *Tucson Citizen*, May 16, 1977: 1D; Steve Weston, "Toros Beaten by Own Tactics," *Tucson Citizen*, May 20, 1977: 1D; "Toros Win in a Walk," *Tucson Citizen*, May 25, 1977: 1E; "Toros' Hitters Silent," *Tucson Citizen*, May 30, 1977: 3D.

34 "Twins Bring Out Best in Toros," *Tucson Citizen*, July 7, 1977: 1D; "Putnam's Hitting Helps Toros Snap Loss String," *Tucson Citizen*, July 12, 1977: 1D; "Toros Get 15 Hits in Rout of Spokane," *Arizona Daily Star*, July 12, 1977: C1; Steve Weston, "Bevacqua Tough on Tacoma," *Tucson Citizen*, July 18, 1977: 1D; Steve Weston, "Inconsistent Pitching Keeps Toros at .500," *Tucson Citizen*, July 23, 1977: 7A; "Hawaii Nicer on This Trip," *Tucson Citizen*, July 29, 1977: 1D; Steve Weston, "Toros Still in Position to Win East," *Tucson Citizen*, August 5, 1977: 1D; Steve Weston, "Toros Looking Better for Run at Phoenix," *Tucson Citizen*, August 8, 1977: 1D.

35 Steve Weston, "Toros Looking Better for Run at Phoenix."

36 "Ranger Notes," *Fort Worth Star-Telegram*, September 1, 1977: 7D.

37 "Toros Close Out PCL Slate Today," *Tucson Citizen*, September 5, 1977: 2D.

38 Jim Reeves, "Twins Pin 9-7 Defeat on Rangers," *Fort Worth Star-Telegram*, September 17, 1977: 1D.

39 Jim Reeves, "Rangers Close with Win," *Fort Worth Star-Telegram*, October 3, 1977: 1D.

40 Matt Michael, "Sharing a Claim to Fame," *Syracuse Post-Standard*, July 20, 1991: F1.

41 "Bosox Trim Roster, Poloni, Bowen Cut," *Hartford Courant*, March 25, 1978: 28; Ken Leiker, "A Look at Baseball," *Arizona Republic*, May 4, 1980: G3; Matt Michael, "Sharing a Claim to Fame," *Syracuse Post-Standard*, July 20, 1991: F1.

42 On July 19, after being on the disabled list for three weeks, Poloni appeared in relief against Charleston and recorded a save. Five days later, the Red Sox reassigned him to Double-A Bristol, where he spent the rest of the season on the disabled list. The Red Sox dropped him from their 40-man roster in November and released him in April 1979. Associated Press, "IL Roundup," *Lancaster* (Ohio) *Eagle-Gazette*, July 20, 1978: 14; Peter Gammons, "Who Pitches? Answer Depends on Campbell," *Boston Globe*, November 26, 1978: 94; John Poloni player contract card, *The Sporting News*.

43 The previous year, Toronto, which began play in 1977, had a rookie-league team, three Class-A teams, and a Triple-A club at Syracuse.

44 "Southern League," *The Sporting News*, August 30, 1980: 44.

45 "Knoxville's Rally Costs O's 2-1 Loss," *Charlotte* (North Carolina) *Observer*, May 27, 1980: 5B.

46 John Poloni player contract card, *The Sporting News*.

47 "Weddings, Poloni-David," *Central New Jersey Home News* (New Brunswick, New Jersey), February 28, 1982: C18.

48 His record: 0-0 in five games with a 0.00 ERA at Wausau in 1983; 0-1 in five games with a 1.93 ERA at Salinas in 1985; and 1-1 in three games with a 1.59 ERA at Salinas in 1986.

49 *Modesto Bee*, August 19, 1986: D1.

50 "Title Escapes Tourists, 3-2," *Asheville* (North Carolina) *Citizen*, September 8, 1987: 1C.

51 "Whited Leads SAL Stars," *Greenville* (South Carolina) *News*, August 28, 1987: 2C.

52 Chris Marti, "Former Top Draft Pick Carpenter Honing Skills in Dunedin," *Tampa Tribune*, May 31, 1995: 5-Polk. The article quoted Poloni's assessment of Carpenter: "He's been pitching up to the potential we projected for him. With a kid his age you have to take things slow. But he's learning quickly." Carpenter, a three-time All-Star, won the Cy Young Award with the St. Louis Cardinals in 2005.

53 The Jays ordered 235 of the $8,000 rings, and general manager Pat Gillick traveled the country to hand out many of them. Before a night game at Syracuse in May 1993, he presented rings to Chiefs manager Nick Leyva, coaches Poloni and Rocket Wheeler, and the star-crossed Bill Buckner, then a hitting instructor in the Toronto farm system. Sean Kirst, "World Series Finally Rings True for Buckner," *Syracuse Post-Standard*, May 13, 1993: C1.

54 John Shea, "As Hudson Nears 200 Wins, Credit A's Scout," *San Francisco Chronicle*, April 21, 2013: B6.

55 Brian Murphy, "Hudson Stands Tall on the Mound," *San Francisco Examiner*, September 10, 1999: D1.

56 Jonah Keri, "Baseball's Big Three: A Look Back at Tim Hudson, Mark Mulder, and Barry Zito in Oakland," *Grantland*, September 23, 2015, https://grantland.com/the-triangle/mlb-oakland-as-big-three-tim-hudson-barry-zito-mark-mulder-billy-beane-moneyball/.

57 Murphy, "Hudson Stands Tall on the Mound."

58 Shea, "As Hudson Nears 200 Wins, Credit A's Scout."

59 Daniel Brown, "Throwback Weekend – The Big Three Reunites at Bay Bridge Series, With Anticipated Hudson-Zito Matchup Saturday," *San Jose Mercury News*, September 25, 2015: 1C.

60 Andrew Zimbalist, *May the Best Team Win: Baseball Economics and Public Policy* (Washington: Brookings Institution Press, 2004), 168. Zimbalist is not alone in these criticisms; e.g., Sheldon and Alan Hirsch, *The Beauty of Short Hops: How Chance and Circumstance Confound the Moneyball Approach to Baseball* (Jefferson, North Carolina: McFarland & Co., 2011), 17-18 ("[The book] distorts the reason for Oakland's success. The team thrived primarily because of superb pitching. ... At the heart of the pitching staff were three dominant starters: Mark Mulder, Tim Hudson, and Barry Zito."); Mike Berardino, "Book on Beane Misses the Mark," *Orlando Sentinel*, June 8, 2003: C12 ("There's also an undercurrent of meanness that surfaces at several

points in the book. The repeated references to the 'Fat Scout' are particularly distasteful, especially when everybody in the game knows it was that very scout, John Poloni, who delivered a skinny Auburn right-hander named Tim Hudson to the A's out of the sixth round in 1997").

61 *2002 Oakland Athletics Information Guide*, 354; *2005 Milwaukee Brewers Media Guide*, 219; *2007 New York Mets Media Guide*, 298; *2008 Texas Rangers Media Guide*, 297; *2010 Cincinnati Reds Media Guide*, 172; *2019 Cincinnati Reds Media Guide*, 220; Fraley, "Rangers' Key Pickup Got His Start in 1977."

62 Poloni is listed as the scout for each of these players at The Baseball Cube: Harville, https://www.thebaseballcube.com/content/player/1097/draft/; Ross, https://www.thebaseballcube.com/content/player/142989/draft/; Wood, https://www.thebaseballcube.com/content/player/7496/draft/; Stephenson, https://www.thebaseballcube.com/content/player/197346/draft/; Trammell, https://www.thebaseballcube.com/content/player/203939/draft/.

63 Fraley, "Rangers Key Pickup Got His Start in 1977."

64 Shea, "As Hudson Nears 200 Wins, Credit A's Scout."

65 Shea, "As Hudson Nears 200 Wins, Credit A's Scout."

ROBERT RAMSAY

BY STEVE FRIEDMAN

The story of Robert Ramsay is one of dedication and love of baseball. He had the rare opportunity to play for his hometown major-league team and his nearby university, and to coach his local high-school baseball team. He was devoted to baseball and to his family. "I think he was a model of humility in a world, in a profession that people don't necessarily know what humility is traditionally about and a society where we glorify and don't always keep what is important in perspective," said his wife, Samantha.[1]

Ramsay's major-league baseball career lasted parts of two seasons, 1999 and 2000, both with the Seattle Mariners. In 43 games pitched, he earned a single victory. His ERA was 4.19 and his weakness was his control; he walked 49 batters in 68⅔ innings.

Ramsay was a native of the Pacific Northwest. Born on December 3, 1973, and raised in Vancouver, Washington, across the Columbia River from Portland, Oregon, he graduated from Mountain View High School in Vancouver, attended Washington State University, and pitched for the Seattle Mariners. During and after his professional baseball career, he primarily lived in the Moscow, Idaho-Pullman, Washington, area where he raised his family with his wife, Samantha.

At the age of 42, Ramsay died of a seizure on August 4, 2016, leaving behind Samantha, his wife of 17 years, and two sons, 11-year-old Ryan and 8-year-old Reidar. Samantha described Rob as honest, sincere, and down to earth.

Growing up in Vancouver, Ramsay pitched for his high-school baseball team. (He became the only player from Mountain View High to pitch in the major leagues.[2]) At age 16, he also pitched in the Babe Ruth League, leading his Vancouver team to the national championship in the Babe Ruth 16-year-old World Series, and was named its most outstanding player.[3]

It was clear that in his high-school years, Ramsay was a well-regarded pitcher. He was 6-feet-5-inches tall and weighed 230 pounds. Scouts rated his fastball as fair, but they suggested that his easy arm action and loose wrist provided potential to add arm speed and a capable curveball, making him a promising starting pitcher.[4] In the 1992 amateur draft, he was taken in the 31st round by the Houston Astros, but did not sign because he planned to attend Washington State University.

Ramsay was a four-year letterman (1993-1996) at WSU.[5] In 1996, his senior year, he led the team in ERA (3.93), innings pitched, and strikeouts, and was co-winner of the Buck Bailey Award as the top pitcher on the team.[6] He became the career leader at WSU in innings pitched. In his junior year, Ramsay was the opening starting pitcher in the Pacific-12 Conference postseason championship series against the nationally seventh-ranked, hard-hitting USC Trojans.[7] "He's been a guy that has been leading off for us most of the year on the mound, and his consistency has been getting better and better with his mechanics, so he's spotting the ball much better," said WSU head coach Steve Ferrington.[8] Ramsay held the Trojans in check before leaving with a 6-4 lead with one out in the eighth inning. Cougar relievers failed to protect the lead as the Trojans rallied to defeat the Cougars.

In the 1996 draft, Ramsay was selected by the Boston Red Sox in the seventh round, the 211th player chosen, just ahead of future major leaguer Mark DeRosa. His teammate, Mike Wetmore, was also drafted in the seventh round that year.[9] Eleven days later, Ramsay signed his first professional contract.

Ramsay's minor-league career was one that showed a consistent movement up the ladder toward the major leagues. After signing, he joined the Red Sox squad in the Gulf Coast League. After just two games, he was promoted to Sarasota of the Class-A Florida State League. He stayed in Sarasota for the entire 1997 season, when he started 22 games and ended up with a 9-9 record. His 4.78 ERA was above the league average, but it earned him a promotion to Trenton of the Double-A Eastern League for 1998.

In Trenton Ramsay showed the potential that would lead him to the major leagues. He compiled a 12-6 record, his 3.49 ERA was among the league leaders, he finished tied for second in strikeouts and walked 50 in 166⅔ innings. He averaged six innings per start and was named the Red Sox' top minor-league pitcher.[10] With this success, Ramsay began the 1999 season at Pawtucket, the Red Sox' Triple-A affiliate. In four months at Pawtucket, he started 20 games and was 6-6. Ramsay suffered from the long ball; he was tagged for 21 home runs in 114⅓ innings. On July 26 Ramsay was traded to the Seattle Mariners for outfielder Butch Huskey, and was assigned to Tacoma, the Mariners' Triple-A affiliate in the Pacific Coast League.[11]

Ramsay's stay in Tacoma was brief. In his five starts, he was 4-1 with an ERA of 1.08, earning him a promotion to the Mariners. Barely a month since he had been traded by the Red Sox, he was making his initial major-league appearance, relieving starting pitcher Gil Meche with one out in the fourth inning against the New York Yankees at Yankee Stadium. "It was pretty crazy," Samantha Ramsay said. "It was like his dream. He always imagined being there and there he was. That's probably when I realized this is a big deal."[12] Upon his call-up, Ramsay became the third former WSU Cougar on the Mariners' roster, joining teammates John Olerud and Aaron Sele.

Adding to the pressure of making his major-league debut, Ramsay entered the game in a stressful situation. The Mariners were trailing 4-0 and the Yankees had runners on first and third. He immediately walked Derek Jeter, loading the bases, then threw a wild pitch to Bernie Williams that advanced all runners, increasing the Yankees' lead to 5-0. After intentionally walking Williams to reload the bases, he struck out former Mariner Tino Martinez for the second out. But Chili Davis followed with a single through the left side, scoring two more runs. When the inning ended one batter later, the Yankees had a commanding 7-0 lead. Ramsay pitched two more scoreless innings.

Ramsay was very low-key and known as a jeans and polo shirt type. Soon after he joined the Mariners, manager Lou Piniella saw him in a hotel lobby and told him, "Son, you can't wear tennis shoes in the lobby. You need to get better clothes. You're going to be in the big leagues, you need to wear better clothes."[13]

Ramsay finished the season with Mariners, ending with a 0-2 record and an ERA of 6.38. He started three games late in the season; his best was a five-inning appearance in which he surrendered only two runs.

After starting the 2000 season in Tacoma, Ramsay was recalled on April 26 to start a game against the Cleveland Indians, replacing the injured Freddy García.[14] It was an emergency start and, after his appearance he was expected to move to the bullpen. "We can use him as a second left-hander in relief," Piniella said.[15] Ramsay represented himself well in the start, holding back a powerful Cleveland lineup for six innings, allowing one earned run on five hits and leaving the game trailing 1-0. He did not get a decision; the Mariners lost 5-3 in 10 innings. It was Ramsay's only major-league start of the season. He remained with the Mariners for the rest of the season, outside of a two-inning injury-rehab start for Class-A Everett.

On June 15 Ramsay entered the game against the Minnesota Twins in the fifth inning in relief of Paul Abbott, who had to leave the game with cramping in his right hamstring.[16] Ramsay was given a 7-1 Mariners lead and became the pitcher of record. After throwing 2⅔ innings, giving up two earned runs, he was awarded the victory in a 12-5 Mariner win. "It's not the typical first win you want to get," said Ramsay, who became the first Mariner reliever to win a game in nearly a month. "You want to earn it a little more, maybe start the game and go six or seven innings."[17]

Ramsay pitched in 37 Mariners games, in 2000 throwing 50⅓ innings, with an ERA of 3.40. With his lone victory, he added one loss. While he generally pitched to contact, striking out only 32 batters during the season, his control continued to be a problem, as he walked 40. He made two relief appearances against the Yankees in the ALCS, facing seven batters in 1⅔ innings without yielding a run.

Ramsay failed to make the major-league roster in 2001 spring training and spent the entire season in Tacoma. During spring training, he was hobbled by a sore knee and didn't appear in a live game until March 10. He was in a battle with veteran Norm Charlton to be the additional left-hander out of the bullpen. "If they decide to go with a second left-hander, that's what I'm aiming for," Ramsay said. "I just have to be myself and not try to strike everybody out."[18] At Tacoma he pitched as a starter all season. With an ERA of nearly 5.00 in 26 games, he continued to struggle with his control and surrendered 26 home runs in 149⅓ innings. He was never called up as the Mariners rolled through a record-setting 116-win season. After the season, he was released.

Ramsay soon found a job with the San Diego Padres, but just after he signed his contract, he began to experience headaches and nausea. One November day, after returning from bird hunting, he told his wife that his headache was severe.[19] She had been urging him to see a doctor, but now she insisted, although she didn't enjoy nagging her husband. "At first I didn't think it was my area to press him on," said Samantha. "He's a grown man, an athlete. He knows his body better than I do. But when we would do things we'd always done, he just wasn't the same. Something was wrong. Finally, I put my foot down. Do something about this or face my wrath."[20]

Ramsay agreed that his wife had persevered in telling him to see a doctor. "I said no. But she persisted and she persisted, and finally after a month and a half I realized I needed to get this thing checked out. It was debilitating. I couldn't work out. I didn't know what it was."[21] His family doctor found a mass on his brain. Then a neurologist in Spokane diagnosed him with glioblastoma multiforme, an aggressive form of brain cancer, one that, even years later, in 2019, offered only a 5.5 percent chance of survival of more than five years.

The standard treatment for the cancerous tumor is surgery, followed by daily radiation and oral chemotherapy for 6½ weeks, then a six-month regimen of oral chemotherapy given five days a month. Ramsay was ready to get to the next step. "I was like, OK, let's go, let's get this thing out," he said, describing his motivation as bordering on excitement. "I just wanted to get after it. I read the Lance Armstrong book, which was very inspirational for me. After reading that, I was like, man, let's go."[22]

Ramsay underwent brain surgery on January 23, 2002, performed by neurosurgeon Mitchell Berger, a 10½-hour operation at the University of California-San Francisco Medical Center.[23] The bulk of the tumor, on the right side of his brain, was removed, but the tumor had sent tentacle-like runners deep into the brain, and they could not be removed.[24] It was then the job of chemotherapy to keep the remaining cancer from retaking the brain.

Ramsay knew he would sit out the 2002 season, as he recovered from the surgery and focused on his chemotherapy. However, he had no intention of giving up on baseball, and one year after the operation, he signed a minor-league contract with the Padres.[25] The Padres had supported him during his surgery and recovery and in November 2002, re-signed him as a minor-league free agent – something they had no obligation to do.

"We are so grateful for the support both teams showed," Samantha said, speaking of both the Padres and the Mariners. "I don't think there's any other team that could have done what the Padres did for us. I'm going to be a Padres fan forever. They absolutely just put their arms around us."[26]

By April of 2003, just a few months after his surgery, Ramsay began working out again. In late spring, he was cleared to go full speed.[27] Gaining confidence, he was considering calling Padres general manager Kevin Towers to discuss his comeback. "I was feeling real good doing that, getting ready to let Kevin know I'm ready to go," Ramsay said.[28]

Then, during a regularly scheduled routine MRI, the cancer was back. "I was feeling really positive, and the recurrence brought me back to earth," he said. "It was like, OK, baseball can wait. Let's worry about my health and deal with that later."[29] He underwent stepped-up chemotherapy to fight the cancer and gradually began to feel better. In October, he took a quail-hunting trip with friends, but had trouble walking a straight line.[30] He returned to the neurologist, who discovered a blood clot. Another brain surgery was performed on November 4.[31]

Since then, despite undergoing chemotherapy treatments every six weeks, he had worked himself back into playing shape, so he signed another minor-league contract with the San Diego Padres, then reported to spring training. From the moment he reported, he went through all the drills with the other players. "It was amazing," said Rick Sutcliffe, the Padres' roving minor-league pitching coach. "He must have gotten tired, but he never showed it."[32]

Ramsay made an early spring-training appearance on March 4, when he was scheduled to pitch an inning against the San Francisco Giants, even though, several days before, he had undergone his regular chemotherapy treatment and could not work out for two days afterward.[33]

Padres manager Bruce Bochy called for Ramsay to start the bottom of the seventh inning. "I ran out to the mound, but bam!" Ramsay said. "I didn't stop to think that our catcher, Wiki Gonzalez, had been the last batter in our half of the inning. He was still putting on his gear, while I'm standing out on the mound without anyone to throw to. I felt kinda silly. I should have waited. I guess I was a little excited. I was pumped."[34]

In the stands down the first-base line sat Samantha Ramsay, two months pregnant. "There was a lot of excitement," she said. "I know Rob was dreaming of this, and while I pray, I pray for health, mainly, but I wouldn't be a pitcher's wife if I wasn't hoping that he'd have a good outing."[35]

As he prepared to face the first Giants batter, an anxious Bochy leaned forward on the dugout bench. "I didn't just want him not to have a ball hit to him," Bochy recalled. "I also didn't want him to get bombed, to have them score five or six runs off him. I know he doesn't have quite his stuff back. I just didn't know how fragile his confidence might be."[36] For protection, Ramsay wore a John Olerud-style helmet while on the mound.

Ramsay retired the side in order, throwing only five pitches. "I think I was floating," he said of how he felt as he walked off the mound. "I appreciated the moment, but, since the diagnosis, I appreciate the little things, like getting out of bed in the morning."[37] Two days later, he began the sixth inning against the Colorado Rockies. After he retired the first two batters, the third reached on an error. A walk and a hit batsman later, Bochy removed him. "He did his job, should've been out of the inning except for the error," Bochy said, "and I just didn't want anything more to happen out there for him."[38]

Soon after his appearance against the Rockies, Ramsay was sent to the minor-league camp. As a minor-league free agent, he was not eligible to pitch in the major leagues until May 15. "Rob needs to get work," Bochy said. "It's hard to get innings now with our starters getting stretched out."[39] Ultimately, Ramsay spent the entire 2003 season in the minor leagues, primarily with the Lake Elsinore Storm of the Class-A California League, where he appeared in 27 games and threw 71 innings with a 3.57 ERA.

As the season concluded and Ramsay approached the continuation of his comeback, he now knew he was cancer-free. He had had clear brain scans for over a year and no longer needed the energy-sapping, intravenous chemotherapy drip treatments.[40] The Baltimore Orioles offered him a minor-league contract, and he reported to spring training. "I've had clear scans for over a year now," he said. "I feel great."[41]

Ramsay noted that he had lost at least 5 mph off his fastball. "Basically, I have to pitch a different way that I used to," he said. "That's fine. If I can still get guys out, that's the name of the game anyhow."[42] It wasn't enough to impress the Orioles, however. On May 7, 2004, his professional baseball career ended when the Orioles released him from extended spring training.[43]

After retiring, Ramsay went back to school and earned his master's degree from the University of Idaho. He taught secondary school for three years and coached baseball at his high school. Despite being cancer-free, the effects of two craniotomies, chemotherapy, and radiation caused seizures that he treated with medication. "Usually, he could feel them coming on and could abate it and recognize it and do things to pull out of it," said Samantha.[44] In 2012, he became a stay-at-home dad.

On August 4, 2016, at the age of 42, Ramsay suffered a seizure that claimed his life.

Before the Mariners game on Monday, August 8, 2016 the Mariners held a moment of silence for their one-time reliever. "It's easy to say that he was valued and loved by all, and he's the kind of person that even before we met in college, people loved him," said Samantha, then a University of Idaho food and nutrition professor. "He was a good guy."[45]

He was a doting father and husband. Samantha said, "With Rob, it didn't matter who you were, what you did, where you were, what you were doing, he would treat you the same. He never wanted fame or recognition or anything, but just to do the things he loved to do, to play the game he loved, to have a family, a wife and healthy kids and go enjoy it. I hope he got what he wanted."[46]

This story would not be complete without a follow-up on Samantha, who was a mountain climber and outdoor enthusiast. Her friend, SeAnne Safaii-Waite, described her as more determined to continue her outdoor activities after the death of her husband. "I would say that she was more intense after that," said Safaii-Waite in a phone interview. "[Being active] was like a lifeline and a way of feeling alive, too. She would always run [in races] for Rob and climb for Rob. It was just part of her spirituality."[47] On July 30, 2017, just five days short of the first an-

Robert Ramsay. Courtesy of the Ramsay family.

niversary of Robert's death, Samantha was struck by lightning and killed as she approached the summit of the Matterhorn, in Switzerland.[48]

SOURCES

All sources for which hyperlinks are provided were accessed on January 6, 2022.

NOTES

1 Anthony Castrovince, "Ramsay's Life Not Measured by Stats," MLB.com, August 8, 2016.

2 Mountain View High School (Vancouver, Washington) – The Baseball Cube.

3 Babe Ruth League (www.baberuthleague.org) Honor Roll of WS Champions.

4 Montreal Expos "N-Z" scouting reports, 1992, National Baseball Hall of Fame. This report was provided to SABR by Roland Hemond, who procured it on behalf of the Scout of the Year Foundation and used it in the Diamond Mines Exhibit at the Baseball Hall of Fame in 2013.

5 "Washington State Cougar History," 07mghistory.pdf (sidearmsports.com).

6 "Washington State Cougar History."

7 Laurence Miedema, "Ramsay Draws Opening Assignment Against USC," *Moscow-Pullman Daily News* (Moscow, Idaho), May 16, 1995: 10.

8 Miedema, "Ramsay Draws Opening Assignment Against USC."

9 Laurence Miedama, "Arizona Picks WSU's Ryan in 26th Round," *Moscow-Pullman Daily News*, June 6, 1996: 1D.

10 Former Baseball Player Robert Ramsay Called Up To Pitch For The Seattle Mariners – Washington State University Athletics (wsucougars.com).

11 Associated Press, "Huskey to Boston for Ex-WSU Pitcher," *Spokane Spokesman-Review*, July 27, 1999.

12 Garrett Cabeza, "Rob Ramsay Left a Lasting Impact on Those Around Him," *Moscow-Pullman Daily News*, August 12, 2016.

13 Cabeza.

14 "Ramsay Gets Call from AAA, Starts vs. Cleveland tonight," *Seattle Times*, April 26, 2000: D11.

15 "Ramsay Gets Call from AAA."

16 Larry Stone, "Cameron Crushes Twins – Outfielder Hits Grand Slam in Easy Road Win," *Seattle Times*, June 16, 2000.

17 Stone: D1.

18 Kirby Arnold, "Mariners Notebook," *Bremerton (Washington) Kitsap Sun*, March 10, 2001.

19 Ira Berkow, "Baseball; for Pitcher, a Spring to Appreciate," *New York Times*, March 17, 2003: D2.

20 David Andriesen, "Rob Ramsay's Game of His Life," *Seattle Post-Intelligencer*, March 3, 2003.

21 Andriesen.

22 Andriesen.

23 Andriesen.

24 Andriesen.

25 Associated Press, "Ramsay Continuing His Comeback from Brain Surgery," *Bremerton Kitsap Sun*, February 25, 2004.

26 Andriesen.

27 Andriesen.

28 Associated Press, "Ramsay Navigates Long Road Back," *Bremerton Kitsap Sun*, March 2, 2003.

29 Andriesen.

30 Andriesen.

31 Andriesen.

32 Berkow.

33 Berkow.

34 Berkow.

35 Berkow.

36 Berkow.

37 Berkow.

38 Berkow.

39 Berkow.

40 Steve Kelley, "Ramsay Again Talks Baseball, Not Cancer," *Seattle Times*, January 28, 2004: D1.

41 Larry Stone, "Postcard from Florida," *Seattle Times*, March 1, 2004: C7.

42 Stone, "Postcard from Florida."

43 Transactions, 2004, Baltimore Orioles Transactions | MLB.com.

44 Castrovince.

45 Cabeza.

46 Castrovince.

47 Cindy Boren, "After Her Husband's Death, She Found Peace in Climbing. A Year Later, She Died on the Matterhorn," *Washington Post*, August 7, 2017.

48 Boren.

HARRY RAYMOND

BY PHILIP H. DIXON

Harry Raymond was a light-hitting third baseman who played mostly for the Louisville Colonels of the American Association in the late 1880s and early 1890s. While his statistical performance as a hitter was hardly exceptional, with a career batting average of only .235, Raymond was at the center of several remarkable events. He was part of what may have been the first strike by major-league players. He was also briefly "permanently" banned for "jumping" his contract. And, when pressed into an emergency stint as a pitcher, Raymond threw a complete-game victory, in his only major-league pitching stint, giving up only two runs (one earned) despite surrendering eight hits and 11 walks.

Although he played his entire baseball career as Harry Raymond, his birth name was John M. Truman.[1] John was born on February 20, 1862, in the hamlet of Sauquoit in the town of Paris, near Utica in upstate New York. His parents, James and Margaret, were of Irish heritage. James was born in Canada and Margaret in New York; but all of John's grandparents were born in Ireland. James was a carriage maker. John was the seventh of the couple's eight children. The 1880 Census listed 17-year-old John as living with his parents in the town of Paris and attending school. By 1883, John had moved to the Midwest. On November 9, 1883, a 21-year-old John and Mary Jane Lane, 19, were married in Jackson County (Kansas City), Missouri.[2]

John began his professional baseball career, as Harry Raymond, in 1887, playing for three Western League teams in the Kansas City area: the Kansas City Cowboys, Leavenworth Soldiers, and Emporia Reds.[3] Raymond broke into the majors late in the 1888 season, appearing in 32 games for the Colonels, all but one at third base. He batted .211 with 13 runs batted in.

In 1889, the 5-foot-9, 179-pound Raymond was the Colonels' regular third baseman throughout the season. The Colonels' season was a disaster. The club compiled a 27-111 record, including a record-setting 26-game losing streak.[4]

In addition to poor performance, the Colonels were plagued by a mercurial and penurious owner, Mordecai Davidson. Undercapitalized and facing low ticket sales, Davidson trimmed the roster and fell behind in meeting the payroll. Then he instituted a system of fines to be imposed on the players for perceived errors. The situation came to a head in mid-June as the team arrived on a road trip to Baltimore. The June 15 *Baltimore Sun* summarized the turmoil: "The trouble which has been brewing in the Louisville club culminated yesterday. When the game was called at the Oriole grounds, only six of the Louisville players put in an appearance. … The players who refused to play say they were short of salary and that on [the previous day] after the game, Shannon and Cook each were fined $25 for errors and stupid base running."[5]

Three local amateurs were recruited to enable the Colonels to field a team, but rain washed out the contest in the second inning. A day before the team left Louisville for the Baltimore road trip, Davidson was presented with a petition signed by the players, including Raymond, stating that unless Shannon's and Cook's fines were rescinded, the players would not play. A copy of the petition was sent to the president of the American Association, C.W. Wikoff. Wikoff, coincidentally, was presiding over a special meeting of the Association's leaders in New York City to determine what to do about the problematic Louisville franchise.

In an attempt to end the players strike, on Saturday, June 15, Davidson and Wikoff traveled to Baltimore to order the players to report for that day's games. Wikoff was reported to have assured the players that their complaints would be fairly considered by the Association. The players were unmoved. They boycotted that day's games, as well.

There were no games on June 16, which was a Sunday, but progress toward a resolution of the stand-off was made. According to the *Baltimore Sun*, the striking players met with Billy Barnie, the Baltimore manager, and followed his advice to file a grievance with the Association, and the two games scheduled for Monday went off with full rosters of players. The *Sun* summarized the resolution: "The trouble in the Louisville Club has ended temporarily. A committee representing the players called upon Manager Barnie, of the Baltimore Club, in whom they have confidence, and accepted his advice to continue playing and lay their grievances before the association for settlement. The sympathy of the public is with the players. The men did wisely in acting upon Manager Barnie's advice."[6]

The American Association's Board of Directors took up the players' grievances at a meeting in Louisville on July 5. The board heard statements from Raymond and the other teammates who had refused to play, as well as from Davidson. The board found that, while the players' refusal to play the June 14 game was "reprehensible and almost unpardonable," they had been "arbitrarily and unreasonably treated in many ways." Accordingly, the board reversed the fines, including those imposed for boycotting the June 14 game. This included $100 levied against Raymond. The board, however, left in place the $100 fines against Raymond and the five other players who boycotted the June 15 game, with the rationale that this refusal came after a direct order by Association President Wikoff.[7] Meanwhile, Davidson turned the franchise back to the Association on July 2. At the meeting on July 5, the board approved the transfer of the Colonels franchise to a new syndicate of local businessmen.

In the midst of this chaos, Raymond contributed an unlikely feat. On July 27 the Colonels faced a game against the Columbus Solons in Columbus without a starting pitcher. Their already barebones roster had been further depleted by injuries to three of the regular starters. Despite having never pitched in the majors and having pitched in only three minor-league games, Raymond took the mound against the Solons.

Raymond threw a complete-game 6-2 victory, a remarkable achievement in itself. Even more remarkable, however, is that he accomplished this despite giving up eight hits, allowing 11 bases on balls, and throwing two wild pitches. One helpful factor was good fielding, which the *Courier-Journal* called "the most brilliant fielding the club has done this season."[8] Three times the Solons loaded the bases without scoring. There were also at least four inning-ending double plays. Raymond's pitching was also solid at crucial times. The *Courier-Journal* summed up his performance: "It is true that he was wild, sending eleven men to bases on balls, but at critical times his judgment was good and his delivery hard to get outside the diamond. Umpire Jack Holland was also very severe in calling balls on him."[9]

Holland did indeed call a severe game on Raymond, while charging Al Mays, the Solons pitcher, with only two walks. Raymond's victory, while inspiring, did not affect the remainder of the 1889 season, which saw the Colonels finish dead last, in eighth place. Raymond improved his batting average to .239 in 130 games, driving in 47 runs.

In 1890 the Colonels and Raymond pulled off a remarkable rebirth, going from worst to first and winning the American Association title.[10] The formation of a third major league – the Players' League – led to the defection of many players to the new league for the 1890 season. The loss of players took a toll on the American Association. The Louisville team nonetheless played well throughout the season. Raymond was the Colonels' regular third baseman. He appeared in 123 games, drove in a career-best 51 runs and hit .259, the highest of his four years in the American Association and one in the National League.

Despite his relatively brief time in the major leagues, Raymond was a central figure in another significant baseball occurrence. It occurred during the 1891 season, a period of labor turmoil in baseball. The Players' League went out of business before the 1891 season and a new national agreement was negotiated by the National League and American Association. A new National Board of Control, chaired by Nick Young, the National League president, was established to oversee relations among the clubs. Disagreements arose, however, over who had the right to sign former Players' League players and even whether Young and the Board of Control had jurisdiction over non-National League clubs.

Raymond started the 1891 season under contract with the Lincoln Rustlers of the Western Association. In June he jumped to the Louisville Colonels. The *Louisville Courier-Journal on* June 21 published a report from a Kansas City newspaper describing Raymond's "jump":

"After a great deal of talk and very little action, the American Association has at length succeeded in stealing one player away from the Western Association. The report of the desertion of third baseman Raymond of the Lincoln Club to the Louisville Club turns out to be true, as Raymond played with the Louisvilles yesterday. ... The question now is what the Western Association is going to do in the way of reprisal or self-protection from the raid of the self-styled pirates. The desertion of Raymond is a serious blow to the Lincoln team."[11]

The National Board of Control quickly acted, ruling that Raymond and another jumping player were permanently ineligible. On June 17, 1891, the Board of Control, in a statement signed by its chairman, Young, declared that Raymond and the other player were "forever ineligible to play with or against another National Agreement club." Lest there be any doubt about the finality of the board's ruling, its statement added that "this order or any other that may be made for the same cause, will never be modified or revoked during the existence of the present board, whose term of office will not expire for five years."[12]

Despite the board's order, Raymond continued to play for the Colonels, logging 14 games at shortstop. Then, despite having just negotiated a two-year contract with Louisville, Raymond jumped back to the Rustlers, along with Louisville pitcher Red Ehret. On July 7 Chairman Young issued a new statement, "clarifying that under the Board's prior order "it was not my intention, nor do I consider I had the authority to thus punish any person whose overt act occurred prior to the issuance of the orders."[13] Young's new order gave jumping players 10 days to return to their prior clubs. Since Raymond had already rejoined the Rustlers, Young's second statement rendered Raymond's case moot.

Harry Raymond, with Louisville in 1899.

In 1892 Raymond played in only 16 major-league games, all in the National League – 12 with the Pittsburgh Pirates and 4 with the Washington Nationals. He also played 12 games for the Spokane Bunchgrassers in the Pacific Northwest League and apparently for the Phillipsburg Burgers in Phillipsburg, Montana.

He was well-traveled and continued playing in the minor leagues, however, until 1899. In 1893 he is seen in 64 games for the Montgomery (Alabama) Colts. In 1894 he played for Binghamton, New York, and (when the franchise was transferred) Allentown, Pennsylvania. He also logged 86 games – batting .342 for the Western League's Detroit Creams (and pitching in one game for Detroit). The Creams changed their name to the Tigers in 1895 and Raymond hit .290 in 121 games.

In 1896 Raymond played for Syracuse, Rochester, and Dubuque – continuing to log an impressive amount of travel for any player in the days before the automobile. Statistics are spotty.

Raymond's 1897 season included stints for Newark and Reading. In 1898 he played in Utica.

In a touch of symmetry, Raymond finished his career in 1899 playing for three New York State League teams – the Utica Pentups, near his childhood home, the Albany Senators, and the Schenectady Electricians.[14]

Harry Raymond/John Truman disappeared from the public eye after Raymond's career ended. At some point after his playing days, he apparently moved to California, where he died in San Diego at the age of 63 on March 21, 1925.[15] He is buried, as John Truman, at Greenwood Memorial Park in San Diego.[16]

SOURCES

In addition to the sources cited in the Notes, the author consulted Baseball-Reference.com, Retrosheet.org, the *Encyclopedia of Minor League Baseball*, and Ancestry.com.

NOTES

1. It is unclear why John Truman adopted Harry Raymond as his "baseball name," using it from his first game in he minor leagues through more than a decade of playing, contract negotiations, and disciplinary disputes. Perhaps the most logical explanation is that his parents did not view professional baseball as an appropriate occupation, and that he adopted Harry Raymond as his baseball name to mollify his parents.

2. Marriage Records, Jackson County Clerk, Kansas City, Missouri.

3. https://www.statscrew.com/minorbaseball/stats.

4. A thorough discussion of the hapless Colonels' season and losing streak is found in Bob Bailey, "Sad-Sack Colonels" in Bill Felber, ed., *Inventing Baseball, the 100 Greatest Games of the Nineteenth Century* (Phoenix: Society for American Baseball Research, 2013) and in David Nemec, *The Beer and Whisky League* (New York: Lyons & Burford, 1994).

5. "LOUISVILLE BASE-BALL CLUB. Six Men Refuse to Play Without Salaries," *Baltimore Sun*, June 15, 1889: 6.

6. "The Louisville Trouble Settled," *Baltimore Sun*, June 17, 1889: 5.

7. "Adjusting the Fines," *Louisville Courier-Journal*, July 6, 1889: 6.

8. "WON THE GAME. At Last Louisville Earns a Victory From a Base Ball Club." *Louisville Courier-Journal*, July 28, 1889: 4.

9. "WON THE GAME."

10. For an account of the losing streak see Jimmy Keenan, "The First Worst to First," in *Inventing Baseball, the 100 Greatest Games of the Nineteenth Century*

11. *Louisville Courier-Journal*, June 21, 1891: 13.

12. "Oh, Come On, Nick Young," *Louisville Courier-Journal*, June 18, 1891: 6.

13. "YOUNG EXPLAINS. Of Course Black Listed Players Can Return to Their Clubs," *Louisville Courier-Journal*, July 8, 1891: 6.

14. Statscrew.com/minorbaseball/stats.

15. California Department of Health and Welfare, Vital Records.

16. Author's 2022 telephone interview with Greenwood Memorial Park representative.

C.J. RIEFENHAUSER

BY PETER M. GORDON

Charles Joseph Riefenhauser was born on January 30, 1990, in Yonkers, New York, to Chuck Riefenhauser, an elevator mechanic, and Mary Lou, a nurse. He was raised in Mahopac (population 7,755), 47 miles north of New York City. Unlike some ballplayers who get their nicknames after establishing a career, Riefenhauser was named for his father, Chuck, but called C.J. from an early age.

Riefenhauser grew up throwing and batting left-handed. He was small for a professional baseball player, listed at 6-feet and 195 pounds during his major-league career. Even in high school, he didn't have a blazing fastball, but still dominated his league during his senior season in 2008. He pitched 52 innings (a typical high-school pitcher in a warm climate like Florida would pitch at least twice that number) for a record of 9-1 and an ERA of 1.88. Riefenhauser said, "At Mahopac High School, every coach I had from freshman to senior year was always teaching the basics, having fun and getting after it."[1]

Riefenhauser didn't play summer ball, but his high-school team traveled to the Carolinas for tournaments against stronger teams that played fall and spring baseball. The Mahopac team's stats for the year listed him as a pitcher-first baseman, but his batting average of .148 suggests that most of his value to the team was as a pitcher.

Riefenhauser's performance wasn't strong enough to entice a major-league team to draft him out of high school. He looked for a college where he could showcase his pitching skills. He told an interviewer, "I wasn't much of a student. I just wanted to play ball."[2] He first attended Iona College in New Rochelle, New York, not very far from his home in Mahopac. After a semester, he transferred to Guilford Community College in Guilford, North Carolina, before finding his way to Chipola College in Marianna, a small town in Florida's panhandle, for the 2009-2010 season. Chipola's baseball team won the 2006-2007 JUCO national championship, and in 2009 was ranked third in the nation, a much better showcase for his talents. He said going to Chipola was "the greatest decision of my life," since both professional and college scouts followed Chipola, and could see him pitch.[3]

That season, Riefenhauser pitched 64 innings in 17 games, with a strikeout-to-walk ratio of 56/27. He finished with a 4-5 won-lost record and a 4.92 ERA. He showed enough to become one of the top recruits for the 2010-2011 season for Elon College, a small North Carolina school. Riefenhauser signed a letter of intent for Elon, but the Tampa Bay Rays drafted him with their 20th-round pick in the 2010 draft. At first, he thought he'd honor his commitment to attend Elon, but after he went home for the summer, he said, "I talked it through with my family and decided there might not be another shot and you never know what's going to happen, every pitch might be your last. So I decided to start my career, give it my all and see what happens."[4]

Riefenhauser pitched 11 games in the summer of 2010 for the Princeton (New Jersey) Rays in the Rookie Appalachian League, with a record of 1-0 and an ERA of 2.84. The Rays moved him up to the Bowling Green (Kentucky) Hot Rods at the end of the season, and he earned one win in two games pitched with an ERA of 1.00.

He started the 2011 season at Bowling Green. He pitched 101⅓ innings, primarily as a starter, and went 6-5 with a 2.31 ERA. That earned him a promotion to the Advanced-A Port Charlotte Stone Crabs, where he faltered a little, going 1-3 with a 4.14 ERA.

Despite a losing record, 7-8, with a 4.76 ERA in the first part of the 2012 season, the Rays promoted Riefenhauser to the Double-A Montgomery Biscuits, where he posted a 1-1 record with a 3.44 ERA. Sometime during the 2012 season, the Rays coaching staff decided to convert Riefenhauser, who had been a starting pitcher since high school, into a reliever.

Riefenhauser said the Rays organization gave him all the support and help he needed to succeed. "They will never give up on you," he said. "They always try their best to get the best out of you. They make you a better pitcher."[5]

He started the 2013 season in Montgomery and dominated opposing batters. Pitching in relief, he went 4-0, with 11 saves and a minuscule 0.51 ERA. His performance earned him a promotion to the Triple-A Durham Bulls and an appearance in the 2013 Futures Game, which features minor-league stars from around the country.

Pitching in the Futures Game marked an important milestone in Riefenhauser's career. He was not originally slated to be on the roster, but when Rays prospect Taylor Guerrieri dropped out due to fatigue, Riefenhauser got the call. He was still thrilled.

"I'm not mad about taking his place, let me tell you that, Riefenhauser told a reporter at the game. "It's an honor to be included, to be recognized."[6] In 2013 the Futures Game was played at Citi Field in Queens, the home of the New York Mets. Since that was less than 100 miles from his hometown of Mahopac, a group of over 100 fans from Mahopac joined the crowd and cheered wildly when Riefenhauser entered the game in the eighth inning to preserve his team's 3-2 lead. He retired the side one-two-three on six pitches.

"I was just trying to throw strikes and hope I didn't leave one right over the middle so they didn't hit me too hard," he said. "My goal going into it was trying not to be nervous or overwhelmed. I haven't been the first- or second-round guy, the top prospect kind of thing. I'm just going in there and battling all the time."[7] Rays farm director Mitch Lukevics gave a scouting report on his pitching prospect at the game: "C.J. Riefenhauser has good stuff, 91-92 MPH (fastball), he has the ability to spin (a curveball) and he's trying to work on a changeup for right-handed hitters. But what this kid brings, he has some inside toughness. He loves to compete. He's a great story because he's another young guy that will will himself to the big leagues."[8]

After the Futures Game, Riefenhauser was sent to Triple-A Durham for the rest of the season, finishing his first stint in Triple-A ball with a 2-1 record and 3.05 ERA in 20⅔ innings pitched.. The Rays added him to their 40-man roster in 2014. He started at Durham, but the Rays called him to the majors in early April. Riefenhauser told interviewer Milo Kaminsky how he heard about it:

"My manager called me at midnight after a game in Norfolk, Virginia. He got a text at dinner with his whole family saying I'm getting called up. I was sitting in the hotel room watching something, I can't remember and when he told me, his whole family is screaming in the phone congratulating me. I was just speechless, I had no emotions and I didn't know what to do. I called my parents and that's when it hit me. Then the next day I have to wake up early, but I barely got any sleep because I was staring at the ceiling all night thinking. They flew me first class on a flight to Florida and I'm looking around and thinking, 'This is the life.' Everything is taken care of for you, you have a driver taking your suitcase and you don't pick up your bag from when you land

C. J. Riefenhauser. Courtesy of the Tampa Bay Rays.

until you get to the field. It's a pretty unbelievable feeling."⁹

Riefenhauser made his debut on April 19, in the seventh inning of a laugher against the New York Yankees at Tropicana Field. The Rays were up 14-1 and manager Joe Maddon saw a low-pressure opportunity for his new rookie. He entered the game after two outs in the seventh and got Alfonso Soriano to ground out to third. He then pitched a perfect eighth, retiring the Yankees on three fly balls.

The next day didn't go as well. The Rays and Yankees were tied 1-1 going into the top of the 12th. Heath Bell, pitching for the Rays, started the inning by walking Yangervis Solarte, and Maddon called once more for Riefenhauser. He got Brett Gardner to hit back to him for a force at second, and the next batter, Brian Roberts, on a lineout to short. Still one on, but two out, he needed one more batter to get out of the inning. He didn't get it.

Brian McCann singled to put runners on first and third. Riefenhauser walked Jacoby Ellsbury intentionally to load the bases, and then walked Dean Anna unintentionally to score the go-ahead run for the Yankees. That was all for him, and Josh Lueke came in from the bullpen and gave up three more runs, all of which were charged to Riefenhauser. His first two days in the majors, which started so full of promise, ended with him having an ERA of 13.50, and a ticket back to Durham.

Riefenhauser earned another call-up by pitching well, with a record of 3-3 and a 1.40 ERA, with one save over 30 games. The Rays have a history of developing a stable of solid Triple-A relievers, but that has meant over time that if a pitcher doesn't make a positive impact soon, the team tries someone else. In April 2014, the Rays were coming off four straight 90-win seasons and expected to get back to the postseason. They didn't have time to let a young pitcher make mistakes.

By September the Rays were out of the pennant race (they finished fourth in the AL East, with a 77-85 record), and the team brought Riefenhauser back. Between September 16 and the end of the season he pitched 3⅓ innings over five games, He gave up five hits and two earned runs, finishing with a 0-0 record and a 5.40 ERA. That was an improvement over his short stint in April. His Fielding Independent Pitching average was only 2.83, and as a 24-year-old pitcher who proved he could pitch well at Triple A and battle in the majors, Riefenhauser had a chance to make the major-league club in 2015.

That season was a transitional year for the Rays organization. Manager Joe Maddon took advantage of a contract clause that allowed him to opt out of his deal if general manager Andrew Friedman left the club. Maddon became manager of the Chicago Cubs, and in 2016 led the Cubs to their first World Series win since 1908. Kevin Cash took the Rays' reins, and led the team to an 80-82 record, an improvement over 2014.

Riefenhauser again started the year on the Durham roster but joined the Rays on April 17. He pitched in relief on April 17 and 18, giving up three earned runs in 1⅓ innings. On April 19 he joined over a dozen Rays on the disabled list. Left-shoulder inflammation was the reason, and while Riefenhauser hoped to get back on the mound after the minimum 15-day stay, he remained on the DL for 41 days with a pulled oblique muscle. When he was activated in May, the Rays sent him to Durham for a rehab stint. They recalled him on June 12.

Two days later, on June 14, Riefenhauser earned his only major-league win. Nate Karns started for the Rays and Chris Sale for the Chicago White Sox. Both hurlers pitched well through six innings. At the end of the sixth, the Rays were behind 1-0, after a run-scoring single by Yolmer Sánchez in the top of the second that drove in Gordon Beckham.

Rays manager Cash sent Riefenhauser to the mound to start the seventh inning, and he held the White Sox scoreless. He got Sanchez to ground out, then gave up a single to catcher Tyler Flowers. Riefenhauser now faced center fielder Adam Eaton, the leadoff hitter. Eaton forced Flowers at second base for the second out, and Rays catcher René Rivera threw out Eaton trying to steal. Riefenhauser's clean inning kept the Rays close.

The Rays went ahead in the bottom of the seventh. Sale walked Steven Souza, and Asdrúbal Cabrera followed with a two-run homer to put Tampa Bay ahead. They put two more runners on but could not convert them into runs. Now that the Rays had the lead, Maddon sent Kevin Kiermaier in to play center field in the top of the eighth, and Steve Gelz to the mound. Gelz retired the White Sox one-two-three.

The Rays threatened again in the bottom of the eighth on singles by Evan Longoria and Logan Forsythe, but Souza grounded into a double play and Cabrera flied out to end the inning. Kevin Jepsen pitched a scoreless ninth for the save, and Riefenhauser earned his first and only major-league victory. The Associated Press story of the game focused on Chris Sale, who struck out 12 in his losing effort, and Cabrera's home run.[10] If the reporter got a quote from Riefenhauser, it didn't make the story.

Reflecting on the win in 2023, Riefenhauser said, "It's great to tell everyone I beat Chris Sale, but it was Asdrubal Cabrera who beat Chris Sale with a homer, and the rest of the bullpen that shut them down. In the clubhouse after the game, we all had a great time, and they gave me the scorecard because it was my first win."[11]

The next day, June 15, the Washington Nationals came to town and the Rays started Erasmo Ramírez. Riefenhauser relieved Ramírez in the seventh and pitched another scoreless inning, giving up only a walk. Ramírez got the win. Riefenhauser made his third appearance in three days in the third inning of the Rays' next game against the Nationals. Alex Colomé started for the Rays and gave up six runs in the first two innings. Manager Cash sent Riefenhauser out to start the third inning, and he held the Nationals scoreless in the third and fourth innings.

Pitching two innings for a third straight day of relief would tax any pitcher, and when Cash sent Riefenhauser out to start the fifth, he gave up a homer to Bryce Harper, got Wilson Ramos to ground out, and then walked a man. Cash sent Enny Romero in to relieve, and he gave up two runs in the rest of the fifth, one of which was charged to Riefenhauser. The Rays ended up losing 16-4.

The Rays sent Riefenhauser back to Durham, and recalled him on July 1, once again putting him in to relieve Colome in a losing effort. Cleveland was beating the Rays 5-0 going into the top of the eighth. Riefenhauser gave up a walk (after a foul pop was dropped), a double, and a three-run homer before getting two outs, after which Cash replaced him. Riefenhauser returned to Durham; he returned to Tampa Bay in September. In between he spent more time on the disabled list with a strained oblique muscle.

The Rays took a good look at Riefenhauser in September. He pitched 8⅓ innings over 11 games, with a decent 2.16 ERA. He reduced his ERA for the year from 9.95 to 5.52, which gave him final 2015 stats of 1-0, 5.52 ERA, but with a FIP of 6.27. Although he couldn't have known it at the time, 2015 was Riefenhauser's last year in the majors.

He pitched well in Durham in mostly a middle relief role, earning a 4-2 record and a 2.86 ERA with one save. Riefenhauser was only 25, and some major-league teams looking for a lefty specialist thought he could help them.

The Rays were not one of those teams in 2015. In November they packaged him with pitcher Nate Karns (who started Riefenhauser's only major-league victory) and minor-league center fielder Boog Powell to the Seattle Mariners for shortstop Brad Miller, first baseman Logan Morrison, and pitcher Danny Farquhar. The trade turned out well for the Rays. Morrison had his best year ever in 2017, hitting 38 homers. Brad Miller hit 30 home runs in 2016, and after a down year in 2017, was traded to Milwaukee for Ji-Man Choi, who became one of the Rays' fan favorites.

In December Seattle traded Riefenhauser and right fielder Mark Trumbo to Baltimore for catcher Steve Clevenger. Perhaps to sharpen his skills, Riefenhauser pitched for Margarita in the Venezuelan Winter League. He strained his shoulder, but tried to rehab and pitch through it. He struggled through four games, ending up with an 0-1 record and an ERA of 11.57. The Orioles released him in February of 2016.

Joe Maddon was managing the Chicago Cubs, and may have remembered good reports about Riefenhauser when he was in the Rays system. The Cubs claimed him off waivers and sent him to Triple-A Des Moines, where he went 2-1 with a 4.55 ERA and one save. On August 10 the team placed him on the disabled list because he hurt his shoulder. Riefenhauser didn't see a future with the

C. J. Riefenhauser. Courtesy of the Tampa Bay Rays.

Cubs and asked for his release. When he came off the disabled list on August 22, the Cubs obliged.

During the offseason Riefenhauser had shoulder surgery and rehabbed to get in shape to try one more time to pitch in the majors. The Houston Astros signed him to a minor-league contract in December and invited him to spring training in 2017 but released him on March 26. They had other prospects with more promise, and even though he pitched well in spring training, Riefenhauser knew the team made a business decision.

Knowing that this would probably be his last year to pitch, he returned to the New York area and joined the Rockland Boulders of the independent Frontier League, Can-Am Division. Rockland County, New York, is southwest of where Riefenhauser grew up in Putnam County. He finished with a record of 5-1 and an ERA of 3.81 in 54⅓ innings pitched. He did not draw interest from any major-league teams. He did get a taste of coaching, acting as pitching coach for the Boulders when the pitching coach left the team in the middle of the season.

Riefenhauser's pitching shoulder was too damaged to allow him to keep pitching on a major-league level. He was only 27 years old and needed to find a new career. He decided to finish his education and stay in baseball. He attended Mercy College in Dobbs Ferry, New York, a small town on the Hudson River in Westchester County, finished his physical education degree, and helped coach the baseball team for two years. In 2018 Riefenhauser moved to Manhattanville College in Harrisonville, New York, to earn his master's degree in physical education.

Riefenhauser said his time coaching the Mercy College team made him "fall in love with coaching."[10] About the time the former pitcher started looking, Sean Kennedy, the baseball coach at Yorktown High School in Yorktown Heights, New York, was retiring after 25 years. Yorktown Heights, in Westchester County, was not very far from his hometown of Mahopac, and as he told a reporter for a local news site, "with Yorktown, it was actually right time, right place. I am done pitching. It was a great run. There are no regrets, ever, in my life." His goal was "to coach Yorktown as long as I can."[12]

In the twentieth century, it was common for major leaguers to spend their offseasons and retirement in their hometowns. That's not as common these days, but Riefenhauser married a woman who went to high school with him, and enjoyed living near friends and both of their extended families in his hometown. As of 2023, Riefenhauser was still teaching physical education and coaching baseball for the Yorktown Huskers. He also owned an indoor sports training facility in Mahopac. He has good memories of his career in professional baseball. He said, "It's cool to be undefeated in the major leagues."[13]

SOURCES

In addition to the sources cited in the Notes, the author consulted a number of other sources, including Baseball-Reference.com and Retrosheet.org.

NOTES

1. Milo Kaminsky, "Interview With C.J. Riefenhauser," newyorknine.org, August 8, 2014. http://newyorknine.org/interview-with-cj-riefenhauser/. Accessed March 10, 2023.
2. Author interview with C.J. Riefenhauser, January 27, 2023, hereafter referred to as Riefenhauser interview.
3. Riefenhauser interview.
4. Kaminsky.
5. Riefenhauser interview.
6. Marc Topkin, "Futures Pitcher Appreciates His Present," tampabaytimes.com, July 13, 2013. https://www.tampabay.com/sports/baseball/rays/futures-pitcher-appreciates-his-present/2131405/. Accessed March 10, 2023.
7. Topkin.
8. Topkin.
9. Kaminsky.
10. Associated Press, "Chris Sale First Since '01 to Fan 12 in 4 Straight, but White Sox Fall to Rays," ESPN.com, June 14, 2015. https://www.espn.com/mlb/recap/_/gameId/350614130. Accessed March 10, 2023.
11. Riefenhauser interview.
12. Brian Marschauser, "Former MLB Player, C.J. Riefenhauser, Tabbed as Yorktown Coach," tapinto.net, July 30, 2019. https://www.tapinto.net/articles/former-mlb-player-c-j-riefenhauser-tabbed-as-yorktown-s-head-coach. Accessed March 10, 2023.
13. Riefenhauser interview.

RALPH "BLACKIE" SCHWAMB

BY GLEN SPARKS

Tried and convicted of murder in a court of law, Ralph "Blackie" Schwamb hurled his best pitches from behind prison walls. The tall, lanky right-hander with a nasty temper and a taste for booze won just a single game as a major leaguer. He won 131 games while playing for teams based at the San Quentin and Folsom state penitentiaries in California.

Schwamb threw a fastball and a curveball that could baffle hitters. He also found his way into frequent trouble and heard the click of handcuffs more than once. Blackie claimed, with some exaggeration, "I always had an angle. Things were too easy for me. It seemed that whatever I decided to undertake, I could make work."[1]

Born on August 6, 1926, in Los Angeles, Ralph Richard Schwamb grew up in a neighborhood south of downtown. His mother, Jeannette (née Tarling), was born in 1904 in Montana. Ralph's father, Chester Hinton Schwamb, was two years older than Jeannette and hailed from Colorado. The couple got married in 1921 and set out for Southern California, along with so many others.

Just over 100,000 people lived in Los Angeles in 1900. That number had grown to nearly 600,000 by 1920 and would top 1.2 million in 1930. Bulldozers ran over acres of orange groves and wildflowers to meet the demand for new housing. Chester Schwamb built a successful career working in the local construction industry as a "carpenter and master builder."[2]

Ralph and his older brother, Chester Jr. (born in 1923), attended 68th Street Grade School. One day, while watching a Western movie with friends at a local theater, Ralph noticed that the bad guys wore black. He decided to do the same. Young Ralph liked the look. Friends started calling him Blackie.

He was a gangly kid and a good all-around athlete who competed at the local parks against future big leaguers like Gene Mauch, Al Zarilla, and George Metkovich. Schwamb made himself a sandlot sensation with his intimidating fastball. He could always throw hard. Once, on a dare and from a reported 300 feet away, Schwamb picked up a rock and broke a "big pane" of glass that workers were hauling away from a nearby factory.

Blackie quit Washington High School at the age of 16. He was already a big drinker and a nasty drunk. Mauch recalled that even as a teenager, "When sober, Blackie was one great kid. With alcohol, he actually pursued daring and trouble."[3]

Schwamb turned 17 years old on August 6, 1943. He celebrated by joining the Navy. Patriotic fervor, though, even during this time of world war, could never trump Schwamb's habit of getting into mischief. He spent more time fighting fellow servicemen than he did the Germans or Japanese. Just a few months into his tour, while on leave in Los Angeles with thousands of other soldiers and sailors, Blackie slugged a military officer and was jailed.

After a few more unpleasant incidents, Schwamb left the Navy with a bad-conduct discharge from the Great Lakes Naval Training Center in Chicago and headed back home. Blackie, who had grown to 6-feet-5-inches, asked about joining one of the local baseball leagues. Evo Pusich, a recreation supervisor at the Manchester Playground and a part-time scout for the New York Giants, called Schwamb "an awfully nice kid."[4]

On March 8, 1946, Blackie married Nellie Ann Eisen, a Minnesota native. Ralph and Nellie, or Nell, were both 19 years old. The couple's son, Richard Page Schwamb, was born on December 6, 1946.

At some point, Blackie met a diminutive (5-foot-5) tough guy named Meyer Harris "Mickey" Cohen. Born in 1913 in Brooklyn, New York, to Jewish immigrants from Kiev, Russia, Cohen grew up in the Boyle Heights area of East Los Angeles and quickly built a nasty rap sheet. At the tender age of 7, he picked up a hot plate and assaulted a police officer. Two years later he robbed the Columbia Theater in downtown LA.[5] Police nabbed Cohen and a judge ordered him to the local reform school.

Later, Cohen took up boxing but rarely strayed from a life of crime. Through the years, in California and elsewhere, he got to know other gangsters, including Al Capone, Meyer Lansky, and Bugsy Siegel. Cohen also made himself into a minor celebrity. Readers often saw his picture in the local newspapers. Cohen owned an armor-plated car and a house in the upscale Brentwood section of West LA.

Schwamb met Cohen in late 1945. The hoodlum put Blackie to work as a so-called leg-breaker. The young right-hander collected debts from gamblers who had run into a streak of bad luck.[6] He also hooked on with a local semipro baseball team as a pitcher and occasional shortstop.

Both the Cleveland Indians and St. Louis Browns kept an eye on Schwamb. St. Louis signed him in September 1946 and gave him a $600 bonus. Jack Fournier, the former first baseman-outfielder for the Brooklyn Robins and other teams and now a Browns scout, liked the slender hurler. Well, Fournier liked Blackie in the way that many other baseball people liked Blackie. That is, with a certain amount of reserve. "He's a screwball, but he can pitch," Fournier said.[7]

Schwamb began his brief tour in professional baseball as a member of the Aberdeen (South Dakota) Pheasants of the Class-C Northern League. He won five games in as many decisions and posted a 1.62 ERA. As usual, he spent many of his off-hours at local bars, and the Browns shipped him to the Globe-Miami Browns, another of the organization's Class-C affiliates, based in the old silver-mining town of Globe, Arizona. Blackie pitched and drank, this time with the desert as a blurry backdrop.

To the surprise of many, Globe advanced to the Arizona-Texas League championship series and played the Tucson Cowboys. Manager Lloyd Brown called on Schwamb to be his ace. First, though, Brown bailed him out of the local jail following one more of the pitcher's drunken escapades. It was a decision the skipper did not regret. Blackie won two games in a best-of-five series and recorded a save in the championship matchup. He struck out 23 batters over a combined 19 innings. Still, it wasn't easy. Browns pitcher Ned Garver heard several stories about Schwamb, including this one: "The only way they kept him sober for the championship series was that every night after the games, they would take him back to jail and lock him up until the morning."[8]

Blackie began the 1948 campaign with the Toledo Mud Hens of the Triple-A American Association, the Browns' top farm team. Bob French from the *Toledo Blade* noted Schwamb's great height and wrote, "[A]ccording to reports, he has a wild and carefree idea about how a baseball player should conduct himself. But he has so much speed they say that he can throw an egg through a bullet-proof safe."[9]

As is the fate of most pitchers, especially those toiling away in the minor leagues, Schwamb sometimes suffered from a poor defense behind him, and he rarely took those error-filled affairs in stride. Frank Mancuso, the Toledo catcher, said, "After one game, he wanted to fight the entire team. Man, he was hot. I don't blame him, but you gotta get along with your teammates."[10]

Nothing Schwamb did for Toledo indicated that he held star potential. He won one game and lost nine in 25 appearances, with a 5.14 ERA over 77 innings. He also walked 52 batters and struck out just 45. The Browns called him up in late July, anyway.

Blackie made his big-league debut in the second game of a doubleheader against the Washington Senators on Saturday, July 25, at Griffith Stadium. The Senators won the opener, 5-1, behind Ray Scarborough. Fred Sanford took the loss.

Schwamb started against Earl Harrist, a third-year right-hander from Louisiana. St. Louis scored twice in the first inning and added two more runs in top of the third. Washington got to Schwamb for one run in the bottom half of the third.

Washington added two more runs in the seventh inning. Mickey Vernon began the rally with a one-out single. Junior Wooten lined another base hit, and both runners advanced an additional base on center fielder Paul Lehner's throw into the infield. Jake Early's two-run single to right field ended Blackie's afternoon.

Blackie Schwamb. Courtesy of Ed Wheatley.

Besides giving up three runs – two earned – Schwamb allowed seven hits and struck out three. Washington tied the score in the ninth inning on an unearned run with Bryan Stephens pitching. St. Louis won, 6-4, on a Don Lund two-run double in the 11th. The following day, the *St. Louis Globe-Democrat* reported that Blackie "pitched great ball for the first six innings."[11]

Schwamb earned his lone major-league victory six days later. Once again, he faced the Senators. This time, he took the mound at Sportsman's Park. The game drew 4,556 fans on a warm summer day. Schwamb started against Walt Masterson. Washington scored two runs, one unearned, in the opening frame. St. Louis fought back and scored twice in the third, once in the fifth, and seven times in the sixth to blow open the game, 10-2.

Blackie, though, made the game interesting. He allowed four runs in the seventh inning on two walks and four singles. Bryan Stephens, who attended the same high school as Schwamb, entered the game with one out and wiggled out of the jam. The Browns went on to win, 10-8. Schwamb's pitching line – eight hits, six runs with five of them earned, four walks, and just two strikeouts – wasn't pretty but it was good enough to put him into the win column, thanks to a lively St. Louis offense.

In the *St. Louis Post-Dispatch*, Robert Morrison wrote, "Brownie bats, which have had an occasional habit of speaking with authority lately, did it again last night" and added that while Washington nearly staged a comeback, "everything turned out all right."[12] Blackie said later, "I had my first major-league win. I was just a week shy of my twenty-second birthday. I had the world by the tail."[13]

As happened so often with Blackie, though, the good times ended fast. He struggled from the get-go in his next game, on August 4 at home, and lasted just one-third of an inning, in which he "was kayoed"[14] by the Boston Red Sox. He allowed five hits and six runs, all of them earned. The Browns, though, scored seven times in the bottom of the first and won, 9-8.

Four days later, Schwamb started at home and lost to the Philadelphia Athletics, 7-5. He gave up two runs and got the hook with two out in the fourth inning. The Browns ordered him to the bullpen. In his first two relief appearances, Schwamb gave up a combined nine runs (eight earned) in 3⅓ innings but then managed two scoreless efforts.

Blackie's final month in the big leagues began with another poor outing. He surrendered three runs in three innings against the Tigers on September 6 and, in his last career start, on September 12, he pitched just two innings and allowed three runs against the Cleveland Indians. Two days later, the Philadelphia Athletics roughed up Schwamb for two runs in two innings.

Oddly enough, Blackie's farewell game, at home vs. the Red Sox on September 18, may have been his best. Manager Zack Taylor sent him in as a reliever with two outs in the sixth inning and Boston already ahead, 11-4. Blackie "checked the Red Sox the rest of the way."[15] He pitched 3⅓ innings of shutout ball, allowing three hits and a walk, with one strikeout. The Browns lost, 11-6. "Schwamb did nice work," the *Globe-Democrat* noted.[16] About two weeks remained in the season. Blackie watched the rest of the action from a seat on the dugout bench.

The rookie made few friends among his fellow Browns. He often snarled and tossed around insults. He dished out unkind words better than he took them. Fellow pitcher Fred Sanford recalled how Schwamb "acted like a big tough guy, but when players started to get on him, razz him, he couldn't take it.… We'd call him things like 'Ears' or 'Dumbo.' He had big ears."[17] St. Louis first baseman Chuck Stevens assessed Schwamb in blunt fashion: "He seemed to go out of his way to break the rules.… Frankly, he was a cancer on that team."[18]

St. Louis put together a 59-94 won-lost record and finished in sixth place. Veteran catcher Les Moss led the team with 14 home runs. Sanford topped the Browns with 12 wins; he lost 21 times. Schwamb went 1-1 and had an ERA of 8.53 in 31⅓ innings. He gave up 44 hits and 21 walks and struck out just seven.

After the season Blackie boarded a train for Los Angeles. He needed some offseason money and went to see Cohen, who was by now a key player in the LA underworld. In fact, as Bugsy Siegel turned his attention to the future gambling mecca of Las Vegas, "Mickey had taken over his old boss's Los Angeles operations – as well as Siegel's organized crime connections back East."[19]

Schwamb did unsavory work for Cohen throughout the fall of 1948. He also prepared for the coming baseball season. The Browns held spring training in the Los Angeles suburb of Burbank. St. Louis, still not bullish on the erratic pitcher's future, offered Blackie a $5,000 contract, the big-league minimum. An angry Schwamb signed on the dotted line.

Jack Graham, a first baseman and second-generation big leaguer, drove Schwamb to practice every day. Not that Schwamb made things easy. Sometimes, Graham had to go looking for his wayward teammate, who was often lying down outside a local bar, sleeping off a bender from the previous night. "That's the way it went all spring," Graham said. "Just about every day, he looked like he hadn't slept, and he smelled like a brewery. Not a pretty sight."[20]

Even so, Browns executive Bill DeWitt gave Blackie the good news. Schwamb had made the big-league club. Sorta. DeWitt wanted his hard-living hurler to pitch a few minor-league games before joining the Browns. Schwamb stormed out of the room and soon cut a deal with the Little Rock Travelers, a Detroit Tigers affiliate in the Southern League, where he won two games and had a 2.37 ERA in three appearances. Schwamb, though, missed the team bus to Chattanooga and caught a ride to New Orleans for liquor and the nightlife. He soon found himself an ex-Traveler.

Next, Schwamb went to Sherbrooke, Quebec, about 100 miles east of Montreal, where he pitched in 12 games for the Athletics in the Provincial League. He went 4-4 with an unpleasant 5.73 ERA. Blackie's baseball future looked bleak, and he needed money, so he pulled a string of offseason robberies in Los Angeles and "took on all the jobs he could get from Mickey Cohen."[21]

(Just a few months earlier, on July 20, 1949, outside a popular nightclub on Sunset Boulevard called Sherry's, Cohen and his cronies traded gunfire with another set of bad guys in what local newspapers dubbed The Battle of Sunset Strip. "Members of Mickey's party started to drop," according to John Buntin's authoritative book on Cohen and the Los Angeles Police Department, *L.A. Noir*.[22] Neddie Herbert, "one of Cohen's top thugs,"[23] took a fatal bullet.)

On the night of October 12, 1949, Schwamb left home for a corner bar named Jimmy's, where he was a regular. Two friends, Ted and Joyce Gardner, had stopped for drinks at the nearby Colony Club. Dr. Donald Buge, a dentist from Long Beach, also went to the Colony Club that night. His wife, Violet, spent the evening playing poker across the street at the Normandie Card Club.

For unknown reasons, and willingly or not, Dr. Buge left the Colony Club in a car with the Gardners, while Violet Buge stayed at the Normandie. Ted Gardner drove a few minutes away to Jimmy's. There, the trio met up with Blackie and ordered drinks. Following a round of libations, all four left together in Gardner's car.

The stories diverge from that point. The bottom line is that Buge was beaten to death, and $53 was stolen from his wallet. Police detectives arrested Ted and Joyce on October 14. Ted confessed and implicated Schwamb, who also was arrested. The district attorney charged Blackie and Ted with first-degree murder.

Blackie told the court that he was "too intoxicated"[24] to remember any of the grisly details. Gardner said that he and Blackie had planned to rob Buge. The jury convicted Schwamb of first-degree murder and first-degree robbery. Los Angeles Superior Court Judge Charles W. Fricke sentenced him on December 23 to life in prison. He could apply for parole in 10 years. Gardner, three years older than Schwamb and with a criminal past of his own, also got a life sentence. Neither man said whether Mickey Cohen had ordered the robbery or murder.

Nellie Schwamb left the courtroom, along with her husband's lawyer, David Silverton. Outside, a friend greeted her with a cheerful "Merry Christmas" but quickly realized the blunder. "Gosh, is that the thing to say at a time like this?" Nell smiled. "Well," she decided, "in spite of a thing like this, we have to go on living, you know."[25]

Schwamb began his prison term at San Quentin. Opened in July 1852, The Arena – as some called it – lies in a picturesque spot in Marin County, just a few miles north of San Francisco. Cold water from the famous Bay spills onto the nearby shore. Clinton Duffy, the prison's warden from 1940 to 1952, wrote in his memoir that San Quentin occupies "one of the prettiest pieces of real estate."[26] The prison also has held some of the country's most notorious criminals, including Sam Shockley, who killed a prison guard during the 1946 Battle of Alcatraz, and the serial killer Gordon Stewart Northcott.

Duffy took the job of warden with reform in mind. He recalled, "San Quentin itself in the old days was often a hell-on-earth, and even today, despite what all of us have tried to do, it is no summer resort."[27] Duffy requested more books for the prison library, added more vocational education courses, and, in maybe his most popular move, ordered the kitchen staff to serve bigger cuts of meat.

Blackie, not long removed from his days as a major leaguer, still wanted to pitch, and San Quentin fielded a team that competed in the San Francisco Recreation Department League. After a series of psychological exams – "He seems very reluctant toward understanding himself and his problems,"[28] according to one report – Schwamb suited up, grabbed a glove, and played his first prison-house baseball game for the San Quentin All-Stars on March 11, 1950.

He struck out three batters against Modesto Junior College, and repeated that performance in his next game, versus Marin Junior College. Blackie fanned eight of 10 batters he faced against Reliable

Drugs of San Francisco and struck out 14 Galileo Salami batters.

Schwamb was Prisoner Number A-13670. Inmates called him Slick. The team played each weekend on the lower yard at San Quentin. In time, crowds gathered to watch Slick pitch. "After we got the team going and winning," Schwamb recalled, "you could fire a machine gun in the upper yard on Sunday and not hit anybody."[29]

The one-time big leaguer boasted a 2.04 ERA as a San Quentin rookie and struck out 281 batters in 203 innings. When Blackie wasn't pitching, he played in the field, often at third base, where he could take advantage of that strong arm. He topped the team with a .457 batting average. Plus, he enjoyed his own jailhouse hootch, using yeast, sugar, and a handful of oranges. "It was like cheap wine," he said.[30]

Schwamb got a job in the prison's athletic office. He ordered equipment and uniforms for San Quentin's various sports teams. At least one guard recalled Schwamb as a "polite"[31] inmate, who liked to read everything from the Western writer Louis L'Amour to philosopher Friedrich Nietzsche.

Baseball practice began in February, and the season lasted until November. Rosters turned over fast, sometimes due to injury, sometimes because a player made parole. Schwamb remained the team's star. He pitched 32 straight scoreless innings during one stretch in 1951 and kept a .371 batting average. In 1952, the same year that Nell filed for divorce, Blackie threw 162 innings, struck out 261 batters, and fashioned a 1.55 ERA. Plus, he hit at a .377 clip.

In time, Schwamb asked for a transfer to Folsom, another tough prison in the California system, located more than 100 miles from San Quentin and less than 25 miles from the state capital of Sacramento. Prison gangs and gamblers at San Quentin had wanted him to throw games.[32]

While at Folsom, Blackie competed in the Tri-County League, and, as he did at San Quentin, worked in the athletic office. At one point, he wrote a letter to San Francisco Giants manager Bill Rigney and offered a splendid scouting report on himself.

Clearly, Schwamb hoped to get out of prison soon and return to the big leagues. Rigney recalled, "(He was) telling me what a great prospect he is, how he's striking out everybody there in prison." The skipper still shook off any idea of signing Blackie. "Are you kidding? He murdered a guy," Rigney said to team owner Horace Stoneham. "Don't we have enough troubles on the team without signing a murderer?"[33]

The prison gates finally opened for Schwamb in January 1960. The state board had granted him parole. He was 33 years old. According to an article in the *San Francisco Examiner*, "Prison officials said it was their understanding [Schwamb] already had written Baseball Commissioner Ford C. Frick for reinstatement."[34]

Schwamb had completed his career as maybe the greatest prison-house pitcher of all time, with an estimated won-lost record of 131-35 and an ERA of 1.80 in nearly 1,500 innings of work. He struck out 1,565 batters and walked 240. Schwamb once said, "I was a lousy gangster, but I was a great pitcher."[35] He certainly was, at least at San Quentin and Folsom.

Back in Los Angeles, Blackie learned how to navigate the complicated freeway system of an ever-growing metropolis. Nearly 2.5 million people were living in the city by 1960. Schwamb found work at a warehouse in Long Beach and got married to Nancy Black in November. He hoped to pitch for the Los Angeles Angels, an expansion franchise set to debut in the American League and which took its name from the city's former Pacific Coast League team. Frick, though, had suspended Schwamb for one year.

Los Angeles Examiner columnist Bob Hunter wrote several pieces in support of Schwamb, and Frick reinstated the pitcher in early 1961. Blackie signed a deal with the Honolulu Islanders, a Kansas City Athletics affiliate.

That final attempt at professional baseball ended, as it often did for Schwamb, with a subpar won-lost record and other bad stats. He drank less, but in 21 innings, he allowed 27 hits and had a 5.14 ERA with one win and two losses. Professional hitters handled Blackie's fastball much better than the cons ever did. Even so, Dave Thies, one of the Islanders' best pitchers, said, "Everybody was cheering that he would go well. He had a demeanor about him that was very likable, no pretense."[36]

His body, though, had begun to tire. His legs felt weak, and the Islanders left him behind at spring-training camp in San Bernardino the following March. Blackie's baseball career was over. Months later, he and Nancy decided to divorce.

Blackie got married again, this time to Judy Norris, in August of 1964. He also worked construction jobs, both in Los Angeles and Sacramento. He still drank, although he told parole agents that he had quit. Judy sued for divorce in the spring of 1969, not long after police threw Blackie behind bars for public drunkenness. In 1971 Schwamb spent two months in LA County Jail and nearly seven months at the Chino minimum-security prison for illegal possession of a firearm.

Jeanette Schwamb picked up her son at the prison gate. A few days later, Blackie began working at a freight company near Los Angeles International Airport. He also began dating his boss, Bea Franklin. The two, along with Bea's daughter Denise, moved into a trailer home in Palmdale, California, a community in the Antelope Valley on the western edge of the Mojave Desert. Blackie wanted to get married. Bea, though, had soured on matrimony. Her former husband had been abusive, she said. Blackie mulled over one final assault. Wisely, he decided against throwing any punches. "I was on the Dudley-Do-Right kick," he said. "I probably would have lost her if I'd beat him up or hurt him."[37]

Blackie battled numerous health problems. He developed a bad cough from all that cigarette smoking and suffered a serious back injury while on a boat trip with Bea to the Channel Islands. Denise recalled about her stepdad, "He mostly tried to steer me certain ways, not boss me around. He was strict about curfew and who I hung out with. But I could always sit down with him and tell him something."[38]

Eric Stone wrote a biography of Schwamb titled *Wrong Side of the Wall*. Blackie invited Stone into his trailer. The two men spoke for a bit. Soon enough, Schwamb told his guest to leave. Now. "That's it," Blackie said. "Get the hell out of here before I (mess) you up."[39]

The felon and former ballplayer died December 21, 1989. He was 63 years old. Just a few years earlier, Blackie said to a friend, with clear lament, "I really could have been someone."[40]

SOURCES

In addition to the sources cited in the Notes, the author consulted baseball-reference.com.

NOTES

1. Eric Stone, *Wrong Side of the Wall: The Life of Blackie Schwamb, the Greatest Prison Pitcher of All Time* (New York: Lyons Press, 2004), 29.
2. Stone, 18.
3. Stone, 33.
4. Stone, 53.
5. John Buntin, *L.A. Noir: The Struggle for the Soul of America's Most Seductive City* (New York: Harmony Books, 2009), 21.
6. Stone, 45.
7. Stone, 63.
8. Stone, 83.
9. Stone, 180.
10. Stone, 182.
11. Harry Mitauer, "Lund's Double Gives Browns Even Break," *St. Louis Globe-Democrat*, July 26, 1948: 17.
12. Robert Morrison, "Browns Gain 10-8 victory for Schwamb," *St. Louis Post-Dispatch*, August 1, 1948: 23.
13. Stone, 114.
14. "Early Touchdown, 9th-inning Safety Decide Night Game," *St. Louis Post-Dispatch*, August 5, 1948: 21.
15. Neal Russo, "Red Sox Rout Browns, 11-6, Boost Lead over Yanks to Two Lengths," *St Louis Post-Dispatch*, September 19, 1948: 57.
16. Glen L. Waller, "Red Sox Win, Gain Ground; Cardinals Bow 3 to 2," *St. Louis Globe-Democrat*, September 19, 1948: 48.
17. Stone, 122.
18. Stone, 122.
19. Buntin, 4.
20. Stone, 139.
21. Stone 158

22 Buntin, 9.
23 Buntin, 9.
24 "Schwamb Beats Death Penalty in Buge Slaying," *Long-Beach* (California) *Press-Telegram,* December 21, 1949: 19.
25 "Life Terms Given in Doctor's Murder," *Los Angeles Times*, December 24, 1949: 15.
26 Clifton T. Duffy as told to Dean Johnson, *The San Quentin Story* (New York: Greenwood Press, 1968), 9.
27 Duffy, 9.
28 Stone, 196.
29 Stone, 202.
30 Stone, 200.
31 Stone, 203.
32 "Chris Rich, Was He the Best Ever?," Sanquentinnews.com, Was He the Best Ever? (sanquentinnews.com).
33 Stone, 236.
34 Walter Judge, "San Quentin's Big Leaguer Leaves Prison," *San Francisco Examiner*, January 6, 1960: 50.
35 Stone, 86.
36 Stone, 259.
37 Stone 279.
38 Stone, 282.
39 Stone, X.
40 Stone, 283.

ATAHUALPO SEVERINO

BY LUIS BLANDÓN

Baseball and history are uncanny bedfellows in language, traditions, and mythology. The ties that bind. Sixteenth-century Peru and the modern Dominican Republic.

Atahualpa (ca. 1502-1533) was the last indigenous Inca emperor of Peru, whose capture and execution by Francisco Pizarro enabled the Spanish conquistadores to secure the Inca lands for the Spanish crown.[1] Vicente Valverde, a Dominican friar sent by the king to accompany Pizarro's expedition, pleaded with Atahualpa to convert to Catholicism and accept Spanish King Charles V as the Inca's sovereign ruler. He showed Atahualpa a Bible and asked him to read from the prayer book of his people. Atahualpa was unimpressed, throwing the sacred tome to the ground and shouting to his troops to prepare for battle.[2] Atahualpa was captured by the Spaniards, convicted of plotting against Pizarro, and executed by garrote on July 15, 1533. The Inca had no written language. So is the legend.[3]

Baseball's Atahualpa Severino was a career minor leaguer from the Dominican Republic, a left-hander who pitched in relief in six major-league games in an all-too-brief September 2011 call-up with the Washington Nationals. There is no legend around the achievements of baseball's Atahualpa, just perhaps individual memories. He was a lefty-throwing 5-foot-9 170-pounder with bright oval eyes. (With time and age, the weight increased to 220.)[4] His major-league career ledger stood out for its brevity. Severino evolved as one of the countless who had the dream, and succeeded early in his career in the minors to earn a brief visit to the majors. The taste of success devolved into bouncing around the minor-league landscape in the United States and Mexico.

Severino was born on November 6, 1984, in Cotuí (population 80,000), located in the fertile La Vega Real region on the Yuna River, where the November weather is a steady 85 to 90 degrees, endemic to tropical rain-forest climes. Cotuí is one of the oldest cities in the Western Hemisphere, founded in 1505. The Spanish colonists named it after the existing Taíno settlement. In the Inca language, the name Atahualpa means "bird of fortune."

Like almost all Dominicans, Cotuíans played baseball and several made it to the major leagues.[5] Severino was like any typical young Dominican boy. He had an affinity and talent for tossing the ball. He played the traditional street game of *vitilla*, the popular variation of stickball that evolved in the Dominican Republic. The rules are simple. A broomstick is a necessity. Two makeshift bases and a manhole cover as home plate with two or three fielders. A ball is hard to find. A bottle cap called "la vitilla" is used as the "ball." "Vitilla is good training in the Dominican, but it's different than baseball," Rafael Devers said.[6] The cap is hard to see and hit. Wilmer Difo said vitilla helped his development: "The vitilla isn't a ball," he said. "It moves many ways. It's hard to hit. To hit it, you really have to see well."[7] Cotuían life meant working in the bauxite and nickel mines, in the plantain, pineapple, or rice fields or in the tourist trade. If you showed talent and skill, baseball was a way out. Severino excelled and was spotted by local scouts.

Severino pitched in the minor leagues for the Expos/Nationals, Royals, Pirates, Braves, and Angels organizations from 2004 through 2015 and in Mexico and the Dominican Republic into the 2019 season. He was briefly called up twice by Washington. He did not appear in a game during a brief stay in 2010 and one in 2011. He was recalled for a third and final time from Syracuse on September 6, 2011. From the 6th through the 26th, Severino appeared in relief in six games. His major-league career totaled 4⅔ innings of pitching with a 3.86 ERA and seven strikeouts. And a career record of 1-0.

Back to beginnings. On February 13, 2004, the recently-turned 19-year-old Severino attended a tryout camp and was signed by Montreal Expos scouts Ismael Cruz and Dana Brown as an international free agent for a $6,000 bonus.[8] He became part of an organization that was in limbo with limited capital to spend on players and by 2005 relocated to Washington. He made his pro baseball debut with the Dominican Summer League Expos in the summer of 2004.[9] Severino suffered an injury that resulted in Tommy John ligament replacement surgery on September 8, performed by orthopedic surgeon Dr. Wiemi Douoguih.[10] He missed the 2005 season as he rehabbed.

The Nationals kept Severino with their Dominican Summer League affiliate for the 2006 season. He dominated the league with a 0.99 ERA and 0.77 WHIP in 45⅓ innings. Hitters batted a meager .121 against Severino and he averaged 15.7 strikeouts per nine innings. After three quality starts in the DSL to start the 2007 campaign, the Nationals promoted Severino to the rookie league Gulf Coast Nationals in 2007. In 13 games and five starts, he pitched well, with hitters batting a minuscule .208 against him.

Severino split the 2008 season first with the low Class-A Potomac Nationals (4-2), and then with the high Class-A Hagerstown Suns (0-4). He allowed

Atahualpa Severino with the Omaha Storm Chasers at Werner Park in Omaha on April 13, 2013. Courtesy of Minda Haas Kuhlmann.

four homers in 72 innings with a 4.00 ERA.[11] The Nationals were enamored with Severino's 95 MPH velocity with a propensity to be a groundball pitcher and a potential profile as a LOOGY specialist – a situational reliever who can get lefties out.[12] But as Severino went up the organizational ladder, the Nationals were increasingly troubled by his control.

A *Baseball America* 2009 scouting report on Severino said he threw at 89-94 MPH with a five-seam and two-seam fastballs with a groundball rate of around 50 percent. Improvement continued in 2009. He started the season with Potomac, going 4-0 with a 2.54 ERA in 29 games and earned a promotion to the Double-A Harrisburg Senators, where he was 6-0 in 15 games in relief with a 2.78 ERA. For the season, Severino had a career-high 15 saves. After the 2009 season the Nationals added Severino, fellow Dominican Juan Jaime, and Aaron Thompson to their 40-man roster to prevent them from being selected in the Rule 5 Draft.[13] Severino remained on the 40-man roster through August 6, 2012.

Coming into the 2010 season at the age of 25, Severino was projected as a sleeper major-league prospect. This expectation was evident when he was selected as one of the Nationals' top prospects whom the team hoped would pitch in the majors in 2010. He attended the Nationals' Rookie Career Development Program along with pitchers Drew Storen and Thompson and second baseman Danny Espinosa. (The team's top pitching prospect, Stephen Strasburg, was excused from attending because he had just got married.[14]) Severino was reassigned to Triple-A Syracuse in spring training. According to the *Washington Post*, "several members of the Washington's front office believe he can contribute out of the Nationals' bullpen this season."[15]

Severino was 4-2 at Syracuse with one save and a 3.55 ERA in 40 games when the call came from the Nationals on July 29, 2010. He was called up when Nationals closer Matt Capps was traded to Minnesota and pitcher Yuniesky Maya was optioned to Syracuse. Severino put on a uniform but did not get into a game, spending three days in the big leagues before being sent back to Syracuse in favor of outfielder Justin Maxwell. Completing the season in Syracuse, he tied Jason Bergmann for the team lead with six relief wins and led the team with 54 appearances. Hitters batted .212 against him, and Severino allowed only one homer when facing left-handed batters.

By the 2011 season, Nationals scouts' opinions of Severino evolved: They now saw him as a middle-inning relief pitcher who could help take some of the workload off the rest of the bullpen. In its end-of-2010 analysis of the Nationals, *Baseball Prospectus* saw the side-arming Severino as a "sleeper" major-league prospect. However, as he progressed through the system, Severino had mounting control problems. There were concerning questions as "his peripherals failed to impress and his splits show he won't be a LOOGY" as the Nationals envisioned.[16] The profile on Severino showed an 89-95-MPH fastball and inconsistent control.

Not making the team in spring training, Severino started the 2011 season with Syracuse, pitching in 35 games in the role of a situational lefty. When called up in September, he had a 4.50 ERA with 38 strikeouts, averaging 10.68 K's per 9 innings; 28 of his game appearances with the Chiefs were scoreless. However, he had 23 walks in 32 innings of pitching.

In his physical appearance, Severino was viewed as "a short guy with a big but erratic arm."[17] In his scouting analysis of Severino for his *FanSided* blog, Aaron Somers described Severino with a touch of realism: "While he's just 5'9", Severino operates with a very high arm slot that gives his fastball explosive late life up in the zone. He works at 91-96 mph, and constantly is trying to climb the ladder with the pitch"[18] Somers concluded that Severino was a pitcher with a good fastball, but that because of his habit of missing his target and throwing outside the strike zone, "[O]nly 34.9% of his pitches were in the zone, one of the lowest rates in baseball, as he's constantly throwing the fastball too high and the slider too far outside.... Imagine Aroldis Chapman's 2011 with slightly less velocity, and slightly fewer strikeouts and walks, in fewer innings – that's what Severino's upside is. He could be a nice asset if put in situations he can succeed in."[19]

The Nationals recalled Severino on July 30, 2011. He did not get into a game, and was optioned back to Syracuse on August 2. On September 6, he was brought back as a September call-up. He wore uniform number 59. His base salary was $414,000. When Severino was recalled, manager Davey Johnson planned to use him in the middle relief role. He made his major-league debut that evening. From his six appearances, *Washington Post* writer Thomas Boswell saw Severino as part of the 2012 bullpen mix intrigued with his 95 mph fastball and situational possibilities.[20]

Severino's September 2011 voyage in the major leagues:

September 6, vs. Los Angeles Dodgers:

Severino made his major-league debut at Nationals Park. He was one of five Nationals who made their major-league debut that season. The game was highlighted by Stephen Strasburg's return from Tommy John surgery, making his first start in 382 days, and pitching five scoreless innings. Severino came into the game in the seventh inning and faced one batter, James Loney, with two outs and Dee Strange-Gordon on first via a single. On a 1-and-1 count, Gordon stole second. Severino struck out Loney swinging on a 3-and-2 count. Two other Nationals made their debut as well: Corey Brown and Stephen Lombardozzi.

September 10, vs. Houston Astros:

With the score 8-3 in visiting Houston's favor, Severino entered in the top of the eighth inning. The second and fourth batters he faced, Jason Michaels and Jason Bourgeois, each singled. Severino struck out Carlos Corporán and Jordan Schafer swinging. He induced J.D. Martinez to pop out to Ian Desmond at shortstop to end the rally. The Astros won 9-3.

September 13, vs. New York Mets:

With one out and a Mets runner on first, Severino replaced Craig Stammen in the seventh and faced one batter, Lucas Duda, in a lefty/lefty matchup. Duda fouled out to first. Washington won, 3-2.

September 21, vs. Philadelphia Phillies:

With Nationals ahead 7-3, Severino was summoned to start the bottom of the eighth. He faced three batters and gave up the first runs charged to his record. He walked Chase Utley, then John Mayberry hit a home run. Raúl Ibañez struck out swinging. Severino was then pulled in favor of Coffey. The Nationals won 7-5.

September 23, vs. Atlanta Braves:

On September 23 at home, Severino came into the game in the fifth after Collin Balester, in relief of Strasburg, gave up one run and left two men in scoring position to widen the Atlanta lead to 4-1. Severino faced Brian McCann. On a full count, Severino allowed the two inherited runners to score when McCann doubled to deep right-center for a 6-1 Braves lead. Severino then induced Freddie Freeman to ground out to second and struck out Jack Wilson swinging. He also pitched the sixth inning, facing three batters yielding only a single to Jason Heyward, who was doubled up on a Tim Hudson weak groundball. At 1⅔ innings, it was longest outing of Severino's major-league career. The Braves won 7-4.

September 26, vs. Florida Marlins:

Playing under wet conditions in Miami and with Florida ahead 4-3, Severino entered the game in the bottom of the eighth, finishing the inning scoreless with two strikeouts. In the top of the ninth with two runners on base, Nationals cleanup hitter Michael Morse connected with on a 89-mph splitter from Marlins reliever Edwin Mujica and the ball flew "over the scoreboard and rattled around the seats."[21] Severino got the win, his only major-league decision. Unbeknownst to Severino his big-league career was over.

The 27-year-old Severino was no longer considered a prospect as spring training commenced in 2012. Younger arms were moving ahead of him. He was now seen as organizational depth in the minors. He came into 2012 spring training on the 40-man roster believing he had an opportunity to make the Nationals given his six appearances in 2011. Severino was a long shot to make the Nationals' bullpen for 2012, who had three bullpen spots earmarked for three other lefties, Tom Gorzelanny, Ross Detwiler, and Sean Burnett. Caught up in a numbers game and pitching ineffectively, Severino was optioned to Syracuse at the end of spring training on March 29.

The Nationals designated Severino for assignment on August 6, 2012, to make room on the 40-man roster for the recently acquired infielder César Izturis. Clearing waivers, Severino was outrighted to Syracuse. The signs were apparent that his career with the Nationals organization was ending. At the time he was waived, Severino was battling with control issues.

At age 28 after the 2012 campaign, Severino was one of the dwindling number of former Expos and one of the few Latinos in the Nationals organization. Though he pitched to a 3-0 record and a 2.81 ERA with three saves, he struggled with his control, walking 36 batters in 48 innings.[22]

The *Washington Post's* James Wagner observed "While [Severino] had the ability to strike out batters, Severino struggled allowing too many walks and hits."[23]

The Nationals let him become a free agent on November 3. Being a lefty situational reliever meant that teams with a need for help in the bullpen might take a flyer on him. What followed was a series of minor-league deals with invitations to major-league camps. For the next three seasons, Severino signed with three organizations with nonroster invites in minor-league contracts. He was a minimal investment.

Severino signed a minor-league deal with the Kansas City Royals on November 14, 2012. At the conclusion of camp, the Royals assigned him to their Triple-A team, the Omaha Storm Chasers, where he made six appearances, allowing three earned runs over nine innings.

On May 31, 2013, the Royals sent Severino to the Pittsburgh Pirates for cash considerations. The Pirates assigned him to Triple-A Indianapolis; for Pittsburgh, Severino represented depth in Triple A. With Omaha and Indianapolis, Severino posted a 3.60 ERA in 39 games (two starts) with 58 strikeouts and 19 walks in 55 innings. Severino dominated against left-handed batters, holding them to a .171 batting average. Nonetheless, the Pirates saw no future for him, letting him go after the season.

On December 18, 2013, Severino signed a minor-league deal with Atlanta as a nonroster invitee to compete for an available left-hander relief slot. He struggled in spring training. Braves manager Fredi González made it clear that he would carry only one left-hander out of the bullpen because righty Jordan Walden had better splits against left-handed batters.[24] Severino spent the 2014 season with Triple-A Gwinnett. The pattern continued as the Braves released him after the season.

Severino's next attempted path back to the majors saw him sign a minor-league deal with the Los Angeles Angels of Anaheim for 2015. He was 30 years old, having spent nine seasons in the minors. He had pitched effectively with Gwinnett with a 3.22 ERA and 1.18 WHIP in 40 appearances, mostly situational. Whatever chance he had to make the Angels' major-league roster were further diminished by his arrival at camp two weeks late because of visa issues in the Dominican Republic.

On March 16 the Angels sent Severino to the Triple-A Salt Lake City Bees. He pitched ineffectively. Severino's 26th game of the season and last game in the minors was a forgettable and brief outing in a 17-0 beatdown by the Fresno Grizzlies on June 14. It was the worst shutout defeat in Bees' history; they surrendered 27 hits in the loss. Relieving Bees starting pitcher Alex Sanabia (5 runs, 10 hits) in the fifth inning, Severino was ineffective, giving up four runs on four hits in an inning of work.[25] He was released two days later.[26] No other major-league organization needing pitching depth in the minors reached out. It was over for him the United States.

Severino pitched in 2016 for the Sultanes de Monterrey of the Mexican Baseball League. He was a free agent after the season. He sat out the 2017 season, playing winter ball in Mexico. He signed with the Diablos Rojos del Mexico on December 7, 2017, but was released on April 8, 2018. Five days later the Sultanes brought Severino back, then on June 17 traded him to the Tigres de Quinta Roo, who released him on July 27 after he pitched in seven games to a 13.50 ERA and a 0-2 record.

Dominican winter ball was always a constant for Severino for 10 seasons. He started two games for the Gigantes del Cibao in 2006-07. He pitched for the Tigres del Licey from 2009 through 2019 except for the 2016-17, when he pitched for the Navegantes del Magallanes of the Venezuelan Winter League, and 2017-18 when he pitched for Aguilas de Mexicali of the Mexican Winter League.

His last professional game was played far away from Washington, D.C. On October 23, 2018, Severino signed with Tigres del Licey in the Dominican Republic for the 2018-19 season. On November 20, Licey placed him on the reserve list, then put him the active roster on December 11. He pitched in two games. In 1⅓ innings, he gave up three runs on four hits. Licey released the 33-year-old Severino on December 16, 2018.

Severino was selected to the champion Dominican Republic national team in the 2013 World Baseball Classic, appearing in three games in relief. He was selected for the Dominican national team in the 2019 Pan American Games.

In 13 professional seasons at all levels and in all countries, Severino was a durable matchup reliever. According to Baseball-Reference.com, he appeared in 662 games (18 starts) with 25 saves and a 3.41 ERA. His record was 47-29. For six games, Severino was a major-league pitcher. Severino's time with the Nationals was so fleeting and nondescript that longtime Nationals beat writer Mark Zuckerman noted, "[I]f you blinked, you might have missed … Severino's time here."[27] Severino did make it to the majors, no matter the longevity of his stay. The odds were against him to even make it to "The Show," but Severino defeated the odds to achieve his major-league dream.

SOURCES

In addition to the sources cited in the Notes, the author consulted baseball-reference.com, retrosheet.org, mlb.com, Baseball America, Fangraphs, and the Kansas City Royals and the Washington Nationals websites.

NOTES

1. Ataphualpa pronunciation: \ah-tuh-WAHL-puh seh-ver-EE-noh\.
2. Kim MacQuarrie, *The Last Days of the Incas* (New York: Simon & Schuster, 2007), 76-85.
3. Ataphualpa is revered figure in Peruvian history and culture and throughout Spanish-speaking Latin America as a heroic and inspirational character.
4. *2010, 2011,* and *2012 Washington Nationals Media Guides.*
5. Cotui is also the hometown of major leaguers Pedro Liriano, Rafael Roque, Duaner Sánchez, José Capellán, and Teoscar Hernández.
6. James Wagner, "Dominican Players Sharpen Their Skills with a Broomstick and Bottle Cap," *New York Times*, October 7, 2017: Section SP, 1.
7. Wagner.
8. As of June 1, 2022, Ismael Cruz was in his sixth season as the Dodgers' vice president of international scouting. See https://www.mlb.com/dodgers/team/front-office/ismael-cruz. Starting in 2002 Cruz was the Expos' director of international scouting and development, and served until 2005 with the Nationals. Dana Brown was the director of scouting for the Expos/Nationals for eight seasons, from 2002-09. As of 2022 he was vice president, scouting for the Atlanta Braves, overseeing the team's amateur scouting process.
9. Severino appeared in 15 games, starting four. He went 2-5 with an ERA of 4.46 in 38⅓ innings pitched.
10. *2012 Washington Nationals Media Guide,*122. See https://www.medstarhealth.org/doctors/wiemi-abell-douoguih-md, accessed May 1, 2022.
11. *2012 Washington Nationals Media Guide.*
12. "LOOGY" is an acronym for "Left-Handed One Out Guy."
13. Dave Sheinin, "Three Added to 40-Man Roster, but Not Reliever Wilkie," *Washington Post*, November 20, 2009: D2.
14. David Sheinin, "Nationals Journal: Just Married: Strasburg Tied the Knot Two Weeks Ago," *Washington Post* January 12, 2010: D2.
15. Adam Kilgore, "Nationals Journal: Villone Released: Balester Reassigned," *Washington Post*, March 16, 2010: D5.
16. Kevin Goldstein, "Future Shock – Top 11 Review – NL East," *Baseball Prospectus*: October 8, 2010. See https://www.baseballprospectus.com/prospects/article/12182/future-shock-top-11-review-nl-east/, accessed April 6, 2022.
17. Aaron Somers, "The Stuff that Dreams Are Made of: Atahualpa Severino," *FanSided's Calltothepen.com*, November 1, 2011. See https://calltothepen.com/2011/11/01/the-stuff-that-dreams-are-made-of-atahualpa-severino/, accessed April 6, 2022.
18. Somers.
19. Somers.
20. Thomas Boswell, "For Nationals, Third Place Would Be a Great Place to Start," *Washington Post*, September 15, 2011: D5.
21. Adam Kilgore, "Morse's Blast in Ninth Rallies Washington," *Washington Post,* September 27, 2011: D3.

22 Patrick Reddington, "Will Sean Burnett Be a Part of the 2013 Washington Nationals Bullpen," *SB Nation Federal Baseball,* November 24, 2012. See: https://www.federalbaseball.com/2012/11/24/3687098/will-sean-burnett-be-a-part-of-the-2013-washington-nationals-bullpen, accessed March 22, 2022.

23 James Wagner, "Nationals Journal: Another Connection to Team's Past Moves On," *Washington Post*, November 22, 2012: D2.

24 David O'Brien, "Braves Undecided on Matter of 2nd Lefty Reliever," *Atlanta Journal-Constitution*, February 21, 2014. See https://www.ajc.com/sports/baseball/braves-undecided-matter-2nd-lefty-reliever/OkszWp1a5tL20Mq6LTNaPN/, accessed March 11, 2022.

25 Vincent Peña, "PCL: Fresno Demolishes Salt Lake, 17-0," *Salt Lake Tribune* (Salt Lake City, Utah), June 14, 2015.

26 Severino had a 8.44 ERA in 26⅔ innings in 26 relief appearances.

27 Mark Zuckerman, "All the Ballplayers Whose Careers ended in D.C.," masnsports.com, January 2, 2021. See https://www.masnsports.com/nationals-pastime/2021/01/all-the-ballplayers-whose-careers-ended-in-dc.html, accessed May 15, 2022.

JOE STRONG

BY JOE SCHUSTER

Joe Strong's journey to the major leagues resembled one of those animated maps in old adventure movies, the sort with lines and arrows madly crisscrossing the world. His 16-year trek took him through seven US cities and five different countries on two continents. When he finally toed the rubber in a major-league game – on May 11, 2000, at the age of 37 years and 245 days – he became one of the oldest players ever to make his major-league debut.

Strong – in his prime a 6-foot, 200-pound right-hander – was born Joseph Benjamin Strong IV on September 9, 1962, in Fairfield, California, the son of Joseph B. Strong III, a baker, and Mandy Lou (Blount) Strong, who at one point worked for an ambulance company; census records show that Strong's parents divorced in 1971. His mother died in 1994.[1] His father died in 2008.[2]

Growing up, Strong was extremely active in sports, playing Little League and Pony League baseball. At St. Patrick's High School in Vallejo, California (now St. Patrick – St. Vincent High School), he played three sports, baseball, basketball, and football. After graduating in 1981, he spent two years at Contra Costa College, where he played baseball and was second-team Camino Norte all-league in 1982.[3] The next season, he earned first-team all-league honors, when he was 8-4 with a 2.29 ERA, on a team that went 14-16-1.[4] The following year, 1984, he enrolled at the University of California-Riverside, then an NCAA Division II school in the California Collegiate Athletic Association, and was one of two players on the team to earn All-Conference honors.

In the June draft that year, on the recommendation of scout Dick Weincek, the Oakland A's chose Strong in the 15th round, the 376th pick overall, and assigned him to Medford in the Class-A Northwest League. Managed by Dennis Rogers, the team was the defending league champion. Strong made his professional debut on June 21, pitching the ninth inning of a 6-0 win over the Bend Phillies. He recorded his first professional win on July 4, when he came into a tie game against the Bellingham Mariners in the seventh inning and threw three shutout frames while Medford was scoring three runs.[5] In all, he appeared in 20 games that season (nine as a starter) and ended with a 5-6 record, a 3.88 ERA, and 66 strikeouts against 36 walks in 72 innings. Medford ended up winning its division but lost the one-game league championship game to the Tri-Cities Triplets of the Texas Rangers organization.

Strong spent two more seasons in the Oakland system, principally as a reliever. In 1985 he was at Modesto in the Class-A California League on a team that featured, among other future major leaguers, several players who would be key pieces of Oakland's 1989 World Series champions, including Mark McGwire, Mike Gallego, and Walt Weiss. Appearing in 42 games – second most among the team's pitcher's – Strong went 7-7 with a 5.06 ERA and 82 strikeouts in 110⅓ innings. He started the

319

1986 season back at Modesto, but in August, after he'd put up a 2-2 record with a 3.42 ERA in 36 games (all in relief), the A's promoted him to Huntsville of the Double-A Southern League, where he appeared in six games in relief, finishing at 1-1 with a 5.40 ERA. At the end of the season, Oakland released him.

For 1987, Strong went to spring training with the independent league San Bernardino Spirit, but while he initially made the roster, in early April the Spirit released him before Opening Day.[6]

He spent that year in Seattle, staying in shape playing ball in a semipro beer league.[7] The following season, Strong latched on with the Reno Silver Sox, an independent co-op team in the Class-A California League, "assembled at nearly the last minute with a combination of unwanted free agents and castoffs from major league organizations."[8] Managed by one-time major-league infielder Nate Oliver, the team came about after the San Diego Padres ended an 11-season affiliation in Reno at the end of the previous season, and a nonprofit organization, the Washoe Youth Foundation, decided to try to keep professional baseball in the city.[9] To help fill its roster, the Silver Sox held a tryout camp on March 12-13, which drew 80 hopeful players, including Strong. Less than three weeks later – on April 8 – he got the nod as starting pitcher for the team's opener, on the road against the Fresno Suns, and went 5⅓ innings, allowing four runs on six hits and two walks, leaving with the game tied at 4-4, on the way to a Reno 7-4 loss. Reno finished the season a league-worst 39-103. As for Strong, who made the California League All-Star team – he appeared in 31 games (24 as a starter) and finished 4-13, with a 4.79 ERA and 107 strikeouts in a team-leading 161⅔ innings.

Strong was back with Reno for 1989, where new manager Eli Grba used him exclusively in relief. He appeared in 53 games, compiling an 8-1 record and 18 saves (second best in the league), with a 3.58 ERA, and 79 strikeouts in 73 innings, earning yet another selection to the California League All-Star team.

For the next three seasons, Strong played in Taiwan, for the Wei Chuan Dragons of the Chinese Professional Baseball League (CPBL), where he was one of the circuit's top pitchers. In 1990 his 1.92 ERA led the league, while his 16 wins ranked second. The following year, he tied for the league lead in victories, with 15, and ranked fifth in strikeouts (116). In 1992 he tied for the league lead in strikeouts (131) and ranked in the top 10 in wins (12) and ERA (3.15).

In November 1992 Strong and a team of CPBL All-Stars faced a traveling contingent of San Diego Padres minor leaguers in an exhibition game; after Strong held his opponents to six hits, the Padres asked him to spring training as a nonroster invitee and afterward signed him to a contract and assigned him to the Las Vegas Stars in the Pacific Coast League. Reportedly the team wanted him to get his arm in condition for long relief.[10] Just as he had reached his highest level of professional ball to that point, however, he developed a sore elbow. In July, when he stood 1-3 with a 5.67 ERA, the Padres sent him on a two-week rehab assignment to the Rancho Cucamonga Quakes of the California League, where, in 10 innings over seven relief appearances, he went 1-0 with a 2.70 ERA and 13 strikeouts. When he finished that assignment, he closed out the season at Wichita of the Double-A Texas League, where in four games (three as a starter), he went 1-0 with a 6.75 ERA; his sole victory came in six innings of one-hit, shutout ball.

When the season ended, Strong decided to return to Wei Chuan, along with a friend and former teammate, Milt Harper, with whom Strong had played at both Reno in 1989 and Wei Chuan in 1991. But on the day they planned to sign their contracts, Harper died in a fall from a 14th-floor window of his apartment building in what was initially ruled a suicide; police later suspected homicide, and investigated the building owner (also a teammate of Harper's and Strong's), but he was later cleared. Police were unable to discover the cause of the fall.

Strong came home, where, a sportswriter later noted, he struggled for two months with survivor's guilt over his friend's death before finally deciding to return to baseball in some fashion, saying he would dedicate his season to Harper's memory.[11] He landed back in the California League, with the independent San Bernardino Spirit, for whom he was the Opening Day starter, as well as the starter for the home opener, going five innings in each game, although he didn't gain a decision in either game. In the third inning of his third start, he had to leave the game when he injured his arm.[12] After missing six weeks, he returned in mid-June but in July suffered another injury that led to his missing the remainder of the season. At the time, he and the team were talking with a club in Taiwan about their acquiring Strong's contract, but because of the persistence of the injury, that never came to pass.[13]

For 1995, Strong appeared set to pitch for the Sonoma County Crushers of the Western League but instead took an opportunity to join the Chicago Cubs as a replacement player during the Major League Players Association strike that year.[14] Details of his performance during spring training appear scarce – the writer found only one reference to an appearance in a Cactus League game, on March 24, when he allowed three runs on three hits in two innings against the California Angels.[15] However, he clearly impressed the Cubs sufficiently that as late as March 29 – four days before the season was scheduled to begin – Chicago cited him as a key piece of their bullpen, assuming the strike remained unresolved.[16] However, two days later, the strike was over and Strong ended up playing with the independent Surrey Glaciers, also of the Western League. Hurling 131 innings for a team that finished next to last, he had a stellar season, making the All-Star team and posting an 8-9 record that concealed his effectiveness; his 2.75 ERA ranked fourth among hurlers with at least 70 innings pitched, and his 129 strikeouts tied for second best.

Surrey folded after that season, and in a reassignment draft of Glaciers players, the rights to Strong's contract went to the Grays Harbor Gulls of Aberdeen, Washington.[17] Strong, however, ended up back overseas, pitching for the China Times of the Chinese Professional Baseball League, where he went 4-4 with a 4.00 ERA in 11 starts.

In 1997, at the age of 34, Strong temporarily left baseball to work in a Seattle Sears warehouse as a forklift operator. He kept in shape by lifting weights "stone-cold hard" and playing catch in the aisles; by the time the year was up, his fastball was in the mid-90s.[18]

He decided to give baseball yet another shot, and for 1998 was back in Asia, pitching for the Hyundai Unicorns (Korean Baseball Organization), going 6-5 in 65 innings, with a 2.95 ERA and 54 strikeouts. The next year, he latched on with the Tampa Bay Devil Rays organization, splitting time between three teams, the Triple-A Durham Bulls, the Double-A Orlando Rays, and the Mexico City Tigers of the Mexican League (on loan from the Tampa Bay organization). His combined record was 2-6, with a 6.00 ERA and 56 strikeouts in 66 innings. At the end of the year, Tampa Bay released him, but Strong persisted, pitching for the Obregon Yaquis in the Mexican Winter League.

There, he ran into Tim Schmidt, a former coach at California-Riverside, who was then working as a scout for the Florida Marlins. As Schmidt later recounted, in a brief pregame chat, Strong told him that he was throwing in the mid-90s, a fact that Schmidt doubted, telling him, "Come on. I coached you."[19] However, when Strong later got into the game in relief, Schmidt took notice: "The first pitch was 94 MPH. Next one was 95, then 96. I'm the only scout in the stands, and I'm sitting there thinking, 'God almighty.'"[20]

Schmidt recommended Strong to the Marlins, who signed him and sent him to the Calgary Cannons of the Pacific Coast League, where Strong had immediate impact, coming in as a reliever on Opening Day, entering the game in the seventh inning after starter Jason Grilli had no-hit the Las Vegas Stars through six. Strong pushed the no-hitter into the ninth, throwing two perfect innings, striking out two.[21] (The no-hitter came to an end in the ninth when reliever Ryan Creek allowed three runs on two hits and two walks, but closed out the 7-3 victory.)

On May 11, with Strong at 1-1 with three saves, a 4.67 ERA and 19 strikeouts over 17⅓ innings in 10 games, the Marlins (who had two injured hurlers) called him up to the major leagues.[22] Wearing number 50, he made his debut that same day, at home against Atlanta, coming on with two outs in the seventh inning, with a runner on second and the Marlins leading 5-4. Coincidentally, he was relieving Grilli, who had made his debut that same day as the starter. The first batter Strong faced was one-time All-Star Wally Joyner, who was just shy of three months older than Strong, but in his 15th major-league season. On a 3-and-2 pitch, Joyner flied out to short left field to end the inning. Strong went one more inning, walking Quilvio Veras leading off the eighth, but then inducing Andruw Jones to ground into a double play before closing out the inning on a groundout by Chipper Jones.

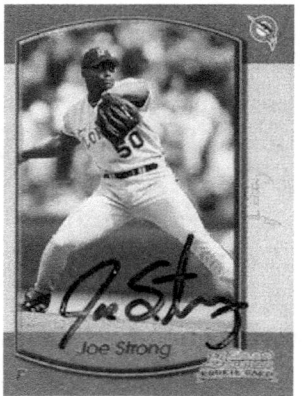

Joe Strong with the 2000 Marlins. Courtesy The Topps Company, Inc.

With the game, he became the oldest player in 40 years to make his debut, since the Pirates' Diomedes Olivo made his initial appearance in the major leagues at age 41 in 1960. As of 2022, Strong was the 32nd oldest player to make his debut in the major leagues.

Initially, Strong seemed nearly untouchable: Over four appearances during his first week, he pitched 3⅔ scoreless innings, allowing only two hits and three walks but no runs, recording his first strikeout (of the Padres Damian Jackson in a 6-2 Marlins loss on May 18).

Then he showed that he was not, after all, invincible. In his fifth game, in 2⅓ innings on May 20 against the Los Angeles Dodgers, he surrendered four runs on two hits and two walks, including a Gary Sheffield grand slam. In that game, he also had his first major-league plate appearance, when he struck out against Carlos Pérez in the sixth inning. On May 25, with his ERA at 5.63, the Marlins sent him back to Calgary.

Strong vowed to return, saying, "I know I'll be back. It's like giving a dog his first taste of meat or giving a vampire his first taste of blood."[23]

A week later, he was back, when reliever Dan Miceli went on the disabled list; Strong was effective in his first three appearances after returning, allowing only one run on three hits and three walks over six innings, while striking out six. On June 13 he marked his first major-league decision, a loss, against Philadelphia, when he came on in the seventh inning with the Marlins leading 2-1 and gave up three runs on three hits in a third of an inning.

However, he bounced back, earning his first major-league save four days later when he recorded the final out in a Marlins 4-3 road victory against Pittsburgh, striking out Jason Kendall with runners on first and third in the bottom of the 11th.

A week later, on June 24, Strong earned his first major-league win, when he came into a home game against the Chicago Cubs with two outs and a runner on first in the top of the eighth with the Marlins trailing 3-2. He gave up a run-scoring double to the first hitter he faced, José Nieves, but then retired Glenallen Hill on a groundout to end the inning. In the bottom of the eighth, the Marlins scored five runs, and when reliever Antonio Alfonseca retired the Cubs in order in the ninth, Strong had his victory.

After that, however, Strong saw little action over the next three weeks, managing only three appearances between his win and July 16, and his rustiness showed, as he gave up six runs on eight hits and two walks in 2⅓ innings, pushing his season's ERA to 7.58. On July 19, when Miceli came off the disabled list, the Marlins sent Strong back to Calgary. He faulted himself: "I probably should have thrown more often between games I pitched. I spent a lot of time sitting in the bullpen watching the game instead of throwing."[24]

Strong returned to the Marlins when the team expanded its roster in September, and appeared in one more game that year, throwing a scoreless two-thirds of an inning against Houston on September 5. His final stats for his major-league season: 18 games, 19⅔ innings, 26 hits, 16 runs (all earned), 12 walks, and 18 strikeouts, with a record of 1-1 with one save, and a 7.32 ERA. For Calgary, he appeared in 29 games, throwing 44⅔ innings, allowing 21 runs (all but one earned), on 44 hits and 20 walks, with 33 strikeouts, with a 2-1 record with nine saves, and a 4.03 ERA.

Strong went to spring training with the Marlins in 2001, but the team ended up sending him to Calgary among its final roster moves just before the start of the season. Florida ended up recalling him less than two weeks later, and he appeared in four games in April, pitching effectively, allowing only a single earned run on three hits and three walks in six innings, with four strikeouts. Despite that, the team sent him back to Calgary on May 6 to make room on the roster for starter A.J. Burnett, who was coming off the disabled list.

That marked the end of Strong's major-league tenure. His final numbers: 23 games, 26⅓ innings pitched, a 1-1 record, with one save, and a 5.81 ERA, with 22 strikeouts and 15 walks. His final strikeout came in his next-to-last game, on April 23, against Arizona, when he fanned Matt Williams. That game also saw his second, and last, career plate appearance in the major leagues, when he struck out against Randy Johnson in the sixth inning.

Strong finished the season with Calgary, going 6-3 in 59 innings over 46 games, with 48 strikeouts and 18 walks, and a 6.25 ERA. In October the Marlins made him a free-agent and the latched on with the Milwaukee Brewers organization just before the 2002 season. They sent him to Indianapolis of the International League. However, on June 6, after Strong had appeared in 19⅓ innings over 15 games, with a record of 0-0 and one save, and an ERA of 4.19, the team released him. He finished out the season with the Bridgeport of the independent Atlantic League, where he went 7-0 with a 1.04 ERA in 34⅔ innings over 30 games, recording 35 strikeouts against 14 walks.

Strong's professional career lasted two more seasons. In 2003 he pitched for Reynoso in the Mexican League, compiling a 6-4 record with a 2.71 ERA, throwing 66⅓ innings 46 games, and recording 44 strikeouts against 28 walks. In 2004, he closed out his professional career 20 years after it began, with the Camden Riversharks of the independent Atlantic League, where he was the team's closer, finishing second in the league with 15 saves, while going 3-0 with a 2.20 ERA.

After leaving professional ball, Strong worked as a coach and instructor. In late 2022 he was listed as the principal owner of Evergreen Sport Center of Federal Way, Washington.

SOURCES

In addition to sources cited in the Notes, the author consulted ancestry.com, baseball-reference.com, retrosheet.org, and sabr.org/bioproject.

NOTES

1   "Mandy L. Strong-Satcherwhite: Highland Resident," *San Bernardino County* (California) *Sun*, November 29, 1994: 21.

2   Joseph Benjamin Strong III Obituary, https://www.legacy.com/us/obituaries/timesheraldonline/name/joseph-strong-obituary?id=23230062. Accessed April 27, 2022.

3   "For the Record," *Sacramento Bee*, May 18, 1982: C4.

4   "Cubs Named to All-CNC Baseball," *Santa Rosa* (California) *Press Democrat*, June 1, 1983: 4D.

5   "Spokane Loses in 17-innings," *Tri-City Herald* (Kennewick, Washington), July 5, 1984: 26.

6   David Bristow, "Four Players Join Spirit; 2 Others Cut," *San Bernardino County Sun*, April 6, 1987: C7.

7   Mike Berardino, "Strong Commitment," *South Florida Sun Sentinel* (Fort Lauderdale, Florida), May 16, 2000: 6C.

8   John Schumacher, "And on the Eighth Day, the Reno Silver Sox Won," *Reno Gazette-Journal,* April 17, 1988: 3B.

9   Don Cox, "Silver Sox Open Season in Fresno," *Reno Gazette-Journal,* April 8, 1988: 19.

10 Doug Padilla, "Playing in Pain," *San Bernardino County Sun,* April 12, 1994: 12.

11 Padilla, "Playing in Pain."

12 Pete Marshall, "Spirit Gets the Hits, Quakes Get the Win." *San Bernardino County Sun,* April 18, 1994: C2.

13 Doug Padilla, "Cervantes Good Night Almost Lost in 8-4 Loss," *San Bernardino County Sun,* August 26, 1994: C2.

14 Dave Williams, "Crushers Name Coaches," *Santa Rosa Press Democrat,* March 9, 1995:C5.

15 "Baseball," *Naples* (Florida) *Daily News,* March 25, 1995: 2C.

16 Joseph Reaves, "Cubs Rotation All 'Right,' but Bullpen a Big Concern," *Chicago Tribune,* March 29, 1995: 4-3.

17 Jeff Morrow, "Posse Picks Up Two Players from Surrey in Dispersal Draft," *Tri-City Herald,* January 9, 1996: C3.

18 Israel Gutierez, "Dad Enjoys Improbable Journey," *Palm Beach Post,* May 14, 2000: 43.

19 Berardino, "Strong Commitment."

20 Berardino.

21 Fred Collins, "Grilli Takes Twinkle Out of Stars," *Calgary Herald,* April 8, 2000: F-1.

22 Joe Capozzi, "Marlins Make Pitching Moves," *Palm Beach Post,* May 12, 2000: 5C.

23 "What's Up in Sports," *Louisville Courier-Journal,* May 27, 2000: E-2.

24 Chuck Otterson, "Miceli's Return Exiles Strong," *Palm Beach Post,* July 20, 2000: 5C.

DENNIS TANKERSLEY

BY GERARD KWILECKI

Right-hander Dennis Tankersley took the mound at Miller Park in Milwaukee on May 26, 2002, in search of his first major-league victory. It was a cool 69 degrees and the wind was whipping at 14 mph. The 6-foot-2 right-hander had started three previous games for the San Diego Padres, getting three no-decisions. But on this day, Tankersley earned his only major-league win and hit a home run to boot.

Dennis Lee Tankersley Jr., was born on February 24, 1979, in Troy, Missouri. His father, Dennis Sr., known as "Big D," was a standout in baseball, football, and basketball. Dennis Sr. married his high school sweetheart, Brenda, and they had two children – Dennis Jr. and Nicole. Dennis Sr. worked as a construction drywall hauler and his mother was an office manager for an electronic material company. Big D died in March 2020.

In an email interview, Dennis wrote, "I had a great childhood. Somewhat of a small-town feel. My days were filled with sports. It was football, basketball, and baseball daily."[1] Dennis grew up in St. Charles, Missouri, and attended St. Charles High School. He was a standout pitcher and hitter for the St. Charles Pirates. He had 77 hits, 22 doubles, 10 home runs, and 60 RBIs during his three-year varsity career. As a pitcher in his junior and senior seasons, he won 15 games and struck out 224 batters. He was drafted in the 38th round of the 1997 draft by the Boston Red Sox. He did not sign and instead went to Merrimack College in North Andover, Massachusetts. The next year the Red Sox again selected Tankersley in the 38th round. This time he agreed, signing a Red Sox contract with scout Steve McCallister.

Tankersley spent his first professional season in 1999 with the Red Sox' rookie Gulf Coast League team in Florida. With a 5-3 record for the low Class-A Augusta GreenJackets in 2000, he was traded to the San Diego Padres on June 30 along with a fellow minor leaguer for veteran infielder Ed Sprague. In 2001 *Baseball America* in its *Prospect Handbook* listed Tankersley as the Padres' number-nine prospect. "Tankersley's out pitch is a two-seam fastball that arrives at 91-92 mph and dives towards the plate," the publication wrote.[2] The Padres sent their newly acquired pitcher to Fort Wayne of the low Class-A Midwest League, where he was 5-2. He split the 2001 season with high-A Lake Elsinore, Double-A Mobile, and Triple-A Portland. He was impressing the Padres scouts with his strikeouts.[3] He was deemed ready to break into the major leagues in 2002.

After Tankersley's impressive 2001 campaign *Baseball America* jumped him to the number-two prospect in the Padres' system. He was listed in the top 20 prospects in all of baseball. Its scouting report noted that "hitters can't sit on his fastball because he has a mid-80s slider that was rated the best breaking ball in the Cal League."[4]

Tankersley was pitching for Double-A Mobile when on May 10, 2002, when he was promoted to the Padres. He didn't have to wait long to make his debut. He took the mound that day in Atlanta facing the Braves. Tankersley quickly recorded his first major-league strikeout, dispatching Gary Sheffield in the first inning. Wearing jersey number 45, Tankersley exited the game with two outs in the sixth inning and the Padres leading 3-2. The Braves came back to win, 7-3, giving the rookie a no-decision. His final line was four hits, two runs, four walks, and five strikeouts. He gave up a two-run home run to Braves outfielder Andruw Jones.

Tankersley started again on May 15, against the Montreal Expos. He had another strong outing, going 6⅔ innings and striking out six, but had another no-decision. His third start, against the Colorado Rockies on May 21, was again a no-decision. Next came the Brewers on May 26 in Milwaukee.

The Padres came into the game with a 22-27 record, riding a five-game losing streak and stuck in fifth place in the National League West Division. The Brewers, also struggling with a 17-32 record, were in sixth place in the Central Division. The Brewers' starter was right-hander Nelson Figueroa. Tankersley took the mound in the bottom of the first inning staked to a 2-0 lead, thanks to a two-run home run by first baseman Ryan Klesko. He walked the first batter he faced, Álex Sánchez, who then stole second base. Sanchez scored on a single by Tyler Houston, and Richie Sexson smacked a two-run homer to center field. Tankersley struck out the next two batters but the Brewers led 3-2 at the end of the inning.

Tankersley helped his own cause in the top of the second inning with a leadoff ground-rule double to center field. He scored on Mark Kotsay's home run to right field. Klesko then hit his second home run of the game, a solo shot to deep right field. The Padres had taken a 5-3 lead. Tankersley had a three-up and three-down second inning.

The gods of baseball may have been shining down on Tankersley in the top of the third inning. He walked to the plate for his second at-bat of the

Dennis Tankersley with the Padres. Photograph Chris Hardy/San Diego Padres.

game. The Padres had already scored a run. Facing right-handed reliever Mike Buddie with two outs, Tankersley, who hit 10 home runs in high school, did not have many professional at-bats. But on a 2-and-0 count, he drove the ball to deep left field for a solo home run that gave the Padres a 7-3 lead.

Tankersley said after the game, "I'm a little disappointed in my pitching performance, but my hitting was more than anything I could have expected coming to the yard."[5] Years later, when asked if he was always a good hitter, he said, "I'd like to think so. I always hit and played right field in college when wasn't pitching. It was something I continued to take seriously at the pro level."[6]

Tankersley lasted until the bottom of the sixth inning when, on his 88th pitch of the game, he hit Alex Ochoa. He exited the game with the Padres leading 8-5. He had to put his first win in the hands of the bullpen. Three relief pitchers paved the way for future Hall of Fame closer Trevor Hoffman to close out the ninth inning. Hoffman struck out three to give Tankersley his first major-league win. The final score was 8-7. Tankersley gave up five of the runs, all earned, and five hits. He struck out six.

Tankersley described the win years later in an interview. "That whole month was a whirlwind. I got my initial call-up while at the hospital when my middle daughter was born on May 6. I remember feeling a huge sense of pride and relief, honestly. I also remember thinking it would be the first of many … missed on that one."[7]

Tankersley finished the season with the Padres. He struggled in his next few starts and then was moved to the bullpen. He finished the 2002 season with a 1-4 record. He began the 2003 season with the Padres, starting against San Francisco on April 9. He took the loss, neither making it out of the first inning nor recording an out. He gave up three hits, four walks, and seven runs (all earned). Sent back down to the minors, he spent the remainder of the 2003 season with Triple-A Portland, where he was 8-11 with a 4.65 ERA. In June 2004 he told a sportswriter the game "was 15 minutes I will never forget."[8]

Tankersley hoped for a better year in 2004 but it was not meant to be. He made his first major-league appearance of the season in the sixth inning on May 22 at Philadelphia. He made three relief appearances, then four starts before being sent back down to the minors in mid-June. When he rejoined the Padres in late August, the results were no different. He finished the 2004 season with a 0-5 record, giving up 35 hits in 35 innings.

After the season Tankersley was traded by the Padres to the Kansas City Royals. Padres general manager Kevin Towers said Tankersley "is a much better pitcher than what his major-league numbers are." (Tankersley's career major-league pitching record was 1-10 with a 7.61 ERA.)[9] He pitched for Triple-A Omaha in 2005, then in three other organizations, pitching in Triple A for the Cardinals, Tigers, and Natonals. After a 4-4 record and a 5.10 ERA with the Nationals' Columbus Clippers, he was released by the Nationals and was out of baseball. He recalled the trade to the Royals: "It was much harder being traded that time. I was traded from the Red Sox to San Diego but that was so quickly in my career I didn't mind. San Diego was my team that I grew up in. I got my first real taste of minor-league baseball there. The good and the bad."[10]

Tankersley made a brief attempt to return to baseball when he signed a minor-league contract with the Padres on March 3, 2012, saying, "I'm a baseball player. I felt like I could still play."[11] He was released on April 2. Of the comeback attempt, he said, "It was something I felt I needed to do. I don't want to say that I retired the first time on my terms but I kind of did. I was having knee trouble which made me feel like I just couldn't do the same things on the mound anymore. Plus, I had three kids and was ready to see them every day. I had some interest from teams on a minor-league deal but I was just mentally done. Then about three years later I was having a conversation with my kids about not quitting something. I don't even remember what now, but a light bulb went off in my head. So I told them that I would prove to them that if you wanted something you just had to work hard for it. So I spent the next seven months training and got hold of my old [Padres] pitching coach, Darren Balsley. Told him what was going on and asked if he would just let me throw for him. No promises or guarantees. So I went to Arizona and threw for him, along with some front-office guys, wasn't expecting all of them! But I threw well enough to stay and was in spring training until the end. At the end we had discussed a possible start in Double A as they had no room in Triple A out of camp. I had kind of accomplished what I set out to do, so decided to head back home and be a dad."[12]

Many men would sell their souls to get a chance to make one appearance in a major-league game. Tankersley's stats were certainly not Hall of Fame-worthy, a 1-10 record, with 97 hits in 86⅓ innings, but he was able to put on a major-league uniform and pitch in 27 games over a three-year period. Tankersley can tell his children and grandchildren about the day he won his first ballgame *and* hit a home run. That is a day many kids playing Little League can only dream of.

As of early 2023, Tankersley resided in Wentzville, Missouri, near St. Louis. He and his wife have five children. He has been a licensed real estate broker since 2013. He plays golf and hunts in his free time. His left knee still causes him some trouble, but he said, "It doesn't affect my golf game so I am good."[13] He misses the ballpark, the camaraderie, and the competition. His kids are active in sports so he says that has helped. At the time of the interview, his 17-year-old son planned to play college baseball. His 20-year-old daughter played soccer at the University of Arkansas. Two younger kids were just getting into sports and his 4-year-old already loved baseball.

SOURCES

In addition to the sources cited in the Notes, the author consulted Baseball-Reference.com and a number of other publications.

NOTES

1. Email interview with Dennis Tankersley, February 8, 2023.
2. *Baseball America 2001 Prospect Handbook* (Baseball America, 2001), 356-57.
3. For his three teams in 2001, Tankersley struck out 173 batters in 136⅓ innings.
4. *Baseball America 2002 Prospect Handbook* (Baseball America, 2002), 378.
5. "Padres End Five-Game Losing Streak," espn.com, May 26, 2002. https://www.espn.com/mlb/recap/_/gameId/220526108. Accessed January 21, 2023.
6. Tankersley interview.
7. Tankersley interview.
8. Bill Center, "Tankersley Toughens Up, Leaves Mistakes Behind," *San Diego Times-Union*, June 19, 2004: D-10.
9. Tom Krasovic, "Lefty May to Padres in Trade for Long – L.A. Believed to Be Interested in Wells," *San Diego Times-Union*, November 9, 2004: D-1.
10. Tankersley interview.
11. Corey Brock, "Tankersley Tries to Make Long Climb Back," MLB.com, March 15, 2012.
12. Tankersley interview.
13. Tankersley interview.

Álex Sánchez

JAY TESSMER

BY ALAN RAYLESBERG

Jay Tessmer pitched in parts of four seasons in his major-league career. Although he won only a single game, he was a member of three World Series championship teams, playing for the New York Yankees in 1998, 1999, and 2000. Appearing in 22 games during his major-league career, Tessmer pitched 23⅓ innings and finished with a perfect won-lost record of 1-0. His only win came in his first major-league appearance, when he got the victory in relief as the Yankees won their 96th game during their record-breaking 1998 season.[1]

Tessmer's story is a Hollywood-style tale about a player who was a walk-on to his college baseball team, after failing to make the cut on his first three tries. Playing for one of the all-time-great college programs at the University of Miami, Tessmer became an All-American, one of the best relief pitchers in the storied history of the Miami Hurricanes and a member of the University of Miami Hall of Fame. He was drafted by the Yankees, became a top prospect in their minor-league system, and had stints in the majors during four seasons, playing on some of the best teams of his era.

Jay Weldon Tessmer was born on December 26, 1971, in Meadville, Pennsylvania, a city in Crawford County in the northwestern part of the state, 90 miles from Pittsburgh. His parents grew up in the area and his family had longtime roots there. Some of Tessmer's ancestors on his father's side emigrated from Germany in the late nineteenth century, settling first in Wisconsin before ending up in Crawford County. Other paternal ancestors date back to the Revolutionary War, living in Virginia, then West Virginia, and eventually Meadville. Tessmer's paternal grandfather, an engineer, was the county surveyor for Crawford County. His paternal grandmother taught in the Meadville school system for 30 years and was a member of the Crawford County Women's Bowling Association Hall of Fame.[2]

Tessmer attended Cochranton High School in Meadville, where he was a three-time all-conference pitcher as well as a standout basketball player.[3] He went to West Virginia for college where he tried out for the baseball team, but did not make the cut. In 1991, after his freshman year, Tessmer transferred to the University of Miami. Tessmer had ties to Florida and the University, as his parents had a home in Port St. Lucie and his father was a Miami alumnus. At Miami, Tessmer tried out for the baseball team, but failed to make the cut in each of his first two years.

A coaching change in Tessmer's third year presented him with a new opportunity, one that would change his life. In 1994 Jim Morris, the legendary college baseball coach, left Georgia Tech and became the new coach at Miami.[4] With a new coach in place, Tessmer decided to give it one more shot. "I love playing baseball," he said. "As long as I was here going to school, I thought, 'Why not give it another chance'?"[5] Miami's pitching coach, Lazaro "Lazer" Collazo, saw something in Tessmer the year before, urging then-coach Brad Kelley to keep him on the team. Kelley, however, was not enamored of Tessmer's side-arm style and didn't think a walk-on pitcher would help the team.[6] With Morris as the coach, Tessmer benefited not only from Collazo's support but also from the fact that Morris had success at Georgia Tech with a walk-on, Kevin Brown, who went on to become a major-league All-Star.[7] On what was now his fourth try to make a college baseball team, Tessmer finally made it. Excited to have finally done so, Tessmer was even more excited when Morris named him to be the set-up man for All American reliever and future major leaguer Danny Graves.[8]

A 6-foot-3 right-hander with a side-arm delivery reminiscent of Kent Tekulve,[9] Tessmer made the most of his opportunity, beginning his college career with a school-record 32⅔ consecutive scoreless innings to start the season. He also led the NCAA in ERA with a 1.16 mark and a record of 6-2 with three saves in 70 innings over 40 relief appearances, as the Hurricanes advanced to the 1994 College World Series.[10] Tessmer was an honorable-mention All-American and played for Team USA in the 1994 Baseball World Cup tournament.[11] Interviewed toward the end of Tessmer's standout 1994 season, Collazo reflected on the improbability of a walk-on pitcher becoming an All-American. "It's an incredible story," said Collazo. "It shows what can happen if you keep the faith."[12] And yet the story had only just begun.

In 1995 Tessmer was named the team captain and became the closer. He was a first team All-American and led the nation with 20 saves. He had a 1.31 ERA and a 3-2 record in 70 innings over 45 appearances. He was named the MVP of the Coral Gables Regional tournament, getting a save in all four Miami wins as the Hurricanes advanced to their second consecutive College World Series.[13] The holder of numerous University of Miami pitching records, Tessmer was inducted into the University of Miami Sports Hall of Fame in 2013.[14]

Congratulating Tessmer at the induction ceremony, Coach Morris said that when he thought of Jay Tessmer, he thought of "perseverance," saying that "nothing was going to stop him." Morris recounted how he told Tessmer's story to many of those he coached since it is "a great story about a guy that had a goal and was going to do everything he could" to achieve it.[15]

After his college career, Tessmer was drafted by the Yankees in the 19th round of the June 1995 amateur draft.[16] He promptly signed with the Yankees, who projected him as a potential major-league closer. Tessmer was not a hard thrower. As one reporter observed, his "side arm delivery produces fastballs with velocity comparable with other pitchers' change-ups."[17] Despite the lack of speed, his unusual motion and excellent control made him effective at getting hitters out, especially right-handers.[18]

Tessmer got off to a great start in professional baseball, debuting with a sensational 0.95 ERA and 20 saves in his rookie season with the low Class-A Oneonta Yankees. He struck out an impressive 52 batters in 38 innings. In 1996, moving up to high Class-A Tampa, Tessmer was the Florida State League MVP with a record of 12-4, exclusively as a reliever, with 35 saves in 68 games and an ERA of 1.48. He again struck out more than a batter an inning with 104 strikeouts in 97⅓ innings. When he advanced to Double-A Norwich in 1997, his career hit a bump as he struggled to a 5.31 ERA with 17 saves in 55 games.

Given his disappointing 1997 season, it was not surprising that Tessmer was still in the minors when the 1998 season began. Indeed, there was not much room on the 1998 Yankees for Tessmer in any event. Those Yankees, one of the greatest teams of all time, ended up winning 114 regular-season games. They had a powerful offense with stars like Derek Jeter, Jorge Posada, Tino Martinez, Bernie Williams, and Paul O'Neill. The starting rotation was top-notch with Andy Pettitte, David Wells, David Cone, Hideki Irabu, and "El Duque" Orlando Hernández. Mariano Rivera was the closer. There were two other established right-handed relievers on the roster in Jeff Nelson and Ramiro Mendoza, together with lefties Mike Stanton and Graeme Lloyd. Lesser-known right-handed relievers Darren Holmes and Mike Buddie were also part of the bullpen. The right-handed-throwing Tessmer gave the Yankees added bullpen depth if reinforcements were needed.

Splitting time in 1998 between Double-A Norwich and the Triple-A Columbus Clippers, Tessmer again excelled as a reliever, with a 0.93 ERA and 34 saves in 57 games. In August 1998, opportunity came his way. The first-place Yankees had suffered a four-game losing streak, ending only with a dramatic walk-off 7-6 win in the second game of a day-night doubleheader on August 26 against the Anaheim Angels. After the game, manager Joe Torre told the press: "Now all of a sudden, the questions aren't about who we're going to play in the World Series. … Now we're concerned about getting there. It's funny what a week does. W-e-a-k, weak."[19] Yankees pitcher Scott Bradley had a bad game in the opener of the doubleheader and was sent to the minors immediately after the game. To replace him, the Yankees called up Tessmer.[20] Tessmer arrived at Yankee Stadium before the night portion of the doubleheader started, "eagerly" looking forward to having an opportunity to pitch in the big leagues.[21]

Tessmer got that opportunity the next night, August 27, 1998, when the Yankees again faced the Angels. Cone started the game but left in the sixth after walking four and allowing four runs. Trailing 4-3 after six innings, the Yankees took a 5-4 lead and left it to Mendoza, who gave up the tying run in the ninth. Stanton then pitched 1⅔ shutout innings as the game went to the 11th inning tied at 5-5. As reported in the New York Times, "the game [now] belonged to Tessmer [and] all the rookie did was retire the Angels 1-2-3 with two strikeouts."[22] Then, in the bottom of the 11th, Bernie Williams doubled off the center-field fence to score Derek Jeter and give the Yankees a thrilling 6-5 win.

Writing in the Times, Jack Curry noted the significance of the victory, commenting that the Yankees' "usually precise starter [Cone] failed miserably, their usually reliable middle reliever [Mendoza] stumbled as a closer, but their unreliable setup man [Stanton] and a rookie [Tessmer] making his major league debut finally pitched sharply enough for the Yankees to erase some of their concerns and give them life last night."[23] As Torre explained, "We needed to win this game. We didn't need it for the standings. But we needed this game for our psyche and our pride."[24]

Tessmer had never been in Yankee Stadium until he arrived from Columbus the day before. And now he had "pitched a scoreless inning to win his first major league game on a memorable night."[25] When Williams hit his game-winning double, Tessmer could not have been more excited. "I'd have to say I'm the happiest guy in the Stadium,'" said Tessmer. "'When [Williams] hit the ball, I was praying [center fielder Edmonds] didn't catch it. I can't explain how it felt. It was unbelievable.'"[26] In the excitement of the moment, few if any would have predicted that this would be the last time that Tessmer was the winning pitcher in a major-league game.

The season ended on September 27, exactly one month after Tessmer's winning performance. After having won the World Series in 1996, and then losing to Cleveland in the 1997 ALDS, the 1998 Yankees

Jay Tessmer. Courtesy of the University of Miami.

were returning to the postseason. They had finished the regular season with an American League-record 114 wins. Yet, as Buster Olney wrote in the *New York Times*, it was the "post-season [that would] define what is remembered 50 years from now."[27] Although Tessmer would not be on the postseason roster, he appreciated the role he had played, however small, in getting the Yankees there. Interviewed after the final game of the regular season, the "soft spoken and earnest" Tessmer recalled how "when he was credited with the victory [in his first major-league appearance], all of the veterans congratulated him warmly, as if he had been around the entire season."[28] With his season over, Tessmer packed his jersey, number 62. "'I want my jersey,' he said, laughing a bit. 'I don't know if I have to pay for it but I'm taking it.'"[29] Olney observed that Tessmer "has thought about the days when he can hand a framed picture of the 1998 Yankees to one of his grandchildren and point to that serious-looking young man with the protruding ears standing in the second row of the team picture, between David Cone and Luis Sojo. That was me, Tessmer might say. That is me."[30]

After appearing in a total of seven games for the Yankees in 1998, with a 3.12 ERA in 8⅔ innings, Tessmer was on the Yankees radar going into the 1999 season. He was considered a top 10 Yankees prospect, projected as a possible "11th man on the staff in 1999."[31] He was included in the 1999 *Yankees Yearbook*.[32] *The Sporting News* remarked about how much depth the Yankees bullpen had going into the season, with Rivera, Lloyd, Nelson, Stanton, Holmes, and Mendoza, adding that "if that isn't enough the Yankees also have a young righthanded relief prospect, Jay Tessmer, who dominated in Class AA and Class AAA last year and pitched well at the major league level in September."[33]

Given the Yankees bullpen depth, Tessmer opened the 1999 season back in Columbus. When Nelson was placed on the disabled list on May 3, Tessmer was called up to replace him. Tessmer made six relief appearances between May 3 and 19, all in games the Yankees were losing. While he pitched well in three of those games, he was banged around in the other three.[34] On May 21, when Nelson returned from the DL, the Yankees returned Tessmer to Columbus.[35] Back in Triple A, Tessmer continued to dominate, finishing the 1999 season with 28 saves in 56⅓ innings with a 3.34 ERA. His 1999 minor-league performance was good enough that *The Sporting News* speculated that the Yankees should fill their need for a left-handed reliever by trading Tessmer to the Twins for Eddie Guardado, remarking that Tessmer "is a submarine pitcher who has had a lot of success in the minors and currently is the closer at AAA Columbus."[36]

After repeating as World Series champions in 1999, the Yankees looked to make it three in a row in 2000. Going into the season, there was concern about their pitching depth "at the higher levels of the minor leagues." Tessmer's stock had fallen and he was part of the first round of spring-training cuts.[37]

Back in Columbus for the 2000 season, Tessmer finished second in the International League in saves with 34 and was called up to the Yankees in September. It was the first year that the Summer Olympics included professional baseball players. The US Olympic team wanted Tessmer. However, the Yankees turned down the request. Tessmer was disappointed, stating, perhaps diplomatically, "It's tough. … It would have been nice to go to the Olympics but it's great to be here [with the Yankees]."[38] The decision by Yankees owner George Steinbrenner was surprising given that Tessmer was no longer considered one of the club's top prospects.[39] Tessmer tried to put the situation in perspective, stating that "just to be considered for the Olympics is an honor. … Hopefully it means that [the Yankees] have plans for me."[40]

Whatever those plans might have been, they changed after the 2000 season. In need of right-handed relief pitching,[41] they traded Tessmer to the Colorado Rockies for another righty reliever, David Lee.[42] After he started the season in Triple-A Colorado Springs, the Rockies sent Tessmer to the Milwaukee Brewers as part of a conditional deal.

He spent the rest of the 2001 season with Triple-A Indianapolis.

Granted free agency after the 2001 season, Tessmer re-signed with the Yankees. Competing with Randy Choate and Adrián Hernández for the final two bullpen spots in 2002, he made the Opening Day roster.[43] *The Sporting News* noted that Mendoza started the season on the disabled list and that Tessmer "is filling the roster spot for the moment," adding that "Tessmer impressed the team during camp with strong movement on his fastball."[44]

Tessmer pitched in relief on Opening Day in Baltimore, relieving Roger Clemens after Clemens was injured and had to leave the game. He appeared again three days later, against the Orioles. With a 4-0 lead in the ninth inning, Tessmer entered at the start of the inning. After he walked two batters, Rivera replaced him and got the save in a 4-1 win. It would be Tessmer's last appearance in a major-league game.[45] For a player who failed three times to make his college baseball team, it must be a good memory to have, that his final major-league appearance was sandwiched between two of the greatest pitchers of all time.

Back in Columbus, Tessmer pitched in 63 games, all in relief, with a 4.37 ERA and four saves. The 2002 season was Tessmer's last in professional baseball, at the age of 30. In his career between the majors and minors, he appeared in 455 games, all in relief. And while he won 41 games (35 losses) in the minors, he finished his major-league career with that single win and no losses.

The University of Miami was good for Tessmer in more ways than one: He met his wife there and found, in South Florida, a place that became his permanent home after retiring as a player.[46] In retirement, Tessmer stayed involved with baseball, teaching youngsters how to pitch, giving private lessons[47] as well as being an instructor at the Players Edge Academy in Boca Raton[48] and the Legends for Youth Clinic Series in Orlando.[49]

In 2018 Tessmer played in the University of Miami Alumni Game, between the current Hurricanes and a team of alumni. Tessmer, then 46 years old, got to pitch one inning in relief. Jim Morris, entering his final season as Miami's coach, said he was "really happy for Tessmer," recalling the "great story" of how he went from a college walk-on to a major leaguer. Tessmer's 12-year-old son, a left-handed pitcher, was at the game. "I doubt if Jay Tessmer pitches in another game," Morris said, "but his son got to see him pitch. … I just think that's great. I was rooting so hard for him."[50]

Tessmer also became a successful businessman. Possessing a B.S. degree in chemistry, Tessmer found work with Joe Taylor Restoration, a company based in Delray Beach, Florida, that provides emergency services for water, fire, mold, and biohazard restoration. After starting as a technician, Tessmer was promoted to the position of estimator. In 2018 he became a branch manager for the Central Florida Region, based in Orlando, and he continued in that role as of 2022.[51]

While Tessmer had a relatively short career in professional baseball, he got to live out his childhood dream of playing in the major leagues. And even though he had only a single win in his big-league career, that win came in an unforgettable game in an unforgettable season. The words he used on the night of August 27, 1998, to describe his first (and only) major-league win could easily be used to describe his baseball career, from a college walk-on to an All-American to a member of one of the greatest major-league teams in history. "It was unbelievable."

SOURCES

In addition to the sources cited in the Notes, the author relied on Baseball-reference.com and Ancestry.com.

NOTES

1   The 1998 Yankees won 114 games, at the time the second-most regular-season wins in history and the most by an American League team. New York went on to win the

World Series, the first of three consecutive championships for the team. As of March 2022, only the 1906 Chicago Cubs and the 2001 Seattle Mariners, who each won 116 games, had more wins in a regular season. By winning 11 postseason games, the Yankees' total of 125 wins in a season were the most in baseball history.

2   Obituary, Wald-Coleman Funeral Home, https://www.waidcolemanfh.com/obituary/Doris-Tessmer.

3   University of Miami Sports Hall of Fame, https://www.umsportshalloffame.com/jay-tessmer.html.

4   Morris was one of the most successful coaches in college baseball history. His teams qualified for the NCAA Regionals for 32 consecutive years, nine at Georgia Tech and 23 at Miami.

5   Jorge Milan, "Canes See Era of Their Ways," *South Florida Sun-Sentinel* (Fort Lauderdale), May 3, 1994.

6   Milan.

7   Milan, "Pitching Propels," *South Florida Sun-Sentinel*, April 15, 1994.

8   Tessmer spoke about this, and his career more generally, during his speech upon his induction into the University of Miami Hall of Fame, available at https://www.umsportshalloffame.com/jay-tessmer.html. In addition to Graves, whom he played with in 1994, Tessmer played with future major-league player and manager Alex Cora in 1994 and 1995. Graves was drafted by Cleveland in the fourth round of the 1994 June amateur draft and had an 11-year career in the majors. Cora was drafted by the Dodgers in the third round of the 1996 draft and had a 14-year career as a player before becoming a coach and later a manager.

9   Tekulve pitched in the majors for 16 years, mainly with the Pirates, before retiring at age 42 after the 1989 season.

10 Miami was seeded number 1 but lost in the second round to 8th-seeded Arizona State.

11 The 1994 World Cup tournament was the last one to exclude professional players. It was held in Nicaragua in August of that year. Team USA lost to Cuba in the quarter-final round.

12 Milan.

13 Seeded number 3, the Hurricanes advanced to the semifinal round before losing to 6th-seeded USC.

14 Website for University of Miami Sports Hall of Fame, https://www.umsportshalloffame.com/jay-tessmer.html. The page for Tessmer includes a video about his career, a congratulatory video by Coach Morris, and Tessmer's acceptance speech.

15 "Hurricanes Baseball Coach Jim Morris talks about Jay Tessmer," available at https://www.youtube.com/watch?v=qClli64Ek1s.

16 In the next round, the Yankees drafted infielder Mike Lowell from Florida International University. Lowell went on to have a 13-year career in the majors, including seven years with the Florida Marlins. Lowell was MVP of the 2007 World Series for the Boston Red Sox. In self-deprecating fashion, during his induction speech, Tessmer referred to his being drafted by the Yankees immediately before Lowell as his "claim to fame."

17 Buster Olney, "Yankees Notebook," *New York Times,* August 29, 1998: C3.

18 John Benson, *Benson's A to Z Baseball Player Guide 1999* (Diamond Library 1998).

19 Jack Curry, "Jeter Applies Band-Aid to Salve Yankees' Wounds," *New York Times*, August 27, 1998: C1.

20 *The Sporting News* referred to it as a "surprise promotion" since Bradley had been promoted only days earlier. Jon Heyman, "New York," *The Sporting News*, September 7, 1998: 67.

21 Curry, "Yankees Notebook; Tired of Team's Funk, Joe Torre Talks Soul," *New York Times*, August 27, 1998: C5.

22 Curry, "Yankees Are Now Working Harder for Their Victories," *New York Times*, August 28, 1998: C1.

23 Curry, "Yankees Are Now Working Harder for Their Victories."

24 Curry, "Yankees Are Now Working Harder for Their Victories."

25 Curry, "Yankees Are Now Working Harder for Their Victories."

26 Curry, "Yankees Are Now Working Harder for Their Victories."

27 Olney, "Yankees' Glittering Regular Season Is a Mere Prelude," *New York Times,* September 28, 1998: D7. Those words were prophetic, as the Yankees went on to win 11 postseason games, sweeping the San Diego Padres to win the World Series. The achievements of the 1998 team gained them recognition as one of the all-time greats. In contrast, when the 2001 Seattle Mariners won 116 regular season games, their loss to the Yankees in the ALCS greatly diminished their regular-season accomplishment.

28 Olney, "Yankees' Glittering Regular Season Is a Mere Prelude."

29 Olney, "Yankees' Glittering Regular Season Is a Mere Prelude."

30 Olney, "Yankees' Glittering Regular Season Is a Mere Prelude."

31 Benson, *John Benson Presents Future Stars – The Rookies of 1999-2000* (Diamond Library 1998). Benson ranked Tessmer as the number 8 Yankees prospect. Mike Lowell, who was drafted by the Yankees immediately after their selection of Tessmer, was ranked number 3. In his scouting report, Benson wrote that, despite not having "exceptional velocity," Tessmer "changes speeds and locations well" with a "high 80's fastball [that] moves sharply," and his "motion confounds righthanded hitters."

32 The *Yearbook* described Tessmer as a player who "already stands out among the Yankee pitchers." After recapping his 1998 performance, the *Yearbook* added "Side-arm delivery notwithstanding, Tessmer will make a direct run at breaking

33 Peter Schmuck, "Insider," *The Sporting News*, February 22, 1999: 53.

34 On May 8, 1999, pitching against the Mariners, Tessmer gave up a home run to Ken Griffey Jr. The homer was Griffey's 361st, tying him with Joe DiMaggio for what was then 45th on the career list. After the game, when asked about Tessmer, Griffey did not know who Tessmer was. As Tom Verducci wrote, "[I]t wasn't Tessmer's pitches that fooled him. … It was only the mention of the name Tessmer," to which Griffey replied "Who is that?" Verducci, "Joltin' Junior," *Sports Illustrated*, May 17, 1999: 32.

35 The *New York Times* predicted the move, stating, "The Yankees' bullpen is due for a complete restructuring in the next week" and noting that Mendoza was likely to move back into a relief role with Clemens returning from his injury and rejoining the rotation. With Nelson about to be activated from the DL, "either Jay Tessmer or Tony Fossas could be shipped out to make room." In fact, both were. Buster Olney, "Yankees Notebook; Torre Is Keeping His Return Date Close to the Vest," *New York Times*, May 17, 1999: D3.

36 "Slap Hitters," *The Sporting News*, August 2, 1999: 24. The Yankees needed a lefty reliever because they had traded Graeme Lloyd.

37 Olney, "Yanks' Top Prospects Are, Well, Minor League," *New York Times*, March 20, 2000: D7.

38 George King and Joel Sherman, "Yanks Tell Tessmer: Forget About Sydney," *New York Post*, September 9, 2000.

39 King and Sherman. Steinbrenner did allow Columbus infielder Mike Coolbaugh to play for the USA Olympic team.

40 King and Sherman. Steinbrenner also refused MLB's request to have Bernie Williams participate in an all-star team tour of Japan in November 2000.

41 The Yankees had lost veteran Jeff Nelson to Seattle in free agency and had released Jason Grimsley after two seasons with the team.

42 Lee was expected to be the Rockies closer for the 2000 season but ended up spending most of the season in the minors. He was "disgruntled" and the Rockies felt that they needed to trade him. Jack Etkin, "Lee Traded to Yankees for Two Minor League Players," *Denver Rocky Mountain News*, January 4, 2001. Lee never pitched for the Yankees, who traded him before the 2021 season for another right-handed reliever, Carlos Almanzar.

43 Tessmer was not on the 40-man roster when spring training began. Choate also made the Opening Day roster. Hernandez did not.

44 Ken Davidoff, "New York Yankees," *The Sporting News*, April 8, 2002: 59.

45 On April 8, 2002, Clemens returned from his injury, Mendoza was reinstated from the disabled list, and Tessmer was sent to the minors.

46 After meeting his future wife, Tamara, at the University of Miami, they married in 1997, when Tamara graduated. At Miami, Tamara was a member of the Sugarcanes, the ball and bat girls for the Miami team.

47 https://pro4mer.com/pros/jay-tessmer/.

48 https://www.groupon.com/deals/players-edge-baseball-academy.

49 2021 LFY Road Trip-Florida Edition https://lessonswithlegends.mlblogs.com/2021-lfy-road-trip-florida-edition-687655b78758 Tessmer wore his old Yankees number 62 at the clinic while also wearing a face mask to protect against the coronavirus.

50 Christopher Stock, "McKendry Sharp as Over 90 Former Players Attend Alumni Game," *Inside the U*, February 10, 2018. https://247sports.com/college/miami/Article/Miami-Hurricanes-RHP-Evan-McKendry-Sharp-as-Over-90-Former-Players-Attend-Alumni-Game-114988870/.

51 https://www.jtrestoration.com/meet-the-team/.

CARL THOMAS

BY TIM OTTO

"Has a pitcher ever made his major league debut as a pinch-hitter?" asked Cleveland sportswriter Harry Jones in his column after the Indians' 1960 Opening Day 4-2 loss to the visiting Detroit Tigers.[1] Detroit scored two runs in the top of the 15th inning to take the lead. After a one-out double in the bottom of the inning, Cleveland manager Joe Gordon, who had used all his position players, called on rookie Carl Thomas to pinch-hit for the Indians reliever. Thomas, a decent hitter during his college career as a three-time All-America hurler for the University of Arizona, struck out.

Although his accomplishments at the collegiate level were not duplicated in his professional baseball career, during his short time at the major-league level with Cleveland, Thomas did play in two games of significance to Indians fans of the late 1950s. His pinch-hitting opportunity occurred during Rocky Colavito's first appearance in a game at Cleveland Stadium after being traded to the Tigers. Less than a month later against the visiting Chicago White Sox, Thomas received credit for his one big-league victory. It was the only time Herb Score, who had been traded by Cleveland to Chicago and took the loss, pitched against the Indians in Cleveland.

Carl Leslie Thomas was born on May 28, 1932, in Minneapolis, the only child of Carl F. and Alberta Thomas.[2] Carl F. pitched for minor-league teams in St. Paul and Louisville during the 1920s.[3] By 1940, the Thomas household included not only the 8-year-old Carl and his two parents, but also his aunt and uncle, their two daughters, ages 6 and 15, and his grandmother Lena Thomas. His father worked at a tractor factory.[4]

Thomas attended Central High School in Minneapolis. At 6-feet-5 and 225 pounds by his senior year, he competed in football, basketball, and baseball, and was a teammate of future major leaguer Johnny Blanchard, a year behind Thomas in school. In 1949 they starred on Central's basketball team, which qualified for the state tournament. Thomas scored a season-high 16 points, including his team's last five points, in the 37-34 win that put Central into the semifinal game, which they lost to the eventual state champion.[5]

In 1950 the pair led Central to its first-ever Twin Cities baseball championship. The right-handed Thomas pitched a no-hitter in the 1-0 win that clinched the Minneapolis high-school title.[6] Two days later, with Blanchard pitching and Thomas playing third base, he hit two home runs in Central's 7-1 win over the St. Paul champion.[7]

After graduating in June of 1950, Thomas attended the College World Series in Omaha as a guest of the Pittsburgh Pirates. It was reported that several other scouts had shown an interest in him and that he had received a scholarship offer from the University of Colorado.[8] After attending Colorado in the fall, he enrolled at the University of Minnesota.[9] Coach Dick Siebert, assessing his baseball team in November of 1950, mentioned

Thomas as one of his promising group of freshmen pitchers.[10]

Thomas never played for the Gophers. According to his father, he quit after about three weeks when he saw one of his friends sign a "big money" pro-baseball contract. Thomas didn't have a scholarship at Minnesota, but when another friend told him he could get a basketball scholarship at Santa Ana Junior College in California, he decided to enroll there for the 1951-52 school year.[11]

Thomas played football, basketball, and baseball for Santa Ana, although an injury cut short his football season. He was 10-2 as a starting pitcher for the baseball team, including a 3-0 no-hit win and another game in which he struck out 18.[12] Santa Ana won the Southern California junior college championship. Thomas was selected as a member of the 15-player Pacific Coast all-star team that, after a stop in Honolulu, toured Japan during the summer of 1952.[13]

The Boston Red Sox and Detroit Tigers both offered to sign Thomas at the end of Santa Ana's season, but he decided to continue his college baseball career, choosing the University of Arizona over the University of Southern California.[14] In a 2013 interview, his wife, Eunice, said, "Carl came to Tucson on a baseball scholarship, but he had played basketball at Santa Ana, and he was a high school football star in Minneapolis. The UA gave him a job hashing for the football team at the stadium dormitory. Well, he got tired of doing it and said, 'If I play football, I won't have to do it anymore, they'll feed me.' So, he did. After the football season, [basketball coach] Fred Enke told Carl he wanted him to play basketball. Carl planned to, but at the last minute he said, 'I want to go home for Christmas.' Coach Enke wouldn't let him, so he stuck to baseball."[15]

Before the start of Arizona's 1953 baseball season, Thomas was involved in an incident that cost him the chance to pitch for the Wildcats that spring. He was a passenger in a car driven by a freshman on the football team who had taken two tires from a car parked at Hi Corbett Field. Thomas and the driver were arrested after an eyewitness to a similar incident the day before had given police the car's license number, and the two tires were found in the back seat.[16] The driver admitted full responsibility and the charges against Thomas were eventually dropped.[17] The university placed Thomas on probation and he was not permitted to participate in any extracurricular activities for the semester.[18]

In 1954 Arizona made its first-ever trip to the College World Series. Thomas headed a strong pitching staff that included future major-league hurler Don Lee. The Wildcats beat Oregon, 12-1, in the first round of the double-elimination tournament played in Omaha. Thomas pitched a complete game, striking out 11 and allowing only four singles. He also drove in an NCAA World Series record seven runs, hitting two home runs and a double.[19]

Arizona lost to Michigan State, 2-1, the next day, setting up a must-win game against Oklahoma A&M. When the Wildcats' starter ran into trouble in the fourth inning, Thomas relieved. He stayed on the mound as the game entered extra innings with the score tied, 4-4. In the 14th inning Thomas, pitching with only two days' rest, gave up a run on two walks and a single.[20] The 5-4 defeat eliminated Arizona and was Thomas's only loss of the season after 12 wins. Thomas was named a third-team All-American for 1954.[21]

In March of 1955, Thomas participated in the second Pan American Games in Mexico City. He was the winning pitcher in the game that clinched a silver medal for the United States, allowing one hit and striking out six over seven innings in a 13-2 win over Venezuela. The Dominican Republic, with future big-league players Felipe Alou and Julián Javier on their roster, won the gold medal.[22]

Arizona returned to the College World Series in 1955. After losing, 4-1, to Western Michigan in the first round, the Wildcats beat Springfield, 6-0, as Thomas yielded only two hits and struck out 15 batters, tying an NCAA World Series record.[23] Arizona won its next game, emerging from the losers' bracket to face the team that had eliminated them the prior year, Oklahoma A&M. The Wildcats again lost to the Aggies, 5-4, this time in 12 innings. Thomas relieved Arizona starter Lee in the 12th with two on and one out. The bases were loaded after a throw to second on a grounder failed to get a force out. An infield roller toward second scored the winning run.[24]

Selected as a first team All-American for 1955,[25] Thomas returned to Arizona for his final year of eligibility. He pitched back-to-back no-hitters against Arizona State and UCLA.[26] The Wildcats returned to the College World Series for the third straight year. After Arizona's first-round win, Thomas started against Minnesota. He allowed only five hits and struck out 10 Gophers, but took the loss as five Wildcat errors led to two unearned runs in Minnesota's 3-1 win.[27]

Wins against New Hampshire and Mississippi gave Arizona and Thomas a second chance against previously unbeaten Minnesota. He equaled his 15-strikeout record set in 1955 as the Wildcats won, 10-4. (Thomas contributed a single, double, and triple in four trips to the plate.[28]) Both Thomas and Don Lee, whose win against Mississippi was his second tournament complete game, were unavailable to pitch for Arizona in the next day's deciding contest. Minnesota won the 1956 NCAA baseball championship, beating the Wildcats, 12-1.[29]

Thomas (13-3) became a three-time All-American when he was named to 1956's second team. Lee (15-0) was selected as a first team All-American.[30] In 2020 NCAA.com picked Arizona's all-time starting nine, based on their college statistics. Thomas and Lee were both chosen for the pitcher's spot, as their numbers were so similar. They held the top two places in Arizona history for wins (Lee had 36 and Thomas 35). Thomas held the Wildcats' record for strikeouts (422, with Lee third at 398) and fewest hits allowed per nine innings (5.59, with Lee third at 6.01).[31]

Thomas worked out with the Cleveland Indians after the College World Series ended, but initially failed to reach agreement on a contract with Cleveland general manager Hank Greenberg. Reportedly some in the organization were concerned that Thomas lacked the blazing fastball needed at the major-league level.[32] The Kansas City Athletics also expressed an interest in Thomas, but front-office officials questioned his age (he turned 24 that May); the A's rebuilding plans emphasized youth.[33] Thomas and Greenberg ultimately agreed on a contract, which was reportedly under the major-league bonus limit of $4,000.[34]

Thomas was assigned to Cleveland's Double-A farm team, Mobile, in the Southern Association, for the balance of the 1956 season. In 13 starts he compiled a 5-4 record, with a 2.61 ERA.

In 1957 he was scheduled to report to San Diego (Triple A) of the Pacific Coast League, and was invited to attend Cleveland's rookie camp in Tucson for the start of spring training.[35] "We always get the cream of the crop from our minor league farms here for the rookie training camp," said pitching coach Mel Harder. "I think Carl has got a lot of ability.

Carl Thomas. Courtesy of Cleveland Guardians.

He's the type of fella who picks up things fast and is eager to learn. He had a wonderful earned run average at Mobile last year and he's taking a big step up going to San Diego."[36]

In two spring training appearances for San Diego against PCL competition, Thomas gave up six runs, including four homers, in three innings against the Los Angeles Angels,[37] and five runs in five innings against the Hollywood Stars.[38] He was sent back to Mobile for the 1957 season, where he posted a 13-13 record, with a 3.25 ERA.

Carl Thomas and Eunice Stark were married on October 19, 1957, in Douglas, Arizona. Her father, Harold Stark, was a well-known and respected Arizona rancher.[39] Eunice attended the University of Arizona and graduated from Arizona State College. Prior to their wedding date Thomas had enlisted in the Arizona Air National Guard. The couple spent the next 10 weeks in Rantoul, Illinois, where he was sent for training at Chanute Air Force Base, before returning to Tucson to live.[40]

Thomas began 1958's spring training with the Indians in Tucson, one of 12 farm system prospects invited to train with the parent club.[41] He pitched well enough to be included on the major-league team's roster when the Indians began their trip back east for the start of the season. Assessing the chances of Thomas being with Cleveland on Opening Day, pitching coach Harder said, "He's been working hard this spring and has shown quite a bit of improvement, but whether or not he will stick, I can't say. If he doesn't make it with the Indians, he'll be pitching Triple A ball. … A year in Triple A would do him a world of good."[42]

Thomas pitched in two exhibition games against the Giants in Texas during the Indians' trip to Cleveland, and was hit hard. He was sent to San Diego when the team was cut to 30 players a week before the start of the regular season.[43] After appearing in four games for San Diego (1-2 record), Thomas was optioned to Indianapolis (Triple A in the American Association).[44] There he was 9-9, with a 2.82 ERA.

Thomas was one of seven farm-club pitchers invited to Tucson for spring training in 1959.[45] Before heading east with the Indians on a five-game exhibition tour, he pitched 12⅓ innings, striking out 10, and giving up two runs on seven hits.[46] Manager Gordon considered Thomas "the best-looking pitcher in camp."[47]

For a second year Thomas was sent to San Diego, this time two days before the regular season began. "We feel that Carl is a good prospect and should be pitching regularly," said Cleveland general manager Frank Lane. "If we kept him with us, he wouldn't get the work he needs. … I talked to [general manager] Ralph Kiner in San Diego and told him to give Thomas a lot of work, especially in relief."[48]

Thomas was 2-2 after pitching only 11 innings for San Diego when he was optioned to Indianapolis in mid-May.[49] Just prior to learning of his reassignment, Thomas made a quick trip back to Arizona to be with his wife for the birth of their twin daughters, Susan and Cynthia.[50]

Pitching in 13 games (12 as a starter) for Indianapolis, Thomas was 7-2 with a 2.75 ERA. He was selected for the American Association's July 13 All-Star Game but was reassigned to San Diego before it was held.[51] In his two separate stints with the Padres, he compiled a 4-5 record.

"I decided last winter that if I didn't make the ball club this year, I'd either ask to be traded or quit baseball altogether," said Thomas as spring training came to a close in 1960.[52] He was the Indians' most impressive pitcher in Tucson, allowing only five runs on 14 hits in 22 innings of work.[53]

"My confidence is much better this spring," said Thomas. "I've convinced myself that I'm no fast ball pitcher and I can't blow the ball by the hitters. … Mel Harder [Cleveland pitching coach] and Ted Wilks [Indianapolis manager] have always told me play within yourself … don't force it. That's what I've been trying to do this spring. I've had good springs before, but near the end I've always tried a little harder to make the team. When I started to put something extra on the ball, I always got myself in trouble and ended up back in the minors."[54]

Thomas was on the Indians' roster when they began their 1960 season at home against the Detroit Tigers on April 19. Two days before the opener, the teams traded All-Star outfielders, with Rocky Colavito going to Detroit in exchange for Harvey Kuenn. On Opening Day, 52,756 spectators saw Cleveland fan favorite Colivito take the field in a Tigers uniform. In what turned out to be a pitchers' duel, neither team scored in regulation. Detroit's two runs in the top of the 11th inning were matched by the Indians in the bottom half of the frame.

In the top of the 15th, Al Kaline drove in two runs to put the Tigers ahead 4-2. Colavito hit into a double play to end Detroit's at-bat, capping a 0-for-6 day that included four strikeouts. With the Indians out of position players, Thomas made his big-league debut as a pinch-hitter in the bottom of the inning, striking out.

The next day Thomas made his debut as a pitcher. Kaline's ninth-inning leadoff homer broke a 4-4 tie. After starter Jim Perry walked the next batter, Thomas relieved him. The first hitter he faced, Steve Bilko, tripled to score another run. Thomas escaped further damage after a lineout to third, a walk, and a line-drive double play, second to first. Perry was charged with the loss in the Indians' 6-4 defeat.

Thomas did not see any action after the Detroit series for almost two weeks. On May 3 in Washington, he entered the game at the beginning of the home half of the sixth with the score tied, 4-4. Thomas retired the side in order, striking out the first two batters he faced. Cleveland scored a run in the top of the seventh to take a 5-4 lead. Thomas walked the leadoff batter in the bottom of the inning, but retired the next three on a foul out, a strikeout, and a fly ball.

Thomas was relieved with one out in the eighth after a single and a triple tied the score at 5-5. He was charged with a second run when the runner at third scored after a two-out single, putting the Senators ahead, 6-5. He was not charged with the loss as Cleveland tied the score in the ninth. Washington scored with one out in its half of the ninth to win, 7-6.

In Baltimore on May 6, Thomas started the bottom of the fifth with the Indians trailing 7-0. Working two innings in a game Cleveland lost 9-2, he was responsible for one run in the sixth when the leadoff batter reached on a hit-by-pitch, moved to second on a wild pitch, and scored on a two-out single.

The Indians were carrying 12 pitchers on their 28-player squad, but were likely to keep only 10 after the May 18 deadline to cut the roster to 25 players. "We've got to evaluate our pitching," said manager Gordon on May 8. "We have to cut down in about 10 days and we have to decide who to keep and who to let go."[55]

Thomas made his next appearance against the White Sox in Cleveland on Saturday, May 14. Barry Latman started for the Indians. Chicago countered with Herb Score, who had been traded by Cleveland for Latman the day before the season began. The matchup didn't last long; both pitchers were removed before two innings were completed.

Thomas relieved Latman in the second with one out and the score tied, 3-3. He entered the game with the bases loaded, but ended the threat by retiring the next two batters on fly balls to center and left field. Score was removed with two outs in the bottom of the inning after Jim Piersall hit a two-run homer to give the Indians the lead, 5-3.

Thomas held the White Sox scoreless over the next three innings, allowing only one hit, an infield single, while walking five. By the end of the fifth inning, Cleveland had increased its advantage to 10-3. Thomas contributed at the plate with a single and a walk, scoring one of the Indians' runs.

Thomas walked Nellie Fox to start the top of the sixth inning. One out later he issued another walk, his seventh of the game. A single, a ground-out, and another single scored three runs. The next batter, Dick Brown, hit a two-run homer, cutting Cleveland's margin to 10-8. Thomas was relieved by Johnny Klippstein, who finished the game as the Indians outlasted the White Sox by a final score of 10-9.

Thomas was awarded the win, but his manager was not happy with the rookie's wildness.[56] In 4⅓ innings he had given up five runs on four hits and seven walks while striking out only one batter. The next day he was sent back to Indianapolis.[57] During his one month with Cleveland, he had worked 9⅔ innings, giving up eight hits and eight runs (7.45 ERA), with five strikeouts and 10 walks.

At Indianapolis Thomas posted a 5-8 record (5.09 ERA) in 16 starts. At the end of July, Cleveland general manager Lane announced that the Indians had obtained Don Newcombe from Cincinnati for Thomas and a "considerable amount of cash."[58] Assigned to the Reds' Double-A affiliate in Nashville, Thomas was 6-5 (4.42 ERA), with eight starts in 11 games.

In March of 1961, Thomas announced his retirement from professional baseball. He said he couldn't reach agreement with Cincinnati on a contract and had received an attractive job offer as a commercial representative with a Tucson home-decorating firm.[59]

Thomas worked out with the Arizona Wildcats' baseball team in 1962. In June he returned to pro baseball with San Diego.[60] In six games he was 1-1 (8.36 ERA). That November the Thomases' third daughter, Lisa, was born.[61]

By 1963, Thomas, definitely finished with professional baseball, was working for a building supply company.[62] In August he was appointed the Tucson sales representative for Phoenix Cement Company, covering southern Arizona.[63] In 1965 the family moved to Phoenix when Thomas was transferred to the company's home office.[64]

In 1966 Thomas began pitching batting practice for the Phoenix Giants when they were in town. "I enjoy the pitching," said Thomas, who provided the service for free. "Sometimes I have to scramble to make it to the park (after work), but I wouldn't be doing it if I didn't enjoy it." Phoenix manager Clyde

Carl Thomas. Courtesy of Cleveland Guardians.

King commented, "We consider Carl as our 22nd man. A batting practice pitcher with his ability can make a big difference."[65]

After 15 years as a sales executive with Phoenix Cement, Thomas opened his own business in 1981, SCL Equipment. The company performed subcontracting and aggregate work in Phoenix and central Arizona.[66]

Thomas was inducted into the University of Arizona Sports Hall of Fame in 1977.[67] In 1994 he was named, along with Wildcats teammate Don Lee, to Baseball America magazine's All-Time College Baseball team for the 1947-64 era.[68]

Thomas became close friends with Arizona State University Hall of Fame coaches Bobby Winkles (baseball), Frank Kusch (football), and Baldy Castillo (track and field). All three were his regular handball partners and fishing buddies. "Carl had a lot of respect for the Sun Devils, but he loved the Wildcats," said his wife. "That's where his heart was."[69]

The Thomases' youngest daughter, Lisa Thomas, died on February 6, 2006, after enduring a mitochondrial disease for 15 years. She was 43 and living with her parents at the time of her death. She was buried in the Riggs Family Cemetery, near Dos Cabezas, Arizona. Her maternal grandparents, her great grandparents, and her great-great-grandparents were all buried there.[70]

Carl Leslie Thomas died at the age of 80 on March 7, 2013, due to advanced Parkinson's disease. He was survived by his wife of 55 years, Eunice; their twin daughters, Susan and Cynthia; and four grandchildren. He was buried in the Riggs Family Cemetery.[71]

SOURCES

The author accessed Baseball-Reference.com and Retrosheet.org. for box scores/play-by-play information, player, team, and season pages, pitching game logs, and other data:

https://www.baseball-reference.com/players/t/thomaca01.shtml

https://www.retrosheet.org/boxesetc/T/Pthomc102.htm

The author used Ancestry.com to access the 1940 United States Federal Census.

NOTES

1. Harry Jones, "Batting Around," *Cleveland Plain Dealer*, April 20, 1960: 33.
2. Carl L. Thomas obituary, *Arizona Republic* (Phoenix), March 24, 2013: B8.
3. "'Boy Has Heart,' Says Dad of Central's No-Hit Ace," *Minneapolis Star Tribune*, June 8, 1950: 19.
4. 1940 United States Federal Census: S.D. No. 5, E.D. No. 89-241, Sheet No.1A.
5. "Central Rallies to 37-34 Win," *Minneapolis Star Tribune*, March 25, 1949: 25.
6. Tom Briere, "Thomas, Central Win No-Hitter," *Minneapolis Star Tribune*, June 8, 1950: 19.
7. Tom Briere, "Thomas Raps Two Homers; Central Wins T-C Title," *Minneapolis Star Tribune*, June 10, 1950: 13.
8. "Prep Notes," *Minneapolis Star Tribune*, June 21, 1950: 20.
9. "Thomas Moves to Minnesota," *Minneapolis Star*, October 25, 1950: 75.
10. "The Roundup," *Minneapolis Star Tribune*, November 4, 1950: 24.
11. Abe Chanin, "The Greatest Thrill a Dad Could Ever Have," *Arizona Daily Star* (Tucson), June 14, 1955: 12.
12. "Pint-Sized Jap Batters 'Menace,'" *Arizona Daily Star*, September 18, 1952: 26.
13. Jim Byrne, "Carl Thomas Off on Pacific Tour," *Minneapolis Star*, July 30, 1952: 38.
14. Byrne, "Carl Thomas Off on Pacific Tour."
15. Greg Hansen, "Couldn't Get a Hit Off Wildcat Thomas in Late April '56," *Arizona Daily Star*, July 8, 2016: B1- B4.
16. "UA Football Hero Held for Theft," *Tucson Daily Citizen*, March 14, 1953: 4.
17. "Public Records," *Arizona Daily Star*, May 12, 1953: 18.
18. "University Cracks Down on Six Students Afoul of Law," *Tucson Citizen*, March 18, 1953: 28.
19. Abe Chanin, "Wildcats' Thomas Mauls Oregon Nine, 12-1," *Arizona Daily Star*, June 11, 1954: 20.
20. Abe Chanin, "Aggies Outlast UA in 14 Frames," *Arizona Daily Star*, June 13, 1954: 15.
21. "Thomas, Gragg Named All-Americans," *Arizona Daily Star*, June 24, 1954: 26.
22. "Thomas Hurls Pan-Am Win," *Arizona Daily Star*, March 23, 1955: 18.
23. "Thomas' 6-0 Win Keeps UA Hopes Alive," *Arizona Daily Star*, June 13, 1955: 9.
24. Abe Chanin, "Aggies Nip Arizona, 5-4, in 12 Innings," *Arizona Daily Star*, June 15, 1955: 29.
25. "Arizona Hits All-American 'Jackpot,'" *Arizona Daily Star*, June 19, 1955: 35.
26. Greg Hansen, "Couldn't Get a Hit Off Wildcat Thomas in Late April '56."
27. Abe Chanin, "Minnesota, Errors Whip UA 'Cats 3-1," *Arizona Daily Star*, June 11, 1956: 9.
28. Abe Chanin, "Arizona Wallops Minnesota, 10-4," *Arizona Daily Star*, June 14, 1956: 1.
29. George McLeod, "Minnesota Smashes Wildcat Title Dream," *Tucson Citizen*, June 15, 1956: 17.
30. "Lee Named All-American," *Arizona Daily Star*, June 24, 1956: 23. Jerry Kindall, Minnesota's shortstop, was also selected as a first team All-American. After a nine-year major-league career with the Cubs, Indians, and Twins, Kindall became the head baseball coach at Arizona, winning NCAA championships in 1976, 1980, and 1986.
31. Wayne Cavadi, "We Picked Arizona Baseball's All-Time Starting Nine," NCAA.com, August 19, 2020: https://www.ncaa.com/news/baseball/article/2018-04-23/we-picked-arizona-baseballs-all-time-starting-nine.
32. "Thomas Still Seeks Pact," *Arizona Daily Star*, July 2, 1956: 13.
33. George McLeod, "Injury, Age Cause A's to Drop Lee, Thomas," *Tucson Citizen*, Jul 12, 1956: 35.
34. "Thomas Signs Tribe Pact," *Arizona Daily Star*, July 4, 1956: 13.

35 Abe Chanin, "Carl Thomas Moving Up," *Arizona Daily Star*, February 13, 1957: 25.

36 Ed Gallardo, "Yankees Getting No Concessions," *Arizona Daily Star*, February 24, 1957: 40.

37 "Thomas Shelled for Six Runs, but Pads Win," *Arizona Daily Star*, March 20, 1957: 16.

38 "Thomas Pitches as San Diego Loses, 9-5," *Arizona Daily Star*, March 28, 1957: 31.

39 "Phoenix Cement Co. Appoints Former Baseball Star," *Williams* (Arizona) *News*, August 22, 1963: 7.

40 "Thomas-Stark Rites Read," *Tucson Daily Citizen*, October 21, 1957: 11.

41 "Thomas Invited to Tribe Camp," *Tucson Daily Citizen*, January 14, 1958: 13.

42 Tom Foust, "Tribe Gives Carl Another Look," *Arizona Daily Star*, April 3, 1958: 36.

43 Harry Jones, "Batting Around," *Cleveland Plain Dealer*, April 9, 1958: 25.

44 Max Greenwald, "Tribe Drops Behind Early, Loses 5-3 Tilt," *Indianapolis Star*, May 9, 1958: 28.

45 "Lemon Bids for Indians' Relief Job," *Cleveland Plain Dealer*, February 24, 1959: 27.

46 Tom Foust, "Leek, Thomas Head East with Tribe," *Arizona Daily Star*, April 3, 1959: 35.

47 Abe Chanin, "Gordon Pleased with Fine Spring Training," *Arizona Daily Star*, March 26, 1959: 31.

48 Harry Jones, "Batting Around," *Cleveland Plain Dealer*, April 10, 1959: 32.

49 "Carl Thomas to Rejoin Tribe," *Indianapolis Star*, May 17, 1959: 28.

50 "Twin Daughters Born to Mr. and Mrs. Carl Thomas," *Arizona Daily Star*, May 16, 1959: 16.

51 Lester Koelling, "A.A. Directors May Slice '60 Schedule," *Indianapolis Star*, July 13, 1959: 13.

52 Harry Jones, "No Detour This Trip for Tribe's Thomas," *Cleveland Plain Dealer*, April 10, 1960: 50.

53 "Mammoth Thomas to Stick," *Arizona Daily Star*, April 8, 1960: 47.

54 Tom Foust, "Thomas Working on New Theory," *Arizona Daily Star*, April 3, 1960: 48.

55 Harry Jones, "2 Indian Pitchers Face Ax," *Cleveland Plain Dealer*, May 9, 1960: 35, 39.

56 Chuck Heaton, "Gordon Finds a Stopper," *Cleveland Plain Dealer*, May 15, 1960: 44.

57 "Carl Thomas Sent to Indianapolis by Indians," *Arizona Daily Star*, May 18, 1960: 27.

58 Harry Jones, "Indians Obtain Newcombe to Bolster Mound Staff," *Cleveland Plain Dealer*, July 30, 1960: 17.

59 "Carl Thomas Retires," *Arizona Daily Star*, March 7, 1961: 27.

60 "Thomas Bids for Return to Baseball," *Tucson Daily Citizen*, June 11, 1962: 41.

61 "Births, St. Joseph's Hospital," *Arizona Daily Star*, November 29, 1962: 27.

62 Abe Chanin, "Lee Ticketed by Big Year with Angles," *Arizona Daily Star*, March 12, 1963: 16.

63 "Phoenix Cement Co. Appoints Former Baseball Star," *Williams* (Arizona) *News*, August 22, 1963.

64 "Thomas, Carl L. Obituary," *Arizona Republic*, March 24, 2013: B8.

65 Bob Eder, "Thomas in New but Vital Role," *Arizona Republic*, April 29 1968: 29.

66 "Where Are They Now," *Tucson Citizen*, August 7, 1981: 66.

67 "Arizona Sports Hall will add former Cats," *Tucson Citizen*, October 25, 1977: 35.

68 Greg Hansen, "Playing Watchdog Is No Easy Task for Livengood," *Arizona Daily Star*, May 24, 1994: 42.

69 "Couldn't Get a Hit Off Wildcat Thomas in Late April '56."

70 "Thomas, Lisa Mary Obituary," *Arizona Republic*, February 9, 2006: 11.

71 "Thomas, Carl L. Obituary."

GEORGE TSAMIS

BY CHRIS HICKS

George Tsamis, a 6-foot-2, 190-pound former left-handed pitcher, made his mark on the diamond managing in the independent leagues. Tsamis described himself as a "players manager" who asks "players to give 100 percent and run out every ground ball, and hustle, show up on time. If you don't, you'll be disciplined; but if you can't play for me, you can't play for anybody."[1] The New Jersey press nicknamed Tsamis's strategy "Tsamis-ball" for his prioritizing pitching and defense.[2] His strategy worked. He managed multiple teams but is best known for his 18 years with the St. Paul Saints and his subsequent position with the Kane County Cougars.

George Alex Tsamis was born on June 14, 1967, in Campbell, California, to Deno and Mina Tsamis, Greek immigrants to the United States. Deno Tsamis left Greece in 1956 and first settled in London, Ontario, with his brother.[3] Mina Giannkipoulos came to the United States via New York on the *TSS Olympia* on May 15, 1958, listing her occupation as seamstress, and then settled in California. The pair met in 1962. On March 25, 1963, Deno moved to the United States, and he and Mina married on June 23, 1963, in Alameda, California. The oldest son, Bill, was born in 1966, followed by George, born in Campbell, California, south of the San Francisco Bay area, in 1967 and Nick, born in 1969. All three of the Tsamis children grew up playing baseball.

In 1979 George played Little League ball in Campbell as a starting pitcher, first baseman, and shortstop (unusual since he threw left-handed). His team made it to the Little League World Series and reached the national championship final against Taiwan, which was making its eighth Little League World Series appearance since 1969. Campbell's coach, Bubby Agliolo, said that Taiwan had "promised to score 12 or 14 runs. ... Our guys proved they belonged by playing as perfect a defensive game as you will ever see anywhere."[4]

The next year, the Tsamis family moved across the country to Clearwater, Florida. The brothers continued to participate in youth baseball. George spent his freshman year at Countryside High School on the bench for the baseball team. His sophomore year, he played first base and pitched, his victories including the school's first full-game no-hitter.[5] Tsamis was already drawing high praise from Countryside's coach, Rick Misenti: "He's an intelligent ballplayer and he pays attention to detail. He mixes up his pitches very well."[6]

Despite being thought of as a pro prospect, Tsamis "was leaning toward staying in school," even if he was drafted by a major-league club upon graduation.[7] Tsamis enrolled at Stetson University in nearby DeLand, Florida, and impressed the coaches enough to be placed in the starting rotation.[8] He showed them they had made the right call by notching 19 strikeouts in a 19-0 win against Bethune-Cookman, breaking the school's previous single-game strikeout record of 16. Tsamis became one of the top three starters in the rotation.[9] His role was starting in the weekend series games and pitching in relief during the week.[10] Tsamis entered his junior year considered one of the best pitchers in the nation.[11] He was also named the number-one starter for the year. In this role, he started the first game of the series against conference opponents[12] His younger brother Nick began his freshman year and joined George on the pitching staff.[13] Tsamis struggled as a junior, at one point losing six straight decisions. Over the summers, he played in the Cape Cod League for the Falmouth Commodores. His first year, 1986, he went 6-2. In 1988, he was selected to the West Division all-star team and was voted team MVP.[14] He finished with a 7-2 record with a 2.77 ERA. Tsamis enjoyed his time playing in the wood-bat league. "You can work inside there and the ball travels farther off an aluminum bat. I broke eight bats up there.... I broke three in one inning."[15]

After his junior year, Tsamis was drafted by the Toronto Blue Jays in the 33rd round of the 1988 amateur draft. The two sides didn't come to an agreement after Tsamis declined Toronto's initial offers and he returned to Stetson for his senior season.[16] That year, he was out for redemption from an uncharacteristically poor performance his junior year, going 7-9 with a 3.62 ERA.[17] "I have to show myself; I have to show everybody that I'm a good pitcher."[18] His coach, Pete Dunn, saw the issue as mental because Tsamis shone against top teams, but tended to struggle against others.[19] Tsamis had a record-setting senior year: for strikeouts in a season;[20] for most wins in a season when he picked up his 11th against Rollins College; and for most complete games in a season (9).[21] One accomplishment was missing: a trip to the College World Series. He graduated with a degree in sports management, but without making the College World Series.[22]

On June 5, 1989, Tsamis was taken in the 15th round of the draft by the Minnesota Twins. He signed a contract the next day with his father and agent, Deno. He spent the first three years of his career moving between levels in the minors and between starting and the bullpen. His career would

George Tsamis. Courtesy The Topps Company, Inc.

be defined by injuries – his and others. At his first team, Visalia of the Class-A California League,[23] general manager Bruce Bucz considered Tsamis "to be a real prospect."[24]

One of Tsamis's assets was a great pickoff move to first that cemented him in the top of the league in picking off baserunners. "Everybody complains about my move," Tsamis said. "They say it's not even close to a pickoff. They think it looks like a balk. The key is that I do the same thing whenever I go to first base or home. Everything is exactly the same."[25] Tsamis struggled as a starter and was sent to the bullpen. After a rocky start, he rebounded to end the season 6–3 with a 3.05 ERA.

Tsamis started the 1990 season once again at Visalia and ended with a 17–4 record with a 2.21 ERA. In 1991, Tsamis started the season promoted to the Double A Orlando SunRays. He then moved up again to Triple-A Portland, Oregon on April 12, because of Denny Neagle's injury.[26] It was supposed to be a short stay with Portland, but he pitched well enough for Portland to keep him for the rest of the season. "They told me it would only be two or three starts and I would be sent back. It got to be three or four starts then I was leading the league in ERA. It showed me I could pitch," he said in midseason.[27]

In the offseason Tsamis pitched in the Venezuelan Winter League, starting 12 games with Cabimas to finish with a record of 4-7.[28] He began 1992 spring training on the major-league roster. The Twins considered him a middle reliever and a "once through the lineup guy."[29] According to Rob Antony, director of media relations, Tsamis impressed the Twins players and Tsamis was "one of the three pitchers at Portland we expect to make it here someday."[30] It was not to be that year. He was optioned back to Portland but missed 10 days due to a pulled abdominal muscle. Tsamis struggled when he was moved to the bullpen, which manager Scott Ullger expected, saying, "It can be a tough adjustment at first."[31] Paul Abbott was called up to the Twins, allowing Tsamis to take his place as starter.[32] He finished the season as the league's leader in wins at 13, tied with Zak Shinall of the Albuquerque Dukes.[33]

In 1993 Tsamis again started at big-league camp, but was reassigned to Portland.[34] Scott Leius injured his rotator cuff, so the Twins recalled Tsamis on April 25, giving him his shot.[35] Tsamis made his debut pitching in relief April 26, against the Milwaukee Brewers, allowing four hits and surrendering a run in four innings. He also hit the very first batter he faced.[36] Even so, Tsamis "surprised club officials with his ability to throw strikes, change speeds, and keep hitters off balance," extending his stay in the majors.[37] Tsamis picked up his first major-league win at Oakland Coliseum on May 26, 1993, in a rain-soaked game full of errors and wild pitches.[38] He was brought into the game with two outs in the eighth inning and the A's leading, 10-9. The Twins were able to give him a 12-10 lead. Tsamis kept the lead, despite giving up a solo homerun to Marcos Armas, giving the Twins a 12-11 victory.

Tsamis went on the disabled list from minor abdominal pain just as the Twins were to send him back to Triple-A.[39] While he recovered, pitcher Mark Guthrie went on the DL.[40] With American League approval, Tsamis was taken off the DL and kept on the major-league roster.[41] On August 14, he earned his only save, pitching four innings in relief against the Oakland A's.[42] Tsamis finished the season 1-2 with a 6.19 ERA, and after the season the Twins sent him outright to Portland.[43] Tsamis spent the winter of 1993-94 playing in the Dominican Winter League. He started two games with a 1-0 record and a 0.77 ERA.[44]

The Twins released Tsamis just two days before the season began, despite him giving up only three earned runs all spring. The Kansas City Royals, New York Mets, Chicago Cubs, and Seattle Mariners, were interested. Tsamis chose the Seattle Mariners based on their lack of left-handed pitching depth. They sent him to Double-A Jacksonville, where he appeared in 13 games (five starts), going 3-3 before landing on the disabled list with a strained left shoulder.[45] A month later Tsamis was promoted to Triple-A Calgary.[46] He struggled in his debut, giving up four runs on six hits in two innings.[47] Another injury, this time a torn rotator cuff put him back on the disabled list.[48]

On August 12, 1994, the major-league players went on strike, and the rest of the 1994 season, including the World Series, was canceled.[49] Tsamis married Kelly Ann Henaghan the next day. On August 18 the Mariners released him.[50] He then returned to the Winter League, appearing in three games with two starts and a 0-1 record with a 12.79 ERA.[51] In December he underwent shoulder surgery to repair his rotator cuff. He never told team officials about his shoulder pain because he thought he had a shot to play in the big leagues again with the Mariners.[52] Tsamis signed a minor-league contract with the Los Angeles Dodgers because they "gave me a big-league camp invitation even if the strike ends. I didn't sign as a replacement player. I signed as a minor leaguer."[53] He told reporters he had been contacted by 20 teams to be a replacement player.[54] Dodgers general manager Fred Claire verified this strategy.[55]

As the strike wore on, the Players Association announced that it would "consider anyone playing exhibition games a strikebreaker." This angered many, including Tsamis. He knew the minor leaguers were "in a no-win situation. If you play, you're considered a scab. If you don't play, you don't have a prayer of making the team."[56] The union was asking them to give up their livelihoods while not supporting or representing them.

To make things even more difficult at camp, the Dodgers offered each player "a guaranteed job for the entire season" if they signed a replacement contract. This only guaranteed a spot in the system, likely placement in the minors. They would also receive a $5,000 signing bonus, and even more money if the strike canceled the season. The Dodgers handed out questionnaires to the players, who had 24 hours to return them. Tsamis said the situation "really stinks," adding, "This is a decision that affects your whole life, your whole future, and you've got 24 hours to decide."[57]

Tsamis accepted the replacement offer. In his first exhibition win, on March 18, he gave up three runs in 1⅔ innings in relief but got a 9-5 win over the Tigers.[58] On April 2 the strike concluded, with major-league players returning on April 3 after 232 days.[59] The Dodgers sent Tsamis to Bakersfield of the California League.[60] He was subsequently released and never returned to the majors.

Tsamis said that he "tried to come back from shoulder surgery too soon. … It wasn't the Dodgers fault."[61] He spent the next few years bouncing from team to team in the minors and independent leagues, occasionally picking up odd jobs to make ends meet. Tsamis said, "After pitching in the majors in 1993, I was ashamed to play in this league (Double-A) last year. Now, considering my situation, I couldn't be happier."[62] He also missed a good portion of the 1996 season.[63] He needed a second shoulder surgery, this time for a torn labrum.[64]

In 1997 and 1998, Tsamis played in the Northeast League, where he pitched and became a pitching coach.[65] He became a father during his first year there. His daughter Casey was born on July 16, 1997. Tsamis knew teams shied away from him because of his two shoulder operations, but still believed he could pitch in the majors. He thought he would be fully healed by spring training in 1998.[66] After the season, he hung up his pitcher's mitt for good and retired with an overall record of 58-33 over 10 seasons of professional baseball: 51-26 in Organized Baseball and 7-7 in the independent leagues. In February 1999, Tsamis was inducted into the Stetson Athletic Hall of Fame.[67]

He then took on his first managerial role with the Waterbury Spirit. The Northeast League merged with the Northern League, which became the team's home. Tsamis managed the team to a 36-50 record.[68] The performance led the team to offer him a contract extension.[69] The team improved in 2000, making the playoffs with a 40-46 record. However, Waterbury ceased operations after the season.[70] According to Northern League commissioner Miles Wolff, the team was, "a victim of low fan support and a decrepit stadium."[71]

For the 2001 season, Tsamis signed on as the manager of the New Jersey Jackals. He was excited to manage what he called "the Yankees of the Northern League." Tsamis expected the team to go further and compete for the Northern League championship.[72] Going into his third year as manager, Tsamis had pinpointed his management style as a "players manager."[73] To help with baserunning and fielding, he added former major leaguer Jackie Hernández.[74] His strategy worked: The team made the playoffs as a wild card and progressed to the Northern League championship, winning the series 3-1.[75] Tsamis was named manager of the year.[76] The playoffs were postponed and attendance sharply declined in the wake of the terrorist attacks on September 11, 2001. Both Tsamis and the team expressed a desire for Tsamis to return to the Jackals in 2002.[77]

During the offseason, three organizations contacted Tsamis, including an offer from the Minnesota Twins.[78] January of 2002 started off with Tsamis agreeing to a three-year extension with the Jackals.[79] The Jackals had an outstanding 2002 season, setting franchise records in total, home, and road wins en route to defending their title in the playoffs. Tsamis was named the East Division manager of the year.[80] The Jackals picked up their second consecutive championship, winning the series three games to one.[81]

In November 2002, Tsamis resigned from the Jackals to take a three-year deal as the manager and "head of player personnel" with the St. Paul Saints.[82] The team had been underachieving in the last few seasons; attendance, still highest in the league, had begun to decline. The Saints hired Tsamis to get them back to their winning ways.[83]

Tsamis recruited players for the Saints in the offseason, including Rickey Henderson. Henderson had no offers from a big-league team despite spending the previous season with the Boston Red Sox.[84] While this attempt was unsuccessful, Tsamis started the season fielding 17 new signees out of 21 roster spots.[85] The 2003 Saints completed just their second 50-win season since the team's inception. Tsamis took them to the playoffs and the Saints gave him a contract extension that would keep him in St. Paul through 2008.[86] For the third year in a row, Tsamis was facing the Winnipeg Goldeyes in the playoffs.[87] The Saints jumped out to a two-games-to-one series lead, but were eliminated when Winnipeg won the next two games.[88]

The 2004 Saints made it to the playoffs with an overall record of 61-34, winning their first championship since 1996 in dramatic fashion.[89] With two outs in the bottom of the ninth, the Saints were trailing the Schaumburg Flyers by three runs when the team rallied to tie the score. Marc Marizzi unloaded on a 1-and-1 pitch to break the tie with a grand slam. This was Tsamis's third championship in four years.[90] The 2005 season saw change in the Northern League as two new teams were added, the Edmonton Cracker-Cats and the Calgary Vipers. These additions caused the league to place the Saints in the Southern Division. The Saints earned a place in the playoffs by winning the first half. They were tied for the second-half title, but the Gary SouthShore RailCats won the tiebreaker.[91]

In September 2005 it was announced that the Saints would leave the Northern League, which they had been a part of since 1993, and join a new league, the American Association. This new 10-team league had teams as far south as Florida, Louisiana, and Texas. This geographic spread meant another change; the Saints began flying to some away games.[92] The Saints struggled their first five years in the league. In the 2006 season, they got a playoff berth with an overall record of 54-42. In 2007 they earned a spot by finishing first in the second half of the season. The 2008 season saw the Saints not make the playoffs for the first time since Tsamis took over as manager, with a losing record of 42-54. The Saints also missed the playoffs in 2009 and 2010 with records of 49-47 and 45-51. Despite the struggles, in July 2007 the team extended Tsamis's contract through 2009.[93] On July 27 Tsamis became the Saints' all-time leader in victories with his 265th win.[94]

After the 2010 season, four of the remaining eight Northern League teams left and joined the American Association.[95] This growth caused restructuring. The 14 teams were divided into three divisions: Central, North, and South. The schedule went to a 100-game single season. The playoff teams were the winners of each division, plus a wild card.[96]

In 2011 the Saints rebounded and made the playoffs as the wild card. Only 11 players who suited up on Opening Day were still with the team at season's end because of injuries and opportunities in MLB.[97] The Saints lost in the finals to the Grand Prairie AirHogs in five games.[98] On July 20, 2012, during his 10th season as manager, the Saints defeated the Sioux City Explorers for Tsamis's 500th win with the team.[99] The Saints finished the season 52-48 without a playoff appearance. On November 21, 2012, Tsamis's father, Deno Tsamis, died at the age of 76.[100]

The Saints finished the 2013 and 2014 seasons with sub-.500 records. In 2014 they played their final season in Midway Stadium, their home since 1993. CHS Field, located in downtown St. Paul, opened in 2015.[101] Able to use the brand-new ballpark to recruit, Tsamis brought in higher-tier players. Only eight of the players from the 2014 team appeared on the 2015 roster.[102] The team Tsamis built christened their new ballpark with an 8-7 win.[103] They set several franchise records and won 74 games, one shy of setting the league's record for most wins in a season. They finished first in their division, making it to the playoffs.[104]

Early in 2016, from May 30 through June 13, the team covered 3,063 miles by bus on the longest road trip in franchise history. The Saints continued winning, despite the long bus rides, going 9-5.[105] They finished out their season in walk-off fashion, beating Lincoln 5-4, and ending tied for the best record in the league at 61-39.[106] However, they were unable to get to the championship after being eliminated by the Winnipeg Goldeyes in the first round of the playoffs.[107] In 2017 the Saints got off to a good start, going 27-13, but the team struggled in the second half and again missed the playoffs. After going 48-52, Tsamis and the Saints hoped for a rebound in 2018.[108]

The American Association realigned in 2018, placing teams in the North or South Division.[109] June 12 brought Tsamis his 1,000th career win in a come-from-behind victory.[110] The Saints returned to the playoffs in the wild-card position after going 59-41 and tying for first in the North Division.[111] They beat the RailCats in the playoff series[112] but lost to the Kansas City T-Bones for the championship.[113]

On August 23, 2019, Tsamis reached another milestone, managing in his 2,000th career game in a 2-1 victory.[114] The Saints returned to the playoffs, staging a huge comeback in the first round by winning the last three games in the series. The Saints quickly defeated Sioux City in three straight games. Chesny Young came up with the bases loaded, swung on the first pitch, and turned it into a grand slam, putting the Saints ahead 5-3. That became the final score, and the Saints won their first American Association championship, but the second championship under Tsamis.[115] Local celebrations included a one-block championship parade. Tsamis and some of the players attended the Twins game, where Tsamis threw out the first pitch.[116]

The 2020 season was unlike anything anyone had ever seen. As coronavirus spread around the world, large gatherings such as concerts and sporting events were canceled or presented with very small audiences. Some leagues, such as the affiliated minor leagues, canceled their seasons altogether. The American Association carried on, albeit with a shortened schedule. Games were played in three "hub cities" that allowed fans to be spectators at the games: Sioux Falls, South Dakota; Milwaukee; and Fargo, North Dakota.[117] The Chicago Dogs were allowed to play in their home stadium.[118] Only six teams, including the Saints, participated in the season. A special draft was held for players who were on inactive teams. Those players would then return to their respective teams in 2021.[119] The Saints lived out of a hotel in Sioux Falls for the first part of the season. The first home game allowed at CHS Field was played on August 4, and the seating was limited to 1,500 to follow social distancing guidelines.[120] The Saints failed to make the playoffs, and Milwaukee beat out Sioux Falls for the title.[121]

In December of 2020, a reorganization of minor-league baseball was announced. Some 40 teams would no longer be part of the minor leagues, but a few teams were added. The St. Paul Saints became the Triple-A affiliate of the Minnesota Twins, only 10 miles away. For Tsamis, this meant that, after 18 years, his role with the Saints would change. He was notified on November 13 that he would no longer be manager.[122] Tsamis understood but was "devastated" by the news yet "happy" for the team and its owners.[123] He did accept the position of director of youth sports and clinics that the club offered.[124]

For "four long painful months," there were no contract offers. Then in February 2021, the phone rang. The Kane County Cougars were a minor-league affiliate for 30 years. With realignment they became independent.[125] They had no players and were responsible for paying for everything: equipment, coaches, and players. The Cougars joined the American Association, the former home of the Saints. The team hired Tsamis, giving him the challenge of putting together a team, including coaching staff, before the start of the season in May.[126] The Cougars experienced some growing pains in their first independent season with a sub-.500 record.

Because of COVID-19, the American Association champion 2019 Saints had not yet been formally honored by the team. On August 5, 2021, the Saints honored the team and Tsamis personally. They retired his jersey (22), and he threw out the first pitch.[127]

The 2022 season showed a big turnaround by the team as it made the playoffs with a 54-46 record. But it was eliminated in the first playoff round by the Cleburne Railroaders.[128] Tsamis was named the 2022 American Association Manager of the Year. The 2023 campaign with Kane County was his 25th season as a manager.[129]

SOURCES

In addition to the sources cited in the Notes, the author consulted Ancestry.com and Baseball-Reference.com.

NOTES

1. Darren Cooper, "Jackals to Usher In Tsamis Time," *Montclair (New Jersey) Times,* November 22, 2000: C3.
2. "NJ Jackals Journal," *Montclair Times,* May 31, 2001: C3.
3. "Tsamis, Deno," *Tampa Bay (Florida) Times,* November 24, 2012: 7B.
4. Don West, "Little Leaguers Big in Campbell," *San Francisco Examiner,* August 29, 1979: 49.
5. Kevin Thomas, "Sophomore Pitcher Has Already Established Himself," *Tampa Bay Times,* March 17, 1983: 10C.
6. "Sophomore Pitcher Has Already Established Himself."
7. Don Banks, "Suncoast High School Stars Await Pro Calls," *Tampa Bay Times,* June 3, 1985: 5C.
8. Beth Rhoden, "Woide to Get Call in Stetson Opener," *Orlando (Florida) Sentinel,* February 14, 1986: 5.
9. "Stetson Baseball Opener Set Feb. 13 Against FIU," *Orlando Sentinel,* February 6, 1987: 13.
10. Creig Ewing, "Stetson Setting Torrid Pace in TAAC Race," *Orlando Sentinel,* March 18, 1987: 12.
11. Darrell Proctor, John Romano, Brian Landman, Holt Hackney, and Scott Alan Salomon, "College Baseball Preview '88," *Tampa Bay Times,* February 3, 1988: 4C.
12. Creig Ewing, "Hatters Lose Lumber, Will Rely on Quick Feet," *Orlando Sentinel,* February 7, 1988: C12.
13. Darrell Proctor, John Romano, Brian Landman, Holt Hackney, and Scott Alan Salomon, "College Baseball Preview '88,"
14. Creig Ewing, "Hatters Have World Flavor," *Orlando Sentinel,* July 31, 1988: 19.
15. Creig Ewing, "Tsamis Plans to Return to Stetson for His Senior Year," *Sentinel,* August 10, 1988: 7.
16. "Tsamis Plans to Return to Stetson for His Senior Year."
17. Creig Ewing, "Hatters Have World Flavor," *Orlando Sentinel,* July 31, 1988: 19.
18. Alan Schmadtke, "Tsamis Out to Prove His Pitching Worth," *Orlando Sentinel,* January 18, 1989: 6.
19. Alan Schmadtke, "Tsamis Out to Prove His Pitching Worth," *Orlando Sentinel,* January 18, 1989: 6.
20. "Naples Catcher Is 4th Recruit Signed by Dunn," *Orlando Sentinel,* May 7, 1989: 15.
21. Alan Schmadtke, "Tsamis Backs 18-Hit Attack as Stetson Cruises," *Orlando Sentinel,* May 10, 1989: B4.
22. Dave Theall, "Northwest Grad Roberts Draws Raves at USF," *Tampa Bay Times,* April 9, 1990: 8.
23. Alan Schmadtke, "Twins Send Tsamis to Visalia," *Orlando Sentinel,* June 7, 1989: 5.
24. George Hostetter, "Clark Worshiper Has Own Identity with Oaks," *Fresno (California) Bee,* April 26, 1990: 7.
25. Jon Flick, "Visalia's Tsamis Blanks Spirit 9-0," *San Bernardino County (California) Sun,* August 5, 1990: C2.
26. Jeff Lenihan, "Rookie Knoblauch Also Showing Qualities of a Leadoff Hitter," *Minneapolis Star-Tribune,* April 15, 1991: 8C.
27. Derek Catron, "Tsamis Follows Advice: Quit Worrying and Get Batters Out," *Orlando Sentinel,* July 4, 1991: I12.
28. Registro stadísti stadístico Del Beisbol Profesional Venezolano, www.pelotabinaria.com.ve/beisbol/mostrarlphp?ID=tsamgeooo1.
29. "Dave Theall, "Tsamis Awaits Call from Big Twins," *Orlando Times,* June 14, 1992: 4.
30. "Dave Theall, "Tsamis Awaits Call from Big Twins."
31. Scott Purks, "Tsamis Looking for Right Stuff in Middle Relief," *Tampa Tribune,* July 15, 1992: 8.
32. Jeff Lenihan, "Reboulet Shaky on Basepaths," *Minneapolis Star Tribune,* July 23, 1992: 5C.

33 Dave Theall and Wayne McKnight, "Pro Baseball," *Orlando Times,* January 30, 1993: 5.

34 Kevin Kaminski, "Twins-Red Sox Recap," *Fort Myers* (Florida) *News-Press,* March 23, 1993: 4C.

35 "Leius Goes on DL; Twins Recall Tsamis," *Saint Cloud* (Minnesota) *Times,* April 26, 1993: 2B.

36 Jim Souhan, "Tapani Gets Rocked Again, Twins Fall 10-3," *Minneapolis Star Tribune,* April 27, 1993: 1C.

37 Jim Souhan, "Garces Out as Willis Activated," *Minneapolis Star Tribune,* May 15, 1993: 7C.

38 Associated Press, "It Rains: Hits, Runs, Blown Saves, Raindrops," *Reno* (Nevada) *Gazette-Journal,* May 27, 1993: 2E.

39 Jim Souhan, "Tsamis Takes Detour to Doctor's Office on His Way to Portland," *Minneapolis Star Tribune,* May 29, 1993: 5C.

40 Dennis Brackin, "McCarty, Twins, Stay Hot," *Minneapolis Star Tribune,* May 31, 1993: 1C, 7C.

41 Jim Souhan, "McCarty, Mack Appear Together, but Not for Long," *Minneapolis Star Tribune,* June 1, 1993: 5C.

42 "Baseball," *Vancouver* (British Columbia) *Province,* August 15, 1993: A57.

43 Sid Hartman, "Purdue, Gophers Similar," *Minneapolis Star Tribune,* October 9, 1993: 3C.

44 "George Tsamis," LIDOM, http://estadisticas.lidom.com/Miembro/Detalle?idMiembro=7160.

45 Dave Theall, "Tsamis Eyeing a Return to Majors as New Mariner," *Tampa Bay Times,* June 26, 1994: 4.

46 Gyle Konotopetz, "The Game Story," *Calgary* (Alberta) *Herald,* July 27, 1994: C2.

47 "The Game Story."

48 Kevin Thomas, "Tsamis Won't Give Up Dream," *Tampa Bay Times,* August 20, 1997: 6C.

49 Tom Verducci, "Sham Spring," *Sports Illustrated,* February 23, 2015: vault.si.com/vault/2015/02/23/the-sham-spring.

50 Gyle Konotopetz, "Game Story," *Calgary Herald,* August 19, 1994: C4.

51 "George Tsamis," LIDOM, http://estadisticas.lidom.com/Miembro/Detalle?idMiembro=7160.

52 Kevin Thomas, "Tsamis Won't Give Up Dream," *Tampa Bay Times,* August 20, 1997: 6C.

53 Jim Souhan, "Rockies Express Interest in Tapani," *Minneapolis Star Tribune,* January 20, 1995: 8C.

54 "Rockies Express Interest in Tapani."

55 Steve Dilbeck (Associated Press), "Dodgers Will Wait to Pop the Question," *Vancouver Sun,* February 11, 1995: C14.

56 "Union Throws Curve to Minor League Players," *Reno Gazette-Journal,* February 21, 1995: 1D.

57 Bob Nightengale, "Play With Us, Stay With Us," *Newport News* (Virginia) *Daily Press,* February 24, 1995: 4.

58 Associated Press, "Dodgers Top Tigers, 9-5," *Lansing* (Michigan) *State Journal,* March 19, 1995: 8G.

59 Tom Verducci, "Sham Spring."

60 "The Day in Sports," *Los Angeles Times,* April 3, 1995: C14.

61 Dave Theall, "Tsamis Seeks Another Chance," *Tampa Bay Times,* June 25, 1995: 8.

62 Peter Thomson, "Nifty Pitching Stops Orlando," *Orlando Sentinel,* July 22, 1995: B-5.

63 Kevin Thomas, "Tsamis Won't Give Up Dream," *Tampa Bay Times,* August 20, 1997: 6C.

64 Nancy Morgan, "Ex-Countryside Star Is Manager in Minors," *Tampa Bay Times,* October 14, 2001: 26.

65 "Deals," *Great Falls* (Montana) *Tribune,* May 17, 1998: 2S.

66 Kevin Thomas, "Tsamis Won't Give Up Dream," *Tampa Bay Times,* August 20, 1997: 6C.

67 Bill Buchalter, "5 to be Inducted in Stetson's Hall," *Orlando Sentinel,* January 8, 1999: C8.

68 John P. Cleary, "Northern League East Teams at a Glance," *Elmira* (New York) *Star-Gazette,* May 26, 2000: 2B.

69 "Transactions," *Kokomo* (Indiana) *Tribune,* August 24, 1999: B4.

70 "Tsamis Named Jackals Manager," *Montclair Times,* November 16, 2000: C7.

71 Eric M. Weiss, "Peters Renews Pitch for Baseball," *Hartford Courant,* October 23, 2000: A4.

72 Darren Cooper, "Jackals to Usher In Tsamis Time," *Montclair Times,* November 22, 2000: C3.

73 "Jackals to Usher In Tsamis Time."

74 "Jackals Add Jackie Hernandez to Staff," *Clifton* (New Jersey) *Journal,* April 5, 2001: A22.

75 Darren Cooper, "Jumping Jacks!," *Montclair Times,* October 4, 2001: C1.

76 Jim Saip, "Story Behind Signing One of League's Elite," *Glen Falls* (New York) *Post-Star,* July 7, 2002: D3.

77 Darren Cooper, "Jumping Jacks!" *Montclair Times,* October 4, 2001: C1, C3.

78 Darren Cooper, "Tsamis' Plan Is the Same," *Montclair Times,* May 23, 2002: C1-C2.

79 "Tsamis Agrees to Three-Year Extension," *Montclair Times,* January 24, 2002: C3.

80 Angela Daidone, "Jackals Manager Earns League Honor," *Hawthorne* (New Jersey) *Gazette,* September 4, 2002: H47.

81 "Back to Back Jacks," *Montclair Times,* September 26, 2002: C1.

82 "Jackals Shake-Up," *Montclair Times,* November 14, 2002: C2; "Francona Picked as A's Bench Coach," *La Crosse* (Wisconsin) *Tribune,* November 7, 2002: B-8.

83 "St. Paul Saints Focus on Winning Again," *La Crosse Tribune,* May 5, 2003: B-4.

84 La Velle E. Neal III, "Saints Show Interest in Signing Henderson," *Minneapolis Star-Tribune,* April 10, 2003: C2.

85 John Millea, "Fireworks Start Quickly for Saints," *Minneapolis Star-Tribune,* May 24, 2003: C2.

86 "Saints Reward Tsamis with 3-Year Contract Extension," *Minneapolis Star-Tribune,* September 1, 2003: C2.

87 John Millea, "Saints Make a Return to Playoff Ball," *Minneapolis Star Tribune,* September 2, 2003: C10.

88 Greg Di Cresce, "Goldeyes Savour Victory Over Tsamis and the Saints," *Winnipeg Sun,* September 8, 2003: S7.

89 "Northern League Division Playoffs," *Kansas City Star,* September 7, 2004: C5.

90 Adam Wazny, "Grand Slam Gives Saints N.L. Title," *Winnipeg Sun,* September 21, 2004: 49.

91 "Breaking Down the Northern League," *Munster* (Indiana) *Times,* September 6, 2005: C3.

92 John Millea, "Saints Venture Out as Part of New Baseball League," *Minneapolis Star Tribune,* May 12, 2006: C10.

93 Brandenburg Wins His Fifth, Helps Saints Top Explorers," *Minneapolis Star Tribune,* July 20, 2007: C6.

94 "Johnnies Senior Charged with Sexual Assault," *Minneapolis Star Tribune,* July 28, 2007: C5.

95 Christopher Burbach, "'Wait Till Next Year' May Be Too Optimistic for Downtown Park," *Omaha World-Herald,* September 14, 2011: 1, 2.

96 "Pheasants Release Schedule," *Sioux Falls* (South Dakota) *Argus-Leader,* December 31, 2010: 3C.

97 Brian Stensaas, "There's No Season Like Postseason," *Minneapolis Star Tribune,* September 1, 2011: C2.

98 "AirHogs Down Saints to Clinch Championship," *Minneapolis Star Tribune,* September 13, 2011: C7.

99 Terry Hersom, "Saints' Tsamis Hits Milestone in Win Over X's," *Sioux City* (Iowa) *Journal,* July 21, 2012: B1, B2.

100 "Tsamis, Deno."

101 Jason Gonzalez, "Aging Midway, Home of Saints, Takes Last Bow," *Minneapolis Star Tribune,* May 15, 2014: C1, C8.

102 Chip Scoggins, "Saints on the March," *Minneapolis Star Tribune,* June 30, 2015: C1, C6.

103 Jim Souhan, "If 'Fun Is Good,' Opening a New Ballpark Is Better," *Minneapolis Star Tribune,* May 22, 2015: C1.

104 Jason Gonzalez, "Saints Hope Playoffs Put Icing on Magical Season," *Minneapolis Star Tribune,* September 9, 2015: C3.

105 Chip Scoggins, "For Well-Traveled Saints, 'Friendly Confines' Is a Bus," *Minneapolis Star Tribune,* June 14, 2016: C1.

106 "Saints Finish Atop League," *Minneapolis Star Tribune,* September 6, 2016: C2.

107 "Goldeyes Eliminate Saints in Fifth Game," *Minneapolis Star Tribune,* September 13, 2016: C7.

108 Jim Paulsen, "Saints Start on the Road," *Minneapolis Star Tribune,* May 18, 2018: C3.

109 "Northwestern Ends U's Soccer Win Streak at Five," *Minneapolis Star Tribune,* October 13, 2017: C9.

110 "Saints' Tsamis Posts 1,000th Career Win," *Minneapolis Star Tribune,* June 13, 2018: C9.

111 "Gophers Are No. 1 in Volleyball," *Minneapolis Star Tribune,* September 4, 2018: C7.

112 "Saints Edge Gary, Win Playoff Series," *Minneapolis Star Tribune,* September 9, 2018: C11.

113 "Saints Lose Finals in Four Games to K.C.," *Minneapolis Star Tribune,* September 16, 2018: C14.

114 "Truax Fight Called Off," *Minneapolis Star Tribune,* August 23, 2019: C3.

115 Randy Johnson, "It's a Grand Slam Finish to Saints' First League Title in 15 Years," *Minneapolis Star Tribune,* September 15, 2019: C3.

116 Jim Souhan, "Saints Get Their Moment in the Sun," *Minneapolis Star Tribune,* September 18, 2019: C1, C4.

117 "St. Paul Saints to Start July 3rd," *Winona* (Minnesota) *Daily News,* June 14, 2020: B2.

118 Randy Johnson, "Saints Up, Play Ball!" *Minneapolis Star Tribune,* July 2, 2020: C1.

119 Tim Gray, "Dogs Strike Out," *Lincoln* (Nebraska) *Journal Star,* June 13, 2020: B1, B3.

120 Randy Johnson, "Coming Home for the Homestretch," *Minneapolis Star Tribune,* July 31, 2020: C4.

121 Curt Hogg, "Champs! The Milwaukee Milkmen defeat Sioux Falls to Win the American Association Championship," *Milwaukee Journal Sentinel,* September 17, 2020. https://www.jsonline.com/story/sports/2020/09/17/milwaukee-milkmen-win-2020-american-association-baseball-championship/3489912001/.

122 Dan Hayes, "After 'Crushing' Departure, Ex-St. Paul Saints Legend George Tsamis Is Finding His Way with Kane County Cougars," *Athletic,* August 6, 2021, www.theathletic.com/2756498/2021/08/06/after-crushing-departure-saints-legend-george-tsamis-is-finding-his-way-with-kane-county-cougars/?redirected=1.

123 Patrick Reusse, "Tsamis Now an Outsider, but Only on Paper," *Minneapolis Star Tribune,* December 13, 2020: C2.

124 "After 'Crushing' Departure, Ex-St. Paul Saints Legend George Tsamis Is Finding His Way with Kane County Cougars."

125 "After 'Crushing' Departure, Ex-St. Paul Saints Legend George Tsamis Is Finding His Way with Kane County Cougars."

126 Chelsea Janes, "Minors League Teams Adjust to Major Shifts," *Spokane* (Washington) *Spokesman-Review,* February 28, 2021: B3.

127 "After 'Crushing' Departure, Ex-St. Paul Saints Legend George Tsamis Is Finding His Way with Kane County Cougars."

128 "Kane County Cougars Yearly Results," Stats Crew, https://www.statscrew.com/minorbaseball/standings/t-kc12296.

129 Robert Pannier, "Kane County Cougars George Tsamis Named American Association Manager of the Year," *Minor League Sports Report*, September 9, 2022. https://minorleaguesportsreport.com/index.php/kane-county-cougars-george-tsamis-named-american-association-manager-of-the-year/#:~:text=On%20Friday%2C%20This%20Week%20in,the%20club%20finished%2054%2D46.

WILSON VALDÉZ

BY LEN PASCULLI

Wilson Valdéz played in 439 major-league games from 2004 through 2012. He was an archetypical utilityman: He played five different positions in the field over parts of seven seasons with seven different major-league teams from 2004 through 2012: the Chicago White Sox, Seattle Mariners, San Diego Padres, Los Angeles Dodgers, New York Mets, Philadelphia Phillies, and Cincinnati Reds. Until one game in 2011. When the Phillies ran out of relief pitchers in the 19th inning, he was called upon to pitch to the heart of the Reds' order. He held the Reds scoreless and his teammates rewarded him with the victory by scoring in the bottom of the inning. Of all the players in major-league history who earned a victory in the only game they pitched, Valdéz is one of only three players who got the victory in the only game he pitched without allowing a hit or a run.[1]

Born on May 20, 1978, in Nizao, a small city on the southern coast of the Dominican Republic, Wilson Antonio Valdéz was the youngest of Angel and Juana's seven children. His father, Angel, worked as a farmer.[2] He died of lung cancer in 1991.[3] His mother worked as a housekeeper; as of 2023, she no longer worked but still lived in the Dominican Republic near Valdéz.[4]

The population of Nizao City is a little more than 6,000 while the population of the entire Nizao Municipality including rural districts is about 30,000. Nizao is about 75 miles west of San Pedro de Macoris (pop. approx. 200,000), a major city that sports historian Rob Ruck called the breeding ground for the best Dominican-born ballplayers.[5] Yet, nine major leaguers, including Valdéz, Vladimir Guerrero Sr., one of three Dominicans in the National Baseball Hall of Fame as of 2021,[6] and All-Star Ketel Marte, who is Valdéz's nephew, were born in little Nizao.[7]

Valdéz attended Aliro Paulino High School (now known as Lucila Mojica High School) in Nizao. Scouts Arturo DeFreitas and Fred Ferreira[8] signed him at age 18 for the Montreal Expos on February 4, 1997, as an undrafted amateur free agent.

The 5-foot-11, 170-pound infielder reported to the Dominican Summer League Expos, where he batted .303 (244 at-bats) in 1997 and .300 (247 at-bats) in 1998. In 1999 he advanced to the Gulf Coast League Expos in Jupiter, Florida, where he accumulated 24 hits and 10 stolen bases in just 82 at-bats (22 games) before he was promoted to the Class-A Vermont Expos in the New York-Penn League for the remainder of the summer and batted .246 in 36 games (130 at-bats).

Over the next two seasons, Valdéz steadily advanced from short-season Class A (the Vermont Expos in 2000), to regular Class A (the Cape Fear Crocs in the South Atlantic League in 2000 and the Clinton (Iowa) LumberKings in the Midwest League in 2001), to Advanced Class A – the Jupiter (Florida) Hammerheads in 2001.

In February 2002 Expos principal owner Jeffrey Loria bought the Florida Marlins and took with him most of the Expos' top brass and staff, including general manager Larry Beinfest; senior vice president and director of international operations Fred Ferreira; field manager Jeff Torborg; and coach Ozzie Guillén. When the Expos released Valdéz in 2002, the new Marlins talent hunters quickly snatched him up. He was assigned to the Double-A Portland (Maine) Sea Dogs and had a good season as their regular shortstop: 98 hits, 19 doubles, 5 triples, and 18 stolen bases.

In 2003, his age 25 season, Valdéz turned a corner. He began with the Marlins' Double-A affiliate, the Carolina (Raleigh, North Carolina) Mudcats, where his batting average swelled to .313, followed by a promotion to the Triple-A Albuquerque Isotopes for the remainder of 2003 and the beginning of 2004. Over the two seasons with Albuquerque (682 plate appearances), Valdéz batted .302 with 23 doubles, 7 triples, 43 runs batted in, 81 runs scored, and 52 stolen bases. He was named Albuquerque's Defensive Player of the Year in 2003.[9]

But Valdéz's path to the Marlins infield was blocked by All-Stars Álex González at shortstop and Luis Castillo at second base, and by capable backups Damion Easley and Lenny Harris. Valdéz was expendable. The Marlins needed bullpen help and the Chicago White Sox would be losing their starting shortstop, José Valentín, to free agency at the end of the 2004 season, so on June 17, 2004, the Marlins traded Valdéz with cash to the White Sox for reliever Billy Koch. Who was the new manager of the White Sox that season? Ozzie Guillén. Valdéz was assigned to the Triple-A Charlotte Knights, where he batted .302 and stole 13 bases, earning him a call-up when the major-league rosters expanded in September 2004.

Valdéz made his major-league debut with the White Sox on September 7, 2004, with a start against the Texas Rangers. He played second base and grounded out three times in as many at-bats against Kenny Rogers. He notched his first big-league hit and RBI off Nate Robertson in a victory over the Detroit Tigers on September 17. Although he got an extended look that month with 46 plate appearances, he was released after the season. The following spring he was claimed off waivers by the Seattle Mariners, who had lost shortstop Rich Aurilia to free agency and his replacement, Pokey Reese, to injury.[10]

Valdéz was the Mariners' starting shortstop in April and May 2005. However, on June 9 he was traded once again, this time to the San Diego Padres for two minor-league relievers, Mike Bumstead and R.D. Spiehs. He reported to the team's Triple-A affiliate, the Portland (Oregon) Beavers. Valdéz was called up by the Padres on August 16 to fill in at shortstop for the injured Khalil Greene and was released on August 30 when Greene returned to the lineup.

Valdéz was signed as a free agent on October 11, 2005, by the Kansas City Royals and he was

Wilson Valdéz. Courtesy of the Philadelphia Phillies/Miles Kennedy.

assigned to Triple-A Omaha; however, before the new season began the Los Angeles Dodgers traded minor-league pitcher Jarod Plummer to the Royals for Valdéz. With much foresight, the Dodgers established the first baseball academy in the Dominican Republic in 1987 and installed a coach (Manny Mota, 1980-2013) to be the "shoulder on which the Dodgers' Latin American players could lean."[11] The Dodgers' strategy during those years was to find and develop, or as they did in 2006 with Rafael Furcal, Wilson Betemit, Julio Lugo, and Valdéz, to sign or trade for versatile Dominican players to add to the organization's depth behind Jeff Kent and Ramon Martinez.[12]

Valdéz did not make it out of the Dodgers farm system in 2006. The "baseball vagabond," as he was labeled by local sportswriter Joe Hawk,[13] had a fine season playing 137 games with the Triple-A Las Vegas 51s. He played second base, shortstop, third base, and the outfield. "It doesn't matter where I play. I want to help the team win and I want to play," said Valdéz.[14] On offense, 51s manager Jerry Royster crowed, "He's a smart baseball player. If I want him to hit and run, if I want him to bunt, if I need him to move a runner over, I can tell him to do it."[15]

Valdéz batted .297 for the 51s in 2006 (.365 at home at Cashman Field[16]) with 6 home runs and 53 RBIs. He led the team in hits (157), stolen bases (26), runs scored (94), and walks (56). He was named the team's Most Valuable Player and was chosen for the Pacific Coast League All-Star team.[17]

In the offseason, Valdéz tried something different. He returned to the Dominican Republic to play winter ball for his old friend, Arturo DeFreitas, the manager of the Gigantes del Cibao. Beginning with the 2006-2007 season, Valdéz played Dominican winter-league ball for 10 consecutive seasons, the first seven with the Gigantes, then three with their rival, the Tigres del Licey. In that first winter he led the team with 68 plate appearances, four doubles, and seven stolen bases. He batted .263. His second winter in the DWL was his best, when he tallied a .287 batting average, .368 on-base percentage, and a .317 slugging average.

Winter ball in the Dominican Republic had lost some of the player attraction it once enjoyed before free agency. Popular major leaguers no longer needed the money or fanfare, nor did they want to risk injury.[18] Valdéz played in the league not for celebrity; he played to get better. "I think of how hard it was [to play in the major leagues]," he said. "I just wanted to show people that I could play."[19]

Valdéz broke camp with the Dodgers in the spring of 2007 with fresh hope. While Furcal nursed an ankle he sprained during spring training and with Lugo lost to free agency, Valdéz filled the reserve role. He had three hits in his first start with the Dodgers and enjoyed a streak of 10 hits in 23 at-bats over seven games in April. However, he collected only three more hits after that and was sent down to Las Vegas on May 16, replaced by the hot-hitting minor leaguer Tony Abreu (another Dominican infielder in the Dodgers' organization). Valdéz slashed .343/.413/.435 and belted four home runs for the 51s before getting recalled by the Dodgers in September.

The new year ushered in a new, albeit short-lived, experience for Valdéz: baseball in the Pacific rim. Valdéz found the adjustment to be difficult. His Dodgers contract had been purchased by the Kia Tigers of the Korean Baseball Organization in January 2008. The Tigers were looking for American players to round out their roster and thought that Valdéz could supply improved defense at shortstop and some punch at the plate.[20] He played in 47 games but batted only .218 in 176 plate appearances. One day he made a barehanded play from his shortstop position on a slow grounder. He got the out but manager Cho Beom-Hyun immediately pulled him from the game, telling Valdéz, "We don't play that kind of baseball. You have to follow the rules." A perplexed and unhappy Valdéz asked to be released and soon he was.[21]

On June 12 Valdéz was picked up by the Yakult Swallows of Tokyo in Japan's Central League[22] to fill in for Shinya Miyamoto, the team's shortstop, who left to play for Japan's national team in the 2008 Beijing Olympics.[23] But there, too, Valdéz became a bit flummoxed when he lost playing time: "I was enjoying it, but now it's like, I don't know. … I know I can play, but they don't think I can play."[24] Valdéz came home to play in the Dominican Winter League once again, then signed a minor-league deal with the Cleveland Indians that included an invitation to spring training in 2009.[25]

Valdéz's real value as a movable piece to fill a team's immediate middle-infield need became apparent again in May 2009. With New York Mets shortstop José Reyes and backup Álex Cora both sidelined with injuries, the Mets acquired Valdéz from Cleveland for cash. Upon Cora's return, Valdéz was shuffled off to the Triple-A Buffalo Bisons on June 25. He was recalled on August 19 because Cora got hurt again. After one season with the Mets, Valdéz filed for free agency.

Before the 2010 season began, with Jimmy Rollins and Chase Utley each entering his age-31 season, the Philadelphia Phillies signed three infielders as free agents: Plácido Polanco, Juan Castro, and Valdéz. After a short stint with the Lehigh Valley IronPigs in Triple A (where he had 10 hits in 22 at-bats), Valdéz the Vagabond found himself playing regularly for a first-place contender. He played in 210 games in 2010 and 2011 – the most he played for any major-league team – as Utley, Rollins, and Polanco missed large swaths of time with injuries.

Valdéz enjoyed several individual highlights and career-best performances during his two seasons with the Phillies. He hit home runs two nights in a row (June 19 and 20, 2010) against the Minnesota Twins at Citizens Bank Park in Philadelphia (he had a total of only six home runs in his career); he drove in 65 runs; scored 76 runs; slugged 30 doubles and 7 triples; and stole 10 bases.

On May 29, 2010, with one out in the third inning, Valdéz singled to center off Florida Marlins pitcher Josh Johnson. The next batter, Utley, sent a 2-and-2 pitch to straightaway center field that Cameron Maybin misjudged for a three-base error scoring Valdéz from first. It was the only run of the game, and all that pitcher Roy Halladay needed as he pitched a perfect game, the 20th perfect game in major-league history.[26]

Valdéz knocked in a career-best four runs on June 29, 2010, with a three-run homer and a fielder's choice to help the Phillies defeat the Cincinnati Reds, 9-6.[27] A month later, on July 29, he smacked a single in the bottom of the 11th inning – his third hit of the night – to lift the Phillies over the Arizona Diamondbacks, 3-2, walk-off style.

Despite the personal heroics, the brass ring for Valdéz was that, with the Phillies, he finally got the chance to play in a postseason game. "We won something like 18 straight to get there," Valdéz remembered.[28] He contributed greatly to the Phillies' first-place finish in the NL's East Division in 2010 as he batted .352 (19-for-54) over his final 18 games and .400 (14-for-35) with runners in scoring position in his last 27 games.[29]

When a backache prevented Polanco from playing in the first game of the National League Division Series against the Cincinnati Reds, Valdéz drew the start at third base and was on the field for Halladay's second gem. In the second inning, Valdéz collected an infield single and scored the third run in a 4-0 Phillies victory – another no-hitter by Halladay.[30] It was Halladay's first postseason game and one of only three no-hitters in postseason history; Don Larsen's perfect game in 1956 was the first and the combined no-hitter by four Houston Astros pitchers in Game Four of the 2022 World Series was the third.

The Phillies swept the Reds in three games before losing to the San Francisco Giants in six games in the National League Championship Series. Valdéz's only appearances in the NLCS were two pinch-running assignments.[31]

On Opening Day, April 1, 2011, against the Houston Astros (a game Halladay started), Valdéz collected two hits, including a single that tied the game at 4-4 in the bottom of the ninth inning. The next batter was John Mayberry Jr., who singled home the winning run.

In the only four-hit game of his career, Valdéz went 4-for-4 with two doubles, three RBIs, and three runs scored against the New York Mets on April 7, 2011 (coincidentally, another Halladay game), capping off a 9-for-21 hitting streak to open the season.

Valdéz's career was exemplified by his versatility, reliability, and ardor, so it came as no surprise that Phillies manager Charlie Manuel called on him to pitch one night in 2011. On May 25 the team was out of relief pitchers and the score was tied 4-4 going into the top of the 19th inning at Citizens Bank Park. What was a surprise, however, was the outcome. In his only pitching appearance in his professional career, Valdéz set down the heart of the Cincinnati Reds' lineup with ease. He got Joey Votto to fly out on a 3-and-1 count. After he hit Scott Rolen with a slow curve, both Jay Bruce and relief pitcher Carlos Fisher popped out. When the Phillies scored in the bottom of the 19th, Valdéz was the winning pitcher – the first player since Babe Ruth to get a win as a pitcher in a game he started in the field. (Ruth did it on October 1, 1921.)

After the 2011 season, the popular Valdéz avoided arbitration and signed a one-year deal with Philadelphia for $930,000. But with second-year man Michael Martínez, free agent Kevin Frandsen, and newly purchased Ty Wigginton available to serve as utility infielders, Valdéz was traded on January 25, 2012, to the Cincinnati Reds for pitcher Jeremy Horst.

The Reds needed Valdéz behind 31-year-old Brandon Phillips and 37-year-old Scott Rolen but mostly to back up rookies Zack Cozart and Todd Frazier. He even logged in some innings behind Drew Stubbs in center field. Valdéz batted only .206 in 208 plate appearances, his lowest batting average since his rookie year, but not without some highlights. On June 8, 2012, his pinch-hit squeeze

Wilson Valdéz. Courtesy of the Philadelphia Phillies/Miles Kennedy.

bunt in the 10th inning with Miguel Cairo on third base lifted the Reds over the Detroit Tigers for a walk-off 6-5 victory. On October 3 against the St. Louis Cardinals, he singled in the sixth inning against September call-up Shelby Miller to break up Miller's no-hitter. It was Miller's first major-league start. This was Valdéz's last hit and his last major-league regular-season game.

The Reds were National League Central champs that year but lost to the San Francisco Giants three games to two in the NLDS. In Game Two Valdéz flied out in his only at-bat in the series for his final major-league at-bat.

Valdéz was granted free agency on November 7, 2012, and was signed by the San Francisco Giants but he was released on March 22, 2013, as the team opened its season with reserve infielders Nick Noonan and Joaquín Árias instead.

The day after he was released by San Francisco, the Miami Marlins signed Valdéz to a minor-league contract with the Triple-A New Orleans Zephyrs. He was released by the Marlins, however, on May 19, 2013, the day before his 35th birthday.

Valdéz's agent hooked him up with the Camden (New Jersey) Riversharks in the Atlantic League of Professional Baseball, an independent but official MLB partner league. Valdéz led the team in three categories: .310 batting average, 37 stolen bases, and 6 triples in 90 games. (A full regular season in the Atlantic League is 140 games.)

When he returned to the Dominican Republic to play winter-league ball later in 2013, Valdéz switched from the Gigantes del Cibao to the Tigres del Licey, with whom he played three seasons. And when he came back to the Atlantic League the following summer, he signed with the York (Pennsylvania) Revolution for the 2014 and 2015 seasons. He played all of his 233 games with York at shortstop and batted .292 in 2014 and .262 in 2015. The 88 bases he stole in his York career stand as the all-time mark for the club, as do his 55 SBs in a single season (2014). He was selected as the starting shortstop for the league's 2014 all-star game.

On August 18, 2015, the crafty batsman helped the Revolution squeeze out a victory via the bunt. In the top of the 11th inning with the score tied 4-4, former major leaguer José Constanza was on third base following a double and a passed ball. Valdéz laid down a perfect bunt to plate the go-ahead and ultimate winning run[32] – shades of his extra-inning walk-off squeeze bunt with the Cincinnati Reds in 2012.

Three nights later, on August 21, Valdéz went from bunt to long ball. He smacked a grand slam in a losing effort for his only home run in 2015 (he hit two in 2014) on a night when he went 4-for-5.[33] His final year playing organized and professional baseball was 2015, after which he returned to the Dominican Republic to coach on a limited basis but he did not play ball. "I was tired," he said.[34]

Wilson married his wife, Kamie, on May 1, 2004; they are divorced. He has three children: Viktor, who was born in 2012, Veronika, born in 2005, and Wilson Andres Valdéz, who was born in 1999 and was signed as an undrafted free agent in 2018 by the Philadelphia Phillies. The younger Wilson played on the Phillies' DSL team for three seasons[35] but he was released from the Phillies organization after the 2022 season.[36]

SOURCES

In addition to the sources cited in the Notes, the author consulted www.baseball-reference.com, https://stathead.com/baseball/, www.retrosheet.org, www.thebaseballcube.com, www.sabr.org, www.newspapers.com, www.facebook.com/yorkrevolution, and www.deanscards.com/wilson+Valdéz.

NOTES

1. Two of the three – John Baker (Chicago Cubs catcher pitched one inning in 2014) and Valdéz – were position players; the third, Tom Dougherty, was a pitcher (pitched two innings for the Chicago White Sox in 1904).

2. Wilson Valdéz, telephone interviews with Len Pasculli on February 17, 2021, and May 18, 2023 (edited for clarity), and several follow-up text messages (hereafter Pasculli-Valdéz interview).

3   "Better Know a Dodger … Wilson Valdez," LAist.com, April 7, 2007. https://laist.com/news/better-know-a-dodger-wilson-Valdez-1. Retrieved August 12, 2021.

4   Pasculli-Valdéz interview.

5   Rob Ruck, "Winter Leagues: Dominican Real Fan and Talent Hotbed," *Baseball Research Journal* (SABR), 1984, https://sabr.org/journal/article/winter-leagues-dominican-real-fan-and-talent-hotbed/.
Pedro Guerrero, Joaquín Andújar, George Bell, Rico Carty, Tony Fernández, Sammy Sosa, Robinson Canó, Alfonso Soriano, Luis Castillo, Johnny Cueto, and both Fernando Tatíses (Senior and Junior) are among the more than 100 major-league players born in San Pedro de Macoris.

6   The other two Dominican Hall of Famers are Juan Marichal (inducted in 1983), born in Laguna Verde and Pedro Martínez (inducted in 2015), born in Manoguayabo. Santo Domingo native Albert Pujols, who retired after the 2022 season, is considered a lock to be a Hall of Famer.

7   In addition to the nine major leaguers born in Nizao, two were from Don Gregorio, an unmerged municipal section of Nizao (including Vladimir Guerrero's older brother Wilton Guerrero), and 32 were from nearby Bani, Peravia Province's capital city (including Miguel Tejeda, Mario Soto, Timo Pérez, Rafael Landestoy, Deivi Cruz, and brothers Erick Aybar and Willy Aybar, and their nephew Wander Franco).

8   Fred Ferreira, who claimed to have signed 61 players who played in the major leagues including Vladimir Guerrero, Bernie Williams (Puerto Rico), and Orlando Cabrera (Colombia), was a longtime scout, first in Florida and Puerto Rico for the California Angels, then Florida, Puerto Rico, and the Dominican Republic for the New York Yankees, Cincinnati Reds, Montreal Expos, and Florida Marlins. Ferreira finished his career as the executive director of international recruiting for the Baltimore Orioles. See Ferreira's interview video at https://www.youtube.com/watch?v=SOMn36s0Gzo.

9   Philadelphia Phillies, "Wilson Valdez," *2011 Philadelphia Phillies Media Guide*, 165.

10 Valdéz was actually selected off waivers by the New York Mets from the White Sox on March 29, 2005, and three days later he was selected off waivers by the Seattle Mariners from the Mets after New York acquired infielder Benji Gil from the Seattle Mariners on March 28, 2005. "Transactions," *New York Times*, https://www.nytimes.com/2005/03/30/sports/transactions.html. Retrieved August 12, 2021.

11 Bill Shaikin, "Dodgers' Manny Mota Enters a New Mode," *Los Angeles Times*, April 22, 2013. https://www.latimes.com/sports/la-xpm-2013-apr-22-la-sp-0423-dodgers-manny-mota-20130423-story.html. Retrieved August 12, 2021.

12 Ned Colletti, "Colletti: Dodgers' Latin American Legacy Still Strong," Spectrum SportsNetLA, June 17, 2015. http://www.sportsnetla.com/articles/2015/06/18/colletti-dodgers-getting-back-to-rich-legacy-in-latin-america-june-18-2015.html. Retrieved August 12, 2021.

13 Joe Hawk, "Season Looks Bright as Valdez Lights Way," *Las Vegas Review-Journal*, April 7, 2006: 1C.

14 Todd Dewey, "Valdez Keeps Hitting as 51s Keep Winning," *Las Vegas Review-Journal*, July 19, 2007: 5C.

15 Joe Hawk, "Royster Sold Dodgers on Acquiring Valdez," *Las Vegas Review-Journal*, April 7, 2006: 9C.

16 Andrew, "The Last Time I'll Complain About Wilson Valdez … For a While," truebluela.com, April 9, 2007. https://www.truebluela.com/2007/4/9/14024/37617. Retrieved August 12, 2021.

17 Todd Dewey, "Valdez Keeps Hitting as 51s Keep Winning."

18 Rob Ruck, *The Tropic of Baseball* (Lincoln: University of Nebraska Press, 1991), 186.

19 Pasculli-Valdéz interview.

20 Kim Tong-hyung, "Kia Tigers Close to Signing Lima," *Korea Times*, January 3, 2008. https://www.koreatimes.co.kr/www/sports/2020/12/600_16664.html. Retrieved August 12, 2021.

21 John E. Gibson, "Hard Drives: Transition Game Hard to Swallow," japanesebaseball.com, July 30, 2008. https://www.japanesebaseball.com/writers/display.gsp?id=19660, retrieved August 12, 2021.

22 Rotowire.com, "Wilson Valdez News." https://www.rotowire.com/baseball/player.php?id=7416.

23 David Watkins, "Say Hello to Valdez (a.k.a. Shiroishi Is Useless)," June 10, 2008. https://tokyoswallows.com/2008/06/say-hello-to-Valdez-a-k-a-shiroishi-is-useless/, retrieved August 12, 2021.

24 John E. Gibson, "Hard Drives."

25 Rotowire.com, "Wilson Valdez News." https://www.rotowire.com/baseball/player.php?id=7416.

26 Alan Cohen, "May 29, 2010: 27 Up and 27 Down for Phillies' Roy Halladay." https://sabr.org/gamesproj/game/may-29-2010-27-up-and-27-down-for-phillies-roy-halladay/.

27 The Phillies TV color commentator's call on the home run was: "When you hang 'em, somebody's gonna bang 'em!" YouTube.com, February 17, 2016. https://www.youtube.com/watch?v=F6y9QiezRpk.

28 Pasculli-Valdéz interview. It was actually 19 wins, 5 losses, with 11 straight wins.

29 Philadelphia Phillies, "Wilson Valdez," *2011 Philadelphia Phillies Media Guide*, 165.

30 See https://sabr.org/gamesproj/game/october-6-2010-phillies-roy-halladay-throws-postseason-no-hitter/; the YouTube video of the game can be found at https://www.youtube.com/watch?v=1BgAIIoGX6s.

31 The Phillies made it back to the postseason in 2011 but were eliminated by the St. Louis Cardinals in Game Five of the best-of-five NLDS; Valdéz did not make an appearance in that series.

32 "Revs Squeeze Out Nail-Biter in Extras," OurSports Central, August 19, 2015. https://www.oursportscentral.

com/services/releases/revs-squeeze-out-nail-biter-in-extras/n-5034988

33 Tom Sixeas, "Wilson Valdez' Grand Slam Can't Save York Revolution in Loss to Somerset Patriots," *York (Pennsylvania) Daily Record*, August 21, 2015. https://www.ydr.com/story/news/2015/08/21/wilson-Valdezs-grand-slam-cant-save-york-revolution/72260818/.

34 Pasculli-Valdéz interview.

35 George Stockburger, "Phillies News: What Happened to Wilson Valdez, Father of Phillies Prospect Wilson Valdez Jr?" thatballsouttahere.com, May 24, 2020. https://thatballsouttahere.com/2020/05/24/phillies-news-wilson-Valdez/ Retrieved August 12, 2021.

36 Pasculli-Valdéz interview.

CHARLIE VAUGHAN

BY ERIC A. SIMONSEN

Charles Wayne Vaughan was born the third son of Gene and Judy Vaughan of Weslaco, Texas, on October 6, 1947 in the nearby hospital at Mercedes. Married in 1941, Judy gave birth to their first son, Richard, in 1944 and bore a second son, Eddie, in 1946. Gene was successful in sales for Burton Auto Supply and was promoted and transferred to Brownsville in September 1948 to be the branch manager for that location.

The United States of the 1960s found baseball continuing to expand its role as "America's Game." While a broadening of television enabled the population to occasionally watch other professional sports, baseball was the leader and growing stronger. The Giants and Dodgers had left the New York City area, placing major-league teams on the West Coast for the first time. In the short span from 1960 to 1962, the number of major-league franchises grew 25 percent, with the creation of another West Coast team, the Angels, as well as the Senators, Colt 45's, and Mets. Daily newspapers in cities large and small reported detailed information about an area's favorite major-league team, as well as results of nearby minor leagues and high-school games. So it is not surprising that baseball became an important part of each of the Vaughan brothers' lives as they grew.

Little League Baseball flourished in Brownsville in the 1950s and '60s. Richard began playing at age 9.[1] Eddie and Charlie followed suit. Gene, their father, had been a quarterback on his high-school football team and received a scholarship his freshman year to play football for Southwest Texas State Teachers College (now Texas State University). His athletic talents apparently passed on to his three sons.

As he grew, Richard became increasingly interested in the fundamentals and strategy of baseball. With Dad busy building the business, Richard happily became the informal coach for his two younger brothers, continuously teaching them and practicing with them many aspects of the game. Charlie notes that Richard "really got our juices flowing with excitement over the game of baseball." With Charlie throwing lefty, Richard guided him to the roles of pitcher and first base.

When he turned 13, Charlie moved up to the local Pony League baseball program and followed that into the related Colt League and American Legion. He recalled pitching successfully for competitive teams at these levels.

The local high school started in 10th grade. Thus, Charlie's sophomore year was his first time playing at that level. He did some pitching, but mostly played first base as brother Eddie led the pitching rotation. By his junior year, Charlie filled the number-two spot in the rotation. The two brothers picked up the nicknames Big Ace and Little Ace, which had more to do with age than physical size. That season ended when the Border Bandits, as the team was nicknamed, lost a sudden-death playoff game for the South Zone championship.

In 1965, his senior year, Charlie combined with Tony Barbosa as a dominating one-two left-handed pitching combination for the Brownsville Eagles, leading his school to the 1965 District 16-4 A (now 5 A) South Zone championship.² Vaughan's regular-season statistics were staggering. With a pitching record of 13-3, he threw 107 innings with 203 strikeouts, an average of 1.89 per inning, He walked 32 batters and allowed only 40 hits for a WHIP of 0.67. He gave up only six earned runs for an ERA of 0.39 and was selected the 4A All-State Tournament left-handed pitcher. With these credentials, Charlie was offered a scholarship to attend and pitch for the University of Texas-Austin.

The Brownsville Eagles won the District championship, taking two games out of three from Corpus Christi Ray. They then swept the Regionals, defeating Waco Richfield and San Antonio Lee two straight each. Charlie pitched the opening game in each series. All three opponents came from much bigger schools than Brownsville. Finishing on top in their region advanced them to the state tournament in Austin. Charlie pitched the semifinal game, eliminating Galena Park (Houston), 7-1. This set up a winner-take-all game for the Texas high-school championship.³

Prior to 1965, amateur baseball players were free to sign a contract with any major-league club they chose. However, in 1965 the major leagues introduced the Rule 4 draft, the first structured methodology for recruiting players from high schools, colleges and other amateur baseball clubs. As a high-school graduate, Charlie was eligible to be selected. He knew that scouts had watched him pitch his senior year, suggesting he could be selected. Deep inside, Charlie had long wanted to be a Yankee.

On June 8, 1965, Charlie was drafted by the Milwaukee Braves in the fourth round with the 64th overall pick. Rick Monday was the first selection in the draft, followed in the first round by other future major leaguers such as Joe Coleman, Billy Conigliaro, Ray Fosse, and Bernie Carbo. Later round selections included Johnny Bench (36th), Larry Hisle (38th), Andy Messersmith (53rd), Ken Holtzman (61st), Ken Boswell (66th), Stan Bahnsen (68th), Graig Nettles (74th), Amos Otis (95th), Sal Bando (119th), and – 190th in the 10th round – Tom Seaver. Nolan Ryan was selected in the 12th round, likely that late because of concern that he would continue his education rather than sign.

Charlie's focus on winning the state championship had pushed the draft to the back of his mind. However, after winning the first game, some uncertainty arose as to whether he would pitch at all in the final game. The subject was never addressed directly with Charlie. Yet, to this day, he has a sense that his being drafted gave Coach Joe Rodriguez and others concerns as to Charlie's availability. Thus, Brownsville's number-two starter was on the mound as scheduled. It was a close contest for the first three innings but began to slip away from Brownsville in the fourth. Charlie was called in to get the last two outs of that inning. However, when Brownsville took the field in the fifth, senior Sergio Munzano took

Charlie Vaughan with the Atlanta Braves. Courtesy of Charlie Vaughan.

the mound. Munzano faltered and was replaced on the mound by sophomore Ruben Delgado. Neither had pitched since March. They could not stop the Dallas Samuel team from taking the championship.

There was an unspoken difference of opinion in the Vaughan family as to what the future held for Charlie. It was impressed on him that pitching with a scholarship would remove the family's financial burden of going to college while providing him with four more years of solid competition on the diamond. Gene believed this would be Charlie's direction, to the point that he discouraged a Houston Astros scout from drafting Charlie at all. For Charlie, starting a career in professional baseball, while attending college in the offseason, would be the first step of a dream come true. Two weeks later, and still some three months shy of his 18th birthday, Charlie and his parents met with Milwaukee Braves scout Al La Macchia. Charlie signed a contract. The terms included a $25,000 signing bonus, which was designed to compensate for the college costs the family would now have to bear.

Charlie was sent to Sarasota, Florida, to play for the Braves' Rookie League team. With Paul Snyder as manager, the Braves finished the 1965 season with 34 wins and 25 losses. Charlie started eight games on the mound, tying him for most starts on the team. He also relieved in six games. His overall record was seven wins and two losses with an ERA of 3.09 in 64 innings pitched. He gave up 42 hits and 37 walks while hitting six batters, resulting in a WHIP of 1.234 and placing him third on the team in this category among the 13 pitchers. When the season finished in late August, Charlie skipped Class A and was promoted to the Austin Braves in the Double-A Texas League. There he pitched in two games, both as the starter. He threw 11 innings, striking out seven while giving up eight earned runs on 15 hits, and seven walks for an ERA of 6.55 and a 2.00 WHIP. He was charged with the loss in one of the games. In early September, he returned home to Brownsville to begin his first semester at Texas Southmost College.

During that offseason, the Milwaukee Braves became the Atlanta Braves. Vaughan was on the 40-man roster. When the Braves broke camp, he returned to the Austin Braves. He was part of the rotation, starting 14 games, fourth most on the roster. He also appeared in relief eight times. In 83 innings he had a surprisingly poor won-lost record of 2-7, despite an ERA of 2.93. While his motion resulted in his occasionally overthrowing, he realized that the fastball that worked so well in Sarasota needed "more" at the Double-A level. So he began to modify his motion and his grips. This experimentation culminated in his allowing 86 hits and 39 walks, for a WHIP of 1.506, along with 11 wild pitches. Despite finishing with a 67-73 won-lost record, Austin made the playoffs and won the Texas League championship. However, by the time that took place Vaughan had been promoted.

Before the Texas League playoffs began, Vaughan was called up to Atlanta. On September 3, barely one month before his 19th birthday, his dream of pitching in the major leagues became a reality. Due to an earlier rainout, doubleheaders against the Astros were scheduled on Saturday and Sunday. Vaughan was named the starting pitcher for the first Saturday game.

The Houston Astros Vaughan was to face struggled through the 1966 season, as they had in recent years. They won only 72 games, finishing in eighth place in the 10-team National League, 23 games out of first. The Braves of the 1960s typically played slightly better than .500 ball. The 1967 season was no exception. They won 85 games and finished in fifth place. Yet, as Vaughan took the mound that day, among others, he saw Joe Torre catching, Eddie Mathews at third base, Felipe Alou at first, and Hank Aaron in right field.

Houston manager Grady Hatton opened with Dave Giusti on the mound. Giusti started 33 games for the Astros that year, picking up 15 victories, tops for the team, despite an ERA of 4.20. With back-to-back doubleheaders, Hatton started only four of his regulars in the game. Vaughan began auspiciously, striking out leadoff batter Ron Davis. Catcher Ron Brand singled. But two force plays ended the top half of the first inning with no score. In the bottom half, the Braves put together two runs on hits by Rico Carty and Torre, a Houston error, and a wild pitch.

In the top of the second, Vaughan gave up only a single to Lee Maye. He struck out big-swinging Dave "Swish" Nicholson and got outs from a fly ball and a grounder. Frank Bolling flied out to open the bottom of the second for the Braves. That brought Vaughan to the plate for his first major-league at-bat. As he recalled, Giusti put a fastball down the middle of the plate. Vaughan jumped on it and drove the pitch out over second base for a single. Felipe Alou bounced into a double play, but the Braves still held the lead at the end of the second inning, 2-0.

Vaughan gave up two hits in the top of the third, but a double play erased any possible scoring.

The bottom of the inning, the Braves jumped on Giusti for five runs. Mathews opened with a solo home run and Denis Menke hit a three-run shot after an RBI single by Carty to give the Braves a 7-0 lead after three innings.

Vaughan continued to hold the Astros in check in the fourth. When the Braves came to bat, Jim Ray relieved Giusti. Ray walked Alou to open the inning and was promptly pulled for Carroll Sembera. Mathews fouled out but Aaron and Torre singled, scoring Alou. After Carty flied out, Mack Jones hit a three-run shot, giving the Braves an 11-0 lead.

At the start of the fifth inning, Gene Freese was announced as the pinch-hitter for the pitcher. Vaughan recalled no pregame discussion as to whom he might face or how he should pitch to each batter. He basically threw whatever Joe Torre called. But when Freese was announced, Vaughan recalled, he was struck by a sudden dose of reality, saying to himself, "Hey, I've got this guy's baseball card!" Charlie struck him out. In the bottom of the inning, the Braves tacked on one more run from consecutive singles by Geiger, Torre, and Carty, making it 12-0.

Neither team scored in the sixth. In the top of the seventh, the Astros picked up two runs on three singles and a sacrifice fly. As Vaughan came into the dugout, manager Billy Hitchcock asked him if he was tired. He acknowledged that he was. Hitchcock congratulated him for pitching a great game and told him Jay Ritchie would take over on the mound. There was no more scoring in the game. The Braves won, 12-2. Little did anyone suspect that this game not only made Charlie Vaughan, at 18 years and 332 days the youngest "one-win wonder" of major-league baseball, but that he would retain the distinction well over 50 years later.

Atlanta sportswriter Wayne Minshew wrote, "Vaughan, a handsome youngster with a big curve ball, worked several strong innings in the opener, scattered 8 Astro hits, and pitched shutout baseball for the first half-dozen innings. He became tired and departed for more experienced Jay Ritchie after the seventh."[4]

He hadn't had his curve working at its best, though, reported sportswriter Wilt Browning.[5] Vaughan told him he wasn't "as nervous as I thought I was going to be. After I got that first guy out in the first inning, I felt a lot better." Vaughan added, "I just wish I had my big curve, because that is my strikeout pitch. I guess 70 percent of my pitches tonight were fast balls and they could have been a lot better too."[6]

Catcher Joe Torre had come out to the mound several times during the game. Vaughan said, "He kept making me take deep breaths before each pitch before getting too nervous. And he kept telling me not to aim the ball, just throw it."[7]

In seven innings Vaughan faced 31 batters. He gave up eight hits and walked three while striking out six. At the plate he was 1-for-4. This was a day he hoped would be the first of many in the years to come. The Braves swept the doubleheader, making it 11 consecutive wins over the Astros and 14 out of 19 games for the season.

Vaughan did not pitch any more that season. However, he returned to Brownsville with high hopes for 1967. Given his performance, he was comfortable that he would again be on the 40-man roster and might have a shot at more major-league experiences in the coming season. During the fall he met and began to date a young woman from Brownsville, Carol Carnesi.

When the 1967 season started, still only 19 years old, Vaughan was pitching for the Richmond Braves of the Triple-A International League. This is the season, he said, that he looks back on in so many ways as his favorite. The team did not get off to a strong start under manager Lum Harris, sitting in seventh place in the eight-team league. However, when summer arrived, the ball started to bounce the Braves' way. An 11-game winning streak across June and July moved them up in the standings, aiming toward the first-place Rochester Red Wings. When the season ended, the Braves owned 14 victories in 20 games against the Red Wings and found themselves tied with Rochester for first place. The Braves won the one-game playoff over Rochester but lost the opening round best-three-out-of-five series to third-place Toledo.

Vaughan did not appear in any of the playoff games. However, for the 1967 season his 24 starts were second-most on the roster. He notched 9 wins against 10 losses and threw three complete games, of which two were shutouts. He struck out 81 in 135 innings pitched but gave up 133 hits, walked 67 and hit 9 batters for a WHIP of 1.48. It was a solid season for Vaughan, especially considering his young age and still somewhat limited experience.

Vaughan returned home for the offseason and headed back to college. Being back home allowed him to continue to build his relationship with Carol. His outlook was bright, but he knew he needed to continue to get stronger if he was to be successful, hopefully in Atlanta. The Braves had not provided any offseason training guidance. So when a college friend went to the campus weight room to train, Charlie went along. His first low squat was at the weight level his friend had lifted. It was far too heavy for Charlie. Immediately he could feel a problem in his groin that stayed with him. This was the first of several major injuries that would change the trajectory of Vaughan's path in baseball.

Upon arrival at 1968 spring training, the initial team physical diagnosed bilateral hernias. Despite that, Vaughan was the starter for the opening spring-training game, against the Washington Senators. He threw three scoreless innings. However, when he went out to warm up for the fourth, his left elbow locked up. He was diagnosed with bone chips – unknown in size or quantity – and put on light duty. When camp broke, Vaughan went to Atlanta to have surgery for the hernia and to rest his elbow. The Braves hoped the elbow chips were small and/or few and might "settle" in a way to allow him to pitch effectively without requiring an operation.

In May the hernia recovery was complete. Vaughan was sent to the Greenwood Braves of the Class-A Carolina League for rehabilitation. However, the elbow problems would not go away. He spent the remainder of the season there, pitching in only seven games, six of which were starts. As a rehab assignment, he threw only 21 innings, with little in the way of effective results. At season's end he went to Houston for elbow surgery; 13 bone chips were removed. Now 20 years old, Vaughan had two surgeries to go along with issues developing in his pitching shoulder and the middle finger of his left hand, resulting from attempts to alter his arm angle and ball grip to improve the effectiveness of his pitching. From his perspective, Charlie termed the 1968 season as "down the drain."

Vaughan headed home for the offseason. His relationship with Carol continued to grow. No longer on the 40-man roster, he was assigned out of spring training to the Braves' new Double-A affiliate at Shreveport, Louisiana, in the Texas League. In late May, Atlanta general manager Paul Richards remarked that Vaughan was "beginning to look like the pitcher the Braves thought he could be."[8] At the beginning of June, Vaughan was called up to Atlanta to fill a weekend roster spot for Ron Reed, who had military duty. On June 1 he entered a game against the Cubs in the bottom of the eighth inning with the Braves trailing, 11-4. He struck out one and gave up one hit, but he walked three, which resulted in two more runs for the Cubs. He spent the entire remainder of the season in Shreveport, starting 21 games, second most on the team. He had 5 wins and 10 losses with 110 innings on the mound but an ERA of 3.27. However, control remained an issue. While he struck out 82, Vaughan allowed 101 hits, walked 55 and hit 5 batters for a WHIP of 1.418. When the season ended, the Braves sent him to two months of winter ball in Phoenix to continue to work his way back. However, Vaughan did not believe he was seeing the improvement he sought in his pitching effectiveness.

Clearly the highlight of 1970 for Charlie was his marriage to Carol on January 30. Together they headed to spring training and then to Shreveport, where he pitched for the Double-A Braves. In the ensuing two months, Vaughan appeared in 13 games, starting eight of those contests. He was 2-4 with an ERA of 4.73 and a WHIP of 1.90. He was told that Kansas City was searching for a left-handed reliever. Thus, he was "loaned" to the Omaha Royals, Kansas City's Triple-A affiliate. While there, Vaughan pitched in five games with little effectiveness. In early August he returned to the Braves at Triple-A Richmond. He pitched only two innings. When September arrived, Vaughan was called up to Atlanta but never made a game appearance. Domestic tranquility aside, 1970 had been yet another disappointing season.

He and Carol returned to Texas, wondering what the coming season might hold for them. Contract negotiations began early in 1971 and soon were at a stalemate. Vaughan requested to be traded to Houston, whose minor-league affiliates were in Texas, closer to Carol and their home. Atlanta declined. Vaughan was offered the major-league minimum salary of $12,000. With offseason jobs difficult to find, economics put him in a stalemate. When training camp opened, he was still in Texas.

With a real estate boom underway in the state, he entered the real estate business and experienced immediate success. His baseball days were over.

On November 12, 1971, Carol gave birth to their first child, Scott. As timed passed, they both became more active in the Brownsville community and purchased their first home. Charlie continued to be successful in the real estate business until early 1976, when he joined his father and two brothers in the family-owned Burton Auto Supply business. On June 28, 1976, their second son, Ryan, was born. They joined a new local church, St Pius X Catholic Church, and became further involved in several community organizations associated with the church and their beliefs.

As time moved on, Charlie assumed more responsibilities at Burton Auto Supply. He and Carol became grandparents of Hannah Grace (born in 2002) and Gunnar Scott (born in 2003), while continuing to deepen ties to their community. Charities, such as the growing Rio Grande Valley Hall of Fame – to which Charlie had been elected – as well as the Fellowship of Christian Athletes, Charlie's high-school alumni group and several pro-life not-for-profit organizations filled their schedules.

Charlie continued to play tennis, his favorite sport second to baseball. However, rotator cuff operations and knee replacements in the 10 years from 2010 reduced those activities.

Despite all the physical talents Charlie Vaughan's body possessed, but which had begun to fail him, Charlie did not quit. He quickly recalled many instances where the concept of "giving back," a philosophy he learned from his first manager in professional baseball, Paul Snyder, resulted in meaningful, positive experiences for himself and his family. Charlie readily offered that this concept, his faith, his 50-plus years of marriage to Carol, and his interactions with his two sons and their families have provided and continue to provide all with enriching lives.

NOTES

1. Author interview with Charlie Vaughan, one of a series of interviews conducted over the second half of 2021. Unless otherwise indicated, any direct quotations come from one or another of these interviews.
2. "Texans, Brownsville Open 14-A Playoff," *Corpus Christi Caller*, May 14, 1965: C1.
3. "Texans, Brownsville Open 14-A Playoff."
4. Wayne Minshew, "Vaughan, Johnson 'Two-Time' Astros," *Atlanta Journal and the Atlanta Constitution*, September 4, 1966: 73, 75.
5. Wilt Browning, "Braves Go Boom for Vaughan," *Atlanta Journal and the Atlanta Constitution*, September 4, 1966: 77.
6. Browning.
7. Browning. Torre said after the game, "You can expect him to be better, because you know he was nervous and wasn't free and easy like we know he can be. When he is free and easy, he'll be a lot more effective." Pitching coach Whitlow Wyatt said Vaughan's back tightened up somewhat late in the game.
8. Wayne Minshew, "Jackson's Homer Tops Braves, 6-2," *Atlanta Constitution*, May 24, 1969: 31.

WILBUR "BIGGS" WEHDE

BY WILLIAM H. JOHNSON

Wilbur Wehde was born on November 23, 1906, in the hamlet of Holstein, Iowa. The town, roughly 45 miles east of Sioux City, was at the time home to fewer than 1,000 residents, mostly first- or second-generation German immigrants. Wehde's father, Gustave, managed a creamery and brokered other farmers' produce, while his mother, Frieda, managed the array of daily tasks that provided the metronome for life on the frontier.[1] Wilbur had four full siblings, brother Gus and sisters Margaret, Florence, and Mabel. Their lives changed dramatically when Frieda died in 1918. Wilbur was only 11 years old. Gustave remarried, and he and his new wife added four more children to the brood: brothers Ray and Roy, and sisters Evelyn and Fern.

The loss of his mother, and the family's adaptation to a new normal, had no discernible effect on Wehde's athletic skills. Starting as a boy, Wilbur played on a variety of local baseball teams, and then later for several semipro and town teams in the Holstein area.[2] Not only did Wehde pitch,[3] but he was one of the better hitters on some of his teams as well.[4] He played for town teams throughout northwest Iowa and even across the border into Minnesota. By 1929, he was referred to as some variant of "Bugs," "Bigs,"[5] or "Biggs" in the newspapers, ostensibly due to his physical size. It was "Biggs" that stuck throughout his future baseball life.

Wehde clearly loved baseball, but with only a high-school diploma and still without any professional prospects, the 21-year-old took the figurative plunge and married Cora Mae Vance in 1928. That happy union lasted until Cora's death in 1961, and produced a son, Jerry, along with daughters Delores and Joanne.

On the baseball diamond, Wehde's longest, and most successful, pre-professional time was spent with the Sioux City Cowboys, and in 1929 the right-hander was so well regarded throughout Iowa that he earned a contract with the Dubuque (Iowa) Tigers of the Class-D Mississippi Valley League. On July 7, 1929, he won his first professional decision when he tossed a three-hitter against the Keokuk Indians.[6] He continued to pitch well that year, and the local paper credited him with helping Dubuque to the 1929 league championship.[7] Overall, Wehde threw 131 innings for Dubuque throughout the summer, enough to entice the Tigers to rehire him for 1930.[8]

In 1930, despite a won-lost record of 11-13 over 220 innings and an earned run average of 5.11, the pitching-starved Chicago White Sox bought Wehde's contract and brought him to the Windy City for the final weeks of the big-league campaign.[9] Wehde made his major-league debut on September 15, 1930, when he took the mound for the sixth inning in a game against the Washington Senators. Facing four batters, he yielded one hit in what proved to be a 14-9 loss to the visitors. The following day he pitched 1⅓ innings, closing out a 10-2 loss to the Philadelphia Athletics. Two more two-inning stints on September 18 and 19, both mopping up losses to the Athletics and Yankees, respectively, constituted the rest of Wehde's season. Overall, he pitched 6⅓ innings, gave up seven hits and seven earned runs (along with one unearned run), and had an ERA of 9.95. The team, despite having three future Hall of Famers on the roster – 41-year-old Red Faber, Ted Lyons, and newcomer Luke Appling – finished the American League season in seventh place, 30 games below .500 with a 62-92 record.

In January, Chicago sent Wehde to the Dallas Steers in the Class-A Texas League.[10] By July, however, he was back with the White Sox, and made his 1931 debut on July 12 in the ninth inning of the first game of a doubleheader against Cleveland. Five days later he pitched a scoreless inning in Washington, and then appeared in four more blowout losses to the Athletics, the Red Sox, and the Yankees.

On July 28, 1931, Wehde finally earned a victory.

Biggs Wehde. Courtesy of Encyclopedia Dubuque.

Tuesday afternoon in the Bronx found a moribund 35-59 Chicago White Sox team visiting the 55-38 Yankees. The latter sported a lineup that included an infield of immortals, including Lou Gehrig at first, Tony Lazzeri at second, and Joe Sewell at third base, along with Bill Dickey behind the plate and Babe Ruth in right field. As might be expected, the home team had a 2-0 lead after one inning, and a 5-3 advantage entering the bottom of the sixth.

In the sixth, Chicago starting pitcher Tommy Thomas let in five more runs and with two outs, manager Donie Bush replaced him with Wehde. After walking Lyn Lary and allowing a run-scoring single by Dickey, Wehde escaped when Lary failed to evade a rundown between second and third. The visitors failed to score in the top of the seventh, so Bush left his blowout specialist Wehde in to try to eat a few innings in what looked like a certain defeat. Wehde walked a batter and gave up one hit and one run in the otherwise uneventful inning. The score stood 12-3, Yankees. Chicago then scored 11 runs in the top of the eighth – off three future Hall of Famers (Herb Pennock, Red Ruffing, and Lefty Gomez) – and held on to win 14-12, making Wehde the pitcher of record for the victorious White Sox. It was one of the more improbable decisions that season, and it proved to be the sole win of Wehde's big-league career.

Wehde did not bat in the big inning. After the first four runs had scored, he was due up with one out and runners on first and second. Smead Jolley pinch-hit for him and doubled to drive in the fifth run of the rally.

Biggs Wehde made one more appearance in the majors, one-third of an inning in a 7-2 Chicago loss to the Detroit Tigers on August 3. On August 16 he and catcher Hank Garrity were sent down to the Minneapolis Millers in the American Association.[11] The 24-year-old pitcher never returned to a major-league pitching mound.

In 1932 Dubuque managed only 47 wins, and a last-place finish, in the Mississippi Valley Leagues.

Wehde's ERA soared to 5.94 over 150 innings, and when the league folded due to the hardship imposed by what was becoming the Great Depression, he returned to Holstein and resumed play in the Sioux City environs, primarily with the independent Nebraska All-Stars in South Sioux City.[12] In 1934 and 1935, Wehde was able to remain near home and play in Organized Baseball by joining the Sioux City Cowboys of the Class-A Western League. Given the level of the competition, 1934 may have been the best season of Wehde's career. Supporting his 10-2 record, his Runs-Against-per-Nine-Innings (RA/9) dropped below 4.00 (3.98). He was one of the first players re-signed for 1935, but the local paper noted that he was finally serious about returning to the White Sox. "Baseball experts are unanimous," the reporter wrote, "in declaring the big right hander would still be in the majors except for a tendency to take things lightly. But his hard work after joining the Cowboys … and his promise … that he'll 'win at least 20 ball games in 1935 and get back up to that big show again' indicates his serious intent."[13]

In 1935 Wehde's pitching was inconsistent, and his RA/9 bloated to 5.61. It appeared his career might have ended, and he did not play in 1936.

Intermittently working at the local stockyards,[14] Wehde spent some time mining and playing semipro baseball in the Black Hills, in Lead, South Dakota.[15] In 1938 he signed with the new Sioux City Cowboys, this time in the Class-D Nebraska State League. In 1939 he helped pitch the team to Sioux City's first championship in a quarter of a century, defeating Lincoln in the Western League championship series.[16] He remained with the team until 1940, even as it relocated to Mitchell, South Dakota, and rejoined the Western League. In 1941 Wehde pitched for the Pueblo (Colorado) Rollers, the St. Louis Browns affiliate in the Western League. He went 8-5 that year, and joined the Sioux Falls (South Dakota) Canaries in the slightly better Northern League for the 1942 season.

At age 35, and with war raging around the world and a number of minor leagues suspending play, Wehde left baseball and enlisted in the United States Navy. In retrospect, Wehde's minor-league time was successful. In addition to his 1-0 record in the major leagues, he logged an 83-66 record in the minors, and threw 1,443 professional innings. He had been able to play near home since 1934, sparing Cora and the family the burden of cross-country moves every year or two.

In 1944 the Navy assigned Wehde to a newly commissioned attack transport ship, the *USS Missoula* (APA-211), built at a shipyard in Richmond, California. He and most of the rest of the crew reported aboard in October 1944,[17] a month after the ship was commissioned, and immediately began abbreviated training prior to heading to the Pacific Theater. In January 1945 Supply Clerk (Petty Officer 3rd Class, SK3) Wehde and the ship sailed toward Japan. *USS Missoula* delivered part of the 5th Marine Division to the invasion of Iwo Jima (including the men who famously raised the American flag on Mount Suribachi). In March, after hostilities died down, the ship and crew headed to the Philippines, and later in the year to Okinawa, where they participated in that final large-scale invasion of the Pacific war. In early 1946, the ship returned to California, and Wehde was released from active duty.

The ship's participation in those two significant military actions netted every eligible crew member the American Campaign medal, the Asiatic-Pacific Campaign medal, and the World War II Victory medal, among others. Wehde's obituary noted that he was a member of both the American Legion and the Disabled American Veterans.

Back home in Correctionville, Iowa, with Cora and the family, and too old for baseball, Wehde returned to work in the Sioux City stockyards. Before the war, he had started as basic yardman. From there he advanced to general labor, then to meat packing. After the war, he worked the animal chutes, and was eventually promoted to chute foreman.[18] He remained there for the rest of his working life, until an on-the-job accident forced him into early retirement.[19] His wife, Cora, died in 1961, and Wehde retired from the stockyards three years later, in 1964. In 1969 he was diagnosed with an undisclosed illness, and he died on September 21, 1970, at the Veterans Affairs Hospital in Sioux Falls, South Dakota. He was buried next to Cora at Calvary Cemetery in Sioux City, Iowa.

SOURCES

In addition to the sources cited in the Notes, the author relied on Baseball-Reference.com. The *Sioux City Journal* provided most of the reporting on Wehde, and the Navy Historical Center generated the information on *USS Missoula* and its achievements during World War II.

NOTES

1. "Holstein Warehouse Burned," *Sioux City* (Iowa) *Journal*, April 3, 1926: 2.
2. "Death Takes Former Hurler for White Sox and Cowboys," *Sioux City Journal*, September 23, 1970: 9.
3. "Holstein Is Winner," *Sioux City Journal*, August 19, 1925: 11.
4. "Holstein Beats Rats," *Sioux City Journal*, July 20, 1926: 11.
5. "Cowboys Appear Stronger This Season," *Sioux City Journal*, April 14, 1929: 21.
6. "Dubuque Takes Pair of Games in Sunday Bill," *Courier* (Waterloo, Iowa), July 8, 1929: 10.
7. "Dubuque Valley Champion Team Well-Balanced," *Sioux City Journal*, September 11, 1929: 20.
8. Statistics from baseball-reference.com, online: Biggs Wehde Minor Leagues Statistics & History | Baseball-Reference.com. Accessed May 17, 2021.
9. "Dubuque Sells Hurler to ChiSox," *Des Moines Tribune*, September 13, 1930: 9.
10. Irving Vaughan, "Now the Draft's Settled, Traffic Should Improve," *Chicago Tribune*, January 21, 1931: 23.
11. "Wehde Sent Away," *Chicago Tribune*, August 16, 1931: 24.
12. Dan Desmond. "All Stars Defeat Vermillion, 11-6," *Sioux City Journal*, August 18, 1933: 11.
13. "Wehde Signs Contract for Next Season," *Sioux City Journal*, January 9, 1935: 13.
14. "Death Takes Former Hurler for White Sox and Cowboys."
15. Dan Desmond. "Sport Static," *Sioux City Journal*, May 2, 1937: 29.
16. "Cowboys Snare Loop Pennant; Whip Links, 8-3," *Sioux City Journal*, September 17, 1939: 17.
17. U.S. Navy Muster Roll of the Crew, *USS Missoula* (APA-211), pg. 9. Filed: March 31, 1945.
18. Wilbur Wehde in Sioux City, Iowa, directories in 1939, 1941, 1943, 1947, and 1957. Online: Ancestry.com - U.S., City Directories, 1822-1995 Accessed: May 19, 2021.
19. "Death Takes Former Hurler for White Sox and Cowboys."

AL YEARGIN

BY BILL NOWLIN

Right-hander Al Yeargin's first game in the big leagues was at the Polo Grounds on Sunday afternoon, October 1, 1922. Working for the Boston Braves, he started the second game of a doubleheader against the reigning World Series champion New York Giants. The Giants had already clinched the 1922 National League pennant and held a seven-game lead over second-place Pittsburgh. The Braves were in last place, 39½ games behind the Giants. The Braves won the first game, 3-0, a two-hit shutout by rookie Tim McNamara, bringing his record to 3-4. Yeargin pitched well in the second game, a seven-inning game, limiting the Giants to five hits and two walks. One of the hits was an inside-the-park two-run home run by rookie Mahlon Higbee, and Yeargin and the Braves came up on the short end of another 3-0 score. Three Giants pitchers worked in sequence, just getting a little work in preparation for the World Series. Art Nehf (19-13) got the win. The Boston papers took little notice, but the *New York Daily Tribune* observed, "The Giants didn't do much with Yeargin, a big chap with a free overhand swing."[1]

Yeargin did go to spring training with the Braves in St. Petersburg in 1923, but his next major-league start wasn't until May 16, 1924, in Cincinnati. He won that one, a complete-game 8-3 win – but then lost his next 11 decisions.

Though he pitched in the minors through the 1931 season, Yeargin never won another game in the major leagues.

Yeargin was born in Mauldin, South Carolina, on October 16, 1901.[2] He died quite young, at age 35. Yeargin was born into a farming family as James Almond Yeargin to parents Isaiah and Anna (King) Yeargin. He was the fourth of seven children, his oldest and youngest siblings being girls; the other four were boys. Two other children in the family had died, perhaps in childbirth or at a young age.

Isaiah Yeargin was a carpenter in Greenville at the time of the 1900 census, but was listed as J.B. Yeargin, a farmer engaged in general farming in 1910. His wife was listed as Narcisy A. Yergan. (That was the spelling of the surname used by the census enumerator.)[3] Both parents were native South Carolinians. The family lived in the community of Austin, in Greenville County, at the time of the 1910 census.

His listed height and weight show that Al Yeargin stood 5-feet-11 and weighed 170 pounds.

Before joining the Boston Braves, Al was a "recruit from Mauldin" who had pitched locally in 1922, in Greenville for the Class-B Southern Atlantic Association (Sally League) Greenville Spinners under manager Cliff Blankenship.[4] The team finished last in the six-team league with a record of 50-82. Yeargin appeared in 29 games with a record of 10-12 in 173 innings and an earned-run average of 3.23. On July 24 the Braves announced the purchase of his contract and their plan to bring him up, as they did, in September.[5]

Fred Mitchell and the Boston Braves finished last in 1922. The October 1 game was their last of the season.

It was reportedly Yeargin's choice to play the 1923 season in Greenville. He had impressed Mitchell and coach Duke Farrell, and Mitchell promised him before the season began that the Braves would keep him all year and not farm him out. As spring training wore on, Yeargin became "sad and low in his mind," dubbed "the man who never smiled." Farrell diagnosed the problem and Yeargin admitted it: he was homesick for his young bride – the former Noette Hawkins.[6]

Al Yeargin played again for Greenville in 1923 and had a good year, with a record of 18-3 and an ERA of 3.65 over a very full 281 innings in 42 games. One of the losses was a 16-inning 3-2 loss to Charlotte. On August 10 he pitched 17 innings in a game ending in a 2-2 tie with Augusta. The Spinners manager was Zinn Beck. The team finished in second place. Not surprisingly, Yeargin's winning percentage was the best in the league.[7]

Yeargin spent the full 1924 season with the Braves. Dave Bancroft was the team's manager. Perhaps Yeargin was quiet and kept to himself; the Boston Herald's Burt Whitman often referred to him as Jim Yeargin. Whitman wrote, "If he has more self confidence and aggressiveness he may stick with the Tribe this year."[8] Two days later, Whitman suggested that Farrell was getting "Yearg" – as he was called – to become more outgoing: "He actually is blooming. He has been seen smoking, going to movies and staying out after 10 o'clock at night."[9] A news story circulated nationally said he was pitching to make the big leagues and suggested, "Somehow or other a year or so in the Matrimony League seems to make a difference."[10]

Yeargin's first three appearances were in relief. He worked the final four innings in a 9-1 loss to the Giants on May 1, allowing the final two runs. He pitched two scoreless innings against the Robins in Brooklyn on May 4. On May 13 against Pittsburgh, he again closed the game, working two innings without allowing any of the Pirates to reach base.

Bancroft gave Yeargin a start on May 16. If Yeargin had the chance to see the next day's Boston Herald, the headline beginning "Rookie Jim Yeargin Is Hero" might well have been pleasing.[11] The game this day in Cincinnati proved to be his one major-league victory. The opposing pitcher was Dolf Luque, who in 1923 had built a record of seven wins and no losses against the Braves. His streak had been snapped the day before, when he was banged out of the box early. Luque was a veteran righty in his seventh season with Cincinnati. He had led both the NL and AL in 1923 in wins (27) and ERA (1.93).

The Braves got on the board with a run in the first, but Yeargin gave up a run to the Reds in the bottom of the second. In the fifth, the Braves got to Luque again, scoring four runs and knocking him out of the game for the second day in succession. Leading off the inning was Yeargin himself, who doubled to left field (his first base hit in the big leagues). The last batter Luque faced was center fielder Casey Stengel, who doubled to right and drove in Boston's fourth and fifth runs.

The Braves added one run in the seventh and two more in the top of the ninth. Yeargin yielded solo runs in the eighth and the ninth. Though tagged for 11 hits in all, he gave up only the three runs and won a complete game, 8-3.

Nine days later, on May 25, Yeargin was himself battered by the Cubs for six runs in 5⅔ innings, and the headlines weren't as kind.[12]

He was "Jim Yeargin" all year long in the Herald. The paper treated him like any other pitcher, not commenting negatively as the losses began to mount. Indeed, as it happens, his season ERA of 5.09 wasn't that much worse than the team ERA of 4.46, and better than two of the regular starters – Joe Genewich (10-19, 5.21) and Tim McNamara (8-12, 5.18). He showed up well at times; after he dropped a 3-2 game to the Pirates on August 23, the Herald headline read, "Jimmy Yeargin Pitches Well but Braves Drop Pittsburgh Final, 3 to 2."[13]

A couple of stories that ran nationally noted that Yeargin had won his first game, but then lost 11 straight. The Boston newspapers made little of the fact. On December 3, however, the Braves dealt him to the Seattle Indians of the Pacific Coast League. They were after outfielder James D. Welsh and sent Seattle both Yeargin and pitcher Sterling Stryker as well as the very sizable sum of $50,000.[14]

Both Stryker and Yeargin reported to Santa Maria, California, in late February for spring training with Seattle. One sportswriter called Yeargin "a clever kid, who seemed always on the point of breaking into the elite, but never quite made it," adding, "He has a good chance to grow up out here in the West."[15] He was, after all, still only 23 years old. As late as March 8, however, Yeargin – called "Jim" by the Seattle papers, too – was reportedly "as weak as a cat" with influenza.[16] As late as April 21, it was still uncertain when he might be ready to pitch. A week later, though, he had developed a sore arm and wasn't expected to be ready for another week. On May 8, Seattle sold Yeargin's contract to the Atlanta Crackers of the Class-A Southern Association. Baseball-Reference.com shows him as having pitched three innings in one game for Seattle.

Yeargin next turned up back in Greenville in 1926, earning headlines with a 1-0 five-hit victory over Augusta on May 12.[17] A brief note at the time indicated that Commissioner K.M. Landis had reinstated Yeargin from the voluntarily retired list of the Boston Braves.[18] Perhaps he had been returned on paper from Atlanta to Seattle, and from Seattle to Boston. No record of him pitching for Atlanta turned up in the press. Yeargin pitched again and lost on May 21, in Greenville, but then he disappears from the newspapers.

His younger brother Russell "Rush" Yeargin from Greer was a shortstop who appeared in some games for the Waycross (Georgia) team in 1926 and tried out for the Alexandria (Louisiana) Reds in 1927. He made the Class-D Cotton States League team and hit .300. Rush Yeargin played through 1933 for Evansville, Mobile, and Des Moines, never getting

Al Yeargin (unnumbered), with the 1927 Greenville Spinners, from the *1928 Spalding Baseball Guide*.

higher than Class-A baseball with Des Moines, where he played his final three seasons. The Des Moines Demons won the Western League championship in 1931.[19]

In 1927, 1928, and 1928, Al Yeargin (he was typically called Alvin or Al in regional newspapers) put in three full seasons for the Greenville Spinners.

His 1927 record was 19-7 with a 3.75 ERA in 32 games. The Spinners were Sally League champions and played against the Virginia League champion Portsmouth Truckers in a postseason matchup. Yeargin held Portsmouth to just two hits in the second game of the series on September 17. He did it again a week later, on the 24th, a 1-0 win over the Jacksonville Tars – another two-hitter – in a game for the "Class B championship of the south."[20] Jacksonville prevailed in the series.

Yeargin's 1928 season started out with a shock. Pitching against the Knoxville Smokies on April 19, he threw four pitches and gave up four runs: a double, a single, a double, and a home run. Smokies manager Gabby Street had instructed his batters to swing at Yeargin's first pitches and Yeargin seemed to have put them all right over the plate.[21] They were the only four pitches he threw in the game, but the Spinners won the game in the end.

Yeargin was never much of a hitter. From such batting averages as are available, his best season may have been 1928, when he hit .267 for Greenville. In one home game, on June 26, he won the game for himself with a double in the bottom of the 10th inning against Columbia. It was his second RBI of the game.[22]

On July 10 the Atlanta Crackers announced that they had purchased Yeargin's contract from Greenville. This was Atlanta's second attempt to acquire him. He pitched for Atlanta on July 22, and again a few times in the days that followed. He lost a complete game to Birmingham on the 25th, then pitched the final 6⅔ innings of a game against Chattanooga the very next day, getting the win. By August 17, however, he was back in Greenville box scores. His record was 2-1 for Atlanta. His record for Greenville is shown as 10-9 (5.08).

Yeargin had one fine stretch in early August 1929. He threw a five-hit 1-0 shutout against Charlotte on August 2, then lost a 1-0 four-hitter against Columbia on August 6, and won a 4-0 five-hit game in Charlotte on the 10th. On the 14th, he shut out Spartanburg, allowing just four hits. His record for the year shows as 15-11 (3.28), at age 27 the best season of his career.

He might have gone elsewhere. Realizing his team had no realistic shot at the second-half title, manager Frank Walker offered around the services of some of his best players. On August 17, he gave Shreveport an option to buy Yeargin's contract.[23] Yeargin was not summoned and played out the season with the Spinners.

Yeargin began the 1930 campaign with Greenville once again. On April 25 he allowed Augusta just four hits while seeing his teammates rack up 22 hits and humiliate Augusta, 20-1, in Augusta. Yeargin was the only one on the Spinners not to get a base hit.

On May 12 he threw a three-hitter in Columbia. On June 22 the Augusta Wolves signed Yeargin, as part of a push at the second-half title. There's no indication that his acquisition directly helped and, in any event, Augusta finished fourth with a 68-70 losing record.

Yeargin's record for the year was 11-13 in 180 innings of work for the two teams combined and an ERA of 4.45. He struck out 93 and walked 55.[24]

Yeargin was with the Raleigh Capitals in the Class-D Piedmont League in 1931, finishing the year with a record of 10-9 in 26 games.

It was his last year in professional baseball and he was only 29 years old.

Yeargin had apparently struggled for some time with stomach pains and other internal problems. He lent his name to an advertisement for a medicinal product named Malva, which ran in the *Henderson (North Carolina) Daily Dispatch*. The advertisement said that "Honest Al" Yeargin praised this new medicine, giving it full credit for restoring his health: "Pitcher Yeargin almost had to give up baseball for good. He was bothered with stomach pains, gas bloating, heavy feeling after eating, constipation, sour stomach and poor appetite. His blood was bad, pimples and boils broke out on his face and body." He walked into a Greenville drugstore and "treated himself to a bottle of Malva. The result was instantaneous. He went back for more. And now Yeargin, feeling once more like the old 'Mauldin Marvel' who mowed them down in the Sally League, in the Piedmont League and for the Boston Braves, is again proving that he still has 'the stuff' in him that makes big leaguers and in time will give a good account of himself."[25]

Yeargin did not return to baseball, however. He went back to farming. He and his wife, Noette, lived in Butler, South Carolina.

On May 8, 1937, Al Yeargin died, at the young age of 35. He took ill and died a week later, after a couple of days in Greenville General Hospital. The cause of death was given as general peritonitis and he had been said to have suffered a ruptured duodenal ulcer. His occupation at the time of death was given as "farmer and ret. base ball player."[26]

Al and Noette Yeargin had two children, shown in the 1940 census as Dorothy, 8, and Alton, 5, and living in Butler. Noette died in 1976.

SOURCES

In addition to the sources cited in the Notes, the author consulted Baseball-Reference.com, Retrosheet.org, and SABR.org.

NOTES

1. W.B. Hanna, "Giants Tune Up for Big Series While Dividing Double Bill with Braves in Season's Final Games," *New York Daily Tribune*, October 2, 1922: 11.
2. His gravestone shows 1902 as his birth year. His name in the 1910 census was rendered as Almont Yeargin, and he was said to be 9 years old.
3. The two eldest children, born before 1900, match up – Shirley and Avery.
4. Jacob H. Monte, "Greenville Spinners Are Anxious for Sally to Open; Blankenship Will Pilot the Club this Season," *Augusta Chronicle*, April 16, 1922: 5, 6. Monte called Yeargin the "Mauldin Marvel" in a May column. Jacob H. Monte, "Yeargin in Form and Greenville Defeats Spartans," *Augusta Chronicle*, May 9, 1922: 6.
5. Burt Whitman, "Braves and Cubs to Mingle Today," *Boston Herald*, July 25, 1922: 8. Several stories of the day called him Alvin Yeargin. He left for Boston the night of September 1.
6. "Pitcher Bridegroom Preferred Carolina to Major League Berth," *Omaha Morning Bee*, March 1, 1924: 9.
7. Baseball-Reference.com shows Yeargin with a record of 18-3, but the September 16 *Augusta Chronicle* shows him as 19-10, with four shutouts and 22 complete games. Confusingly, he is listed as Rush Yeargin, with a record of 18-9, in the Lloyd Johnson and Miles Wolff *Encyclopedia of Minor League Baseball*. Rush was the nickname of his younger brother, Russell. At least as confusingly, the playoffs were shown as between first-place Charlotte and fifth-place Macon.
8. Burton Whitman, "Fred Lucas Prominent as Dick Rudolph Shows the Youngsters How It's Done," *Boston Herald*, March 4, 1924: 10.
9. Burton Whitman, "Condition of Tribe Box Staff Surprising and Gratifying, Says Banny," *Boston Herald*, March 7, 1924: 20.
10. NEA Service, "Al Yeargin Courts Fame," *Charleston* (South Carolina) *Evening Post*, April 1, 1924: 9.
11. Rookie Jim Yeargin Is Hero of Braves's Third Straight Win over Reds," *Boston Herald*, May 17, 1924: 9.
12. "Cubs Hammer Yeargin and Cooney and Trounce Banny's Braves, 11 to 0," *Boston Herald*, May 26, 1924: 8.
13. *Boston Herald*, August 24, 1924: 14.
14. "This sum far exceeds any that the Boston Nationals have expended for a player in recent years." See Burton Whitman, "Braves Give $50,000 in Players and Cash for Coast Outfielder," *Boston Herald*, December 4, 1924: 1.
15. John B. Foster, "Salt Lake Is Paradise for batters," *Washington Evening Star*, February 27, 1925: 31.
16. Cliff Harrison, "Homer Nearly Wrecks Tribe in Hot Battle," *Seattle Daily Times*, March 8, 1925: 21. Harrison also wrote, "Yeargin hasn't shown as much as Stryker because of his physical condition." See Cliff Harrison, "Seattle Stronger in Defensive Way," *The Sporting News*, March 26, 1925: 7. Another correspondent added, regarding spring 1925, "Yeargin arrives in no condition to pitch." Ed Danforth, "Niehoff Upholds Great Record in Southern with Atlanta Team," *The Sporting News*, November 12, 1925: 5.
17. The headline in the *Augusta Chronicle* spanned seven of the eight columns on the page. See "Yeargin Whips Tygers in Last Game, 1 to 0," *Augusta Chronicle*, May 13, 1926: 6.
18. *Rockford* (Illinois) *Register-Gazette*, May 15, 1926: 13.
19. Russ Yeargin is shown in the team photograph on page 5 in the November 19, 1931, issue of *The Sporting News*.
20. "Spinners Open with Victory," *Charleston* (South Carolina) *Evening Post*, September 24, 1927: 6.
21. Bob Wilson, "Smokes and Spins Play Two Games This Afternoon," *Knoxville News-Sentinel*, April 24, 1928: 14.
22. Associated Press, "Yeargin Doubles to Win His Own Game from Comers," *Augusta Chronicle*, June 28, 1928: 6.
23. Carter Latimer, "Greenville Farms Out Stars," *Augusta Chronicle*, August 29, 1929: 21.
24. "Pitching Records for 1930 of the South Atlantic League," *The Sporting News*, November 6, 1930: 8.
25. Advertisement for Malva in *Henderson* (North Carolina) *Daily Dispatch*, November 25, 1932: 4.
26. Standard Certificate of Death, State of South Carolina. Thank to SABR member Dr. Stephen D. Boren for providing thoughts regarding Yeargin's death.

CONTRIBUTORS

MALCOLM ALLEN lives in Brooklyn, New York, with his wife, Sara, and their two daughters. Originally from Baltimore, the University of Maryland graduate spent three years as an usher at the Orioles' Memorial Stadium, where Fred Besana earned his lone big-league victory in 1956.

GARY BELLEVILLE is a retired information technology professional living in Victoria, British Columbia. He has written a variety of articles for the *Baseball Research Journal,* the Games Project, and Baseball BioProject. Gary has also contributed to several SABR books, including *Jackie: Perspectives on 42* and *Our Game, Too: Influential Figures and Milestones in Canadian Baseball.* He grew up in Ottawa, Ontario, and graduated from the University of Waterloo with a Bachelor of Mathematics (computer science) degree.

LUIS A. BLANDÓN, a Washington, DC native, is a producer, writer and researcher in video and documentary film production and in archival, manuscript, historical, film and image research. His creative storytelling has garnered numerous awards, including three regional Emmys®, regional and national Edward R. Murrow Awards, two TELLY awards and a New York Festival World Medal. He was Senior Researcher and Manager of the Story Development Team for two national programs for Retirement Living Television. He served as the principal researcher for several authors including for *The League of Wives* by Heath Hardage Lee and her current biography project on First Lady Pat Nixon. He has a Masters of Arts in International Affairs from the George Washington University.

RICHARD BOGOVICH was the author in 2022 of *Frank Grant: The Life of a Black Baseball Pioneer.* His previous books were *Kid Nichols: A Biography of the Hall of Fame Pitcher* and *The Who: A Who's Who.* He has contributed chapters to such SABR books as *The First Negro League Champion: The 1920 Chicago American Giants.* He has degrees from Northern Illinois University, and is office manager of the Wendland Utz law firm in Rochester, Minnesota.

WILLIAM H. "BILL" BREWSTER holds a master's degree in history from the State University of New York at Albany, and has been a SABR member since 2013. He's written two baseball history books, *The Workingman's Game,* which was a 2020 Seymour Medal finalist, and *That Lively Railroad Town.* He and his wife, Maria, reside in South Carolina.

ALAN COHEN has been a SABR member since 2011. He chairs the BioProject fact-checking committee, serves as vice president-treasurer of the Connecticut Smoky Joe Wood SABR Chapter, and is a datacaster (MiLB stringer) with the Eastern League Hartford Yard Goats, the Double-A affiliate of the Colorado Rockies. He also works with the Retrosheet Negro Leagues project. A major area of his research is the

Hearst Sandlot Classic (1946-1965), from which 87 players, including one-win wonder Ralph Mauriello, advanced to the majors. He has four children and nine grandchildren, and resides in Connecticut with wife Frances, their cats, Morty, Ava, and Zoe, and their dog, Buddy.

MIKE COONEY never had the opportunity to throw a pitch in a major-league ballpark, but he did start one game while in high school. After he walked four and hit one batter, and got no outs, his career as a pitcher came to an end. With baseball in the rear-view mirror, Mike earned a master's degree in journalism, worked in the automotive industry for 40 years and for 10 years as an adjunct professor teaching English composition at Ivy Tech Community College (Indiana). As a hobby, he wrote over 500 "A Stone's Throw" columns for the *Vevay* (Indiana) *Reveille-Enterprise*. Now retired for the fourth time, Mike lives on a bluff overlooking the Ohio River with his wife, Jade, and two rescued German Shepherds.

RORY COSTELLO is a lifelong Mets fan who has enjoyed the peaks, such as 1986 and 2015, and endured the valleys … such as 1993, in which the Kenny Greer game was one of the bright spots. He lives in Brooklyn, New York, with his wife, Noriko, and son, Kai.

RAY DANNER lives in Cleveland Heights, Ohio, where he is a local real estate investor specializing in the area's beautiful century homes. When he is not fixing toilets, he can be found underwater at the Greater Cleveland Aquarium as part of the dive team. He was on the sports beat for *The Cauldron* at Cleveland State University while completing his MBA and was a contributing writer at "It's Pronounced Lajaway," a member of the ESPN SweetSpot Network. Ray also plays rover on a vintage base ball club, the Whiskey Island Shamrocks. A SABR member since 2012, he is a lifelong Strat-O-Matic fan and enjoys contributing to SABR's Games Project and BioProject.

DENNIS D. DEGENHARDT retired after 40 years as a credit union professional, including chief executive the final 14, to do what he wanted when growing up, baseball. The difference now is researching and writing instead of making the big leagues. He has previously contributed to three SABR Bio-books, authoring five SABR Bios and two Game Projects. In addition, he has been an active member serving as an officer in the Ken Keltner Badger State Chapter since 2001, including president since 2019, where he publishes a monthly newsletter, the *Keltner Hot Corner*. Dennis and his spouse, Linda, have four children, six grandkids, and one great-grandson.

PHILIP DIXON is a former politics reporter for United Press International, a current environmental attorney in Albany, New York, and a lifelong Chicago Cubs fan. He has been a SABR member since the 1980s.

JEFF FINDLEY has been a member of SABR since 2009. A native of Eastern Iowa, he did the only logical thing growing up in the heart of the Cubs/Cardinals rivalry – he embraced the 1969 Baltimore Orioles and became a lifelong fan. When he's not watching baseball, he works as an information security professional for a Fortune 50 financial services company in central Illinois. He enjoys doing historical research and contributing to both the SABR BioProject and the Games Project.

JOHN FREDLAND is an attorney and retired Air Force officer. As an undergraduate at Rice University, he covered Rice's nationally ranked baseball teams for the school newspaper, the *Rice Thresher*. John received his law degree at Vanderbilt University, then served as an active-duty attorney in the Air Force's Judge Advocate General's Corps for 20 years. He lives in San Antonio, Texas, and chairs SABR's Baseball Games Project Research Committee. John grew up in a suburb of Pittsburgh; his interest in Western Pennsylvania sports history drew him to the life and career of Jordan Jankowski, the all-time home-run king of Pittsburgh-area high school baseball.

STEVE FRIEDMAN has been a SABR member since 1990. He has contributed articles for SABR publications and the BioProject. He resides in the Pacific Northwest and has been a season ticket holder of the Seattle Mariners since 1995. His youth was spent in the San Francisco Bay Area where he followed his beloved Giants. Steve retired after a career as an operator of cable television systems.

PETER M. GORDON has written biographies, historical articles, and poems for more than 20 SABR publications. He's a member of the Nineteenth Century and Deadball Era committees, and of the Central Florida SABR chapter. His baseball poetry is collected in the chapbook *Let's Play Two: Poems About Baseball*. Peter lives in Orlando, Florida, and teaches in the film production MFA program at Full Sail University.

TOM HAWTHORN is a speech writer for British Columbia Premier David Eby. Hawthorn's most recent book is *The Year Canadians Lost Their Minds and Found Their Country: The Centennial of 1967* (Douglas & McIntyre, 2017). He served as archival researcher for the 2003 National Film Board documentary *Sleeping Tigers: The Asahi Baseball Story*. He is an honorary member of Havana's Peña Deportivo. Born in Winnipeg, he moved to Montreal as a boy, where he used earnings from two paper routes to attend Montreal Expos games at Jarry Park. He is completing a commissioned history of baseball in Vancouver, British Columbia, Canada.

Although **STEVE HEATH** was a sportswriter for two metropolitan daily newspapers for more than a decade, some would say his career has been on the decline (when it comes to the excitement factor) since he was earning $2 a game and getting to meet the likes of Willie McCovey, Brooks Robinson, and Maury Wills as the 11-year-old visiting team batboy for the Sacramento Solons of the Pacific Coast League. Also an accomplished public relations professional and nonprofit executive who still lives in Sacramento, these days Steve is pursuing publication of a book that uses a set of baseball cards as the framework for a look back at the historic 1981 season. So it was only natural for Steve to take on the story of former Cincinnati Reds pitcher Scott Brown, whose one quirky career win was achieved in 1981 against Fernando Valenzuela and the Dodgers.

TIM HERLICH has been a member of SABR since 1995. In addition to his work on the O'Brien twins, he has contributed biographies of Ryne Sandberg, Bill North, Ray Washburn, Joe Staton, and Tom Cheney to the SABR BioProject. He has delivered several research presentations at annual SABR conventions, receiving the Doug Pappas Research Award for best oral presentation in 2009. He was a featured speaker at the National Baseball Hall of Fame in 2012 commemorating the 50th anniversary of Cheney's record-setting 21-strikeout game. Tim and his wife, Leslie, reside in Seattle, Washington. Their favorite teams are the Seattle Mariners and Philadelphia Phillies.

BILL HICKMAN was the long-serving chair of SABR's Pictorial History Committee. He currently maintains the "near major leaguers" database on the SABR website. He is the team historian for the Bethesda Big Train club in the Cal Ripken Collegiate Baseball League and serves as the secretary for the board of directors of the organization that operates that team. He has published numerous baseball articles; this is his third for a SABR baseball book. He is a graduate of Northwestern University and the Harvard Business School. He has served on the faculty of the US Naval Academy.

CHRIS HICKS began watching baseball with his grandfather as a child, which led to a lifelong passion for the game and his local Kansas City Royals. A wheelchair user since childhood, Chris became interested in the history of the game and the baseball card collecting hobby. His uncle took him to a Monarchs reunion in the early 1990s. This began years of learning independently about the history of the game. He joined SABR in 2020.

JOHN PAUL HILL teaches history at Toccoa Falls College in northeast Georgia. His articles and reviews on baseball history have appeared in *Nine: A Journal of Baseball History and Culture* and the *Register of the Kentucky Historical Society*. Formerly a Florida resident, he is a Tampa Bay Rays fan.

MARK HODERMARSKY, a retired English teacher at St. Ignatius High School in Cleveland, where he taught a course in baseball literature for 25 years, is the author of *A Treasured Legacy: Baseball in Cleveland, 1865-1900*, his ninth book. He has written articles for a variety of publications, including the *Cleveland Plain Dealer* and SABR.

BILL JOHNSON has contributed over 40 articles to SABR's BioProject, and presented papers at the 2011 Cooperstown Symposium on Baseball and American Culture, the 2017 Jerry Malloy Negro League Conference, and the inaugural Southern Negro League Conference. He has published a biography of Hal Trosky (McFarland and Co., 2017) and most recently an article about Negro American League All-Star Art "Superman" Pennington in the journal *Black Ball*. Bill and his wife, Chris, reside in Georgia.

JOSH KAISER is an educator and baseball enthusiast living with his wife and daughter in South Bend, Indiana. He is the head of school at Good Shepherd Montessori School and enjoys reading, traveling, and playing a weekly game of Strat-O-Matic baseball.

NORM KING (1957-2018) of Ottawa, Ontario, joined SABR in 2010 and became a prolific contributor to the SABR BioProject and Games Project until his untimely death from a rare form of bile duct cancer in 2018. He was the lead editor and author of *Au jeu/Play Ball: The 50 Greatest Games in the History of the Montreal Expos*, published in 2016, and wrote chapters for a number of other SABR books, including *That's Joy in Braveland: The 1957 Milwaukee Braves; Winning on the North Side: The 1929 Chicago Cubs;* and *A Pennant for the Twin Cities: The 1965 Minnesota Twins*. He was an active member of SABR's Quebec Chapter and a friendly face at the SABR national convention each year.

SEAN KOLODZIEJ, a SABR member since 2018, is a lifelong Cubs fan. He was born, raised, and still lives in Joliet, Illinois, with his wife, Amy. His greatest moment at Wrigley Field was watching Glenallen Hill hit a home run onto the rooftop of a building on Waveland Avenue.

GERARD KWILECKI, a lifelong Atlanta Braves fan, was born and raised in Bainbridge, Georgia. He earned his bachelor's and master's degrees from Valdosta State University. He resides near Mobile, Alabama, with his family. He currently works for the University of South Alabama.

DAVID LAURILA grew up in Michigan's Upper Peninsula and now writes about baseball from his home in Cambridge, Massachusetts. A contributor to numerous publications over the years, he has written regularly at FanGraphs since May 2011. He was at Tiger Stadium for Steve Ellsworth's lone big-league win.

LEN LEVIN is a longtime newspaper editor in New England, now retired. He lives in Providence with his wife, Linda, and an overachieving orange cat. He now (Len, not the cat) is the grammarian for the Rhode Island Supreme Court and edits its decisions. He also copy-edits many SABR books, including this one. He is just down the interstate from Fenway Park, where he has spent many happy hours.

CHAD MOODY is a nearly lifelong resident of the Detroit area, where he has been a fan of the Detroit Tigers from birth. An alumnus of the University of Michigan and Michigan State University, he has spent 30 years working in the automotive industry. Chad has contributed to numerous SABR and Professional Football Researchers Association (PFRA) projects. He and his wife, Lisa, live in Plymouth, Michigan, with their dog, Daisy.

JACK V. MORRIS is the head of a large pharmaceutical company's research library. He lives in suburban Philadelphia with his wife and is the father of two adult daughters. His baseball biographies have appeared in numerous books, including *The Team That Forever Changed Baseball and America* (1947 Brooklyn Dodgers) and *Scandal on the Southside* (1919 Chicago White Sox). He is not the Jack Morris of World Series fame but, every once in a great while wishes he was.

JIM MOYES has been a member of SABR for more than 30 years after being encouraged to join by his close friend, the late Marc Okkonen. Moyes, who has written bios in SABR publications *Deadball Stars of the National and American League*, first began working for the media as a stringer for the *Muskegon* (Michigan) *Chronicle* in 1956. Moyes has also written stories in the *Traverse City* (Michigan) *Record* and more recently has written a number of columns called "Moyes Memories" for both the *Muskegon Chronicle* and the *Local Sports Journal*. Moyes is primarily known for his work in broadcasting that began in 1967 in Traverse City doing play-by-play for the local Traverse City High School teams. Beginning in 1976, until he retired to Florida in 2009, he was the "voice" of high-school sports in Muskegon for many years. He has been inducted into the Muskegon Sports Hall of Fame and was the first member of the media to be inducted into the Michigan Basketball Coaches Hall of Fame. Moyes has continued his work in broadcasting, as well as writing for the local newspaper in Ponte Vedra, Florida. He continues his love affair for the sport of baseball where he has worked as the PA announcer since 2013 for the University of North Florida baseball program.

JERRY NECHAL is a retired former administrator at Wayne State University, residing in Sylvan Lake, Michigan. He has written articles for the *Baseball Research Journal* and has made several contributions to the SABR Biography Project and the Games Project. Other interests include hiking, architecture, theater, and gardening. He still longs for a bleacher seat in old Tiger Stadium.

TIM NEWBY is a writer and educator. He is the author of two books, 2015's *Bluegrass in Baltimore: The Hard Drivin' Sound & Its Legacy*, and 2019's *Leftover Salmon: Thirty Years of Festival*. Newby's work has appeared in a variety of publications including *Bluegrass Unlimited*, *Paste*, *Relix*, *AmericanaUK*, *Inside Lacrosse*, and *Honest Tune*. His next book, a biography of nineteenth-century slugger Pete Browning, will be published in 2024 by the University Press of Kentucky.

BILL NOWLIN never pitched in major-league baseball but he did go 1-for-3 in a charity game held at Fenway Park back around the year 2002, a single over shortstop into left field. He has written or edited a lotta books, many available free to SABR members. He lives in both Cambridge, Massachusetts, and at Fenway Park.

TONY S. OLIVER is a native of Puerto Rico currently living in Sacramento, California, with his wife and daughter. While he works as a Six Sigma professional, his true love is baseball and he cheers for both the Red Sox and whoever happens to be playing the Yankees. He is fascinated by baseball cards and is currently researching the evolution of baseball tickets. He believes there is no prettier color than the vibrant green of a freshly mown grass on a baseball field.

TIM OTTO grew up in northeast Ohio, 35 miles from Cleveland's Municipal Stadium. His first memories of major-league baseball date to the spring of 1960 when, as a second grader, he was fascinated by the controversy surrounding the trade of Rocky Colavito to the Tigers for Harvey Kuenn. Shortly thereafter he started monopolizing the sports section of the *Cleveland Plain Dealer* each morning at breakfast and that June attended his first major-league game. Carl Thomas, the subject of Tim's article for this book, was optioned to the minors in May of 1960 after winning his only big-league game. In researching that game, Tim had a feeling he might have watched it on TV. That feeling was confirmed when he found it listed as NBC's "Game of the Week" in the *Plain Dealer*'s entertainment section.

LEN PASCULLI is a retired lawyer and adjunct professor born in one of baseball's alleged birthplaces, Hoboken, New Jersey. He has been a SABR member since 2001. Len's article on Wilson Valdez in this collection marks the 10th biography he has written for SABR. (Len's biography of Scott Service can be found in SABR's companion publication, *One-Hit Wonders*.) Len is a one-win wonder himself, having pitched a complete game (seven-inning) victory in 2004 at the age of 49 at Doubleday Country Inn and Farm Baseball Fantasy Camp in Carlisle, Pennsylvania. Besides playing pickleball and pulling out what's left of his curly hair while managing his Rotisserie League baseball teams, Len enjoys cooking and traveling with his wife, Jan.

MARK PESTANA has been a SABR member since 1990, and a baseball fan since 1967, when he moved to the Boston area during the summer of the Impossible Dream Red Sox. He lives in Williamstown, Massachusetts, and his focus is on nineteenth-century baseball history. He has contributed to the following SABR books: *Inventing Baseball: The 100 Greatest Games of the 19th Century; Boston's First Nine: The 1871-75 Boston Red Stockings; The Glorious Beaneaters of the 1890s; Base Ball's 19th Century Winter Meetings 1857-1900; The World Series in the Deadball Era; Whales, Terriers & Terrapins: The Federal League 1914-15; Braves Field: Memorable Moments at Boston's Lost Diamond*; and *From the Braves to the Brewers: Great Games & Exciting History at Milwaukee's County Stadium*.

PAUL PROIA is a lifelong Cubs fan with a journalism degree from the University of Kansas. He is the author of *Just a Big Kid: The Life and Times of Rube Waddell* and has written scores of essays on mostly obscure baseball players. A SABR member for nearly 20 years, he is an active member of the BioProject team in an editing role. He and his wife, Jeanne, live in South Florida.

ALAN RAYLESBERG is an attorney in New York City. He is a lifelong baseball fan who enjoys baseball history and roots for the Yankees and the Mets. Alan also has a strong interest in baseball analytics and is a devotee of baseball simulation games, participating in both draft leagues and historical replays. Alan has written many articles for SABR, including other biographies. Before going to law school, Alan was the sports director of his college radio station and dreamed of a career in sports broadcasting or journalism. Now after many years practicing law, he is grateful for the opportunity that SABR has provided to allow him to realize at least some of that dream from many years ago.

CARL RIECHERS retired from United Parcel Service in 2012 after 35 years of service. With more free time, he became a SABR member. Born and raised in the suburbs of St. Louis, he became a big fan of the Cardinals. He and his wife, Janet, have three children and he is the proud grandpa of two.

RICHARD RIIS (1958-2021) wrote more than a dozen articles for SABR, both player biographies and game accounts. He worked in libraries throughout his professional life, devoting more than 40 years to work as a librarian and department head.

JOE SCHUSTER is the author of the novel *The Might Have Been* (Ballantine), a finalist for the CASEY Award for best baseball book of the year, and two baseball-related titles in Gemma Media's series of books for adult literacy programs, *One Season in the Sun* and *Jackie Robinson*. He has contributed to numerous SABR books, including *20-Game Losers, Bridging Two Dynasties, Sweet 60, Drama and Pride in the Gateway City,* and *One-Hit Wonders,* among others. A lifelong St. Louis Cardinals fan, he is married and the father of five and grandfather to three, all of whom share his passion for the Redbirds.

ERIC A. SIMONSEN is a lifelong baseball fan who, with his wife, Suzanne, has lived in Utah for the past 13 years. He joined SABR the day after he read about its creation in *The Sporting News*. Eric quickly became SABR treasurer, a position he held for several years until international demands on his financial career required him to resign. Eric has been a member for the past 50-plus years. Always an avid reader of SABR publications, Eric had never conducted any original baseball research until the search for authors for *One Win Wonders* was posted on the SABR website.

STEVE SISTO is a lifelong New York Mets fan who has written several SABR biographies for Mets players of the late-1990s and early-2000s teams that he grew up watching. In addition to his work with SABR's BioProject, he is also co-chair of the Origins Research Committee. He and his father are nearly halfway complete in their goal to see a game in every major-league ballpark. A native of Brooklyn, New York, Steve currently lives in Framingham, Massachusetts, with his wife, Caroline, and their two dogs, Monty and Benji.

After receiving master's degrees in chemistry and library science, **BRUCE SLUTSKY** pursued a career as a science/engineering librarian. He retired in 2017 after working 25 years for the New Jersey Institute of Technology. He joined SABR in 2016 and for several years has coordinated fact-checking for the Games Project. He also assists Andy McCue by indexing Games Project and BioProject articles for The Baseball Index. Bruce has been a diehard fan of the New York Mets since the team's inception in 1962. He wrote three articles for *Metrospectives: A Collection of New York Mets Greatest Games* (SABR, 2018).

GLEN SPARKS grew up in Santa Monica, California, and is a lifelong Dodgers fan. He wrote a biography of Hall of Fame shortstop Pee Wee Reese, published in 2022 by McFarland, and has co-edited SABR books about Roberto Clemente, Willie Mays, Jackie Robinson, and Babe Ruth. He and his wife, Pam, live in Cardinals country with their cats Buster, Kasper, and Lucy.

CLAYTON TRUTOR is the chair of SABR Vermont. He's the author of *Loserville: How Professional Sports Remade Atlanta – and How Atlanta Remade Professional Sports* and *Boston Ball: Rick Pitino, Jim Calhoun, Gary Williams, & the Forgotten Cradle of Basketball Coaches*. He'd love to hear from you on Twitter: @ClaytonTrutor.

MICHAEL TRZINSKI is retired from his day job and now works summers as the "Lawnmower Man" at a cranberry marsh. He lives in Port Edwards, Wisconsin. He has been married to Kelli since 2001 and has three children (Corey, Bronson, and Emily) and nine grandchildren. He also has a cat (Hudson) and a grandpup (Ellie). Michael has written three SABR bios in addition to contributing to two SABR books, and looks forward to doing many more.

ERIC VICKREY, a native of Illinois, is the author of the book *Runnin' Redbirds: The World Champion 1982 St. Louis Cardinals* and has contributed dozens of articles to SABR's BioProject. He lives in Seattle with his wife, Gina.

JOHN WATKINS, a retired law professor, has been a St. Louis Cardinals fan as long as he can remember. His great-uncle, George Watkins, was a major-league outfielder with the Cardinals in the 1930s.

BOB WEBSTER grew up in northwest Indiana and has been a Cubs fan since 1963. After moving to Portland, Oregon, in 1980, Bob spends his time working on baseball research and writing and is a contributor to quite a few SABR projects. He worked as a stats stringer on the MLB Gameday app for three years and is a member of the Pacific Northwest Chapter of SABR and the Oregon Sports Hall of Fame, and is on the board of directors of the Old-Timers Baseball Association of Portland.

PAUL WHITE, a SABR member since 2001, is a native of Boston and lifelong fan of the Red Sox. He earned a degree in history and political science from the University of Kansas in 1990, as well as several professional designations during a 33-year career in the insurance industry. Paul began publishing a blog called "Lost in Left Field" in 2002, and his writing about Jim Rice's Hall of Fame case was cited in articles on ESPN.com and in SABR's biography of Rice that has appeared in several SABR publications. His work can still be found at www.lostinleftfield.com or www.pauldwhite.substack.com. Paul has contributed several entries to the SABR Games Project and the SABR BioProject and is contributing an essay about Sandy Koufax's final season to SABR's Koufax book project. He is writing a book for McFarland Publishing on the history of the Hall of Fame's recognition of Negro Leagues players, scheduled for publication in 2024. Paul and his wife live near Kansas City.

PHIL WILLIAMS lives in Oreland, Pennsylvania, and has been a SABR member since 2007. He has contributed numerous articles to SABR's BioProject and is working on a book on Philadelphia baseball during the Deadball Era.

GREGORY H. WOLF was born in Pittsburgh, but now resides in the Chicagoland area with his wife, Margaret, and daughter, Gabriela. A professor of German studies and holder of the Dennis and Jean Bauman Endowed Chair in the Humanities at North Central College in Naperville, Illinois, he has edited more than a dozen books for SABR. Since January 2017 he has been co-director of SABR's BioProject, which you can follow on Facebook and Twitter.

Friends of SABR

You can become a Friend of SABR by giving as little as $10 per month or by making a one-time gift of $1,000 or more. When you do so, you will be inducted into a community of passionate baseball fans dedicated to supporting SABR's work.

Friends of SABR receive the following benefits:
- ✓ Recognition in This Week in SABR, SABR.org, and the SABR Annual Report
- ✓ Access to the SABR Annual Convention VIP donor event
- ✓ Invitations to exclusive Friends of SABR events

SABR On-Deck Circle - $10/month, $30/month, $50/month

Get in the SABR On-Deck Circle, and help SABR become the essential community for the world of baseball. Your support will build capacity around all things SABR, including publications, website content, podcast development, and community growth.

A monthly gift is deducted from your bank account or charged to a credit card until you tell us to stop. No more email, mail, or phone reminders.

Josh Gibson

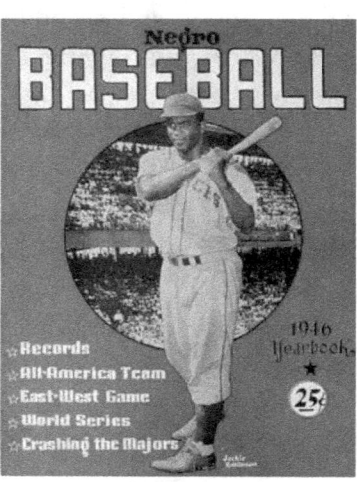
Jackie Robinson

Cool Papa Bell

Join the SABR On-Deck Circle

Payment Info: __Visa __Mastercard __ Discover   ○ $10/month

Name on Card: _____   ○ $30/month

Card #: _____   ○ $50/month

Exp. Date: _____ Security Code: _____   ○ Other amount _____

Signature: _____

Go to sabr.org/donate to make your gift online

The SABR Digital Library

Available wherever books are sold

The First Negro League Champion: The 1920 Chicago American Giants

Edited by Frederick C. Bush and Bill Nowlin

Paperback $29.95 244 pages • Ebook $9.99

This book chronicles the team which won the title of champion in the Negro National League's inaugural season. Rube Foster, a Hall of Famer, and his White business partner John Schorling are featured along with biographies of every player on the team include Cristóbal Torriente, a member of both the National Baseball Hall of Fame and the Cuban Baseball Hall of Fame, as well as early Blackball stalwarts Dave "Lefty" Brown, Bingo DeMoss, Judy Gans, Dave Malarcher, Frank Warfield, and Frank Wickware. A comprehensive timeline of the 1920 season and a history of the founding of the Negro National League are included.

We Are, We Can, We Will: The 1992 World Champion Toronto Blue Jays
Edited by Adrian Fung and Bill Nowlin

Forewords by Buck Martinez and Dave Winfield

Paperback US $34.95/Canada $41.95 394 pages • Ebook $9.99

The 1992 Toronto Blue Jays will always be remembered as the first World Series-winning club from Canada. After a near miss in 1991, the 1992 club confidently adopted "We Are, We Can, We Will" as their team motto. This book features biographies of every player who played for the 1992 Toronto Blue Jays including Hall of Famers Dave Winfield, Jack Morris, and Roberto Alomar. Manager Cito Gaston, Hall of Fame general manager Pat Gillick, and radio broadcaster Tom Cheek are also included, as well as a "ballpark biography" of SkyDome. Ten reports describe significant games from the 1992 season illustrating Toronto's championship journey from Opening Day to the last game of the World Series.

From Shibe Park to Connie Mack Stadium: Great Games in Philadelphia's Lost Ballpark
Edited by Gregory H. Wolf
Paperback $39.95 398 pages • Ebook $9.99

This collection evokes memories and the exciting history of the celebrated ballpark through stories of 100 games played there and several feature essays. The games included in this volume reflect every decade in the ballpark's history, from the inaugural game in 1909, to the last in 1970.

Shibe Park was the home of the Philadelphia A's from 1909 until their relocation to Kansas City and the Philadelphia Phillies from 1938 until the ballpark's closure at the end 1970. In 1953 it was renamed Connie Mack Stadium. The ballpark hosted big-league baseball for 62 seasons and more than 6,000 games—over 3,500 games by the A's and 2,500 by the Phillies—and was home to Frank Baker, Del Ennis, Chief Bender, and Robin Roberts.

¡Arriba!: The Heroic Life of Roberto Clemente

edited by Bill Nowlin and Glen Sparks

Paperback $34.95 338 pages • Ebook $9.99

2022 marks the 50th anniversary year of Roberto Clemente's passing. This book celebrates his life and baseball career. Named to 15 All-Star Game squads, Clemente won 12 Gold Gloves, four batting titles, and was the National League's Most Valuable Player in 1966. The first Latino inducted into the National Baseball Hall of Fame, Clemente played 18 seasons for the Pittsburgh Pirates and became the 11th player to reach the 3,000-hit milestone, hitting number 3000 on the season's last day. At the time no one knew he would never play baseball again. Clemente was known for his charitable work. He lost his life on the final day of 1972 while working to provide relief for victims of an earthquake in Nicaragua.

SABR publishes up to a dozen new books per year on baseball history and culture. Researched and written by SABR members, these collaborative projects cover some of the game's greatest players, classic ballparks, and teams.

SABR members can download all Digital Library publications for free or get 50% off the purchase of paperback editions.

www.ingramcontent.com/pod-product-compliance
Lightning Source LLC
LaVergne TN
LVHW060151080526
838202LV00052B/4133